Taiwan

Taiwan Strait
Islands
p302

...thern
Taiwan
p132

Western
Taiwan
p210

Eastern Taiwan
& Taroko
National Park
p165

Southern
Taiwan
p249

Piera Chen

Mark Elliott, Dinah Gardner, Thomas O'Malley

PLAN YOUR TRIP

ON THE ROAD

Contents

LANDSCAPE NEAR HUALIEN (P173)

EFIRED / SHUTTERSTOCK ©

**YOUBIKES (P117), NEAR TAIPEI 101 (P83)
BY ARCHITECT CY LEE, TAIPEI**

Contents

RAOHE STREET NIGHT
MARKET (P101), TAIPEI

FAZON1 / GETTY IMAGES ©

Welcome to Taiwan

Generous like its 23 million people, Taiwan offers wondrous vistas, lively traditions and a culture as luxuriant as Jade Mountain on a sunny day.

The Beautiful Isle

Famed for centuries as Ilha Formosa (Beautiful Isle; 美麗島; Měilìdǎo), this is a land with more sides than the 11-headed Guanyin. Towering sea cliffs, marble-walled gorges and tropical forests are just the start of your journey, which could take you as far as Yushan, Taiwan's 3952m alpine roof.

In Taiwan you can criss-cross mountains on colonial-era hiking trails or cycle a lone highway with the blue Pacific on one side and green volcanic arcs on the other. And if you simply want classic landscapes to enjoy, you'll find them around every corner.

Have You Eaten?

'Have you eaten?' The words are used as a greeting here, and the answer is almost always 'yes', as there's just too much nibbling to do. Taiwan offers the gamut of Chinese cuisines, the best Japanese outside Japan, and a full house of local specialities from Tainan milkfish and Taipei beef noodles to indigenous barbecued wild boar. Night markets serve endless feasts of snacks including oyster omelettes, shrimp rolls and shaved ice. When you're thirsty you can indulge in juices from the freshest fruits, local craft beer, fragrant teas and, in a surprising twist, Asia's best gourmet coffee and drinking chocolate.

Asian Values On Their Terms

Defying those who said it wasn't in their DNA, the Taiwanese have created Asia's most vibrant democracy and liberal society, with a raucous free press, gender equality, and respect for human rights and, increasingly, animal rights as well. The ancestors are still worshipped, and parents still get their dues, but woe betide the politician who thinks it's the people who must pander, and not them. If you want to catch a glimpse of the people's passion for protest, check out Taipei main station on most weekends, or just follow the local news.

The Tao of Today

Taiwan is heir to the entire Chinese tradition of Buddhism, Taoism, Confucianism and that amorphous collection of deities and demons worshipped as folk faith. Over the centuries the people have blended their way into a unique and tolerant religious culture that's often as ritual heavy as Catholicism and as wild as Santería. Taiwanese temples (all 15,000) combine worship hall, festival venue and art house under one roof. Watch a plague boat burn at Donglong Temple, go on a pilgrimage with the Empress of Heaven, study a rooftop three-dimensional mosaic, and learn why a flag and ball have come to represent prayer.

Why I Love Taiwan

By Piera Chen, Writer

When I first visited Taiwan aged six, the hotel's pork cutlets impressed me. Later, as a fan of director Hou Hsiao-hsien, I went to Jiufen and Fengkuei, the settings for his films; I was hooked. Many trips and obsessions later, I now live in Taiwan, and am in love with Kaohsiung's flamboyant culture. Taiwan never ceases to surprise, like the night I waited for a meteor shower in Kenting. I had expected a crowd to show up, but found myself completely alone – not even a hint of a shadow. Then I looked up: the whole sky was moving.

For more about our writers, see p416

Above: Festival performer, Tainan (p272)

Taiwan

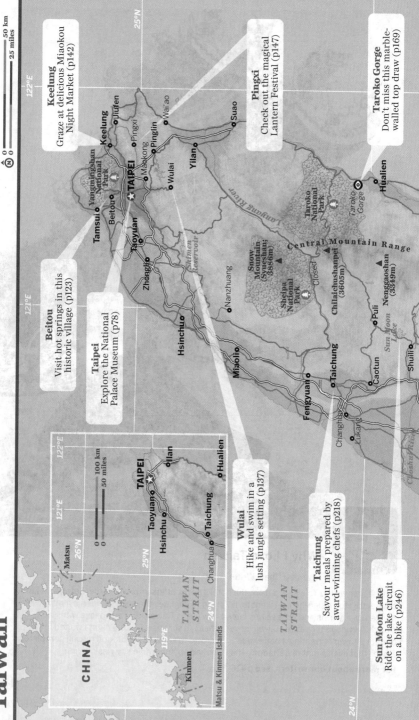

Keelung
Graze at delicious Miaokou Night Market (p142)

Pingxi
Check out the magical Lantern Festival (p147)

Taroko Gorge
Don't miss this marble-walled top draw (p169)

Beitou
Visit hot springs in this historic village (p123)

Taipei
Explore the National Palace Museum (p78)

Wulai
Hike and swim in a lush jungle setting (p137)

Taichung
Savour meals prepared by award-winning chefs (p218)

Sun Moon Lake
Ride the lake circuit on a bike (p246)

CHINA

Matsu & Kinmen Islands

TAIWAN STRAIT

Central Mountain Range

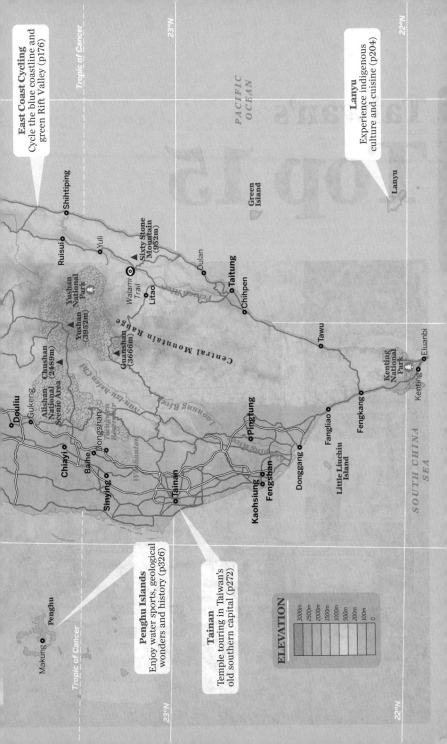

East Coast Cycling
Cycle the blue coastline and green Rift Valley (p176)

Lanyu
Experience indigenous culture and cuisine (p204)

Penghu Islands
Enjoy water sports, geological wonders and history (p326)

Tainan
Temple touring in Taiwan's old southern capital (p272)

Tropic of Cancer

PACIFIC OCEAN

SOUTH CHINA SEA

Shihtiping

Ruisui

Yuli

Sixty Stone Mountain (952m)

Dulan

Green Island

Lanyu

Walami Trail

Taitung

Litao

Chihpen

Yushan National Park

Yushan (3952m)

Central Mountain Range

Guanshan (3666m)

Tawu

Dookiu

Gukeng

Alishan National Chushan (2489m) Scenic Area

Chiayi

Baihe

Dongshan

Tsengwen Reservoir

Wushanto

Sinying

Lounung River

Kaohsiung

Fengshan

Pingtung

Fengliao

Kenting National Park

Kenting

Eluanbi

Tainan

Dongang

Little Liuchiu Island

Fengkang

Makung

Penghu

Tropic of Cancer

ELEVATION

| 3000m |
| 2500m |
| 2000m |
| 1500m |
| 1000m |
| 500m |
| 200m |
| 100m |
| 0 |

23°N

22°N

Taiwan's
Top 15

Temple Treasures

1 There are 15,000 official temples in Taiwan, three times as many as there were 30 years ago. Still the focus of local culture, temples play the role of community centre as much as house of worship. Both Tainan and Lukang boast a wealth of old buildings, from understated Confucius temples to Mazu temples rich in examples of southern folk decorative arts. But if you can only visit one temple in Taiwan, head to Bao'an Temple (p74) in Taipei, a showcase of traditional design, rites and festivities.

Below left: Bao'an Temple (p74), Taipei

Gourmet Taiwan

2 Besides being one of the world's street-food capitals, Taiwan is steadily making a mark on Asia's fine-dining landscape. Twenty restaurants received stars in the inaugural Michelin Star Taipei in 2018, rising to 24 in 2019. The lists don't just include European-style establishments, or expensive Japanese or Cantonese kitchens, but also restaurants that specialise in traditional or contemporary Taiwanese cuisine. Besides this, there are an increasing number of chefs in Taichung and other cities – with or without culinary awards – who have done inspiring things with Taiwanese ingredients, like JL Studio (p220).Below right: Braised fish in soy sauce (紅燒魚; *hóngshāo yú*)

R. NAGY / SHUTTERSTOCK ©

LOCS4613 / GETTY IMAGES ©

The Penghu Archipelago

3 The collection of islands known as Penghu (澎湖; Pénghú; p326) is distinctive yet hard to pin down. Its wave-whipped coastlines feature coral stone-walled settlements, charming sea-facing temples and beaches suitable for water sports – in winter it becomes a wind-surfing paradise for top-class athletes the world over. Added to this mix are geological wonders, handsome military sites, a large aquarium, remnants of ancient sea trade and a banyan from dynastic times. Penghu cuisine is celebrated for its delicious simplicity and abundance of seafood. Top: Twin Hearts Stone Weir (p337)

Tainan on Foot

4 The Tainanese are proud of their past as Taiwan's oldest city and justifiably so – Tainan (台南; Táinán; p272) is full of gems that offer a multifaceted experience of history. Besides temples and markets, there are fascinating streets with repurposed shophouses and entire districts built around old military sites; all these can be easily explored on foot, with a bus ride in between to tide you over. When you're tired, take a break at a cafe frequented by Nobel Prize–winning poets or sip a cocktail in a former medical clinic.

Cafes & Coffees of Taiwan

5 Blessed with good soil, and a climate and altitudes conducive to Arabica trees flourishing, Taiwan has become the coffee mecca of Asia, winning worldwide awards for its beans that range from nutty to tea-like. You can sip them at their source in Gukeng and Dongshan, but it's more interesting to go to a cafe that serves an excellent cup of coffee, and also roasts and sells beans. A bonus is the setting, which can range from retro coffee houses to delightful scrapyards (p221).

Taroko Gorge

6 Taiwan's top tourist draw is a walk-in Chinese painting. Rising above the froth of the blue-green Liwu River, the marble walls (yes, marble!) of Taroko Gorge (p169) swirl with the colours of a master's palette. Add grey mist, lush vegetation and waterfalls seemingly tumbling down from heaven, and you have a truly classic landscape. Walk along the Swallow Grotto to see the gorge at its most sublime or brave the Jhuilu Old Trail, a vertiginous path 500m above the canyon floor.

ROETTING / POLLEX / AGE FOTOSTOCK ©

Cycling the East Coast

7 Cycling fever has taken over the island, and the unspoiled and sparsely populated east coast has emerged as the top destination for multiday trips. Like the sea? Then ride the stunning coastline on Hwy 11, between Hualien (p173) and Taitung (台東; Táidōng; p194), the east coast's two largest cities. You'll pass beaches, fishing harbours and art villages. Love the mountains? Try the Rift Valley, bounded by lush, green ranges. On both routes there are enough roadside cafes, campgrounds, homestays and hot springs to ensure your cycling trip won't be an exercise in logistics.

National Palace Museum

8 Taiwan houses what is often believed to be the greatest collection of Chinese art in the world. With ancient pottery, bronzes and jade, Ming vases, Song landscape paintings and calligraphy that even those who are not art lovers can appreciate, Taipei's National Palace Museum (p78) isn't merely a must-visit, it's a must-repeat-visit. Why? Out of the nearly 700,000 pieces in the museum's collection – spanning every Chinese dynasty, in addition to prehistory and the modern-age – only a tiny fraction is ever on display at the one time.

A Stationary Feast: Night Markets

9 Taiwan's night markets are as numerous as they are varied. Fulfilling the need for both food and entertainment the markets bring happy crowds almost every night of the week to gorge on a bewildering array of snacks and dishes. Check out the Miaokou Night Market (pictured top right; p142) in Keelung, in many ways the grandaddy of them all, for the quintessential experience of eating and people-watching. The night market snacks in Tainan are copied everywhere, but are still best enjoyed on their home turf.

The Mazu Pilgrimage

10 This mother of all walks across Taiwan is, appropriately enough, dedicated to Mazu (literally, old granny), the maternal patron deity of the island. For nine days, hundreds of thousands of the faithful (and visitors) follow a revered statue of Mazu (p231) over 350km across Taiwan, while several million more participate in local events like elaborate ceremonies, theatrical performances and feasting. This is Taiwan's folk culture at its most exuberant and festive, with crowds, wild displays of devotion and a whole lot of fireworks.

JUTINAN JUJNDA / SHUTTERSTOCK ©

Hiking Jungles & High Mountains

11 Taiwan is 50% forested and the urban jungle gives way to the real thing astonishingly quickly. In mountainous Wulai (pictured below; p137), old indigenous hunting trails cut through tropical forests. Take a break from your trek to enjoy crystal-clear streams or deep swimming pools and repeat all over the island. Taiwan is also two-thirds mountainous: hundreds of mountains soar above 3000m, and well-established hiking routes run everywhere.

Sun Moon Lake National Scenic Area

12 Sun Moon Lake (p244) is the largest body of water in Taiwan and has a watercolour background, ever-changing with the season. Although the area is packed with tour groups these days, it's still easy to get away from the crowds on the trails and cycling paths. For diverse fun, loop down to the old train depot at Checheng or visit the Chung Tai monastery in nearby Pul. No matter what, don't miss the region's high-mountain oolong tea: it's among the world's finest.

CHEN MIN CHUN / SHUTTERSTOCK ©

WENLIQU / SHUTTERSTOCK ©

The Magic Lights of the Lantern Festival

13 One of the oldest of the lunar events, the Lantern Festival celebrates the end of the New Year's festivities. The focus of course is light, and everywhere streets and riversides are lined with glowing lanterns, while giant neon and laser displays fill public squares. Making the mundane surreal and the commonplace magical, the little mountain village of Pingxi (pictured above left; p147) takes simple paper lanterns and releases them en masse into the night sky. There are few sights more spectacular or mesmerising.

Indigenous Taiwan

14 Though long suppressed, tribal culture and pride has made a remarkable turnaround in the 21st century. Begin your understanding at the Shung Ye Museum of Formosan Aborigines in Taipei, and then check into a homestay run by Yami islanders on Lanyu (p205) during the flying fish season. Or consider a visit to the communally run Smangus, a high-mountain centre of Atayal culture and language. In the summer, head to the east coast around Taitung for exuberant festivals celebrating harvests, coming of age and a deep love of live music. Top right: Formosan Aboriginal Culture Village (p245)

Hot Springs Wild & Tamed

15 Taiwan's surface has plenty of fissures, and the abundance of spring sources is hard to match anywhere in the world. The waters boil and bubble but cause no trouble; they are effective for everything from soothing muscles to conceiving male offspring. Nature lovers heading to hot springs in Beitou (pictured above; p124) and Tai'an will find them a double happiness: stone, wood and marble coupled with mountain views. If you're willing to walk in, you'll discover there are still quite a few pristine wild springs deep in the valleys.

Need to Know

For more information, see Survival Guide (p383)

Currency
New Taiwan dollar (NT$)

Language
Mandarin, Taiwanese

Visas
Tourists from most European countries, Canada, USA, New Zealand, South Korea and Japan are given visa-free entry for stays of up to 90 days (www.mofa.gov.tw).

Money
ATMs are widely available (except in villages), while credit cards are accepted at most midrange and top-end hotels and at top-end restaurants.

Mobile Phones
Most foreign mobile phones can use local SIM cards with prepaid plans, which you can purchase at airport arrival terminals and top up at telecom outlets or convenience stores.

Time
National Standard Time (GMT/UTC plus eight hours)

When to Go

Taipei
GO Year-round

Taichung
GO Oct–Jun

Hualien
GO Mar–May, Sep–Jan

Tainan
GO Oct–Mar

Kaohsiung
GO Apr–May, Oct–Jan

Hot summers (warm to cool at elevations), cold to mild winters

High Season (Jul & Aug)
➡ Tourist accommodation costs increase 30% to 50%.

➡ Saturday nights (year-round) and Chinese New Year also see increases.

Shoulder (Sep & Oct, Apr–Jun)
➡ Good discounts on accommodation midweek.

➡ Crowds at major sights on weekends.

➡ Best time to visit outer islands.

➡ Typhoon season (June to October) could mean disruptions to flights, sailings and access to remote areas.

Low Season (Nov–Mar)
➡ Few crowds except during January and Chinese New Year.

➡ Best discounts on accommodation at major tourist sights (up to 50%).

➡ High season for hot-spring hotels.

Useful Websites

Forumosa (www.forumosa.com) Expat community site.

Information For Foreigners (www.immigration.gov.tw) Visa regulations and daily life matters.

Lonely Planet (www.lonely planet.com/taiwan) Destination information, hotel bookings, traveller forum and more.

Taiwan Tourism Bureau (www. taiwan.net.tw) Official website of the Taiwan Tourism Bureau.

English in Taiwan (www.english intaiwan.com) Site for expat teachers in Taiwan.

Taiwan Reporter (www.taiwan reporter.de) Observations of a German journalist in Taiwan.

Important Numbers

When calling local long-distance numbers, the '0' in the area codes is used. When dialling from overseas, it's dropped.

Fire and ambulance services	✆	119
Police	✆	110
Country code	✆	886
International access code	✆	002
24-hour toll-free travel information hotline	✆	0800-011765

Exchange Rates

Australia	A$1	NT$20.96
Canada	1C$	NT$23.44
Euro zone	€1	NT$33.82
Japan	¥100	NT$28.70
New Zealand	NZ$1	NT$19.43
UK	UK£1	NT$38.11
USA	US$1	NT$31.03

For current exchange rates, see www.xe.com.

Opening Hours

Many restaurants, cafes and museums are closed on Monday.

Banks 9am–3.30pm Mon–Fri

Cafes Noon–8pm

Convenience stores Open 24 hours

Department stores 11am–9.30pm

Government offices 8.30am–5.30pm Mon–Fri

Museums 9am–5pm Tue–Sun

Night markets 6pm to midnight

Offices 9am–5pm Mon–Fri

Post offices 8am–5pm Mon–Fri

Restaurants 11.30am–2pm & 5pm–9pm

Shops 10am–9pm

Supermarkets To at least 8pm, sometimes 24 hours

Daily Costs

Budget:
Less than NT$2500

➡ Dorm bed: NT$550–800

➡ Noodles and side dish: NT$80–200

➡ MRT: NT$40

➡ Convenience store beer: NT$40

Midrange:
NT$2500–4000

➡ Double room in a hotel: NT$1400–2800

➡ Lunch or dinner at a restaurant: NT$250–500

➡ Taxi rental per day: NT$1600–3000

➡ Gourmet coffee: NT$120–260

Top End:
More than NT$4000

➡ Double room at a four-star hotel: NT$4000–12,000

➡ Meal at a top restaurant: NT$800–2000

➡ Private guided tour: NT$9000

➡ Cocktail at a high-end bar: NT$300–400

Arriving in Taiwan

Taiwan Taoyuan International Airport (✆03- 273 3728; www. taoyuan-airport.com) Buses run every 15 minutes to the city centre (NT$110 to NT$140, about 60 minutes); most routes operate from 6am to 12.30am, and route 1819 runs 24 hours. A taxi (40 to 60 minutes) to the city costs NT$1200 to NT$1400. Taoyuan Airport MRT (rapid transit) line, running every 10 minutes between the airport and Taipei (NT$160, 35 minutes for express train and 50 minutes for commuter train, 6am to 11.30pm), is the faster and more convenient option.

Kaohsiung International Airport (www.kia.gov.tw) KMRT trains leave every six minutes from am to midnight (NT$35). A taxi costs NT$350 to the city centre.

Getting Around

Air Only really useful for getting to the outlying islands.

Bicycle Cycling around the island is a popular tourist activity.

Bus Slower but cheaper than trains, buses also connect passengers to more destinations than the trains.

Car or scooter A fun option, but you will need an International Driver's Permit.

Train Fast, reliable and cheap, Taiwan has both a High Speed Rail (HSR) and a regular rail link.

For much more on **getting around**, see p393

What's New

Taiwan's tourism landscape is changing as we speak. From cacao farms and gourmet restaurants to private museums, flea markets and music dives, there are plenty of new and exciting attractions to impress visitors, whether you are travelling solo, with friends or with a family in tow.

Cacao Farms

Chocolate farms have sprung up all over the southernmost county of Pingtung, growing beans and crafting some of the finest chocolates in Asia and the world. You can tour the premises, learn about drying and fermentation, make your own sweets, and indulge at Fu Wan Chocolate (p294), Choose Chius (p291) and Cocosun (p291).

Private Museums

There are three top-notch but under-the-radar private museums in southern Taiwan: in Kaohsiung, Museum 50 (p251) houses exquisite artefacts created by Japanese masters connected to Taiwan, and Alien Art Centre (p252) displays contemporary art by Taiwanese and international masters in a former guesthouse for military recruits; while in Tainan, the uplifting Thousand Fields Seed Museum (p273) shows you wondrous indigenous flora inside a lovely residence.

Gourmet Dining

The number of Michelinstarred restaurants and eateries with other prestigious culinary awards is growing in Taiwan, and not only in Taipei. Book a table at JL Studio (p220) in Taichung, or Le Palais (p100) and RAW (p100) in Taipei; or head to Tu Pang (p220) in Taichung or House of Crab (p264) in Kaohsiung for a chefy and memorable meal sans stars.

Craft Beer

Craft beer is all the rage on the island and is available almost everywhere, from breweries to bookshops. Proper pubs where you can down a Taiwanese brew or four include Craft Beer Taproom (p105), ChangX (p221), Three Giants (p221) and 58 Bar (p103).

Markets

Taiwan's nocturnal food bazaars may be world famous but there are other markets that provide an equally immersive experi-

---

LOCAL KNOWLEDGE

WHAT'S HAPPENING IN POLITICS

On the cusp of the 2020 presidential election, China remains the top issue in the race between KMT candidate Han Kuo-yu and incumbent Tsai Ing-wen. Han pledges to make Taiwan richer and better friends with Beijing, while Tsai advocates progressive values and keeping China at arm's length.

Taiwan is plagued by low salaries and high housing costs, and some Taiwanese see China as a way out. But here's the dilemma: is it possible to have profitable economic relations with China and still enjoy political autonomy? Opinion polls have shown that most Taiwanese are not in favour of rule by China. Hong Kong's anti-extradition protests have also fuelled sentiments against the 'One Country, Two Systems' mode of governance.

In August China suspended issuing permits to independent tourists to Taiwan. While the move will further strain Taiwan's economy, it remains to be seen whether the Taiwanese will give in to such blatant pressure tactics.

ence, like Kaohsiung's fabulous Neiwei Flea Market (p251), which offers everything under the sun plus a huge chunk of local life; Taipei's Maji Square (p99), with its farmers' market, stylish bistros and live music; and Taichung's Audit Village (p215), known for beautiful handicrafts and tempting desserts.

Cultural Venues

Three major cultural centres of high architectural and artistic interest have opened their doors. Kaohsiung's sleek, Dutch-designed Weiwuying National Centre for the Arts (p265) offers a rich program of music and performing arts as the premier cultural centre in southern Taiwan. The quirky Japanese-designed National Taichung Theater (p221) is a state-of-the-art opera house in Taichung. And Tainan's Art Museum Bldg 2 (p276) by Japanese Shigeru Ban shows artworks by southern Taiwanese masters.

Military Tourism

Kaohsiung, a port of strategic importance in WWII, is opening its former military sites to the public. For starters, check out the Military Dependants' Village Museum (p257) and the Story House of Naval Base Zuoying (p257). If hands-on excitement is what you are after, make your way to the Houlin Military Base Laser Shooting Simulation (p314) on the former military island of Kinmen.

Latest Dives

As always, the best music dives are a pain to find – and that's half the fun. For great indie sounds and a unique vibe, try to find your way to Taichung's cavernous the Cave (p221), and the amicable Forro Cafe (p218); to Chiayi's elusive Fake Qoo (p230) and its sister venue Moor Room (p230); or to Changhua's mysterious FDLC (p235).

LGBTIQ+

You can find LGBTIQ+-friendly places all over Taiwan, but Taipei certainly has the lion's share. Happening favourites in the capital include Red House Bar Street (p103), Abrazo (p105), Commander D (p104) and H*ours Cafe (p103); while in Lukang in western Taiwan, Fang Kofi (p239) serves excellent coffee.

LISTEN, WATCH & FOLLOW

For inspiration and ideas, visit www.lonelyplanet.com/taiwan/travel-tips-and-articles and www.lonelyplanet.com/news/taiwan.

Taiwan Everything (www.taiwaneverything.cc) Mainly food, accommodation and the outdoors.

A Hungry Girl's Guide to Taipei (www.hungryintaipei.blogspot.com) Food is an obsession with Taiwanese and this blog highlights just why.

twitter.com/triptotaiwan Taiwan's official tourism guide (@TriptoTaiwan).

twitter.com/kaohsiungcity Kaohsiung's official twitter account (@KaohsiungCity).

FAST FACTS

Food trend Refined Taiwanese cuisine; gourmet restaurants

Number of registered temples 12,106

Number of mountains over 3000m 165

Population 23.6 million

POPULATION PER SQ KM

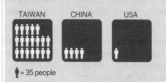

TAIWAN   CHINA   USA

= 35 people

Cafes

The coffee-drinking trend seems to continue unabated in Taiwan, with cafes materialising on every street in major urban areas. Some would say that it's harder to find bad coffee than good coffee in Taiwan. Here are a few gems that offer a solid cup of joe in a memorable setting: Tainan's Ubuntu (p289), L'Esprit Cafe (p286), and Narrow Door (p287), Lukang's Fang Kofi (p239), Taipei's Bok Su Lao (p122), Hytte (p148) in Sandiaoling, Taitung's Taimali (p197) and Chiayi's Saint Tower Coffee (p229).

If You Like...

Temples

With 12,000 and counting, there is a temple for every god and occasion.

Longshan Temple This graceful walled temple in Lukang is a treasure house of woodcarving and design. (p235)

Bao'an Temple A top example of southern temple art and architecture that won Unesco recognition for its restoration. (p74)

Tzushr Temple The temple's post-WWII reconstruction was overseen by an art professor – and it shows. (p135)

Lu'ermen Temples The Orthodox Lu'ermen Mazu Temple and the Lu'ermen Tianhou Temple are two of the most important temples in Taiwan, with relics from Koxinga's original battleship. (p268)

Tainan Confucius Temple Taiwan's first Confucius temple and a model of graceful design and dignified atmosphere. (p277)

City God Temple Your moral character will be scrutinised at the home of Taiwan's most famous temple plaque: 'You're here at last'. (p275)

Chung Tai Chan Temple The casino-meets-mosque exterior belies an interior filled with tradition-inspired decorative arts. (p247)

Food

Chi Fan Shi Tang A proper sit-down meal of good old Taiwanese cuisine, done well. (p97)

House of Crab Some of Taiwan's top-quality seafood can be had in Kaohsiung and Penghu Islands, and of course Taipei. (p264)

Da Dong Night Market You'll find unique street food all over Taiwan, but don't miss Tainan for its milkfish and beef broth. (p285)

Guo's Chiayi's delicious fowl, like turkey and braised goose, are well worth trying. (p229)

Le Palais Michelin-starred and award-winning restaurants in Taipei, Taichung and Kaohsiung. (p100)

One Bar Taiwanese home cooking given a modern twist; enjoy it in Taipei, Kaohsiung and Tainan. (p264)

Flower Space Taste proof of Taiwan's reputation for being an Asian mecca for vegetarians. (p177)

Dian Shui Lou You'll find Chinese regional dumplings, noodles and hotpots in Taipei, Taichung and even Cingjing. (p101)

Mu-Ming Sumptuous indigenous fare can be enjoyed along the east coast and in Pingtung. (p177)

Outdoor Activities

Hiking is outstanding and scenic cycling routes are endless. And for water sports, there's scuba diving, river tracing, surfing and one gusty archipelago for world-class windsurfing.

Taroko Gorge Cycling along a 19km-long marble-walled canyon, backed by cliffs and peaks right next to the Pacific Ocean. (p169)

Penghu Islands One of the windiest places in the world in autumn, Penghu offers Asia's finest windsurfing. (p326)

Wulai Just a short ride from Taipei, this expanse of subtropical forest and wild rivers is one of the north's top spots for hiking, cycling and river tracing. (p137)

Yangmingshan National Park This national park in urban Taipei offers scenic trails dotted with hot springs and, in spring, cherry blossoms. (p127)

Yushan National Park Hiking trails cross 1050 sq km of high mountains and deep valleys. (p55)

Lanyu An abundance of fish life and a unique island culture make this a perfect spot for scuba and snorkelling fans. (p205)

Houfeng Bicycle Path A breezy ride through history that passes

an old train station, courtyard houses, a Japanese-era train tunnel and suspension bridge and even a horse farm. (p217)

Night Markets

Da Dong A nifty market offering everything from Tainan beef soup to spring rolls in a city famous for its street snacks. (p285)

Wenhua Road Think braised goose, bowls of turkey over rice, and all the other goodness that make Chiayi one of Taiwan's most delicious cities. (p229)

Raohe Street The cognoscenti's night market, Raohe is Taipei's oldest, and unrivalled in snacking opportunities. (p101)

Ruifeng Kaohsiung's largest night market is stuffed with stalls and sit-down areas; the deliciousness includes duck wraps, mochi and even steak and paella. (p263)

Miaokou Nightly offerings from the bounty of the sea at Taiwan's most famous snacking destination. (p142)

Fengjia Make a pilgrimage to this frenetic market, the birthplace of many quirky yet popular snacks in Taiwan. (p219)

Traditional Festivals

Rising living standards and economic prosperity haven't killed folk culture in Taiwan: it just means there is more money than ever to fund extravagant and sometimes outlandish festivals.

Mazu Pilgrimage Taiwan's largest religious festival is a nine-day, 350km walk around the island for Mazu believers – which is almost everyone. (p231)

Burning of the Wang Yeh Boats A sublime week-long religious

Top: Longshan Temple (p235), Lukang

Bottom: Street snack, Raohe Street Night Market (p101), Taipei

festival that concludes with the torching of a 'plague ship' on a beach. (p292)

Yenshui Fireworks Festival Like Spain's Running of the Bulls, only they let fireworks loose here and you're not supposed to run from them. (p282)

Neimen Song Jiang Battle Array Martial arts meets religion; you'll find Taiwanese opera and roadside banqueting at this exhilarating annual extravaganza. (p259)

Keelung Ghost Festival A mesmerising month-long Taoist and Buddhist spectacle bookended by the symbolic opening and closing of the Gates of Hell. (p144)

Flying Fish Festival A virile coming-of-age ceremony celebrated in Lanyu during spring, with costumed young men engaging in a fishing contest. (p206)

Beaches

Nanao This wide-crescent bay has a black-sand beach and looks down a stunning coastline of high, steep cliffs. (p153)

Jibei Sand Tail The finest white-sand beach in Taiwan, with an ever-changing shape. (p337)

Shanshui Swim, surf, snorkel or just hang out at this superb beach next to a pretty village. (p329)

Baishawan Clear blue tropical waters, coconut palms and a white-crescent beach make this the south's top beach. (p141)

Wai'ao A long black-sand beach with the north's most happening surf scene. (p151)

Hot Springs

Taiwan has more than 100 hot springs ranging from common sulphur springs to rare seawater springs on an offshore volcanic isle.

Guanziling Soak in a rare and therapeutic mud hot spring in the mountains of Tainan. (p288)

Green Island Indulge yourself in an exceptional seawater hot spring by the ocean. (p201)

Lisong This wild spring, deep in a remote river valley, sprays down on you from a multi-coloured cliff face. (p193)

Beitou In the wooded mountains surrounding Taipei, these springs are reachable by a quick MRT ride. (p123)

Mountain Retreats

With over two-thirds of Taiwan being mountainous, there's a lot of space to get away from the crowds and the heat in summer.

Nanzhuang In the stunning foothills of the Snow Mountains, the villages here are a mix of Hakka, Taiwanese and indigenous. (p159)

Dasyueshan In the heart of Taiwan's pine-and-hemlock belt, this high-mountain reserve is a prime birding venue. (p223)

Retreats in Yuli Inspiring retreats, not necessarily right in the mountains but raised high enough to count, in scenic Yuli. (p191)

Alishan National Scenic Area Lures travellers with its indigenous culture, an alpine railway, ancient cedars and phenomenal sea of clouds. (p223)

Tea

The country has ideal conditions for growing tea, so it has the goods to satisfy everyone from the novice looking for a flavourful brew to the connoisseur willing to pay thousands of dollars for a few ounces of dry leaves

High mountain oolongs Grown above 1000m in moist but sunny conditions, these teas have a creamy texture and a lovely bouquet. (p114)

Oriental Beauty Unique to Taiwan, this sweet reddish-coloured tea has a fruity aroma and lacks all astringency. (p265)

Lei cha A field-worker's drink; rich and hearty with added puffed rice and pounded nuts. (p158)

Antique Assam Tea Farm Sun Moon Lake black-tea growers spent a decade reviving their industry. Drink straight without sugar or milk. (p244)

Unique Wildlife

Taiwan has a rate of endemism far higher than the world average, which means there are lots of critters and plants you won't find anywhere else.

Birds Taiwan's range of habitats supports over 650 species, including 150 endemic species. (p379)

Butterflies Taiwan isn't known as the 'Kingdom of Butterflies' for nothing – it's home to over 370 species; 56 of which are endemic. (p379)

Fish Check out the Formosan salmon: it never leaves the rivers of its birth. (p379)

Mammals Of 120 species, about 70% are endemic, including the Formosan rock monkey and the giant flying squirrel. (p378)

Month by Month

January

Generally wet and cool
in the north and dry and
sunny in the south. There
are few people travelling,
unless the week of Lunar
New Year falls in this month.

🏃 Southern Beaches

If you want to swim in the
winter months, head south
to Kenting National Park.
Beaches in the north, the
east and on Penghu will
be closed and the waters
choppy and chilly. (p295)

🎎 Lunar New Year

Held in January or Febru-
ary, Lunar New Year is
mostly a family affair until
the end, when spectacular
Lantern Festival activities
are held. There are bazaars
in cities like Kaohsiung,
lasting from around the
28th night of the old year to
the 3rd of the new. (p360)

February

Also very wet and cool
in the north and dry and
sunny in the south, with the
possibility of cold fronts
and sandstorms. Travelling
during the Lunar New Year
is difficult but usually easy
before and after.

🎎 Lantern Festival

One of the most popular
traditional festivals, with
concerts and light shows
across Taiwan (p360). However, the simplest of all, the
Pingxi sky lantern release
(p147), is the most spec-
tacular. On the same day,
Yenshui holds a massive
fireworks festival (p282),
and Taitung has its Bomb-
ing Master Handan (p197).

🎎 Mayasvi

The dramatic Tsou indig-
enous festival of Mayasvi
thanks gods and ancestral
spirits for their protection.
It's held on 15 February in
Tsou villages in Alishan.
(p224)

March

The start of spring
brings rain and rising
temperatures, but it's
still pleasantly cool in the
north. Tourists are few and
discounts are available.

🎎 Megaport

Southern Taiwan's wild and
raucous rock music festival
takes place on a weekend in
March at Pier-2 Art Centre,
right by the beautiful Kaohsiung Port. (p259)

🎎 Neimen Song
Jiang Battle Array

An exciting folk festival in
Kaohsiung that is mostly
martial arts, but also part
religion and part talent
show, supplemented by
much traditional-style
feasting. (p259)

April

It's usually wet and warm in
the north and wet and hot
in the south. Generally it's
low season for individual
travel but peak time for
Chinese tour groups.

☉ Youtong Flowers

The tall branching youtong
tree is found all over the
north. In spring its large
white flowers make entire
mountainsides look as if
they are dusted with snow.
Check them out at Sansia,
Sanyi, Taian Hot Springs
and Sun Moon Lake.

🎎 Baoan Folk
Arts Festival

Bao'an Temple won a
Unesco heritage award for
reviving traditional temple

fare, and this is your chance to see lion dancing, god parades, folk opera, fire walking and god birthday celebrations. The festival runs from early April to early June. (p74)

🎎 Spring Scream

Taiwan's largest and longest-running outdoor music event is held in the bright sunshine of Cijin Beach on Kaohsiung's Cijin Island. (p259)

🎎 Mazu Pilgrimage

This annual religious pilgrimage is Taiwan's premier folk event. Hundreds of thousands of believers follow a Mazu statue on a nine-day, 350km journey, with a million more participating in local events (www.dajiamazu.org.tw; p231)

🎎 Penghu Fireworks Festival

The two-month Penghu Fireworks Festival kicks off in April. It features fireworks, food and music two or three times a week over the coastal stretch of Makung and, occasionally, a couple of beaches further out. (p334)

👁 Blue Tears

The start of the 'Blue Tears' season in Matsu; the warmer months are best for viewing the legendary glowing algae, but you can spot them in April and May too.

May

It's the start of 'plum rain'; expect heavy afternoon showers. Travel picks up across the island and on outer islands.

🍴 Start of Mango Season

Taiwan's mangoes are rated highly for good reason: they are sweet, succulent, fleshy and nearly sublime. Prices vary each year depending on the rains. The season ends around September.

🎎 Welcoming the City God

A smaller-scale pilgrimage than the Mazu, Welcoming the City God brings unique and colourful parades across the charming landscape of Kinmen. (p311)

June

It's getting warmer everywhere – already low 30s in the south. Heavy showers are possible. Major destinations are crowded on weekends.

🎎 Dragon Boat Festival

Honouring the sacrifice of the poet-official Qu Yuan, the Dragon Boat Festival is celebrated all over Taiwan with flashy boat races on the local rivers and tasty sticky-rice dumplings. (p238)

🎎 Taipei Film Festival

One of the highest-profile international cultural events in Taipei, with 160 film from 40 countries. Venues include Huashan 1914 Creative Park and Zhongshan Hall. Held in June and July (www.taipeiff.org.tw).

July

Hot and humid everywhere. Heavy afternoon showers in the north, plus the

possibility of typhoons, which can disrupt travel. Major destinations are very busy, especially on weekends.

🎎 Taiwan International Balloon Fiesta

Held in Taitung County's stunning Luye Plateau (Luye), this two-month balloon festival is becoming one of the summer's biggest draws. (p194)

🎎 Indigenous Festivals

Every July and August a number of traditional indigenous festivals are held along the east coast. Themes include coming of age, ancestor worship, courting, harvest and displays of martial and hunting skills.

August

It's hot and humid but generally drier than July, with a high possibility of typhoons. Many student and family groups are travelling. Major destinations are very busy.

🎎 Ghost Month

Ghost Month is one of the most important traditional festivals in Taiwan. Events include the opening of the gates of hell, massive offerings to wandering spirits, and a water-lantern release. Biggest celebrations are held in Keelung. (p144)

👁 Day Lily Season

Orange day lilies are grown for food in the mountains of the east coast, and their blooming in late August and early September in places such as Sixty Stone

Mountain is an enchanting sight that attracts flower lovers and photographers. (p187)

September

The weather is cooling but it's still hot during the day. There's a high possibility of typhoons but generally dry and windy.

🏃 Windsurfing in Penghu

There's world-class windsurfing from September to March across the Penghu archipelago. Wind speeds can reach 40 to 50 knots, attracting windsurfers from all over the world. (p326)

🏃 Sun Moon Lake International Swimming Carnival

The world's largest mass open-water swim takes place every September in Taiwan's largest body of water, Sun Moon Lake. The 3.3km swim is not meant to be challenging, but fun. Expect tens of thousands of swimmers. (p246)

🎎 Confucius Birthday

Held on 28 September with elaborate early-morning celebrations at Confucius Temples across Taiwan. Those at Taipei's Confucius Temple are the most impressive. (p75)

🎎 Taipei Arts Festival

A month-long extravaganza of theatre and performance art by Taiwan and international artists, the Taipei Arts Festival runs from August to September or from September to October. (p86)

October

October has the most stable weather across the island if there's no typhoon – dry, warm and windy. It's the best time of year in the north. There are few travellers except for tour groups.

🎎 Taichung Jazz Festival

Taichung Jazz Festival is a nine-day jazz fest that attracts fans from all over Asia with its strong local and international line-ups. (p217)

👁 Grey-faced Buzzard Migration

Tens of thousands of buzzards, and other raptors, appear over the Hengchun Peninsula (Kenting National Park) during autumn for the grey-faced buzzard migration, described as one of the world's great avian migrations. The birds appear in Taiwan again in the spring over Changhua (www.birdingintaiwan.com/gray-facedbuzzard.htm).

🎎 Burning of the Wang Yey Boats

Held for one week every three years (autumn 2021, 2024 etc), this spectacular display of folk faith concludes with a 14m-long wooden boat being burned to the ground on the beach. Attended by tens of thousands, it's both a celebration and a solemn ritual. (p292)

🏃 Penghu Triathlon

An annual Ironman race (www.ironman.com) and a short-course triathlon held in Makung. The archipelago's famously strong winds in winter makes this one of the tougher races in Asia.

December

Cooling in the north but still warm during the day; there's the possibility of cold fronts and wet, humid weather. In the south it's dry with temperatures in the 20s. The travel season is generally low except for tour groups.

🎎 Art Kaohsiung

Southern Taiwan's only international art fair, Art Kaohsiung lasts approximately three days and showcases the works of mostly Taiwan and Asian artists. (p261)

🎎 Kaohsiung Lion Dance Competition

Teams from Taiwan, China, Malaysia, Singapore and around the world compete in various traditional temple dance routines. This lively and colourful contest is held in Kaohsiung once every two years. (p262)

👁 Purple Butterfly Valleys

This mass overwintering of purple butterflies in the valleys stretching across southern Taiwan can be seen in Maolin Recreation Area from December to March during the morning hours. (p381)

🏃 Hot Springs

You can, of course, visit hot springs year-round but the days are cooling, especially in the mountains where many springs are located. It's a good chance to avoid the big crowds in January and February at outdoor pools.

Itineraries

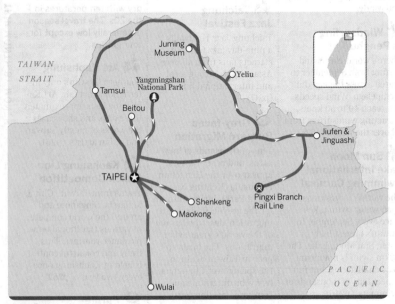

1 WEEK Taipei and the North

Start with four days in **Taipei** being awestruck by the National Palace Museum collection and sensorially overloaded at Longshan and Bao'an Temples, as well as shopping and snacking at night markets and local shops. Activities around Taipei abound. If you like tea, take the gondola to mountainous **Maokong** and experience a traditional teahouse. For hot springs, historic **Beitou** is just an MRT ride away. Or spend an afternoon on a stinky tofu tour along the restored old street of **Shenkeng**. Then rent a bike and ride along the river paths in Taipei or hike the trails in **Yangmingshan National Park** or **Wulai**, a mountainous district with natural swimming pools.

On day five take a bus further afield to the old mining towns of **Jiufen and Jinguashi** for sightseeing and a little hike. The next day head to nearby Ruifang and catch the **Pingxi Branch Rail Line** down an 18km wooded gorge to photograph the old frontier villages and hike paths cut into steep crags.

On day seven round off the trip: head back up the coast, stopping at the bizarre rocks of **Yeliu** and renowned sculptures at **Juming Museum**. From **Tamsui**, a seaside town with beautiful colonial houses, the MRT takes you back to Taipei.

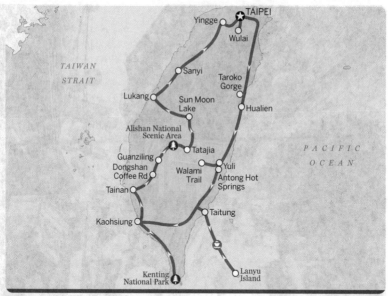

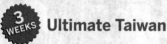 **Ultimate Taiwan**

Start with a few days in **Taipei** to see the sights and catch the groove of this dynamic Asian capital. It has one of the best Chinese art collections in the world, a thriving street-food and coffee scene, a living folk-art heritage, and some world-class cycling and hiking in **Wulai** and other on-the-doorstep locations.

Then hop on a train to **Hualien** and spend two days wandering the dazzling marble-walled **Taroko Gorge**. More scenic delights await down Hwy 9, which runs through the lush Rift Valley. Take a train to **Yuli** and hike the nearby **Walami Trail**, an old patrol route running deep into subtropical rainforest, then recuperate at **Antong Hot Springs**. Next, head to **Taitung** and catch a flight or ferry to **Lanyu**, an enchanting tropical island with pristine coral reefs and a unique indigenous culture.

Back on the mainland, another train ride – across Taiwan's fertile southern tip – takes you to **Kaohsiung**, Taiwan's buzzing second-largest city, where the best of urban Taiwan mingles with southern hospitality. Check out the museums and the uplifting Pier-2 Art Centre, and indulge in excellent seafood, followed by a night of jazz. Then for beaches or scootering along beautiful coastline, head down to **Kenting National Park**.

Continue by train up the coast to the old capital of **Tainan** for a couple of days of temple touring and snacking on local delicacies. Rent a vehicle for the drive up the winding **Dongshan Coffee Road** then spend the evening in rare mud hot springs in **Guanziling**. The following day continue up into the wild expanse of mountain ranges in the **Alishan National Scenic Area**. Spend some time touring postcard-perfect Alishan. If there's time, hike around **Tatajia** in the shadow of Yushan, Taiwan's highest mountain.

From Alishan or Yushan, take the bus to **Sun Moon Lake** the following morning. At the lake, stop to sample oolong tea and maybe catch a boat tour. Heading north, fans of traditional arts and crafts will enjoy the following days' stops in **Lukang**, home to the magnificent Longshan Temple and many traditional crafts; and **Yingge**, a town devoted to ceramics, before returning to Taipei.

Top: Jiufen (p143)

Bottom: Lotus Pond (p254), Kaohsiung

SEAN PAVONE / SHUTTERSTOCK ©

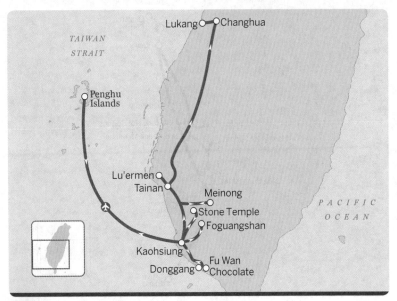

2 WEEKS — Explore Southern Taiwan

Start your tour in **Kaohsiung**. Spend a few days here visiting exquisite private museums, exploring industry-turned-art-spaces, flea markets, historic neighbourhoods and music dives, indulging in seafood meals and drinking cocktails, and relaxing on Cijin Island. Make side trips to the centre of Buddhism in southern Taiwan, **Foguangshan**, and to the fantastical **Stone Temple** in the northern district of Tianliao.

Next head to the fishing port of **Donggang** in Pingtung County by taking the Kenting Express to Dapeng Station. Pay a visit to **Fu Wan Chocolate** to tour the cacao farm and stuff your face with award-winning chocolates. Return to Kaohsiung and fly to the **Penghu Islands** for a few days of windswept fun – sightseeing, water sports, island hopping and feasting on seafood.

Return to Kaohsiung and take the high-speed train to **Tainan**. Take it easy for a few days checking out museums, ancient forts and Taiwan's oldest temples. Alternate sightseeing with cafe crawling, souvenir shopping and snacking. End your nights with cocktails and live music. If you're into history and old temples, make a side trip to **Lu'ermen** for the Luer'men Mazu Temple and the Orthodox Lu'ermen Mazu Temple.

From Tainan, cab it to the bucolic Hakka village of **Meinong**. Stay in a courtyard house for a couple of days, and spend your time cycling in paddy fields, visiting traditional craftspeople and historic sights, and eating your fill of Hakka fare.

Take the bus to **Changhua**. There are a couple of laudable temples downtown, but mainly use Changhua as a base to visit the historic town of **Lukang**. Spend a full day in Lukang, sampling traditional cakes and wandering through cobbled streets, majestic temples and grand mansions.

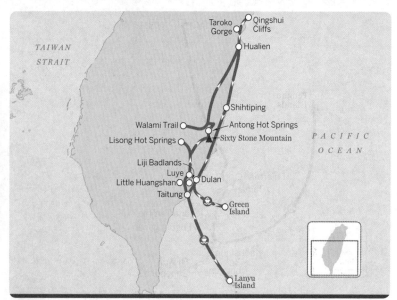

The East Coast Loop

2 WEEKS

The best way to negotiate this route is to have your own vehicle. You can also hire a car and a driver. From **Hualien**, a low-key coastal town with good eating and seaside parks, it's a quick hop to **Taroko Gorge**, Taiwan's premier natural attraction. After a couple of days hiking, biking and marvelling at the marble walls, head up Hwy 11 to the **Qingshui Cliffs**, among the world's highest.

Return to Hualien and take Hwy 11 to **Taitung**. It's three days on a bike alongside some of Taiwan's best coastal scenery; otherwise, rent a car or scooter. Plan to stop often, but in particular at **Shihtiping** for seafood and jaw-dropping views, and **Dulan**, Taiwan's funkiest town, for an art scene centred on a reclaimed sugar factory, or for surfing when the waves are up. From Taitung, catch a ferry or flight to **Green Island** and/or **Lanyu** for a couple of days of snorkelling, hot springs and exploring the island culture of the indigenous Tao.

To head back north, take Hwy 11乙 (aka Hwy 11B) west and connect with 東45 (aka East 45) and later County Rd 197 for a scenic drive up the Beinan River valley, with the crumbling **Liji Badlands** on one side and the jagged cliffs of **Little Huangshan** on the other.

The 197 drops you off on Hwy 9, near **Luye**, a bucolic pineapple- and tea-growing region with a stunning plateau. Just north, connect with the South Cross-Island Hwy for some yodel-inducing high-mountain scenery, and the chance to hike to **Lisong**, a wild hot spring that cascades down a multicoloured cliff face.

For more scenic eye candy, stop at the flower fields of **Sixty Stone Mountain**. Spend the night at **Antong Hot Springs** so you are fully rested for a cycle the next day out to historic **Walami Trail**, a Japanese-era patrol route.

Opportunities to indulge in local indigenous foods are numerous along this route. You'll be well fed for the final stretch back to Hualien, which you should do along quiet County Rd 193.

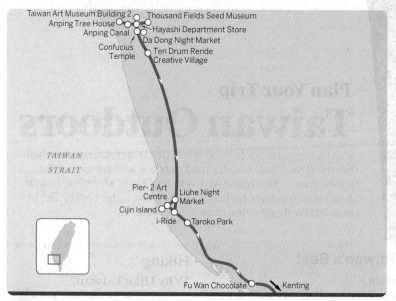

 Southern Taiwan with Kids

Southern Taiwan with its tropical weather, proximity to the sea and colourful history can be a wondrous place for children. This route explores the child-friendly side of eclectic Kaohsiung, historic Tainan and leafy Pingtung.

Spend a couple of days in Tainan. Make an appointment with the eye-opening **Thousand Fields Seed Museum** a few days before your arrival. Head east to central Tainan and visit the modern **Tainan Art Museum Building 2**. Its criss-crossing staircases, multiple entrances and airy atrium make it a pleasant space to explore when you tire of the art. There are plenty of fruit stalls and cafes around this area. **Hayashi Department Store** has beautifully packaged Taiwanese snacks, handicrafts and stationery. Be sure to check out the art deco lift. The **Confucius Temple** nearby has a lovely park where the dogs are timid and the squirrels bold; bring nuts. For dinner **Da Dong Night Market** has an assortment of delicious options.

Next morning, go south to **Ten Drum Rende Creative Village**. Watch drum performances, go on long slides and rooftop swings, and launch a sky lantern in a chimney. Have something to eat in the cafe. Head back to Tainan proper and explore **Anping Tree House** and the scenery. A cruise on the **Anping Canal** is an option if you have the energy. Head to Kaohsiung and stay two days. Mornings can be spent on virtual-reality theatre **i-Ride,** and the mechanical and laser thrills of **Taroko Park**. **Pier-2 Art Centre** and **Cijin Island** are better visited in the afternoon. Depending on your schedule, you can have lunch at Taroko Park or Pier-2. Cijin Island is great for coastal cycling for the whole family, and swimming and watching the sunset on the beach. Kaohsiung has plenty of excellent restaurants, but for range of options, you can't beat **Liuhe Night Market**.

From Kaohsiung head to **Fu Wan Chocolate** in the fishing port of Donggang in Pingtung. A tour and shopping at the chocolate farm's boutique should take a couple of hours. You can spend the night in one of the villas here, but can also head straight to **Kenting** for two days of sun and beach, and some sightseeing thrown in.

Plan Your Trip
Taiwan Outdoors

With its rugged mountainous spine, dense forest cover over half the island, vast backcountry road network, which includes the highest pass in Northeast Asia, and 1566km of shoreline, Taiwan abounds with venues for hiking, cycling and water sports. Get to know Ilha Formosa at the pace it deserves.

Taiwan's Best

Hiking

There are hundreds of well-maintained natural trails in Taiwan. Some of the best low-altitude trails are within an hour of Taipei. The best high-mountain trails are in Yushan and Shei-pa National Parks. In most cases, you don't need a guide.

Cycling

Taiwan has good roads with wide shoulders in popular biking areas. There are also hundreds of kilometres of bike-only routes around cities. Bikes are allowed on the Mass Rapid Transit (MRT), trains and some buses, and day and multiday rental programs are widely available.

Hot Springs

Springs are located all over the island. The most accessible are in Beitou, reachable by Taipei MRT.

Water Sports

The offshore islands are top spots for diving. Hundreds of clean mountain streams make the island an ideal river-tracing destination. There is beginner-to-advanced surfing around northern Taiwan, the east coast and Kenting National Park. In winter, head to Penghu for world-class windsurfing.

Hiking

Why Hike Taiwan?

Taiwan's landscape is striking, and with multiple biogeographical zones ranging from tropical to alpine, the flora and fauna is ever-changing. It's possible to hike year-round on a well-developed trail network from sea level to 3952m. You don't need a guide for most hikes, and it's possible to go for days without seeing others. National park trails feature inexpensive cabins with water and bedding (but usually no food).

National Parks & Other Hiking Venues

Over 50% of Taiwan is mountainous and heavily forested, and about 20% is protected land divided between national parks, forest recreation areas, reserves and various state forests.

National parks and forest recreation areas (FRAs) have excellent trails. Within the boundaries of each you'll find a visitor information centre and often a small village with basic accommodation and food. Paved trails lead to scenic spots, while unspoiled areas with natural paths may be further into the park. Forestry reserves may have good trails, but usually offer few facilities for hikers.

Many trails are also maintained at the regional level and offer excellent day and sometimes overnight hikes. Both national and regional trails are usually signposted in English and Chinese.

Planning Your Hike

You can hike year-round, but the best weather is from September to December and March to May. Midweek is best for popular trails, but many are never busy. Winter hiking above the snowline is possible, though Yushan National Park requires that a team leader be certified for winter hiking. Shei-pa National Park simply asks to see that hikers are adequately prepared (such as having crampons and an ice pick).

Weather

Afternoon fogs are common year-round, as are thunderstorms in summer. Typhoons affect the island from early summer to late autumn, while monsoon rains batter the island in May and June. Obviously you should not go out hiking during storms or typhoons, but also avoid going to the mountains in the few days afterwards as landslides, swollen rivers and streams can wash out roads and trails. Always be prepared for a change of weather and for the weather in the mountains to be different from the weather in the city.

Natural Disasters

Earthquakes are common all over the island and are especially strong along the east coast – don't hike for a few days after a big earthquake. Taiwan is also prone to massive landslides (it has been called the landslide capital of the world) and huge sections of trail are often washed out after earthquakes and typhoons. Trails can be closed for months or even years (sometimes forever) – don't attempt trails that have been closed.

Plants & Animals

Māo yǎo rén (貓咬人, cat bite people) Taiwan's version of poison ivy. Grows at mid elevations.

Rabies In 2013 Taiwan had its first rabies outbreak in 50 years. At the time of writing, the disease was limited to ferret-badgers, bats and house shrews. The risk of getting rabies is low unless you'll be spending lots of time in the wilderness or around such animals.

Snakes Most are harmless but Taiwan has its share of deadly venomous snakes, which often have triangular-shaped heads, very distinctive patterns, thin necks and tapered tails. Large, fat python-like snakes are usually harmless rodent eaters. You won't find snakes at higher elevations. For more, check out www.snakesoftaiwan.com.

EMERGENCY PHONE NUMBERS

Even in high mountains it's often possible to get mobile-phone reception, but remember that phones lose power quickly in the cold and in areas with low signals. Hiking maps highlight good reception areas. If you can't communicate by voice, try texting.

➡ Basic emergency numbers: ☑119 or ☑112

➡ Dial ☑112 to connect to available signals, even if your mobile phone doesn't have a SIM card

➡ National Rescue Command Centre: ☑0800-077 795

➡ Ministry of Defence Rescue Centre: ☑02-2737 3395

➡ Emergency radio frequencies: 145MHz, 149.25MHz, 148.74MHz or 148.77MHz

Ticks A possible problem at lower altitudes, even around cities. Be careful in summer and always check yourself after hiking.

Wasps Most active in autumn, these dangerous insects kill and hospitalise people every year. In danger areas you will often see warning signs. Avoid wearing perfumes and bright clothing.

Getting Lost

It's easy to get lost hiking in Taiwan if you are not on a well-made trail. The forest is extremely thick in places, and trails are sometimes little more than foot-wide cuts across a steep mountainside with many unmarked branches. Trails also quickly become overgrown (some need teams to come in every year with machetes just to make them passable). Never leave a trail, or attempt to make your own. If you plan to hike alone, let someone know.

Lower-Altitude Trails: Below 3000m

There are low-altitude trails all over Taiwan. Trails run through subtropical and tropical jungles, broadleaved forests, temperate woodlands and along coastal bluffs. Some are a few hours' long, while others go on for days. All three major cities – Taipei,

Kaohsiung and Taichung – have mountains and trails either within the city limits or just outside.

Permits are not needed for most low-altitude hikes, except for areas that restrict the number of hikers who can enter per day. For these areas you may need to register at a police checkpoint on the way into the area – this is a simple process but you'll need a passport.

Great places to hike include Wulai (p137), Maokong (p128), the Pingxi Branch Rail Line (p150) and Yangmingshan National Park (p127) in the north; and Taroko National Park (p172) in the east.

What to Pack

➡ Clothes made of lightweight moisture-wicking material are best. Gortex is not much use at lower altitudes because of the humidity and heat (a small umbrella is more useful if it rains).

➡ Running shoes are better on jungle trails and ridge walks because of their superior grip.

➡ Plenty of water (at least 3L to 4L per day if hiking in the warmer months).

➡ Also bring a torch (flashlight); trails are notorious for taking longer than you think.

Trail Conditions

Trail conditions vary greatly, from a foot-wide slice through dense jungle to a 2m-wide path with suspension bridges over streams that was once used as a transport route. Most trails have signposts and map boards, but if you encounter overgrown sections it's best to turn back. Few lower-altitude trails are flat for any distance: many, in fact, are so steep that ropes or ladders (always pre-existing) are needed to climb certain sections.

While it is common in most parts of the world to hike 3km to 4km an hour, on Taiwan's trails 1km an hour progress is not unusual because of the extremely steep conditions.

Water

On some trails you can use small streams and springs as a water source (treat before drinking), but it is advisable to bring what you need for the day.

Sleeping

Camping on the trail is mostly a DIY thing (there are few established sites on trails). Some forest recreation areas and national parks forbid it at lower elevations.

Transport

Public transport (usually bus) is available to the majority of lower-altitude trails.

High-Mountain Trails: Above 3000m

Taiwan has some genuinely world-class high-mountain hikes and anyone in decent shape can conquer them. Few demand any technical skills (in part because rougher sections already have ropes and ladders in place), but many routes are closed in the winter months or require a certified leader. You need to apply in advance for permits (p37) for most high-mountain trails.

Trails are generally clear of overgrowth, have good bridges over streams and have frequent distance and direction markers. However, landslides and washouts of sections are very common, so always be prepared for a bit of scrambling. For sleeping, there are usually sturdy unstaffed cabins and campgrounds.

PRACTICAL TIPS

➡ Don't be tempted to head to the summit of a mountain in light clothing and with limited supplies simply because the weather looks good. Always be prepared with wet- and cold-weather gear and plenty of food and water. Deaths are not uncommon on Taiwan's high mountains and they are often related to hikers being unprepared for fast-changing conditions.

➡ When it comes to a good night's sleep in a cabin, snoring can be a terrible nuisance, as can Taiwanese hikers' habit of getting up at 3am so they can catch the sunrise on the peak. Bring earplugs!

➡ Ribbons are placed on trails by hiking clubs to indicate the correct path to take on a complicated or easily overgrown system. If you aren't sure where to go, following the ribbons is usually a sound approach.

HIGH-MOUNTAIN PERMITS

Permits are largely a holdover from martial-law days, but they do prevent overcrowding on the trails and let authorities know who is in the mountains in case of an emergency (such as an approaching typhoon). Restrictions have eased in recent years (eg you no longer need a guide and solo hikers can apply), but if you are caught without a permit you will be fined. If a rescue is required you will have to pay the full costs. Note that everything mentioned here is subject to change.

First off, permits are required to hike the high mountains. Anyone can apply (foreigners, locals, groups or individuals), but the process is complicated and many people pay to have the permits done for them. Permits are nontransferable and valid only for the date for which you apply. If a typhoon cancels your hike, permits cannot be changed to another date (you have to reapply). Note that Taroko National Park only allows Taiwanese to apply for permits (though foreigners can join a local hiking group).

There are two kinds of permits that may be required, depending on where you hike: national park permits (入園, rù yuán) for entering restricted areas in a national park and police permits (入山, rù shān) for entering a restricted high-mountain area. Hiking in national parks requires both kinds of permits. Non-national-park hikes usually require only a police permit.

National park permits must be applied for at least seven days in advance (for the Yushan main route, at least a month in advance). It is best to apply online, although the process is tedious. National parks will usually also process police permits for you. The Shei-pa National Park website (www.spnp.gov.tw) has a sample of a completed form in English. The bilingual website npm.cpami.gov.tw/en has details on the requirements of all the trails, as well as instructions on how to apply for a national park permit.

Police permits can be applied for at the Ministry of the Interior (www.moi.gov.tw), at a police station in the same county as the hike, or at the police squad within the national park. You'll need triplicate copies of your itinerary written out, the trail map, a name list of group members (including their dates of birth and emergency contacts) and a national park permit (you must have this before applying for a police permit). Make sure you have ID and/or your passport.

Paths generally begin in a dense mixed forest that turns coniferous higher up. The treeline ends around 3300m to 3600m. After this, short Yushan cane spreads across the highlands until the very highest elevations. Alpine lakes are surprisingly rare. High-altitude terrain tends to be strikingly rugged with deep V-shaped valleys and steeply sloped mountain ranges. Long exposed ridgelines are common obstacles to cross.

Some excellent hikes include the Yushan Peaks (p213), Snow Mountain (p163), the Holy Ridge (p162), the Batongguan historic trail (p214), Jiaming Lake (p192), Hehuanshan (p242), Dabajianshan (p161) and Beidawushan (p301).

The Top 100 (百岳, Bǎiyuè) are all peaks over 3000m and considered special or significant because of elevation, beauty, geology or prominence. Taiwanese hikers dream of completing the full list (available at Wikipedia).

What to Pack

➡ Wet- and cold-weather gear is essential even in summer. Because of altitude gains of 2000m to 3000m, most hikes take you through a range of climatic conditions. Temperatures can get down close to 0°C even in summer, and in autumn and winter to -10°C at night.

➡ Bring all the food and snacks you will need, and cooking gear.

➡ Also take a walking stick. Trails are steep and these help with balance and to spread the weight of a pack.

Trail Conditions

In general, high-mountain trails are well made and clear to follow. Solid metal or wood bridges will be in place where needed. Almost all trails require a great deal of steep uphill climbing, often more than 1000m of elevation gain a day. Many trails require at least some rope or chain climbs (these will be fixed in place and are generally not especially demanding).

Water

Most high-altitude trails will have a water source (eg streams or rainwater-collecting tanks at cabins). Maps show water sources, but always ask at the national park headquarters for the latest; they sometimes dry up in winter. Water should be filtered or chemically treated before drinking.

Sleeping

Cabins and campgrounds are available on most trails. Cabins can range from boxy concrete structures to stylish wood A-frames offering bunk beds with thick foam mattresses, solar lighting and eco-toilets. Water sources are usually available at the cabin or nearby. With the exception of Paiyun Cabin on Yushan, cabins are usually unstaffed and do not provide sleeping bags, meals or snacks.

Campgrounds are flat clearings in the forest (sometimes the sites of former police outposts). Water sources are sometimes available.

Transport

There are public buses to Shei-pa, Yushan, and Taroko national parks, as well as Hehuanshan. For most other hiking areas you will need your own vehicle or to arrange transport.

Need to Know

Websites, Blogs & Books

➡ The government-operated Forest Recreation Areas website (www.forest.gov.tw) is comprehensive.

➡ An expat writer who's published books on hiking in Taiwan runs Taiwan Off the Beaten Track (www.taiwanoffthebeatentrack.com).

Maps

➡ For northern Taiwan maps, Taiwan Jiaotong Press (台北縣市近郊山圖) publishes a series of 14 maps at a scale of 1:25,000, covering the north from Sansia/Wulai. These are available at mountain-equipment shops around the Taipei Main Station. These shops will also carry variously scaled topographic maps of popular trails.

➡ National park maps are available at park visitor centres or mountain-equipment shops. Most national park websites have basic maps (in English) of the climbing routes. Topographic maps may be available at national park bookshops.

Hiking & Tour Agencies

➡ 523 Mountaineering Association (www.523org.blogspot.com) is a nonprofit that offers free day hikes around Taipei.

➡ Taiwan Adventures (www.taiwan-adventures. com) organises hiking trips around Taiwan, including free hikes. Also offers mobile apps with photos.

Cycling

Taiwan is one of Asia's top cycling destinations. And don't the locals know it! Cycling fever struck the island around 2005, and all ages and levels of society now participate in the sport. You'll find yourself well treated by fellow cyclists and also passers-by.

Much of the riding focus is on the more sparsely populated east coast, but there are excellent routes everywhere. In addition to world-class road cycling minutes from urban centres such as Taipei, Taiwan has challenging high-mountain and cross-island routes, as well as leisurely paths through rice and tea fields with no end of dramatic mountain and coastal scenery to enjoy.

Planning Your Bike Trip

The best time to cycle in Taiwan is from September to December for generally good weather island-wide. Winter in the south and coastal west sees warm and dry conditions. Riding after a typhoon (assuming there has been no road damage) is usually a good way to ensure clear weather. Other than directly during a typhoon or sandstorm, you can ride all year.

Sleeping & Eating

Quality and reasonably priced accommodation is easy to find everywhere on the island. Hostels hotels are used to cyclists and will find a place to store your bike safely. There are also plenty of campgrounds on the east coast. Cheap restaurants are everywhere in rural areas and only on the cross-island highways would you ride more than a few hours without finding food or lodging.

Convenience stores are ubiquitous, again except on cross-island roads. They provide drinks, decent food and washrooms. On popular cycling routes, they usually have bicycle pumps and repair kits.

WHERE TO CYCLE

Taiwan has three types of cycling venues: bike-only paths, roads and mountain-biking trails. Mountain biking is quiet, but there are still popular routes around Taipei. Bike-only paths are concentrated in Taipei, Kaohsiung and down the east coast. There are about 1000km of such paths and the network is growing as the government works on a round-the-island path. Roads in Taiwan are generally in good condition, with wide shoulders (often marked as exclusively for bikes and scooters) on many popular routes.

LOCATION	CYCLING OPPORTUNITIES	DESCRIPTION	CYCLING ROUTES
Northern Taiwan	plenty	Road cycling either along steep mountain or flat coastal routes; hundreds of kilometres of riverside paths in Taipei; some mountain-biking trails	North Cross-Island Hwy, Wulai, Hwy 9, Hwy 2, Taipei, Hsinchu
Eastern Taiwan & Taroko National Park	plenty	Range of routes along the coast, in inland valleys and up rugged gorges; some exceptionally challenging rides up to the high mountains	Hwy 11, Hwy 9, Taroko Gorge, Hwy 14 (Mugua River Gorge), County Rds 193 and 197
Western Taiwan	plenty	Mostly road cycling on mountain routes in the interior; challenging grade in many areas	Sun Moon Lake circuit, Hwy 21, Daxueshan FRA road, Houfeng Bicycle Path
Southern Taiwan	plenty	Mostly gentle road riding on quiet country routes; some coastal riding and mountain biking on old trails	County Rd 199, Dongshan Coffee Rd
Taiwan Strait Islands	fair	Mostly flat coastal ring roads; often windy conditions; difficult to transport bikes to islands but some have free rentals	Refer to individual islands

On many popular cycling routes the local police station functions as a rest stop for cyclists. Inside you are welcome to use the bicycle pump, repair kit, water and rest area. Some stations even allow camping out the back.

Bikes on Public Transport

➡ You can take a bagged folding bike on practically any form of transport.

➡ The government-run Kuo Kuang Bus Company (www.kingbus.com.tw), and most county bus companies, will usually take a full-sized bagged bike as luggage (for half the fare).

➡ Train policy on full-sized bikes is confusing and inconsistent. For longer distances, it's still best to ship the bike (remove anything that might break or fall off and bag the bike or secure it with cardboard) to your destination train station one day before. You only need to give your phone number, ID number, the value of the bike and the destination in Chinese. You cannot ship from Taipei Main Station – go to Wanhua or Songshan.

➡ The baggage room is called xínglǐ fáng (行李房). Tell the attendant: Wǒ yào tuōyùn jiǎotàchē (我要托運腳踏車; I want to ship a bike).

➡ You can take a nonbagged bike on designated slow local trains, and a bagged (full-sized) bike on any local train. Some fast Tze-chiang trains have a 12th car with bike storage so you can ride on the same train as your bike. Visit www.railway.gov.tw and look for the bike symbol next to the schedule (note that the English website is not as comprehensive as the Chinese).

➡ The High Speed Rail (HSR) network allows you to take bagged bikes on as luggage.

Dangers & Annoyances

Feral dogs are common in the mountains. If one runs after you, the best approach is simply to stop, place your bike in front of you, and remain calm or indifferent. Dogs may snarl and bark, but they will quickly grow tired if you don't give them any reason to get excited. Throwing rocks or squirting dogs with water is counterproductive. More extreme measures can result in a fine and/or social-media shaming.

Drivers are used to scooters so you won't encounter aggression for being a two-wheeled vehicle on the road. However, in Taiwan general driving skills are poor and vehicles cutting across lanes when rounding bends, passing on the outside lane on blind corners and driving too fast and carelessly are all common potential hazards for cyclists.

Need to Know

Websites & Blogs

➡ Check out Taiwan in Cycles (www.taiwanincycles.blogspot.tw) for a serious cyclist's interesting commentary.

Renting Bikes

➡ City bike-rental programs are available in Taipei (www.youbike.com.tw) and Kaohsiung (p258), while day rentals are available in many towns down the east coast, on the outer islands, and in rural tourist areas.

➡ For multiday rentals, Giant Bicycles (www.giantcyclingworld.com) has the best program: three days for NT$1200, then NT$200 for each additional day. These are good-quality road bikes and include saddle bags and repair kits. As it's best to reserve in advance, you'll need someone to call first in Chinese.

➡ For mountain-bike rentals (and weekend rides) around Taipei check out Alan's Mountain Bike (p83).

Tours

➡ In Motion Asia (www.inmotionasia.com) is a foreign-run company focusing on small group mountain- and road-biking tours into remote areas. Giant Adventure (www.giantcyclingworld.com) also runs a program of round-the-island trips with full backup.

Water Sports

Water sports are popular at beaches on the north coast, the east coast and in Kenting in southern Taiwan. The Japanese influence has spawned interest in river tracing and surfing. Scuba diving, snorkelling and windsurfing are less popular but top notch.

General dangers to be aware of include the fact that Taiwan has no continental shelf. The deep blue sea is just offshore, and dangerous currents and rip tides flow around the island. Do not swim at a beach unless you know for certain it is safe.

Hot Springs

Taiwan is ranked among the world's top 15 hot-spring sites and harbours a great variety of springs, including sulphur springs, cold springs, mud springs and even seabed hot springs. Hot springing was first popularised under the Japanese and many of the most famous resort areas were developed in the early 20th century. In the late 1990s and early 21st century hot-spring fever struck Taiwan a second time and most of the hotels and resorts you'll find today are of recent vintage.

Before entering public hot springs, shower thoroughly using soap and shampoo. Mixed pools require a bathing suit (there are no nude mixed pools in Taiwan). Bathing caps must be worn in all public pools.

Random health checks show overuse at many hot-spring areas, with hotels and resorts often diluting natural hot-spring water, and even recycling water between bathers. This is common around the world, even in Japan, and if you want to avoid it, remember that, in general, the less developed the area, the purer the water quality. In popular spots go midweek when there are fewer bathers.

Wild Springs

There are still probably a hundred wild springs deep in the mountains. Some can be hiked into relatively easily while others require several days. A wild spring worth checking is Lisong (p193) on the South Cross-Island Hwy.

Hotels & Resorts

The best developed springs are set in forested valleys, in meadows or overlooking the ocean. Private rooms and public spas in these areas are usually both available. Rooms featuring wood or stone tubs can be basic or very luxurious and are rented out by the hour (NT$600 to NT$1500). Rooms with beds can also be rented for the night (NT$2800 to NT$9000). Public spas are sometimes just a few stone-lined pools, but some are a whole bathing complex. The average cost for unlimited time at a public spa is NT$300 to NT$800.

Check out hot springs in Beitou (p124), Yangmingshan National Park (p127), Wulai (p137) and Guanziling (p288).

WHAT'S IN THE WATER?

Water bubbling up from underground picks up a variety of minerals that offer a veritable bouquet of supposed health benefits (some more believable than others), according to aficionados.

WATER TYPE	BENEFICIAL FOR	WHERE TO FIND
alkaline	making good coffee	Antong
alkaloid carbonic	nervousness, improving skin tone	Tai'an
ferrous	conceiving a male child	Ruisui
mud spring	improving skin tone	Guanziling
sodium bicarbonate	general feelings of malaise, broken bones	Jiaoxi
sodium carbonate	improving skin tone	Wulai
sulphurous	arthritis, sore muscles	Beitou

River Tracing

River tracing (suòxī) is the sport of walking and climbing up a riverbed. At the beginning stages it involves merely walking on slippery rocks. At advanced stages it can involve climbing up and down waterfalls. Taiwan has hundreds of fast clean streams and rivers, some just minutes from the cities. There are no dangerous animals in the water and the landscape is exotic.

The general season for tracing is June to September. On the hottest days of summer many people simply trace up to deep waterfall-fed pools for swimming. Be aware that afternoon thundershowers in summer are common in the north and central mountains, and water levels can rise fast.

River-tracing sites worth checking out include Wulai, which is one of the best venues for amateurs (it has deep river pools for swimming, endless waterfalls and a jungle landscape), and various locations in Hualien, including the Golden Canyon, a full-day trip into a beautiful gorge. Contact Hualien Outdoors (p175) for guided tours.

Equipment required for river tracing includes a life jacket, a helmet, ropes or climbing slings, and a waterproof bag. Felt-bottomed rubber shoes are necessary for gripping the slippery rock – you can pick up a pair for between NT$300 and NT$400 at a mountain-equipment shop. Neoprene can be useful even in summer as it can get chilly in higher mountain streams, especially when you've been in the water all day.

Scuba & Snorkelling

Taiwan has an excellent range of venues for scuba diving and snorkelling, with good visibility and warm waters year-round in the south. There are well-preserved deep- and shallow-water coral reefs off Lanyu, Green Island, Kenting and the east coast. Green Island alone has 200 types of soft and hard corals and plenty of tropical reef fish. It also has a yearly hammerhead shark migration during the winter months (for advanced divers only).

In the north there's good diving from Yeliu down to Ilan, including off Turtle Island. With the Kuroshio Current (north-flowing ocean current) running close to shore, you'll find an intriguing mix of tropical and temperate sea life, including some gorgeous soft coral patches.

In Taiwan, currents are strong and have been known to sweep divers out to sea. Exits on shore can be hard. The biggest problem, though, is usually sunburn, so wear a shirt with SPF protection even when snorkelling. Sharks and jellyfish are not usually a problem but caution is advised.

The best time to dive is during the shoulder season, which runs before and after summer. Winter is also a good time to escape the crowds, with visibility in the south and the east still very good (20m).

Contact Taiwan Dive (p202) for serious dives, such as going out to watch the hammerhead shark migration.

Windsurfing

Taiwan has two main windsurfing venues: Penghu, and the west coast of Hsinchu and Miaoli counties. Penghu is Asia's top-rated windsurfing destination and the windiest place in the northern hemisphere during autumn. The unique topography of the archipelago keeps the waves down and advanced windsurfers can reach some impressive speeds.

Taiwan Outdoors

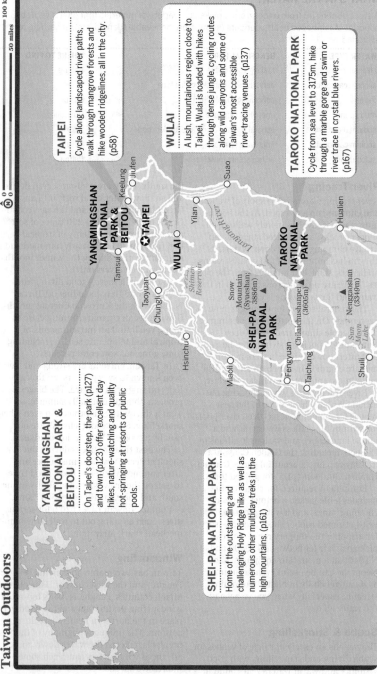

TAIPEI

Cycle along landscaped river paths, walk through mangrove forests and hike wooded ridgelines, all in the city. (p58)

WULAI

A lush, mountainous region close to Taipei, Wulai is loaded with hikes through dense jungle, cycling routes along wild canyons and some of Taiwan's most accessible river-tracing venues. (p137)

TAROKO NATIONAL PARK

Cycle from sea level to 3175m, hike through a marble gorge and swim or river trace in crystal blue rivers. (p167)

YANGMINGSHAN NATIONAL PARK & BEITOU

On Taipei's doorstep, the park (p127) and town (p123) offer excellent day hikes, nature-watching and quality hot-springing at resorts or public pools.

SHEI-PA NATIONAL PARK

Home of the outstanding and challenging Holy Ridge hike as well as numerous other multiday treks in the high mountains. (p161)

THE EAST COAST

In this lightly populated region you'll find Taiwan's best cycling routes, some superior hikes and an emerging surf scene. (p181)

YUSHAN NATIONAL PARK

Climb Taiwan's highest peak or set out on the week-long historic Batongguan trail. (p212)

KENTING NATIONAL PARK

Taiwan's beach playground also has some sweet cycling on quiet rural roads and along coastal bluffs, and exceptional surfing at Jialeshui. (p295)

PENGHU ISLANDS

This is one of the world's top spots for windsurfing. You'll also find a wealth of swimmable beaches and pristine snorkelling and diving sites at dozens of small coral islands. (p326)

GUANZILING

Soak in rare mud hot springs and then ride the beautiful Dongshan Coffee Road south to Tainan. (p288)

THE EAST COAST

○ Shihtiping

Ruisui ○

Sixty Stone Mountain (952m) ▲

○ Taitung

YUSHAN NATIONAL PARK

Chushan (2489m) ▲   Yushan (3952m) ▲

○ Litao

Guanshan (3666m) ▲

○ Douliu

Alishan National Scenic Area

GUANZILING

Wushantou

○ Pingtung

Chiayi ○

Sinying ○

Tainan ○

○ Kaohsiung

KENTING NATIONAL PARK

○ Kenting

PENGHU ISLANDS

Plan Your Trip
Family Travel

The Taiwanese adore kids, but they are also conscious about disturbing other people, so young children are generally well behaved in public. That said, with some imagination and the following pointers, you won't have much difficulty finding ways to keep your kids amused in Taiwan.

Keeping Costs Down

Transport

Children under six (or 115cm) can ride the MRT for free. Same for high-speed rail and intercity trains, provided you hold them on your lap; if your child needs a seat, buy a children's ticket – half-price for kids between six and 12 years (or 115cm to 150cm).

Activities

Even in the big cities like Taipei and Kaohsiung, there's no shortage of nature in city centres – riversides, gentle hikes, corner parks with play facilities and big parks for frisbee, ice cream and ducks.

Museums, zoos and many other attractions are free for children under six. Museums and libraries have children's play and reading rooms; and there is always a water machine near the toilets to refill your bottle.

Eating

Children under 6 (sometimes older) can eat for free at Western-style buffet restaurants at hotels. To take a break from restaurants, pack a picnic with nuts for squirrels and fruit for birds and spend a good part of an afternoon in a park.

Children Will Love...

Museums

National Museum of Natural Science (p215), **Taichung** Exhibit areas cover rainforests, dinosaurs, botany and space; there are also theatres and a botanical garden.

National Taiwan Museum (p65), **Taipei** Lots of hands-on games and a museum shop with stuffed animals and colourful rocks.

Thousand Fields Seed Museum (p273), **Tainan** Educational and fascinating place where exotic-looking seeds can be admired, touched and experimented with.

Postal Museum (p68), **Taipei** Pretend you're a postal employee and make your own stamp with your face.

DIY Experiences

Chun Shui Tang Teahouse (p221), **Taichung** Make your own bubble tea!

Puppetry Art Centre (p83), **Taipei** Find out all about puppets and learn how to make one.

Museum of Old Taiwan Tiles (p227), **Chiayi** Try painting your own tiles; buy lovely tile stickers and plaster them over the walls back home.

Choose Chius (p291), **Pingtung** Make your own chocolate while eating lots of it at a cacao farm.

Ten Drum Rende Creative Village (p277), **Tainan** Paint then release your own sky lantern in a century-old chimney.

Places with Animals

Whale watching (p184), **Chenggong** You'll see dolphins too if you're lucky.

Penghu Aquarium (p326), **Penghu** Mesmerising collection of sea life.

Cat Village (p147), **Houtong** A village where (vaccinated) cats roam free.

2-28 Peace Memorial Park (p64), **Taipei** Squirrels, water fowl and people walking their dogs (and cats!)

Black-faced Spoonbill Reserve and Exhibition Hall (p279), **Tainan** Visit the habitat of the endangered water fowl and watch them through binoculars.

Parks & Arty Outdoor Spaces

Pier-2 Art District (p253), **Kaohsiung** Repurposed warehouses by the harbour offer interactive art experiences, book and stationery shopping, and lawns for running and napping.

Xihu Sugar Refinery (p234), **Changhua** A disused factory in an attractive park where you can picnic and cycle; locomotive rides and ice cream are bonuses.

Alishan Forest Railway Chiayi Garage (p227), **Chiayi** An urban park where you can play hide-and-seek and check out old steam locomotives.

Da'an Forest Park (p73), **Taipei** A large urban park where you can rollerblade, shoot hoops and watch the ducks go by, with a cafe and a amphitheatre to boot.

Rides

Maokong Gondola (p128), **Taipei** Gondola ride with great views.

i-Ride (p111), **Taipei** Pricey 5-D virtual-reality cinema taking you above the clouds and deep into the oceans of Taiwan; there's another one in Kaohsiung.

Miramar Entertainment Park (p85), **Taipei** A huge mall, cinema and amusement park complex.

Taroko Park (p258), **Kaohsiung** A mini-amusement park for young children and an indoor centre with laser and sports games for older kids.

Kids' Corner

Say What?

Hello.	您好 *Nín hǎo*
Goodbye.	再見 *Zàijiàn*
Thank you.	謝謝 *Xièxie*
My name is ...	我叫... *Wǒ jiào ...*

Did You Know? ℹ

• Rubbish bins are practically nonexistent in Taiwan – the island recycles 55% of its waste.

Have You Tried?

ELWYNN / SHUTTERSTOCK ©

Stinky tofu (臭豆腐; *chòu dòufu*) Street snack food.

EXPERIMENTING WITH TAIWANESE FOOD

Travel is an opportunity to expand the palate, so while you can easily find good pizzas, burgers and salads in Taiwan, why not persuade the kids to try something new? Taiwanese cooking is varied and portions are generally not big. Plus you can always fall back on a good ol' plate of pasta when you need to. Besides easy-to-like spring-onion pancakes (蔥抓餅, *cōng zhuābǐng*), beef noodles (牛肉麵, *niúròu miàn*) and braised pork rice (滷肉飯, *lǔròu fàn*), here are some Taiwanese foods that children are likely to enjoy, and how to eat them.

Dumplings

You'll find all kinds of dumplings (餃子, *jiǎozi*) – dough pockets stuffed with ground meat and vegetables – in Taiwan. They may be boiled, steamed or panfried into 'potstickers' (鍋貼, *guōtiē*). While they are all delicious, the popular soup dumpling (小籠包, *xiǎo lóng bāo*) is the hardest to eat because of the juice from the steamed meat. The proper way to do it is to pinch the top where the skin is thickest with your chopsticks while supporting the body with a spoon underneath. Nibble a little off the top to release the steam; blow into it for faster cooling. Add in a few drops of vinegar and put the whole thing in your mouth. Soup dumpling restaurants also serve steamed vegetarian dumplings (素餃, *sù jiǎo*) with a mix of veggies, rice vermicelli and shiitake mushrooms.

Boiled dumplings have a thicker wrapping than steamed dumplings and less complex pleating, which makes them easier to eat. The most popular fillings for boiled dumplings or potstickers are pork and cabbage (白菜豬肉, *báicài zhūròu*) and pork and leek (韭菜豬肉, *jiǔcài zhūròu*); you can also buy them frozen at supermarkets. Locals usually eat boiled dumplings with a dipping sauce made from mixing vinegar (醋, *cù*), soy sauce (醬油, *jiàngyóu*) and, if you dare, chilli (辣椒, *làjiāo*). Din Tai Fung (p97), Zilin Steamed Dumpling House (p97) and Dian Shui Lou (p101) make sumptuous dumplings.

Hotpots

Many children enjoy hotpots (火鍋, *huǒ guō*) or steamboats because the variety of food is mind-blowing – and they get to cook. Most pots have a divider down the centre to hold two

Best Regions

Taipei

Abundant children's attractions from museums and puppetry to mechanical rides and playgrounds, many are free, too; also gentle hikes and riverside cycling.

New Taipei City

Sky lanterns, a scenic train, a cat village and interactive mining exhibits await, if the little legs don't mind walking.

Taichung

Fancy cakes and ice cream in fun settings, a handicraft village with loads of sweet treats and, further afield, a wetland teeming with marine life, and cycling for the whole family.

Kaohsiung

Child-friendly museums and cultural programs, theme-park and virtual-reality rides and entertaining industry-art crossovers.

Tainan

Hands-on speciality museums from salt to seed; a fort and a water fowl reserve; quaint walkable streets; canal cruises; and products of the Tainanese famous sweet tooth.

Pingtung

Cacoa farms galore and year-round sun-and-beach fun on the southernmost coast.

kinds of soup bases, eg chicken broth and spicy Sichuan. Ingredients include sliced meats, seafood, radish, greens, noodles and 'balls' (meat or seafood processed into springy bite-sized spheres).

After ordering, go to the fancy condiments table or tray to customise your dipping sauce. Pick from soy sauce, vinegar, garlic puree, sesame paste, sesame oil, chillies and spring onions. Put whatever you want in your bowl and mix it up. When cooking, slide the food into the soup or lower it with a strainer. After it's done, take it out with the strainer, then dip and eat.

There are plenty of hotpot places in Taiwan and, come winter, the queue for a table at **Old Sichuan** (老四川, Lǎo Sìchuān; Map p72; ☑02-2515 2222; www.oldsichuan.com.tw; 112 Chang'an E Rd, Sec 2, 長安東路二段112號; dishes NT$128-488; ⏰11.30am-1am; ✳; Ⓜ Songjiang Nanjing) in Taipei, and Old Uncle's Hotpot (p220) in Taichung, are long.

Desserts

Taiwanese love their sweets and the good news is much of it is quite healthy. Silken tofu (豆花; dòuhuā), grass jelly (燒仙草, shāo xiān cǎo), red bean soup (紅豆湯, hóng dòu tāng) and mung bean and Job's tears soup (綠豆薏仁湯, lǜdòu yìrén tāng) are all very common; sometimes eaten as is, but more often with the addition of toppings: seasonal tropical fruits, boiled peanuts or taro, tapioca pearls and even ice cream, crème brûlée and pineapple cake.

In many shops, you can see the toppings behind the ordering counter or there are pictures of the toppings on the menu; you can simply point to whatever you like.

If you're thirsty in a night market, refreshing aiyu jelly (愛玉, àiyù) or fig-seed jelly, often with lemon juice added, or creamy papaya milk (木瓜牛奶, mùguā niúnǎi) might do the trick.

Night markets such as Ruifeng (p263), Raohe (p101) and Da Dong (p285) have desserts, as do shops such as Ice Monster (p98), Shuanglian Sweet Rice Ball (p99) and North Pole Soft Ice Special Shop (p126).

Good to Know

➡ Look out for the 👪 icon for family-friendly suggestions throughout this guide.

➡ You're not likely to find high chairs or booster seats at low-end restaurants, but they are common at midrange and high-end places.

➡ Car seats are required by law for children aged under 4, except when they travel in taxis. Major car rental companies have a limited number of car seats you can hire. Uber has vehicles with car seats.

➡ Pushchairs are welcome on buses, trains, high-speed rail and the MRT. In cities outside Taipei, pavements can be uneven and overrun by parked scooters. The best time to visit a night market is from 5pm to 6pm, before crowds make keeping track of kids or manoeuvring pushchairs difficult.

➡ There are free-to-use nursing rooms in metro, train and bus stations, shopping malls, museums and parks. Breastfeeding in public is not common.

➡ You can find baby formula, food and nappies (diapers) at supermarkets. All-natural products are available at upmarket grocery stores like Jason's Market Place (www.jasons.com.tw) and the big Carrefour stores (www.carrefour.com.tw).

➡ Simple medication can be bought at pharmacies. Hospitals have paediatricians and you can make an appointment to see them without a referral from a general practitioner.

Useful Resources

➡ The Community Services Centre (www.communitycenter.org.tw) has information for families relocating to Taiwan.

➡ For all-round information and advice, check out Lonely Planet's *Travel with Children*.

Plan Your Trip
Eat & Drink Like a Local

The Taiwanese are a force to be reckoned with when it comes to round-the-clock eating. There's a lot to love about Taiwanese food, and a lot of it to love. Follow the sound of lips smacking and let the food extravaganza begin.

The Year in Food

Top-quality victuals are available year-round, but certain foods are associated with particular seasons.

Spring (Mar–May)

Lanyu's Flying Fish Festival (April/May), a traditional coming-of-age ceremony for the island's young men, is the only time of the year that flying fish can be eaten.

Summer (Jun–Aug)

Try refreshing drinks made from local favourites such as winter melon, lotus root, pickled plums and mesona (a type of mint). Alternatively, down a few bowls of shaved-ice desserts with colourful sweet toppings.

Autumn (Sep–Nov)

Grapefruit, persimmons, dragon fruit, star fruit and pears are all in season in autumn. Crabs too.

Winter (Dec–Feb)

This season is dedicated to the Taiwanese love of Chinese medicinal ingredients, chiefly dāngguī (當歸, Angelica root or female ginseng), in their cooking. The two classic winter dishes, cooked with ginseng and rice wine, are a soothing mutton stew (羊肉爐, yángròu lú) and a ginger-heavy duck stew (薑母鴨, jiāngmǔ yā). An aromatic dish of chicken cooked in lots of sesame oil and rice wine (麻油雞, máyóu jī) is another favourite.

Food Experiences
Meals of a Lifetime

House of Crab (p264), **Kaohsiung** A formal restaurant known for its masterful seafood dishes.

JL Studio (p220), **Taichung** Award-winning nouvelle Singaporean cuisine.

Smart Fish (p228), **Chiayi** Best known for fried fish heads in milky broth with greens.

Mu-Ming (p177), **Hualien** Inventive multicourse indigenous fare.

RAW (p100), **Taipei** Taiwanese ingredients, Euro approach, Michelin-crowned, too.

Vegan Project (p219), **Taichung** Exquisite vegan dishes beautifully plated.

Zhuxin Residence (p286), **Tainan** Seven-course Taiwanese meals in a century-old house.

Cheap Treats

Visit any night market in Taiwan for a filling meal that's light on your wallet, including the following.

Black pepper bun (胡椒餅, hú jiāo bǐng) Peppery baked bun with a pork and leek filling, commonly found in markets.

Danzai noodles (擔仔麵, dànzǎi miàn) Ever-reliable noodle snack, served with pork in shrimp stock in Tainan and available all over the island.

Fluffy spring-onion pancakes (蔥抓餅, *cōng zhuābǐng*) Chewy, flaky pancakes with spring onions and a plethora of toppings including corn and basil; try Ju Tang (p263) in Kaohsiung.

Fried mackerel in soup (土魠魚羹, *tǔtuō yúgēng*) Deep-fried Spanish mackerel served dunked in a thick soup at hawker stands.

Seaweed-wrapped rice ball (飯糰, *fàn tuán*) Taiwan's answer to Japan's onigiri, available at convenience stores.

Steamed pork sandwich (刈包, *yì bāo*) Lan Jia (p92) in Taipei sets the standard.

Sweet peanut soup (花生湯, *huāshēng tāng*) A speciality of Ningxia Night Market (p99) in Taipei.

Taiwan bubble tea Sweet, milky tea with giant tapioca balls, available throughout the country.

Dare to Try

Chicken testicles (雞腰子, *jī yāozi*) Also known as jī fú (雞佛), these tiny sausage-shaped organs can be had sautéed at Kaohsiung's Liuhe Night Market (p264) or hotpot restaurants.

Coffin toast (棺材板, *guāncái bǎn*) Tainan's fat, deep-fried-in-egg toast planks, hollowed out and filled with a thick chowder of seafood and vegetables.

Fried sandworms (炒沙蟲, *chǎo shāchóng*) A speciality of Kinmen; best served hot.

Iron eggs Braised and dried eggs with a black rubbery consistency.

Medicinal drinks Try Herb Alley (p103) in Taipei for Chinese traditional herbal drinks – the bitter tea (sans sugar) is extremely bitter.

Milkfish guts (虱目魚腸, *shīmù yúcháng*) The fried intestines and offal of milkfish – a Tainan delicacy.

Stir-fried pig intestines (薑絲炒大腸, *jiāngsī chǎo dàcháng*) Hakka-style: stir-fried with ginger.

Local Specialities

Taiwanese cuisine can be divided into several styles of cooking, though the boundaries are often blurred: there's Taiwanese, Hakka, Fujianese and of course the gamey fare of the indigenous peoples. Most regional Chinese cuisines can also be found as well, the most popular being Cantonese.

Taiwanese

Taiwanese cooking has a long, storied and complex history, with influences ranging from all over China mixed with a unique indigenous/Polynesian base. In general, food that you see people enjoying at roadside markets and restaurants tends to emphasise local recipes and ingredients – seafood, sweet potatoes, taro root and green vegetables cooked very simply are at the heart of most Taiwanese meals. *Xiǎoyú huāshēng* (小魚花生, fish stir-fry with peanuts and pickled vegetables) is one example of a Taiwanese favourite.

Chicken rates second in popularity to seafood, followed by pork and beef. *Kézǎi* (蚵仔, oysters) are popular, and *kézǎi tāng* (蚵仔湯, clear oyster soup with ginger) is an excellent hangover cure and overall stomach soother.

Hakka

Hakka dishes are very rich and hearty; sensible for a people who historically made their living as farmers and needed plenty of energy to work the fields. Dishes are often salty and vinegary, with strong flavours. Pork, a favourite of the Hakka, is often cut up into large pieces, fried and then stewed in a marinade. Our favourite Hakka dish is *kèjiā xiǎo chǎo* (客家小炒, stir-fried cuttlefish with leeks, tofu and pork).

Hakka cuisine is also known for its tasty snacks, including *zhà shūcài bǐng* (fried, salty balls made from local mushrooms and flour), *kèjiāguǒ* (客家粿, turnip cakes with shrimp and pork) and *kèjiā máshǔ* (客家麻糬, sticky rice dipped in sugar or peanut powder).

PRICE RANGES

The following food price ranges generally refer to the cost of a meal rather than a single dish (unless a single dish is what is usually ordered, such as beef noodles).

$ less than NT$200

$$ NT$200–600

$$$ more than NT$600

BEST LISTS

One Bar (p264), **Kaohsiung** Modernised grannie's cooking meets slick retro decor.

Daxi Fishing Harbour (p153), **Toucheng** Glorious seafood right by the harbour.

Flower Space (p177), **Hualien** Well-made vegetarian in a curious dining room.

Cauliflower Old Memory (p335), **Penghu Islands** Penghu specialities in a fun environment.

Shumin Kitchen (p264), **Kaohsiung** Excellent Taiwanese food complemented by a nice booze selection.

La Table de Moz (p335), **Penghu Islands** Top-quality East–West fusion fare; prebooking is a must.

Fujianese

Much of Taiwanese cuisine has Fujianese roots, as the earliest wave of Han Chinese immigration to the island in the 18th century comprised primarily Fujian mainlanders. Fujianese cuisine particularly abounds on the Taiwan Strait islands of Matsu and Kinmen (both of which are a stone's throw away from Fujian province), but you'll find Fujianese cuisine all over Taiwan.

One of the most popular dishes is *fó tiào qiáng* (佛跳牆, 'Buddha Jumps Over the Wall'), a stew of seafood, chicken, duck and pork simmered in a jar of rice wine. Allegedly the dish is so tasty that even the Buddha – a vegetarian, of course – would hop over a wall to get a taste.

Cantonese

Cantonese is what non-Chinese consider 'Chinese' food, largely because many émigré restaurateurs in other countries originate from Guangdong (Canton) or Hong Kong. Cantonese flavours are generally more subtle than other Chinese styles – almost sweet, with very few spicy dishes. Cantonese cooking emphasises the use of fresh ingredients, which is why so many restaurants are lined with tanks full of live fish and seafood.

Cantonese *diǎnxīn* (點心, dim sum) snacks are famous and can be found in restaurants around Taiwan's bigger cities. As well as *chāshāobāo* (叉燒包, barbecued pork buns), you'll find *chūnjuǎn* (春卷, spring rolls), *zhōu* (粥, rice porridge) and, of course, *jī jiǎo* (雞腳, chicken feet) – an acquired taste.

Indigenous

Travellers who visit Taiwan without sampling the dishes of the tribal peoples who called the island home millennia before the first Han sailor ever laid eyes on Ilha Formosa are definitely missing out. The product of hunters, gatherers and fishing people, indigenous dishes tend to be heavy on wild game and mountain vegetables, as well as a variety of seafood.

One must-try dish is *tiěbǎn shānzhūròu* (鐵板山豬肉, fatty wild boar grilled, sliced, and grilled again with onions and wild greens). A staple that's easy to carry and an excellent source of calories to bring along on a hike is *zhútǒng fàn* (竹筒飯, steamed rice – with and without meat – stuffed into a bamboo stalk); these bamboo-inspired energy bars are a speciality of the Tsou tribe in Alishan, who are also known for their love of bird's-nest fern, tree tomatoes and millet wine.

Over in Sandimen, millet is the staple of the Rukai diet, while *qínàbù* (奇那步), or taro and meat dumplings, and grilled wild boar with papaya (木瓜拌山豬肉, *mùguā bàn shānzhūròu*) can also be tasted in many Rukai villages. The Baiyi in Cingjing, who originally came from Yunnan, infuse their mushroom and meat dishes with herbs such as mint, chillies and stinging 'flower peppers'.

Vegetarian

Taiwanese vegetarian cuisine has plenty to offer any traveller, vegetarian or not. The country's Buddhist roots run deep, and while only a small (but still sizeable) percentage of Taiwanese are vegetarian, a fair chunk of the population abstains from meat for spiritual or health reasons every now and again, even if only for a day or a week.

Buddhist vegetarian restaurants are easy to find. Just look for the gigantic *savastika* (an ancient Buddhist symbol that looks like a reverse swastika) hanging in front of the restaurant. Every neighbourhood and town will generally have at least one vegetarian buffet. The Taiwanese are masters at adding variety to vegetarian cooking, as well as creating 'mock meat' dishes made of tofu or gluten on which veritable miracles have been performed.

How to Eat & Drink
When & Where

Most breakfast places open at about 6am and close by 11am or noon. A traditional breakfast in Taiwan usually consists of watery rice with seaweed (鹹粥, *xián zhōu*), clay-oven rolls (燒餅, *shāobǐng*) and steamed buns (饅頭, *mántóu*), served plain or with fillings; the meal is generally washed down with plain or sweetened hot soybean milk (豆漿, *dòujiāng*). Other popular breakfast foods include rolled omelettes (蛋餅, *dàn bǐng*), egg sandwiches (雞蛋三明治, *jīdàn sānmíngzhì*) and turnip cakes (蘿蔔糕, *luóbo gāo*).

The Taiwanese generally eat lunch between 11.30am and 2pm, many taking their midday meal from any number of small eateries on the streets. *Zìzhù cāntīng* (自助餐廳, self-serve cafeterias) are a good option, offering plenty of meat and vegetable dishes to choose from. Some self-serve cafeterias are vegetarian.

Dinner in Taiwan is usually eaten from 5pm to 11pm, though some restaurants and food stalls in bigger cities stay open 24 hours. Taiwan's cities – especially the larger ones – all have a fair-to-excellent selection of international restaurants. Don't be surprised to run into a small Indonesian, Indian or even Mexican eatery in a back alley.

The most important thing to remember in Taiwan when it comes to food is that some of the best eats are found on the street – gourmets know that some of Asia's best street eats are found in night markets in and around Taiwan's cities.

Bars often keep long hours in Taiwan, opening in the afternoon and closing late at night. Most bars offer a limited menu, while some offer full-course meals. Expect to pay at least NT$120 for a beer and NT$200 and more for imported or craft beer.

Etiquette for Dining Out

➡ In restaurants, every customer gets an individual bowl of rice or a small soup bowl. It is quite acceptable to hold the bowl close to your lips and shovel the contents into your mouth with your chopsticks. If the food contains bones, just place them on the tablecloth (it's changed after each meal), or into a separate bowl if one is provided.

➡ Remember to fill your neighbours' teacups when they are empty, as yours will be filled by them. You can thank the pourer by tapping your middle finger on the table gently. On no account should you serve yourself tea without serving others first. When your teapot needs a refill, signal this to the waitstaff by taking the lid off the pot.

➡ Taiwanese toothpick etiquette is similar to that of neighbouring Asian countries: one hand wields the toothpick while the other shields the mouth from prying eyes.

➡ Probably the most important piece of etiquette comes with the bill: although you are expected to try to pay, you shouldn't argue too hard, as the one who extended the invitation will inevitably foot the bill. While splitting the cost of the meal is fashionable among the younger generation, as a guest you'll probably be treated most of the time. Return the favour if you have a chance or buy the host a gift.

THE BASICS

The Taiwanese love to eat out and you won't go hungry if you start by 8pm; many restaurants tend to wind down by 9pm. Booking a few days to a week in advance is necessary for popular and upmarket establishments, and often months for award-winning places.

Night markets A cheap and boisterous experience of everything from snacks and sweets to seafood and noodle soups.

Restaurants Asian cuisine, particularly Japanese, dominates, along with local fare.

Cafes Growing rapidly in number, they offer almost ubiquitously good brews or pour-overs along with cakes and pastries.

Oolong tea

Drinks

Tea

Tea is a fundamental part of Chinese life. In fact, an old Chinese saying identifies tea as one of the seven basic necessities of life (along with fuel, oil, rice, salt, soy sauce and vinegar). Taiwan's long growing season and hilly terrain are perfectly suited for producing excellent tea, especially high-mountain oolong, which is prized among tea connoisseurs the world over (and makes a great gift for the folks back home).

There are two types of teashops in Taiwan. Traditional teashops (more commonly called teahouses) are where customers brew their own tea in a traditional clay pot, choosing from several types of high-quality leaves, and sit for hours playing cards or Chinese chess. These places can be found tucked away in alleys in almost every urban area, but are best visited up in the mountains. Taipei's Maokong is an excellent place to experience a traditional Taiwanese teahouse. Then there is the stands found on every street corner. These specialise in bubble tea – a mixture of tea, milk, flavouring, sugar and giant black tapioca balls. Also called pearl tea or *boba cha,* the sweet drink is popular with students, who gather at tea stands after school to socialise and relax, much in the way that the older generation gathers at traditional teahouses.

Coffee

Taiwan is home to a world-class coffee culture – certainly the best in Asia. Not only is Taiwan big on coffee consumption – good-quality coffee can be easily found in big cities such as Taipei, Taichung, Tainan and Kaohsiung – but the island also grows its own beans and exports it in limited amounts.

The main coffee-growing regions are mountainous areas in the south, including Dongshan in Tainan, Dewen in Sandimen, Pingtung, Gukeng in Yunlin and Alishan in Chiayi. The two main factors limiting Taiwan coffee exports are costs (labour is more expensive here than, say, Vietnam) and land in the mountains often belongs

NOCTURNAL FOOD FUN

One Taiwan experience you can't miss out on is eating at a night market. All cities in Taiwan have at least a few of their own, and even a medium-sized town will have a street set up with food stalls selling Taiwanese eats, alongside clothes, sundries and sunglasses late into the night.

So what kind of food can you expect to find on the fly in Taiwan? Some items won't surprise people used to eating Asian food back home. Taiwanese dumplings (餃子, *jiǎozi*) are always a good bet, especially for those looking to fill up on the cheap. Stuffed with meat, spring onion and greens, they are served by the plate.

Other snacks include braised goodies, from tofu (豆腐, *dòufu*) to coagulated duck's blood (鴨血, *yā xuè*) and pig's intestines (大腸, *dà cháng*); fried taro balls (炸芋丸, *zhá yùwán*) with pork floss and optional egg yolk; deep-fried chicken cutlets (雞排, *jī pái*), some bigger than your face; savoury rice pudding (粿, *guǒ*) in all forms, steamed in a bowl with pork, radish or pumpkin, as in Tainan, or in a herbal broth, as in Chiayi; and sesame oil chicken (麻油雞, *má yóu jī*), a warming soup infused with aromatic sesame oil, with chicken pieces or pork offal.

Probably the most recognisable Taiwanese street snack is *chòu dòufu* (臭豆腐, stinky fermented tofu). This deep-fried dish is something of an acquired taste, like certain European cheeses. That said, many eaters find the smell stronger than the taste. What's really pungent is steamed stinky tofu, which you can find in Shanghainese restaurants. Another unusual food to watch for is *pídàn* (皮蛋, 'thousand year eggs'), duck eggs that are covered in straw and stored underground for six months – the yolk turns green and the white becomes like jelly. It's often served as a cold dish with tofu and sesame sauce; its alkalinity also allows it to work like cheese on the palate when paired with red wine.

to indigenous peoples who often prefer to protect the land from development, so plantations are limited in area.

Juices

Fresh-fruit stands selling juices and smoothies are all over Taiwan – these drinks make wonderful thirst quenchers on a hot summer day. All you have to do is point at the fruits you want (some shops have cut fruit ready-mixed in a cup) and the person standing behind the counter will whiz them up in a blender for you after adding water or milk. Especially good are iced-papaya milkshakes.

Popular juices include *hāmìguā* (哈密瓜, honeydew melon), *xīguā* (西瓜, watermelon), *píngguǒ* (蘋果, apple) and *gānzhè* (甘蔗, sugar cane).

Sugar-cane juice is usually sold at speciality stands selling raw sugar cane rather than ordinary fruit stands.

Harder Stuff

The Taiwanese tend to be fairly moderate drinkers (with some exceptions, such as banquets, which are a time when much drinking occurs), but Taiwan is the proud creator of a world-class whisky. Kavalan Distillery in Yilan produces a smooth, tropical-fruity whisky that has bagged over 200 international awards since its launch in 2008 and is now available in 60 countries. You can visit the distillery and find the liquor in bars all over the island.

Another locally produced inebriant well worth trying is *gāoliáng jiǔ* (高粱酒, *gaoliang* liquor). Made from fermented sorghum, gaoliang is usually associated with Kinmen Island, though much of it is produced in factories in Chiayi. Another local favourite is *wéishìbǐ* (維士比, whisbih), an energy drink with a fine mixture of Angelica, a medicinal herb (當歸, *dānggui*), ginseng, taurine, various B vitamins and caffeine – and some ethyl alcohol to give it a kick.

Regions at a Glance

Taipei is surrounded by forested hills and heritage towns that make the best day trips. Within the city limits are world-class museums and never-ending opportunities for snacking and shopping. Heading out towards the coast or the mountains puts the traveller in northern Taiwan, with its hot springs, and many cycling and hiking routes. The dusty plains of western Taiwan hold vibrant temple towns, while heading east, the unspoiled Central Mountains rise quickly to over 3000m. Over the mountains lies eastern Taiwan with a landscape that's pure eye candy. In tropical southern Taiwan, foodies and ecotourists brush against culture vultures taking in magnificent festivals and cool cityscapes. Finally, scattered on both sides of the mainland are Taiwan's islands, boasting a Cold War legacy, seaside villages and a top windsurfing destination.

Taipei

Food
History
Shopping

Food Capital

With hundreds of restaurants incorporating culinary influences from every corner of China, some of the best Japanese outside Japan, hands down Asia's best coffee, and a night-market scene loaded with unique local snacks, Taipei definitely has it all foodwise.

Varied Legacies

You'll find temples and markets dating back centuries coexisting with Taipei's flashy modernity, as well as neighbourhoods and parks from the Japanese colonial era now being revived as cultural and entertainment centres.

Locally Made

Taipei shines in locally designed products such as ceramics, glassware, clothing, tea sets, jade, home furnishings and knick-knacks. You'll also find a host of enticing agricultural products, from designer desserts to organic teas.

p58

Northern Taiwan

Outdoor Activities
Hot Springs
Museums

Hiking & Cycling

The north's network of trails crosses landscapes that vary from tropical jungles to alpine meadows above 3000m. The roads offer some first-class cycling, with day and multiday options along coastal routes, riverside paths and cross-island highways.

Hot Springs

With dozens of hot springs dotting the north, there's always a place for a dip somewhere close by. And with facilities ranging from five-star resorts to natural pools deep in the mountains, there's something for every taste and style.

Museums

Once a centre for traditional cottage industries such as tea, pottery and woodcarving, as well as gold and coal mining, the north boasts a small yet rich collection of museums highlighting them all. Master carver Juming and his internationally acclaimed works have their own outdoor park.

p132

Eastern Taiwan & Taroko National Park

Landscapes
Cycling
Culture

Gorge, Coast & Valley

Much of the east has hardly changed its face for modern times. It's still a land of 1000m seaside cliffs, marble gorges, subtropical forests and vast yellow rice fields nestled between blue-tinged mountain ranges.

Cycling

The scenery that makes the east a draw for nature lovers is best viewed at cycling speeds. The premier challenge is an 86km route from sea level to 3275m through Taroko Gorge, but most opt for all or part of the 400km loop down the coastline and back through the Rift Valley.

Indigenous Festivals & Art

Hunting, fishing and coming-of-age festivals dot the summer calendar. Woodcarvers operate small studios up and down the driftwood-rich coastline, while Dulan's weekly bash at a former sugar factory is keeping the music alive.

p165

Western Taiwan

Mountains
Culture
Wildlife

Hiking & Landscapes

The 3000m-plus spine of Taiwan runs through the west, with three ranges competing for scenic supremacy. Yushan (3952m), the highest mountain in Taiwan, is just one of many worthy hiking opportunities.

Folk Culture

As one of the first areas settled by Chinese immigrants, the west is home to some of Taiwan's oldest temples. Exuberant yearly festivals such as the week-long Mazu Pilgrimage honour a pantheon of traditional folk gods.

Bird- & Butterfly-Watching

With its wealth of protected reserves and national parks, the west is a haven for endemic species such as the Mikado pheasant and several hundred butterfly species. Vast numbers of purple milkweed butterflies pass through each year.

p210

Southern Taiwan

History
Culture
Food

Temples & Festivals

In the south, the legacy of the faith that sustained Taiwan's earliest immigrants is evident in a wealth of magnificent temples, and spectacular rituals and festivals like Donggang's Burning of the Wang Yeh Boats and Kaohsiung's Niemen Song Jiang Battle Array.

Urban Sights

Kaohsiung's intriguing mix of cultures – port, military and fishing – and Tainan's rich heritage as Taiwan's oldest city have translated into thoroughly unique and enjoyable urban experiences, from museums in former military settlements to highly walkable streets with all things chic.

Night Markets & Seafood

Tainan's traditional snacks are famous throughout Taiwan: milkfish and savoury rice pudding are just a couple of mouth-watering highlights. Kaohsiung has some of the freshest seafood in Taiwan, from grilled oysters at night markets to sophisticated crab dishes at classy establishments.

p249

Taiwan Strait Islands

Landscapes
Activities
History

Beaches & Coastal Scenery

Penghu's beaches are Taiwan's finest, and the traditional villages are a nice backdrop. The volcanic origins of Lanyu, Green Island and Penghu have left stunning coastal formations. Kinmen's landscape includes lakes, mudflats and fine beaches.

Windsurfing & Snorkelling

As the windiest place in the northern hemisphere in late autumn, Penghu attracts windsurfers from all over the world. For snorkellers, the easily accessed coral reefs off Lanyu and Green Island burst with marine life and colour year-round.

Civil War

Former frontiers of the civil war, Matsu and Kinmen have a rich legacy of old military tunnels, memorials and museums. More interesting to many are the traditional villages, wonderfully preserved because of their frontier status.

p302

On the Road

Taiwan Strait Islands
p302

Taipei
p58

Northern Taiwan
p132

Western Taiwan
p210

Eastern Taiwan & Taroko National Park
p165

Southern Taiwan
p249

Taipei

02 / POP 2.7 MILLION

Best Places to Eat

➡ Yongkang Beef Noodles (p98)

➡ RAW (p100)

➡ Thai Food (p96)

➡ Addiction Aquatic Development (p100)

➡ Din Tai Fung (p97)

Best Places to Stay

➡ Grand Hotel (p90)

➡ Flip Flop Hostel Garden (p90)

➡ Play Design Hotel (p90)

➡ three little birds (p89)

➡ W Hotel (p91)

Why Go?

For a 300-year-old city, Taipei has been having a very late coming-of-age party. But then again, this unhurried but vibrant capital has taken a while to become comfortable in its own skin. With Chinese, Japanese and western influences in its food, culture, folk arts and architecture, Taipei has finally decided that it's a mix, and all the better for it.

As with the multifarious street food, the traveller is advised to try as much as possible when it comes to exploring. Day trips are particularly recommended, and a quick MRT ride takes you to tea fields, hot springs, river parks and colonial towns backed by a mountainous national park. Within the city don't miss the Minnan-style temples beautified with unique decorative arts, the heritage lanes turned art hubs, and gourmet cafes and boutique centres, the buzzing neon neighbourhoods or the nightlife scene, growing in reputation yearly

When to Go
Taipei

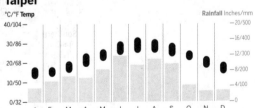

Jan & Feb The weeks bracketing the Lunar New Year are a great time to visit.

June–Sep Fresh tropical fruits are readily available.

Oct–Dec The perfect time to visit, with the heat gone and the chill yet to begin.

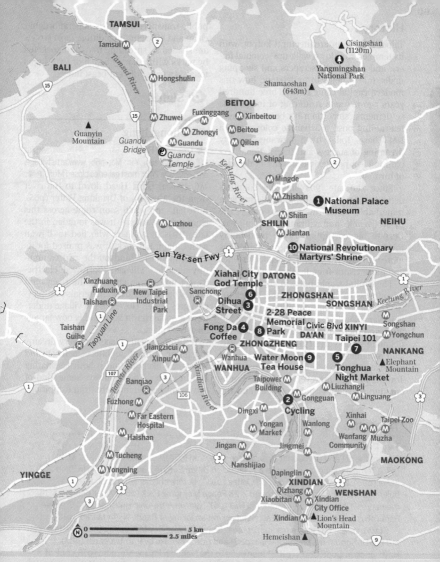

Taipei Highlights

1 National Palace Museum (p78) Enjoying an art legacy spanning millennia.

2 Cycling (p130) Pedalling around the city and the river.

3 Dihua St (p74) Exploring the the Japanese-era architecture.

4 Fong Da Coffee (p104) Savouring a rich slice of Taipei's coffee culture.

5 Tonghua Night Market (p113) Jostling with the locals for mouthfuls of yum.

6 Xiahai City God Temple (p76) Feeling the spirituality and praying to the matchmaker god.

7 Taipei 101 (p83) Seeing Taipei from the clouds at the city's iconic building.

8 2-28 Peace Memorial Park (p64) Contemplating history under lovely old trees.

9 Water Moon Tea House (p106) Sipping tea and buying gear for brewing back home.

10 National Revolutionary Martyrs' Shrine (p79) Watching the pomp and pageantry at the changing of the guards.

History

Taipei is such an architectural hotpot, with its temples, run-down walk-ups, colonial finery, and modern skyscrapers and shopping malls, that it helps to understand how this modern capital came to be. Three hundred years ago it was a scattering of indigenous settlements; since then it's been a Chinese tea-trading post, a Japanese colony, and a KMT base. Today it's a Taiwanese society dreaming of success and international recognition – a perplexing product of decades of turmoil.

Since the late '90s and the country's democratisation, the capital has made a remarkable transformation into one of the most liveable and vibrant cities in Asia. Despite big corruption cases, particularly involving infrastructure projects, Taipei has more visible heritage, and is cleaner, greener and more visitor-friendly, than ever before.

The capital would not win any prizes for an impressive cityscape but the Taipei 101 (p83) area clearly has ambitions. The futuristic Nanshan Plaza (p115) was completed in 2018, and there are plans to convert the Taipei main station area (p117) into a local version of Times Square; it will also have two massive structures called the Taipei Twin Towers. You will, however, never go far without finding spotless public toilets, and the public-transport system is superaffordable, clean and efficient. In addition, most streets are shaded by spreading trees and pocketed by parks with a handy bench or two. Taipei today is a very different beast indeed.

⊙ Sights

◉ Zhongzheng

⭐ **Treasure Hill** VILLAGE
(寶藏巖, Bǎozàng Yán; Map p66; www.artistvillage.org; ⊙village 24hr, most galleries closed Mon; P 🐾; MGongguan) FREE Head down to the river from the Museum of Drinking Water (p65), turn left, and you'll soon come across this charming art village. It was founded in the late 1940s by soldiers who fled to Taiwan with Chiang Kai-shek. It was praised for its 'living memories' and off-the-grid community lifestyle – villagers 'borrowed' electricity, set up organic farms by the river, built homes out of discarded materials and recycled grey water. However, the village underwent a makeover in 2010 and is now largely an artist village.

It's a photogenic place, and very dreamy to explore at night; architects, activists and artists are likely to find it both fascinating and inspiring. There's always some kind of arty event happening here from exhibitions

---

TAIPEI IN...

Two Days

Admire the art and devotional atmosphere at Bao'an (p74), Longshan (p69), and Xiahai (p76) Temples, shop for ceramics and fabric on Dihua St (p74), and then lunch in Zhen Siwei (p96). Enjoy a latte at Fong Da Coffee (p104) before checking out Japanese-era buildings and small museums around 2-28 Peace Memorial Park (p64). After pondering the meaning of Chiang Kai-shek Memorial Hall (p61), dine in retro-chic Huashan 1914 Creative Park (p61) and end the day with some late-night snacking at Raohe Night Market (p101).

Start the next day with a traditional breakfast at Fuhang Soy Milk (p93), then take the MRT to Dr Sun Yatsen Memorial Hall (p83) and ride a Youbike over to Taipei 101 (p83). Have lunch at Good Cho's (p102) then head to the National Palace Museum (p78), one of the world's best for Chinese art. For dinner try dumplings or beef noodles on Yongkang St (p98), followed by a stroll in Da'an Park (p73) and a nightcap at Another Brick (p102) or tea at Wistaria (p104).

Four Days

Follow the itinerary above and then plan for a full day in historic Tamsui (p118) with its temples, forts and colonial neighbourhoods. For dinner, head back to town to your pre-booked table at Le Palais (p100) or RAW (p100), followed by jazz at Blue Note (p110).

The next morning hike through Yangmingshan National Park (p127), then catch a quick bus down to Beitou's Hot Spring Museum (p124). From here wander down past hot springs, temples and museums. Head back to Taipei for snacking at Ningxia Night Market (p99) and winning cocktails at Indulge Experimental Bistro. (p104)

DECODING TAIPEI STREET NAMES

Taipei street, lane and alley signs are all bilingual, but most locals can neither read nor write a romanised address. In most cases, showing someone that you want to go to '14 Zhongxiao Rd' is going to elicit blank stares. Another problem is that while officially Taipei uses Hanyu Pinyin, you will run into varying romanisations, especially on name cards.

Below are some major streets with their characters, Hanyu Pinyin and possible alternative spelling.

EAST–WEST ROADS	PINYIN	POSSIBLE ALTERNATIVE
和平路	Heping Rd	Hoping Rd
信義路	Xinyi Rd	Hsinyi Rd
仁愛路	Ren'ai Rd	Jen-ai Rd
忠孝路	Zhongxiao Rd	Chunghsiao Rd
八德路	Bade Rd	Pateh Rd
市民大道	Shimin Blvd	Civic Blvd

NORTH–SOUTH ROADS	PINYIN	POSSIBLE ALTERNATIVE
中華路	Zhonghua Rd	Junghua Rd
延平路	Yanping Rd	Yenping Rd
重慶北路	Chongqing Rd	Chungching Rd
承德路	Chengde Rd	Chengteh Rd
中山路	Zhongshan Rd	Chungshan Rd
建國路	Jianguo Rd	Chienkuo Rd
敦化路	Dunhua Rd	Tunhua Rd

to light shows to outdoor movie screenings. Check the website to see what's on.

★ **National 2-28 Memorial Museum** MUSEUM
(二二國家紀念館; Èr'èr Guójiā Jìniànguǎn; Map p66; http://228.org.tw; 54 Nanhai Rd, 南海路54號; ☉10am-5pm Tue-Sun; ⓂChiang Kai-shek Memorial Hall) FREE This graceful memorial to the victims of the 2-28 Incident is housed in a beautiful Japanese building dating back to 1931. The permanent exhibition, which is excellent, charts in detail the tragic events of February 1947 and the subsequent years of White Terror. The English audio guide (free) is essential as there is little written in English. Many of the stories are brutal and moving.

★ **Huashan 1914 Creative Park** CULTURAL CENTRE
(華山1914, Huàshān Yījiǔyīsì; Map p66; ☎02-2358 1914; www.huashan1914.com; 1 Bade Rd, Sec 1, 八德路一段1號; ☉park 24hr; Pⓗ; ⓂZhongxiao Xinsheng) FREE Borrowing from western urban-regeneration models, this early-20th-century wine factory has been restored as Taipei's most retro-chic venue. Remodelled warehouses now hold live-

music performances and pop-up shops sell innovative Taiwanese-designed products, there are ever-changing exhibitions, and a host of stylish restaurants, cafes and bars will have you loving the ambience as much as the food. Many of the exhibitions are aimed at children and take over the giant spaces. Don't forget SPOT around the back, Taipei's best independent cinema. The factory opened in 1916 as a private wine-making facility, and was finally shuttered in 1987.

★ **Chiang Kai-shek Memorial Hall** MONUMENT
(中正紀念堂, Zhōngzhèng Jìniàn Táng; Map p66; ☎02-2343 1100; www.cksmh.gov.tw; 21 Zhongshan S Rd, 中山南路21號; ☉9am-6pm; P; ⓂChiang Kai-shek Memorial Hall) FREE This grandiose monument to authoritarian leader Chiang Kai-shek is a popular attraction and rightly so. It is a sobering feeling to stand in the massive courtyard. Chiang's blue-roofed hall is a prime example of the neoclassical style, favoured by CKS as a counterpoint to the Cultural Revolution's destruction of genuine classical culture in China. Note the main hall shuts at 6pm, but the surrounding park is open 5am to midnight.

Greater Taipei

TAMSUI
See Tamsui Map (p120)

Danhai Light Rail

Baliaka Rd

Datunshan ▲

101

11

26
23

BALI

9

Mangroves

Hongshulin M

Tamsui River

6 18
27

Shamaoshan ▲
(643m)

Guanyin
Mountain ▲

25

15

Zhuwei M

Fuxinggang M

BEITOU
See Beitou Map (p124)

Guandu
Bridge

Zhongyi M

Beitou M

Guandu M

Qilian M

1
7
Guandu Temple

Shipai M

2

*National
Palace
Museum*

Keelung River

4 10

SHILIN

Luzhou M

See Shilin Map (p84)

13

Taiwan Taoyuan
International ✈
(23km)

Sun Yat-sen Fwy

1

See Zhongshan & Datong
Map (p80)

Sanchong Loop

Xinzhuang
Fuduxin

New Taipei
Industrial
Park

ZHONGSHAN

Taishan M

Sanchong

DATONG

Taishan
Guihe M

1

See Ximending &
Wanhua Map (p70)

DA'AN

Taoyuan Line

1

Jiangzicui M

Xinpu M

Wanhua M

ZHONGZHENG

107

Tamsui River

1

WANHUA

See Zhongzheng
Map (p66)

Banqiao M

3

Xindian River

Lin Family
**Mansion
& Garden**
2

Fuzhong M

106

Gongguan M

Dingxi M

Far Eastern
Hospital M

8
Yongan
Market M

Wanlong M

Haishan M

*National Human
Rights Museum*

YINGGE

Tucheng M

Jingan M

3
Jingmei M

114

Yongning M

3

**LITTLE
BURMA**

Nanshijiao M

20

Dapinglin M

XINDIAN

Qizhang M

Xiaobitan M

Xindian City Office

5 M

19

Xindian

16

24

21

12

Hemeishan

Greater Taipei

◎ **Top Sights**
- 1 Guandu Temple B3
- 2 Lin Family Mansion & Garden........... B6
- 3 National Human Rights Museum D6
- 4 National Palace Museum D3

◎ **Sights**
- 5 Bitan Suspension Bridge..................D7
- 6 Grass Mountain Chateau D2
- 7 Guandu Nature Park........................ C3
- 8 Museum of World Religions D6
- 9 Shihsanhang Museum of Archaeology A2
- 10 Shung Ye Museum of Formosan Aborigines D3
- 11 Wazihwei Nature Reserve A1

✪ **Activities, Courses & Tours**
- 12 Hemeishan D7
- 13 Jiantan Mountain D4
- 14 Jinbaoli Trail E1
- 15 Lengshuikeng.................................... E1
- 16 Lion's Head Mountain........................D7
- 17 Miramar Entertainment Park............E4

🛏 **Sleeping**
- 18 International Hotel............................ D2
- 19 New California Hotel...........................D7

🍴 **Eating**
- 20 Hoe Hoe Kyaw Restaurant D6
- 21 Loving Hut D7
- 22 RAW E4
- 23 Twin Sisters......................................B1

🍷 **Drinking & Nightlife**
- 24 Bi Ting...D7
- 25 Mommouth Coffee B2

🛍 **Shopping**
- National Palace Museum Shop.. (see 4)

ⓘ **Transport**
- 26 Bali Ferry Pier...................................... B1
- 27 Yangmingshan Bus Station D2

Entrance to the main hall is made via a series of 89 steps (Chiang's age when he died). Inside the cavernous hall is an artefact museum with Chiang's two Cadillacs, various documents and articles from his daily life. The hourly changing of the honour guard is probably the most well-received sight with most visitors. The flag raising at dawn and lowering at dusk is also conducted with pomp and is popular with local tourists.

Some eclectic and excellent exhibitions are held in two halls next to Chiang's, which are generally ticketed.

LOCAL KNOWLEDGE

JAPANESE LEGACY

Visitors to Taipei today can see the Japanese influence in remnants of their architecture, such as Zhongzheng District's government buildings in the centre of the city, and the wooden villas in the hot-spring resort of Beitou (p123). The amazing variety of excellent Japanese restaurants is also considered the best in the world outside of Japan.

The country is Taiwan's closest ally in Asia, despite its role as the colonial master and its WWII atrocities. Contemporary links also influence culture, from the popularity of *kawaii* cuteness among teenaged girls and young women to the sharp design aesthetic, which is becoming ever more prevalent. Some observers contend that Taiwan's legendary politeness is also partly a derivative of that colonial past. In 2018, Japanese announcements were added to some MRT stops, including Taipei main station, in addition to Mandarin, Hokkien (Taiwanese), Hakka and English.

Botanical Gardens   GARDENS
(植物園, Zhíwùyuán; Map p66; 53 Nanhai Rd, 南海路53號; ⊗5.30am-10pm; MXiaonanmen) FREE An oasis in the city, this 8-hectare park has well-stocked greenhouses, literature- and Chinese-zodiac-themed gardens, a lotus pond and myriad lanes where you can lose yourself in quiet contemplation. The gardens were established by the Japanese in 1921 and are part of a larger neighbourhood that maintains an old Taipei feel. Within the park, look for the Qing administrative office, built in 1888, and a herbarium from 1924 (both only open 9.30am-4pm Wed-Sun)

National Taiwan Craft
Research and Development
Institute   ARTS CENTRE
(Map p66; www.ntcri.gov.tw; 41 Nanhai Rd, 南海路41號; ⊗9.30am-5.30pm Tue-Sun; P; MChiang Kai-shek Memorial Hall) FREE This striking redand-white building, with its circular neoclassical Chinese-style roof, dates back to just 1956. It now houses the Craft Research and Development Institute. The 2nd floor showcases Taiwanese-designed and -made gift products – everything from stylish chopsticks to ceramics. The 3rd and 4th floors are used for free craft exhibitions and craft

workshops (jewellery, leather and fabrics). There's an organic buffet restaurant on the rooftop. Don't miss the circular lift, the spiral staircases and the glazed roof tiles.

2-28 Peace Memorial Park   PARK
(二二八和平紀念公園, Èr'èrbā Hépíng Gōngyuán; Map p66; MNTU Hospital) FREE Established in 1908, this was the first urban public park in Taiwan built on European models. Known as Taihoku (Taipei) Park under the Japanese, then Taipei New Park under the Kuomintang (KMT), its present name hails from 1996 in recognition of one of the pivotal events in Taiwanese modern history, which began here: the killings known as the 2-28 Incident (p352). The incident involved an uprising in which Taiwanese protested against the post-WWII Chinese government set in place by Chiang Kai-shek. Tens of thousands were killed in the following months.

In the centre of the park stands a memorial to 2-28 and at the southern end of the park is a **museum** (二二八紀念館, Èr'èrbā Jìniànguǎn; Map p66; ☑02-2389 7228; www.228.org.tw; 3 Ketagalan Blvd, 凱達格蘭大道3號; NT$20; ⊗10am-5pm Tue-Sun; MNTU Hospital) dedicated to the event. Otherwise this lovely little area of old trees, ponds, pavilions, pathways, bandstands, shrines and a large outdoor stage is used just as its founders intended: as a meeting place, a hang-out and a general refuge from the city. In the days before smartphone dating apps, this park also used to be a cruising area for gay men. Today it's overrun by bold brown squirrels.

There are multiple entrances to the park; the two main ones are off Ketagalan Blvd and Xiangyang Rd. In addition, two exits of NTU Hospital MRT station open onto the park.

Land Bank
Exhibition Hall   MUSEUM
(土銀分館, Tǔyín Fēnguǎn; Map p66; ☑02-2314 2699; https://en.ntm.gov.tw; 25 Xiangyang Rd, 襄陽路25號; NT$30; ⊗9.30am-5pm Tue-Sun; ♿; MNTU Hospital) Evolution is the theme at this museum, set in a 1930s former bank: evolution of life, evolution of money and banking, and evolution of the bank from the Japanese colonial era to modern Taipei. It's an odd juxtaposition but the displays, from soaring sauropod fossils to the open bank vault, are well presented and rich in details. Ticket includes admission to the National Taiwan Museum. Recent additions of virtual- and

augmented-reality displays make it a good choice for children.

Shandao Temple
BUDDHIST TEMPLE

(善導寺, Shàndǎosì; Map p66; 23 Zhongxiao E Rd, Sec 1,忠孝東路一段23; ⊙8am-5pm; P; MShandao Temple) FREE This Japanese-era temple is an imposing, hushed edifice in dark-pink and brown marble, and is in sharp contrast to the flashy bling of most of Taiwan's other temples. It is looked after by resident nuns.

Taipei Guesthouse
HISTORIC BUILDING

(臺北賓館, Táiběi Bīnguǎn; Map p66; www.mofa. gov.tw/entgh; 1 Ketagalan Blvd, 凱達格蘭大道1號; ⊙8am-4pm on scheduled days; MNTU Hospital) FREE Surrounded by a high grey concrete wall just to the south of NTU Hospital MRT station, Taipei Guesthouse is a two-storey Renaissance-style building dating back to 1901. Throughout its life it has mostly been used to host visiting dignitaries. The interior decorations are sumptuous and ornate. Common folk can take a gander roughly once a month on open days (check the website for dates).

Mitsui Warehouse
HISTORIC BUILDING

(記憶倉庫, Jìyì Cāngkù; Map p66; ☑02-2371 4957; 265 Zhongxiao W Rd, Sec 1,忠孝西路一段265號; ⊙10am-6pm Tue-Sun; MBeimen) FREE This faded red-brick warehouse has been carefully restored (70% of the bricks were cleaned and reused) and sits on a highway-flanked scrap of land opposite the North Gate (p75). Dating from 1914, it's an attractive building, with the displays inside all in Mandarin. Do, however, have a try of the virtual-reality experience, which will have you loading baskets with butter and flour back in the old warehouse.

Jinan Presbyterian Church
HISTORIC BUILDING

(濟南基督長老教會, Jǐ'nán Jīdū Zhǎnglǎo Jiàohuì; Map p66; 3 Zhongshan S Rd, 中山南路3號; ⊙open during services; MNTU Hospital) FREE This lovely red-brick church with its arched Gothic windows dates from 1916 and is fronted by a row of palm trees. Inside is dominated by white wood. The church is right next to the Legislative Yuan.

Taipei Artist Village
ARTS CENTRE

(臺北國際藝術村, Táiběi Guójì Yìshùcūn; TAV; Map p66; www.artistvillage.org; 7 Beiping E Rd, 北平東路7號; ⊙11am-9pm Tue-Sun; MShandao Temple) FREE This yellow-and-white striped building that looks like municipal offices is home to a small gallery, a garden and a cafe. It runs an artist-residency programme and there's usually an exhibition or workshop going on. Check the website before you go.

Museum of Drinking Water
MUSEUM

(自來水園區, Zìláishuǐ Yuán Qū; Map p66; ☑02-8369 5104; https://waterpark.water.gov.taipei; 1 Siyuan St, 思源街1號; adult/child Sep-Jun NT$50/25, Jul & Aug NT$80/40; ⊙9am-6pm Sep-Jun, to 8pm Jul & Aug; P; MGongguan) Located next to a water park (open in summer only), this museum covers the history of water treatment in Taipei and is set in a rather beautiful former pump station built in baroque style in 1908. It's more interesting than it sounds. The surrounding parkland and woodland, spread over a small hill, are also well worth exploring and very picnic-able.

Presidential Office Building
HISTORIC BUILDING

(總統府, Zǒngtǒng Fǔ; Map p66; www.president. gov.tw; 122 Chongqing S Rd, Sec 1, 重慶南路一段122號; with passport free; ⊙9-11.30am Mon-Fri; MNTU Hospital) FREE Built in 1919 as the seat of the Japanese governor-general of Taiwan, this striking building has housed the offices of the Taiwan president since 1949. Its classical European-fusion style includes many Japanese cultural elements, such as a sunrise-facing front, and a shape in the form of the character 日, part of 日本 (Japan), as seen from the air. You can visit the building Monday to Friday if you turn up before 11.30am. Bring your passport. Twelve times a year, the office is fully opened to the public, usually for a full day. Check the website for dates.

National Taiwan Museum
MUSEUM

(國立台灣博物館, Guólì Táiwān Bówùguǎn; Map p66; ☑02-2382 2566; https://en.ntm.gov.tw; 2 Xiangyang Rd, 襄陽路2號; NT$30; ⊙9.30am-5pm Tue-Sun; MNTU Hospital) Established in 1908 as Taiwan's first public museum; the present location in 2-28 Park hails from 1915. Reopened in 2017 after an upgrade, it has been transformed from its formerly dreary state into an engaging and atmospheric walk through Taiwan's natural history and indigenous cultures. Apart from some dodgy taxidermy, the exhibits are rich, informative and well explained in English. The 1st floor is reserved for special exhibits, which are often world-class and usually focus on the natural world.

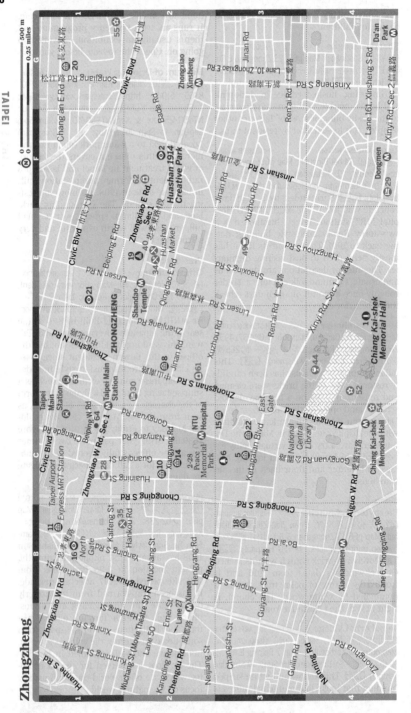

Map continues on
Gongguan Area Inset

Da'an
Forest
Park

DA'AN

Xinsheng S Rd 新生南路

Wenzhou St

National
Taiwan
University

Lane 4,
Yongkang St

Yongkang St

Lane 31,
Yongkang St

Qingtian St

Heping E Rd 和平東路

Xinhai Rd

Wenzhou St

Lane 86

Yongkang
Park

Lane 243 (Cafe Lane)

Yongkang St

50
42
32
Lane 10
58
38
41
33
25

Jinhua
Elementary
School

Jinshan S Rd 金山南路

Chaozhou St

Jinhua St

Lishui St

Foreign
Language
School

Chaozhou St

National Taiwan
Normal University
(Shida)

Lane 101

39
Shida Rd
51

Shida
Night
Market

Lane 93
Lane 105

Longquan St

Lane 283

Roosevelt Rd 羅斯福路

240
Lane
210

Lane 210

49
60
59
48

Taipower
Building
43

Puchang St

Aiguo E Rd 愛國東路

Nanchang Rd

Jinjiang Rd

Shida Rd

Guting

26

Shuiyuan Rd

Pedestrian/Bike Bridge

Xindian River

Chaozhou St

Roosevelt Rd 羅斯福路

57
47

Heping W Rd 和平西路

Tongan St

9

Nanchang Rd

36

Guling St

Tingzhou Rd

Chongqing S Rd 重慶南路

Nanhai Rd

Chongqing S Rd

17
3
National 2-28
Memorial Museum

13

重慶南路

Ningbo W Rd

Sanyuan St

31

Quanzhou St

Botanical
Gardens
7

Ningbo W St

Heping W Rd 和平西路

Ningbo Rd

Zhonghua Rd 中華路

Juguang Rd
Xizang Rd

Gongguan Area

(Same scale as main map)

400 m
0.2 miles

National
Taiwan
University

Gongguan

Roosevelt Rd

Ziyoushan Rd

56
23

Lane 24
37

Tingzhou Rd

27
4
Treasure
Hill

12

Siyuan St

Shuiyuan Rd

45
53
24

Xindian River

Zhongzheng

**Kishuan Forest
of Literature** HISTORIC BUILDING
(紀州庵文學森林, Jìzhōu An Wénxué Sēnlín; Map p66; ☎02-2368 7577; www.kishuan.org.tw; 107 Tongan St, 同安街107號; ☺Tue-Sun 10am-6pm, to 9pm Fri; P; MGuting) FREE This sleepy wooden lodge was built by a Japanese family in 1917 and was lovingly reconstructed after two fires in the 1990s almost destroyed it. Visitors can tour the inside and chill on the open verandahs, provided they slip off their shoes and wear socks to protect the polished floors. It is managed by the Taiwan Literature Development Foundation, and occasional art exhibitions and film showings are held here.

Postal Museum MUSEUM
(郵政博物館, Yóuzhèng Bówùguǎn; Map p66; 45 Chongqing S Rd, Sec 2, 重慶南路二段45號; NT$10; ☺9am-5pm Tue-Sun; ✦; MChiang Kai-shek Memorial Hall) This oft-overlooked museum has had a massive makeover and is now bags of fun if you're a young kid, into stamps or even mildly interested in them. It contains five floors of intensely detailed information imaginatively and beautifully presented through images, interactive exhibits, models, videos, photographs and games. Children can pretend to be a postie and pedal a bicycle, for example. Look out for the special exhibition on rare stamps of the world.

Ximending & Wanhua

Wanhua is where Taipei first started out as a trading centre, growing rich by selling tea, coal and camphor. Over time the area lost its importance as the city spread eastwards, leaving behind marvellous pockets of living history in its temples and heritage buildings.

To its north is Ximending (西門町; Xīméndīng, and usually shortened to 'Xi-men') pedestrian area, an eight-branched intersection chock-full of young people, fast food and shops selling novelties, cosmetics and designs. There's an entire street (Wu-chang) devoted to cinemas, and a lane populated by piercing and tattoo parlours (Lane 50 Hanzhong).

★**Longshan Temple**   BUDDHIST TEMPLE
(龍山寺, Lóngshān Sì; Map p70; www.lungshan.org.tw; 211 Guangzhou St, 廣州街211號; ⊙6am-10pm; Ⓜ Longshan Temple) Founded in 1738 by Han immigrants from Fujian, this temple has served as a municipal, guild and self-defence centre, as well as a house of worship. These days it is one of the city's top religious sites, and a prime venue for exploring both Taiwan's vibrant folk faith and its unique temple arts and architecture. The temple can get very congested with tourists; try coming early in the morning (before 8am) or late in the evening (after 8pm) to avoid the crush.

Longshan is dedicated to the bodhisattva of mercy, Guanyin, though in true Taiwanese style there are over 100 other gods and goddesses worshipped in the rear and side halls. Matsu, goddess of the sea, is enshrined in the back centre; Wenchang Dijun, the god of literature, to the far right (come during exam period to see how important he is); red-faced Guan Gong, the god of war and patron of police and gangsters, is enshrined to the far left; and in front of that is the Old Man Under the Moon, known as the Matchmaker or the Chinese Cupid.

As with most temples in Taiwan, Longshan has been rebuilt multiple times after destruction by earthquakes, typhoons and even bombing in the last days of WWII. The present structure (with elements from the masterful 1920s and post-WWII reconstructions) doesn't have the same flow and elegance as Bao'an Temple (p74), but it is still an impressive structure with sweeping swallowtail eaves, colourful *jiǎnniàn* (mosaic-like temple decoration) figures on the roof, and elaborate stone- and woodcarvings.

TAIPEI SIGHTS

CINEMATIC INSIGHTS

The Great Buddha+ (Huang Hsin-yao; 2017) An excellent satire on inequality, corruption and religion in Taiwan.

A Brighter Summer Day (Edward Yang; 1991) A masterpiece about tensions between mainland migrants and local Taiwanese in 1960s Taipei.

City of Sadness (Hou Hsiao-hsien; 1989) A taboo-breaking classic about events around the 2-28 Incident.

Stray Dogs (Tsai Ming-liang; 2013) Venice Film Festival prize-winner about poverty in Taipei.

Millennium Mambo (Hou Hsiao-hsien; 2001) Award-winning romantic drama starring Shu Qi.

Check out the two-of-a-kind bronze pillars outside the front hall and the incense holders outside the main hall. The handles depict a common temple motif: The Fool Holding up the Sky. The western-style appearance of the 'fools' is no coincidence. They are said to represent the Dutch (or sometimes Dutch slaves), who occupied Taiwan in the 17th century.

The best times to visit Longshan are around 6am, 8am and 5pm, when crowds of worshippers gather and engage in hypnotic chanting. Or try Guanyin's birthday on the 19th day of the second lunar month, or the weeks before and during Lunar New Year.

★**Zhongshan Hall**   HISTORIC BUILDING
(中山堂, Zhōngshān Táng; Map p70; ☎02-2381 3137; https://english.zsh.gov.taipei; 98 Yanping S Rd, 延平南路98號; ⊙9.30am-9pm; Ⓟ; Ⓜ Ximen) ᴳᴿᴱᴱ This handsome four-storey building, constructed in 1936 for the coronation of Emperor Hirohito, is where the Japanese surrender ceremony was held in October 1945, and later where Chiang Kai-shek delivered public speeches from the terrace following his four 're-elections'. On the 3rd floor stairwell hangs the masterwork *Water Buffalo* by Huang Tu-shui (1895–1930), the first Taiwanese artist to study in Japan.

Zhongshan Hall was one of the most modern buildings in Taiwan at the time it was built, and it blends modernist and western-classical styling. Note the filings on the bricks, custom-made by a kiln in Beitou: the design scatters direct sunlight, making

Ximending & Wanhua

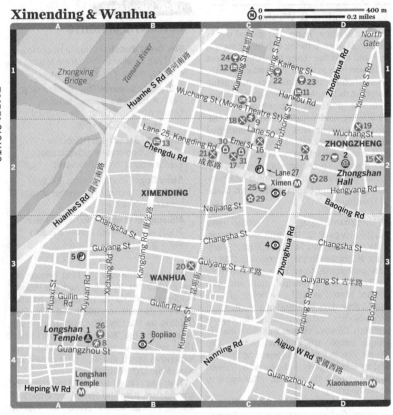

the building difficult for enemy bombers to see (a concern as Japan had been skirmishing with China since 1931).

The hall has an auditorium and frequently hosts music and drama performances. You can explore the whole building freely, even the rooftops, at any time during opening hours. Working from the top down, there's an excellent cafe, Le Promenoir Coffee (p104), on the 4th floor, a teahouse on the 3rd, and a restaurant, The Fortress Room on the 2nd, where you can drink or dine on the balcony from which Chiang delivered his public addresses. Free historical or cultural exhibitions, often very good, fill the rooms and hallways throughout.

Qingshan Temple
TAOIST TEMPLE

(青山宮, Qīngshān Gōng; Map p70; 218 Guiyang St, Sec 2, 貴陽街二段218號; ⏰5.30am-9pm; ⓂLongshan Temple) Along with Longshan, this elegant temple, built in 1856, is one of Wanhua's top houses of worship. There is

an abundance of top-quality wood, stone and decorative artwork to see here, and the god's birthday festival is one of Taipei liveliest religious events. Called the Night Patrol (夜間出巡; Yèjiān Chūxún), this parade takes place from 5pm to 9pm over two nights (the 20th and 21st days of the lunar 10th month; around the end of November or early December).

Qingshan's resident god (Qingshan Wang; 青山王) is credited with saving the people of Wanhua from a deadly plague. During the days of his birthday celebrations, he sets out on a pilgrimage to expel evil from the neighbourhood. There are fireworks, gongs, lanterns and a colourful parade of people dressed up as gods, giant Infernal Generals, and other Taoist and folk figures. What makes this pilgrimage particularly dramatic and worth attending is that it takes place at night.

The temple is worth a visit any time to examine the stonework in the main hall,

Ximending & Wanhua

the octagonal plafond ceilings (built without nails), the lively cochin pottery figures on either side of the worship hall, and the striking multicoloured *jiǎnniàn* (mosaic relief) work on the roof, which you can admire up-close by climbing the stairs at the back of the temple.

Tianhou Temple   TAOIST TEMPLE
(天后宮, Tiānhòu Gōng; Map p70; 51 Chengdu Rd, 成都路51號; ⊙6am-10pm; ⓂXimen) **FREE** This small, atmospheric temple appears from the outside as a narrow, elaborate shopfront in the Ximending area. But walk through the gate and you'll find one of Taipei's most intriguing temples, a place where Japanese and Chinese worship patterns existed, and still exist, side by side.

The original Tianhou Temple (devoted to the goddess Matsu, also known as Tianhou, or the Empress of Heaven) was built in 1746, and demolished during the last years of Japanese rule to make way for a roadway. The current structure was erected in 1948 on the grounds of a former Japanese temple devoted to Hongfa Dashi. As you face the exit you can see a statue of Hongfa Dashi to the right, while on the left is a group of Jizō (the Ksitigarbha bodhisattva) statues. Even today many local worshippers will pray to the

Japanese deities as they make their way round the temple.

Bopiliao Historic Block   AREA
(剝皮寮, Bō Pí Liáo; Map p70; www.bopiliao. taipei/en; Lane 173, Kangding Rd, 康定路173巷; ⊙9am-9pm Tue-Sun; ⓂLongshan Temple) **FREE** One of the best-preserved historic sections of Wanhua, Bopiliao covers both Qing and early Japanese-era architecture. Some of the buildings house art galleries (generally open from 9am to 6pm, Tuesday to Sunday) showing experimental works, mostly by young local artists. Although reconstruction work is impressive, the street lacks life; it's more like a museum compared with the atmospheric Dihua St (p74) that is still used by the community. But it's worth a look if you're in the area.

During the Japanese era, the narrow Qing-built street and shops became the back alley to new, wider Guangzhou St. As such the eras neatly divide themselves, with Japanese buildings to the south and Qing to the north. The differing styles are easy to spot: Qing-era buildings are commonly red brick, and shopfronts are set back from arcades. Japanese buildings incorporate western baroque designs, and facades are embellished with flowers and other common motifs.

Da'an

Bopiliao was the setting for many scenes in the 2010 Taiwanese gangster flick *Monga*.

Red House CULTURAL CENTRE
(西門紅樓; Xīmén Hónglóu; Map p70; ☏02-2311 9380; www.redhouse.org.tw; 10 Chengdu Rd, 成都路10號; ⊙11am-9.30pm Tue-Sun, to 10pm Fri & Sat; ⓜXimen) FREE Ximending's most iconic building was built in 1908 to serve as Taipei's first public market. These days it's a multifunctional cultural centre, with regular live performances in the theatre upstairs. There's a small cafe and gift shop at ground level. Towards the back of the building is the Creative Boutique, two floors of craft and design stalls. Look out for the Taiwanize clothing brand and the gorgeous gifts based on designs from Taiwan traditional tiles, once used by the aristocracy to adorn doorways.

◉ Da'an

Da'an (大安; Dà'ān) is an important commercial and residential area (property prices are among the highest in the city) with several major universities. You'll find some of Taipei's ritziest shopping areas here, the classiest bars and also lovely, leafy Da'an Park.

Da'an

Taiwan Contemporary Culture Lab CULTURE PARK
(C-Lab, 臺灣當代文化實驗場, Táiwān Dāngdài Wénhuà Shíyànchǎng; Map p72; ☎02-8773 5087; www.clab.org.tw/en; 177 Jianguo S Rd, Sec 1, 建國南路一段177號; ⊙7am-9.30pm Tue-Sun; Ⓜ Zhongxiao Xinsheng, Ⓜ Zhongxiao Fuxing) FREE This sprawling complex, formerly the Air Force Command Headquarters, was turned over to the Ministry of Culture in 2018 to develop as a space for young innovators and for hosting art and cultural events. At the time of writing, not much was going on but it's a lovely huge space to walk around; fairly eerie at night. Several of the red-brick and whitewashed buildings, typical of Taiwan's institutional architecture from the 1950s to 1960s, still bear their Air Force insignia.

Da'an Forest Park PARK
(大安公園, Dàān Gōngyuán; Map p72; Ⓟ♿☺; Ⓜ Da'an Park) This is Taipei's Central Park, where the city comes to play. And play it does, from kids rollerblading to teens shooting hoops to old men engaged in *xiàngqí* (Chinese chess). The park is a great place to stroll around after a meal on nearby Yongkang St or for a summer picnic. There's a little outdoor cafe, a sandpit, a firefly pond and a towering statue of Guanyin, the Buddhist goddess of mercy. Joggers do laps around its perimeter.

Taipei Grand Mosque MOSQUE
(台北清真寺, Táiběi Qīngzhēnsi; Map p72; 62 Xinsheng S Rd, Sec 2, 新生南路二段62號; Ⓜ Da'an Park) Built with money from the Saudi government and other Middle Eastern countries back in the 1950s, this modest, traditional structure is set in its own gardens; note the golden crescent moons topping the railings. Friday prayers attract a number of food vendors outside. Since this is an active place of worship, visitors are advised to admire it from the outside.

◎ Zhongshan & Datong

Datong (大同; Dàtóng) is one of the oldest areas of the city but there's a new vibe to the Dihua St area, which still retains its Qing- and Japanese-era mansions and shops. You don't want to miss the temples in this district either – they are Taipei's finest. Zhongshan (中山; Zhōngshān) was once a centre for finance and international business; today it is still loaded with hotels and endless eateries (especially Japanese). There are also numerous small but excellent museums, plus Taipei Expo Park and Miramar, the city's version of the London Eye.

★ **Dihua Street** HISTORIC SITE
(迪化街, Díhuà Jiē; Map p80; MBeimen, MDaqiaotou) This former 'Centre Street' has long been known for its Chinese medicine shops, fabric market and lively Lunar New Year sundry market. It has attracted numerous restoration and cultural projects and is now a magnet for young entrepreneurs, eager to breathe new life into the neighbourhood with cafes, restaurants, art studios and antique shops.

Thankfully, this gentrification hasn't squashed the original atmosphere – fancy ceramic shops sit side by side with long-term tenants selling sacks of dried mushrooms and agricultural produce.

Díhuà Jiē was constructed in the 1850s. Merchants from the Wanhua area were on the losing side of an ethnic feud (over different groups' ancestor origins – all too common in Taiwan's history), and fled to Dadaocheng (now a neighbourhood inside Datong). The merchants prospered here while the Wanhua port, further downstream, eventually silted up. Some might say they got their revenge.

After Taiwan's ports were opened following the Second Opium War (1856–60), western tea merchants flooded into the area and built handsome mansions and trading stores. Later, during the Japanese era, baroque and modernist architectural and decorative touches were added to many shops, making Dihua Taipei's most historically diverse street. The first house/shop on the street is at 156 Dihua St, Sec 1. Notice its low profile and narrow arcades. Further up the street, near Mingquan W Rd, are typical shops from the late 19th century with arched windows and wide arcades. Closer to Yongle Market are the western-style merchant houses and shops renovated during Japanese times.

On the 8th and 9th floors of Yongle Market is DaDaoCheng Theater (p110), a popular venue for traditional performances.

Note: the Lunar New Year bazaar here is extremely bustling and popular. If you don't like crowds, it is best to avoid this area.

★ **Ama Museum** MUSEUM
(阿嬤家, Āmā Jiā; Map p80; ☑02-2553 7133; www.twrf.org.tw/amamuseum; 256 Dihua St, Sec 1, 迪化街一段256號; NT$100; ⊙10am-5pm Tue-Sun; MDaqiaotou) Set in a restored heritage house at the top end of Dihua St is this permanent exhibition showcasing the history of Taiwanese 'comfort women' – sex slaves for soldiers – during Japanese rule in WWII. Run by the Taipei Women's Rescue Foundation, the museum makes use of the foundation's meticulous research over many years, interviewing and collecting materials from almost 60 survivors. In addition, Ama puts on temporary exhibitions focusing on women in history.

★ **Bao'an Temple** TAOIST TEMPLE
(保安宮, Bǎoān Gōng; Map p80; www.baoan.org.tw/english; 61 Hami St, 哈密街61號; ⊙7am-10pm; MYuanshan) FREE Recipient of a Unesco Asia-Pacific Heritage Award for both its restoration and its revival of temple rites and festivities, the Bao'an Temple (also called Dalongdong Bao'an Temple) is a must-visit when in Taipei. This exquisite structure is loaded with prime examples of the traditional decorative arts, and the yearly folk arts festival (April to June) is a showcase of traditional performance arts.

The temple was founded in 1760 by immigrants from Xiamen, Fujian province, and its modern size and design began to take shape in 1805. The main resident god is Emperor Baosheng (or Wu), a historical figure revered for his medical skills. The rear shrine is dedicated to Shennong, the god of agriculture.

From 1995 to 2002, the temple underwent its largest renovation project ever. Under sound management, skilled artisans were employed and top-quality materials used. In addition, the temple began holding an annual folk-arts festival (called Baosheng Cultural Festival), which includes the Five Day Completion Rituals to Thank Gods (essentially to transform the temple from an everyday to a sacred space), the gods' birthday celebrations, lion dances, parades, Taiwanese opera performances and even free Chinese-medicine clinics. See the temple's website for dates of events, all of which are free.

There's an information office, with a brochure on Bao'an and a small selection of English-language books, at the rear of the temple's inner courtyard.

Museum of Contemporary Art Taipei ARTS CENTRE
(台北當代藝術館, Táiběi Dāngdài Yìshùguǎn; Map p80; ☑02-2552 3731; www.mocataipei.org.tw; 39

Chang'an W Rd, 長安西路39號; NT$50; ⊙10am-6pm Tue-Sun; Ⓜ Zhongshan) Very bright, very modern, and often fun and very experimental art is showcased here. The long red-brick building dates back to the 1920s. It started life as an elementary school then became Taipei City Hall, before its current incarnation as the city's modern art museum. Well worth a visit. Bags must be checked in, and English audio guides are available.

Taipei Confucius Temple   CONFUCIAN TEMPLE
(孔廟, Kǒng Miào; Map p80; www.ct.taipei.gov.tw; 275 Dalong Rd, 大龍街275號; ⊙8am-9pm Tue-Sat; ⓐ; Ⓜ Yuanshan) FREE Constructed by the famous Fujian craftsman Wang Yi-shun in the late 1920s, this temple is a beautiful example of Minnan-style architecture and of Taiwan's delightful decorative arts. There are no statues or imagery of the great sage – where you would expect one there is a spirit tablet. There are informative displays (in English) on the history of Confucius, the temple and the Six Confucian Arts (including archery and riding); many are interactive and fun for inquisitive children (open 9am to 5pm).

Also recommended are the free Confucius-themed shows in the 4D cinema. Nine screenings (first one at 10am, last at 4pm) are held throughout the day. On Saturdays at 10am, the temple stages traditional performances in the main hall (Dacheng Hall). English audio guides are also available.

Confucius' birthday is celebrated on 28 September with a 6am ceremony presided over by the mayor of Taipei. It's a colourful event and free tickets are handed out several days before the event. If you miss out, you can line up at 5.30am on the day itself to try and bag a spare.

The grounds and main temple hall are open until 9pm, but the exhibitions in the side rooms close at 5pm.

Su Ho Paper Museum   MUSEUM
(樹火紀念紙博物館, Shùhuǒ Jìniàn Zhǐ Bówùguǎn; Map p66; ☑02-2507 5535; www.suhopaper.org.tw; 68 Chang'an E Rd, Sec 2, 長安東路二段68號; NT$100, with paper-making session NT$180; ⊙9.30am-4.30pm Mon-Sat; ⓐ; Ⓜ Songjiang Nanjing) Fulfilling the lifelong dream of Taiwanese paper-maker Chen Su-ho, this stylish four-storey museum displays a working traditional paper mill and temporary exhibits. It has a focus on paper sculpture and installation art, as well as good overviews of paper-making around the world and in

Taiwan. For a DIY experience, join the daily paper-making classes for kids at 10am, 11am, 2pm and 3pm.

museum207   CULTURAL CENTRE
(Map p80; ☑02-2557 3680; www.museum207.org; 207 Dihua St, Sec 1, 迪化街一段207號; ⊙10am-5pm Wed-Mon; Ⓜ Daqiaotou) FREE This lovely corner building from the 1960s has been converted into a historical-cultural museum with great English explanations, by the same people behind Taipei Story House (p75). museum207, though, appears to be much less twee. At the time of writing, for example, there was an excellent display of old slides of Taiwan street scenes. Clamber to the top floor to get a bird's-eye view of the Qing dynasty rooftops.

Taiwan Comic Base   MANGA
(台灣漫畫基地, Táiwān Mànhuà Jīdì; Map p80; https://tcb.culture.tw; 38 Huayin St, 華陰街38號; ⊙10am-8pm Tue-Sun; Ⓜ Taipei Main Station) FREE Taiwan Comic Base is a Ministry of Culture initiative to show off and support the island's vibrant manga industry. This small centre has a graphic-novel bookshop on the ground floor (Mandarin language only). The main attractions here are the occasional exhibitions and events on graphic novels, sometimes incorporating virtual-and augmented-reality displays on the 2nd and 3rd floors. Check their website to see what's on.

North Gate   GATE
(北門, Běimén; Map p66; Ⓜ Beimen) Comparisons with the Arc de Triomphe may be a bit exaggerated, but the russet-red, newly restored Qing Dynasty North Gate is rather photogenic, especially when it is illuminated at night. Originally constructed in the 1880s, it is the biggest of the city gates, through which the common folk could gain entry into the government quarter during imperial times.

The gate stands in the middle of Zhongxiao W Rd, just east of Zhonghua Rd. Take MRT Exit 2 and walk towards Zhongxiao W.

Taipei Expo Park   PARK
(花博公園, Huābó Gōngyuán; Map p80; www.taipei-expopark.tw; Ⓟ; Ⓜ Yuanshan) This expansive park covers three linked-up sections – stroll around or take a YouBike. It has a lively food court called Maji Square (p99), and Eco Ark (a giant structure of recycled bottles). Across Zhongshan N Rd you'll find the Fine Arts Museum (p78), and Taipei Story House in

the Fine Arts Park. Further east, Xinsheng Park has innovative pavilions, a maze and Lin Antai Historic House (p78). The main park entrance is directly outside Yuanshan MRT station.

Xiahai City God Temple
TAOIST TEMPLE

(霞海城隍廟, Xiáhǎi Chénghuáng Miào, Hsiahai City God Temple; Map p80; www.tpecitygod.org; 61 Dihua St, Sec 1, 迪化街一段61號; MBeimen) This lively and well-loved temple on Dihua St was built in 1856 to house the City God statue that the losers in the Wanhua feud took as they fled upstream. Little has changed since those days. The temple is a terrific spot to witness folk-worship rituals as well as admire some gorgeous pieces of traditional arts and crafts. If you want to pray to the deities yourself, the temple's website has a step-by-step guide on how to go about it.

The temple management deserves kudos for the clear English signs about the temple introducing the City God, the City God's Wife (known as a Chinese Cupid and the recipient of devotees' pleas concerning affairs of the heart) and the Matchmaker (said to have brought together thousands of couples), as well as some of the temple's outstanding decorative pieces.

Two of the most interesting are clay sculptures in the main hall just before the altar, demonstrating the Chinese talent for using homonyms in art. The sculpture on the left, for example, shows a man on an elephant holding a pike and chime. Since the Chinese for pike is *ji* and chime is *qing,* together these form the homonym *jiqing* meaning 'auspicious' (note that different characters would represent the different meanings, but the sounds are the same). The other sculpture shows a man riding a lion while holding a flag and ball. Flag is *qi* and ball is *qiu,* which together sound like *qiqiu,* or to 'pray for'.

On the City God's Birthday (the 14th day of the fifth lunar month), dozens of temples around Taipei send teams here to entertain the City God. The procession stretches over a kilometre and performances include lion dances, god dances and martial arts displays. Things get going around 2pm to 3pm and all the festivities last five days.

Xingtian Temple
TAOIST TEMPLE

(行天宮, Xíngtiān Gōng; Map p80; 109 Mingquan E Rd, Sec 2, 民權東路二段109號; ⊙4am-10pm; MXingtian Temple) FREE This newish temple,

---

City Walk
Through Qing- & Japanese-era Taipei

START LONGSHAN TEMPLE
END HUASHAN 1914 CREATIVE PARK
LENGTH 5KM; FOUR HOURS

The tour begins at ❶ **Longshan Temple** (p69) in Wanhua, Taipei's oldest district. Restored numerous times over the centuries, Longshan remains the spiritual heart of this district, as it was when Fujian immigrants first established it in 1738. From Longshan head to ❷ **Bopiliao** (p71), a formerly thriving commercial area with excellent examples of both late-Qing and Japanese-era shops. The red-brick arcades here are popular spots for photographs.

Returning to Longshan, head north. At Guiyang St check out the exquisite Qing-era stone pillars, hanging lanterns and ceramic figures at ❸ **Qingshan Temple** (p70), built in 1856, then head to ❹ **Qingshui Temple**, founded in 1787. Note the fine Qing-era temple design: single-storey halls and a sweeping swallowtail roof. Both the outer dragon pillars and dragon and tiger side carvings date to the 18th and early 19th centuries.

Cut up to Changsha St and follow it to the site of the ❺ **Nishi Honganji** (西本願寺廣場; Xīběnyuànsì Guǎngchǎng; Map p70; cnr Changsha St & Zhonghua Rd; M Ximen) FREE, once the largest Japanese Buddhist temple in Taiwan. Retrace your steps and head down Hanzhong St, followed by Neijiang St. At No. 25 turn right into the back of the ❻ **Red House** (p72), an octagonal structure built in 1908 as Taipei's first public market. The area you are now in is called Ximending (or Ximen for short), a reference to the former *ximen* (west gate) of the old Qing-era city walls. Now cross Zhonghua Rd (take note of how the streets have widened) and zig-zag to ❼ **Zhongshan Hall** (p69), built in 1936 at a time when architectural tastes were changing from western–classical hybrids to more modernist designs. The hall is a mix of both.

Continue up Yanping S Rd to ❽ **Taipei Futai Street Mansion**. The two-storey former office, built in 1910 in a western style, is the only surviving building on Futai St from that era. Just up from here is the ❾ **North Gate** (p75) – the only remaining

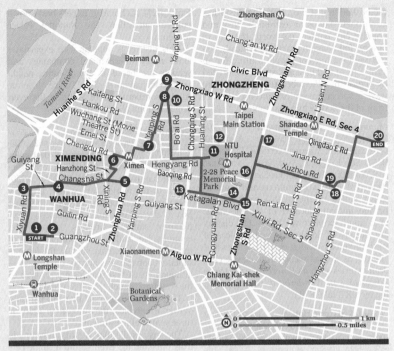

Qing-era gate that has its original appearance – and the **10 Taipei Post Office**, built in 1930. Head back down Bo'ai Rd and then along Hengyang Rd, noting the Japanese-era shops and the pleasant arcades (covered walkways, a traditional Taiwanese design). At 2-28 Park check out the **11 National Taiwan Museum** (p65). Built in 1915, it was the first major public building constructed under Japanese colonial rule. The **12 Land Bank Exhibition Hall** (p64) across the way was the most architecturally advanced structure in Taiwan when completed in 1933, and yet it still incorporated traditional arcades into the outer structure.

Next is the **13 Presidential Office Building** (p65), to the southwest of the 2-28 Park, completed in 1919 and restored in 1947. Originally the office of the Japanese colonial governor, the building faces east to the rising sun, and the design (as seen from the air) forms the character 日 (sun), part of 日本 (Rìběn, which means Japan in Mandarin).

Now head to **14 Taipei Guesthouse** (p65), built at the turn of the 19th century and widely considered the most beautiful baroque-style building from the Japanese era. Note again how wide the boulevards are in this area: this is Taipei as the Japanese wanted it to be, modelled on Paris of the 1890s. Head up to

the **15 East Gate** and then turn in to the old **16 National Taiwan University Hospital** (國立台灣大學醫學院附設醫院; Guólì Táiwān Dàxué Yīxué Yuàn Fùshè Yīyuàn; Map p66; 1 Changde St, 常德街1號; M NTU Hospital), built in 1912. The next few blocks along Zhongshan N Rd have a wealth of beautiful Japanese-era buildings, including the **17 Jinan Presbyterian Church** (p65), built in 1916 and an unusual example of Gothic architecture in Taipei.

Retrace your steps to Xuzhou Rd and stop in at the **18 Mayor's Residence Art Salon** (p103), one of the best-preserved wooden Japanese houses in Taiwan. Then cut through the **19 College of Social Sciences National Taiwan University**. These buildings, completed in 1919, are a good example of how the Japanese often blended eastern and western elements: the buildings are largely classical in style, with Grecian pillars and semicircular arches, but have roofs in traditional Japanese black tiles. The pond and gardens (both originals) are also Japanese in style.

End your journey at **20 Huashan 1914 Creative Park** (p61) on Zhongxiao E Rd, a restored wine factory from the 1920s that now houses chic restaurants, cafes, performance halls and excellent gift shops.

established in just 1967, lacks that historical atmosphere but is an extremely busy and popular city temple. It's worth the trip to observe folk religion practices. Typically, you will see long lines of people waiting for an 'exorcism' of bad luck and spirits conducted by one of the blue-robed temple staff, who wave a special low-smoke incense stick in front of the body while chanting.

Miniatures Museum of Taiwan MUSEUM
(袖珍博物館, Xiùzhēn Bówùguǎn; Map p80; ☎02-2515 0583; www.mmot.com.tw; 96 Jianguo N Rd, Sec 1, 建國北路一段96號; adult/child NT$200/160; ⊙10am-6pm Tue-Sun; ⓂSongjiang Nanjing) Whimsical, wondrous and fantastically detailed are the creative works at this private museum located in the basement of a nondescript tower block. On display are dozens of doll-house-sized replicas of western houses, castles, chalets, palaces and villages, as well as scenes from classic children's stories such as *Pinocchio* and *Alice's Adventures in Wonderland*. If you're coming by MRT, take Exit 5.

Lin Antai Historic House HISTORIC BUILDING
(林安泰古厝, Lín Āntài Gǔ Cuò; Map p80; https://english.linantai.taipei; 5 Binjiang St, 濱江街5號; ⊙9am-5pm Tue-Sun; ⓂYuanshan) FREE This Fujian-style 30-room house, Taipei's oldest residential building, was first erected between 1783 and 1787, near what is now Dunhua S Rd. As was typical in those times, the house expanded as the family grew in numbers and wealth, reaching its present size in 1823. Today the historic house is notable for its central courtyard, swallowtail roof and period furniture.

Fine Arts Museum MUSEUM
(市立美術館, Shìlì Měishùguǎn; Map p80; www.tfam.museum; 181 Zhongshan N Rd, Sec 3, 中山北路三段181號; NT$30, free Sat after 5pm; ⊙9.30am-5.30pm Tue-Fri & Sun, to 8.30pm Sat; Ⓟ; ⓂYuanshan) Constructed in the 1980s, this airy, four-storey box of marble, glass and concrete showcases contemporary art, with a particular focus on Taiwanese artists. Exhibits include pieces by Taiwanese painters and sculptors, from the Japanese period through to the present. Check the website to see what's currently showing.

Shilin

North of Taipei city centre, Shilin (士林; Shìlín) is an affluent residential area sitting at the base of Yangmingshan National Park (p127). It's home to Taipei's best-known cultural attraction, the National Palace Museum.

This district is popular with expatriates since many international companies and schools are based in the Tianmu neighbourhood, just north of the Palace Museum. At the southern end of Shilin is the ever-popular Shilin Night Market.

★National Palace Museum MUSEUM
(故宮博物院, Gùgōng Bówùyuàn; Map p62; ☎02-6610 3600; www.npm.gov.tw/en; 221 Zhishan Rd, Sec 2, 至善路二段221號; NT$350; ⊙8.30am-6.30pm Sun-Thu, to 9pm Fri & Sat; Ⓟ; 🚌R30) Home to the world's largest and arguably finest collection of Chinese art, this vast hoard covers treasures in painting, calligraphy, statuary, bronzes, lacquerware, ceramics, jade and religious objects. Some of the most popular items, such as the famous Jadeite Cabbage, are always on display – although check first that it's not on loan to the southern branch (p225) in Chiayi.

There are controversial plans to partially or even wholly close the museum in 2020 for three years' refurbishment.

The historical range at this museum is truly outstanding. Even within a single category, such as ceramics, pieces range over multiple dynasties, and even back to Neolithic times.

➡ Level 1 includes rare books, special exhibits, Qing and Ming dynasty furniture, religious sculptures, and a great orientation gallery to give you an overview of dynasties.

➡ Level 2 includes painting, calligraphy, a history of Chinese ceramics with abundant examples, and an interactive area with videos and a virtual tour of 20 famous paintings.

➡ Level 3 contains bronzes, weapons, ritual vessels, and Ming and Qing dynasty carvings. There is also the stunning jade collection, covering weapons, teapots, jewellery, ritual objects and the renowned Jadeite Cabbage.

➡ Level 4 was closed at the time of writing. Previously a teahouse, there are plans to convert it into more exhibition space.

The classy Silks Palace restaurant is in the building to the left of the main hall. Also on the left is the second Exhibition Hall that occasionally hosts special shows.

The museum offers free guided tours in English at 10am and 3pm (book online or register in person about 20 minutes before, limited to 30 people). If you prefer to move about at your own pace, try an English **headphone guide** (NT$150). There is also a **museum gift shop** (Map p62; www.npmshops. com; basement, National Palace Museum, 221 Zhishan Rd, Sec 2, 故宮博物院, 至善路二段221 號; ⊘9am-7pm Sun-Thu, to 9.30pm Fri & Sat; 🛜; 🚇R30) worth exploring.

To reach the museum from Shilin MRT station, head out Exit 1 to **Zhongzheng Rd** (Map p84; Zhongzheng Rd, 中正路) and catch the R30 (red 30), minibus 18 or 19, or bus 255, 304 or 815. It's about 15 minutes to the museum. From Dazhi MRT station take bus B13 (brown 13).

Cixian Temple TAOIST TEMPLE
(慈諴宮, Cíxián Gōng; Map p84; www.facebook. com/mazu1796; 84 Danan Rd, 大南路84號; ⊘6am-10pm; 🚇Jiantan) Dedicated to the worship of Matsu, this 1927 reconstruction of the original 1864 design sits at ground central for Shilin Night Market. It's worth a visit (even if you aren't already in the area to snack) in order to examine the masterful cochin ceramic panels above the arched doors in the main hall, as well as the exquisite stone- and woodcarvings throughout.

★**Shilin Night Market** MARKET
(士林夜市, Shílín Yèshì; Map p84; www.shi-lin-night-market.com.tw; ⊘5pm-midnight; 🅿; 🚇Jiantan) Taipei's most famous night market is hugely popular with travellers – and many young locals – who come to enjoy the carnival of street-side snacking, shopping and games. In 2011, the government moved much of the action inside a covered market: the food vendors were relegated to the basement, while clothing, toys and games were given ground level, diluting all the fun. However, there are still lanes and lanes full of food stalls outside, and they retain the original buzz.

National Revolutionary Martyrs' Shrine SHRINE
(國民革命忠烈祠, Guómín Gémìng Zhōngliècí; Map p80; https://afrc.mnd.gov.tw/faith_martyr; 139 Beian Rd, 北安路139號; ⊘9am-5pm; 🚇Dazhi, 🚇Jiantan) **FREE** This large shrine marks the memory of almost 400,000 soldiers who died for Taiwan (mostly within China). The bulky complex, built in 1969, is typical of the northern 'palace-style' architecture popu-

LOCAL KNOWLEDGE

TAIWAN TUNES

Growing (野生) **by Lin Sheng-hsiang** (林生祥) Singer-songwriter and social activist who performs in the Hakka dialect.

Insects Awaken (驚蟄) **by Lim Giong** (林強) Musician known for pop and electronic music, and film scores.

Story Thief (偷故事的人) **by A-Mei** (張惠妹) Puyuma pop diva who sings in Mandarin and Hokkien.

Takasago Army (高砂軍) **by Chthonic** (閃靈) 'The Black Sabbath of Asia' adapt folk songs and use traditional instruments.

A City (城市) **by Deserts Chang** (張懸) Singer-songwriter with an urban sensibility.

larised during Chiang Kai-shek's reign. The hourly changing of the guards is a popular attraction, especially with Japanese tourists. It takes almost 20 minutes for the white-clad soldiers to march from the gate to their posts in front of the memorial, giving plenty of time to get a good photo.

Walk 1.5km, grab a YouBike from Dazhi station, or else take a bus or taxi from Dazhi or Jiantan MRT stations. The shrine is also one of the stops on the Taipei Sightseeing Bus route.

Shung Ye Museum of Formosan Aborigines MUSEUM
(順益台灣原住民博物館, Shùnyì Táiwān Yuán-zhùmín Bówùguǎn; Map p62; ☎02-2841 2611; www.museum.org.tw; 282 Zhishan Rd, Sec 2, 至善路二段282號; adult/child NT$150/100; ⊘9am-5pm Tue-Sun; 🚇R30) There are currently 16 recognised indigenous tribes in Taiwan, and the exhibits at this private museum cover the belief systems, festivals, geographic divisions, agriculture and art of them all. Fine examples of tribal handicrafts can be seen on each level, and videos relate the tribes' histories and other aspects of tribal life. English guided tours at 2pm on Saturday and Sunday.

The museum is across the road and up a short distance from the entrance to the National Palace Museum; a joint ticket is NT$400, saving you NT$100. If you forget to buy the joint ticket, just show your Palace

Zhongshan & Datong

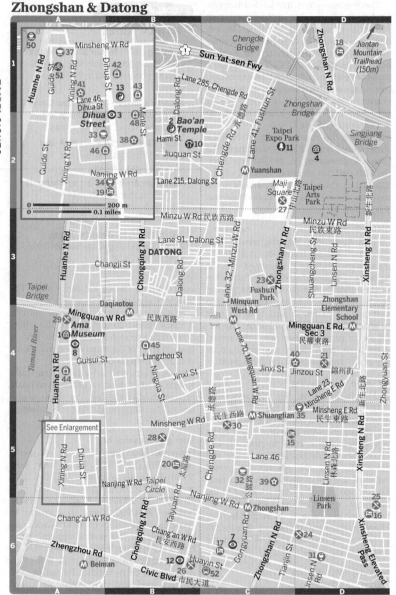

museum ticket stub for the same day and you'll get 80% off.

Taipei Astronomical Museum MUSEUM
(天文科學教育館, Tiānwén Kēxué Jiàoyùguǎn; Map p84; https://en.tam.gov.taipei; 363 Jihe Rd, 基河路363號; adult/child NT$40/20, IMAX & 3D

theatres NT$100/50, Cosmic Adventure NT$70/35; ⏰9am-5pm Tue-Fri & Sun, 9am-8pm Sat; 🅿🚻; Ⓜ Shilin) This children's museum houses four floors of constellations, ancient astronomy, space science and observatories. Although fun, there is a dearth of English-language content. More English-friendly attractions

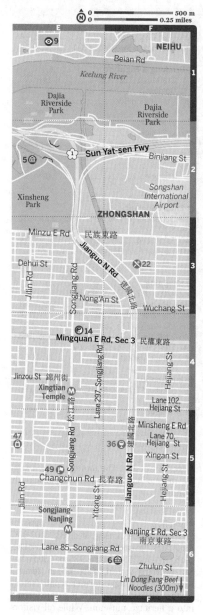

National Taiwan Science Education Center MUSEUM

(國立台灣科學教育中心, Guólì Táiwān Kēxué Jiàoyù Zhōngxīn; Map p84; ☑02-6610 1234; http://en.ntsec.gov.tw; 189 Shishang Rd, 士商路189號; adult/child NT$100/70; ⊙9am-5pm Tue-Fri, to 6pm Sat, Sun & school holidays; ℙ💪; ℳShilin) Interactive exhibits at this children's museum cover the gamut of scientific knowledge, from anatomy (a walk-through digestive tract!) to zoology (a cat-head-shaped helmet that gives the wearer feline hearing powers) to chemistry, life science and physics. There are good English translations at every point. The 3D theatre (turbo ride and regular), sky cycling and special exhibits are not covered by the general admission ticket.

You can take the R30 bus from here straight to the National Palace Museum (p78) or Jiantan MRT station.

Shilin Official Residence GARDENS

(士林官邸, Shìlín Guāndǐ; Map p84; 60 Fulin Rd, 福林路60號; gardens free, house NT$100; ⊙9.30am-noon & 1.30-5pm Tue-Sun; ℙ; ℳShilin) For 26 years, this two-storey mansion and its elaborate Chinese- and western-style gardens were part of the official residence of Chiang Kai-shek and his wife Soong Mei-ling. Today the entire estate is a lovely **public park** (⊙8am-5pm Tue-Sun), often with flower exhibitions. The house, though interesting enough, merely displays the rather humdrum domestic life, and middlebrow tastes, of the Chiangs. The free audio guide is more than a little obsequious about the house's master and mistress.

◎ Songshan

Songshan (松山; Sōngshān) is a rectangular district in the middle of Taipei whose northeastern curve is bounded by the Keelung River.

South of the airport is the genteel Minsheng Community, a grid of tree-lined peaceful lanes of low-rise buildings dotted with parkland, funky cafes, cute shops and art galleries.

The tourist hotspots are clustered around the train station, home to the heaving Raohe Street Night Market, the clothing bargain bins of Wufenpu and the ostentatious Ciyou Temple. Cultural attractions, including the Puppetry Art Center, lie along the Civic Boulevard highway.

(at an extra charge) are the IMAX and 3D theatres. Cosmic Adventure is a space journey simulator that trundles pod riders past the planets of the solar system. You can sky- and star-gaze through the optical **telescope** (⊙10am-noon & 2-4pm Tue-Sun, 7-9pm Sat) on the 4th floor for free.

Zhongshan & Datong

Minsheng Community   AREA
(民生社區, Mínshēng Shèqū; Map p88; MSong-shan Airport, MNanjing Sanmin) This is the place to watch Taiwan's hipsters while enjoying a street-side coffee or browsing upcycled designer wear or exclusive art galleries. It's a secret little oasis from the traffic-choked streets full of malls and towers. In recent years it has gained fame from being the set of many TV shows and films.

Ciyou Temple   TAOIST TEMPLE
(慈祐宮, Cíyòu Gōng; Map p88; www.facebook.com/Songshanciyou; 761 Bade Rd, Sec 4, 八德路四段761號; ⊙6am-10pm; MSongshan) FREE This 18th-century triple-tiered temple is dedicated to Matsu, the black-faced Chinese goddess of seafarers. It marks the start of the Raohe Street Night Market (p101) and is one of Taipei's busiest and most-colourful

places of worship. The rooftop *jiǎnniàn* (剪黏, mosaic-like decoration) is particularly vibrant.

Taipei Railway Workshop   WORKSHOP
(臺北機廠, Táiběi Jīchǎng; Map p88; ☎02-8787 8850; https://trw.moc.gov.tw/Default; 50 Civic Blvd, Sec 5, 市民大道5段50號; ⊙9.30am-4.30pm Tue-Sat; MNanjing Sanmin, MSun Yat-sen Memorial Hall) FREE This huge former repair factory for the country's trains is being transformed into a heritage museum. While all visitors can enter and peek from the main gate, a full exploration of the cavernous workshops – four stories high, complete with dusty tools and rusting diesel and steam engines – is by prebooked two-hour tour Wednesday and Saturday only. Register online (no English). A highlight is the arc-shaped bathhouse for

engineers. A remarkable project that is well worth a visit.

Puppetry Art Center of Taipei　MUSEUM
(台北偶戲館, Táiběi Ǒuxìguǎn; Map p88; ☑02-2528 9553; www.pact.org.tw; 2nd fl, 99 Civic Blvd, Sec 5, 民大道五段99號2樓; ⊗10am-5pm Tue-Sun; ♿; Ⓜ Nanjing Sanmin, Ⓜ Sun Yat-sen Memorial Hall) This small and fun museum (set aside about 40 minutes) showcases a medley of magical string, hand and shadow puppets, many with embroidered robes and fiery beards. The displays could do with a bit more English explanation, but interesting snippets abound. String puppets, for example, were originally used more than 1000 years ago in exorcisms.

◎ Xinyi

Taipei's financial and city-government district, Xinyi (信義; Xìnyì) is the 'bright lights, big city' part of town. It has the tallest buildings – Taipei 101, of course, as well as new-kid-on-the-block Taipei Nanshan Plaza – plus the swankiest malls and the hottest nightclubs. And yet, nicely, it is also a casual place, a sporting place even. There are hiking trails to Elephant Mountain starting a stone's throw from Taipei 101, and wide pavements circulating through the area where cyclists pedal along on city YouBikes.

★ Taipei 101　TOWER
(台北101, Táiběi Yīlíngyī; Map p92; ☑02-8101 8800; www.taipei-101.com.tw; 7 Xinyi Rd, Sec 5, 信義路5段7號; adult/child NT$600/540; ⊗9am-10pm, last ticket sale 9.15pm; Ⓟ; Ⓜ Taipei 101) Towering above the city like the gigantic bamboo stalk it was designed to resemble, Taipei 101 is impossible to miss. At 508m, Taipei 101 held the title of 'world's tallest building' for a number of years. Until 2011, it also held the title of the world's tallest green building. Ticket sales are on the 5th floor of the Taipei 101 Shopping Mall. The pressure-controlled lift up is quite a rush; at 1010m per minute it takes a mere 40 seconds to get from ground level to the 89th-floor observation deck. Observation decks are on the 88th and 89th floors, with an outdoor deck on the 91st floor opened on some occasions, weather permitting.

Songshan Cultural &
Creative Park　CULTURE PARK
(松山文創園區, Sōngshān Wénchuàng Yuánqū; Map p92; www.songshanculturalpark.org; 133 Guangfu S Rd, 光復南路133號; ⊗9am-6pm;

Ⓟ♿♨; Ⓜ Sun Yat-sen Memorial Hall) FREE Set in a former tobacco factory (or more accurately an industrial village) from the 1930s, this lovely park is part lush gardens, part frog-filled lake, part industrial chic, part workshop and part design studio. The place is dotted with pop-up creative shops, cafes and galleries.

The long, steel grey-painted corridors of the factory have a wonderful, institutional throwback feel. The outdoor areas of the park are open until 10pm. Entrance is off Guangfu S Rd on Yangchang Rd.

Taiwan Design Museum　ARTS CENTRE
(台灣設計館, Táiwān Shèjì Guǎn; Map p92; www.songyancourt.com/en/tdm; Songshan Cultural & Creative Park, 133 Guangfu S Rd, 光復南路133號; NT$150; ⊗9.30am-5.30pm Tue-Sun; Ⓜ Sun Yat-sen Memorial Hall) Housed in one wing of an atmospheric former tobacco factory, this exhibition space showcases modern designs by local and international artists.

National Dr Sun Yat-sen
Memorial Hall　CULTURAL CENTRE
(國父紀念館, Guófù Jìniànguǎn; Map p92; http://en.yatsen.gov.tw; ⊗9am-6pm; Ⓟ; Ⓜ Sun Yat-sen Memorial Hall) FREE The hall and its surrounding gardens occupy an entire city block. The latter are well used by picnickers, kite flyers, breakdancers and the early morning taichi crowd, while the cavernous interior serves as a cultural centre with regular exhibitions and performances. There's a large, though sparsely informative, museum on the life of Sun Yat-sen, the founder of modern China. The elaborate changing of the guards, with their extremely shiny boots, takes place every hour.

✦ Activities

Gongguan Riverside
Bike Path　CYCLING
(Map p66; Gongguan Waterfront Plaza, Zhongzheng; ♨; Ⓜ Gongguan) With a bike rental station and access to the riverside via a path rather than steps, this is one of the best places to get onto the bike trails, with their avenues of trees, wild birds and scenic views of the river. Facing the river, cycle left to Bitan (40 mins), right all the way to Tamsui (3-4 hours) or anywhere in between.

Alan's Mountain Bike　CYCLING
(Map p66; ☑02-2933 4319; www.alansmountain bike.com.tw; 34 Roosevelt Rd, Sec 5, 羅斯福路五段34號, Zhongzheng; ⊗noon-8.30pm Mon-Fri,

TAIPEI ACTIVITIES

TAIPEI ACTIVITIES

Shilin

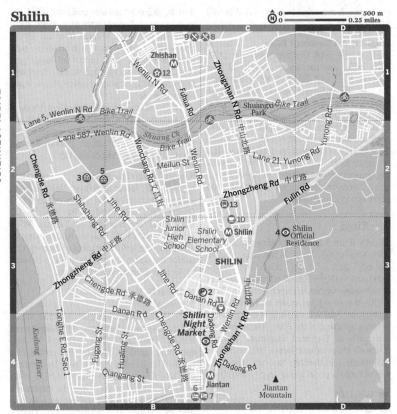

Shilin

◎ **Top Sights**
1 Shilin Night Market C4

◎ **Sights**
2 Cixian Temple.......................................C3
3 National Taiwan Science Education
   Center...A2
4 Shilin Official Residence......................C3
5 Taipei Astronomical Museum.............A2

🛏 **Sleeping**
6 Tango Inn...B4
7 Tango Taipei Jiantan C4

🍴 **Eating**
8 Din Tai Fung C1
9 MiaCucina B1

🍷 **Drinking & Nightlife**
10 A Loving Cafe C3
11 Funky Fresh Bar..................................C3

🎭 **Entertainment**
12 Taiwan Traditional Theatre Center B1

🚍 **Transport**
13 Buses to National Palace Museum C2

1-7pm Sat; Ⓜ Gongguan) This long-standing bike-repair and -rental shop offers road bikes at NT$600 a day for round-the-island trips, or mountain bikes for off-road action for NT$1500 a day or NT$200 an hour. Owners speak fluent English, run weekend trips and offer tours.

Hidden Taipei   WALKING

(Map p70; ☏ 02-2331 5992; www.hiddentaipei.org; Longshan Temple, 211 Guangzhou St, 廣州街211號, Wanhua; NT$400 per tour; Ⓜ Longshan Temple) Hidden Taipei's tour guides are former homeless people who lead exploration of the backstreets around Longshan Temple (p69), and relate stories about their experiences living rough. Run by the NGO Homeless Taiwan, the group currently doesn't run tours in English but they can organise volunteers to interpret if you call ahead of time. Tours always meet outside Longshan Temple MRT Exit 1.

Light Project Ximending MASSAGE
(光光光, Guāng Guāng Guāng; Map p70; www.facebook.com/lightprojectximending; 72-7 Wuchang St, Sec 2, 武昌街二段72-7號, Ximending; NT$1500 for 70 mins; ⊙1-10.30pm; Ⓜ Ximen) This tiny, serene space offers spiritual and energising massages with the use of two blunt, yet daunting-looking cleavers. 刀療 (dāoliáo), literally knife therapy, is an ancient Chinese art and is still popular in Taiwan. Hailing from the US, practitioner Olivia Wu speaks fluent English, making this a good place to experience knife massage for the first time.

Blue Highway CRUISE
(Map p80; ☑02-2618 2226; www.riverfun.net; Dadaocheng Wharf, 大稻埕碼頭, Datong; NT$270; Ⓜ Beimen) Weekend boat trips between Dadaocheng and Tamsui. Tickets must be booked in advance through the website, which is only in Chinese (best to get your hotel to help you). Alternatively, you can head to the Dadaocheng Wharf (大稻埕碼頭, Dàdàochéng Mǎtóu; Map p80; Ⓜ Beimen) around 2pm and try to buy a ticket. The view from the river is not particularly stunning but it's refreshing to be out on the water.

Miramar Entertainment Park FERRIS WHEEL
(美麗華百樂園, Měilìhuá Bǎilèyuán; Map p62; www.miramar.com.tw; 20 Jingye 3rd Rd, 敬業三路20號, Zhongshan; tickets adult/child Mon-Fri NT$150/120, Sat & Sun NT$200/150; ⊙11am-11pm Sun-Thu, to midnight Fri & Sat; Ⓜ Jiannan Rd) Part mall, part amusement park, all fun. There's an enormous Ferris wheel, located on the 5th-floor roof. It takes 17 minutes to make one complete revolution, offering leisurely panoramic views of the city. There's also an IMAX cinema and a busy food court.

Jiantan Mountain HIKING
(劍潭山, Jiàntánshān; Map p62; Shilin; Ⓜ Jiantan) The mountain rises behind the Grand Hotel and has great views over the Keelung River basin and city, including Taipei 101 (p83). To access the trailhead, cross Zhongshan N Rd from Jiantan MRT; look for the steps up the hillside just to the left of the little temple. The main route runs to Neihu and

takes about two hours to finish if you don't get lost!

Elephant Mountain HIKING
(象山, Xiàngshān; Map p92; Xinyi; Ⓜ Xiangshan) This mountain has its own MRT station (Xiangshan, which means Elephant Mountain). The trailhead is about an eight-minute walk south. The vantage point of many classic shots of Taipei 101 (p83), it's a steep climb up. Weekends it gets crowded, especially around sunset. Don't forget to take water. Various trails take you to different viewpoints; there are bilingual maps at key points.

🎓 Courses

Taipei Language Institute LANGUAGE
(TLI; Map p66; ☑02-2367 8228; www.tli.com.tw; 4th fl, 50 Roosevelt Rd, Sec 3, Zhongzheng, 羅斯福路三段50號4樓; Ⓜ Taipower Building) This long-running, very well-regarded, private Mandarin-language school offers immersion courses, both long-term and short-term as well as one-on-one and group classes.

Mandarin Training Center LANGUAGE
(MTC; Map p66; ☑02-7734 5130; https://mtc.ntnu.edu.tw; National Taiwan Normal University, 129 Heping E Rd, Sec 1, 和平東路一段129號, Da'an; Ⓜ Guting) This is one of the most popular centres at which to learn Mandarin. Many language learning materials and textbooks in Taiwan are written and published by this university.

International Chinese Language Program LANGUAGE
(ICLP; Map p72; ☑02-2363 9123; https://iclp.ntu.edu.tw; National Taiwan University, 4th fl, 170 Xinhai Rd, Sec 2, 辛亥路二段170號四樓, Da'an; Ⓜ Gongguan; Technology Building) Small classes and an intensive learning environment at Taiwan's top university. Studying here, though, will cost you top dollar.

CookInn Taiwan COOKING
(Map p72; ☑02-2775-5375; https://cookinn.tw/en; 2nd fl, 5 Lane 290, Guangfu S Rd, 光復南路290巷5號2樓, Da'an; ⊙9.30am-1pm, 2-4.30pm Tue-Fri; 9.30-1pm Sat & Sun; ♿; Ⓜ Sun Yat-sen Memorial Hall) Morning classes (from NT$2,300) include a trip to a market to shop for ingredients to traditional Taiwanese dishes such as three-cup chicken. Afternoons (from NT$1,800) are more about tea ceremonies, dumplings and pastries. Very competitively priced considering you get to eat

everything you make. Children and vegetarians welcome.

Festivals & Events

★ Taiwan LGBT
Pride Parade   LGBT
(台灣同志遊行, Táiwān Tóngzhì Yóuxíng; www.
facebook.com/Taiwan.LGBT.Pride; ☉last Sat in
Oct; ⓘ) **FREE** Asia's largest and most vibrant
pride parade has been running since 2003.
The family-friendly, sometimes-political,
always-fun march passes through the capital's main avenues. According to organisers, 130,000 people took part in 2018. For
information on the many afterparties check
Formosa Pride's website (www.formosapride.
com/en).

★ Taipei Golden Horse
Film Festival   FILM
(臺北金馬影展, Táiběi Jīnmǎ Yǐngzhǎn; www.golden
horse.org.tw; ☉Nov) This month-long film
festival is part of the Mandarin-speaking
world's biggest film-awards event. Venues
vary but usually include cinemas on Wu-
chang St in Ximen and SPOT in Huashan
1914 Creative Park (p61). Often called Taiwan's Oscars.

Taiwan International
Festival of Arts   PERFORMING ARTS
(台灣國際藝術節, Táiwān Guójì Yìshù Jié; http://
tifa.npac-ntch.org; National Theater & Concert Hall,
21 Zhongshan S Rd, 中山南路21號; ☉Feb-Apr;
ⓂChiang Kai-shek Memorial Hall) This festival
includes dance, theatre, Shakespeare, music
and mime; all performances are held at the
National Theater & Concert Hall (p109). The
festival attracts local, Asian and global acts
and is usually a real mixture. Many shows
sell out quickly, so book early.

Dream Parade   PARADE
(夢想嘉年華, Mèngxiǎng Jiānniánhuá; www.face
book.com/DreamCommunityCarnival; ☉Oct) This
colourful event is sponsored by the Dream
Community, a collective of artists and families in the Xizhi area of New Taipei City.
Expect elaborate floats, stilt walkers, fire
breathers, puppeteers, dancers, indigenous
performers and lots of great costumes and
painted faces. It's a one-day Mardi Gras–
type event in the streets of central Taipei.

Taipei Film Festival   FILM
(臺北電影節, Táiběi Diànyǐng Jié; http://eng.
taipeiff.org.tw; ☉Jun-Jul) This influential festival showcases over 200 local and international films through the end of June through

---

ⓘ WHAT'S ON & WHERE

Local Acts

Chinese opera DaDaoCheng Theater
(p110), Taipei Eye (p111), Taiwan Traditional Theatre Center (p111)

Music National Theater & Concert
Hall (p109), Taiwan Traditional Theatre
Center (p111), Zhongshan Hall (p69)

Puppet shows DaDaoCheng Theater
(p110), **Nadou Theatre** (台原亞洲偶戲博
物館, Táiyuán Yàzhōu Ǒuxì Bówùguǎn; Map
p80; ☎02-2556 8909; www.taipeipuppet.
com; 79 Xining N Rd, 西寧北路79號; museum adult/child NT$80/50; ☉10am-5pm
Tue-Sun; ⓘ; ⓂBeimen)

Indie, rock, club, techno Revolver
(p109), Riverside Live House (p110),
Wall Live House (p110), Pipe Live Music
(p109)

Mandopop Taipei Arena (p111)

International Performers

Theatre, dance and music National
Theater & Concert Hall (p109)

Pop Taipei Arena (p111)

Jazz Blue Note (p110), Sappho Live
(p110)

---

to July. Venues include SPOT at Huashan
1914 Creative Park (p61) and Zhongshan
Hall (p69).

Taipei Lantern Festival   LIGHT SHOW
(臺北燈節, Táiběi Dēngjié; ☉Jan or Feb) At designated locations around the city, lanterns,
light displays, music and performances
are staged for one week. It all takes place
around the 15th day of the first lunar month.
Check local English-language media for
information.

Taipei Children's
Art Festival   ART
(臺北兒童藝術節, Táiběi Értóng Yìshù Jié; www.
taipeicaf.org; ☉Jul-Aug; ⓘ) This festival has
films, interactive exhibits, storytelling,
puppetry, live theatre and more from local
and international troupes and performers.
There are venues all over the city. Most
performances are free, others cost around
NT$300.

Taipei Arts Festival   ART
(臺北藝術節, Táiběi Yìshù Jié; www.artsfestival.
taipei/index.aspx; ☉1 month btwn Aug & Oct)

Experimental theatre, dance and performance art by local and international artists. Events are held in various locations including Zhongshan Hall (p69) and Taipei Artist Village (p65).

🛏 Sleeping

🛏 Zhongzheng

★UINN Travel HOSTEL $
(悠逸旅館, Yōuyì Lǚguǎn; Map p66; ☎02-2333 1277; http://travel.uinnhotel.com; 38 Chongqing S Rd, Sec 3, 重慶南路三段38號; dm from NT$600; ☯❋@☎; ⓂChiang Kai-shek Memorial Hall) This traveller-focused hostel located in an old part of Taipei has colour-coded dorm rooms – pink for women, blue for men, purple for mixed – all with windows as well as underground capsules. Beds come with a mini-TV each. There's a games room with darts, movie projector and bar. Facilities are spotless and staff couldn't be more helpful. It's about 700m from the MRT station, and you'll spot it by its bright-yellow painted facade.

★Attic LODGE $
(閣樓, Gélóu; Map p66; http://attic.artist village.org/en; Treasure Hill; dm/s/d from NT$800/1200/1600; ☯02-2364 5313; P☯❋☎; ⓂGongguan) This lovely village house in Treasure Hill (p60) has massive picture windows and great views of the river. There are a variety of rooms with shared bathrooms – dorms, singles and doubles – all simply but beautifully decorated in wood, white and beige. Basic breakfast included, and 10% discount Sunday to Thursday. Access is via a long walk up steps so it's not suitable for those with heavy luggage.

Once you enter the village, ask for directions. Note there are no roads inside Treasure Hill, it's all stone paths and steps.

Taiwan Youth Hostel & Capsule Hotel HOSTEL $
(台灣青旅; Táiwān Qīnglǚ; Map p66; ☎02-2361 3000; www.taiwanyh.com/en; basement, 11, Qingdao W Rd, 青島西路11號B1; d from NT$750; ☯❋@☎; ⓂTaipei Main Station) This place pushes all the right buttons. It's superfriendly, spotless and has some of the biggest bunk spaces in Taipei, each equipped with a small desk and locker. Women-only and mixed dorms have tons of room for luggage, and there's a lounge with a small stage for live music. The only downside is it's all underground, so no natural light.

This is as central as you can get, just round the corner from Exit M8 of Taipei main station.

CityInn Hotel HOTEL $$
(新驛旅店, Xīnyì Lǚdiàn; Map p66; ☎02-2314 8008; www.cityinn.com.tw; 7 Huaining St, 懷寧街7號; r from NT$1800; ☯❋☎; ⓂTaipei Main Station) One of six CityInns in central Taipei; this branch offers much the same fresh, friendly appeal as the others. Rooms are on the cramped side but cheerfully decorated and spotless. Add an extra NT$500 on weekends. Note that not all rooms have a window and there's no breakfast provided.

🛏 Ximending & Wanhua

Meander Taipei HOSTEL $
(漫步旅店, Mànbù Lǚdiàn; Map p70; www.meander.com.tw; 163 Chengdu Rd, 成都路163號; dm/s/d from NT$550/1380/2080; ☯❋@☎; ⓂXimen) Reworked from an old hotel, this hostel ticks all the boxes when it comes to services and facilities for independent travellers – massive lounge space, games, free tours and superhelpful staff. Dorms and doubles though, have a greyish institutional feel to them, a kind of prison chic perhaps, and some rooms have no windows.

★Hotel Papa Whale DESIGN HOTEL $$
(Map p70; ☎02-2331 1177; www.papawhale.com; 46 Kunming St, 昆明街46號; s/d from NT$1500/1700; ☯❋@☎; ⓂXimen) It's easy to spot this place by the giant blue whale on its facade. Crammed with retro chic, from 1930s radio sets to a 1950s coke machine, this hotel is one of Taipei's hippest. The building is like a boat: none of the smallish rooms – and there are 335 of them – have an exterior window, though they are wonderfully stylish.

East Dragon Hotel HOTEL $$
(東龍大飯店, Dōnglóng Dà Fàndiàn; Map p70; ☎02-2311 6969; www.east-dragon.com.tw; 23 Hankou St, Sec 2, 漢口街二段23號; d from NT$1800; ☯❋@☎; ⓂXimen) The lobby of this 50-year-old hotel has old-world charm; check out the marble flooring and spiral staircase. Rooms, renovated in 2019, are more pedestrian but are some of the best value in town, with all expected fittings. Add another NT$500-1000 for extra space and a view. This is an old favourite for repeat guests.

Songshan

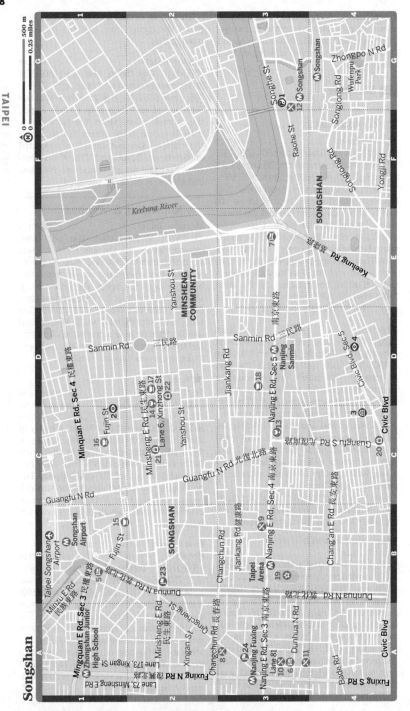

TAIPEI

500 m
0.25 miles

Keelung River

MINSHENG
COMMUNITY

SONGSHAN

SONGSHAN

Sanmin Rd 三民路

Sanmin Rd 三民路

Yansheng St

Yanshou St

Yanshou St

Minsheng E Rd 民生東路

Minsheng E Rd 民生東路

Lane 6, Xinzhong St

Fujin St

Fujin St

Guangfu N Rd

Guangfu N Rd 光復北路

Jiankang Rd

Jiankang Rd 健康路

Nanjing E Rd, Sec 5 南京東路

Nanjing E Rd, Sec 4 南京東路

Nanjing
Sanmin

Guangfu S Rd 光復南路

Civic Blvd, Sec 5

Civic Blvd

Civic Blvd

Civic Blvd

Chang'an E Rd 長安東路

Changchun Rd

Changchun Rd 長春路

Dunhua N Rd 敦化北路

Dunhua N Rd

Qingcheng St

Xingan St

Xinyi St

Dunhua N Rd

Taipei
Arena

Nanjing E Rd, Sec 3 南京東路

Nanjing Fuxing

Lane 81

Dunhua N Rd

Bade Rd

Fuxing S Rd

Fuxing N Rd 復興北路

Lane 73, Minsheng E Rd

Lane 173, Xingan St

Zhongshan Junior
High School

Minzu E Rd
民族東路

Taipei Songshan
Airport

Songshan
Airport

Minquan E Rd, Sec 4 民權東路

Mingquan E Rd, Sec 3 民權東路

Minsheng E Rd, Sec 3 民生東路

Keelung Rd 基隆路

Songlong Rd

Songjiong Rd

Zhongpo N Rd

Wufenpu
Park

Yongji Rd

Songhe St

Raohe St

Songshan

Songshan

Songshan

AMBA   BOUTIQUE HOTEL **$$**
(Map p70; ☎02-2375 5111; www.amba-hotels.com; 5th fl, 77 Wuchang St, Sec 3, 武昌街二段77號5號; d & tw from NT$2900; ❋@🛜; Ⓜ Ximen) AMBA, run by the **Ambassador Hotel** (國賓大飯店; Guóbīn Dàfàndiàn; Map p80; ☎02-2551 1111; www.ambassadorhotel.com.tw; 63 Zhongshan N Rd, Sec 2, 中山北路二段63號; r from NT$4000; Ⓟ❋@🛜; Ⓜ Shuanglian), is clearly aimed at young, savvy 'lifestyle' travellers. The interior sports an industrial-chic design, curious art and surprising use of splashes of colour. Lots of nice little touches like separate toilet and shower stalls, funky flip-flops, silent minifridges, and a very cool cocktail lounge.

As you walk down Wuchang St (Movie Theatre Street) look for the stylish Eslite Mall. The lifts to AMBA are located past the outdoor cafe along the side with the wooden deck.

Use the code 'shengba' to get a discount when you book on their website.

🛏 Da'an

★ **three little birds**   HOSTEL **$**
(美好日子, Měihǎo Rìzi; Map p72; ☎0987-320 724; www.threelittlebirdstpe.com; 10-1 Lane 62, Taishun St, 泰順街62巷10-1號; dm/d from NT$550/NT$1200; ❋@🛜; Ⓜ Taipower Building) This fabulous LGBT-run hostel has singles, doubles and dorm rooms. The owners, one gay guy and a lesbian couple (the three little birds) are superfriendly and happy to take guests out to LGBT+ venues. Comfortable

and cosy, with a kitchen area. A little tricky to find; look for the three-bird motif on the wall and ring the bell.

Dongmen 3 Capsule Inn   HOSTEL **$**
(Map p66; ☎02-2356 3299; www.dongmen3.com.tw; 110 Xinyi Rd, Sec 2, 信義路二段110號; dm s/d from NT$650/1000; ⊜❋🛜; Ⓜ Dongmen) Fronted by Two Shot coffee shop, this very well-run capsule inn offers single and double bed nooks, each with its own locker, minitable inside, lamp, and pull-down blind to create a private space. Add NT$150 for Friday and Saturday nights. Lots of space, seating and light and a hard-to-beat location.

Rido Hotel   BOUTIQUE HOTEL **$$$**
(麗都唯客樂飯店, Lìdōu Fàndiàn; Map p72; ☎02-2706 5600; www.rido.com.tw; 11 Xinyi Rd, Sec 3, 信義路三段11號; r from NT$3000 incl breakfast; Ⓟ⊜❋@🛜; Ⓜ Da'an Park) The Rido is a kooky little boutique hotel with very classy rooms that are elegantly furnished in modern, old-Shanghai or European styles. Rooms are spacious and comfortable and include nice touches such as a separate bathtub and shower. The glass lift glides past curious giant paintings. Carpets are great to sink into and there's a lot of polished brass and dark wood.

The Corner House   APARTMENT **$$$**
(安居, Ānjū; Map p72; ☎02-2704 5888; www.thecornerhouse.com.tw; 10 Lane 157, Xinsheng S Rd, Sec 1, 新生南路一段157巷10號; r from NT$3450; ❋@🛜; Ⓜ Da'an Park) Set back in a quiet lane,

The Corner House offers modern, tasteful rooms – they call them serviced apartments – each with a little kitchenette and sofa space; some have minibalconies. There's a basement gym and a rather elegant path up to the reception area with Chinese character motifs.

Zhongshan & Datong

★Flip Flop Hostel Garden HOSTEL $
(夾腳拖的家, Jiājiǎotuō de Jiā; Map p80; ☎02-2558 5050; www.flipflophostel.com; 122 Chang'an W Rd, 長安西路122號; dm/s/d from NT$450/950/1200; ⊗@🛜; ⓂZhongshan, ⓂTaipei Main Station) The use of an open central courtyard, balconies on every floor, architectural tricks, lots of white and huge windows gives Flip Flop an inconceivably large amount of space for central Taipei. This is a fantastic option: rooms are light and airy, there are tons of events and cultural connections with local groups, plus a huge hangout area to meet other travellers.

★Chill Roof BOUTIQUE HOTEL $$
(好得文旅, Hǎodé Wén lǚ; Map p80; ☎02-2571 8875; www.facebook.com/ChillRoof; 11th fl, 11 Nanjing E Rd, Sec 2, 南京東路二段11號11樓; r from NT$2700; ⊗🌼🛜; ⓂSongjiang Nanjing) Chill Roof is a quirky little boutique hotel whose more than 10 rooms feel more like someone's real bedroom, with patterned rugs, bright paints, beanbags, wigwams, hammocks and funky wallpaper. Bathrooms are big and elegant, with clawfoot tubs. Another plus is that rooms are huge, something pretty rare in squashed Taipei. There's no breakfast; the room, albeit gorgeous, is all you get.

Entrance is through a rather shabby commercial building and old lift, but once you reach the 11th floor, the hotel is very smart. One of the rooms does not have a window; check when you book.

★Play Design Hotel DESIGN HOTEL $$$
(玩味旅舍, Wànwèi Lǚshě; Map p80; www.playdesignhotel.com; 5th fl, 156-2 Taiyuan Rd, 太原路156-2號5樓; r from NT$3600; ⊗🌼🛜; ⓂZhongshan) This hotel is a shrine to design. Each one of its six enormous bedrooms is meticulously put together. There's a Japanese room, a Taiwanese room, one dedicated to the art of tea drinking and another to science (a virus lampshade and petri-dish ornaments). For NT$100 you can even select items of furniture to place in your room. A totally unique experience.

The staff are warm and welcoming and very passionate about this project. Every detail has been considered, and the price reflects that. They do not provide breakfast but have hand-drawn maps of the surrounding streets showing where to eat and what to see.

OrigInn Space HERITAGE HOTEL $$$
(Map p80; ☎02-2558 8843; www.facebook.com/OrigInnSpace; 247 Nanjing W Rd, 南京西路247號; r from NT$3200; ⊗🌼🛜; ⓂBeimen) Unlike other heritage hotels, this restored home close to Dihua St keeps the smallest heritage details in its four huge rooms. Beautifully furnished and decorated, and with towering ceilings, staying here is an atmospheric, historical experience. That experience is what you're paying for, since there's no lift or breakfast and some rooms come with the bathroom down the hall.

Shilin

Tango Inn BOUTIQUE HOTEL $$
(Map p84; ☎02-2885 6666; http://jh.tangoinn.com.tw; 18 Jihe Rd, 基河路18號; d from NT$2550; ⊗🌼@🛜; ⓂJiantan) This black-painted building just outside Exit 2 of Jiantan MRT has 50 rooms that are sleek little numbers in plum purple and slate grey. They have some of the comfiest mattresses in the city. While bedroom space is fairly squashed, bathrooms are massive. Ask for a rear-facing room to avoid noise pollution from the main road.

★Grand Hotel HERITAGE HOTEL $$$
(圓山大飯店, Yuánshān Dàfàndiàn; Map p80; ☎02-2886 8888; www.grand-hotel.org; 1 Zhongshan N Rd, Sec 4, 中山北路四段1號; r from NT$4480 mountain view, NT$7000 city view; 🅿⊗🌼@🛜🌼🌼; ⓂJiantan) This landmark Taipei hotel is a pleasant if kitsch place to stay, with excellent English service, a range of top-notch restaurants, and dreamy views over the whole city. Recently refurbished in 2016, the rooms are immaculate, humungous, and royal with polished wooden floors. You will certainly feel like an emperor when you arrive in the lobby!

The hotel was first established in 1952 as Chiang Kai-shek felt Taipei had no proper hotels for hosting foreign dignitaries. The main building was completed in 1973 on the grounds of the former Taipei Grand Shrine, though it underwent major renovations after a fire in 1995. Today there are three main sections, including the Golden Dragon and the Chi Lin. Note that breakfast is not included. If you just want the experience of staying at the Grand, but don't have the budget, elegant doubles, albeit with no windows, start from NT$3,000.

Tango Taipei Jiantan HOTEL $$$

(Map p84; ☑02-2885 0999; http://jt.tango-hotels.com; 16-6 Jihe Rd, 基河路16-6號; d from NT$3600; P❖❄@🛜❄; MJiantan) This is the more luxurious brother of the Tango Inn next door. The swimming pool shimmers through the far glass wall as you enter the cathedral-like lobby. Opened in December 2018, rooms are elegant and medium-sized, with huge windows that set off the dark wood and mauve paint of the walls and furnishings. Lovely marshmallow squashable bedding.

🛏 Songshan

★Sleepy Dragon Hostel GUESTHOUSE $

(杜萊根國際青年旅舍, Dùláigēn Guójì Qīngnián Lǚshě; Map p88; ☑02-8787 0739; www.sleepydragonhostel.com; 7th fl, 399 Nanjing E Rd, Sec 5, 南京東路5段399號7樓; dm incl breakfast from NT$520 Sun-Thu, NT$630 Fri & Sat; ❖❄@🛜; MNanjing Sanmin) Husband-and-wife team Shelley and Satoru lovingly crafted this place of four roomy 12-bed dorms (three mixed, one female only) almost by hand. Bunk beds have pull-out trays for laptops and curtains for privacy. In the same building as NK Hostel, and close to the back entrance of Raohe Street Night Market and nearby access to the riverside for biking.

NK Hostel GUESTHOUSE $

(Map p88; ☑02-2769 0200; www.nkhostel.com; 5th fl, 399 Nanjing E Rd, Sec 5, 南京東路5段399號5樓; dm from NT$680 Sun-Thu, NT$780 Fri & Sat; ❖❄@🛜; MNanjing Sanmin) This very plush guesthouse has big, white, comfy dorm beds, and the shiny shared bathroom facilities are spotless. There's a coffee lounge and laundry, and a simple breakfast is included in the price. There are beds for about 100 guests spread over a number of floors.

NK also has ensuite private rooms with some great views of the river or Taipei 101. However, they are quite pricey (around NT$2700 a night) considering there are none of the typical hotel facilities such as a restaurant or gym.

Mandarin Oriental Taipei HOTEL $$$

(Map p88; ☑02-2715 6888; www.mandarinoriental.com/taipei; 158 Dunhua N Rd, 敦化北路 158號; r from NT$11,500; P❖❄@🛜❄; MSongshan Airport) An opulent five-star experience on a sleepy boulevard near Songshan Airport. Rooms are richly furnished in an eastern–modern meld. Facilities include an enormous spa, a 20m pool and a string of top-notch restaurants with tastes from Italian to traditional Chinese.

Simple Hotel DESIGN HOTEL $$$

(Map p88; ☑02-6613 1300; www.fwhotel.tw; 52 Lane 4, Dunhua N Rd, 敦化北路4巷52號; d from NT$3000 incl breakfast; P❖❄@🛜; MNanjing Fuxing) Located on a quiet side street, this newish hotel has a sleek wooden design and clever mood lighting. Snag a south-facing room for great views of Taipei 101 from your balcony. Cheaper rooms are considerably smaller, but there's lots of light and clean lines.

🛏 Xinyi

Formosa101 HOSTEL $

(Map p92; ☑0955-780 359; www.hostelformosa.com; 5th fl, 115 Keelung Rd, Sec 2, 基隆路二段115號9樓; dm/s/d from NT$550/1000/1500; ❖❄@🛜; 🚇1960, MTaipei 101) Ticks most of the boxes: clean, efficient, kitchen, laundry, lounge and a good location near Taipei 101 and across the road from Tonghua Night Market (p113). There's a mixture of private rooms, some with bathroom, including a four-bed family suite and four eight-bed dorms (three mixed, two women's). Windowless rooms are a bit glum but the linen is crisp and flowery.

★Eslite Hotel DESIGN HOTEL $$$

(誠品行旅, Chéngpǐn Xínglǚ; Map p92; ☑02-6626 2888; www.eslitehotel.com; 98 Yanchang Rd, 菸廠路98號; d from NT$8,000 incl breakfast; P❖❄@🛜; MTaipei City Hall) Run by the very successful book chain of the same name, Eslite Hotel has 104 hush, plush rooms in white and olive green. Rooms are very spacious and those facing the park also have good views of Taipei 101 in the distance. Taipei's most tasteful hotel.

Rooms with city skyline views are NT$500 extra. The wonderful lounge, on the ground floor, is like a luxurious library. .

★W Hotel HOTEL $$$

(Map p92; ☑02-7703 8890; www.wtaipei.com; 10 Zhongxiao E Rd, Sec 5, 忠孝西路五段10号; d from NT$10,000; P❖❄@🛜❄; MTaipei City Hall) The W gets Taipei. It gets the naive, fun, technology-intoxicated vibe of this city that's

also surrounded by lush nature. So expect lots of wood, stone and cutting-edge light installations. Also expect cityscape views that are just as stunning as the views of nearby hills gleaming with greenness on a sunny day. This hotel is so hip, it hurts.

Humble House Taipei DESIGN HOTEL **$$$**
(寒舍艾麗酒店; Hánshè Àilì Jiǔdiàn; Map p92; ☎02-6631 8075; www.humblehousehotels.com; 18 Songgao Rd, 松高路18號; d from NT$10,000; P☁☀@☎☎; MTaipei City Hall) This newish luxury residence is anything but humble; rather it's hush and hip in beige and purple. Impeccable service, plush rooms, a tad smaller than you'd think for this price but still spacious enough.

It also has a gorgeous rooftop swimming pool, large gym and spa, while the more expensive suites come with sweeping views of Taipei 101 and city skyscrapers. Reception is on 6th floor.

✖ Eating

✖ Zhongzheng

⭐ **Snow King** ICE CREAM **$**
(雪王; Xuě Wáng; Map p70; 2nd fl, 65 Wuchang St, Sec 1, 武昌街一段65號2樓; bowls from NT$95; ☉noon-8pm; ✳🚫; MXimen) Snow King is a legend, serving intensely flavoured home-made ice cream for more than 70 years. There are scores of wild tastes, from the expected (chocolate) to the downright bizarre (wasabi, pork knuckle or Taiwan Beer). Grab a window pew to enjoy your bowl and admire the view of Zhongshan Hall (p69) across the way. It's closed on Tuesdays between November and February.

⭐ **Lan Jia** TAIWANESE **$**
(藍家; Lán Jiā; Map p66; ☎02-2368 1165; 3 Alley 8, Lane 316, Roosevelt Rd, Sec 3, 羅斯福路三段316巷8弄3號; steamed buns NT$60; ☉11am-

Xinyi

midnight Tue-Sun; Ⓜ Gongguan) Lan Jia is widely regarded as having the best *yì bāo* (刈包) in Taiwan. What's *yì bāo*? Think of a savoury slow-braised pork hamburger with pickled mustard and ground peanuts stuffed inside a steamed bun. You'll find this place by the long queue snaking outside.

Take the MRT Exit 4 and turn left at the second lane (Lane 316).

Jinfeng Braised Meat Rice TAIWANESE $
(金峰滷肉飯, Jīnfēng Lǔròu Fàn; Map p66; 10 Roosevelt Rd, 羅斯福路10號; dishes NT$30-60; ⏰8am-1am; Ⓜ Chiang Kai-shek Memorial Hall) This long-running and often hectic place serves Taiwanese comfort food quickly and cheaply, without fuss or atmosphere. Try the *lǔròu fàn* (魯肉飯, rice and meat strips); *hōng ròu fàn* (焢肉飯, slow-braised pork belly and rice) or *fènglí kǔguā jī* (鳳梨苦瓜雞, bitter melon pineapple chicken).

Heritage Bakery & Cafe DESSERTS $
(Map p66; ☎02-2311 1079; www.heritage.com. tw; 73-2 Hankou St, Sec 1, 漢口街一段73-2號; cakes from NT$150; ⏰10.30am-8pm, closed last Mon of month; ✳🛜✍; Ⓜ Ximen) This two-storey, airy cafe set in a refurbished heritage house with exposed brickwork is an Insta-grammer's delight. As are the scrumptious cakes. Cinnamon rolls are their bestseller but there are also brownies, pies and tarts flavoured with fruit, crammed with chocolate and covered in cream. We recommend the red-guava cheesecake. The only downside is that service is a bit scatty. It's closed on the first Monday of the month.

Fuhang Soy Milk BREAKFAST $
(阜杭豆漿, Fùháng Dòujiāng; Map p66; 2nd fl, Hushan Market, 108 Zhongxiao E Rd, Sec 1, 忠孝東路一段108號 華山市場; items NT$25-60; ⏰5.30am-12.30pm Tue-Sun; ✳✍; Ⓜ Shandao Temple) A popular shop in the Huashan Market for a traditional Taiwanese breakfast. Be prepared to wait – the queue regularly snakes down the stairs, and since the *Michelin Guide* gave them a nod in 2018, well down the street. Tasty it may be, but it's not a friendly experience if you don't speak Mandarin, and the wait time can get ridiculous.

If you're determined, try to get here before 6.30am; take Exit 5 from Shandao Temple MRT station, and look for the queue that leads upstairs in Huashan Market.

Best sellers include *dòujiāng* (豆漿, soy milk), *yóutiáo* (油條, fried bread stick), *dàn bǐng* (蛋餅, spring onion–filled crepes and egg) and *shāobǐng* (燒餅, stuffed layered flatbread).

Food Spotters' Guide

Taiwan is a foodies' heaven. Offering arguably the best Japanese food outside Japan, as well as a full range of Chinese cuisines and its own local specialities, you wont go hungry in this country.

1. Braised pork rice
Taiwan's ultimate comfort food is freshly steamed rice drizzled with luscious, melt-in-your-mouth braised pork. It's called *luroufan* (滷肉飯) or *rouzaofan* (肉燥飯) in the south.

2. Oyster omelette
Gooey in the middle and crisp on the edges, omelettes of small juicy oysters and crunchy vegetables are typically eaten at night markets with a sweet and hot sauce.

3. Soup dumplings
Steamed in bamboo baskets, these translucent mini-lanterns sag with minced pork and broth; variations may be laced with crab roe, basil or black truffle.

4. Turkey rice
Slivers of tender turkey and jus on rice, with a sprinkle of fried shallots, this dish originated with US solders who imported the fowl to Chiayi after WWII.

5. Milkfish
This unctuous fish of legendary status in Tainan comes pan-fried to golden brown, basking in broth, or with slippery rice noodles.

6. Taiwanese spring rolls
A plethora of toppings like finely shredded meat and veggies, and sweet peanut powder, makes for an explosion of textures in a pillow-soft wrap.

7. Beef noodles
The quintessential Taipei dish of braised beef and al dente noodles in a tangy broth, allegedly brought here by Sichuanese veterans, now features Wagyu and sous-vide versions.

8. Grass jelly
Silken jelly made from a nutritious mint-like plant is combined with sweetened pulses, taro balls, mangoes, and a tonne of other goodies in refreshing desserts and drinks.

9. Ginger duck stew hotpot
A warming duck stew simmered with plenty of ginger and rice wine, to which you add hotpot ingredients like cabbage and bean curd as you eat.

10. Cured mullet roe
A delicacy once presented to royalty, amber-hued Taiwanese caviar – eaten sliced and grilled with a splash of rice wine – is a popular and delectable souvenir.

Shirakawago
SUSHI $$

(合掌村, Hézhǎng Cūn; Map p66; Hushan Market, 108 Zhongxiao E Rd, Sec 1, 華山市場忠孝東路一段108號; nigiri set NT$380; ⏰11.30am-2pm & 5pm-7.30 Tue-Sat, 11am-1.30pm Sun; 🖼; Ⓜ Shandao Temple) With long queues that compete with the other darling of Huashan market, Fuhang (p93), this cute little sushi and sashimi-platter place offers well-priced sets, hand rolls and rice bowls paired with a jostling market experience.

Auntie Xie's
TAIWANESE $$

(謝阿姨, Xiè Āyí; Map p70; 📞02-2388 1012; basement, 122 Bo'ai Rd, 博愛路122號B1; set menus NT$430; ⏰11.30am-2pm & 5.30-8.30pm; 🖼; Ⓜ Ximen) This very traditional basement restaurant is a secret local favourite. There's no menu: each diner chooses fish or meat, and dishes are decided by the kitchen that day. The signature dish is the taro congee (芋頭粥, yùtou zhōu).

🍴 Ximending & Wanhua

⭐ Thai Food
THAI $

(泰風味, Tài Fēngwèi; Map p70; 25 Lane 10, Chengdu Rd, 成都路10巷25號; dishes NT$120-340; ⏰2-10pm Tue-Sun; 🍴; Ⓜ Ximen) Don't overlook this unassuming place in the courtyard in the Red House Bar Street (p103). A one-woman show (a Chinese lady born in Thailand), Thai Food serves some of the most delicious Southeast Asian curries, soups and noodles in Taipei for those on a budget. At night, with the fairy lights alight and the people coming out to party, it has a great atmosphere.

Ai Laksa
MALAYSIAN $

(艾叻沙, Ài Lèshā; Map p70; www.facebook.com/isarawaklaksa; 124 Zhonghua Rd, Sec 1, 中華路一段124號; NT$90-120; ⏰11.30am-10pm; Ⓜ Ximen) Snuck among the T-shirts and beauticians along busy Zhonghua Rd is this cheery, yellow-fronted hole in the wall with a few outdoor stools and tables. It serves some of the tastiest and freshest food in Ximending for rock-bottom prices. Their signature dish is the spicy Sarawak Laksa, a noodle soup filled with chicken strips and prawns, and tangy with lime juice.

Lao Shan Dong Homemade Noodles
NOODLES $

(老山東牛肉家常麵店, Lǎoshāndōng Niúròu Jiācháng Miàndiàn; Map p70; shop 15, basement, 70 Xining S Rd, 西寧南路70號地下室15; noodles from NT$90; ⏰10.30am-9.30pm; 🖼; Ⓜ Ximen) Superpopular with locals, this unpretentious canteen in the basement of Wannian Commercial Building (p112) has been serving up handmade, thick, floury, Shandong-style noodles since it opened in 1949 (a momentous year for Taiwan!). You can watch the noodle makers in their puffs of flour while you eat. The noodles are firm and bouncy, and the beef broth is light and tangy.

Since it was given a mention by Michelin, this humble noodle joint has upgraded its sign to include English, so it will be easy to find.

Yong Fu Ice Cream
ICE CREAM $

(永富冰淇淋, Yǒngfù Bīngqílín; Map p70; 68 Guiyang St, Sec 2, 貴陽街二段68號; NT$40 per bowl; ⏰10am-10pm; 🍴; Ⓜ Ximen) This corner store (with no English sign) has been serving customers since the 1940s and is easy to spot – there'll be gaggles of people outside eating ice cream. More like sorbet, this handmade traditional dessert comes in nine flavours such as taro, red bean and peanut. The lemon is satisfyingly sharp.

Da Che Lun Restaurant
JAPANESE $$

(大車輪餐飲企業, Dà Chēlún Cānyǐn Qǐyè; Map p70; www.dcl1976.com; 53 Emei St, 峨嵋街53號; plates from NT$140; ⏰11am-9.30pm Sun-Thu, to 10.30pm Fri & Sat; 🖼; Ⓜ Ximen) Plates of raw fish and assorted sushi are pulled past customers by tiny trains, and Taiwanese pop music from the '50s fills the air. This is a fun throwback to a time when Emei St was a major commercial centre. Taipei's first conveyor-belt sushi joint, Da Che Lun still serves pretty good seafood in this narrow, near-subterranean hideout.

Modern Toilet Restaurant
INTERNATIONAL $$

(便所主題餐廳, Biànsuǒ Zhǔtí Cāntīng; Map p70; 📞02-2311 8822; www.moderntoilet.com.tw/en; 2nd fl, 7 Lane 50, Xining S Rd, 西寧南路50巷7號2樓; mains NT$280-540; ⏰11.30am-10pm; 🖼🛜; Ⓜ Ximen) Greeted by the sound of a toilet flushing and a sign proudly claiming 'crappy food', guests at this novelty restaurant need a certain sense of humour. Diners sit on toilets (lid down), hotpots bubble in their own toilet bowl, and the lampshades are shaped like pyramids of poo. The menu is bland international – curries, pasta and hotpots – but urine for a laugh!

Zhen Siwei
SICHUAN $$

(真四味, Zhēnsìwèi; Map p70; 39-1 Lane 25, Kangding Rd, 康定路25巷39-1號; dishes NT$130-300; ⏰11am-2pm & 5-9pm Tue-Sun; 🖼;

EATING LARGE IN LITTLE BURMA

In the western suburb of Zhonghe is a small but vibrant community of immigrants from Thailand and Myanmar. Huaxin St (華新街) is the centre of this community and, not surprisingly, a great place to go for food. To get here take Exit 4 of Nanshijiao MRT station, turn right and walk for 550m until you reach Huaxin St. There are at least a dozen restaurants and canteens to choose from here, with dishes averaging NT$60 to NT$100. Don't miss exploring the score of small grocery shops with Southeast Asian food staples and oddities, such as durian-filled Oreos. There won't be any English-language menus, but almost everyone has a picture menu on the wall. Cuisine is roughly split between the fresher Yunnanese food (from southern China) and spicy Burmese.

Huaxin Street is more lively at breakfast and lunch times, and many places aren't open for dinner. One which does stay open is **Hoe Hoe Kyaw Restaurant** (南國風味泰緬小吃, Nánguó Fēngwèi Tàimiǎn Xiǎochī; Map p62; Lane 1, 43 Zhongxiao Jie, 忠孝街1巷43號; dishes NT$100-200; ⊙10am-2.30pm & 5-9pm Wed-Mon).

Ⓜ Ximen) Lane 25, Kangding Rd is packed with Sichuan restaurants, and this one, at the head of the lane, has the craziest queues at peak mealtimes. This place with its lazy Susans has been around for 40 years. Expect no-nonsense, authentic Sichuan fare.

✕ Da'an

★ Soypresso   ICE CREAM $
(二吉軒豆乳, Èrjíxuān Dòurǔ; Map p66; ☑02-2396 7200; www.soypresso.com.tw; 34-6 Yongkang St, 永康街34-6號; desserts/drinks from NT$60; ⊙7am-10pm; ❈☑; Ⓜ Dongmen) This place is buzzing. Complementing their heavenly soy soft scoop (NT$60) are a range of soy milks, soy puddings and soy yoghurt. There is seating inside and outside on cute stools with tofu-shaped cushions. Flavours on offer are taro (recommended), matcha, red bean and cocoa, among others.

Chi Fan Shi Tang   TAIWANESE $
(喫飯食堂, Chīfàn Shítáng; Map p66; ☑02-2322 2632; 5 Lane 8, Yongkang St, 永康街8巷5號; dishes NT$180-320; ⊙11.30am-2pm & 5-9pm; ☎; Ⓜ Dongmen) Taking homestyle Taiwanese cooking to a higher level of freshness and presentation is this popular eatery. Chi Fan's dim lighting and grey-slate-and-wood interior complement the modern approach, though the boisterous clientele keep the atmosphere down to earth. Try the cold chicken plate, the superb pumpkin and tofu (南瓜豆腐, nánguā dòufu) or the oysters in garlic sauce (蒜泥蚵, suànní hé).

Zilin Steamed Dumpling House   DUMPLINGS $
(紫琳蒸餃館, Zǐlín Zhēngjiǎo Guǎn; Map p72; ☑02-2752 0962; Dinghao Mall, basement, 19 Zhongxiao E Rd, Sec 4, 忠孝東路四段97號頂好名店城B1; 10-dumpling basket from NT$90; ⊙11am-9pm; ❈☑; Ⓜ Zhongxiao Dunhua) In the basement of tiny Dinghao Mall is this secret gem – the best-value juicy dumplings in the city. It's always heaving, but the line moves fast and the friendly staff will seat you swiftly. Watch the cooks mould the dumplings in a cloud of flour then enjoy them steaming, straight from the basket.

Shida Night Market   MARKET $
(師大路夜市, Shīdà Lù Yèshì; Map p66; ⊙3-11.30pm; Ⓜ Taipower Building) Though the market has been reduced in scale because of noise complaints from local residents, it's still a lively place for a cheap feed of traditional snacks washed down by fruit juices and teas. There are also tons of inexpensive boutiques to browse, as well as little restaurants and cafes to hang out in. A nice young studenty vibe.

Vege Creek   VEGAN $
(蔬河, Shū Hé; Map p72; www.facebook.com/vegecreek; 2 Lane 129, Yanji St, 延吉街129巷2號; noodles about NT$180; ⊙noon-2pm & 5-9pm; ❈☎☑; Ⓜ Sun Yat-sen Memorial Hall) The novelty here is you choose the ingredients for a tongue-banging noodle broth – fill the canvas bag with your choice of vegetables, fake meats, tofu, noodle and bundles of fresh leafy goodness. Inexpensive, healthy and filling. The brand has been so successful that you can also find them in most Eslite shopping malls around the city.

★ Din Tai Fung   DUMPLINGS $$
(鼎泰豐, Dǐngtàifēng; Map p72; ☑02-2321 8928; www.dintaifung.com.tw; 194 Xinyi Rd, Sec 2, 信義路二段194號; dishes NT$90-260; ⊙10am-9pm; ❈; Ⓜ Dongmen) Taipei's most celebrated

hai-style dumpling shop – the *New ...mes* once called it one of the 10 best ...rants in the world – is now a world-...de franchise. This is the place that started it all, and daily meal-time queues attest to its enduring popularity. Try the classic *xiǎolóng bāo* (小籠包), steamed pork dumplings), done to perfection every time. Take Exit 5 from Dongmen MRT.

★Toasteria Cafe   MEDITERRANEAN $$
(Map p72; ☑02-2752 0033; www.toasteriacafe.com; 3 Lane 169, Dunhua S Rd, Sec 1, 敦化南路一段169巷3號; mains NT$195-295; ◎11am-1am Mon-Fri, from 9am Sat & Sun; ❉⃝🛜⃝✍⃝; Ⓜ Zhongxiao Dunhua) A marvellous Mediterranean kitchen with a massive menu that's heavy on the cheese. Tapas, hummus, big eggy breakfasts, pasta, grilled fish, salads and paninis. Try the apple brie with honey-mustard toasted pocket. Also doubles as a pub, with Hoegaarden on tap and a cupboard full of cocktails.

Yongkang Beef Noodles   NOODLES $$
(永康牛肉麵, Yǒngkāng Niúròumiàn; Map p66; ☑02-2351 1051; 17 Lane 31, Jinshan S Rd, Sec 2, 金山南路二段31巷17號; small/large bowl NT$220/240; ◎11am-3.30pm & 4.30-9pm; ❉; Ⓜ Dongmen) Open since 1963, this is one of Taipei's top spots for beef noodles, especially of the *hóngshāo* (紅燒, red spicy broth) variety. Beef portions are generous, and melt in your mouth. Other worthwhile dishes include steamed ribs. Expect queues at lunch and dinner.

Ice Monster   DESSERTS $$
(Map p72; ☑02-8771 3263; www.ice-monster.com; 297 Zhongxiao E Rd, Sec 4, 忠孝東路四段297號; dishes NT$180-250; ◎10.30am-11.30pm; ❉⃝🛜⃝✍⃝; Ⓜ Sun Yat-sen Memorial Hall) A superpopular shaved-ice joint with a wide menu of flavours, including strawberry, kiwi fruit and, most famously, mango. So busy that customers are limited to one hour seating time and a minimum order of NT$100. In winter, hot sweet soups are also served.

Red Dragonfly   JAPANESE $$
(紅蜻蜓, Hóng Qīngtíng; Map p66; ☑02-2394 7517; 35-1 Yongkang St, 永康街35-1號; ◎6-11.30pm; ❉; Ⓜ Dongmen) Hugely popular, this Taiwan-influenced Japanese izakaya (gastropub) is a rowdy, happy place, where skewers of fish, mushrooms, squid and chicken are washed down by draught beer. There are lots of small dishes, try the steaming wobbly-egg rolls or the fried oysters. There's

no English sign but you'll spot it by the crowds waiting outside.

Ooh Cha Cha   VEGAN $$
(Map p72; ☑02-2737 2994; www.oohchacha.com; 4 Lane 118, Heping E Rd, Sec 4, 和平東路四段118巷4號; dishes NT$240-280; ◎10am-10pm Sun-Thu, to midnight Fri & Sat; ❉⃝🛜⃝✍⃝❉; Ⓜ Technology Building) Quite possibly the best international vegan food in town. This small funky cafe with glass walls offers scrumptious salads, brown-rice bowls, coconut-tempeh curries and naughty burgers as well as cakes and life-sustaining smoothies. Wonderfully, there's even beer on tap, plus wine and cocktails. Who says vegans can't have fun?

Du Hsiao Yueh   NOODLES $$
(度小月, Dù Xiǎo Yuè; Map p72; ☑02-2773 1344; www.noodle1895.com; 12 Alley 8, Lane 216, Zhongxiao E Rd, Sec 4, 忠孝東路四段216巷8弄12號; dishes NT$200-450; ◎11.30am-9.30pm; ❉; Ⓜ Zhongxiao Dunhua) An upscale branch of a famous Tainan-based snack restaurant. 'Slack Season' (which refers to the style of tangy noodles served during the fishing low season) serves a long menu of southern dishes including mullet roe, bamboo shoots with pork, outrageously good fried-shrimp rolls, and of course the noodles (a mere NT$55 per bowl). Look for the sign reading 'Since 1895'.

NOMURA   JAPANESE $$$
(Map p72; ☑02-2707 7518; 4 Alley 19, Lane 300, Ren'ai Rd, Sec 4, 仁愛路四段300巷19弄4號; lunch/dinner from NT$1500/3000; ◎noon-2.00pm & 6pm-10pm Tue-Sun; ❉⃝🛜; Ⓜ Xinyi Anhe) Outside of Japan, Taipei is the best place in the world for Japanese food. Several restaurants serving Edomae-style sushi (sushi that follows the Tokyo traditions) have a great reputation for Michelin-level quality of food and presentation. Among these is NOMURA, named after the Japanese chef who founded the restaurant in 2011. Indeed, it earned a Michelin star in 2018.

Dayin Jiushi   TAIWANESE $$$
(大隱酒食, Dàyǐn Jiǔshí; Map p66; ☑02-4890 7622; 65 Yongkang St, 永康街65號; dishes NT$180-360; ◎5pm-midnight Mon-Fri, 11.30am-2pm, 5pm-midnight Sat & Sun; ❉⃝🛜; Ⓜ Dongmen) Formerly called James Kitchen, this top spot for Taiwanese food seems to have regained its favoured status after an ownership change. Try the oysters with breadsticks, the bamboo shoots or the tofu-mushroom rolls.

Warm and cosy inside. Reservations are recommended.

Zhongshan & Datong

★Kanokwan
THAI $

(Map p80; 24 Lane 21, Nanjing E Rd, Sec 2, 南京東路二段21巷24號; dishes NT$50-120; ◷10.30am-9pm Mon-Sat; ✲; Ⓜ Songjiang Nanjing) Ask a Thai expat for Taiwan's best street restaurant from their home country, and they'll say Kanokwan. This no-frills place with metal tabletops is always jammed. Don't mind the shouting and jostling, it's worth it for the delicious stir-fried, authentic Thai fare. No English menu, so point at a photo pasted on the front window.

Ningxia Night Market
MARKET $

(寧夏夜市, Níngxià Yèshì; Map p80; cnr Ningxia & Nanjing W Rds; ◷6pm-midnight; Ⓜ Zhongshan) This is an excellent venue for sampling traditional snacks, not least because most stalls have tables. The food here is very fresh, and dishes to try include fish soup, oyster omelette, satay beef, sweet peanut soup (花生湯, huāshēng tāng) and fried taro cake (芋餅, yùbǐng). If you're brave try the bitter tea (苦茶, kǔchá).

Shuanglian Sweet Rice Ball
DESSERTS $

(雙連圓仔湯, Shuānglián Yuánzǐtāng; Map p80; www.sweetriceball.tw; 136 Minsheng W Rd, 民生西路136號; bowls NT$90-120; ◷10.30am-10pm; ✲⚘; Ⓜ Shuanglian) This smart Taiwanese dessert place has been in business since 1951 and serves up high-quality, classic sweet-bean soups and shaved ice. Their signature dish is *moji* balls dusted in peanut and sesame powder that taste like chewy bundles of joy. The staff clearly take great pride in their freshly made food.

#21 Goose & Seafood
TAIWANESE $

(21號鵝肉海鮮, 21 Hào É'ròu Hǎixiān; Map p80; ☎02-2536 2121; 21 Jinzou St, 錦州街21號; dishes NT$40-150; ◷4.30pm-4am; ✲; Ⓜ Zhongshan Elementary School) Loud, rustic and fun, #21 offers great food that's very fresh and very Taiwanese. The place gets its name from its two specialities: roasted goose meat and an assortment of fried and stewed fish dishes.

Maji Square
MARKET $

(Map p80; www.majisquare.com; Taipei Expo Park, 花博公園; ◷11am-10pm; 🛜; Ⓜ Yuanshan) A huge covered food court with lots of choice – burgers, fried rice, a couple of Indian eateries (one vegetarian), and local meat noodle dishes. Midway there's a carousel and **Crafted** (Map p80; www.crafted.tw; Maji Square; ◷4.30-11pm Tue-Sat, to 9.30pm Sun; 🛜), a craft-beer bar, while at the back are several western-style gastropubs and a stage for live music. There's also a health-food supermarket that has cheaper, chilled craft beer.

The area is a great place to take the family. Watch the planes heading in to Songshan Airport – every few minutes one will roar past overhead.

Maji Square is on the right as you enter Taipei Expo Park from Yuanshan MRT.

Blossom Rena Vegan Cafe
VEGAN $$

(貝多蕾納, Bèiduō Lěinà; Map p80; ☎02-2585 8626; www.facebook.com/BlossomRenaVeganCafe; 26-1 Zhongshan N Rd, Sec 3, 中山北路三段26-1號; meals NT$230-320; ◷11.30am-9pm Tue-Sun; ✲🛜⚘; Ⓜ Mingquan W Rd) Imaginative Taiwanese and western cuisine using tofu and lots of vegetables. The three-cup lion's mane mushroom is a delicious bowl of big meaty mushroom cushions; the desserts are also to die for. The vegan waffle with fruit and cream is big enough to share and is indistinguishable from dairy. Inside is relaxed, like a home kitchen with sprays of white orchids.

Lin Dong Fang Beef Noodles
NOODLES $$

(林東芳牛肉麵, Líndōngfāng Niúròu Miàn; Map p72; ☎02-2752 2556; 322 Bade Rd, Sec 2, 八德路二段322號; dishes NT$170/240; ◷11am-2am; ✲; Ⓜ Nanjing Fuxing) This long-running family favourite (and famous restaurant) serves up bowls of noodles steeped in a light bone stew tempered with medicinal herbs. Following its Michelin blessing, it has moved to new fancy digs. The street-side kitchen is now gone and diners head upstairs to neat rows of wooden tables in air-conditioned comfort.

Fei Qian Wu
JAPANESE $$

(肥前屋, Féiqián Wū; Map p80; ☎02-2561 859; 13-1 Lane 121, Zhongshan N Rd, Sec 1, 中山北路一段121巷13-1號; small/large bowl NT$250/480; ◷11am-2.30pm, 5-9pm Tue-Sun; ✲; Ⓜ Zhongshan) There's no English sign for this extremely popular *unagi* (eel) restaurant; you'll spot it by the long lines waiting outside. The queue moves quickly, and you can scan the menu while you wait. Almost everyone orders the eel rice (which comes in ready-prepared lidded boxes) and egg rolls. The grilled squid is delectable and a steal at NT$90.

LOCAL KNOWLEDGE

VEGAN TAIPEI

There's been a huge explosion in vegetarian and vegan restaurants, on top of the vegetarian buffets which you can find everywhere. Marvellously they encompass all kinds of cuisines from burgers to Burmese. There are also some exquisite vegan dessert places and nut-milk bars. If you're buying bread or packaged food look for the characters 純素 (chúnsù) or 全速 (quánsù); they both mean vegan. There's no doubt Taipei is a great place if you don't eat animal products.

As well as Happy Cow's listings (www.happycow.net/asia/taiwan/taipei), It's a Vegan Affair (www.facebook.com/groups/veganaffair) produce an annual map of vegan restaurants in the capital.

★ **Le Palais**   CANTONESE $$$
(頤宮, Yí Gòng; Map p80; ☑02-2181 9985; www.palaisdechinehotel.com/en/restaurant.php; 17th fl, 3 Chengde Rd, Sec 1, 承德路一段3號17樓; dishes from NT$580-2280; ⏰11.30am-2.30pm & 5.30-9.30pm; P🅿️❄️; Ⓜ️Taipei Main Station) The only restaurant in Taipei to be awarded three Michelin stars is an elegant, romantically lit space that serves excellent Cantonese cuisine, including softly steamed dim sum. Their signature dish, the roast baby duck, must be ordered two days in advance. Reservations essential and there's a smart dress code. It's within the five-star Palais de Chine hotel next to Taipei main station.

★ **RAW**   MODERN FRENCH $$$
(Map p62; ☑02-8501 5800; www.raw.com.tw; 301 Lequn Rd, Sec 3, 樂群路三段301號; for 2 people set meal NT$3500; ⏰11.30am-2.30pm & 6-10pm Wed-Sun; ❄️; Ⓜ️Jiannan Rd) RAW is all the rage in Taipei. You'll need to make reservations online at least a month in advance for this place owned by Taiwanese celebrity chef André Chiang. Multicourse set dinners of concept food have been variously called imaginative, creative, multiflavoured and perfectly presented. The decor matches the decadent air with secret drawers and a boat-shaped bar. Bookings are taken for a minimum of two people.

★ **Addiction Aquatic**
Development   SEAFOOD $$$
(上引水產, Shàng Yǐn Shuǐchǎn; Map p80; www.addiction.com.tw; 18 Alley 2, Lane 410, Minzu E Rd, 民族東路410巷2弄18號; ⏰10am-midnight, fish market opens 6am; ❄️; Ⓜ️Xingtian Temple) Housed in the former Taipei Fish Market – you can't miss it, it's a huge blue-and-slate-grey building – is this collection of chic eateries serving the freshest seafood imaginable. There's a stand-up sushi bar, a seafood bar (with wine available), hotpot, an outdoor grill, a wholesale area for take-home seafood and a lifestyle boutique. This place is popular and doesn't take reservations.

To get there from Xingtian Temple (p76), head east along Mingquan E Rd, then turn north at the funeral parlour following the curve of the Jianguo elevated road. Cross to the other side at Nongan St and continue heading north. Within a couple of minutes you will see a huge blue structure down a side street on your right. The total distance is about 1km.

Qian Tian Xia   CHINESE $$$
(黔天下, Qián Tiānxià; Map p80; ☑02-2557 7872; www.ocg.url.tw; 358-2 Dihua St, Sec 1, 迪化街一段358-2; dishes NT$150-500; ⏰11.30am-2.30pm & 5.30-9.30pm Tue-Sun; ❄️🔊; Ⓜ️Daqiaotou) At the northern end of historic Dihua St (p74) is Taipei's finest Guizhou restaurant. The interior is upscale but relaxed, and dishes are authentic and well presented. The restaurant is in a courtyard off the main street. The waitstaff are trained to explain the dishes to diners.

🍴 Shilin

Din Tai Fung   DUMPLINGS $$
(鼎泰豐, Dǐngtàifēng; Map p84; ☑02-2833 8900; www.dintaifung.com.tw; SOGO mall, basement, 77 Zhongshan N Rd, Sec 6, 中山北路六段77號; dishes NT$90-260; ⏰10.30am-9.30pm Mon-Fri, 10am-9.30pm Sat & Sun; Ⓜ️Zhishan) This branch of the famous Din Tai Fung (p97) dumpling restaurant is a good opportunity to experience their legendary fare without the tourist crush, although you may still have to queue up. At least you can wait in the comfort of the air-conditioned SOGO mall. Good option if you're hungry after visiting the National Palace Museum (p78).

MiaCucina   VEGETARIAN $$
(Map p84; ☑02-8866 2658; www.facebook.com/Miacucinafamily; 48 Dexing W Rd, 德行西路48號; mains NT$250-395; ⏰11am-10pm; P❄️🔊🚲🍴; Ⓜ️Zhishan) Serving Italian food in American portions, this place is best enjoyed with a friend. Superpopular, especially with expats; it's worthwhile booking if you come for

dinner. Panini, fresh pasta, Buddha bowls and salads all without any meat. We recommend the flatbread with blue cheese, cinnamon, apple and caramelised pecans.

✕ Songshan

Angkor Wat Snacks   CAMBODIAN $

(吳哥窟柬泰雲風味小吃, Wúgēkū Jiǎntàiyún Fēngwèi Xiǎochī; Map p88; www.facebook.com/AngkorKitchen; 454 Changchun Rd, 長春路454; dishes NT$90-160; ⏰11.30am-8.30pm Mon-Sat; ❀; Ⓜ Nanjing Fuxing) Tasty Cambodian fare with Thai undertones. There's no English name but the Chinese has a red sign. Try the *jiāomá jī* (椒麻雞, fried chicken on shredded cabbage) or Cambodian curry (柬式咖哩, *jiǎnshì gālí*) with pho noodles (河粉, *héfěn*), rice noodles (米粉, *mǐfěn*) or French bread. There's a picture menu to help you decide. The menu is meat-heavy, although the owners said most dishes could be prepared for a vegetarian.

Raohe Street Night Market   MARKET $

(饒河街觀光夜市, Ráohéjiē Guānguāng Yèshì; Map p88; ⏰5pm-midnight; Ⓜ Songshan) Taipei's oldest night market, Raohe St is a single pedestrian lane stretching between two ornate gates. In between you'll find a great assortment of Taiwanese eats, treats and sometimes even seats. Look for pork ribs in herbal broth, vermicelli and oysters, spicy stinky tofu and steamed buns.

★ NCI Sushi   SUSHI $$

(德相美式加州壽司, Déxiāng Měishì Jiāzhōu Shòusī; Map p88; www.ncisushi.com; 2 Alley 28, Lane 256, Nanjing E Rd, Sec 3, 南京東路三段256巷28弄2號; plates NT$300-400; ⏰11.30am-2pm, 5.30-9pm; ❀❂❀; Ⓜ Nanjing Fuxing) Superb Californian-style sushi joint, notable for their playfully named rolls. Try the Marilyn Monroll with scallops and Parmesan sauce. The Salmonlicious is just that, while vegans are not ignored with soybean, avocado and asparagus-filled choices.

Kunming Islamic Restaurant   INDIAN $$

(昆明園, Kūnmíng Yuán; Map p88; 26 Lane 81, Fuxing N Rd, 復興北路81巷26號; dishes NT$180-300; ⏰11.30am-2pm & 5.30-9.30pm Mon-Fri, 5.30-9.30pm Sat & Sun; ❀❀; Ⓜ Nanjing Fuxing) This halal restaurant serves some of the best, if not the best, Indian with Burmese undertones in town. Try their tandoori chicken. This is a Muslim restaurant and therefore does not serve alcohol. Set meal with salad and Indian milk tea NT$240.

Dian Shui Lou   JIANGSU $$$

(點水樓, Diǎnshuǐ Lóu; Map p88; ☎02-8712 6689; www.dianshuilou.com.tw; 61 Nanjing E Rd, Sec 4, 南京東路四段61號; baskets from NT$150, dishes from NT$320; ⏰11am-2pm, 5.30-9pm; ❀; Ⓜ Taipei Arena) Often compared to the other main dumpling establishment Din Tai Fung (p97), Dian Shui Lou offers well-rated baskets of the delicacy as well as a range of Jiangsu, Zhejiang and Taiwan traditional dishes. The interior is cold and classy, service quite formal. Snag a table near the open kitchen to watch the chefs roll dough as you eat.

✕ Xinyi

He Shun Xiang   VEGAN $

(和順鄉, Héshùn Xiāng; Map p92; ☎02-2767 2016; 46 Alley 5, Lane 147, Keelung Rd, Sec 1, 基隆路一段147弄5弄46號; dishes NT$85-130; ⏰11.30am-2pm & 5-9pm Thu-Tue; ❀❂; Ⓜ Taipei City Hall) Tasty, meat-free noodle and rice dishes from Yunnan and Myanmar. Coconut curry vegetables come recommended, as does the peppery deep-fried tofu in sesame dipping-sauce-goodness. Arrive early, the tofu often sells out. No English sign; look out for the white child's pedal car on the wall, next door to a small pizza place.

Minder Vegetarian   VEGETARIAN $

(明德素食園, Míngdé Sùshí Yuán; Map p92; www.minder.com.tw; basement, Eslite Xinyi, 11 Songao Rd, 松高路11號; price by weight; ⏰11am-9.30pm; ❂; Ⓜ Taipei City Hall) Minder is a chain of buffet-style vegetarian (not vegan) restaurants run by the controversial and very wealthy Tzu Chi Buddhist foundation. The selection and quality of dishes is usually better than the many similar buffets, but the cost is also slightly higher. This branch in the basement of the Eslite Xinyi has a great selection of vegetables, fake meats and crispy salads.

★ Xiang Chu Xiang   THAI $$

(象廚, Xiàng Chú; Map p92; ☎02-2749 1988; 9 Lane 147, Keelung Rd, Sec 1, 基隆路一段147巷9號; dishes NT$150-400; ⏰11.30am-2.30pm, 5.30-9.30pm Tue-Sun; ❀❂; Ⓜ Taipei City Hall) With memorably tasty Thai food, this is a real gem. The yellow crab curry is to die for. Great prices, no-nonsense service. If it's not on the menu you can't have it, and if you arrive less than one hour before closing, they'll tell you to go – but the food is so good that this place is jammed most nights.

Good Cho's
CAFE $$

(好丘, Hǎo Qiū; Map p92; 54 Songqin St, 松勤街 54號; mains from NT$300; ⏱10am-8pm Mon-Fri, 9am-6.30pm Sat & Sun; ❄🅿; Ⓜ Taipei 101)
Inside former military-dependent **Village 44** (信義公民會館, Xìnyì Gōngmín Huìguǎn, Xingyi Assembly Hall; Map p92; cnr Zhuangjing & Songqin Sts; Ⓜ Taipei 101) **FREE** is this lovely cafe/performance space/lifestyle shop with marble floors, retro lighting and great acoustics. The menu is a mixed bag of brunchy bagels, Chinese desserts, savoury pancakes and rice dishes. It's closed on the first Monday of the month.

Drinking & Nightlife

🍷 Zhongzheng

⭐ Another Brick
BAR

(Map p66; ☎02-2365 2371; www.facebook.com/AnotherBrickTaipei; 31 Xinhai Rd, Sec 1, 辛亥路一段31號; ⏱6pm-1am Sun-Thu, to 2.30am Fri & Sat; 🛜; Ⓜ Taipower Building) This laid-back, funky Belgian-run bar has a good stock of Belgian craft beer. Usually more mellow in the early evening, when you can snag a happy-hour bevvie (until 9pm), it tends to get jammed later on. There's cosy, shadowy seating and

Instagrammable decorations such as a fish tank in a retro TV and a wall of LP covers.

Gongguan Riverside Bars
BEER GARDEN

(Map p66; ⏱6pm-late; Ⓜ Gongguan) A string of simple outdoor bars with local and expat owners that offer a range of bottled beers, ciders and spirits. Nothing fancy, but there's a friendly, upbeat atmosphere and a lot of music. No fixed times, and it's often not open in winter if it's too cold. If it's raining, move your table under the shelter of an overhead motorway. It's rare to find outdoor places to drink, away from the road and residential areas where homeowners can complain about the noise.

To get here, head out of the MRT via Exit 4, take the first road left and go straight for about 800m until you hit the riverside. You'll hear the boom of the music before you see the bars, underneath the elevated road.

Jackwell
CAFE

(傑克威爾, Jiékè Wēiěr; Map p66; www.facebook.com/jackwell.cafe; 118 Roosevelt Rd, Sec 2, 羅斯福路二段118號; ⏱8am-9pm Mon-Fri, from 9am Sat & Sun; 🛜; Ⓜ Guting) This snuggly little corner of a coffee shop is basically just a tumble of tables looking out onto a back lane next to Guting MRT station. It's remarkably popular

---

ASIA'S COFFEE CAPITAL

Taipei has emerged as Asia's coffee capital. It seems the Dutch first planted coffee around the Gukeng area (Yunlin county) in the 17th century, but for centuries the red beans were used only for decorative purposes by indigenous peoples.

Things really began in the early 2000s, when Taiwanese living or studying abroad started bringing back new ideas about how to make 'proper coffee'. As is usual here, they found a ready audience eager both to try new things and to learn to appreciate the drink at a higher level. Today you'll find scores of cafes serving gourmet coffee, often from single-origin beans (some locally grown), roasted on the premises and brewed in a slow, labour-intensive way right in front of you.

Where to Get a Good Cup
Passable fresh-brewed coffee is available at any convenience store for NT$40 to NT$60. Some of the best, and ridiculously cheap for the quality, coffee comes from chains like cama café (www.facebook.com/camacafe), which roast on the premises and cater to takeaway. To save the environment, bring your own flask or ask for a mug and drink it on the premises. Another massively successful chain is Louisa (www.louisacoffee.co), which was one of the first to start selling flat whites.

Wilbeck Cafe (p108) is a real local gem. This small, much more intimate chain sells very good, well-priced coffee in cute retro cubby holes. There are a handful across the city, including near Taipei main station and across from City Hall MRT.

Starbucks are ubiquitous here but independent coffee shops serve up much better brews and offer a more interesting experience.

There are high concentrations of cafes on Lane 243 just south of Yongkang Park; the alleys north of Zhongshan MRT Exit 2; and Dihua St, Sec 1. But you will find coffee shops virtually all over the city.

because of its excellent coffee and budget prices – a small and very good Americano is just NT$45. Jackwell is well worth a visit.

Kafka by the Sea
CAFE
(海邊的卡夫卡, Hǎibiān de Kǎfūkǎ; Map p66; ☑02-2364 1996; www.facebook.com/kafka. republic; 2nd fl, 2 Lane 244, Roosevelt Rd, Sec 3, 羅斯福路三段244巷2號2樓; ⏰1-10pm Mon-Fri, from noon Sat & Sun; 🐾; MTaipower Building) A hipster cafe without any of the pretension. Spacious, studious, with a wall of windows, and damn good coffee and cakes. Named after the Haruki Murakami book, *Kafka on the Shore,* the venue often hosts music acts of all genres come evening, when caffeine can be swapped for an alcoholic beverage.

Mayor's Residence Art Salon
CAFE
(市長官邸藝文沙龍, Shìzhǎng Guāndǐ Yìwén Shālóng; Map p66; www.mayorsalon.tw; 46 Xuzhou Rd, 徐州路46號; ⏰9am-5pm; 🐾; MShandao Temple) Built in 1940, this is one of the best-preserved large Japanese-style residences in Taiwan. With its heritage styling, great natural lighting and garden, it's a superb place for a coffee, tea or light meal. Small art exhibitions are frequently held here.

Chun Shui Tang
TRADITIONAL DRINKS
(春水堂, Chūnshuǐ Táng; Map p66; www.chun shuitang.com.tw; ground fl, National Concert Hall, Liberty Sq, 21 Zhongshan S Rd, 中山南路21號; ⏰11.30am-8.50pm; MChiang Kai-shek Memorial Hall) The pearl milk tea (NT$85) here is supposed to be the best in the city – pink, frothy and creamy with small, firm pearls and only lightly sweetened. There are branches across the city, but this one on the ground floor of the National Concert Hall is one of the nicest. Traditional light noodle dishes and Chinese desserts are also available.

H*ours Cafe
CAFE
(Map p66; ☑02-2364 2742; www.facebook.com/ hours.cafe; 12 Alley 8, Lane 210, Roosevelt Rd, Sec 3, 羅斯福路三段210巷8弄12號; ⏰2-11pm; 🐾🍴; MTaipower Building) Lovely little gay-owned cafe serving simple snacks and beverages.

🍷 Ximending & Wanhua

⭐ Driftwood
CRAFT BEER
(Map p70; www.facebook.com/driftwoodxmd; Hotel Papa Whale, 46 Kunming St, 昆明街46號; ⏰5pm-11.30 Sun-Thu, to 1.30am Fri & Sat; 🐾; MXimen) Laid out like a tiki bar with a scattering of wooden benches with thatched shelters, this

is another of Taihu Brewery's outlets and it's excellent. The long, open bar sports 18 craft beers on tap; happy hour is until 9pm every day, when you can get three drinks for the price of two.

⭐ 58 Bar
CRAFT BEER
(Map p70; www.facebook.com/pg/the58bar; 58 Kaifeng St, Sec 2, 開封街58號二段; ⏰6.30pm-1am; 🐾; MXimen) With its bright-red painted front, the 58 Bar is hard to miss. Long and narrow like it has been slipped into the building as an afterthought, this lively joint has more than 100 varieties of craft beer, and all are sourced from Taiwan. Happy hour is until 9pm, when pints of draught pale ale are NT$200. Pub grub is also available.

⭐ Red House Bar Street
GAY
(Map p70; ⏰6pm-late; 🐾; MXimen) This strip of open-air bars behind the historic Red House is a friendly and lively gay district that welcomes everyone. You will often see families with children mixing with the crowd.

⭐ Herb Alley
TRADITIONAL DRINKS
(青草巷, Qīngcǎo Xiàng; Map p70; Lane 224, Xichang St, 西昌路224巷; drinks NT$20-100; ⏰9am-10pm; MLongshan Temple) Just around the corner from Longshan Temple (p69) is this herb-selling area that dates back to Qing times. It's a great place to sample some of the incredible range of Chinese herbal drinks available, though some may truly curdle your liver.

Try the refreshing roselle (洛神花, luòshén huā), the soothing wax-gourd tea (多瓜茶, dōngguā chá) or the incredibly bitter, bitter tea (苦茶, kǔ chá). Herb Alley is just to the right of Longshan as you face the entrance (Lane 209, though the official address is Lane 224, Xichang St). Wander through and as you pop onto Xichang St, you'll see the drink stalls.

Eighty-Eightea
TEAHOUSE
(八拾捌茶, Bāshíbā Chá; Map p70; ☑02-2312 0845; www.facebook.com/88tea; Xibenyuan Temple Sq, cnr Changsha St & Zhonghua Rd; ⏰11.30am-9pm; 🐾; MXimen) Housed in the refurbished wooden quarters of a Japanese priest, this lovely teahouse really catches the afternoon light through its windows. There's a Japanese sitting area, as well as regular tables, where you can enjoy one of their own branded Taiwanese teas. Try the cinnamon oolong. Simple rice dishes are also available.

ℹ️ THE BAR SCENE

There's no lack of bars within the city, although prices are quite high. Typically, beers sell for between NT$150 and NT$350, spirits or cocktails between NT$250 and NT$600. Places that open early (6pm) tend to have happy hours until around 8pm.

Bars are spread throughout the city, although Da'an district probably has more than its fair share, especially of the more upmarket cocktail/speakeasy joints.

Le Promenoir Coffee
CAFE

(4f劇場咖啡, 4F Jùchǎng Kāfēi; Map p70; www.facebook.com/LePromenoirCoffee; 4th fl, 98 Yanping S Rd, 延平南路98號4樓; ⊙10.30am-8.30pm; 🛜; MXimen) This cafe is set in a long gallery with lovely big windows, on the 4th floor of Zhongshan Hall (p69). It's the perfect setting for reading or meeting a friend. Look out for the magnificent, polished, green grand piano with the painted peacocks.

Fong Da Coffee
CAFE

(蜂大咖啡, Fēngdà Kāfēi; Map p70; 🕾02-2371 9577; 42 Chengdu Rd, 成都路42號; ⊙8am-10pm; MXimen) One of Taipei's original coffee shops, Fong Da dates from 1956 and still uses some of the original equipment. Service is brusque – this is a taste of old Taipei after all, and coffees are strong, hot and bitter. It's a nice slice of history, very different from Taiwan's contemporary coffee-culture experience.

Commander D
GAY

(Map p70; www.facebook.com/commander.tw; basement, 36 Kaifeng St, Sec 2, 開封街二段36號B1; NT$200-300; ⊙9pm-3am, to 4am Fri & Sat; 🛜; MXimen) This underground and popular dungeon club is accessed by a vault-like door. Down below it's all hot and steamy, with frequent live acts – for a taster check their Facebook page. The interior is painted black, with cages, chains, ropes, handcuffs and little secret corners.

🍵 Da'an

★ Indulge Experimental Bistro
COCKTAIL BAR

(Map p72; 🕾02-2773 0080; www.indulgebistrotaipei.blogspot.com; 11, Lane 219, Fuxing S Rd, Sec 1, 復興南路一段219巷11號; ⊙6pm-2am Sun-Thu, to 3am Fri & Sat; 🛜; MZhongxiao Fuxing) Taipei's cocktail jewel in the crown was voted one of the world's 50 best bars in 2018. They offer gorgeously and imaginatively designed drinks with fairy-tale names and spices from the east. 'Soldier & Village' is a concoction of sorghum liquor, osmanthus and myrrh, for example. Attentive bar service, the creamy decor and a certain confidence create a warm, welcoming ambience.

★ Wistaria Tea House
TEAHOUSE

(紫藤廬, Zǐténg Lú; Map p72; 🕾02-2363 7375; www.wistariateahouse.com; 1, Lane 16, Xinsheng Rd, Sec 3, 新生路三段16弄1號; ⊙10am-10pm; 🛜; MTaipower Building) History, nostalgia and fine tea combine in this charming former wooden dormitory from the Japanese era. Wistaria was built in 1920 for naval personnel and later used as a hang-out for artists, literati and political dissidents following the 1979 Kaohsiung Incident (which led to the arrest and imprisonment of most of the top democracy advocates in Taiwan).

The teahouse has a fine selection of oolongs, Tieguanyin, green teas and some rare pu'er (dark fermented) tea that could set you back thousands in one afternoon of drinking. Light meals and snacks are also served. Come in the daytime to enjoy views of the koi pond and leafy garden.

★ Cafe Libero
CAFE

(Map p72; 🕾02-2356 7129; 1 Lane 243, Jinhua St, 金華街243巷1號; ⊙11am-11pm, to midnight Fri & Sat; 🛜; MDongmen) Set in a house from the 1950s with vintage furniture and a zelkova parquet floor, this is the perfect place for a romantic date. It also has a touch of the murder mystery about it, with the scarlet sofa chairs and dark wood in the back room. Good coffee and excellent whiskies, with a small outdoor seating area.

Fourplay Cuisine
COCKTAIL BAR

(Map p72; 🕾02-2708 3898; https://fourplaytaipei.com; 49 Dongfeng St, 東豐街49號; ⊙6pm-1am Mon-Thu, to 2am Fri & Sat; 🛜; MDa'an) Walk into Fourplay and ask for a drinks menu – the bartender is likely to say that *he* is the drinks menu. Tell him what you fancy and he'll tailor a tipple. Packed to the gills, even on a weeknight, you'd be wise to reserve a spot. A second branch has opened at number 61 down the street.

Costumice Cafe
CAFE

(Map p72; 🕾02-2711 8086; www.costumice.com.tw; 6 Alley 71, Lane 223, Zhongxiao E Rd, Sec 4, 忠孝東路四段223巷71弄6號; ⊙noon-midnight

Sun-Thu, to 1am Fri & Sat; 🛜; Ⓜ Zhongxiao Dunhua) This ultrahip cafe-bar has a marvellous leafy yard, perfect for a lazy afternoon wine or coffee. This is where the beautiful people flock at night. Craft beer (draught and bottled) is also available.

Abrazo Bistro
GAY

(Map p72; 🗹 02-2731 8282; www.facebook.com/Abrazobistro; 198 Dunhua S Rd, Sec 1, 敦化南路一段198號; ⏱ 11.30am-2am Tue-Sun, to 4am Fri & Sat; 🛜; Ⓜ Zhongxiao Dunhua) The hottest and swankiest gay bar in town, catering to well-groomed and well-heeled professionals. Downstairs has VIP booths, a DJ and a throbbing atmosphere. Upstairs looks a bit like a Roman bathhouse. This place is sardine-tin stuffed on weekends and crowds spill out onto the streets.

Craft Beer Taproom
CRAFT BEER

(啜飲室大安, Chuàiyǐnshì Dà'ān; Map p72; 🗹 02-2773 5565; www.facebook.com/cysdaan; 34 Lane 27, Ren'ai Rd, Sec 4, 仁愛路四段27巷34號; ⏱ 5pm-midnight Mon-Sat, to 11pm Sun; 🛜; Ⓜ Zhongxiao Fuxing) The taproom is packed with locals and expats, an industrial chic space filled with long benches and sporting a buzzing vibe. With 24 beers on tap – half of which are brewed by owner Taihu, and the other half mostly imported IPAs, ales and stouts from the US – there's plenty of choice. A kooky option would be the lethal-in-medium-amounts Long Island Iced Beer.

Trio
COCKTAIL BAR

(三重奏, Sānchóngzòu; Map p72; 🗹 02-2703 8706; 12 Alley 54, Lane 63, Dunhua S Rd, Sec 2, 敦化南路二段63巷54弄12號; ⏱ 6pm-midnight Tue-Sat; 🛜) This well-regarded, chilled cocktail bar focuses on rum blends and is famed for its Earl Grey recipes. There's no menu: simply tell the bartender what flavours you like and they will whip you up a personalised poison. There's a larger seating area downstairs or you can stick to the open-sided, glowing bar nook at ground level.

23 Public
CRAFT BEER

(Map p72; 🗹 02-2363 2387; www.facebook.com/23Public; 100 Xinhai Rd, Sec 1, 辛亥路一段100號; ⏱ 3.30pm-midnight; 🛜; Ⓜ Taipower Building) With 12 kinds of craft beer on tap (eight from their own 23 Brewing Company), this little corner place is a great spot for sampling great beer; 23 IPA, a hoppy brew, is their top seller. Happy hour (NT$150 a glass) is until 7pm daily.

Zhang Men
CRAFT BEER

(掌門, Zhǎng Mén; Map p66; 🗹 02-2395 2366; www.zhangmenbrewing.com/index_en.html; 10 Lane 4, Yongkang St, 永康街4巷10號; ⏱ 1pm-midnight Sun-Fri, to 1am Sat; 🛜; Ⓜ Dongmen) Small on space but big on beer, this local microbrewery has 20 draught varieties. The fruity New England IPA goes down a treat. Can't decide? Go for the six small taster glasses (NT$498). There's outdoor seating in a small front yard. This is the original taproom; there are now four in Taipei, including a rooftop Xinyi branch (p108).

Ounce Taipei
COCKTAIL BAR

(Map p72; www.facebook.com/OunceTaipei; 309 Xinyi Rd, Sec 4, 信義路四段309號; ⏱ 6pm-2am Sun-Thu, to 3am Fri & Sat; 🛜; Ⓜ Xinyi Anhe) This slick speakeasy-style bar is everything you'd expect it to be: behind a secret door, heavy on the dark hardwood, dim lighting, and serving top-rated cocktails. The establishment is fronted by a tiny bar called BS Mini. Ounce has plans to open another branch in Dongmen. Check Facebook for updates.

Cha Cha Thé
TEAHOUSE

(采采食茶, Cǎi Cǎi Shí Chá; Map p72; 🗹 02-8773 1818; www.chachathe.com; 23 Lane 219, Fuxing S Rd, Sec 1, 復興南路一段219巷23號; ⏱ 11am-10pm; 🛜; Ⓜ Zhongxiao Fuxing) A hyper-stylish

ALL THE TEA IN TAIWAN

Tea growing and drinking has a venerable tradition in Taiwan. While most people head to Maokong when they want to enjoy brewing and imbibing, there are a few excellent places within Taipei, many set in beautifully restored Japanese-era residences. Eighty-Eightea (p103), for example, is housed in a refurbished Japanese priest's digs! If bubble tea (boba cha) is your cuppa, good news: you'll find endless roadside stands and stalls throughout the city selling it hot or cold with ice. Most of these places also offer fruit-flavoured teas, such as lemon or passion fruit, and sweetened or unsweetened black- and green-tea-flavoured drinks for between NT$30 and NT$80 a cup. 50 Lan, Comebuy (our favourite) and CoCo are three of the most popular chains; you'll see them everywhere.

If you bring your own flask, you can save on plastic and sometimes get a small discount.

but genuinely serene teahouse designed by chic fashion house Shiatzy Chen. One wall is made of compressed tea bricks, and there's beautifully packaged tea for sale.

Water Moon Tea House
TEAHOUSE

(水月草堂, Shuǐyuè Cǎotáng; Map p72; ☑02-2702 8399; www.teawatermoon.com; 2 Alley 180, Fuxing S Rd, Sec 2, 復興南路二段180巷2號; ☺2-10pm; ☎; ⓂTechnology Building) With some of the city's oldest and finest teas, an elegant design and classes in tea appreciation, this is the place for the serious drinker, or for someone looking to learn more about the art. Sundays see a large expat crowd of qigong enthusiasts, some of whom are volunteers here and can help arrange tea classes (search for 'mindfultaipei' on Facebook).

Drop Coffee House
CAFE

(滴咖啡, Dī Kāfēi; Map p72; ☑02-2368 4222; 1, Lane 76, Xinsheng S Rd, Sec 3, 新生南路三段76巷1號; ☺10.30am-10pm; ☎; ⓂGongguan) Set in an 80-year-old gutted Japanese-era private residence with lovely worn wooden flooring, this coffee house serves single-origin coffee from places such as Rwanda and Brazil. The aroma of coffee hits you as you walk in.

Zhongshan & Datong

★wooo
CAFE

(窩窩, Wō wō; Map p80; ☑02-2555 2056; www.facebook.com/wooo.tp; 404 Minsheng W Rd, 民生西路404號; ☺noon-7pm Mon-Fri, 10am-8pm Sat & Sun; ☎; ⓂBeimen) This fun Hong Kong-style cafe set in a restored apothecary certainly has a lot of retro charm. The original medicine cabinets with their wooden drawers and stoppered jars line one wall. It seems to have a bit of an identity crisis, though, stocking local and Hong Kong bottled IPAs, but shuttering in the early evening. For nostalgia seekers and early drinkers!

Check out what's stuffed in their medicine jars. More black magic, perhaps, than your traditional healing dried herbs.

★Illumination Books
CAFE

(浮光書店, Fúguāng Shūdiàn; Map p80; www.facebook.com/IlluminationBooks; 2nd fl, 16 Lane 47, Chifeng St, 赤峰街47巷16號2樓; ☺noon-10pm Tue-Sun; ☎; ⓂZhongshan) This gorgeous 2nd-floor cafe–bookshop housed in a restored heritage house is full of light and elegance. The shelves of books, exposed brickwork, scattered tables and an armchair by the window make this a lovely place to unwind. Pots

of tea in a dozen different flavours can be topped up with hot water for free.

★Le Zinc
WINE BAR

(Map p80; www.facebook.com/lezinclo; 67 Dihua St, Sec 1, 迪化街一段67號; ☺10am-7pm Sun & Mon, to midnight Tue-Thu, to 1am Fri & Sat; ☎; ⓂBeimen) This warm and stylish cafe/wine bar is at the far back of one of Dihua St's traditional brick shops. Enter via ArtYard67 (p114) to get a look at how these long and narrow buildings were constructed to facilitate air flow and natural lighting. If you arrive late, enter from the back alley. Its wine list now includes choices from Taiwanese vineyards.

Triangle
CLUB

(Map p80; www.facebook.com/TriangleTaipei; Taipei Expo Park; before/after midnight (incl. drink) NT$200/300; ☺10pm-4am; ⓂYuanshan) Packed with foreign students, this smallish club is right next to Maji Square. Eclectic range of tunes – sometimes even reggae – karaoke and live music. Less expensive than the more blingy options in Xinyi, and if the music is right, Triangle promises a fun night. Also hosts a monthly gay party, Werk! (www.facebook.com/werktaipei).

To get here enter Expo Park from Yuanshan MRT and turn right into Maji Square. It's on the left-hand side, near the rear.

Pier 5
BEER GARDEN

(Map p80; www.facebook.com/DOYENPIER5; Dadaocheng Wharf, 大稻埕碼頭; ☺4pm-11pm; ☎; ⓂBeimen) This lively waterfront strip of outdoor pop-up bars offers gorgeous views of the river. Some of the stalls have rooftop areas, or else there are benches and seats all around. There's a decent pizza place, as well as draught beer, whisky and the now-ubiquitous craft brews. Come weekends, performances including live music and puppet theatre are often held here. Watch out for mosquitoes.

Soi 13
GAY

(Map p80; 13 Minsheng E Rd, Sec 1, 民生東路一段13號; NT$500; ☎; ⓂShuanglian) Taipei's new favourite gay sauna. Has a steam room, sauna, Jacuzzi, darkroom, maze, cabins, lounge and cafe. Crowded on nights when locals get a discount.

Mikkeller
CRAFT BEER

(Map p80; www.facebook.com/mikkellertaipei; 241 Nanjing W Rd, 南京西路241號; ☺4pm-midnight Sun-Thu, to 1am Fri & Sat; ☎; ⓂBeimen) There

LGBTIQ+ TRAVELLERS

Foreign-born gay and lesbian travellers will find Taipei friendly and exciting. An open-minded city, Taipei hosts Asia's biggest pride parade (p86) every October. It's common to see LGBT+ couples holding hands on the streets, though not so common to see them kissing. The centre of gay nightlife is the bar and restaurant area around the Red House (p103) in Ximending.

As LGBT+ culture becomes more mainstream and hook-up apps replace cruising sites, the old gay haunts, clubs and bars in Taipei, have dwindled. This might also indicate that there is greater social inclusiveness in that the LGBT+ community feels comfortable going to non-queer venues.

Useful resources include Utopia (www.utopia-asia.com/tipstaiw.htm), Taiwan Tongzhi (LGBT) Hotline Association (http://hotline.org.tw/english) and Taiwan LGBT Pride (www.facebook.com/Taiwan.LGBT.Pride).

In Taipei you can get up-to-date information on gay-nightlife options from Toto at three little birds (p89) hostel. A community of lesbians often meets at Love Boat (p112) and every month, nightclub Triangle (p106) hosts a gay party night called WERK! (www.facebook.com/werktaipei).

Gs Hotel (www.gshome.co) is a men-only guesthouse offering singles, doubles, twins and dorms, some with shared bathrooms, and a steam room in Songshan District.

are 24 craft beers on tap – and always a few local brands – in this famous Danish microbrewery. It's in an enviable location near Dihua St in a lovely refurbished heritage house. Take your glass to the 2nd floor, which looks a bit like a primary-school classroom. A nice mellow option although a tad too brightly lit for a bar.

Taboo   LESBIAN
(Map p80; www.facebook.com/TABOONightClub; 90 Jianguo N Rd, Sec 2, 建國北路二段90號; ⊙9pm-2am Wed, Thu & Sun, 10pm-4am Fri & Sat; MXingtian Temple) This long-running basement lesbian club attracts a young set of women, with the liveliest nights Fridays and Saturdays. There's a dance floor and DJ, and the venue often hosts theme nights.

G*star Club   GAY
(Map p72; www.facebook.com/gstarclub; basement, 23 Longjiang Rd, 龍江路23號; ⊙10pm-late; MNanjing Fuxing) Still going strong, this fairly small but packed dance club puts on lots of parties. Expect a youngish crowd.

Goldfish   GAY
(Map p80; ☏02-2581 3133; www.facebook.com/goldfishtaipei; 13 Lane 85, Linsen N Rd, 林森北路85巷13號; ⊙9pm-late Fri-Wed; ☎; MShandao Temple, MZhongshan) Nice cocktail bar with inventive recipes in the Japanese quarter. Popular with bears and muscled types.

Lugou Cafe   CAFE
(爐鍋咖啡, Lúguō Kāfēi; Map p80; ☏02-2555 8225; www.facebook.com/luguocafeartyard; 1, 2nd

fl, Lane 32, Dihua St, Sec 1, 迪化街一段32巷1號2樓; ⊙11am-7pm; ☎; MBeimen) Speciality coffees, including local choices such as Alishan, on the 2nd floor of a Dihua St heritage building (originally the chemist AS Watson & Co). Mismatched furniture, eclectic decor, Frank Sinatra jazz: grab a window seat and slip back in time. The coffee is a pleasure, the sandwiches not so. Upstairs is the thinkers' theatre. Ask at the cafe for a leaflet to see what's on; very occasionally there are English-language performances.

🍷 Shilin

Funky Fresh Bar   CRAFT BEER
(Map p84; https://funky-fresh.business.site; 89-4 Danan Rd, 大南路89-4號; ⊙7pm-midnight; ☎; MJiantan) Cashing in on Taipei's craft-beer craze is Funky Fresh situated on the cusp of the Shilin Night Market (p79) action. It's a heavenly nook serving a good range of Taiwan-branded craft beer in bottles with an additional six on tap piped through two metallic mannequins. Come before 9pm and happy hour entices at NT$150 a glass.

A Loving Cafe   CAFE
(愛上咖啡館, Àishàng Kāfēiguǎn; Map p84; ☏02-2883 6565; www.facebook.com/alovingcafe; 47 Lane 235, Zhongzheng Rd, 中正路235巷47號; ⊙noon-7pm Mon-Fri, to 6pm Sat & Sun; ☎🍽; MShilin) Rather than queue up at the bland coffee chain round the corner, pop into this cute, mellow cafe just behind Exit 1 of the MRT. Single-origin coffee, lovingly prepared

TAIPEI DRINKING & NIGHTLIFE

desserts and the scrumptious-sounding Cointreau–brown sugar au lait.

 Songshan

★ **Fujin Tree 353** CAFE
(Map p88; ☑02-2749 5225; www.facebook.com/fujintree353cafe; 353 Fujin St, 富錦街353號; ◉9am-6.30pm Mon-Fri, to 7.30pm Sat & Sun; ☜; Ⓜ Songshan Airport) With outdoor seating facing tree-lined Fujin St, this cafe is hard to beat. Inside it's all woodwork, mood lighting and strategically placed twigs. If you want to people-watch Taiwan's hip generation, this is ground control.

Buddha Tea House TEAHOUSE
(吉祥草茶館, Jíxiáng Cǎo Cháguǎn; Map p88; ☑02-2718 7035; www.facebook.com/BuddaTeaHouse; 114 Fujin St, 富錦街114號; ◉11am-11pm; Ⓜ Songshan Airport) The smell of incense and the fluttering of Tibetan prayer flags indicate this charming little teahouse hidden behind trees. Run by the gregarious Mr Hwang, an indigenous artist from the Paiwan tribe, this atmospheric old house also serves Chinese dishes. Share a pot of tea in one of the tatami-mat rooms out back, facing an enchanted garden.

This magic place has been around for three decades. That's quite an achievement in Taipei.

Wilbeck Cafe CAFE
(威爾貝克, Wēiěrbèikè; Map p88; ☑02-2767 2277; www.facebook.com/WilbeckOne; 1 Alley 2, Lane 123, Nanjing E Rd, Sec 5, 南京東路五段123巷2弄1號; ◉7.30am-6pm Mon-Fri, 8am-6pm Sat & Sun; Ⓜ Nanjing Sanmin) Cosy little secret space with outdoor smoking section and some of the best-quality, cheapest brews in town. Their latte with a splash of Baileys (NT$80) is perfect for a winter-morning buzz. Retro curios fill the interior, from a framed copy of the book *Humpty Dumpty* to an old transistor radio. No wi-fi, evidence of its true coffee character.

Rokucyoumecafe CAFE
(六丁目, Liù Dīngmù; Map p88; ☑02-2761 5510; 7 Lane 6, Xinzhong St, 新中街6巷7號; ◉noon-9pm Sun-Thu, to 10pm Fri & Sat; ☜; Ⓜ Nanjing Sanmin) This cute cafe is aiming to be a little bit of Tokyo in Taiwan. Its speciality is matcha, that favoured flavouring from Japan made from powdered green tea. Matcha lattes and home-cooked cakes are so green they look too special to eat. Their coffee is genuinely

excellent and lovingly prepared. Note the shop sign is only in Chinese characters.

This place is packed on weekends, but still feels cosy and welcoming.

Beer & Deer CRAFT BEER
(啤魯麋鹿, Pí Lǔ Mílù; Map p88; ☑02-2760 0920; www.facebook.com/beerndeer; 4 Alley 4, Lane 36 Minsheng E Rd, Sec 5, 民生東路五段36巷4弄49號; ◉4pm-midnight Mon-Fri, from 3pm Sat & Sun; Ⓜ Nanjing Sanmin) Tucked up an alleyway in Minsheng Community, Beer & Deer appears to have no deer but lots of beer – more than 80 craft varieties, mostly imported. It's a small space, a couple of tables, but looks bigger as it opens onto the street. If you're around evening-time, a chilled bottle of Gweilo beer from Hong Kong could hit the spot.

1001 Nights Hookah Lounge Bar CLUB
(一千零一夜水煙館, Yīqiānlíngyī Yè Shuǐyān Guǎn; Map p88; ☑02-2765 1122; www.facebook.com/1001NightsTaipei; 2nd fl, 8 Nanjing E Rd, Sec 5, 南京東路五段8號2樓; ◉9pm-late; ☜; Ⓜ Nanjing Sanmin) One of Taipei's most fun places to dance. Reasonably priced drinks, Latin American and African beats and, of course, fragrant shisha.

 Xinyi

Zhang Men CRAFT BEER
(掌門, Zhǎng Mén; Map p92; www.facebook.com/ZMBTaipei; 4th fl, 16 Songgao Rd, 松高路16號, 4樓; ◉4pm-12am Mon-Fri, 2pm-12am Sat & Sun; ☜; Ⓜ Taipei City Hall) Besides the very tasty and varied craft brews on tap, what makes this place extraspecial is the outdoor rooftop seating with royal views of Taipei 101 and the city skyline. It's a prime location if the weather is good; otherwise the indoor space is cramped, with a weird sports-bar vibe and service below par for Taiwan.

Landmark CRAFT BEER
(啜饮室 Landmark, Chuàiyǐn Shì Landmark; Map p92; www.taihubrewing.com/en-us-taprooms; 68 Zhongxiao E Rd, Sec 5, 忠孝東路五段68號; ◉5-11.30pm Mon-Thur, 3pm-1.30am Fri & Sat, 3-11.30pm Sun; ☜; Ⓜ City Hall) With 13 craft beers on tap, Landmark is great place to sample some tasty brews. Owned by Taihu, a local microbrewery and craft-beer importer, so it's a very slick outfit. All outdoor tables, with no seating. Earlier in the evening, it's popular with suited types just off work – but that's also when happy hour kicks in (second drink half price).

Hanlin Tea House TEAHOUSE
(翰林茶館, Hànlín Cháguǎn; Map p92; www.hanlin-tea.com.tw; 5th fl, ATT4FUN, 12 Songshou Rd, 松壽路12號, ATT4FUN, 5樓; ⊙11am-9pm; 🖘; MTaipei 101) This famous brand from Tainan is one of two big teahouses that claims to have invented the recipe for the sweet tapioca balls-in-tea. Go all out and order the State Banquet Class Bubble Milk Tea! There's no seating but it's fine to walk around the mall and drink.

Yue Yue CAFE
(閱樂書店, Yuèyuè Shūdiàn; Map p92; Songshan Cultural & Creative Park, 133 Guangfu S Rd, 光復南路133號; ⊙10am-8pm; 🖘; MTaipei City Hall) This bookish cafe with a piano, a sofa and green-shaded banker's lamps is open until 2am. The lattice windows, high roof and lazy vibe make it a lovely spot for a coffee and cake. There's also seating facing the lake, but you may want to bring some mosquito repellent.

☆ Entertainment

National Theater & Concert Hall CONCERT VENUE
(國家戲劇院, 國家音樂廳, Guójiā Xìjù Yuàn, Guójiā Yīnyuè Tīng; Map p66; ☎02-3393 9888; http://npac-ntch.org/en; Liberty Sq, 21 Zhongshan S Rd, 中山南路21號, Zhongzhen; 🖘; MChiang Kai-shek Memorial Hall) Located inside Liberty Sq, the National Theater & Concert Hall hosts large-scale concerts and cultural events including dances, musicals, Chinese and western opera, and performances of Chinese and western classical and popular music. The halls, completed in 1987, were among the first major performance venues built in Asia.

Pipe Live Music DANCE
(水管音樂, Shuǐguǎn Yīnyuè; Map p66; www.pipelivemusic.com; Gongguan Waterfront Plaza, Zhongzhen; MGongguan) A grungy industrial-style club next to the river. Hosts an eclectic range of local and international DJs and bands, playing everything from house and techno to indie and hip-hop, and very occasionally holding LGBT+ events. The building was originally a water-pumping station.

Revolver LIVE MUSIC
(Map p66; www.revolver.tw/bar; 1 Roosevelt Rd, Sec 1, 羅斯福路一段, Zhongzhen; live music upstairs NT$300-400; ⊙6.30pm-3am Mon-Sat, to 1am Sun; 🖘; MChiang Kai-shek Memorial Hall) One of Taipei's liveliest spots for drinking and catching live music (usually indie or rock). Very popular with expats, foreign students and backpackers, who start spilling out on

CLAW-CRANE CRAZE

Rivalling convenience stores in their popularity, claw-crane game arcades have taken over Taiwan, and Taipei in particular. You'll find them on high streets, in shopping centres, in night markets, MRT stations, down alleyways, in restaurants and massage parlours. There's even a machine in the swanky five-star W Hotel (p91) lobby.

Where and How to Play

These 24-hour brightly lit, jingle-blaring spaces (some blast upbeat techno) offer customers a cheap attraction. For NT$10 you are given one chance to joystick a metal claw so it snatches one of the prizes inside. Mostly these are soft toys or action figures, but occasionally you'll see fake Ferrero Rocher, underwear, and even sex toys.

Look for a sticker on the side of the machine stating the maximum amount needed before a prize is guaranteed. It's usually in the hundreds or thousands of New Taiwan dollars, but it allows owners to bypass gambling regulations. Even so, judging by how fast the games have proliferated, and watching people spend hours playing for what essentially is cheap (and usually fake) tack, they have become horribly addictive.

The Story of Their Success

With wages mostly depressed, some residents have seen them as opportunities to earn some extra cash. Indeed well-placed machines with attractive prizes can reap the owner or renter of the game several tens of thousands of Taiwanese dollars a month.

Landlords convert their shopfronts to arcades and rent out the individual machines because there is so little outlay. They're popular because of the immediate pleasure of winning something for just NT$10. For many, the prize is not important. Indeed plenty of players just give the toys away – for them it's beating the machine that's important. Plus, there are countless online tutorials teaching you how to win.

to the street by 8pm. They're probably on their way to catch the happy hour that lasts until 9.30pm (mixers and beer NT$80-150).

Wall Music
LIVE MUSIC

(Map p66; www.facebook.com/thewall.tw; basement, 200 Roosevelt Rd, Sec 4, 羅斯福路四段200號B1, Zhongzhen; tickets from NT$500; ⊙Shows 8-11pm; 🚇; ⓂGongguan) The cavernous Wall is Taipei's premier venue for independent music, both local and international. Expect rock, indie, jazz, soul, and pop. Descend the dark stairs and smell the stale beer. There are lockers for your valuables to free you up on the dance floor.

PartyWorld
KARAOKE

(錢櫃, Qiánguì; Map p70; www.cashboxparty.com; 55 Zhonghua Rd, Sec 1, 中華路一段55號, Ximending; ⊙10am-7am next day; 🚇; ⓂXimen) PartyWorld is Taiwan's best-known karaoke chain. They're not the cheapest, but they're the biggest. This branch opposite the Ximending area looks like a hotel from the outside.

Riverside Live House
LIVE MUSIC

(河岸留言, Hé'àn Liúyán; Map p70; ☑02-2370 8805; www.facebook.com/Riverside.Music; 177 Xining S Rd, 西寧南路177號, Ximending; ⓂXimen) One of Taipei's best live-music venues, the 800-seat Riverside sits at the back of the historic Red House (p72) in Ximending. Acts range from local Mandopop (Mandarin pop music) to jazz and straight-up rock 'n' roll.

★ Blue Note
JAZZ

(藍調, Lándiào; Map p66; ☑02-2362 2333; www.facebook.com/bluenote.taipei.1974; 4th fl, 171 Roosevelt Rd, Sec 3, 羅斯福路三段171號4樓, Da'an; from NT$350; ⊙8pm-1am, performances start 9.30pm; ⓂTaipower Building) Taipei's longest-running jazz club, Blue Note has been around since 1974. It's a moody little purple cavern with a fairy-lit ceiling. Very local and friendly atmosphere. Check the Facebook page to see who's playing.

Red Room
LIVE PERFORMANCE

(紅坊, Hóng Fāng; Map p72; www.redroomtaipei.com; Taiwan Contemporary Culture Lab, 177 Jianguo S Rd, Sec 1, 建國南路一段177號, Da'an; 🚇♿; ⓂZhongxiao Xinsheng, ⓂZhongxiao Fuxing) Live music, theatre, poetry readings, dance, lectures, workshops, anything goes in this beautiful space inside Taiwan Contemporary Culture Lab (p73) – first building on left from Jianguo S Rd side gate. Rugs are rolled out on the wooden floor for the audience. It's

run by volunteers who are a mix of expats and locals, and many performances are in English. Check website for schedule.

There are regular drama and arts activities for children.

Sappho Live
JAZZ

(Map p72; ☑02-2700 5411; www.sappholive.com; 1, Lane 102, Anhe Rd, Sec 1, 安和路一段102巷1號, Da'an; shows start 9.30pm, Tue-Sun; 🚇; ⓂXinyi Anhe) This live jazz club is a cosy, purplish underground space with soft lighting. Music extends to blues, reggae and Latin-inspired beats. Their well-organised website has the latest schedule. Cover charge ranges from NT$200-300, with free jam sessions Sundays and Tuesdays.

Bobwundaye
LIVE MUSIC

(無問題, Wú Wèntí; Map p72; ☑02-2377 1772; www.facebook.com/Bobwundaye; 77 Heping E Rd, Sec 3, 和平東路三段77號, Da'an; ⊙6pm-2am Mon-Sat; 🚇; ⓂLiuzhangli) This laid-back neighbourhood bar (the name means 'no problem' in Taiwanese), painted in warm Mediterranean oranges and reds, features regular live music by local and expat bands, and attracts a similarly mixed crowd. See their Facebook page for schedule. Happy hour until 9pm, and with local brew Red Point on tap, you can't go wrong. Also serves hearty fried pub food.

DaDaoCheng Theater
OPERA

(大稻埕戲苑, Dàdàochéng Xìyuàn; Map p80; ☑02-2556 9101; www.facebook.com/dadaochen2011; 8th & 9th fl, 21 Dihua St, Sec 1, 迪化街一段21號8-9樓, Datong; ⓂBeimen) Above Yongle Market (p114), this theatre regularly holds performances of Taiwanese opera. In May and June it hosts free shows in the outside square. On the 8th floor is a small puppet theatre and a pretty good free display with English explanations about the history, drama and practice of puppetry in Taiwan.

Super 346 Livehouse
LIVE MUSIC

(Map p66; www.tw346.com; 85 Bade Rd, Sec 2, 八德路二段85號, Zhongshan; ⊙4-11pm Wed-Sat, to 10pm Tue & Sun; 🚇; ⓂZhongxiao Xinsheng, ⓂNanjing Fuxing) The creepy night-time walk from Bade Rd through the old brewery to get to Super 346 Livehouse is what makes this place worth a trip. Built in 1919 as Taiwan's first brewery, this landmark building has gone through many names, beginning with Takasago. At the back is the large warehouse that serves as a rowdy beer hall with live bands by night.

USEFUL WEBSITES

As well as these sites, the most up-to-date information can be found on venues' own social media or websites, or ask at one of the Visitor Information Centres.

Taipei Travel (www.taipeitravel.net) Lists dates for current and upcoming festivals and other major events.

ArtsTicket (www.artsticket.com.tw) For ticket information and times.

Culture Express (http://cultureexpress.taipei/EN) Also available as a leaflet from Visitor Information Centres; lists venues and some events, mostly art exhibitions.

Ministry of Culture (https://english.moc.gov.tw) Comprehensive news on cultural events, including shows.

Accupass (www.accupass.com) Ticketing site for all kinds of events (in Mandarin only). If you read Mandarin, you can opt to pay via iBon kiosks (payment machines in convenience stores).

SPOT – Taipei Film House
CINEMA

(光點台北, Guāngdiǎn Táiběi; Map p80; ☑02-2511 7786; www.spot.org.tw; 18 Zhongshan N Rd, Sec 2, 中山北路二段18號, Zhongshan; tickets NT$260; ☺11am-10pm, last film 9pm; 🤝; Ⓜ Zhongshan) This excellent art-house cinema is housed in a beautiful white colonial building that was once home to the US ambassador, and which dates back to 1925. The leafy garden has a **cafe** (☺10am-9pm), a perfect place for a prefilm glass of chilled white wine in summer. There is also a branch of SPOT at Huashan 1914 Creative Park (p61).

Taipei Eye
PERFORMING ARTS

(台北戲棚, Táiběi Xìpéng; Map p80; ☑02-2568 2677; www.taipeieye.com; 113 Zhongshan N Rd, Sec 2, 中山北路二段113號, Zhongshan; Mon, Wed & Fri NT$550, Sat NT$880; 🤝; Ⓜ Shuanglian, Ⓜ Minquan W Rd) Taipei Eye showcases Chinese opera together with other rotating performances, including puppet theatre and indigenous dance. This is a tourist show, but it's well regarded and booking can be done online in English. There are three to four shows weekly, usually starting around 8pm.

Taiwan Traditional Theatre Center
THEATRE

(臺灣戲曲中心, Táiwān Xìqǔ Zhōngxīn; Map p84; https://tttc.culture.tw/XiquEn; 751 Wenlin Rd, 文林路751號, Shilin; 🤝; Ⓜ Zhishan) This spanking-new theatre complex plays host to traditional operas and music but looks entirely futuristic – three grey polygonal buildings with coloured stripes like giant barcodes. The main 1036-seater hall is lavishly decorated in gold and chandeliers; next door is the smaller experimental theatre. The Taiwan Music Institute, at the entrance, has a fun free exhibition on Taiwanese folk music.

The exhibition has thousands of CDs you can listen to and a simple mixing system where you can make your own music by combining folk tunes with melodies that can be uploaded to a phone.

The complex is stunning and it's worth checking out performances as they often incorporate modern and avant-garde styles of both music and dance.

Taipei Arena
LIVE PERFORMANCE

(臺北小巨蛋, Táiběi Xiǎo Jùdàn; Map p88; ☑02-2578 3536; https://english.arena.taipei; 2 Nanjing E Rd, Sec 4, 南京東路4短2號, Songshan; 🤝; Ⓜ Taipei Arena) Vast, cavernous and shaped like a flying saucer, the Taipei Arena hosts concerts and sporting events. Some top international names have played here – Madonna performed at the arena in 2016.

i-Ride Taipei
FLYING CINEMA

(Map p92; www.facebook.com/iRideTAIPEI; 6th fl, Breeze Nanshan, 17 Songzhi Rd, 微風南山6樓, 松智路17號, Xinyi; NT$480; ☺11am-10pm, shows hourly on the half-hour; 🤝; Ⓜ Taipei 101) Swoop through the clouds above Taiwan's peaks, float over tea plantations and take a plunge with a turtle: i-Ride Taipei is a 5D cinema where a hemispherical screen and a dipping-and-diving seat give a convincing flying experience. There's no doubt it's a breathtaking way to see Taiwan, but at NT$480, it's a bit steep for a 10-minute show.

 Shopping

🏠 Zhongzheng

Antique Mall
ANTIQUES

(藏舊尋寶屋, Cángjiù Xúnbǎo Wū; Map p66; ☑02-2391 2100; 38 Roosevelt Rd, Sec 2, 羅斯福路二段

LOCAL KNOWLEDGE

SHOPPING TIPS

➡ Bargaining is uncommon except in street markets, and even then discounts of just 10% are possible. If you build a rapport with the shopkeeper and buy extra, then a discount is often offered without asking.

➡ Generally speaking, there is no rip-off culture here. Sellers are usually honest.

➡ Teashops often let you taste the tea before you buy.

➡ Purchase items Made in Taiwan when you can – the country's ambiguous sovereignty status makes it difficult for it to make trade deals.

➡ Take your own bags; say no to plastic!

38號; ⊙11am-9pm; Ⓜ Guting) A rabbit's warren of old gems. You'll find everything here from ornate furniture to kimonos, chinaware, plastic toys, dial-up telephones and rocking horses. There's even a car-sized wooden junk (Chinese boat). Prices seem a bit on the steep side, but rummage through and you might find a bargain.

National Cultural and Creative Gift Center
GIFTS & SOUVENIRS

(國家文創禮品舘; Guójiā Wénchuàng Lǐpǐn Guǎn; Map p66; www.handicraft.org.tw; 1 Xuzhou Rd, 徐州路1號; ⊙9am-6pm; ☏; Ⓜ NTU Hospital) Four floors of jade, ceramics, tea sets, jewellery, scrolls, Kinmen knives, Kavalan whisky and handmade soap are just some of the highlights of the variety on offer here. Colourful Franz porcelain is featured in a special section. There are money-changing facilities and a selection of National Palace Museum Shop (p79) products if you forgot to buy them when you were in Shilin.

Flying Squirrel Culture Studio
ARTS & CRAFTS

(飛鼠文化工作室; Fēishǔ Wénhuà Gōngzuòshì; Map p66; Huashan Market, 108 Zhongxiao E Rd, Sec 1, 華山市場忠孝東路一段108號; ⊙9am-6pm Tue-Sun; Ⓜ Shandao Temple) On the ground floor of compact Huashan Market, this little shop (no English name, look for stall A19) sells some curious indigenous handicrafts, brightly coloured with bold geometric patterns. Many are by prize-winning designer Milay Chou from the Puyuma tribe. High-

lights include bottles of potent sweet rice wine, gorgeous table lamps and men's ties.

VVG Thinking
GIFTS & SOUVENIRS

(好樣思維, Hǎo Yàng Sīwéi; Map p66; ☏02-2322 5573; www.facebook.com/vvgteam; Huashan 1914 Creative Park; ⊙noon-9pm; ☏; Ⓜ Zhongxiao Xinsheng) In the funky loft space above a fusion restaurant in the Huashan 1914 Creative Park (p61), you'll find this quirky, boutique design shop with a rich collection of art books, cookbooks, vintage collectibles and designer products. Don't miss the mechanical tin toys. VVG – which stands for very, very good – is in the last red-brick building to the west of the giant smokestack.

Love Boat
ADULT

(愛之船拉拉時尚概念館, Àizhī Chuán Lālā Shíshàng Gàiniàn Guǎn; Map p66; www.lesloveboat.com; 11 Lane 240, Roosevelt Rd, Sec 3, 羅斯福路三段240巷11號; ⊙2-10pm Tue-Sun; ☒; Ⓜ Taipower Building) A shop for the lesbian community with both in-store and online sales. In recent years it has expanded into a cafe and hosts local events, tarot-card readings and knife massages. There's a good range of merchandise, from sex toys to suits. Love Boat has also opened a store in Ximen.

GinGin Store
ADULT

(晶晶書庫, Jīngjīng Shūkù; Map p66; www.ginginbooks.com; 8 Alley 8, Lane 210, Roosevelt Rd, Sec 3, 羅斯福路三段210巷8弄8號; ⊙1.30-9.30pm Wed-Mon; Ⓜ Taipower Building) GinGin's is a gay-and-lesbian shop offering books and adult magazines (Mandarin only), DVDs, stationery, gifts, posters, sex toys and clothing. See if you can spot the portrait of Sun Yat-sen on a rainbow background! In the summer, small art exhibitions are held in the back room.

🔒 Ximending & Wanhua

Wannian Commercial Building
SHOPPING CENTRE

(萬年商業大樓, Wànnián Shāngyè Dàlóu; Map p70; www.facebook.com/WanNianBuilding; 70 Xining S Rd, 西寧南路70號; ⊙11.30am-10pm; ☏; Ⓜ Ximen) Serving shoppers since 1973, this small mall is old school but aimed squarely at the youth. Four floors of jeans, sneakers, toys, games, bags and shoes, plus Tom's World, an Aladdin's cave of arcade games, shooting, steering, dancing and drumming on the 5th. There's a great basement food court and a late-night cafe up top.

Although the mall opens at 11.30am, some of the shops won't open until the afternoon, especially on a Monday.

Sunmerry
CAKES
(Map p70; 52 Emei St, 峨嵋街52號; ⊙10.30am-11pm; MXimen) The place to get inexpensive boxes of pineapple cakes (NT$180 for 12 cakes), the standard gift to give people when you holiday in Taiwan. This small shop is always packed with tourists from Asia doing just that. Alternatives on sale are nougat-filled cream crackers (another local delicacy), oolong tea cakes and mango treats.

Forbidden
ADULT
(Map p70; 21 Lane 10, Chengdu Rd, 成都路10巷21號; ⊙2pm-midnight; MXimen) One of the best sex shops in the gay bar district, selling underwear, swimwear, T-shirts, lube, condoms, sex toys and one of Taiwan's craziest novelty souvenirs – a giant penis pineapple cake (also comes in others flavours such as blueberry and passion fruit).

Da'an

★Tonghua Night Market
MARKET
(通化夜市, Tōnghuà Yèshì; Map p72; Linjiang St, 臨江街; ⊙6pm-1am; MXinyi Anhe) Taipei's liveliest night market, and all the better for being local and less touristy. Food-wise there are steaks, sushi, animal-shaped biscuits, candyfloss, noodles and the best rice-wine sweet dumplings in the city. There's even a stall pumping out draught beer. Shopping-wise there are lamps, jewellery, underwear, aprons, kitchenware, posters, puzzles and even a hippy shop selling Indian clothing and peace pipes.

Jianguo Weekend Holiday Jade Market
MARKET
(建國假日玉市, Jiànguó Jiàrì Yùshì; Map p72; ⊙9am-6pm Sat & Sun; MDa'an Park) This giant market peddling jade and other semiprecious stones is under Jianguo Overpass. There are also beads, pearls, religious artefacts and copper teapots. Some stalls allow bargaining. Just south is a weekend flower market that smells heavenly and has some fine examples of bonsai bushes and orchids of many colours. To get here, walk in through the flower market where Jianguo Overpass meets Xinyi Rd.

Taiuan-e-tiam
BOOKS
(台灣e店, Táiwān e Diàn; Map p72; www.facebook.com/taiouan.e.tiam; 6 Lane 76, Xinsheng S Rd, Sec 3, 新生南路三段76巷6號; ⊙10.30am-9pm; MGongguan) This lovely independent bookshop, run by Mr Wu, stocks a selection of scholarly history and political books on Taiwan in English, as well as maps, indigenous art and CDs. The store is dedicated to advancing Taiwanese identity.

Deyu Shenyaohang
CHEMIST
(德宇蔘藥行, Déyǔ Shēnyàoháng; Map p66; 32 Yongkang St, 永康街32號; ⊙9am-9pm Mon-Sat; MDongmen) Traditional Chinese medicine store with both dried herbs and prepackaged remedies. There's no English sign. You can spot this place by its old wooden cabinets, rows of porcelain jars and colourful packages.

Eslite
BOOKS
(誠品, Chéngpǐn; Map p72; 245 Dunhua S Rd, 敦化南路245號; ⊙24hr; ☎; MZhongxiao Dunhua) This is Taipei's most renowned bookshop chain, with locations all over town. This branch is the famous 24-hour location. There's a good selection of English books and magazines, and it's worth it just to see all the Taiwanese reading quietly on steps, on the floor, and in all the corners.

TAIPEI SHOPPING

LOCAL KNOWLEDGE

XIMEN SHOPPING

Ximen is often compared to Tokyo's Harajuku district. Neon-spattered buildings, flashing outdoor screens and lanes throbbing with music – all aimed at young people. You'll find dozens of little boutiques, beauticians, hairdressers, tattoo parlours, and shops and shops selling stuffed toys, bags, shoes and bling. You'll also notice the prevalence of claw-crane machines that have become the latest craze to hit the city. Ximen has it bad.

This is tourist town, so you can also find cheap souvenirs and gifts in every street. For more upmarket and imaginative presents, head to the Red House's (p72) design emporium, Creative Boutique.

🏠 Zhongshan & Datong

★ Lao Mian Cheng
Lantern Shop
ARTS & CRAFTS

(老綿成, Lǎomiánchéng; Map p80; 298 Dihua St, Sec 1, 迪化街一段298號; ⊙9am-7.30pm; MDaqiaotou) Handmade lamps with painted dragons, bold flowers, bamboo and calligraphy, are solid red, and as big as a gym ball or small as a fist. There are also concertinaed paper lanterns, purses and cushion covers. This tumbledown marvel of a shop was opened back in 1915 by the current owner's grandfather. It's sometimes closed on Sunday.

★ Lin Hua Tai
Tea Company
TEA

(林華泰茶行, Línhuátài Cháháng; Map p80; ☎02-2557 3506; 193 Chongqing N Rd, Sec 2, 重慶北路二段193號; ⊙7.30am-9pm; MDaqiaotou) The oldest tea-selling shop in Taipei, dating to 1883. The current fourth-generation merchants are more than happy to talk tea and let you sample the wares, which sit in large metal drums about the warehouse. Prices per *jin* (600g measure) are clearly written on the top of each drum. Ask for a tour of the tea factory in the back.

Yongle Market
MARKET

(永樂市場, Yǒnglè Shìchǎng; Map p80; 21 Dihua St, Sec 1, 迪化街一段21號; ⊙10am-6pm Mon-Sat; MBeimen) The rather ugly concrete structure, grafted onto a beautiful colonial-era facade adjacent to DaDaoCheng Theater (p110), houses a huge fabric market on the 2nd and 3rd floors, spruced up in 2019. Cotton, satin, silk, gauze, Japanese prints, bold colours, cat or owl designs, stripes, gingham and feather boas – bolts and bolts of it.

Fabric is sold by the *chi* (尺; about 30cm) or *ma* (碼; 90cm).

inBlooom
ARTS & CRAFTS

(印花楽, Yìnhuālè; Map p80; ☎02-2555 1026; www.inblooom.com; 28 Minle St, 民樂街28號; ⊙9.30am-7pm; MBeimen) This funky fabric shop uses bold and bright designs in cotton canvas to make bags, purses, laptop and book covers, Japanese wall curtains and anything you like. One of their hallmark motifs is repeated mynah birds in silhouette. You can also custom-make any item with their fabric.

Little Garden
SHOES

(小花園, Xiǎohuāyuán; Map p80; ☎02-2555 8468; www.taipei-shoes.com; 2 Lane 32, Dihua St, Sec 1, 迪化街一段32巷2號; ⊙9.30am-7pm; MBeimen) This third-generation shop is the last remaining traditional embroidered shoe outlet in Taipei. Most of the dainty little items (with patterns such as auspicious dragons, peonies and goldfish) are handmade. Tiny, adorable infant slippers start at NT$650.

ArtYard67
CERAMICS

(民藝埕67, Mínyìchéng Liùshíqī; Map p80; ☎02-2552 1367; 67 Dihua St, Sec 1, 迪化街一段67號; ⊙10am-7pm; MBeimen) In a restored long shophouse from 1913, this exceptional ceramic studio carries the Hakka Blue brand, inspired by the indigo colour of Hakka clothing.

Ten Shang's
Tea Company
TEA

(天祥茗茶, Tiānsháng Míngchá; Map p80; ☎02-2542 6542; 156 Jilin Rd, 吉林路156號; ⊙10am-9pm Mon-Sat; MXingtian Temple) 🍃 Hailing from a mountain tea-growing community in central Taiwan's Nantou, Mr and Mrs Chang have been selling organically grown oolong teas from all over Taiwan for a quarter of a century. Visitors are welcome to come in and chat over a pot or two of their exquisite high-mountain tea while shopping for tea and supplies.

🏠 Songshan

SunnyHills
PINEAPPLE CAKES

(微熱山丘, Wéirè Shānqiū; Map p88; ☎02-2760 0508; www.sunnyhills.com.tw/index/en; 1 Alley 4, Lane 36, Minsheng E Rd, Sec 5, 民生東路五段36巷4弄1號; ⊙10am-8pm; MSongshan Airport, MTaipei Arena) Visitors to this famous pineapple-cake maker are seated at a wooden table and given a complimentary tray holding a bowl of black tea and a wrapped cake. If the firm casing and juicy fruit interior is to your liking, there are gift boxes available. The cheapest is a very reasonable NT$420 for 10. There's no pressure to buy.

Chuan-Der
Buddhist Art
BUDDHIST

(全德佛教事業機構, Quándé Fójiào Shìyè Jīgòu; Map p88; www.chuan-der.com.tw; 49 Guangfu S Rd, 光復南路49號; ⊙10am-9pm; MSun Yat-Sen Memorial Hall) This stretch of Guangfu Rd has a gaggle of Buddhist shops, and this is the mother of them all. Three floors of incense, statues, books, scrolls and beads. Most of the stock is Tibetan, but there are Chinese Buddhist artefacts, too. Many of the items also make beautiful gifts. Note: the shop doesn't display its English name.

Wolf Tea
TEA

(Map p88; ☑0970-844 235; www.wolftea.com; 23 Alley 8, Lane 36, Minsheng E Rd, Sec 5, 民生東路五段36巷8弄23號; ⊗1-7pm; M Nanjing Sanmin) A tiny sliver of a shop, easy to overlook – hunt for the wolf-head logo. Gently designed gift boxes and tins in bright colours of Taiwan-grown teas, including black, green and flower infusions. There's a little tatami-mat tasting table upstairs; you'll need to climb cube-like steps to reach it.

Xinyi

Breeze Nanshan
MALL

(微風南山, Wéifēng Nánshān; Map p92; 17 Songzhi Rd, 松智路17號; ⊗11am-10pm; ☎; M Taipei 101) Housed in the new, sleek, sexy black tower in Taipei Nanshan Plaza, the only building (at 272m) to give Taipei 101 a run for its money in the height stakes. This luxury mall is like stepping into the pages of a *Cosmopolitan* magazine. The ground floor boasts top-end brands such as Manolo Blahnik shoe wear and Japanese perfume brands.

Eslite Spectrum
MALL

(誠品生活, Chéngpǐn Shēnghuó; Map p92; Songshan Cultural & Creative Park, 133 Guangfu S Rd, 光復南路133號; cinema tickets NT$290; ⊗11am-10pm; ☎; M Taipei City Hall) Yes, there are lots of Eslite shopping malls around the city, but this one is special because it's set in the gorgeous grounds of Songshan Cultural & Creative Park (p83). It's full of independent brand stores, a glass-blowing studio, a concert hall and a cinema showing arthouse films in the basement.

The shopping mall dominates the park and is easy to spot next to the old factory buildings.

❶ Information

Taiwan Tourism Bureau (www.taiwan.net.tw) has helpful visitor information centres all over the city and run a free 24-hour hotline (☑0800-011 765) with English-speaking staff.

❶ Getting There & Away

As the nation's capital, Taipei is well connected to the rest of the main island by rail, bus and air, and to its outlying islands by air and ferries (weather permitting).

Taipei is also directly connected to most major cities in Asia, and there are daily flights to countries in North America, Europe and Oceania (such as Australia). The number of nonstop flights has been expanding and now includes Amsterdam, London, Paris, Rome, Toronto, New York, Los Angeles, Sydney and Auckland. The most frequent flights are to Japan, South Korea, Hong Kong and China.

Flights, cars and tours can be booked online at lonelyplanet.com/bookings.

AIR

Taiwan Taoyuan International Airport (Map p133; www.taoyuan-airport.com; ☑03-273 3728) is about 40km west of Taipei, in Taoyuan City, and has two terminals. A third is under construction.

The Taoyuan Airport MRT (www.tymetro.com.tw) connects the airport with central Taipei. It's linked by underground walkways to Beimen and Taipei main station MRT stops. Express trains take 40 minutes and cost NT$150. The service runs between 6am until just after 11pm. There's also a commuter service from the same platform that is slower (about 50 minutes) and stops at more stations. Taipei Songshan Airport has its own MRT station on the brown line. This is not near Songshan train station (which is on the green line).

A trip by taxi to Taoyuan Airport from the city centre should cost around NT$1200 and take about 45 minutes depending on traffic. A ride to

TAIPEI BUS SCHEDULES

Buses to all major cities run every 20 to 30 minutes from around 6am to 11pm. Return tickets are usually slightly cheaper than two singles. Services by UBus to Tainan and Kaohsiung are 24 hours. The following are full-fare examples with Kuo-kuang Bus Company from Taipei Main Station.

DESTINATION	FARE (NT$)	DURATION	STATION
Hsinchu	135	1hr 40min	Taipei bus station, City Hall bus station
Kaohsiung	590	5hr	Taipei bus station, City Hall bus station
Keelung	57	50min	Kuo-kuang bus station, City Hall bus station
Sun Moon Lake	470	4hr	Taipei bus station
Taichung	300	2hr 50min	Taipei bus station, City Hall bus station
Tainan	480	4hr 20min	Taipei bus station, City Hall bus station

HIGH-SPEED RAIL (HSR)

High Speed Rail (HSR; www.thsrc.com.tw) trains run from 6.30am to 11pm. Tickets can be purchased at the HSR counter and automated kiosks at basement level 1 of Taipei main station. Bookings can also be made via the HSR website. There are discounts of 10% to 35% for booking eight to 28 days in advance, respectively.

Journey times vary as not all trains stop at all stations.

DESTINATION	STANDARD FARE (NT$)	DURATION
Chiayi	1080	1hr 27min
Hsinchu	290	32min
Kaohsiung (Zuoying)	1490	1hr 34min
Taichung	700	1hr
Tainan	1350	1hr 45min
Taoyuan	160	21min

Songshan Airport will cost around NT$200 and take 20-30 minutes.

Various express bus companies ferry passengers between Taoyuan Airport and stops around the city including Taipei main station (24-hour service, bus 1819), Songshan Airport and City Hall. The trip takes around an hour and costs NT$90-145.

Taipei Songshan Airport (松山機場, Sōngshān Jīchǎng; Map p88; www.tsa.gov.tw/tsa; 340-9 Dunhua N Rd, 敦化北路340-9; Ⓜ Songshan Airport) is just north of the city centre and services direct flights to China, Japan and South Korea, plus domestic routes. The airport has money changers that are open seven days a week and often until late (10.30pm), so it's a useful place to go if you need to change money at awkward times during your stay in Taipei.

BUS

Taipei city is serviced by three major bus stations: Kuo-kuang Bus Taipei Terminal, Taipei bus station, and Taipei City Hall bus station. All are centrally located in the capital, and offer a cheaper but slower option than the trains. They are particularly useful for closer destinations in northern Taiwan and when train tickets are sold out.

Kuo-Kuang Bus Taipei Terminal (Map p66; Ⓜ Taipei Main Station) Just to the east of Taipei main station (Exit M1 and M2) alongside Civic Blvd. This small depot has buses to Taiwan Taoyuan International Airport, Keelung, Jinshan and other destinations in northern Taiwan.

Taipei bus station (台北轉運站, Táiběi Zhuǎnyùn Zhàn; Map p80; Q Square, cnr Chengde Rd & Civic Blvd; Ⓜ Taipei Main Station) Directly to the north of Taipei main station and connected to it by underground walkways through Q Square (a shopping mall). This multi-storey station offers a wide variety of luxury buses to destinations including Yilan, Hsinchu, Sun Moon Lake, Taichung, Chiayi, Tainan and Kaohsiung. The main bus companies servicing

this station are Ubus, Kamalan Bus and King Bus (Kuo-kuang).

Taipei City Hall bus station (市府轉運站, Shìfǔ Zhuǎnyùn Zhàn; Map p92; 6 Zhongxiao E Rd, Sec 5, 忠孝東路五段6號; ⊙ buses 4.30am-1am; Ⓜ Taipei City Hall) Located in the eastern part of the city, and connected to Taipei City Hall MRT station. This station is the fastest way to get to destinations in northeastern Taiwan such as Keelung, Ruifang, Jinshan and Yilan (such as Jiaoxi). There are also services to Taoyuan, Taichung and Tainan.

CAR & MOTORCYCLE

While Taiwan's public transport is so efficient that it seems redundant to hire your own vehicle, it's certainly an option if you want the freedom to tour the island on your own schedule. Roads are of a high standard, but be warned that the route from Taipei to the east of the island (from Su'ao to Hualien) is considered dangerous because it follows some very steep cliffs, so drive with care.

TRAIN

The most convenient way to travel between Taipei and other Taiwanese cities is by High Speed Rail (HSR) or Standard Train (TRA). The HSR can now whizz you from Taipei to the southern city of Kaohsiung, a journey of 345km, in 1 hour and 34 minutes.

Because the road routes connecting Taipei to the east coast are too dangerous for direct buses, most people take the train (sadly, not yet high speed). From Taipei to the furthest stop, Taitung, takes between four and six hours.

ⓘ Getting Around

BICYCLE

Within the city, riding conditions are generally good, as Taipei is mostly flat and many major roads now have wide pavements that can be ridden on (riding with Taipei traffic can be dangerous). There are also hundreds of kilo-metres of riverside paths.

Bicycles are allowed on all MRT lines except the entire brown line (Taipei Zoo to Taipei Nangang Exhibition Centre), and the Taipei Main, Tamsui and Dongmen stations. MRT maps show which stations can be used. There is a NT$80 charge for bike plus passenger to enter the MRT. Folding bicycles are allowed on any train at any time free of charge; they must be fully disassembled and placed in a bag.

Giant is Taiwan's premier bicycle manufacturer (it makes make the YouBikes you see all over the city) and it also has **shops** (捷安特, Jié'āntè; Map p80; ☎02-8771 4045; www.giantcyclingworld. com; 432 Minsheng W Rd, 民生西路432號; ⊙11am-9pm Mon-Thu, from 10am Sat & Sun; ⋗Beimen) that sell, rent and repair machines.

BUS

➡ City buses are generally clean and comfortable and run frequently.

➡ Bus stops always display the schedule (in Mandarin only) and some have LED screens telling you when the next bus will arrive (although they are sometimes mistaken). The most useful app showing bus arrivals for nearby stops and numbered routes is Taiwan Bus (in English).

➡ Most city buses have LED displays at the front in Mandarin and English and also a screen above the driver announcing stops in Mandarin and English.

➡ Fares are NT$15 on most short routes within the city centre. If the sign over the fare box reads 上車 (shàngchē), that means you pay getting on, while 下車 (xiàchē) means you pay getting off. The easiest way is to pay is to swipe your EasyCard, although coins are also accepted (no change is given).

LOCAL KNOWLEDGE

YOUBIKE

The city's excellent shared-bicycle programme, YouBike (https://taipei.youbike.com.tw), offers thousands of bikes at around 400 stations and counting. Bikes can be rented at one location and dropped off at another. Each 30 minutes costs NT$10 (after four hours the price goes up). You will need an EasyCard (register the card on the YouBike website; you'll need access to a phone to accept a code sent by SMS) or a credit card.

Most YouBike stations are outside MRT stations and near major tourist sites. The YouBike app shows the real-time bike situation and location of all stations, as does the YouBike website.

➡ Service times vary according to the route – most run from roughly 5am to around 11pm.

CAR & MOTORCYCLE

An international driving permit is required to rent a car.

GoodCars (www.goodcars.com.tw) One of the cheapest companies, at NT$1380 a day on weekdays. Three locations in Taipei.

CarPlus (www.car-plus.com.tw/en) English-speaking, from NT$2500 a day.

Easy Rent (www.easyrent.com.tw/english) They have a booth in **Taipei main station hall** (台北車站, Táiběi Chēzhàn; Map p66; 49 Zhongxiao

STANDARD TRAINS (TRA)

Taiwan's trains are clean, convenient and mostly on schedule. Unlike the HSR, TRA train stations are almost always in the centre of town (Taitung is an exception). You can find schedules and fares in English at the TRA website (http://twtraffic.tra.gov.tw/twrail).

DESTINATION	FAST/SLOW TRAIN FARE (NT$)	DURATION FAST/SLOW TRAIN
NORTH/EAST LINE		
Hualien	440/340	2/2½hr
Keelung	41	45min
Taitung	783/604	3½/6hr
Yilan	218/140	1½/2½hr
WEST LINE		
Chiayi	598/385	3½/5hr
Hsinchu	177/114	1/2hr
Kaohsiung	843/650	5/7hr
Taichung	375/241	2/3hr
Tainan	738/569	3/5½hr

ℹ️ EASY DOES IT

➡ EasyCard is the stored-value card of the Taipei Rapid Transit Association (TRTA) and can be bought in most MRT stations and convenience stores for NT$100 (nonreturnable).

➡ EasyCards can be used for the MRT, buses, some local trains, nonreserved HSR rides, some taxis, the YouBike programme, and purchases at all convenience stores, Starbucks, and dozens of other shops.

➡ You can add value to the card at any MRT station or convenience store.

W Rd, Sec 1, 忠孝西路一段49號; ☎); from NT$2400 a day.

Bikefarm (www.bikefarm.net) Minimum four days at NT$500 a day for 125cc scooter or motorbike. Book your bike by emailing Jeremy through the website; he speaks English.

MRT

➡ Clean and safe, MRT trains run from 6am until midnight.

➡ Eating, drinking and chewing gum are not allowed in paid areas.

➡ Most places in the city centre are within 1.5km of a station.

➡ Announcements and signs are in Mandarin and English, as are fares and routes at ticket machines.

➡ Coins and bills are accepted and change is provided, though it's more convenient to buy day passes or an EasyCard.

➡ There are five lines: line 1 is brown, line 2 red, line 3 green, line 4 orange, line 5 blue. Both the brown and red lines have stretches that go above ground. The brown line is a driverless train, so head to the front or back carriages for the best view.

➡ Fares depend on length of journey and vary from NT$20 to NT$65.

➡ All stations have clean public toilets, which you can use even if you are not riding the MRT. Most are located outside the turnstiles, and if they're inside just ask the booth attendant to let you in.

TAXI

➡ The flagfall is NT$70 for the first 1.25km plus NT$5 for each 250m thereafter. From 11pm to 6am there is a surcharge of NT$20 on top of the fare.

➡ You can find yellow cabs all over the city and at all hours, but drivers may not be able to speak much English.

➡ Call ☐ 55850 for a taxi (for English service, press 2). There is also a hailing app (search '55850'), but it's only in Mandarin.

➡ Uber has been on-again off-again in Taiwan in a spat over regulations – most recently it has been ordered to register as a taxi company. Check the app to see if the company is currently operating in Taipei. Note that because of restrictions it won't be cheaper than a taxi.

➡ TaxiGo (www.taxigo.com.tw) is a cab-hailing chat bot that uses Facebook messenger.

TAIPEI'S SUBURBS

Tamsui

This historic town at the mouth of the Tamsui River is a popular destination for both tourists and locals due to its seaside atmosphere and fresh air tinged with a salty tang. As you approach on the MRT, the journey runs past mountains and thick mangrove forests, making it feel like a trip well out of town. And when you pop out of the station into the wide riverside park with bike paths, moored boats and views of an emerald volcanic peak (Guanyin Mountain) dominating the skyline it all looks very promising – and it delivers.

◎ Sights

Apart from the riverside views and rowdy seafood-snack stalls, Tamsui's huge selling point is the fantastically restored historic buildings that range from warehouses to forts and churches to missionary schools. Just a walk around these will take the better part of the day. And to top it off there are also three lively temples.

★**Oxford College**   HISTORIC BUILDING

(牛津學堂, Niújīn Xuétáng; Aletheia University; ☉10am-7pm Tue-Sun; Ⓜ Tamsui) **FREE** Oxford College was the first western university in Taiwan and founded by Presbyterian missionary George Leslie Mackay. The original building, built in 1882, fronts a Chinese-style pond and a large, more recent chapel. It forms part of Aletheia University, whose functioning campus is next door.

The row of buildings on the southern side include Mackay's old house and separate residences for male and female missionaries. These have been converted into a lovely cafe (p122), an afternoon teahouse and exhibition spaces with old photos from Mackay's life.

★ Hobe Fort

FORT

(滬尾砲台, Hùwěi Pàotái, Huwei Fort; ☑02-2629 5390; 34-1 Lane 6, Zhongzheng Rd, Sec 1, 中正路一段6巷34-1; NT$80; ⊙9.30am-5pm Mon-Fri, to 6pm Sat & Sun; MTamsui) About 1km beyond Fort San Domingo (p121) on Zhongzheng Rd is the turn-off for Hobe Fort, built in 1886 when then governor Liu Ming-Chuan was attempting to shore up Taiwan's defences to protect it against foreign invaders. If Fort San Domingo was meant to convey authority, Hobe Fort was built for military action.

This prime heritage spot (it has suffered almost no reconstruction) has thick earthen walls, massive gates, four batteries and steep steps to its ramparts to deter intruders. While it was used by the Japanese as a base for artillery firing practice, the fort never saw any military action.

The admission fee includes entry to Fort San Domingo (p121) and the Customs Officer's Residence (p121). The fort is closed on the first Monday of the month.

Tamsui Cultural Park

HISTORIC SITE

(淡水文化園區, Dànshuǐ Wénhuà Yuánqū; ⊙9am-5.30pm Tue-Sun; MTamsui) FREE This handsome and serene collection of old brick warehouses, just behind Tamsui MRT on the riverside, was once the Shell Tamsui Warehouse: as in Royal Dutch Shell. The oil company leased the land in 1897 and held on until the 1990s, when it donated it to the Tamsui Cultural Foundation. Some of the warehouses are used as craft shops and for displaying art. There's a small museum area at the rear showcasing Shell's history in the area.

Longshan Temple

BUDDHIST TEMPLE

(龍山寺, Lóngshān Sì; 22 Lane 95, Zhongshan Rd, 中山路95巷22號; ⊙5.30am-8.30pm; MTamsui) FREE Longshan Temple is one of five Longshans in Taipei, and as such is devoted to the Guanyin Buddha. Built in 1738 and then rebuilt in the 1850s, the temple retains much of its southern architectural roots. The swallowtail roof is particularly elegant. You can find the temple hidden away in the lanes of the traditional market.

Yinshan Temple

BUDDHIST TEMPLE

(鄞山寺, Yínshān Sì; 15 Denggong Rd, 鄧公路15號; ⊙6.30am-5pm May-Sep, 7am-4pm Oct-Apr; MTamsui) FREE This dainty two-hall temple was constructed in 1822 by Hakka immigrants from Guangdong province. The resident deity, the Dingguang Buddha (the guardian of Dingzhou), is only worshipped by the Hakka, and only in this and one other temple in Taiwan.

Yinshan Temple has largely preserved its original appearance. The swallowtail roof epitomises southern elegance, while the *jiǎnniàn* (mosaic-like temple decoration) figures and the interior woodcarvings demonstrate the refined skills of Qing-era craftspeople. On the front wall look for clay sculptures depicting stories of Dingguang quelling the threat of flood dragons and tigers.

The temple only has three front doors (fronted by a traditional wooden picket fence). According to Taiwanese custom, temples that worship emperors, queens and gods are allowed to have five doors; those built to worship generals, ministers and others are allowed only three doors.

Former Residence of Tamsui Township Head Tada Eikichi

HISTORIC BUILDING

(淡水街長多田榮吉故居, Dànshuǐ Jiēzhǎng Duōtián Róngjí Gùjū; ☑02-2620 5092; 19 Mackay St, 馬偕街19號; ⊙9.30am-5pm Mon-Fri, to 6pm Sat & Sun; MTamsui) FREE This attractive 1930s wooden residence was the home of Japanese entrepreneur and public servant,

FOUGHT-OVER FORTS

For centuries, Tamsui (which means 'fresh water') occupied an important trade and defensive post for the various empires that sought to control Taiwan. Its strategic position, at the point where the largest river system in Taiwan's north empties into sea, and its steep terrain made it ideal both as a natural port and a location for forts and cannons. The town's most famous landmark, Fort San Domingo (p121), was established by the Spanish; it was later controlled by the Dutch, Chinese, British and Japanese.

By the 20th century silting had caused Tamsui to lose its importance as a port and the area reverted to a sleepy fishing-and-farming community until the recent boom in tourism. These days, work continues on landscaping and beautifying the riverfront as well as restoring historic sights scattered among the narrow lanes winding up the hillsides.

Tamsui

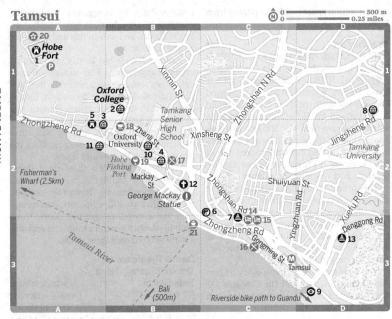

Tamsui

Tada Eikichi. Slip off your shoes and stroll about the tatami mat–covered rooms; you can even rummage about in the cupboards. The porch at the back was built to give its owner enviable views of the river and Guanyin Mountain. Its location is immediately after the pedestrian bridge that crosses Zhongshan Rd, just below the Tamsui Customs Officer's Residence (p121). It's closed on the first Monday of the month.

Tamsui Customs Wharf   HISTORIC BUILDING
(淡水海關碼頭; Dànshuǐ Hǎiguān Mǎtóu; 259 Zhongzheng Rd, 中正路259號; ⊙9.30am-5pm Mon-Fri, to 6pm Sat & Sun, outdoor area 24hr; Ⓜ Tamsui) FREE The buildings here date back to the 1860s and 1870s and include former wharf offices, a warehouse and military barracks. The slabs of the wharf itself were quarried from Guanyin Mountain. The interior is used for art exhibitions and there's a

small shop and tourist information office. The wharf is a lovely place to come and see the sunset. It's just down from Fort San Domingo on the riverside.

The wharf is closed on the first Monday of the month.

Tamsui Customs Officer's Residence HISTORIC BUILDING
(前清淡水關稅務司官邸, Qián Qīng Danshuǐ Guān Shuǐwù Sī Guāndǐ, Little White House; ☑02-2628 2865; 15 Zhenli St, 真理街15號; NT$80; ⊗9.30am-5pm Mon-Fri, to 6pm Sat & Sun; ⓂTamsui) This residence was constructed in 1869 after Taiwan was forced open to foreign trade by China's defeat in the Second Opium War (1856–60). This colonial-style white bungalow, raised to allow humidity to disperse, is framed by a long verandah with arched columns.

The admission fee includes entry to Fort San Domingo and Hobe Fort (p119). The residence is closed on the first Monday of the month.

Former British Consular Residence HISTORIC BUILDING
(英國領事館, Yīngguó Lǐngshìguǎn; 1 Lane 28, Zhongzheng Rd, 中正路28巷1號; included in Fort San Domingo ticket; ⊗9.30am-5pm Mon-Fri, to 6pm Sat & Sun; ⓂTamsui) Inside the Fort San Domingo site is the 1891 Former British Consular Residence, an elegant red-brick Victorian-style house, complete with furnishings re-created from photographic records. The consulate was closed in Japanese times, then reopened after WWII until 1972 when Britain shuttered it. London has recognised the PRC since 1950, and all relations with Taiwan now take place on an unofficial basis. The residence is closed on the first Monday of the month.

Fuyou Temple TAOIST TEMPLE
(福祐宮, Fúyòu Gōng; 200 Zhongzheng Rd, 中正路200號; ⊗6am-8.30pm; ⓂTamsui) FREE Halfway along Zhongzheng Rd is smoky Fuyou Temple. Built in 1782, this beautiful low-lying structure is the oldest temple in Tamsui, and is dedicated to Matsu, Goddess of the Sea. Check out the roof truss over the altar; the topmost posts are carved in the motif 'the fool holding up the sky'.

Tamsui Presbyterian Church CHURCH
(淡水禮拜堂, Dànshuǐ Lǐbàitáng; 8 Mackay St, 馬偕街8號; ⓂTamsui) The Gothic-style Tamsui

Presbyterian Church was reconstructed in 1933. It's a popular backdrop for wedding photos. Open only during services.

Fort San Domingo FORT
(紅毛城, Hóngmáo Chéng; ☑02-2623 1001; 1 Lane 28, Zhongzheng Rd, 中正路28巷1號; NT$80; ⊗9.30am-5pm Mon-Fri, to 6pm Sat & Sun; ⓂTamsui) Fort San Domingo is Tamsui's most famous sight. The original fort, built in 1628 during the Spanish occupation of Taiwan (1626–41), was dismantled by the Spanish before they left. The 13m-high structure seen today is the Fort Anthonio built by the Dutch in 1644. These days the original Spanish name is used, though to locals it's still the Red Haired Fortress (a reference to the colour of Dutch hair).

Maritime Museum MUSEUM
(海事博物館, Hǎishì Bówùguǎn; ☑02-2623 8343; Tamkang University; ⊗9am-5pm Mon-Sat; ☐R27, R28) FREE This four-storey museum (shaped like an ocean liner) is anchored by dozens of large model ships from around the world. Every seaworthy vessel imaginable is here, set in blue velvet-lined display cabinets There are steamers, frigates, aircraft carriers, container ships, wooden junks as well as a collection of nautical equipment, from sextants to steering gear. If you're into ships, you shouldn't miss it.

The museum is on the Tamkang University campus, in the hills above town. Either walk up (it takes about 25 minutes) or catch the R27 or R28 bus from the station outside Exit 2 of Tamsui MRT.

🛏 Sleeping & Eating

Tourist Bunny HOSTEL $
(旅行邦尼, Lǚxíng Bāngní; ☑02-2621 8707; www.facebook.com/TouristBunny; 7 Lane 87, Zhongshan Rd, 中山路87巷7號; dm NT$599/660 weekdays/weekends; ❀❄🤏; ⓂTamsui) A friendly and helpful hostel option. Kevin and Jenny speak good English and run a tight ship. Dorms are six-people rooms: all come with their own separate shower and toilet inside. Simply decorated and freshly painted. You'll spot this place by its bright-blue front door.

Open Room HOTEL $$
(歐朋侖旅店, Ōupénglún Lǚdiàn; ☑02-2621 8333; www.facebook.com/OpenroomTamsui; 9 fl, 93 Zhongshan Rd, 中山路93號9樓; d from NT$2280; ❀❄🤏; ⓂTamsui) One of the best-value places to stay in Tamsui, just up from the MRT

TAIPEI TAMSUI

on a small hill and next to the morning market. All rooms have big picture windows, are well-sized, clean, modern and nicely furnished. When booking ask for room 1 or 2, as these have sweeping river views and padded window seats. No breakfast.

Gongming Street STREET FOOD $
(⊘9am-9pm; MTamsui) This popular market street by the MRT has stacks of stalls and shops selling local snacks such as *a-gei* (fried tofu stuffed with noodles), grilled squid, chicken and corn, sugarcane juice, powdered almond and shelves of cheap toys and souvenirs.

Laopai Wenhua A-gei TAIWANESE $
(老牌文化阿給, Lǎopái Wénhuà Āgěi; 6-4 Zhenli St, 真理街6-4號; a-gei bowls NT$40; ⊘5am-2.30pm; MTamsui) Tamsui's best *a-gei* (阿給, *ā gěi*) is in this old shop just before the beginning of Zhenli St.

🍷 Drinking & Nightlife

★ Bok Su Lao CAFE
(牧師樓, Mùshī lóu; ☑02-2628 1212; www.face book.com/boksulao; 32 Zhenli St, 真理街32號; ⊘10am-7pm; 🛜; MTamsui) One of the most beautifully located cafes in northern Taiwan, Bok Su Lao is set in the grounds of Oxford College (p118) and housed in a former residence for male missionaries. Grab a table under the red-brick arches facing the lawn. A bit on the pricey side, but worth it for the unique atmosphere.

Prost Bar BAR
(233 Zhongzheng Rd, 中正路233號; ⊘5.30pm-late; MTamsui) This simple hole-in-the-wall watering hole is right up against the riverside, perfect for a sunset-bathed drink. There are 42 bottled beers, mostly European but a handful of local craft offerings, too.

☆ Entertainment

Cloud Gate Theater DANCE
(雲門舞集, Yúnmén Wǔjí; www.cloudgate.org.tw; 36 Lane 6, Zhongzheng Rd, Sec 1, 中正路一段6巷36號; 🛜; MTamsui) An experimental contemporary dance group; the theatre also hosts international acts. To get here just walk past Hobe Fort (p119) and follow the signs. This swanky, new building houses a 450-seat theatre, and a 1500-seat outdoor theatre, as well as two studios. There are lovely views from the large wooden deck.

It's worthwhile checking its website:, it often hosts free exhibitions and occasional outdoor music and dance performances by visiting artists.

ℹ Getting There & Away

Ferry The ferry (p123) from Bali takes just five minutes. There's also the weekend Blue Highway (p85) boat trip from Dadaocheng in Datong District.

Light Rail The Danhai LRT line or Green Mountain Line leaves from next to Hongshulin MRT station and loops around Tamsui's suburbs, As a commuter service, this is not of particular interest to overseas tourists.

MRT Tamsui MRT station is the last stop on the red line north, about 45 minutes from Taipei main station.

YouBike The riverside bike route from Guandu Temple (p124) is a pleasant half-hour spin.

Bali

Just at the wide mouth of the Tamsui River, where it pours into the sea, is this little waterfront village (八里; Bālǐ) with landscaped parks, boardwalks and bike paths running north and south.

A fun five-minute ferry ride connects Tamsui with Bali, making it possible to visit both in one day. On weekends and holidays Bali is packed; try to come on a weekday.

The most popular activity is cycling, and there are many bike-hire shops right off the boat dock. Heading south towards Guandu offers open views of Tamsui framed by the Yangmingshan mountains, as well as Bali's own emerald volcanic Guanyin Mountain (which has its own hiking trails).

North, the paths run past a row of food stalls and a scrap of dark-sand beach, then through more landscaped parks and the 60-hectare Wazihwei Nature Reserve. Further along (3.5km from the pier) you will find the Shihsanhang Museum of Archaeology.

◉ Sights

Wazihwei Nature Reserve BIRD SANCTUARY
(挖子尾自然保留區, Wāzǐwěi Zìrán Bǎoliúqū; Map p62; 🚌R13) A mixture of mudflats and mangroves, this quiet section along the Tamsui River is home to migratory birds, abandoned fishing boats, and, at low tide, a carpet of crabs. The easiest way to get here is to cycle from **Bali Ferry Pier** (Map p62;

off Longmi Rd, Sec 2; to Tamsui one-way/return NT$23/45; ☺7am-7pm).

Shihsanhang Museum of Archaeology MUSEUM
(十三行博物館, Shísānxíng Bówùguǎn; Map p62; ☎02-2619 1313; www.sshm.ntpc.gov.tw; 200 Museum Rd, 博物館路200號; NT$80; ☺9.30am-5pm Nov-Mar, to 6pm Mon-Fri, to 7pm Sat & Sun Apr-Oct; 🅿️♿; ⛴R13) This vaguely boat-shaped edifice made from concrete, sandstone and titanium alloy showcases the prehistory of the Shihsanhang culture, which thrived some 500 to 1800 years ago. There are plenty of interactive games for children, and a particular highlight is the examples of Austronesian *tapa* (barkcloth) patterned with beautiful geometric designs.

The museum is a 20-minute cycle from the ferry pier, or catch the R13 from Guandu MRT station.

🍴 Eating & Drinking

Twin Sisters BAKERY $
(姊妹雙胞胎, Zǐmèi Shuāngbāotāi; Map p62; 25 Duchuantou St, 渡船頭街25號; doughnuts NT$20; ☺10am-8pm; ⛴; ⛴Bali Ferry Pier) Join the locals – you can spot this place as it's the only one with a long line – for bags of sugary doughnuts twisted into sticks, puffed into balls or just shaped like a regular ring with a hole. Once the buns are all sold this place shuts up for the day.

Mommouth Coffee CAFE
(媽媽嘴咖啡, Māmāzuǐ Kāfēi; Map p62; ☎02-2618 3205; www.mommouth.com.tw; 9 Longmi Rd, Sec 2, 龍米路二段869號; ☺11am-6pm; 🚻🚲; bicycle from Bali or Guandu) Don't let the name put you off – it literally means Mother's Mouth Coffee – this little cafe is always heaving with locals. It's halfway along the bike path between the ferry pier and Guandu Bridge. With benches on the bank and moist brownie slices, it's a justifiably popular spot to take a break, especially now they have a coffee-infused ale.

ℹ️ Getting There & Away

Bicycle When the weather is pleasant, cycling from Guandu is a popular option. The ride crosses the impressive red-painted Guandu Bridge and then follows the river north.

Bus The R13 bus from Guandu MRT station will drop you off near all the main tourist sites in Bali.

Ferry The easiest way to get to Bali is by **ferry** (tickets to Bali one-way/return NT$23/45, to Fisherman's Wharf NT$60; ☺7am-7pm Mon-Fri,

A DAY OF HIKING & HOT SPRINGS

Both Beitou and Yangmingshan National Park (p127) can be visited together in one superb day trip. Frequent buses connect the two via scenic mountain roads less than an hour away. Visit YMS first for a morning hike, lunch at Grass Mountain Chateau (p127), then bus down to Beitou. From the Chateau, the minibus9 小 (Taiwan Tourism Shuttle Bus Beitou-Zhuzihu route; www.taiwantrip.com.tw) takes you to Beitou Park. Or from opposite the 7-Eleven near the main bus station at YMS, catch minibus 230 down to the Beitou Museum (p125). After exploring this, and having tea in its Japanese-era teahouse, walk down the hill via Youya and Wenquan Rds back to Xinbeitou.

to 8pm Sat & Sun) from Tamsui (which has its own MRT station).

Beitou

Hot springs and history form the major attractions in this mountainous suburb, a 35-minute MRT ride north of central Taipei. Beitou Park is the main strip of green leading uphill towards Yangmingshan National Park from Xinbeitou MRT station. It was formerly one of the largest hot-spring spas under Japanese rule, attracting visitors from around the world (including Sun Yat-sen).

The first hot-spring business was started by a German in the late 1800s, but it was the Japanese who really developed the area, opening Beitou Park in 1911. Today Japanese-built bathhouses and villas, some restored and reworked as museums, are dotted around Beitou Park.

⭕ Sights

⭐Guandu Temple TAOIST TEMPLE
(關渡宮, Guāndù Gōng; Map p62; www.kuantu.org.tw; 360 Zhixing Rd, 知行路360號; ☺6am-9pm; 🅿️; ⛴R35, MGuandu) FREE Dating back to 1661, this gawdy, grand, massive multistorey temple (one of Taipei's oldest) is built right into the side of a mountain. In fact, a 100m-plus tunnel runs through the mountain itself. Take either flight of steps at the rear of the temple and climb as far as you

Beitou

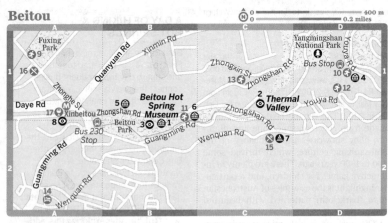

Beitou

can for a panoramic view of the Tamsui riverscape. The temple makes a great stop if you're planning to do a bike trip along the river to Tamsui or Bali.

Guandu Temple is a riot of decorative arts, especially rooftop *jiǎnniàn* (mosaiclike temple decoration), and there are Qing-era stone columns in the worship hall.

★ **Beitou Hot Spring Museum** MUSEUM
(北投溫泉博物館, Běitóu Wēnquán Bówùguǎn; ☑02-2893 9981; www.facebook.com/Beitou Museum1913; 2 Zhongshan Rd, 中山路2號; ⊗9am-5pm Tue-Sun; Ⓜ Xinbeitou) **FREE** Built in 1913 as the Beitou Public Baths, this handsome building is a copy of the bathhouses in Shizuokaken Idouyama in Japan.

It is also a good example of the turn-of-the century fascination among Japanese architects for blending eastern and western architecture and aesthetics.

★ **Thermal Valley** AREA
(地熱谷, Dìrè Gǔ; Hell Valley; ⊗9am-5pm Tue-Sun; Ⓜ Xinbeitou) **FREE** Throughout the Japanese era this geothermal valley was considered one of Taiwan's great scenic wonders. The area has been much altered since, but the stone-lined basin filled with near-100°C green sulphur water is still a fascinating sight, especially on cool winter days when a thick, sulphury-smelling mist can be seen lifting off the waters.

Puji Temple BUDDHIST TEMPLE
(普濟寺, Pǔjì Sì; 112 Wenquan Rd, 溫泉路112號; ⊗8am-5pm; Ⓜ Xinbeitou) **FREE** This Japanese-style wooden temple was built in 1905 and is dedicated to Guanyin. It's home to a couple of nuns and is beautifully preserved. Check out the bell-shaped windows and the intricately carved beams, and if you're lucky, wild pink orchids will be in bloom in the pine-tree garden out front.

Xinbeitou Historic Station TRAIN STATION

(新北投車站, Xīnběitóu Chēzhàn; www.xbths.
taipei; 1 Qixing St, 七星街1號; ◎10am-6pm Tue-
Thu, to 8.30pm Fri-Sun; MXinbeitou) FREE This
light and airy wooden station building dates
back to 1916 and was in service until 1988,
when it was disassembled and packed off
to Changhua to go on display. After locals
campaigned for its return, It was shipped
back and reconstructed close to its original
location using blueprints from its 1930s in-
carnation. Exhibits recounting the station's
story don't have much English but there are
lots of good photos.

Don't miss the hot hand-soaking pool just
before the station.

Plum Garden HISTORIC BUILDING

(梅庭, Méi Tíng; ◉02-2897 2647; 6 Zhongshan
Rd, 中山路6號; ◎9am-5pm Tue-Sun; MXinbeitou) FREE This fairly modest two-storey
residence combines Japanese and western
architectural styles and dates back to the
late 1930s. In the 1950s it was the home of
Chinese master calligrapher Youren Yu. It's
been richly renovated – the original tatami floors have been replaced with deep
polished wooden boards, though the doors
and huge windows are the originals – and
there's not much else to see here. Even so,
it deserves a quick stop to appreciate its elegance. Remember to remove your shoes.

Guandu Nature Park PARK

(關渡自然公園, Guāndù Zìrán Gōngyuán; Map
p62; ◉02-2858 7417; www.gd-park.org.tw; 55
Guandu Rd, 關渡路55號; NT$60; ◎9am-5pm
Tue-Fri, to 6pm Sat & Sun Apr-Sep, to 5.30pm Sat
& Sun Oct-Mar; P; RR35, MGuandu) Ten years
in the planning, this 57-hectare nature reserve opened in 2001 under the control of
the Wild Bird Society of Taipei. There's a visitor centre and good trails and hides, as well
as over 100 species of birds, 150 species of
plants and 800 species of animals.

It's a 1.2km walk from Guandu MRT, or
take the R35 bus from outside the station.

Beitou Museum MUSEUM

(北投文物館, Běitóu Wénwùguǎn; ◉ext 9 02-2891
2318; www.beitoumuseum.org.tw; 32 Youya Rd, 幽
雅路32號; NT$120; ◎10am-6pm Tue-Sun; □230,
MXinbeitou) This museum opened in 2008
in a Japanese-style building constructed in
1921 as a high-class hotel. The 1st floor has
a teahouse serving afternoon tea, displays
on a traditional Japanese home and temporary exhibitions focused on culture. The
2nd floor preserves the look of the original

tatami-floored banquet and performance
hall. Outside are traditional gardens and
decks overlooking the town and mountains.
Ask for the free English audio guide.

Ketagalan Culture Center MUSEUM

(凱達格蘭文化館, Kǎidágélán Wénhuàguǎn;
◉02-2898 6500; www.english.katagalan.gov.taipei;
3-1 Zhongshan Rd, 中山路3-1號; ◎9am-5pm
Tue-Sun; MXinbeitou) FREE This multistorey
centre explores Taiwan's indigenous people's
culture with exhibits, performances, pictures and artefacts. There are crafted pieces
– baskets, ladles and traditional costumes –
and there are also some more curious items,
such as carved wooden cups made for two
people to drink wine at the same time.

The centre underwent extensive renovation in 2019. There's a nice gift shop on the
left as you walk in.

Beitou Library LIBRARY

(圖書館北投, Túshūguǎn Běitóu; ◉02-2897 7682;
251 Guangming Rd, 光明路251號; ◎8.30am-
9pm Tue-Sat, 9am-5pm Sun & Mon; MXinbeitou)
⚑ FREE Opened in 2006, this beautiful
wooden building was Taiwan's first green
construction project. You can go inside and
wander about or just hang out on the decks.
Its ecological credentials in part come from
solar panels on the roof and the use of rain-
water in flushing toilets and watering the
library's pot plants.

🏃 Activities

★ Marshal Zen Garden HOT SPRINGS

(少帥禪園, Shǎo Shuài Chán Yuán; Shann Garden; ◉02-2893 5336; www.sgarden.com.tw; 34
Youya Rd, 幽雅路34號; NT$1200-1500 per hour;
◎11am-8.30pm; □230, MXinbeitou) This gorgeous collection of old Japanese buildings
was once the Xin Gao Hotel, used to wine
and dine kamikaze pilots before their last
flight. It's now a high-end restaurant (set
meals from NT$1800), plus a hot-spring spa
with private rooms sporting black-slate tubs,
tatami floors and dreamy views over Beitou,
all the way to volcanic Guanyinshan.

Marshal Zhang was a famous 20th-
century Chinese commander who kidnapped
Chiang Kai-shek in 1936 to force him into a
united front with the communists against
the Japanese. Never one to hold a grudge (!),
afterwards Chiang held Zhang under house
arrest for the next 40 years.

There is a NT$200 admission fee if you
just want to go in and see the buildings and

TAIPEI BEITOU

grounds. The ticket also allows you to take a hot-spring foot bath. Minibus 230 drops you off right outside the residence, or, if you book a meal or hot-spring soak, you can call for a free pickup from Beitou MRT station.

Fuxing Park Foot-Soaking Pool
HOT SPRINGS

(Zhonghe St, 中和街; ⊙8am-6pm Tue-Sun; MXinbeitou) FREE These three wooden-seat-lined tubs are very popular with middle-aged and elderly locals for soaking their toes. The greenish water is about knee-deep. It's open to the public, including tourists, but it's very much a place for locals.

In the eastern corner of Fuxing Park, diagonally opposite North Pole Soft Ice.

Spring City Resort
HOT SPRINGS

(春天酒店, Chūntiān Jiǔdiàn; ☑02-2897 5555; www.springresort.com.tw; 18 Youya Rd, 幽雅路18號; indoor per hour NT$600, outdoor unlimited time NT$800; ⊙indoor 24hr, outdoor 9am-10pm; MXinbeitou) On the road down from Beitou Museum (p125) is this stylish hotel with a mixed-gender (swimsuit and swimming cap required), outdoor hot-spring garden complexes. There are beautiful views over the town and mountains from the pools – that's volcanic Guanyinshan in the distance. As well as rooms, the hotel offers meal-and-hot-spring packages for NT$1680. There are two restaurants, Taiwanese and Japanese.

Villa 32
HOT SPRINGS

(☑02-6611 8888; www.villa32.com; 32 Zhongshan Rd, 中山路32號; weekday/weekend NT$1980/2580; ⊙10am-11pm; MXinbeitou) One of Beitou's most expensive hot-spring options, Villa 31 offers a very elegant and high-end experience. There are segregated nude pools (swimming cap provided) as well as private pools (weekday/weekend NT$2800/3600 for two people, 90 minutes). Villa 32 is a 700m walk from the MRT up Zhongshan Rd. Reservation is recommended.

Millennium Hot Springs
HOT SPRINGS

(公共露天溫泉, Gōnggòng Lùtiān Wēnquán; 6 Zhongshan Rd, 中山路6號; NT$40; ⊙5.30-10pm; MXinbeitou) This mixed-gender (swimsuit required) public hot spring boasts a number of pools, ranging in temperature from comfortably warm to near-scalding. It can get unpleasantly crowded. The pools are closed for 30 minutes every 1½ hours or so for cleaning. Shorts are not allowed. They sell bathing suits for both men and women at the entrance if your own doesn't make the cut.

🛏 Sleeping & Eating

Solo Singer
BOUTIQUE HOTEL $$

(☑02-2891 8312; www.thesolosinger.com; 7 Lane 21, Wenquan Rd, 溫泉路21巷7號; r from NT$2500; ⊜❋❂; MXinbeitou) 🌿 During the early decades of the post-WWII boom, dozens of small family-run inns dotted Beitou's winding alleys. Solo Singer, the love project of a group of young Taiwanese artists, historians and hotel professionals, is a charming restoration (the owners would say rebirth) of one of these. There are just 10 rooms so book ahead; discounts are common. Triples and four-bed spaces are available.

★ North Pole Soft Ice Special Shop
DESSERTS $

(綿綿冰專賣店, Miánmián Bīng Zhuānmài Diàn; 47 Zhonghe St, 中和街47號; desserts NT$40-55; ⊙noon-9pm Wed-Mon; ☏; MXinbeitou) Open since 1961, and pretty much unchanged since then, this shaved-ice place is no-frills deliciousness. Get a cup of peanut, pearl and red bean shaved-ice delight – their bestseller at NT$50 – and watch the world go by from one of their street-facing tables.

To get here, turn left when you exit the MRT station, cross the road and walk 300m up Zhonghe St. They have an English sign.

Man Ke Wu Hot Spring Noodles
RAMEN $

(滿客屋溫泉拉麵, Mǎn Kè Wū Wēnquán Lāmiàn; ☑02-2894 8348; 110 Wenquan Rd, 溫泉路110號; noodles NT$110-190; ⊙11am-2pm & 5-9pm Tue-Sun; MXinbeitou) This popular restaurant serves fantastic ramen noodles (拉麵, lāmiàn) in a miso base prepared with hot-spring water. Try the standard ramen with pork (正油叉燒, zhèngyóu chāshāo), with kimchi (泡菜叉燒, pàocài chāshāo) or with a side of fried pork ribs (排骨, páigǔ). The soft-boiled hot-spring egg with dried seaweed (溫泉蛋, wēnquán dàn; NT$30) is the simplest of dishes but so tasty.

🍷 Drinking & Nightlife

23 Public Beitou
CRAFT BEER

(☑02-2891 6374; www.facebook.com/23Public.Beitou; 2 Qixing St, 七星街2號; ⊙5.30pm-late; ☏; MXinbeitou) This cosy nook tucked into the side of the MRT (come out and immediately turn right) is a branch of the popular local craft-beer brewery, 23 Public (p105), back in the city.

ⓘ Getting There & Away

Taipei Beitou is easily reached by MRT in 30 minutes from Taipei main station. Take the Tamsui (red) line to Beitou station and transfer to the spur line (deliriously slow!) to Xinbeitou station.

Yangmingshan From the stop just outside Yangmingshan bus station (p128), minibus 230 leaves every 30 minutes or so for Xinbeitou MRT, passing by Beitou Museum on its way (Quanyuan Rd, 泉源路). If leaving from Beitou, catch the bus from the Bus 230 Stop (Guangming Rd, 光明路) opposite Xinbeitou MRT station.

Yangmingshan National Park

Taipei is truly lucky to have this diverse park at its doorstep, complete with forested mountains, hot springs, rolling grass hills, and some spectacular butterfly and bird species. The park covers 11,338 sq km, with a top elevation of 1120m, and is easily accessible from the downtown area by frequent buses.

⊙ Sights

Grass Mountain Chateau　　　　MUSEUM
(草山行館, Cǎoshān Xíngguǎn; Map p62; ☑02-2862 2404; www.grassmountainchateau.com.tw; 89 Hudi Rd, 湖底路89號; NT$30; ☺10am-6pm Tue-Sun, last entry 5pm; [P]; ⊟minibus []9) Built in 1920 and visited by Japanese Crown Prince Hirohito, this handsome building became Chiang Kai-shek's first residence in 1949. The chateau is now a museum, exhibition centre and well-regarded **restaurant** (mains NT$488) serving dishes favoured by the Generalissimo, such as meatballs, braised spare ribs and lamb. There are lovely views of the city from the verandah.

The easiest way to get here is to take the path directly behind Yangmingshan bus station and walk 15 minutes up Hushan Rd (湖山路) towards the flower clock. Look for the sign pointing the way down to the chateau directly before the car park.

⚐ Activities

There's top-class hiking, both gentle and arduous, and some challenging cycling. The higher you go, the more likely you will be surrounded by mountain mists. And when you've finished, you can wallow in the hot springs.

> ⓘ **YANGMINGSHAN TRAILS**
>
> The park has a wide network of trails, most stepped and marked with English signage. The park website (www.ymsnp. gov.tw) lists them all and includes times, distances and maps.

The park is closed on the last Monday of every month.

Tienlai Resort & Spa　　　　HOT SPRINGS
(天籟度假酒店, Tiānlài Dùjià Jiǔdiàn; ☑02-2408 0000; www.tienlai.com.tw; 1-7 Mingliu Rd, 名流路 1-7號; hot springs unlimited time weekdays/weekends NT$600/900; ☺7am-midnight; [🚌1717]) Taiwan's largest outdoor hot-spring resort has more than 20 pools of all shapes and sizes (many scented with essential oils), as well as waterfalls, jet showers, a bubbling spring (that massages you from below), saunas, steam rooms and swimming pools. Women must wear a swimming cap. The sweeping views of green mountains are just icing on the cake.

Jinbaoli Trail　　　　HIKING
(魚路古道, Yú Lù Gǔdào, Fisherman's Trail; Map p62; 🚌S15, []15) This historic trail follows a former fish trade route from Shilin to Jinshan. It begins along one of the most enchanting parts of Yangmingshan: the rolling grass hills of Qingtiangang, a lava plateau and former cattle-grazing area that still has a population of wild water buffalo. The trail is 6.6km and takes about four to five hours.

The trail starts at the Qingtiangang bus stop, reached by shuttle bus 108 from the park headquarters or directly from Jiantan MRT on minibus 15 (小15), and finishes at the Tienlai Hot Springs area. From here you can catch an hourly Royal Bus back to the park headquarters (30 minutes) or on to Jinshan at the coast.

Lengshuikeng　　　　HOT SPRINGS
(冷水坑, Lěngshuǐkēng; Map p62; ☺6am-9pm; 🚌108, S15, []15) **FREE** The public bath on the park's eastern side has naked men's and women's indoor baths (women must wear a hat or secure their hair). Lengshuikeng means 'cold water valley', and it's comparatively chilly at 40°C. High iron content makes the waters reddish brown. The baths close for cleaning every two to three hours for between 30 and 90 minutes.

Shuttle bus 108 drops you off at the springs on its clockwise route around the park. You can also get here directly from Jiantan MRT on minibus 15 (小15). Note there's a helpful visitor centre (9am to 4.30pm) on the opposite side of the road to the baths (this is where the buses stop) with a nice cafe and gift shop. It's closed on the last Monday of the month.

🛏 Sleeping

International Hotel
HOTEL **$$**

(國際大旅館, Guójì Dàlǚguǎn; Map p62; ☑02-2861 7100; http://0228617100.ok99.tw; 7 Hushan Rd, Sec 1, 華山路一段7號; d/tw NT$2310/3190; P❄✳🐾; 🚍R5, 260、230) Built in 1952, the International has maintained its original character with a rustic stone facade and basic rooms. The hotel is close to a hot-spring source and offers both public and in-room hot-spring baths. Three-hour use of rooms (including hot springs) is NT$990. It's just NT$120 for use of the segregated nude public pool (7am to 9pm). Women must tie their hair back.

Tienlai Resort & Spa
RESORT **$$$**

(天籟度假酒店, Tiānlài Dùjià Jiǔdiàn; ☑02-2408 0000; www.tienlai.com.tw; 1-7 Mingliu Rd, 名流路1-7號; r from NT$7800; P❄✳@🐾; 🚍1717) Most guests come here for the hot springs, outdoor pools and the sweeping views of green mountains.

❶ Getting There & Away

R5 (NT$30, 35 minutes, every five to 15 minutes). Starts at Jiantan MRT station and terminates at **Yangmingshan bus station** (Map p62; Shengli St, 勝利街) from 5.30am to 12.40am.

Minibus 15 (小15; NT$30, 45 minutes, every 20 to 60 minutes) This bus goes directly from Jiantan MRT station to Lengshuikeng and Qingtiangang, from 5.40am to 10.30pm.

260 (NT$30, 1 hour, every seven to 15 minutes). This route begins at Taipei train station and ends at Yangmingshan Bus Station, from 6am to 10.30pm.

❶ TIME FOR TEA

Teahouses generally offer a discount if you purchase both tea and a meal. Tea is usually sold in 50-75g packets or tins for around NT$300-400. You then pay a water charge per person (around NT$100, depending on teahouse and time of day) to drink it at their premises. You can bring your own tea for around double the charge per person for hot water.

Minibus 230 (NT$30, 35 minutes, every 15 to 45 minutes) Runs between the Yangmingshan bus station and Beitou MRT, via Beitou Museum (p125), from 5.30am to 10.45pm.

❶ Getting Around

Park Shuttle Bus 108 Does a loop around the park every 20 to 40 minutes starting at Yangmingshan bus station from 7am to 5.30pm. Fares are NT$15 for each ride or NT$60 for a day pass.

Maokong

The lush hilly region of southern Taipei, known as Maokong (貓空; Māokōng), has a long association with tea cultivation. In fact, for a time it was Taiwan's largest tea-growing area. These days the verdant landscape is not just a place to grow tea; it's also somewhere to enjoy drinking it. There are few activities so quintessentially Taiwanese, and the city has made an extra effort to attract visitors to the region. This includes restoring old trails, landscaping roads, building lookouts and adding public transport options such as a scenic gondola ride starting from near the MRT Taipei Zoo station. Cyclists in particular appreciate the low traffic conditions in the hills, and Maokong has emerged as one of the most popular of the many scenic day trips around Taipei.

⊙ Sights

Maokong Gondola
CABLE CAR

(貓空纜車, Māokōng Lǎnchē; ☑02-2181 2345; https://english.gondola.taipei; one-way adult/child NT$120/50; ⊙9am-9pm Tue-Thu (plus 1st Mon of month), to 10pm Fri, 8.30am-10pm Sat, 8.30am-9pm Sun; Ⓜ Zoo) This 4km-long, 30-minute gondola ride is as much an attraction as a mode of transport. On clear days and nights the views across Taipei and up the lush Zhinan River valley are enchanting; on foggy days they are dreamy. The gondola has four stations: near the zoo, Taipei Zoo South, Zhinan Temple and Maokong itself. Paying by EasyCard gives you a NT$20 discount. If you're coming by MRT, get off at the zoo, turn left, and walk for about five minutes. Avoid taking the gondola on weekend mornings or afternoons. Take bus BR15 up instead and catch the gondola down after 9pm.

Tea Research and Promotion Center
MUSEUM

(茶推廣中心, Chá Tuīguǎng Zhōngxīn; ☑02-2234 2568; 8-2 Lane 40, Zhinan Rd, Sec 3, 指南路三段

40巷8-2號; ⊙9am-5pm Tue-Sun; gondola Maokong) **FREE** This lovely red-brick building,
about a 20-minute walk from Maokong
gondola station, has tranquil gardens, free
tea (look for the tap at the far right of the
entrance hall), and a demonstration hall
showing the excruciating process that goes
into making a brew, from picking the leaves,
to drying, spinning and roasting them.

Zhinan Temple TEMPLE
(指南宮, Zhǐnán Gōng; www.chih-nan-temple.org;
115 Wanshou Rd, 萬壽路15號; ⊙5am-9pm; ☐530,
小10, Maokong Tour Bus Left Line, gondola Zhinan
Temple) **FREE** The serene and stately Zhinan
Temple sits high above Wenshan District
in a near feng shui–perfect perch: two rivers converge in the valley below, while lush
wooded hills flank its rear halls. First built
in 1891, the temple is dedicated to Lu Tung
Pin, one of the eight immortals of classic
Chinese mythology.

Note that some signs spell the name Chih
Nan. To get here, take bus 530 from Taipower Building MRT station to Zhinan Temple
station; otherwise take the gondola.

Eleven shrines and three large temples
make up the entire complex. In the far
right temple, dedicated to the Sakyamuni
Buddha, look for a central Thai-style black
Buddha. This was a gift from a Thai prime
minister exiled during a coup and later rein-
stated, it is said, with the help of the Zhinan
Temple pantheon.

Zhinan Temple's final claim to fame is its
resident god's notorious habit of splitting up
unmarried couples (Lu himself was a jilted
lover). Many young Taiwanese still avoid the
place for this reason.

You can hike up to the temple in less than
an hour from National Chengchi University (there's a small drinks and snack stand
in the temple). There is also a long flight of
steps up to the temple (access via Zhinan
Road Section 2) passing tumbledown huts.

✕ Eating & Drinking

★ Yaoyue Teahouse   TEAHOUSE

(邀月茶坊, Yāoyuè Cháfāng; ☑02-2939 2025; www.yytea.com.tw; 6 Lane 40, Zhinan Rd, Sec 3, 指南路三段40巷6號; ⊗24hr; 🚬; ☲🗐10, Maokong Tour Bus Left Line, gondola Maokong) This very popular 24-hour teahouse is set off by itself in a beautiful valley. There are lots of tables with great views, and a busy kitchen serving reasonably priced Chinese dishes (NT$158 to NT$358) and dim sum, including a range of tea-infused recipes. The dumplings are a big favourite. Kitchen hours are 11am to 10pm (until 2am Fridays and Saturdays).

It takes about 25 minutes to walk here from the gondola but it's worth it. It's down its own set of stairs in the mountain side; look for a sign with the Chinese characters in the name. You can also take the Maokong Tour Bus Left Line or 小10 and ask to be dropped off at 邀月茶坊 (Yāoyuè Cháfāng).

★ Sih Ye   TEAHOUSE

(四爺, Sì Yé; ☑02-2234 0140; www.sihye.com; 2nd fl, 16 Lane 38, Zhinan Rd, Sec 3, 指南路三段38巷16-2號2樓; ⊗10am-10pm; 🚬; gondola Maokong) Just a minute's walk downhill from Maokong station. Sih Ye has one of the most beautiful teahouse interiors: a central bodhisattva statue, indoor pond, moon door and great city views. It's also the only place where you can recline on cushions in private booths and watch carp swim beneath glass flooring. Food (stir-fried dishes and seafood, NT$280-320) is available until 9pm.

Zi Zai Tian   TEAHOUSE

(自在田, Zìzài Tián; ☑02-2938 1113; 27 Lane 45, Lao Quan St, 老泉街45巷27號; ⊗11am-6pm Tue-Sun; 🚬; ☲Maokong Tour Bus Right Line, gondola Maokong) This gem is set inside a remodelled traditional stone farmhouse dating from 1831. A 30-minute walk downhill from the gondola past Lioujisiang (六季香茶坊, Liùjìxiāng Cháfāng; ☑02-2936 4371; 53 Lane 34, Zhinan Rd, Sec 3, 指南路三段34巷53號; ⊗10am-late Tue-Sun; 🚬), this teahouse is generally fairly quiet. To get to here by bus, take the Maokong Tour Bus Right Line heading past the Zhanghu Trail.

ⓘ Getting There & Away

Bus There are two public buses, the Brown 15 (BR15), which runs from the Taipei Zoo MRT to Maokong and minibus 10 (小10) from Wanfang Community MRT station (brown line). Both cost NT$15 and run every half-hour to one hour.

Cycling/hiking Cycling involves a reasonably challenging 40-minute bike climb. Hiking up to Maokong will take a couple of hours.

Maokong Gondola (p128) Taking the gondola adds a further experience to the trip.

Shared taxi From the top next to the gondola station, there is a taxi rank which charges a fixed NT$75 fee per person to Taipei Zoo MRT station. The car leaves when full (five passengers).

ⓘ Getting Around

There are two Maokong Tour Buses (called the Right Line and Left Line) that ply the winding roads to some of the trail heads and Zhinan Temple.

Xindian

The main attraction in Xindian (新店; Xīndiàn), a sprawling largely residential district in the southwestern corner of New Taipei City, is Bitan (碧潭; Bìtán; Green Lake), a stretch of dammed river famous since the Japanese era for its grey-green waters and rocky cliffs. There is something tender, lush and romantic about the landscape here.

Bitan sits right across from the Xindian MRT station as you exit (head left). A pleasant wooden walkway hugs the lake. There's a cycling path that links to Taipei, bird-shaped pedal boats, hiking trails leading into the misty hills, and the impressive Bitan Suspension Bridge (p131).

Slightly further afield is the National Human Rights Museum that is well worth a visit if you are interested in Taiwan's recent history.

◉ Sights

★ National Human Rights Museum   MUSEUM

(國家人權博物館, Guójiā Rénquán Bówùguǎn; Map p62; ☑02-8219 2692; www.nhrm.gov.tw; 131 Fusing (Fuxing) Rd, 復興路131號; ⊗9am-5pm Tue-Sun; 🅿; ⓂDapinglin) 🆓 This former detention centre, court and jail was where political prisoners were incarcerated and tried during the White Terror period (1947–87). The English audio guide is highly recommended. These peaceful but sombre grounds include tiny jail cells, shackles, the old commissary and a row of telephones where prisoners could speak for just 10 minutes every week with a visitor. This museum is highly recommended for the insight it gives into the horrors of authoritarianism and just how far Taiwan has come.

To get here, take Exit 1 from Dapinglin MRT station (green line) and walk for about 15 minutes. Head down Mingquan Rd, turn right at the crossroads and carry on past the large Buddhist hospital until you hit Fusing Rd. Turn left; the museum is straight ahead.

The museum is connected to the sprawling National Human Rights Museum (p200) on Green Island. If you have at least 10 people, you can book a guided tour. Call at least one day ahead. Some guides are ex-prisoners of this jail and offer extraordinary insights.

Bitan Suspension Bridge   BRIDGE
(Map p62; **M**Xindian) **FREE** This 200m-long bouncy pedestrian bridge was built by the Japanese in 1937. It offers a great vantage point from which to gaze towards the forested hills of Taiwan's northern mountain range, or back up the river to the concrete jaws of the city.

🏃 Activities

⭐Hemeishan   HIKING
(和美山, Héměishān; Map p62; **M**Xindian) A wonderful oasis, this low mountain affords a couple of hours' hiking in lush forest with genuinely outstanding views of the higher mountains heading south and across Taipei. To find the trailhead simply cross the Bitan Suspension Bridge and look for the stairs to the left just after the map board.

Lion's Head Mountain   HIKING
(獅頭山, Shītóushān; Map p62; **M**Xindian) Sometimes called Little Lion's Head Mountain, this pleasant hill climb starts from a trail head on Zhongxing Rd behind Xindian's post office. Ask at the visitor information centre for directions. There are pagodas to rest in and peek at the view of the city, including Taipei 101 (p83) in the distance. Either loop back down or carry on to Maokong (several hours).

🛏 Sleeping & Eating

New California Hotel   HOTEL **$$**
(新加州景觀旅館, Xīn Jiāzhōu Jǐngguān Lǚguǎn; Map p62; 02-2916 1717; www.new-california.com. tw; 1 Beixin Rd, Sec 1, 北新路一段1號; s/d from NT$1780/2180; 🌬✳@🛜; 🚌1968, **M**Xindian) Directly across from the Xindian MRT station, the busy New California Hotel has 45

clean, modern and compact singles and doubles, although they're decorated a bit like dentist waiting rooms. It's worth it to pay NT$200 extra to get a room facing the lake. The breakfast lounge on the 8th floor also has sweeping views.

You can get directly to the hotel from Taiwan Taoyuan International Airport via airport bus 1968.

⭐Loving Hut   VEGAN **$**
(愛家蔬食, Àijiā Shūshí; Map p62; 02-2910 7656; www.facebook.com/lovinghutBT; 211 Xindian Rd, 新店路211號; ⏰11am-8pm Sat, Sun & national holidays; 🅿✳🛜🍴👶; **M**Xindian) This cute, brightly lit and friendly place with yellow laminate tables offers a Taiwanese twist on pasta and Italian rice dishes using mushrooms, tofu and cashews. It's just behind Xindian MRT station, where the road of food carts begins. The desserts are famous – the vegan tiramisu has won awards. It is only open weekends and national holidays.

🍷 Drinking & Nightlife

Bi Ting   TEAHOUSE
(碧亭, Bì Tíng; Map p62; tea per person NT$250; ⏰noon-10pm; 🕿; **M**Xindian) This almost 60-year-old teahouse sits like a witchy temple on a rocky cliff. Sip a coffee or share a pot of tea while gazing at the lake below. There's no English sign; steps winding up to the teahouse are just before the western end of the Bitan Suspension Bridge. Since no food is served, customers are allowed to bring their own snacks.

ℹ Getting There & Away

The easiest way to get here is to take the green MRT line all the way to the end at Xindian station. If you're coming directly from Taoyuan International Airport, take Bus 1968 (NT$135, 80 minutes), which also terminates at Xindian MRT.

Many locals like to make a day of it by cycling from Taipei to Bitan along the riverside cycle paths.

Bus No. 849 – the stop is around the back of the **Visitor Information Centre** (02-2918 8509; Xindian MRT forecourt; ⏰9am-6pm; **M**Xindian) – takes you to the popular hot-spring resort of Wulai. Note this bus has shockingly long queues on weekends and holidays.

Northern Taiwan

Best Places to Eat

→ Miaokou Night Market (p142)

→ Jishan Street (p144)

→ Daxi Fishing Harbour (p153)

→ Duanchunzhen Beef Noodles (p157)

→ Taiya Popo (p139)

Best Places to Stay

→ The Ore Inn (p145)

→ Louzicuo Guesthouse (p148)

→ Rising Sun Surf Inn (p152)

→ Shanhaiguan Guesthouse (p145)

→ Sol Hotel (p157)

Why Go?

For many travellers, heading outside Taipei into the north gives them their first taste of how big this little island is. It's not just that there are mountains reaching up to 3886m. It's that those mountains – and their valleys and meadows – seem near endless, and that around every corner is a rustic hot-spring village, forest reserve or indigenous hamlet.

Using a mix of coastal trains and tourist buses, you can see much of the north, but having your own wheels, whether two or four, lets you strike closer to the soul of the region, traversing precipitous, cross-island highways, stumbling upon time-warp townships, and pulling over at roadside stalls to taste fruit fresh from the orchards. But remember: the north is a big place. While the blue magpie can fly those few kilometres in no time, the winding road takes a bit longer.

When to Go
Keelung

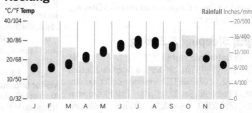

°C/°F Temp — Rainfall Inches/mm

Apr Youtong flowers in bloom.

Sep–Dec Best months for cycling and hiking.

Dec Start of the hot-spring season.

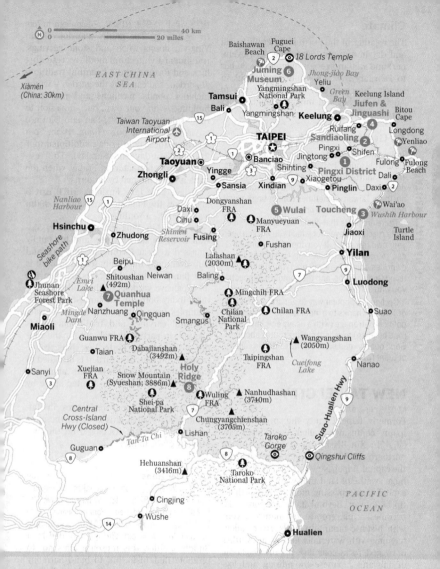

Northern Taiwan Highlights

1 **Pingxi District** (p146) Riding the rails between heritage stations on a beautiful branch line railway.

2 **Sandiaoling Waterfall Trail** (p148) Having your spirits lifted by this trio of gorgeous cascades.

3 **Toucheng** (p151) Summer surf vibes and seafood on a sleepy stretch of coast.

4 **Jiufen & Jinguashi** (p143) Tapping the richness of the area's mining heritage.

5 **Wulai** (p137) Swimming and river tracing through jungle.

6 **Juming Museum** (p142) Enjoying the works of Taiwan's master sculptor in a natural setting.

7 **Quanhua Temple** (p160) Breathing in incense and mountain air at this enchanting temple complex.

8 **Holy Ridge** (p162) Hiking for days along the vertiginous paths of the O' Holy Ridge trail in Shei-pa National Park.

Climate

The weather in the north is generally warm and dry in autumn (September to November) and wet and cool in winter (December to February), with possible sandstorms in spring (March to May). Summers (June to August) are hot and muggy, though cooler in the mountains.

ⓘ Getting There & Around

Trains and buses join up the major towns and cities and ply tourist hotspots along the coastlines. Tourist Shuttle Buses (www.taiwantrip.com.tw) delve inland into the foothills and mountains of northern Taiwan, sometimes connecting several popular destinations on one route.

There are parts that public transport doesn't quite reach, however, for which you will you need your own transport. If you don't fancy hiring a car, you can use an online service such as www.ownrides.com, where you plan your itinerary using Google Maps, and the company connects you with a driver.

Cycling is a popular way to get around this part of Taiwan. Thanks to a mountainous terrain and political patronage (with a heavy emphasis on road building) excellent cycling routes abound. Good quality road bikes can be rented in Taipei at Giant (p117).

NEW TAIPEI CITY

🗘 02 / POP 3,972,000

Formerly Taipei County, the special municipality confusingly called New Taipei City (新北市; Xīn Běishì) takes up most of the northern tip of Taiwan. Not to confused with the capital Taipei, New Taipei City (NTC) is a huge swathe of land that wraps around the capital, encompassing most of the northern tip of Taiwan. Beyond its urban core, NTC becomes a playground for nature lovers, with historic mountain trails, river valleys teeming with waterfalls and great swathes of rugged, rocky coastline. It's also the home of Taiwan's Japanese-era mining and logging industries, nicely preserved for tourists and including the delightfully scenic Pingxi Branch Rail Line, connecting time-warp mining villages and some terrific all-abilities hiking.

⊙ Sights

★ **Lin Family Mansion & Garden** GARDENS
(林本源園邸, Lín Běnyuán Yuándǐ; Map p62; www.linfamily.ntpc.gov.tw; 9 Ximen St, Banqiao District,

板橋區西門街9號; NT$80; ⊙9am-5pm, to 7pm Fri; MFuzhong) The family mansion of Lin Ying-yin boasts wood and stone carvings, traditional architectural motifs representing luck and fortune, and a beautiful traditional garden. You can visit the garden – which includes ponds, pavilions and numerous buildings – on your own, but admission to the residence (三落大厝; Sān Luò Dà Cuò) is via guided tour only (10am, 11am, 2pm and 3pm Tuesday to Friday, additional tour 2.30pm Saturday and Sunday). The residence stays open later on Friday, when the garden is illuminated by lanterns.

To get here take Fuzhong MRT Exit 3 and follow the English signs (about a 600m walk), or take a YouBike.

In 1778 Lin Ying-yin migrated to Taiwan from Fujian province, and his family amassed a great fortune trading rice and salt. Eventually the family settled in what is now Banqiao city, building this mansion and its expansive gardens in the mid-19th century. Today both are the largest remaining examples from that period left in Taiwan. Beautiful carvings and traditional motifs abound: in particular look out for the windows shaped like butterflies, bats, coins, peaches and fans. The garden is designed in the southern-Chinese style with abundant viewpoints created in the limited space by narrow maze-like walkways.

Of all the restored residences in Taipei and New Taipei, this is by far the most worthwhile to visit. It's closed on the first Monday of the month.

Museum of World Religions MUSEUM
(世界宗教博物館, Shìjiè Zōngjiào Bówùguǎn; Map p62; 02-8231 6118; www.mwr.org.tw; 7th fl, 236 Zhongshan Rd, Sec 1, Yonghe District, 永和區中山路一段236號7樓; NT$150; ⊙10am-5pm Tue-Sun; MDingxi) Though founded by a Buddhist order, this museum aims not to promote Buddhism, but to build harmony by showing the communality of all religions. Highlights include detailed scale models of the world's great holy sites such as Islam's Dome of the Rock, Sikhism's Golden Temple and Christianity's Chartres Cathedral; remarkably, the insides of these models can be viewed via tiny cameras.

You can walk to the museum from Dingxi MRT on the yellow line (it's about 1.1km) or take bus 706 from Exit 2.

Eating

Hoe Hoe Kyaw Restaurant
BURMESE $

(南國風味泰緬小吃, Nánguó Fēngwèi Tàimiǎn Xiǎochī; Map p62; Lane 1, 43 Zhongxiao Jie, 忠孝街1巷43號, Zhonghe; dishes NT$100-200; ⊙10am-2.30pm & 5-9pm Wed-Mon; Ⓜ Nanshijiao) One of many fantastic Burmese restaurants near Huaxin St in the western suburb of Zhonghe. This is the first shop on a left-hand alley about 400m down Huaxin St. Service is superfriendly, the space small and bustling. Try samosas (三角, sānjiǎo), fried chicken on shredded cabbage (椒麻雞, jiāo má jī), curry (咖喱, gālí) or ginger salad (兩辦薑絲, liǎng bàn jiāng sī).

❶ Getting There & Away

Surrounding the capital, New Taipei City is well served with buses and trains.

BUS

There are several useful Taipei Tourist Shuttle buses in New Taipei City, including **Route 856** between Fulong and Ruifang, and **Route 795** from Muzha to Pingxi and Shifen. For schedules and fares, go to www.taiwantrip.com.tw.

TRAIN
High-speed Rail

Almost all HSR trains stop at Banqiao station, a transport hub where standard (TRA) and subway (MRT) trains also stop. Journey times from major cities to Banqiao station vary as not all trains stop at all stations.

TO	FARE (NT$)	TIME
Hsinchu	260	25min
Kaohsiung (Zuoying)	1460	1hr
Taichung	670	50min
Tainan	1320	40min
Taipei	40	8min
Taoyuan	130	13min

Standard Trains

➡ The Western Line is the main route between cities from north to south.

➡ The Yilan Line runs to Ruifang, and the Pingxi Line to Shifen, Pingxi and Jingtong.

➡ Schedules and fares in English are available on the TRA website (twtraffic.tra.gov.tw/twrail).

MRT

The Taoyuan International Airport access line opened in 2017, running southwest from the airport as far as Huanbei in Taoyuan city.

TAXI

As in Taipei, the flagfall is NT$70 for the first 1.25km plus NT$5 for each 200m thereafter. From 11pm to 6am there is a surcharge of NT$20.

Yingge & Sansia

📷 02 / POP 200,700

The neighbouring towns of Yingge and Sansia make for an easy day trip from Taipei when combined together. Yingge (鶯歌; Yīnggē) lives by and for the production of ceramic and pottery objects: everything from cups and saucers to elaborate *objets d'art*. The old town of Sansia (三峽; Sānxiá), 3km to the east, has a delightfully ornate Taoist temple and a couple of blocks of well-preserved Qing- and Japanese-era buildings.

Pottery was first introduced to Yingge in 1804, but it remained a cottage industry producing cheap earthenware until the Japanese ramped up production in the 1930s. In addition to daily-life items, the local kilns began to fire ceramic parts for mines and weapons. After WWII ceramicists from all over Taiwan began to settle in Yingge and by the 1970s the town was the third-largest ceramic production centre in the world.

Nearby Sansia prospered as an important transport hub for charcoal, camphor and indigo dye, as evident in Minquan Old Street, a handsome block of red-brick merchant houses and residences dating from the end of the Qing dynasty to the early years of the Japanese colonial era. Sansia's name (Three Gorges) reflects the fact that it sits at the confluence of three rivers.

❷ Sights

Tzushr Temple
TAOIST TEMPLE

(祖師廟, Zǔshī Miào; 📷 tour 02-2671 1031; 1 Zhangfu St, 長福街1號) The centre of religious life in Sansia, the Tzushr Temple honours Qingshui Tsu-Sze, a Song-dynasty general worshipped by the people of Anxi, Fujian, for his power to protect their tea industry. First erected in 1769, the present structure hails from a late-1940s restoration that is still not finished.

In 1947 Tzushr Temple was in near total decay, as were many temples around Taiwan after WWII. Professor Li Mei-shu, scion of a wealthy and politically active family, was given the task of supervising the rebuilding. Li, a trained art professor, was the perfect man for the job. In addition to his formal training, which included a stint in Japan, Li had been a careful observer of temple crafts as a child. Li supervised reconstruction with an obsessive attention to detail and introduced numerous innovations, including bronze doors and wall relief and the use of gold foil over woodcarvings.

After Professor Li's death in 1983, however, the temple committee attempted to go the cheap route with the rest of the reconstruction. The master craftspeople were let go one by one, and a construction company was hired to oversee work. The ensuing public lambasting halted work, and these days everything still seems on hold.

Some standout features to look for include the 126 hand-carved stone pillars (the original design called for 156) and the astonishingly beautiful plafond (decorative ceiling), which recedes into a vortex. On every sculpted surface you'll find traditional motifs and auspicious symbols (such as bats, storks, frogs, crabs, cranes, peonies, pines, vases and turtles) and illustrated stories from history and mythology. Buy a copy of the *Shanhsia Tsu-sze Temple Tour Guide* booklet (NT$200) at the temple for more details, or call for a private tour (in Chinese only).

Manyueyuan Forest Recreation Area
PARK

(滿月圓森林遊樂區, Mǎnyuèyuán Sēnlín Yóulè Qū; ☑ 02-2672 0004; www.forest.gov.tw; NT$80-100; ⊙ 8am-5pm) Once you get past the paved waterfall trails in this scenic park 20km southeast of Sansia, you reach natural hikes that climb for hours through sweet-smelling cedar forests. Public transport to the park is limited; from Yingge train station, it's around a NT$500 taxi ride.

The main trail starts up a short incline to the right of the toilets at the end of the paved route to Manyueyuan Waterfall. There are many side branches but the main route connects Manyueyuan with Dongyanshan Forest Recreation Area. However, there is no public transport to and from Dongyanshan, so if you walk there you must walk back. It's about a four-hour hike one-way.

Two very worthy diversions on the main trail are up to Beichatianshan (北插天山; North Sky-Piercing Mountain; elevation 1727m), the highest peak in the north, and going further afield to a stand of giant ancient cedars (神木, shénmù).

To get to Beichatianshan, take the main trail to its highest point and then turn left,

following the English signs. It's a long day hike to the summit and back (expect 10 to 12 hours), so many people make it an overnight trip. There's a wild campsite near the base, beside a rushing stream.

The trail down to the old cedars follows the same path as to the base of Beichatianshan and then drops down a side trail, but this is not clearly marked in English. Get a map, or follow another hiking group.

You can take bus 807 from Sansia Bus Station to the Manyueyuan Forest parking lot, but it's infrequent (every 1 hour 40 minutes).

Minquan Old Street
AREA

(民權老街, Mínquán Lǎojiē; 37-147 Minquan St, 民權街37-147號; ⊙ 10am-8pm) This block of tastefully restored merchant houses and residences dates from the end of the Qing dynasty. On weekends there's a lively market atmosphere as the little shops sell speciality snacks, tea, vintage toys and souvenirs, and run indigo tie-dye (藍染; lánrǎn) workshops. Street performers also work the area. The best way to get here is to take a taxi from Yingge (about NT$200).

As you walk the Old Street, look for the diversity of styles in the shop facades: they incorporate late-Qing, Japanese and western baroque elements. The mortar used for the bricks is a combination of sticky rice and crushed seashells. The manholes are also beautiful, featuring scroll-like clouds and leaping carp. Many of the stores here used to be coffin shops, which is why some locals believe Minquan Old St to be haunted.

Yingge Ceramics Museum
MUSEUM

(鶯歌陶瓷博物館, Yīnggē Táocí Bówùguǎn; ☑ 02-8677 2727; www.ceramics.ntpc.gov.tw; 200 Wenhua Rd, 文化路200號; NT$80; ⊙ 9.30am-5pm Mon-Fri, to 6pm Sat & Sun, closed 1st Mon of month) This modern museum covers everything from 'snake kilns' and woods used in firing to special exhibitions showing the direction modern Taiwanese ceramics is taking. The flashy videos and occasional humorous displays help to maintain interest as you move around the three floors. The museum is a signposted 1km stroll from Yingge train station.

Yingge Old Street
AREA

(鶯歌老街, Yīnggē Lǎo Jiē) This cobbled street, Yingge's earliest ceramics hub, is lined with dozens of pottery shops selling tea sets, kitchenware, vases, ornaments and much more. Prices start at around NT$50 for a cup or saucer, rising to thousands for high-quality pieces. To get to Yingge Old Street, turn right out of the train station and follow the signs.

Note that the majority of items you see do not come from Yingge, or even Taiwan, but rather from China, Japan and other places in Asia. Most shops close around 6pm or 7pm. A boardwalk halfway along the street crosses the railway tracks and leads to the Yingge Ceramics Museum.

❶ Getting There & Away

Trains from Taipei Main Station (NT$31, 30 minutes) run to Yingge every 30 minutes.

From Yingge, you can take a taxi to Sansia (from Yingge Ceramics Museum to Tzushr Temple it costs around NT$150) or bus 702 (NT$15) from the museum.

Wulai

☑ 02 / POP 6182

This mountainous township 25km south of Taipei is a world apart from its urban neighbour. In the jungle that covers most of the area you'll find spectacular waterfalls, river pools for swimming, hiking trails and the relics of a once-thriving logging industry. Wulai (烏來; Wūlái), which means 'hot spring water', is a beautiful and largely untamed slice of Taiwan.

The main village is a popular place for hot springing. The village area is a bit shabby, but the tourist street is fun for snacking or sitting down to a hearty meal.

◎ Sights

Neidong Forest Recreation Area　　　　　　FOREST

(內洞森林遊樂區, Nèidòng Sēnlín Yóulè Qū; weekdays/weekend NT$65/80; ⊗8am-5pm) About 4km past Wulai Waterfall is this forested area popularly known as Wawagu (Valley of the Frogs). With its hiking trails through broadleaved and cedar forests, bird and insect life, river views and rushing waterfalls (especially the three-tiered Hsinhsian Waterfall; Xīnxián Pùbù), this place is worth a dedicated trip. It's particularly enchanting on a misty winter's day.

You can walk to Neidong from Wulai Waterfall in about 40 minutes. Make your way along the main road beyond the falls for 1.5km, cross the narrow suspension bridge and follow the road on the other side upstream to Neidong. A taxi from the main Wulai tourist area is NT$410.

SOAK & SLEEP

Wēnquán (hot-spring) hotels start a few kilometres before the main village as you ride into Wulai from Taipei. There are more along the tourist street as well as spreading into the hills around the village.

For cheap but decent options head to the end of the tourist street, cross the bridge and turn left. There are a row of small hot-spring hotels facing the river charging NT$200 to NT$300 for private bathing tubs, and NT$700 to NT$1400 for rooms (including bed, bathroom and hot-spring tub) per two hours.

Wulai Waterfall　　　　　　　　　WATERFALL

(烏來瀑布, Wūlái Pùbù; 16 Pubu Rd, 瀑布路16號; ⊗cable car 8.30am-10pm) This 80m-high waterfall is quite a beauty, and the fact that you can fly over it on a cable car is one more reason to come to Wulai. There's a log cart railway (NT$50, until 5pm) to the base, or you can walk the pedestrian route beside the train line (about 1.6km) along a pleasant wooded lane with some mountain scenery.

To get to the log cart railway station, walk to the end of the pedestrian food street in Wulai, cross the bridge and head up the wooden stairs.

Wulai Log Cart Museum　　　　　MUSEUM

(烏來林業生活館, Wūlái Línyè Shēnghuó Guǎn; 1-2 Pubu Rd, 瀑布路1之2號; ⊗9am-5pm Wed-Mon) FREE Facing Wulai Waterfall, this snazzy little museum tells the story of Wulai's old log cart railway, which was only motorised in 1974. Prior to that, loggers pushed the heavily-loaded carts by hand. During the Japanese era, carts were converted to rail-mounted rickshaws to convey tourists to the waterfall.

Wulai Atayal Museum　　　　　MUSEUM

(烏來泰雅民族博物館, Wūlái Tàiyǎ Mínzú Bówùguǎn; ☑02-2661 8162; 12 Wulai St, 烏來街 12號; ⊗9.30am-5pm Mon-Fri, to 6pm Sat & Sun, closed 1st Mon of month) FREE The Atayal are the third-largest indigenous tribe in Taiwan and form a big presence in Wulai (part of their traditional territory). Inside this charming museum are replicas of traditional bamboo and wood houses, and engaging displays on hunting, farming, religious beliefs, musical instruments, facial tattooing and headhunting.

Wulai

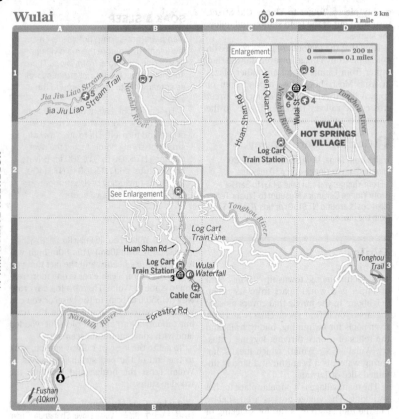

Wulai

◉ Sights

⊕ Activities, Courses & Tours

⊗ Eating

⊕ Transport

🏃 Activities

Jia Jiu Liao Stream   WATER SPORTS, HIKING
(加九寮溪, Jiā Jiǔ Liáo Xī) A popular river-tracing venue, the Jia Jiu Liao Stream features a jungle canopy worthy of a Tarzan film, a natural waterslide (滑水道) and a deep pool large enough for a group to swim in. To get here, take a bus to or from Wulai and get off at Chenggong Village (成功站; Chénggōng Zhàn). It's a 3km walk north from Wulai tourist area.

From Chenggong Village, follow the side road down. Cross the red bridge, go over the hump and, before the second bridge, head up the stairs on the left. When obvious make your way to the stream. The first section is usually very crowded with picnickers and swimmers on summer weekends. The stream has no steep inclines and flows relatively gently, so it's pretty easy going but still great fun.

An average walker can reach the big swimming hole in less than an hour. The natural slide is about 100m downstream. On summer weekends you'll usually see groups here. Serious hikers can keep going along the full 20km Jia Jiu Liao Stream trail. The trail is relatively straightforward these days and, while not signed, the main path is obvious.

Full Moon Spa HOT SPRINGS
(明月溫泉, Míngyuè Wēnquán; ☑02-2661 7678; www.fullmoonspa.net; 1 Wulai St, Lane 85, 烏來街85巷1號; public pools unlimited time NT$390) Just off the main tourist street, Full Moon has mixed and nude segregated pools with nice views over the Tonghou River. Its private rooms feature wooden tubs and can be rented by the hour (from NT$780, minimum two people). Overnight stays (from NT$3900) include breakfast and dinner.

✕ Eating

Indigenous cuisine is the standard fare in Wulai. A few tantalising selections that can be found at any number of shops along Wulai St include mountain vegetables, chicken and boar, *zhútǒng fàn* (竹桶飯, sticky rice steamed and served in bamboo tubes) and freshwater fish. Snacks and alcoholic drinks made from *xiǎomǐ* (小米, millet) can be found at stalls in the village.

★ Taiya Popo TAIWANESE INDIGENOUS **$$**
(泰雅婆婆, Tàiyǎ Pópó; ☑02-2661 6371; www.taiyapopo.com; 14 Wulai St, 烏來街14號; dishes NT$70-300; ⊘10am-9pm) This long-running restaurant on the tourist street, just past the Atayal Museum, serves some excellent if obscure indigenous dishes, such as bird's nest fern, betelnut salad, bamboo partridge and flying squirrel.

❶ Information

If you go river tracing (*suòxī*), plan to be out of the water by 3pm or 4pm. Afternoon showers are a daily occurrence in late spring and summer, and rivers can become swollen very quickly. Also keep an eye open for snakes and leeches on the more overgrown trails.

SWIMMING & RIVER TRACING

Every weekend in the hot summer months, river-tracing clubs or informal groups of friends flock to the rivers and streams around Wulai to practise river tracing, which combines scrambling, swimming and hiking (and true technical climbing and rappelling at higher levels).

---

❶ Getting There & Away

Bus 849 to Wulai (NT$30, 40 minutes, every 15 to 20 minutes) runs from the taxi stand area at Xindian MRT station in New Taipei City to Wulai bus station (烏來總站; Wūlái Zǒngzhàn).

A taxi back to Xindian MRT station is NT$680.

Cihu

Cihu (慈湖; Cíhú; Lake Kindness) is a quiet, scenic area where the remains of Chiang Kai-shek's body are entombed, awaiting an (hopeful) eventual return to China. It's also the site of one of Taiwan's oddest tourism attractions. No, not the mausoleum itself, but Cihu Memorial Sculpture Park, where 152 unwanted Chiang Kai-shek statues have been sent over the past decade to escape being melted down or smashed.

◉ Sights

Cihu Mausoleum MAUSOLEUM
(慈湖陵寢, Cíhú Língqín; 1097 Fuxing Rd, Sec 1, Daxi District, 復興路一段1097號; ⊘9am-5pm Wed-Mon) FREE It's a 15-minute stroll from the arched gate on the main road to Chiang Kai-shek's mausoleum. Time your visit to catch the hourly changing of the guard. Cihu was supposedly chosen for Chiang's final resting place because the scenery here reminded him of his hometown in Zhejiang province.

Cihu Memorial Sculpture Park PARK
(慈湖紀念雕像公園, Cíhú Jìniàn Diāoxiàng Gōngyuán; 大溪區復興路一段1097號; ☑03-388 4437; 1097 Fuxing Rd, Sec 1, Daxi District, 復興路一段1097號; ⊘8am-5pm) FREE Home to 152 unwanted Chiang Kai-shek statues, this open-air sculpture park is a hoot (surely unintentionally), with promenades of Chiang busts and clumps of Chiangs standing facing each other as if in conversation. There are story-time Chiangs reading books to shorter Chiangs, salesmen Chiangs bowed at the waist with hat removed, avuncular Chiangs always smiling, and martial Chiangs, sword in hand, ready to defend the nation.

On a more serious note, the park also gives insight into the cult of personality that was developed (and still exists for hardcore KMT supporters) around Chiang. You'll learn, for example, how his statues were placed at the front of every school, and often in pre-existing popular shrines so worshippers would be forced to pay homage whether they wanted to or not.

The rules on sculpting the Generalissimo were stringent: standing statues couldn't be shorter than 170cm (his height), while busts had to reveal at least the third button on his uniform.

Eating

Go Go Box   FOOD TRUCK **$**
(138 Fuxing Rd, Sec 2, 復興路二段138號; hamburger NT$100; ⊙10am-5pm Thu-Tue) Graze on burgers, burritos and barista coffee from this food truck 3km east up the road from Cihu. The truck is parked in a kitsch roadside space evoking a British pub garden. It's a popular weekend stop for bikers. A taxi here from Cihu costs around NT$200.

ⓘ Getting There & Away

From the Taoyuan Zhongli train station, take a Taiwan Tourist Shuttle bus (route 501, NT$100, hourly from 9am to 4pm, 1¼ hours).

Baling

☑ 03 / POP 1501

Perched on a lofty ridgeline some 60km inland from Taoyuan city, the settlement of Upper Baling (上巴陵; Shàng Bālíng) offers splendid mountain views, rustic country cooking, and most importantly for the day trippers passing through, is on the road into Lalashan Forest Reserve.

Baling is an approximation of 'big tree' in the local Atayal language. About 10km down the mountain, where the road joins the North Cross-Island Highway, is the less interesting Lower Baling.

◉ Sights & Activities

Lalashan Forest Reserve   FOREST
(拉拉山國有林自然保護區, Lālāshān Guóyǒu Lín Zirán Bǎohùqū; Daguanshan Forest Reserve; ⊙8am-5pm) **FREE** This 63.9 sq km expanse of mixed forest holds one of the largest stands of ancient red hinoki cypress trees left in Taiwan. The most ancient of the ancients is over 2800 years old. A 3.7km boardwalk trail winds through the dense forest via a couple of dozen cypresses, with signs indicating the age, species, height and diameter of each giant.

The visitable area of the reserve is small, and you'll see everything within two hours. To make a day (or two) of it, hikers can take on the 18km Fu-Ba National Trail, which starts (or finishes) in the reserve itself.

You'll need your own vehicle to get here, unless you're prepared to catch a (very) slow bus from Taoyuan train station to Lalashan entrance (route 5301 leaves at 6:30am, route 5090 at 6:47am, both taking around four hours).

Fu-Ba National Trail   HIKING
(福巴越嶺古道, Fú-bā Yuèlíng Gǔdào) This 18km national trail is named after the two villages it connects: Fushan and Upper Baling. Two hundred years ago, the Atayal hacked this route up the mountains to facilitate trade and marriage, and it's still common to see Atayal hunting or fishing in the area. Hiking the trail takes 6-8 hours from Lalashan down to Fushan; more if coming up.

The trailhead on the Baling side starts inside the Lalashan Forest Reserve itself, and is clearly marked. Along the trail, there are several good wild campsites (with water from nearby streams). The trailhead coming up is just past Fushan village, 17km south of Wulai.

Note that you'll need to register at the **police station** (巴陵派出所, Bālíng Pàichūsuǒ; ⊙8:30am-5pm) in Upper Baling (or at a checkpoint on route in Fushan if hiking up). Bring your passport.

Magic World can arrange for you to be picked up or dropped off at Lalashan (which is especially helpful if you're hiking up from Fushan to Baling). Request this in advance.

🛏 Sleeping

Goodian Coffee B&B   GUESTHOUSE **$$**
(谷點咖啡民宿, Gǔdiǎn Kāfēi Mínsù; ☑03-391 2415; www.goodian.com.tw; tw from NT$3000; 🖥) On the road between Lower and Upper Baling, this well-run guesthouse has sweeping mountain views from its guestrooms, and brews good-quality Italian coffee (hence the name). Breakfast and dinner included.

**Magic World
Country House**   HOTEL **$$**
(富仙境鄉村度假旅館, Fùxiānjìng Xiāngcūn Dùjià Lǚguǎn; ☑03-391 2668, 03-391 2115; d incl breakfast from NT$2500) Halfway up the hairpin mountain road between Lower Baling and Upper Baling, this mansion-like hotel offers spacious rooms, a lush garden where cherry blossoms bloom in the spring, and awesome views over the mountains from the wooden deck. The hot-water flow may be a little unsteady at times.

NORTHERN TAIWAN BALING

ℹ️ Getting There & Away

Public transport to Upper Baling is long-winded and slow, so it's best to visit if you have your own vehicle.

Two buses leave from just outside Taoyuan train station to Upper Baling and onward to the Lalashan entrance (which is a few kilometres back from the start of the reserve proper). Route 5301 departs at 6:30am, and route 5090 at 6:47am, both taking around four hours.

If driving from Fusing, take Hwy 7 to Lower Baling, and change to Hwy 16 for Upper Baling and Lalashan Forest Reserve.

NORTHEAST COAST

☑ 03

A film roll of captivating natural landscapes unfurls along Taiwan's rugged northeast coast. Rolling grass hills, lofty cliffs, sand and pebble beaches, rocky terraces and windswept peninsulas are interspersed with sleepy coastal villages, tourist-magnet towns like Jiufen and a thriving summer surf scene.

The 166km coastal Provincial Hwy 2 takes it all in, from the mouth of the Tamsui River to the alluvial plains of Yilan, while trains also hug the coast from Fulong southwards through Yilan country.

◉ Sights

Yehliu Geopark   PARK

(野柳地質公園, Yěliǔ Dìzhí Gōngyuán; ☑ 02-2492 2016; www.ylgeopark.org.tw; 167-1 Gangdong Rd, Wanli District, 野柳里港東路167-1號; adult/child NT$80/40; ⊙ 7.30am-6pm May-Sep, to 5pm Oct-Apr, visitor centre 8am-5pm) Stretching far out into the East China Sea, this limestone cape is a geologist's dreamland where aeons of wind and sea erosion can be observed in hundreds of pitted and moulded rocks. The most striking have quaint (but accurate) names such as Fairy's Shoe (仙女鞋; Xiānnǔ Xié) and Queen's Head (女王頭; Nǚwáng Tóu), which truly looks just like a silhouette of the famous Nefertiti bust. Bus 1815 from Taipei City Hall Bus Station stops here (NT$84, 1 hour).

Tourist Shuttle Bus route 862 from Tamsui MRT station stops directly outside the park entrance. Yehliu Geopark gets very crowded on weekends and during holidays, with many tourists swarming around Queen's Head waiting to take pictures. Try to visit early morning on a weekday.

ℹ️ STAYING LONGER

Most of the attractions along Taiwan's northeast coast are doable as a day trip from Taipei, but some travellers choose to overnight in Jiufen, which has an abundance of cute B&Bs, many with sea views. There are also several campsites and one or two hostels en route for budget travellers and cyclists.

New 18 Lords Temple   TEMPLE

(新乾華十八王公廟, Xīngànhuá Shíbāwánggōng Miào; ☑ 02-2638 2453; 52 Pinglin, Maolin village, 茂林村坪林52號) A few kilometres back in the hills from the old 18 Lords Temple is a larger, newer version of the temple with a giant dog statue in the parking lot standing well over 15m high.

Neither the old nor the new 18 Lords Temple is served by the Tourist Shuttle buses, so you'll need your own vehicle. If you're coming to the new temple from the old, cross the bridge above the temple as you head in the direction of Jinshan (金山). You'll see signage for First Nuclear Plant (核一廠) at a traffic light. Turn right into Chanye Rd (產業道路) and walk for 1km, before turning left. You should see the huge canine statue of the new temple up on a hillside.

18 Lords Temple   TEMPLE

(十八王宮, Shíbā Wánggōng; 1-1 Aliban, Ganhua Li, Shimen, 石門區乾華里阿里磅1-1號; ⊙ 24hr) FREE Sometimes called the 'dog temple', this recently restored place of worship has a canine legend attached. After a group of 17 fisherman were lost at sea, the dog of one of the men missed its master so much that it leaped into the sea and drowned. People were so impressed by this act of loyalty that they built the temple in its honour. The temple is just off Provincial Hwy 2 in front of First Nuclear Power Plant (核一廠).

When you arrive, women may try to instruct you in how to light incense or use one of the small red packets for worship – wave it over burning incense, then wipe it on the statue's nose and head (and sometimes genitals) before placing it in the mouth. If you let them show you, they may ask for NT$200 for the materials. Decline politely if you don't intend to engage in worship.

Baishawan Beach   BEACH

(白沙灣, Báishāwān) One of the better beaches in New Taipei City is found at this little bay sometimes called White Haven Beach. The

WORTH A TRIP

TAIWAN'S ICONIC SCULPTOR

Ju Ming (born 1938) is Taiwan's most famous living sculptor, having gained fame here in the 1980s, and internationally a decade later. His works are instantly recognisable despite varying from giant stone abstractions, to delicate wood pieces, to a series of nativist works that includes sculptures of historical figures as well as daily-life scenes. Among the most popular of the artist's works are those in the 'Tai Chi' series, which feature gigantic blocky stone monoliths in various martial arts poses.

The majority of Ju Ming's works can be seen together at the **Juming Museum** (朱銘美術館, Zhūmíng Měishùguǎn; www.juming.org.tw; 2 Xihu, Jinshan, 金山區西勢湖2號; NT$350; ⊙10am-6pm Tue-Sun May-Oct, to 5pm Tue-Sun Nov-Apr; ☒), which lies across a 15-hectare park in the hills above Jinshan. Most works are outdoors so make sure to bring an umbrella or a hat to protect against sun or rain.

Just up the street from the museum is the vast Jinbaoshan Cemetery (金寶山; Jīn Bǎo Shān; Chin Pao Shan), which, odd as it may sound, is a sight not to be missed. This wonderland for the underworld will literally make you feel envious of the deceased for having one of the best living environments in Taiwan. There are well-tended gardens, beautiful carvings by master artists (including Ju Ming), a towering golden columbarium (a building with niches for funeral urns to be stored), and row upon row of intricately carved and decorated graves looking over a gorgeous stretch of the northeast coastline and the East China Sea.

The most famous grave here is that of Teresa Teng (鄧麗君), a silky voiced pop singer who died tragically young in 1995, though not before achieving massive popularity (which endures) in the Chinese-speaking world. Tourist Shuttle buses stop just across from her grave but you wouldn't miss it for the fresh flowers, pilgrims and giant workable keyboard in front.

Both the museum and cemetery are served by the Taiwan Tourist Shuttle buses (www.taiwantrip.com.tw) from Tamsui or Keelung.

Chinese name translates as 'white-sand bay' – though it's definitely more of a brownish colour. Swimming is permitted from May to September, as is surfing. Tourist Shuttle Bus route 862 from Danshui MRT station stops on Hwy 2 just before the entrance.

Laomei Algal Reef NATURAL FEATURE
(老梅海岸, Lǎoméi Hǎi'àn) The flat and fantastical tongue-like protrusions at low tide here are actually wave-sculpted volcanic lava. From March to May, they're carpeted by a thick layer of bright green algae. Tourist Shuttle Bus route 862 from Tamsui MRT stops nearby.

🏃 Activities

Bitou Cape Trail HIKING
(鼻頭角步道, Bítóu Jiǎo Bùdào) For dramatic vistas of sea-eroded cliffs and frothing waves, the Bitou Cape, prodding out into the East China Sea ('bitou' means 'nose tip') has a well-marked circular trail that takes about 1½ hours to hike. The trailhead starts near the Bitou Cape bus stop; to get here from Ruifang train station or Jiufen, take Taiwan Tourist Shuttle bus route 856 (NT$50, 40 minutes) heading to Fulong.

To start the trail, head up the side road to the left of the highway tunnel and you'll pass what must be the nicest setting for a school in Taiwan. At certain points en route it's possible to descend down steps to a rocky platform called the Fisherman's Pathway, where you'll see people fishing. From here you can keep walking south along the coast to Longdong.

CU Surf Paradise Taiwan SURFING
(台湾西元衝浪新樂園, Táiwān xīyuán chōnglàng xīn lèyuán; ☎02-2638 2733; www.facebook.com/cu.surf.taiwan; 1-9 Bajia Rd, Baishawan, 石門區德茂里 八甲一之九號一樓; ⊙8am-6pm) This surf shop on the eastern edge of Baishawan Beach (p141) offers surf lessons, surfboard rental and repair, and surf tours in northern Taiwan. Tourist Shuttle Bus route 862 from Danshui MRT station stops just outside.

🍴 Eating

Miaokou Night Market MARKET $
(基隆廟口夜市, Jīlóng Miàokǒu Yèshì; www.miaokow.org; Rensan Rd; 仁三路; ⊙5-11pm) One of the most famous night markets in Taiwan, Miaokou's moreish mouthfuls are the main reason to find yourself in the rainy port city

of Keelung, unless you're taking the ferry to or from China. Trains from Taipei (NT$41, 45 minutes) leave every 20 minutes or so for Keelung, and the market is a ten-minute stroll east, past the harbour.

❶ Information

Most of the region falls under the auspices of either the **North Coast & Guanyinshan Scenic Administration** (白沙灣遊客中心, Báishāwān Yóukè Zhōngxīn; ☑ 0800-800 380; www.north guan-nsa.gov.tw; 33-6 Xiayoukeng, Demaoli, Shimen District, 石門區德茂里下員坑33-6號; ⊗ 9am-5pm; 🛜) headquartered at Baishawan Beach or the **Northeast & Yilan Coast Scenic Administration** (福隆遊客中心, Fúlóng Yóukè Zhōngxīn; ☑ 03-995 3885; www.necoast-nsa. gov.tw; 36 Xinglong St, 興隆街36號; ⊗ 9am-6pm) in Fulong.

The **English Tourist Hotline** (☑ 0800-011 765) answers enquiries in Mandarin, English or Japanese, and helps to handle travel-related emergencies.

❶ Getting There & Away

BUS

Tourist Shuttle Bus route 862 (www.taiwantrip. com.tw) connects sights along Taiwan's north-east coast from Tamsui MRT station to Keelung, while route 856 goes from Keelung to Fulong via Jiufen.

TRAIN

Direct services from Taipei stop at Fulong and stations in Toucheng, while for other destinations, including Jiufen, travellers alight at Ruifang or Keelung and change to buses.

❶ Getting Around

BICYCLE

Provincial Hwy 2 is popular with road cyclists, as are the picturesque side roads around Sanzhi, Fulong and Daxi.

BUS

There are public buses to most places in the region. Between MRT Tamsui Station and Keelung, the Tourist Shuttle Bus (route 862, www.taiwantrip.com.tw, one-day pass NT$100) runs hourly on weekdays and every 30 minutes on weekends to the main sites, including Juming Museum. The last buses leave/return around 5pm or 6pm. From Keelung heading eastwards, Tourist Shuttle Bus route 856 goes to Fulong via Jiufen.

TRAIN

Local trains provide a useful if slow and infrequent service along the top of the east coast,

from Fulong down to Toucheng and onwards through Yilan County.

Jiufen & Jinguashi

☑ 02 / POP 3100

Clinging to rainswept hillsides overlooking the sea, the former mining towns of Jiufen (九份; Jiǔfèn) and Jinguashi (金瓜石; Jīnguāshí) serve up a captivating mix of yesteryear charm, industrial heritage, whimsical tea houses and enough snacks to feed half the country. Which is about how many tourists squeeze and shuffle their way along narrow Jishan Street (p144), Jiufen's main drag, famous for its snack vendors, on any given weekend.

Fortunately you can skip the worst of the crowds by arriving in the morning and saving the much quieter Jinguashi, with its gold mine-themed attractions, for the afternoon. Equally, the lanes and hillsides here offer opportunities for relaxed wandering, with mountain and sea vistas at every turn.

⊙ Sights

★**Gold Ecological Park**　　　HISTORIC SITE
(黃金博物園區, Huángjīn Bówùyuánqū; Gold Museum; www.gep.ntpc.gov.tw; NT$80; ⊗ 9.30am-5pm Mon-Fri, to 6pm Sat & Sun (closed 1st Mon of month)) 🆓 Jinguashi's big draw is this Japanese-era mining-complex-turned-tourist-park, where hillside paths connect 1930s offices, workshops and dormitories, and you can fondle reputedly the world's largest gold bar at the Gold Museum. The **Beishan Fifth Tunnel** (extra NT$50; ⊗ to 4.30pm) offers a walk-through glimpse of working conditions in the old mine, while high above the park, the ruins of a Japanese shinto shrine appear like something out of Greek mythology. The bus from Jiufen stops beside the ticket office.

The Crown Prince Chalet (太子賓館; Tàizǐ Bīnguǎn), a Japanese-style garden mansion with sweeping sea views, is another draw, though unfortunately you can only wander the gardens and peek through the windows. It was built in 1922 by the mining company to allegedly house the Japanese crown prince (the future Emperor Hirohito) on an inspection tour. He never came, and later the chalet became a hotel for high-ranking Kuomintang officials.

It may be interesting to note as you walk around that not all the gold in this area has been collected. Even today there remains a 250-tonne reserve estimated at more

LOCAL KNOWLEDGE

KEELUNG GHOST FESTIVAL

During the seventh lunar month (usually August or September), the port city of Keelung hosts Taiwan's most renowned **Ghost Festival** (中元節, Zhōngyuán Jié; www.klcg.gov.tw; ⊙ Aug or Sep), a blend of Taoist and Buddhist beliefs and rituals. Each year a different Keelung clan is chosen to sponsor the events. Highlights include folk-art performances, the opening of the Gates of Hell and the release of burning water lanterns.

Keelung's festival began in the mid-19th century as a way to bridge the rift between feuding groups of Hoklo immigrants. However, the belief in ghost month is widespread in Chinese culture. According to popular beliefs, during this month 'hungry spirits' roam the earth and must be appeased and sated with elaborate banquets, festivities and a whole lot of ghost paper burning.

The main events are:

Day 1, seventh lunar month The Gates of Hell are opened at noon at Laodagong Temple (老大公廟), west of Keelung Harbour.

Day 12 Lights are lit on the main altar of Chupu Temple (主普壇), which overlooks Keelung Harbour from Zhongzheng Park.

Day 13 A large parade throughout downtown Keelung honours the 15 clans involved.

Day 14 An elaborate lantern release ceremony takes place (Ghost Month's main event), beginning with an evening street parade of floats which slowly make their way to Badouzi Harbour, southeast of downtown. Sometime around midnight, water lanterns shaped like houses and stuffed with ghost paper are released into the harbour and set alight.

Day 15 During the day, temples and private households hold rituals to deliver the wandering spirits from their suffering – you'll see piles of food and money outside people's homes.

Day 1, eighth lunar month At 5pm, the Gates of Hell are shut again at Laodagong Temple. According to folklore experts, the gates are closed on the first day of the eighth month to allow for potential tardy spirits.

than NT$200 billion (US$6 billion) lying underground.

Remains of the 13 Levels
HISTORIC SITE

(十三層遺址, Shísāncéng Yízhǐ) Just across from the Golden Waterfall, on a sea-facing bluff, are the remains of a massive copper-smelting refinery (十三層; Shísāncéng) whose 13 levels descend towards the sea in rapid progression. The derelict buildings inspire such a heavy, dystopian industrial awe that they have been used as a background for music videos.

If you want to get close, head up the side road just after the Golden Waterfall (on the right as you head down). The road winds up to the top level and then drops down to the village of Changren. There's a short flight of stairs across a car park to a lookout with a perfect vantage point over the remains. You can't take a bad photograph here.

Jishan Street
AREA

(基山街, Jīshān Jiē; Jiufen Old Street) Countless snack stalls and souvenir shops line the narrow 'old street' threading through Jiufen, a mining town so prosperous it became known as 'Little Shanghai' in the 1930s. Hugely popular, the street can become intolerably crowded by the afternoon, so plan accordingly. Shuqi St, with its famously steep steps, Japanese-era theatre and teahouses, intersects a few hundred metres along Jishan St.

Golden Waterfall
WATERFALL

(黃金瀑布, Huángjīn Pùbù) The cascades at this popular tourist stop have stained the rocks a honeycomb yellow due to the pyrite (fool's gold) deposits picked up by the water as it passes through the area. You'll find the waterfall two bus stops from the Gold Ecological Park (p143) as you head towards the sea (which is also a yellowish hue, dubbed 'ying-yang sea', from the river outflow).

Taiwan POW Memorial and Peace Park
MEMORIAL

(國際終戰和平紀念園區, Guójì Zhōng Zhàn Hépíng Jìniàn Yuánqū) Only a single gatepost remains of the Kinkaseki camp where 1000 British and allied soldiers were imprisoned and forced to work in the neighbouring copper mine during WWII. Now a park, there are statues and a wall engraved with all the prisoners' names; at least 10% of them died here. It's one bus stop after the Gold Ecological Park (p143) when coming from Jiufen.

Nanya Peculiar Rocks　　　NATURAL FEATURE
(南雅海岸, Nányǎ Hǎi'àn) This quirky section of coastline has an eroded swirl of rock that genuinely looks like a striped ice-cream cone. The odd shapes and colours were formed by the sea and wind eroding sandstone rocks containing seams of iron and copper. Bus 856 stops at Nanya, 4km east of Jinguashi along Provincial Hwy 2.

Fushan Temple　　　TAOIST TEMPLE
(福山宮, Fúshāngōng; 1 Lunding Rd, 崙頂路1號; ☺6am-6pm) Blending Japanese, Chinese and European decorative motifs (note the angels over the altar), 200-year-old Fushan Temple was where the region's miners would pray to Tudi, the Earth God, to point them to a rich vein of gold. To reach the temple, walk up the main road to the top of the hill, where the road splits. Left goes to Jinguashi and right will take you to Fushan Temple in about 1km.

🏃 Activities

Mt Keelung Hiking Trail　　　HIKING
(雞籠山, Jīlóngshān; Keelung Mountain) You can't miss this 588m peak for the way it soars upwards, making it dizzying to behold from below. Allow half an hour to slog up the steps to the summit. The trailhead is 300m up the main road from Jiufen's 7-Eleven.

🛏 Sleeping

Jiufen and Jinguashi make for an easy day trip from Taipei, but spending the night in a B&B lets you wander about after dark and in the morning when Jiufen is at its most enticing.

★**The Ore Inn**　　　HOMESTAY $$
(九份山經, Jiǔfèn Shānjīng; ☎0971-399 968; 204 Jishan St, 基山街204號; d NT$2000-3000; ⓐ) Renovated in a minimalist style with polished concrete floors and excellent sea views, this guesthouse is well away from the tourist hubbub, despite being on Jishan St. Some rooms are partially built into the side of the mountain, a feature of Jiufen houses. Prices increase on weekends and holidays.

★**Shanhaiguan Guesthouse**　　　HOMESTAY $$
(九份山海觀民宿, Jiǔfèn Shānhǎi Guān Mínsù; ☎0972-887 200; www.jiufenhotel.com; 217 Jishan St, 基山街217號; d NT$1800-NT$2500; ⓐ) This guesthouse is actually a number of individual midrange rooms set in various locations on the hillsides around Jiufen. Most have superb sea views. Check-in and breakfast (included) is at a tea house at 217 Jishan St. Prices go up on weekends and holidays.

🍷 Drinking & Nightlife

★**Jiufen Teahouse**　　　TEAHOUSE
(九份茶坊, Jiǔfèn Cháfǎng; ☎02-2496 9056; www.jiioufen-teahouse.com.tw; 142 Jishan St, 基山街142號; ☺10.30am-9pm; ⓐ) Step back in time at this century-old wooden tea house full of antique furnishings and cosy nooks to hunker down in. The tea selection includes aged pu'ers, roasted Oriental Beauty and Tieguanyin. A pot (with unlimited water refills) starts at NT$600, plus NT$100 per guest, so it's an expensive place to drink solo. Find it just west of the Shuqi St steps on Jishan St.

Shu-ku Tea Store　　　TEAHOUSE
(樹宿奇木樓, Shùkū Qímùlóu; ☎02-2497 9043; 38 Fotang Ln, 佛堂巷38號; teas/snacks from NT$300/50; ☺10am-10pm Sun-Wed & Fri, to midnight Sat) This creaking two-storey teahouse from the Japanese era has the look and feel of a frontier gambling den. Inside you can almost picture the miners squatting on makeshift benches, shuffling cards

NORTHERN TAIWAN JIUFEN & JINGUASHI

JIUFEN NIBBLES

Much of Jiufen's recent fame comes via its association with filmmaker Hayao Miyazaki's *Spirited Away (2001)*, an animated movie set in a place supposedly inspired by the town. In one scene, the protagonist's parents gorge themselves along a snack street and turn into pigs. Fittingly, Jiufen's 'old street' is lined with food outlets. Grazing on local snacks is de rigueur in Jiufen. Look for *yùyuán* (芋圓, taro balls), *yúwán* (魚丸, fish balls), *cǎozǐ gāo* (草仔糕, herbal cakes), *ba-wan* (肉圓, gelatinous dumplings filled with pork or red bean) and *hēitáng gāo* (黑糖糕, molasses cake). If the crowds get too much, you can take refuge in a tea house.

and warming their hands on a metal teapot. There's no minimum order, making it a good spot for an evening beer. Grab a terrace table for views over the twinkling illuminations of Jiufen.

ℹ Information

At the bottom of the Shuqi St steps that link up with Jishan Street, the **Visitor Information Centre** (九份旅遊服務中心; ☑ 02-2406 3270; 89 Qiche Rd, 車路89號; ⊙ 9am-6pm) has history displays and other themed exhibits. From here you can catch the bus to Ruifang Station, or the other way to Jinguashi.

ℹ Getting There & Away

Bus From Taipei, catch the frequent Keelung Bus Company (基隆汽車客運; www.kl-bus. com.tw) bus 1062 at Zhongxiao Fuxing MRT (Exit 1) to Jiufen/Jinguashi (NT$101, 1¼ hours, every 30 minutes from 6:16am to 8.30pm).

Train From Taipei Main Station, trains (fast NT$76, 40 minutes; slow NT$49, 50 minutes) leave every 20 minutes. Exit at Ruifang, go left (east) along the main road for 300m to Ruifang bus interchange, and catch bus 788 or 825 for the last 15 minutes to Jiufen/Jinguashi.

ℹ Getting Around

Buses from the direction of Ruifang train station stop at the Jiufen Visitor Information Centre, followed by Jishan Street (p144) just before the 7-Eleven, before continuing to Jinguashi. The two towns are 3km apart and served by buses every 10 minutes or so, or you can take a taxi between the two for NT$270.

Pingxi District

☑02

Despite Taiwan's heavily urbanised landscape, the north has retained much of its frontier past, where a slower pace of life prevails in the throwback settlements that dot Pingxi District – a wild, wooded gorge served by the Pingxi Branch Rail Line (平溪鐵路支線; Píngxī Tiělù Zhīxiàn). Along this picturesque valley you'll find thrilling hikes, high waterfalls, river pools, a cat village and the remains of what was a thriving coal industry.

The annual sky lantern releases around the first full moon after Chinese New Year, taking place in Pingxi town and Shifen, are a spectacle not to be missed.

Once a sleepy farming community whose residents grew yams and tea and harvested camphor, Pingxi was blasted into modern times with the discovery of 'black gold' in

1907: coal that is, not oil. By 1921 the Japanese Taiyang Mining Company had constructed the 13km Pingxi branch line from Sandiaoling to Jingtong, and there was hardly a moment's rest for the next 60 years. At the height of operations, 18 mines were open, employing over 4000 miners. About 80% of the town's residents made their living directly from the mines.

Conditions were bad, even by the appalling standards of most coal mining. The mine veins ran deep underground, and the narrow pits forced miners to work lying down, often naked because of the oppressive heat and humidity. By the 1970s cheaper foreign coal was already slowing down operations and by the mid-'80s mining ceased altogether in Pingxi. In 1992 the branch line was declared a scenic tourist line, thus saving it, and nicely the local villages too, from decay and closure.

ℹ Information

At the **Shifen Visitor Centre** (十分遊客中心, Shifēn Yóukè Zhōngxīn; ☑ 02-2495 8409; 136 Nanshanping, 南山坪136號; ⊙ 8am-6pm), near Shifen station, you can pick up English-language brochures and consult the large maps on the 1st floor.

ℹ Getting There & Away

BUS

Taiwan Tourist Shuttle buses (www.taiwantrip. com.tw; NT$45) run from Muzha MRT station (walk to the main road and cross for the bus stop) to Shifen Visitor Centre, with stops at Jingtong and Pingxi town every hour or so on weekdays and every 30 minutes on weekends. The last return bus leaves Shifen at 8.35pm.

TRAIN

Most visitors coming from Taipei travel first to Ruifang (NT$49, 40-50 minutes), then change on to the Pingxi Branch Rail Line. You can purchase a day pass for all stops on the line at Ruifang station (NT$80), which is more convenience than cost-saving. The last train back from Jingtong is 8:33pm.

Houtong

☑02 / POP 589

Spread over both banks of the Keelung river, this former coal-mining town is a scenic place to spend an hour or two as a prelude to riding the Pingxi line. The photogenic mining heritage, a mix of derelict and restored buildings, bridges and pits, is genuinely interesting, but... most folks come for the cats.

PINGXI SKY LANTERN FESTIVAL

Of all the ancient Chinese festivals, Pingxi's **Lantern Festival** (平溪天燈節, Píngxī Tiāndēng Jié; ⊘ Feb) has best been re-imagined for the modern age, with spectacular light shows, live concerts and giant glowing mechanical lanterns. Yet one of the best spectacles is still the most traditional: the release of the *tiāndēng* (天燈), or sky lanterns, which occurs en masse at regular intervals throughout the festivities.

A *tiāndēng* is a large paper lantern with a combustible element attached to the underside, that when lit causes the lantern to float into the sky like a hot-air balloon. In Pingxi people have been sending sky lanterns into the air for generations. Long ago, the remote mountainous villages were prone to attacks from bandits and marauders. Sky lanterns were used to signal to others, often women and children, to get packing and head into the high hills at the first sign of trouble. But today it's all about the sublime thrill of watching glowing orbs rising up against a dark sky.

The festival takes place on two or three weekends in February, one of which is likely to coincide with the Spring Lantern Festival (元宵節), which occurs on the 15th day of the first lunar month. The location alternates between Shifen and Pingxi town, so check ahead. During the festival, there are shuttle buses all day to the site, and the trains run later than usual. Just after sunset, lanterns are released en masse every 20 minutes or so until about 8.30pm.

If you wish to take part in one of the official lantern releases, you'll need to queue up and register on the day of the event – aim to seek out the registration desk on site by 10am (some people queue up from much earlier). As your lantern floats away to the heavens repeat your wishes to yourself...and pray your lantern doesn't burn up prematurely and crash down into the crowds, or light a tent on fire, as occasionally happens.

Over the past few years, the local township has allowed the sale and release of sky lanterns at any time, meaning the surrounding forests are dotted with the shells of spent lanterns. At least during the Lantern Festival there are clean-up crews, fire trucks are on hand to deal with any incidents, and it is also a very wet time of the year (making the risk of a forest fire negligible). During the rest of the year there are no such precautions, so act responsibly if you visit the area.

In recent years, Houtong (侯硐; Hóudòng) has become synonymous with its 'Cat Village', a large population of tame wandering strays who, thanks to government largesse, even have their own dedicated bridge.

◉ Sights & Activities

Cat Village VILLAGE
(貓村, Māocūn; ⊞ Houtong) Cross the 'cat bridge' out of the train station to hang out with Houtong's feline divas, who are well used to being doted on by tourists. Similar to Japan's cat islands, there are schmaltzy cat-themed souvenir shops and cafes arranged all over the hillside. Although the cats receive vaccinations, petting is discouraged, and there are disinfectant stations to wash your hands.

Houtong's cats have been central to this former coal-mining village's efforts to revive itself. Villagers here traditionally kept cats because houses were built on the hillside where rats were rampant. After the closure of the coal mines in the 1990s, locals moved out en masse and the area went into decline. Later, cat lovers organised efforts to take care of the strays, which attracted the attention of the media, and outsiders began dropping off unwanted felines here. Now there are estimated to be around 200 cats in the village.

Dacukeng
Historic Trail HIKING
(大粗坑古道, Dàcūkēng Gǔdào) This steep, two-hour ramble connects Houtong with Jiufen via the abandoned gold rush village of Dacukeng. To reach the trailhead from Houtong train station, cross the Coal Transportation Bridge then turn left at the Houtong Mine Site. After 800m you'll see a sign for the hike in Chinese (next to an English sign for the 'Jinzibei Historic Trail').

ⓘ Getting There & Away

The best way to get here is by train, with direct services from Taipei Main Station (1 hour, NT$56).

It's possible to hike between Houtong and Jiufen (2-3 hours) on the Dacukeng Historic Trail (p147).

Sandiaoling

02 / POP 15

The first stop on the Pingxi Branch Rail Line and Taiwan's only station unreachable by car, Sandiaoling (三貂嶺; Sāndiāolǐng) is a charming relic of a village nestled in a bend of the Keelung River. The main reason to alight here is to hike to the trio of waterfalls on the well-marked Sandiaoling trail, but spare half an hour to grab a selfie on the old railway bridge and a coffee in the delightful Hytte Cafe.

To get to Sandiaoling, exit the station and follow the tracks south until they split. Cross underneath the tracks and bear right.

Activities

Sandiaoling Waterfall Trail HIKING
(三貂嶺瀑布步道, Sāndiāolǐng Pùbù Bùdào)
Once part of a trade route between Yilan and Taipei, this well-marked trail passes three beautiful cascades through the up-stream watersheds of the Keelung River. It takes about 2½ hours up and back down, or you can continue along trails and sweet backcountry roads all the way to Shifen station and the 40m-wide Shifen Waterfall, the broadest fall in Taiwan.

The trailhead is well-marked in Sandiaoling village. The first waterfall is the 40m Hegu Falls (合谷瀑布; Hégǔ Pùbù; Joining of the Valleys Falls), which you can view from a distance. After that you can get up close to two 30m falls in quick succession that look almost identical: Motian Falls (摩天瀑布; Mótiān Pùbù) and Pipa Dong Falls (枇杷洞瀑布; Pípádòng Pùbù). You can go behind Motian via a cave formed by the overhang: it's like something out of *The Last of the Mohicans*. Pipa Dong also has a ledge at the top that lets you get behind for great photos.

Drinking & Nightlife

Hytte Cafe CAFE
(113 Yuliao Rd, 魚寮路113號; ⊙11am-5pm) Born from the vestiges of a derelict mining cot-tage, this delightfully hip hangout should be a mandatory stop before or after tackling the Sandiaoling Waterfall Trail. Enjoy pour-over coffee, homemade cakes and cold beer in a gorgeously upcycled space with railway

sleeper flooring and foliage sprouting from the ruined stone walls.

ⓘ Getting There & Away

The first stop on the Pingxi Branch Line, San-diaoling can be reached by direct train from Taipei Main Station (NT$59, 1 hour, hourly). Trains run hourly from Sandiaoling to other stops along the line.

Shifen

02 / POP 956

With its creaking suspension bridges, water-fall trails and old houses hugging the rail-way tracks, Shifen (十分; Shífēn) is easily the most charming stop along the Pingxi Branch Rail Line, and the most popular with visi-tors. It's the only place left in Taiwan where the trains trundle so close to the buildings, and the nostalgic scene seems to tug at people's heartstrings, no matter where they come from.

The town mushrooms in size each year for the Pingxi Sky Lantern Festival (p147), but like in Pingxi town, tourists come in their droves to launch sky lanterns here all year round.

⦿ Sights

Shifen Waterfall Park WATERFALL
(十分瀑布, Shífēn Pùbù; ⊙9am-4.30pm) FREE
Taiwan's 'Little Niagara' can be glimpsed as you chug past on the Pingxi Branch Rail Line, but to get up close to the coun-try's widest, if by no means tallest, falls it's a well-marked 30-minute walk downriver from Shifen train station, taking you over suspension bridges with lush valley views. En route, keep a lookout for peculiar kettle holes worn into the limestone riverbed.

Sleeping

★ Louzicuo Guesthouse GUESTHOUSE $$
(樓仔厝民宿, Lóuzǐ Cuò Mínsù; ☑0966-502 503, 0989-190 160; https://louachu.okgo.tw; Lane 74, 3 Shefen St, 十分街74巷3號; d from NT$2300) Perched on a ledge facing the handsome Jingan suspension bridge, this rambling, century-old house is the best place to stay along the Pingxi Branch Rail Line. Rooms are rustic and tastefully decked out, and a cafe-restaurant serves good if pricey meals, with lovely outdoor seating overlooking the river. Best of all, it's mere steps from Shifen station.

ⓘ Getting There & Away

Shifen train station is 15 minutes along the Pingxi Branch Rail Line from Sandiaoling (NT$15), with trains running every hour.

Jingtong

☑ 02 / POP 284

The village of Jingtong (菁桐; Jīngtóng) marks the end of the Pingxi Branch Rail Line, and it has one of the best-preserved traditional train stations in Taiwan. With nearby coal carts, abandoned buildings strangled by roots, Japanese-era wooden houses and the old pit entrance on the hill above the station, it's a fun place to explore and take pictures. There's also some great hiking in the area.

🏃 Activities

Shulangjian Mt Trail HIKING
(薯榔尖山步道, Shǔlángjiānshān bùdào) A favourite hike is up to the pyramid-tipped Shulong Point (薯榔尖; Shǔláng Jiān, 622m), Jintong's highest peak. To reach the trailhead from the train station, cross the tracks and climb to the first level. Head left, then bear right at the split and go up the narrow lane through tiny Er Keng village. The trail is signposted just past the village.

🛏 Sleeping & Eating

Hokkaido Guesthouse GUESTHOUSE $
(北海道民宿, Běihǎidào Mínsù; ☑ 0910-306 722; 1 Baishijiao, 白石腳1號; d midweek/weekends & holidays NT$1500/1800; ❄ 🛜) A former residence for railway officials, this Japanese-style inn with tatami-mat floors and futons makes for an atmospheric base. It's 300m down the hill from the station, overlooking the river.

Rongyuan Guesthouse GUESTHOUSE $$
(榕園民宿, Róngyuán Mínsù; ☑ 02-2495 2272; 8-1 Erkeng, 二坑8之1號; d NT$2000) This family-run guesthouse has pleasant doubles and views over Jingtong. Breakfast is included, and there's the option of a home-cooked dinner. Limited Chinese spoken. Find it up on the hill behind the large police station.

Jingtong Chongde Vegetarian VEGETARIAN $
(菁桐崇德素食, Jīngtóng Chóngdé Sùshí; ☑ 02-2495 1568; Jingtong station; dishes NT$70-190; ☺10am-5pm; ☑) Trains rumble right past the open door of this eatery run by a sweet old couple, a short stroll up the tracks from the station. Choose from vegetarian dishes like stir-fried greens, bamboo rice, and stewed oyster mushrooms with rice or noodles. And finish with a mug of sour-sweet kumquat tea.

ⓘ Getting There & Away

It takes 40 minutes to ride the length of the Pingxi Branch Rail Line from Sandiaoling to Jingtong (NT$19), with trains running every hour.

Pingxi Town

☑ 02 / POP 270

The old mining settlement of Pingxi town (平溪; Píngxī) feels slightly less touristy than Shifen, with an 'Old Street' that even has a few local shops among the snack vendors as it nears the Keelung River. Like Shifen, Pingxi town is most famous as a launch site for *tiandeng* (天燈), otherwise known as sky lanterns, which visitors purchase from shops and launch into the stratosphere (usually from the railway tracks) all year long, and not just during the Pingxi Sky Lantern Festival (p147). Visitors are also drawn here to scramble up the Pingxi Crags.

🏃 Activities

Pingxi Crags CLIMBING
(平溪岩, Píngxī Yán) These 450m-high crags require you to scramble up metal ladders and steps hewn into the rock for vertigo-inducing views. No technical skill is needed, but it's an adrenaline rush nonetheless. The trailhead is across the Keelung River from Pingxi train station. Cross the bridge from Pingxi Old Street and turn left. Look for the stairs beside a trail map.

ⓘ Getting There & Away

It takes 35 minutes to ride the Pingxi Branch Rail Line from Sandiaoling to Pingxi (NT$16), with trains running every hour.

Fulong

☑ 02 / POP 1984

Fulong Beach, one of the few stretches of golden sand in northern Taiwan (elsewhere it's an ashy charcoal colour), is the main reason visitors make their way to this unprepossessing seaside town. Fulong (福隆; Fúlóng) also has opportunities for surfing, diving and other aquatic pursuits, while for landlubbers it's the start of several excellent cycle routes and hiking trails.

LOCAL KNOWLEDGE

PINGXI BRANCH RAIL LINE

This charming 13km narrow-gauge railway, built in the 1920s, is one of three still-operating branch rail lines from the Japanese era, alongside Jiji Line (Sun Moon Lake) and Neiwan Line (Hsinchu). The trio are the lucky survivors among the systems that lost their original functions as transporters of coal, gold, copper or building materials. Most never made it to the 1990s, when these lines were granted a new lease of life as tourist attractions. An exception is the Tamsui branch, which was developed into a metro line.

The Pingxi spur, extending deep into the former coal country of the northeast, was the shortest of the three and had the fewest passengers. The fact that it survived the demise of the coal mining industry in the 1980s had much to do with its location in the rugged Keelung River Valley. Steep mountains, a winding river and plunging gorges meant that it still had value as a means of transport for villagers, vendors, merchants and anyone whose presence was wanted in another town.

The Pingxi Line starts in eastern Keelung city, branches off the main east-coast trunk at Ruifang, and extends to Jingtong. The most interesting stops are Houtong, Sandiaoling, Shifen, Pingxi town and Jingtong. The entire ride takes about 45 minutes.

◉ Sights

Fulong Beach
BEACH

(福隆海水浴場, Fúlóng Hǎishǔi Yùchǎng; NT$100, NT$40 winter (no swimming); ⊙8am-6pm May-Sep) This 3km sweep of golden sand is the most popular beach in northern Taiwan. You can rent surfboards, kayaks, umbrellas and loungers along the beachfront. Check safety conditions – www.epa.gov.tw/en – before you visit. Fulong Beach is a five-minute walk from Fulong station. The waters are closed from October to May, but you can still access the beach.

🏃 Activities

Caoling Old Tunnel
CYCLING

(舊草嶺隧道, Jiù Cǎolíng Suìdào) This scenic bike jaunt passes through an old 2km train tunnel, cutting through the cape and emerging on the southeast side by the ocean. A coastal bike lane beside the highway (but secure against cars) then takes you back around the cape to Fulong, a 20km loop. Rent bikes from shops near the station; the route starts on the lane running east from the station.

Caoling Historic Trail
HIKING

(草嶺古道, Cǎolíng Gǔdào; Tsaoling) Built in 1807 to provide transport between Tamsui and Yilan, the old Caoling Trail, of which an 8.5km stretch remains today, rises up through wooded hillsides to high, grassy headlands overlooking the Pacific. It's a lovely day hike especially when combined with

sections of the adjoining Taoyuan Valley Trail which offers spectacular sea views. The two most common start and end points are at Fulong and Daxi.

If you start in Fulong, you can take a 10-minute taxi ride to the official trailhead, cutting out a stretch of road walking. The trailhead in Daxi is behind the Caoling Qingyun Temple, just north of the train station.

In recent times, a long addition was made to the trail called the Taoyuan Valley Trail (桃園谷步道; Táoyuángǔ Bùdào) – an emerald grassy bluff grazed by water buffalo and with panoramic coastal views. If you choose to tack on this extra section, it boosts the total length to 16km, taking 5-8 hours to complete.

The trails are well maintained and easy to follow, with signposts and maps (in English). Save the walk for the autumn or spring months; you'll roast at the top during summer, and in winter you'll understand exactly why there is a 10m-long boulder inscribed 'Boldly Quell the Wild Mists'.

Scubar
WATER SPORTS

(☑0981-949 927; 17-2 Dongxing St, 東興街17-2; ⊙11am-7pm) This PADI dive and water-sports equipment rental shop serves Fulong's smaller (free) beach. Scubar also doubles up as a relaxed American-style restaurant on weekends between March and October, serving burgers, poutine, veggie chilli, coffee, beer and cocktails, and excellent homemade ice cream. The restaurant stays open until 11.30pm on Saturdays.

✦ Festivals & Events

Hohaiyan Rock Festival   MUSIC
(貢寮國際海洋音樂祭, Gòngliáo Guójì Hǎiyáng Yīnyuèjì; https://hohaiyan.ntpc.gov.tw; Fulong Beach, Fulong village; 福隆村福隆海水浴場; ☉ Jul) FREE Since 2000, Fulong Beach has hosted the Hohaiyan Rock Festival, which has grown from a small indie event into the largest free outdoor concert in Taiwan, attracting hundreds of thousands over a three- to five-day period. 'Hohaiyan' is a tonal word connected to waves in the Amis language.

🛏 Sleeping & Eating

YMCA Fulong Campsite   CAMPGROUND $
(青年會福隆營地, Qīngniánhuì Fúlóng Yíngdì; ☑ 02-2763 1261; 54 Fulong St, 福隆街54號; dm from NT$300) A YMCA-run campsite right beside Fulong Beach, with 50 barracks-like dorm beds spread over several cabins. You can also rent their barbecue facilities without staying here.

Longmen Riverside Camping Resort   CAMPGROUND $
(龍門露營區, Lóngmén Lùyíng Qū; ☑ 02-2499 1791; www.lonmen.tw; entrance fee NT$100, 4-person sites incl tent from NT$1050, 6/8-person cabins from NT$3000) This 37-hectare campsite by the Shuangshi River has accommodation for up to 1600 people, a swimming pool, barbecue facilities and even paintball. To get here from Fulong train station, turn left at the main road (Hwy 2) after exiting the station. A lane running along the highway leads to the campsite, which is just past the visitor centre. The entire walk is about 10 minutes.

Fullon Hotel Fulong   RESORT $$$
(福容大飯店, Fúlóng Dà Fàndiàn; ☑ 02-2499 1188; www.fullon-hotels.com.tw/fl/en; 41 Fulong St, 福隆街41號; d incl breakfast from NT$11,880; P 🐾) With its distinctive turrets and beachside location, this cream-coloured behemoth has 187 spacious rooms (ask for a sea-facing balcony) and an outdoor pool complex with kids' facilities. An adjoining, resort-like villa has yet more rooms. Rates drop considerably between September and May.

Fulong Biandang   TAIWANESE $
(福隆便當, Fúlóng Biàndāng; Fulong St, 福隆街號; NT$60-80; ☉ 9am-7pm) Several shops all sell the same bento boxes outside Fulong train station. Choose from the standard Fulong bento (福隆便當; Fúlóng biàndāng) with pork, egg, tofu and veggies, the pork cutlet bento (排骨便當; páigǔ biàndāng),

or the chicken leg bento (雞腿便當; jītuǐ biàndāng). The last two sell out fast.

ℹ Information

The waters at Fulong Beach are officially closed from October to May, though you can still access the beach, which is usually pretty dirty at this time unless a crew has been in to clean it up.

The currents at Fulong can be treacherous in places, especially where the river flows into the sea. The Environmental Protection Agency (EPA; www.epa.gov.tw/en) recommends that people not swim for several days after a typhoon, as many contaminants get washed into the sea from the land.

During summer, the EPA makes regular announcements about the water quality here and at other beaches.

ℹ Getting There & Away

To get here from Jiufen, take a Taiwan Tourist Shuttle bus (Route 856, www.taiwantrip.com.tw, NT$50, one hour) heading to Fulong. Buses run hourly from 9am to 5.15pm weekdays and 8am to 4pm weekends.

Trains from Taipei to Fulong (NT$83, 1½ hours); leave every 40 minutes or so.

Toucheng

☑ 03 / POP 29,187

With its ragtag surf community, boulder-strewn beaches and cheap seafood markets, the coastal settlement of Toucheng (頭城; Tóuchéng) is a great place to tune in to a slower pace of life in northern Taiwan. The draw here is **Wai'ao Beach** (外澳海灘, Wài'ào Hǎitān; 230 Binhai Rd, Sec 2; 鎮濱海路二段230號) FREE, a beguiling sweep of black sand facing Turtle Island, and boasting its own surf school and hostel (p152). Local trains trundle up and down this stretch of coast, stopping at unmanned stations and adding to the slow travel vibe.

◎ Sights

Turtle Island   ISLAND
(龜山島, Gūishān Dǎo; ☉ 9am-5pm Mar-Nov) This captivating volcanic islet, 10km off the coast of Yilan, is less than 3km long yet rises up to 398m. Once supporting a population of 750 people, the island was taken over by the military in 1977 then returned to civilian rule in 2000. These days Turtle Island is a protected marine environment and access is very limited, though you can get close on a boat cruise from Wushih Harbour.

In addition to fantastic views from the highest point, the island also has numerous quirky geological features. These include underwater hot springs, volcanic fumaroles, and a 'turtle head' that faces right or left depending on where you stand.

If you just want to circle the island or whale- and dolphin-watch, you don't need permits but you should still make a reservation. Call the **Wushih Harbour Visitor Centre** (☏03-978 9078) or visit in person; it's a short taxi ride from Toucheng station or a 15-minute walk south along the boardwalk from Wai'ao station. Expect to pay around NT$1200 for a three-hour tour cruise or more for a combination cruise involving stops on the island and dolphin- and whale-watching (May to October). Whales are seldom seen, but dolphins are common in summer.

If you wish to land on the island you must apply in advance for a special permit. Download a copy of the application form from the Northeast & Yilan Coast Scenic Administration (p143) website and fax it, along with your passport information, three to 20 days before you wish to sail. Once you get your permit, ask for a list of boat operators and make a reservation (none speak English so ask the Scenic office for help). If you're staying at Rising Sun Surf Inn in nearby Wai'ao, staff can help arrange fast permits for the island.

Stand-up paddleboarding around the island is starting to become popular. Check out www.letsgoplay.com.tw for excursion opportunities (Chinese only).

Lanyang Museum   MUSEUM
(蘭陽博物館, Lányáng Bówùguǎn; ☏03-977 9700; www.lym.gov.tw/ch; 750 Qingyun Rd, Sec 3; 鎮青雲路三段750號; adult/child NT$100/free; ⊙9am-5pm Thu-Tue) Designed to imitate the area's cuesta rock formations, this stunning glass and aluminium-panelled structure is worth a visit for the architecture. Exhibits focus on the ecology and history of the Lanyang (Yilan) Plain, an alluvial fan formed by the Lanyang River. You can walk here from Wai'ao train station in 20 minutes. Cross the street and head right (south) along the boardwalk.

Honeymoon Bay   BEACH
(蜜月灣, Mìyuè Wān) The tiny coastal town of Daxi has a rocky surf beach known as Honeymoon Bay, where, depending on the swells, conditions are suitable for beginners to advanced surfers. You'll find board rental and shops selling food and drink around the beach. To get here from Daxi train station, cross the road and walk south for 600m along the sea wall.

Beiguan Tidal Park   NATURAL FEATURE
(北關海潮公園, Běiguān Hǎicháo Gōngyuán; 10 Binhai Rd, Sec 4, Toucheng; 頭城鎮濱海路10號) FREE This small seaside park has beautiful cuesta and 'tofu' block rock formations, as well as lookouts down the coast. Beiguan Tidal Park is halfway between Wai'ao and Dali, located around the Km127 point of Provincial Hwy 2. You can walk here in 20 minutes from Guishan train station.

🛏 Sleeping

★**Rising Sun Surf Inn**   HOSTEL $
(衝浪背包客棧, Chōnglàng Bèibāo Kèzhàn; ☏03-977 0933; www.risingsunsurfinn.com; 230 Binhai Rd, Sec 2, 鎮濱海路二段230號; dm/tw NT$550/1500; ❋☎; 🚉Wai'ao) Savour postcard-perfect views of Turtle Island from the balcony of this hostel and surf school right on Wai'ao Beach (p151), offering mixed and female-only dorms and one Japanese-style twin. Candy, the ocean-loving Taiwanese owner, knows the area's surf scene, hiking and other attractions in-

---

SURFING AT WAI'AO

Wai'ao is suitable for surfers of all levels nearly all year round; the main beach has a sand bottom. From November to March, northeast winds bring consistent 1.2m to 1.5m waves. From April to October, southerly and easterly tropical depressions bring 1m to 1.5m waves. Summer is a good season for beginners with 0.4m to 0.9m swells, but July to September pre-typhoon weather can occasionally bring 2m to 2.5m perfect barrels.

Rising Sun Surf Inn offers English surfing lessons (and rentals) by experienced coaches. Two-hour lessons including surfboard rental for the day and use of hostel showers cost NT$1500. Groups can negotiate a discount.

For swimming, there's no lifeguard so do so at your own risk, and stick to the beach areas across from the train station, watching for rogue currents.

side out. Simple meals like dumplings and acai bowls are available, along with breakfast.

Dali Yi Hostel HOSTEL $
(大里驛青年旅館, Dàlǐ yì Qīngnián Lǚguǎn; ☑ 0986-328 397; 317-2 Binhai Rd, Sec 6, 濱海路 6段317-2號; dm/tw NT$600/2000; ☎) Steps from Dali's train station, this hostel has spacious, modern dorms (some with sea views) and a shared kitchen. Ask for a room at the rear if you're bothered by road noise. It's a handy base for hikers, right by the trailhead of both the Caoling Historic Trail (p150) and the Taoyuan Valley Trail.

✖ Eating

★ Daxi Fishing Harbour SEAFOOD $
(大溪漁港, Dàxī Yúgǎng; 490 Binhai Rd, Sec 5, 濱海路五段490號; dozen oysters NT$200; ⊙ 10am-6.30pm, closed 2nd & 4th Tue of month) By buying at source in this two-storey food court beside Daxi's fishing fleet, you can gorge on everything from grilled oysters (生蠔; *shēngháo*) to sea urchin (海膽; *hǎidǎn*) to whole fish at bargain prices. The harbour is a 20-minute walk north from Daxi train station.

Most vendors will have the day's catch displayed in tanks to be grilled or fried, or you can buy direct off the boats and take it to the vendors yourself.

Abo Onion Pancake FOOD TRUCK $
(阿伯蔥油餅, Ābó Cōngyóubǐng; 59 Xiangxiang Rd, 纘祥路59號; from NT$35; ⊙ 10am-5pm) The onion-and-fried-egg pancakes (蔥油餅; *cōngyóubǐng*) sold from this truck on the right as you exit Toucheng train station are a local institution – crisp, pillowy and satisfying.

Kakahong CAFE $
(☑ 0920-519 993; https://kakahong.shopage. org; 34 Kailan East Rd, 開蘭東路34號; desserts NT$40-150; ⊙ 11.30am-7.30pm Thu-Tue (daily Jul & Aug); ☎🐾) 🖊 This cool cafe is the centrepiece of 'Happy Together', a creative community of surfers who operate businesses here to support their wave-chasing lifestyle. As well as great coffee, desserts and light meals, the cafe sells locally made products like woven surfboard bags and jewellery. It's a 15-minute walk from Toucheng train station.

🍷 Drinking & Nightlife

Drifters Pizza Pub PUB
(☑ 03-978 9488; 231 Binhai Rd, Sec 2, 鎮濱海路 二段231號; ⊙ noon-10pm Thu-Tue, to midnight

Sat; ☎) Duck in to this lively joint behind Wai'ao Beach (p151) for craft beer, cocktails and hand-tossed Italian-style pizza. Live music every Saturday and holidays. In the off-season (roughly November to March), Drifters opens on weekends only – check ahead.

ℹ Getting There & Away

Express trains from Taipei stop at Toucheng station (NT$184, 1¼ hours), with local trains also calling at Wai'ao (NT$119, 2 hours) and Daxi (NT$101, 1 hour 40 minutes).

ℹ Getting Around

Local trains (hourly) serve destinations up and down this stretch of coastline.

You'll find cheap scooter-hire shops outside Jiaoxi train station, ten minutes south along the rails from Toucheng.

NANAO
☑ 03 / POP 6147

The sleepy coastal town of Nanao (南澳; Nán'ào) spreads out on an alluvial plain between a black sand beach and rugged hillsides, and feels a long way from anywhere. River tracing and canyoning are just starting to take off in the remote mountain valleys here, and Nanao's 'mystery beach' with its sea cave is another draw, though the waters can be perilous.

◉ Sights & Activities

Taipingshan National Forest Area PARK
(太平山國家森林遊樂區, Tàipíngshān Guójiā Sēnlín Yóulè Qū; https://tps.forest.gov.tw; 58-1 Taiping Lane, Nanao, 太平巷58之1號; train NT$180; ⊙ 6am-8pm) This logging-area-turned-mountain-retreat offers easy forest trails along whimsical relics of old railway tracks, and countless lookouts over the snow mountains. Popular with Taiwanese families and retirees, an old logging train takes visitors from Taipingshan Villa (www.tps.forest. gov.tw), the sole accommodation here, to a nature area with boardwalk trails 3km away. If you don't have your own vehicle, it's easiest to visit Taipingshan on a whistle-stop day tour from Taipei or Yilan (www.taiwantour bus.com.tw, from NT$1100).

Nanao Mystery Beach BEACH
(南澳神秘海灘, Nán'ào Shénmì Hǎitān) Hemmed in by impassable cliffs, the black

ATAYAL NANAO

The Atayal settled in the Nanao region about 250 years ago, and throughout the late Qing period were successful in repelling Taiwanese advancement. It was not until 1910, after a five-year campaign by the Japanese to 'pacify' indigenous groups, that Taiwanese settlers were able to begin to develop the land for farming. These days the Atayal presence is still strong, and much of their traditional way of life, including hunting for deer and pigs, is visible as soon as you head off the highway.

sand beach running south of Nanao's river estuary offers dramatic coastal vistas. About 6km along the sand is a waterfall and large sea cave. Note that freak waves can be treacherous here – five people died in 2018, leading to a ban on beach buggies.

Jhaoyang Historic Trail   HIKING
(朝陽步道, Zhāoyáng Bùdào) This easy 2.2km forest hike, along part of a trail dating back to the Qing dynasty, has attractive bay views higher up. The trailhead is well marked just in front of the harbour, beside a row of seafood eateries and shops.

🛏 Sleeping

Nan-Ao Recreation Farm   CAMPGROUND
(南澳農場, Nánào Nóngchǎng; ☑ 03-988 1114) FREE This 64-sq-km campsite is clean, green and free-= of charge. There are shaded sites and hot showers (from 5pm to 10pm). It's a 3km march from Nanao station along Nanao South Road, turning right after you cross the river. From the campground, follow the river to the sea and you'll eventually reach a long black sand beach called Nanao Mystery Beach (p153), which has dramatic views along the rocky coastline.

Man Xueyuan   B&B $
(迎日小築慢學院, Yíngrì Xiǎozhú Màn Xuéyuàn; ☑ 03-998 1858; 23 Xinxi Rd, 新溪路23號; NT$1000 per person) Once serving as digs for railway workers, this stone bungalow has been converted into three comfortable apartments, each with two or three twin bedrooms and a common area for breakfast (included). It's best suited to those with transport, but the owners can collect guests from Nanao train station, or you can walk from tiny Wuta train station close by.

🍴 Eating

Pu Yan Chili Hunter   ICE CREAM $
(樸豔, ☑ 03-998 2898; 276 Suha Lu, 蘇花路二段276號; 1 scoop NT$80; ⊗ 10.30am-7pm) Taro, peanut, green mango and many more ice-

cream flavours have been blended with the region's chillis at this modern store just up from Nanao train station (spot the chilli 'ladies' outside). Dusted with crumbled chilli cookies, it's a fire-and-ice sensation. All flavours have a non-chilli version too.

Good Eats Cafe   TAIWANESE $$
(好糧食堂, Hǎo Liángshí Táng; ☑ 0919-117 273; 13-1 Nan'ao Lu, 南澳路13-1號; meal sets from NT$250; ⊗ noon-8pm Sat & Sun; 🛜) English-speaking owner Pinyu presides over this cute cafe-restaurant with furniture hewn together by a local artist and funky hanging bottle lighting. Healthy Taiwanese meal sets might include fish from the harbour, mountain veggies, rice grown behind the restaurant and homemade sweet peanut tofu.

Although only open on weekends and holidays, Pinyu can sometimes fire up the wok in the week if you call ahead (and do also call ahead for vegetarian meal sets).

ℹ Getting There & Away

There are trains every hour or two to Nanao from Taipei (fast NT$304, 2 hours; slow NT$195, three hours).

HSINCHU & MIAOLI COUNTIES

Stretching from the coast to the foothills of the Snow Mountain Range, the neighbouring counties of Hsinchu (新竹; Xīnzhú) and Miaoli (苗栗; Miáolì) are just far enough away from Taipei that relatively few travellers set their sights on this region. But those who do come will discover Hakka towns, hot springs, mist-shrouded mountain temples and spectacular mountain scenery en route to Shei-pa National Park.

Ethnographically, Hsinchu and Miaoli Counties have large Hakka communities, reflected in the food you'll find in many small towns. It's good to familiarise yourself with some of the staples before heading out.

Atayal and Saisiyat peoples also live here in large numbers.

ⓘ Getting There & Away

Getting around the area by public transport is doable, but this is a region that really suits having your own vehicle. Trains go up and down the coast all day, while the Tourist Shuttle Bus (www.taiwantrip.com.tw) makes a few forays inland as far as Nanzhuang.

HSINCHU COUNTY

High Speed Rail Travel to/from Taipei costs NT$290 (40 minutes, every half-hour).

Tourist Shuttle Buses Route 5700 runs from the train and HSR stations to Shitoushan (NT$100, one hour). Route 5805 runs from Zhudong train station to Nanzhuang (NT$92, one hour).

Train Hsinchu County is on the main west-coast line, which connects Taoyuan city and Miaoli County, so there are trains via Hsinchu city and other stations to major cities. Trains frequently depart from Taipei (fast NT$177, 70 minutes; slow NT$114, 1 hour 40 minutes).

MIAOLI COUNTY

High Speed Rail Travel to/from Taipei costs NT$430 (50 minutes, every half to one hour).

Train Frequent trains leave Taipei (fast NT$255, 1½ hours; slow NT$164, 2¼ hours).

Hsinchu

03 / POP 434,674

The oldest city in northern Taiwan, Hsinchu (新竹; Xīnzhú) is booming, with palatial apartment blocks sprouting among Japanese-era heritage buildings and shabby '70s development. The town centre benefits from a handsome grid of canals bordered by shops and restaurants. Out on the coast, Hsinchu has a scenic ocean-side bike path, and a harbour with a lively restaurant and cafe scene.

Long a base for traditional industries such as glass- and noodle-making, Hsinchu leapt into the modern era in 1980 with the establishment of Hsinchu Science Park, a centre for semiconductors and tech modelled on California's Silicon Valley. Accounting for a hefty slice of Taiwan's GDP, it's also why foreign faces are relatively common in the city.

⊙ Sights

★ **City God Temple**　　　　TAOIST TEMPLE
(城隍廟, Chénghuáng Miào; 75 Zhongshan Rd, 中山路75號; ⊗6am-10pm; 🚌5, 10, 11, 20, 23, 28)

FREE First built in 1748, and masterfully restored in 1924, this Hsinchu landmark has the highest rank of all the city god temples in Taiwan, and is a splendid example of the fine work local artisans were capable of in the early 20th century. A wide selection of food stalls fills the courtyard by the temple entrance.

Examples of this work include the elegant structure itself, with sweeping swallowtail eaves, the shallow but vivid plafond ceiling, and the wealth of carved wooden brackets and beams: look for dragons, phoenixes and melons, as well as panels of birds and flowers (auspicious symbols when placed together). The *jiǎnniàn* (mosaic-like temple decoration) dragons on the roof are superb.

The temple is most lively during the seventh lunar month and on the 29th day of the 11th month, when the birthday of the temple god is celebrated.

Guqifeng Gallery　　　　GALLERY
(古奇峰民俗文物館, Gǔqífēng Mínsú Wénwùguǎn; Guqi Mountain; ☑03-521 5553; 66 Gaofeng Rd, Lane 306, 高峰路306巷66號; ⊙8am-5pm Sat & Sun) FREE If you're in Hsinchu on a weekend, don't miss this fantastic collection of treasures, which includes a four-poster bed of pure jade, dragon boats made of ivory, and even a dinosaur carcass. The artefacts, collected over a 20-year period, are maintained by Pu Tian Temple, on the slopes of Guqifeng about 5km south of town.

To get here, take a taxi from downtown (NT$250) or bus 20 from Zhongzheng Rd (p158), near the train station.

CYCLING AROUND NANLIAO HARBOUR

At Nanliao Harbour, 10km northwest of Hsinchu station, a bike-only route winds its way south through coastal forest and alongside a beautiful stretch of coastline. Consider heading out here for a late afternoon ride and then having dinner.

The BL15 bus takes 40 minutes to connect the harbour with downtown (p158). When you get off the bus, head across the parking lot towards a blue tower, both for the bike rental area and a pleasant enclosed section of harbour with a strip of good-quality eateries. The last bus back is at 8.40pm.

Hsinchu

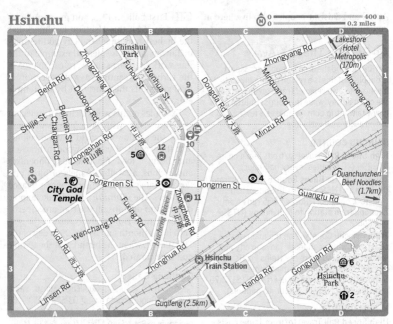

Hsinchu

Confucius Temple CONFUCIAN TEMPLE
(孔廟, Kǒng Miào; 289 Gongyuan Rd, 公園路289
號; ◎8am-5pm Wed-Sun; 🚌1, 2, 31) **FREE** First
built in 1810, this is one of Taiwan's most
elegant wooden structures. As with any temple, don't rush through: stand in place and

tiny treasures such as stone relief panels,
carved plinths, hanging woodcarvings, soft
painted beams and colourful mosaic dragons all begin to appear in rich detail.

The temple is a 15-minute walk from the
south entrance of Hsinchu station.

Hsin Chih-Ping
Residence HOUSE
(辛志平校長故居, Xīn Zhìpíng Xiàozhǎng Gùjū;
32 Dongmen Rd, 東門街32號; ◎10am-6pm Tue-
Sun) **FREE** With tatami floors, sliding screen
doors and antique furnishings, this beautifully preserved Japanese house was the residence of school principal Hsin Chih-Ping
(Xin Zhiping). The school, once attached,
has since relocated to another part of town.
The residence is a five-minute walk east of
Hsinchu train station.

Municipal Glass
Museum MUSEUM
(玻璃工藝博物館, Bōlí Gōngyì Bówùguǎn; ☑03-
562 6091; www.hcccb.gov.tw; 2 Dongda Rd, Sec
1, 東大路一段二號; NT$50; ◎9am-5pm Tue-
Sun) In a heritage building on the edge of a
pleasant wooded park, this newly renovated
museum is dedicated to the local history
of glassmaking, an industry dating back to
1880. It's a 15-minute walk from the south
side of the train station.

Image Museum
HISTORIC BUILDING

(影像博物館, Yǐngxiàng Bówùguǎn; ☑03-528 5840; https://culture.hccg.gov.tw/en; 65 Zhongzheng Rd, East District; 中正路65號; NT$20; ⊙9am-noon, 2-9pm, Tue-Sun) This classical Roman-style building with Arabic details was Taiwan's first air-conditioned luxury cinema when it opened under Japanese rule in 1933. It now houses a cinema and the small Image Museum, which offers a slightly interesting look at Taiwan's image industry, if little else. The entrance to the museum is in a side lane.

🛏 Sleeping

Lakeshore
Hotel Metropolis
BUSINESS HOTEL $$

(煙波都會一館, Yānbō Dūhuì Yīguǎn; ☑03-542 7777; www.lakeshore.com.tw/en/metropolis; 177 Minsheng Rd, 民生路177號; s/tw NT$3600/4600; @🛜) This branch of the Lakeshore chain is not near the lake, but it is an excellent-value, midrange business hotel, with smart modern rooms and a great morning buffet spread. Discounts of up to 30% are available.

⭐Sol Hotel
HOTEL $$$

(迎賓大飯店, Yíngxī Dàfàndiàn; ☑03-534 7266; www.solhotel.com.tw; 10 Wenhua St, 文化街10號; d incl breakfast from NT$4500; @🛜) An upmarket hotel with a superb central location just across from the canal. Business-chic rooms are huge, and the breakfast buffet is bountiful. Great discounts can be found online.

🍴 Eating

The area around City God Temple (p155) has a lively food market and many small eateries nearby. The canal area is good for Japanese, barbecue and western fare. Hsinchu is particularly known for its meatballs (貢丸; gòngwán) and flat rice noodles (粄條; bǎntiáo).

⭐Duanchunzhen
Beef Noodles
NOODLES $

(段純貞牛肉麵, Duànchúnzhēn Niúròumiàn; ☑03-574 8838; 135 Jiangong 1st Rd, 建功一路135號; noodles from NT$80; ⊙11.30am-2pm & 5.30-8.30pm Tue-Sun; 🚌5608) Though some distance from downtown, the Chungking-style beef noodles (重慶牛肉麵; Chóngqìng niúròu miàn) here are a worthwhile pilgrimage for committed foodies. Just as hearty and full-flavored are the stewed beef noodles (紅燒牛肉麵; hóngshāo niúròu miàn), while beef noodles in tomato soup

(蕃茄牛肉麵; fānjiā niúròu miàn) are a tangy, non-spicy option. Expect to queue for a table. A taxi from the main train station (not the HSR) costs about NT$150.

Temple Duck Rice
TAIWANESE $

(廟口鴨香飯, Miàokǒu Yāxiāng Fàn; ☑03-523 1190; 142 Zhongshan Rd, 中山路142號; duck rice NT$70; ⊙10.30am-9.30pm) This clean and efficient little shop close to City God Temple (p155) serves tantalising Taiwan-style roasted duck shredded on a bed of rice (鴨肉飯; yāròu fàn). Embellish with a fried egg (煎雞蛋; jiān jīdàn) and a side of stir-fried water spinach (炒空心菜; chǎo kōngxīncài). The shop is 10 minutes on foot from Hsinchu train station.

🍷 Drinking & Nightlife

Zhangmen Craft Brewery
CRAFT BEER

(掌門, Zhǎngmén; ☑03-535 8816; www.zhangmenbrewing.com; 10 Wenhua St, 文化街10號; ⊙6pm-1am Mon-Fri, from 4pm Sat & Sun; 🛜) A relaxed, convivial craft beer bar with sophisticated bar snacks and an outdoor patio. Zhangmen's clientele is a mix of tech-industry types and Japanese businessmen.

Bar Fly
SPORTS BAR

(☑03-533 5939; 44 Ren'ai St, 仁愛街44號; ⊙7pm-3am, closed last Sun of month) A good place to sink cheap beers, shooters and party pitchers, this rowdy dive has English-speaking staff and a host of games including foosball, pool and e-darts. Bar snacks available. Look for the mural of the dreadlocked gentleman on the wall outside.

ℹ Information

Hsinchu City's website (https://culture.hccg.gov.tw/en) has listings covering the main attractions.

WINDSURFING

The water is not the cleanest along the west coast but conditions are great for windsurfing. For lessons and rentals contact Spot X-Sport (www.spot.com.tw), 20km down the coast from Nanliao Harbour. It also has backpackers-style lodging in the Jhunan Seashore Forest Park (假日之森, Jiàrì Zhī Sēn), 100m from the sea in a quaint little hamlet.

ℹ Getting There & Away

Hsinchu is connected to Taipei by both regular trains and High Speed Rail (HSR). While the latter is faster, Hsinchu's HSR station is 10km outside the city and requires further connections to reach the centre. The regular express train from Taipei is arguably a better option because Hsinchu train station is right in the heart of the city.

High Speed Rail (HSR) Travel to/from Taipei costs NT$290 (40 minutes, every half-hour). At Hsinchu, exit the station and take a train from the adjacent Liujia Station to Hsinchu train station (NT$16, 20 minutes, every half-hour). A taxi from Hsinchu HSR station to the city centre should cost NT$300.

Train Hsinchu is on the main west-coast line so there are trains to all major cities. Frequent trains leave Taipei (fast NT$177, 70 minutes; slow NT$114, 1 hour 40 minutes).

Bus Tourist Shuttle Buses Route 5700 runs from the train and HSR stations to Shitoushan (NT$100, one hour). Route 5805 runs from Zhudong Train Station to Nanzhuang (NT$92, one hour).

ℹ Getting Around

BUS

Bus to Guqifeng (Zhongzheng Rd, 中正路) Hsinchu Bus Company operates Route 20 (NT$15, hourly) from Zhongzheng Rd a few minutes north of Hsinchu train station.

Bus to Nanliao Harbour (Zhongzheng Rd; 中正路) Hsinchu Bus Company operates Route BL15 (NT$15, every 15 minutes) from Zhongzheng Rd, just north of Eastern Gate (東門; Dōngmén; Dongmen Roundabout, 東門圓環).

TAXI

Roaming taxis are not numerous in Hsinchu. Get your hotel to call for a taxi before you head out, and hang on to the number of the driver you've found.

HEARTY HAKKA

Beipu is almost 90% Hakka, and in just about every restaurant you'll find Hakka staples explained with picture menus. Try mountain chicken (土雞; tǔ jī), fried tofu and kèjiā xiǎochǎo (客家小炒; stir-fried strips of pork, squid, veggies and tofu).

Smaller shops sell a variety of good goods. Around town you will also find vendors selling léi chá (擂茶; pounded tea) flavoured ice cream.

Beipu

✓ 03 / POP 9408

The small Hsinchu County town of Beipu (北埔; Běibù) pulls in the visitors with its Hakka cultural heritage, and makes for a pleasant morning or afternoon excursion when travelling to or from Shitoushan. There's an authentic feel to the town, and it's one of the best places to try Hakka pounded tea. Beipu is small and easy to navigate. The bus drops you off in the heart of things.

⊙ Sights

Jiang A-sin Mansion   HISTORIC BUILDING
(姜阿新古宅, Jiāngāxīn Gǔzhái; ✆ 0978-992 425, 03-580 3586; peterhbwu@gmail.com; 10 Beipu St, 北埔街10號; NT$50; ⊙10am-5pm Fri-Sun) This sumptuous mansion, built in the late 1940s, served as the home and reception hall of wealthy Beipu tea merchant and county councillor, Jiang A-sin. It was designed by Taiwanese architect Peng Yuli (彭玉理), who took inspiration from western-style Japanese architecture, and was built using the finest materials, as evidenced by the woodwork and the window embellishments.

Proportions may look a little off to the trained eye as measurements followed Chinese feng shui principles. Although only open to the general public from Friday to Sunday, you can visit from Tuesday to Thursday if you prebook a tour (minimum five people, NT$100 per person). Call or email Mr Peter Wu. The mansion is completely closed on Mondays.

Zhitian Temple   TEMPLE
(慈天宮, Cítiān Gōng; Citian Temple; ✆03-580 1575; 1 Beipu St, 北埔街一號; ⊙6am-7pm) FREE A charming traditional temple (c1835) dedicated to Guanyin. Notable features to look for include the carved stone pillars, both out front and especially within the main hall, which features tales in relief from *The Twenty-four Filial Exemplars*, a classic work promoting Confucian values.

🍷 Drinking & Nightlife

★ **Well Teahouse**   TEAHOUSE
(水井茶堂, Shuǐjǐng Chátáng; ✆03-580 5122; 1 Zhongzheng Rd, 中正路1號; ⊙10am-6pm) This delightfully antique Hakka home has stood here for well over a century, and makes for an atmospheric setting to sample the local staple of *léi chá* (擂茶, NT$100). *Léi chá* is

EMEI LAKE: HOME OF THE ORIENTAL BEAUTY

A short drive from Beipu, pretty Emei Lake (峨眉湖; Éméi Hú) serves as a reservoir for farmers growing Oriental Beauty tea. This highly oxidised oolong is renowned for several things: 1) Queen Elizabeth gave it its name; 2) it's completely lacking in astringency; and 3) it needs small crickets to bite the young shoots for the full flavour to come out.

When brewed, the tea is red in colour and has a naturally sweet and slightly spicy flavour. Like high-mountain oolong, it's one of those teas that is immediately appealing, and countries such as China and India are now getting in on the action. From what we've heard, most of what is sold in the area is actually grown in China. For real Oriental Beauty, it's best to shop in Pinglin.

While the tea is the lake area's claim to fame, visitors will most likely first notice an airport-terminal-sized (and -looking) monastery, and the 72m Maitreya Buddha Statue, built by the World Maitreya Great Tao Organization (www.maitreya.org.tw).

more like sweet porridge than tea – it actually comes with a cuppa on the side.

You can also have a try at making your own *léi chá* (from NT$300), which is cheaper the more people you do it with.

ⓘ Getting There & Away

From the Hsinchu High Speed Rail (Exit 4), catch Tourist Shuttle Bus route 5700 heading to Lion's Head Mountain (www.taiwantrip.com.tw; NT$60, 40 minutes, hourly). The first bus is at 8.19am. The last bus back is 5:17pm.

Trains run daily from Hsinchu train station to Zhudong train station every 10 to 20 minutes between 6am and 10.45pm, from where you can also pick up the Tourist Shuttle Bus or take a taxi (about NT$200).

Nanzhuang

☑ 03 / POP 10,156

A former logging and coal-mining area, Nanzhuang (南莊; Nánzhuāng) is set in the foothills of the Snow Mountains, one of the most enchanting regions in northern Taiwan. Little seems to have changed here since Japanese times, and many streets and villages have retained their signature clapboard facades. The food is also varied, reflecting the diverse ethnic make-up of the residents: Hakka and Taiwanese as well as indigenous Taiya and Saisiyat.

◎ Sights

Nanzhuang Village   VILLAGE
(南庄; Nánzhuāng) The village of Nanzhuang is a low-slung time warp of clapboard houses, shops and tourist stalls that makes for a great couple of hours strolling. Osmanthus

Lane (桂花巷; Guìhuā Xiàng), an impossibly narrow alley packed with stalls selling Hakka food, tea and snacks flavoured with sweet osmanthus, is just behind the main drag.

Saisiyat Folklore Museum   MUSEUM
(賽夏族民俗文物館, Sàixiàzú Mínsú Wénwù Guǎn; ☑ 03-3782 5024; 25 Xiangtian Lake, Donghe village, 東河村向天湖部落; NT$30; ⊙ 9am-5pm Tue-Sun; ☐ 6658, 6659, 6664) On the shore of Xiangtian Lake, this museum is dedicated to the Saisiyat (賽夏族) and their intriguing Festival of the Short People (賽夏族矮靈祭; Sàixiàzú Ǎilíngjì; the Pas-ta'ai Ritual). The Saisiyat ('the true people') are one of the least populous indigenous groups in Taiwan, some 5000 in number. Buses to the lake and museum leave from the visitor centre.

The Festival of the Short People is held in honour of the Ta'ai, a mythical pygmy race. According to legend, the Ta'ai and Saisiyat once lived in peace, but after the Ta'ai began molesting Saisiyat women they were killed off. Famine resulted and the festival arose as a way of appeasing the vengeful spirits who were clearly at the root of the disaster.

The festival takes place at Xingtian Lake on a full moon around the 15th day of the 10th lunar month every two years, with a particularly large event held every 10 years.

Luchang Village   VILLAGE
(鹿場, Lùchǎng) High-altitude Luchang Village is in a stunningly beautiful setting reached via a deep canyon road 15km southeast of Nanzhuang village. There is no bus here, so you'll have to take a taxi from Nanzhuang if you don't have your own transport. A few kilometres further up the road is the trailhead to the 2220m-high Jiali Mountain (加里山; Jiālǐ Shān).

ℹ WHAT & WHERE TO EAT

For meals, head to Osmanthus Lane in Nanzhuang village (p159) or to one of dozens of restaurants off the main roads, which usually have set meals of four to five dishes for two people for NT$400 to NT$500. Locally raised trout is popular.

Xiangtian Lake   LAKE

(向天湖, Xiàngtiān Hú; Hsiang-Tian Lake) Often swathed in mist, this small, high-altitude lake (738m) is sacred to the Saisiyat people. Buses to here leave from Nanzhuang Visitor Centre.

🛏 Sleeping

Pu Yuan Villa   GUESTHOUSE $$

(南江璞園, Nánjiāng Pú Yuán; ☎ 03-782 5925; www.037825925.com.tw; 31-8 Dongjiang, Nanzhuang 3rd village, 3鄰東江31之8號; d from NT$3500; ☎) Just outside Nanzhuang village is this old-fashioned guesthouse with large rooms and a garden setting. Breakfast included. To get here, take the Tourist Shuttle Bus from the visitor centre heading to Xiangtian Lake (p159) and get off at the Dongjiang He Tribe bus stop.

ℹ Information

Nanzhuang Visitor Centre (南庄遊客中心, Nánzhuāng Yóukè Zhōngxīn; ☎ 03-782 4570; www.trimt-nsa.gov.tw; 43 Datong Rd, 大同路43號; ⊘ 8.30am-5.30pm; ☎)

ℹ Getting There & Away

Nanzhuang is best visited from Shitoushan, but if you want to come directly, catch Tourist Shuttle Bus route 5805 from Zhudong train station. Buses (NT$92, 45 minutes) run roughly hourly from 8.20am to 5.20pm. The last return bus is at 6.20pm.

ℹ Getting Around

Nanzhuang is ideally suited to biking or driving. With only a couple of roads running through the region, orienting yourself is easy. County Rd 124甲 makes a big loop off Provincial Hwy 3, covering most of Nanzhuang. If you take a side trip up Township Rd 21苗 to Qingquan Hot Spring, you will have seen everything.

Scooters (per day NT$500) can be rented on the main street in Nanzhuang with an international driving permit.

Shitoushan

ELEV 492M

Beautiful, dense forests and rugged rock faces define the topography of Shitoushan (獅頭山; Shītóushān), a foothill on the border of Miaoli and Hsinchu Counties. But it is the temples here, built into recesses in the sandstone slopes since the late 19th century, that have given the place its fame. Shitoushan is sacred ground for the island's Buddhists and draws big weekend crowds, with people coming to worship or simply enjoy the beauty and tranquillity of the mountain. Give yourself at least three hours to explore the area, or an overnight stay for the full effect.

👁 Sights & Activities

★**Quanhua Temple**   TAOIST TEMPLE

(勸化堂, Quànhuà Táng; www.lion.org.tw; ⊘ 8.30am-5pm) FREE The only Taoist temple on the mountain, Quanhua Temple (c 1897) is dedicated to the Jade Emperor. The elaborate main hall is built into a recess in the sandstone cliff face, overlooking Futian Temple below. From here you can take in a dazzling landscape of soaring swallowtail ridgelines and vivid decorative dragons, carps and phoenixes on the tapering temple eaves.

Futian Temple   BUDDHIST TEMPLE

(輔天宮, Fǔtiān Gōng; ⊘ 8.30am-5pm) FREE This temple is dedicated to the Ksitigarbha bodhisattva, one of the most beloved divinities in Japan (where he is known as Jizō). One level lower down the mountain from Quanhua Temple, Futian Temple is reached via an arched gate up a set of stone stairs from the main car park.

Shitoushan Historic Trail   HIKING

(獅頭山古道, Shītóushān Gǔdào) Starting from the Visitor Centre (p161), this 4km climb on a paved road passes Buddhist temples cut into the hillsides. The walk itself is nothing special until Wangyueh Pavilion, the highest point, where a stone stele marks the Miaoli and Hsinchu county line. Here you can rest up and enjoy country cooking and cold beer, then it's an exciting downhill ascent to magnificent Quanhua Temple.

🛏 Sleeping

Quanhua Tang Lodge   LODGE $

(勸化堂, Quànhuà Táng; ☎ 03-782 2563; www.lion.org.tw; tw NT$1200) Visitors (including non-Buddhists) are allowed to stay overnight in neat twin rooms attached to Quanhua Temple. The old rules forbidding talking during meals or couples sleeping together are no longer enforced, but do be on your best behaviour. The staff at Lion's Head Mountain Visitor Centre can help you book.

Excellent vegetarian meals are included in the rate; if they don't appeal to you, check out the stalls and shops lining the back car park or the cafe on the way up to the hall. The office where you check in if you are spending the night is beside Futian Temple.

ℹ️ Information

Lion's Head Mountain Visitor Centre (獅 頭山遊客中心, Shītóushān Yóukè Zhōngxīn; ☑03-580 9296; 60-8 Liuliao, Qixing village, Emei township; 峨眉鄉七星村六寮60-8號; ⊙8.30am-5.30pm) has trail maps and is the start of several hikes. It's on the other side of the mountain to the main temples.

ℹ️ Getting There & Away

Bus From the Hsinchu High Speed Rail station (Exit 4), Tourist Shuttle Bus route 5700 goes to the Lion's Head Mountain Visitor Centre (www. taiwantrip.com.tw; NT$90, 1 hour, hourly). The first bus is at 8.19am. The last bus back is 5pm.

If you have your own vehicle it's better to head directly to the Quanhua Temple car park.

ℹ️ Getting Around

From the Lion's Head Visitor Centre you can catch the Lion's Head Mountain Nanzhuang Route bus (all day pass NT$50) to Quanhua Temple, the first stop.

Alternatively, you can hike the Shitoushan Historic Trail to the temple area, a two-hour uphill tramp on a tarmac road.

Shei-pa National Park

Home to 51 mountain peaks over 3000m high, Shei-pa National Park (雪霸國家公園; Xuěbà Guójiā Gōngyuán) boasts some of the finest alpine scenery in Taiwan, and a bevy of multiday mountain trails for experienced hikers. Trails like the scenic ascent to Snow Mountain, Taiwan's second-highest at 3866m, with cabins to bed down in en route to the summit. The less energetic, or those simply seeking an escape from the city, can bask in the crisp air and mountain vistas at Wuling Farm recreation area.

Established in 1992, much of the 768-sq-km national park remains inaccessible (in fact, prohibited) to ordinary travellers. The three sections you are permitted to enter are the forest recreation areas of Wuling, Guanwu and Xuejian. In the case of the first two, multiday trails from the recreation areas lead deep into the rugged interior of the park.

🔘 Sights

Wuling Farm FOREST (武陵農場, Wǔlíng Nóngchǎng; Map p163; ☑04-2590 1259; www2.wuling-farm.com.tw; 3-1 Wuling Rd, 武陵路3-1號; weekend/weekday NT$160/130; ⊙24hr; 🅿) Wuling Farm, also known as Wuling Forest Recreation Area (武陵國家森林遊樂區), is a relaxing mountain retreat

---

HIKING DABAJIANSHAN

The most famous climb in the Hsinchu area is to Dabajianshan (大霸尖山; Dàbàjiān Shān; Big Chief Pointed Mountain; 3492m). The barrel-peaked Daba is one of the most iconic high mountain images in Taiwan and is a sacred spot to the Atayal.

Hiking Dabajianshan takes three days to complete, including two overnight stays on the mountain in **99 Cabin** (九九山莊, Jiǔjiǔ Shānzhuāng; https://npm.cpami.gov.tw/en/bed_1.aspx) FREE at 2800m.

The route starts at **Guanwu Forest Recreation Area** (觀霧森林遊樂區, Guānwù Sēnlín Yóulè Qū; https://recreation.forest.gov.tw; Tai'an Township; 泰安鄉; ⊙7am-5pm). To begin, hikers walk a 19.5km (four to six hours) forestry road (closed to vehicles) to the old trailhead. This is followed by a 4km (three- to four-hour) hike to 99 Cabin. The next day, hikers leave 99 Cabin and hike 7.5km (four to five hours) to the base of Dabajianshan peak (you can't climb to the summit any more).

Most hikers return to 99 Cabin the same day, and then head back to Guanwu the following morning. But it is also possible to hike another three days from Dabajianshan to Snow Mountain along what is known as Holy Ridge (p162).

Because Dabajianshan is within Shei-pa National Park, mountain and national-park permits are required to climb it.

popular with Taiwanese families who come for the maples, cherry blossoms, crisp air and high-altitude vistas. During the spring cherry blossom season, the road from Yilan to Wuling is packed with cars, and there are daily limits on entry to the recreation area. Wuling is doable as a day trip from Yilan if you join a group tour operated by Taiwan Tour Bus (NT$1390, www.taiwantourbus. com.tw).

Taoshan Waterfall   WATERFALL
(桃山瀑布, Táoshān Pùbù) Known poetically as the Sound of Mist Waterfall, this 50m-high veil lies at the end of the Taoshan Trail. The 4.3km trail follows a paved footpath that takes a couple of hours to finish one-way. You'll only see why it's called Sound of Mist during spring and summer. In winter, the water flow is weak but you'll still enjoy a cool and invigorating hike through the forest.

Zhaofeng Bridge (兆豐橋; Zhàofēng Qiáo) a suspension bridge over the pristine Chijiawan

River is in a section of Wuling Farm that's celebrated for its beautiful, cherry-blossom-lined walkways. There are a couple of hostels (p164) with uninspired buffet dining here if you wish to spend the night. A better option if you can manage it is the campsite (p164) set high on a gorgeous alpine meadow.

🏃 Activities

★ O' Holy Ridge   HIKING
(聖稜線O型縱走, Shènglíng Xiàn O Xíng Zòngzǒu) The 'O' stands for the circular nature of this advanced, multiday hike (called 'Shengleng Trail' on the national park website), which begins and ends at Wuling Forest Recreation Area. It may also describe the shape of your mouth upon seeing some of the best high-mountain scenery in the country. The trailhead is on the path to Taoshan Waterfall.

This is not a trail for the faint-hearted or the inexperienced. You will be required to

Shei-pa National Park

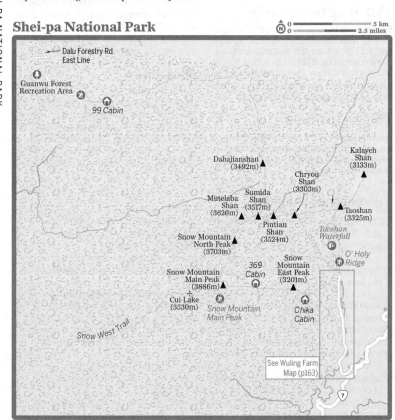

scramble up and down scree slopes, navigate narrow ledges with 1000m drops on either side, and use fixed ropes to climb vertical shale cliff faces. It's a grand adventure, but you need to be prepared.

After a hard push on the first day to the ridgeline, you never drop below 3000m for the next four days as you reach the summit of a half-dozen peaks, including grassy Chryou Shan (池有山; 3303m), crumbly Pintian Shan (品田山; 3524m), black-faced Sumida Shan (素密達山; 3517m), sublime Snow Mountain North Peak (雪山北峰; 3703m), and Snow Mountain Main Peak (雪山主峰; 3886m) on the last day. For a full description of the five-day hike see hikingintaiwan.blogspot.com.

The Holy Ridge (without the O) has several variations. The most popular is a linear path going from Dabajianshan to Snow Mountain.

Snow Mountain Main Peak   HIKING
(雪山主峰, Xuěshān Zhǔfēng) The first recorded climb of Snow Mountain was in 1915 – it was then called Mt Silvia, and is now also spelled Syueshan, Shueshan and Xueshan. Since then this sublime peak (Taiwan's second highest at 3886m) has attracted teams and solo hikers from all over the world.

The trail, from the **ranger station trailhead** (雪山登山口服務站, Xuěshān Dēngshānkǒu Fúwùzhàn; Map p163; www.spnp.gov.tw) in Wuling to the summit, is 10.9km and takes 9½ to 11½ hours to complete (one-way). Because of the altitude gain, and the fact that most people are carrying heavy packs, this usually requires two days (with a third for the return):

➡ Trailhead to Chika Cabin 2km, 1½ hours

➡ Chika Cabin to 369 Cabin 5.1km, five to six hours

➡ 369 Cabin to Main Peak 3.8km, three to four hours

The trail to the main peak is for the most part broad and clear, and requires mere fitness rather than any technical skill (unless you're going in winter). The first day's itinerary is always a bit tricky. If you have taken a bus and walked (or hitch-hiked) the 7.5km to the trailhead (2140m), then you aren't likely to get any further than **Chika Cabin** (七卡山莊, Qīkǎ Shānzhuāng; https://npm.cpami.gov.tw/en/bed_1.aspx) FREE the first night. Nor should you, as it's best to acclimatise at this elevation before going further.

Wuling Farm Area

The second day's hike is a long series of tough switchbacks (one is even called the Crying Slope). But the views on a clear day are stunning, and the landscape is ever-changing: from forested cover to open meadowland, to fields of Yushan cane. The box-fold cliff faces of the Holy Ridge are unforgettable.

At **369 Cabin** (三六九山莊, Sānliùjiǔ Shānzhuāng; https://npm.cpami.gov.tw/en/bed_1.aspx) **FREE**, a sturdy shelter nestled on a slope of Yushan cane, most hikers overnight, getting up at 2am so that they can reach the summit by daybreak. Unless you know the path to the top, it's really not advisable to do this.

So, assuming you get a reasonable start you'll soon be in the Black Forest, a moody stand of Taiwan fir. At the edge of the forest be on the lookout for troops of Formosan macaques. Note that the giant hollow before you is a glacial cirque formed by retreating ice fields.

It's another 1km from here to the summit along more switchbacks. The summit of Snow is rounded and requires no climbing to mount. But you'll want to linger here and take in the Holy Ridge and other surrounding peaks.

Hikers normally reach the summit of Snow and then return to the trailhead (and their vehicles) on the same day. You need to leave 369 Cabin no later than 6am to accomplish this before dark. For reference: from the Main Peak back to the trailhead takes about six hours (two hours back to 369 Cabin and a further four hours from there to the trailhead).

🛏 Sleeping

Before and after hikes you can sleep and eat at Wuling Farm, which has hostels and a campsite. On the trails, there are cabins at the end of each day's hike with bunk beds, eco-toilets, water, solar lighting and sometimes an outside deck. Cabins are unattended, so bring your own food.

Cabins often get snapped up on weekends and holidays, so book your spot (early) on the park's website (https://npm.cpami.gov.tw/en/bed_1.aspx).

Wuling Farm
Campground CAMPGROUND $
(武陵農場露營區, Wǔlíng Nóngchǎng Lùyíng Qū; Map p163; ☑04-259 01470; www.wuling-farm.com.tw; sites NT$500-1300, cabins NT$1600-2200;

⊙7am-9.30pm) Set high on a gorgeous alpine meadow, this campsite offers clean, modern facilities (including showers and a convenience store) with grass sites, platform sites and even platforms with pre-set tents. Sites come unpowered and powered. For ultimate comfort, try the little wooden cabins (without bath). Book up to three months in advance on their website. Discount of 10% on weekends.

Wuling National
Hostel HOTEL $$
(武陵國民賓館, Wǔlíng Guómín Bīnguǎn; Map p163; ☑ext 2001 or 2002 04-259 01259; 3-1 Wuling Rd, 武陵路3-1號; d/tw NT$3750/3420; 🕸) A comfortable place to stay, with forest views all around, the hostel (really a mid-range hotel) offers clean rooms that include buffet-style breakfast and dinner. The rather lacklustre, canteen-style meals here are also available for nonguests (NT$150-350).

ℹ Information

The park's main **headquarters** (雪霸國家公園遊客中心, Xuěbà Guójiāgōngyuán Yóukè Zhōngxīn; ☑03-799 6100; www.spnp.gov.tw; 100 Shuiwei Ping, Fusing village, Dahu township, 大湖鄉富興村水尾坪100號; ⊙9am-4.30pm Tue-Sun) are inconveniently located on the road to Tai'an Hot Springs, though there is a **branch** (雪霸國家公園武陵管理處, Map p163; www.spnp.gov.tw; 7-10 Wuling Rd, 武陵路7-10號; ⊙8am-5pm Mon-Fri) in Wuling Forest Recreation Area, the starting place for most hikes.

ℹ Getting There & Away

All hikes begin in the Wuling Farm (p161) section of Shei-pa National Park. Two Kuokuang Motor Transport buses (ww.kingbus.com.tw) leave daily from Yilan's bus station, a short walk from the back exit of the train station (route 1751, NT$283, three hours, 7.30am and 12.40pm). The return bus from Wuling leaves at 9.10am and 2.10pm.

There are also buses to/from Taipei (four hours) and Taichung via Lishan (seven hours).

Another option is to rent scooters in Jiaoxi and ride the 100km up to the park.

Eastern Taiwan & Taroko National Park

Best Places to Eat

➡ Meet Marlin (p184)
➡ Flower Space (p177)
➡ WaWa (p208)
➡ Mu-Ming (p177)
➡ Ba'le #1 (p176)
➡ Fugang Harbour (p198)

Best Places to Stay

➡ Wisdom Garden (p191)
➡ Leaf Inn (p176)
➡ Toro Oceanview B&B (p203)
➡ Ocean Skyline (p182)
➡ The Gaya (p196)
➡ Meni's Place (p207)

Why Go?

It was sightings of the east that led the Portuguese to call Taiwan *Ilha Formosa*, meaning 'Beautiful Isle'. Steep ridges of thickly forested mountains rise from the Pacific in wave after wave, often leaving only a narrow strip of oceanside land. Or none at all around the Qingshui Cliffs. Between the region's two main cities, Hualien and Taitung, the East Rift Valley provides an alternative north-south inland connection through a valley of rich agricultural land that's at its most picturesque in the expansive rice paddies around Chishang. Mountains, still being created by the pyrotechnics of plate tectonics, edge both sides of the valley, where geological activity also results in several hot springs.

Regional highlights are exploring mountain canyons, cycling the quiet country lanes and meeting the indigenous peoples who give the east a unique cultural appeal. That's most visibly evident on the highly distinctive island of Lanyu.

When to Go
Hualien

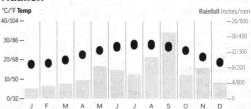

Mar & Apr
Low-season prices; temperature is comfortable pre-summer humidity, but windy.

Jun–Sep Festivals are at their most active, but heat can be draining and typhoons possible.

Sep–Jan Best months for cycling, challenging surfing season.

Eastern Taiwan & Taroko National Park Highlights

1 Taroko Gorge (p169) Getting beyond the tour-bus viewpoints in Taiwan's most celebrated area of spectacular canyonland.

2 Sixty Stone Mountain (p187) Zigzagging up past a monastery viewpoint, through thick woodlands and onto rolling upland fields that blaze orange with blooming lilies in August.

3 Chishang (p192) Meandering through the rice fields and lakesides on gentle, bucolic cycle rides.

4 Moonlight Inn (p185) Surveying the happening little artists' and surfers' getaway of Dulan from this Japanese-style forest cafe.

5 Lanyu (p204) Circumnavigating Taiwan's most culturally distinct island.

6 Grand Cosmos Spa (p189) Wondering whether you've been transported to Las Vegas from the old hot springs area of Ruisui.

7 Amis Folk Centre (p181) Watching the moon rise during a sunset concert from a park that combines contemporary art and indigenous thatched architecture.

History

Archaeological remains found in the Baxian Caves, south of modern-day Shihtiping, date the first human habitation on the east coast as far back as 30,000BC. Settlements at Beinan (Taitung) and in the hills above Dulan recall a culture that was still essentially Neolithic around 3000 years ago, and the region remained isolated and primarily indigenous until the late 19th century. To the Taiwanese, this was the 'land over the mountains', a land essentially cut off from the rest of the island. It was only in the Japanese era that Hualien and Taitung were connected to the railway network, after which the east was gradually opened to fishing, logging, gold mining, tobacco growing and sugar production. Taitung was also built up as an air and naval base for the Japanese empire's expansion into the Pacific.

During the 1950s, further transport connections, including two cross-island roads (now both defunct), helped enable a fresh round of immigration. But today, although the east coast comprises about 20% of Taiwan's land, it remains home to only 3% of the population, around a quarter of them indigenous.

✿✰ Festivals & Events

East Coast Land Arts Festival   CULTURAL
(東海岸大地藝術節, Dōng Hǎi'àn Dàdì Yìshùjié; www.teclandart.tw; ⊙ May-Sep) Every year, ephemeral, contemporary sculptures made out of mostly natural materials appear in public spaces along the east coast, notably at Duli's Amis Folk Centre (p181), where there are also concerts on full moon nights combining sound and vision as the moon rises over the sea during performances.

Amis Harvest Festival   CULTURAL
(阿美族豐年祭, Āměizú Fēngniánjì; ⊙ Jul-Sep) Taiwan's largest indigenous festivities involve much song and dance, with ceremonies to welcome and send away spirits.

The festivals take place in many parts of Hualien and Taitung counties. The exact dates vary from place to place and are chosen by tribal chiefs based on harvest times.

ℹ Information

24-Hour Toll-Free Travel Information Hotline
☑ 0800-011-765 888

Regional Tourism Info www.eastcoast-nsa.gov.tw

TAROKO NATIONAL PARK

☑ 03

Taroko National Park (太魯閣國家公園; Tàilǔgé Gúojiā Gōngyuán), the east coast's top tourist attraction, really puts the *formosa* (beautiful) into Taiwan's historic name. The park covers 1200 sq km, rising from sea level to over 3700m, incorporating 27 peaks over 3000m. Almost all Taiwan's bio-geographical zones are represented here, along with half the island's plant and animal species. But most visitors come to see just one area – the eponymous 18km-long gorge whose marble walls rise out of the blue-green Liwu River with a crowded backdrop of green mountainsides soaring above and several enticing hiking trails clinging to cliff edges. It's one of Asia's scenic wonders.

History

Taroko began as coral deposits, compressed beneath an ancient sea and transformed by aeons of geology into limestone and then marble, schists and gneiss. Some five million years ago, Taiwan started lifting from the sea as the Philippine and Eurasian plates collided. Water erosion then carved out softer deposits to leave the towering canyon walls of harder rock.

Humans are known to have inhabited the park as long as 3000 years ago. However, the ancestors of today's Truku (Taroko) indigenous tribe only began to settle along the Liwu River in the 17th century. The Truku were known for their hunting and weaving skills, the use of facial tattoos, and ritual headhunting.

The tribe lived in isolation until 1874 when the Qing began to build a road from Suao to Hualien to help open the area to

CLIMATE

Summers in the east are drier than in the north, which makes the area more suitable for outdoor activities, but June to October is steamy hot and typhoon season means that the coast can be frequently battered by severe storms. April and May are wet and warm, often overcast with winds that can interfere with hopper flights to Lanyu. Winters, while cold and damp in the mountains, can be fine and clear, and waters at Green Island are still likely to be warm enough for diving in wetsuits.

EASTERN TAIWAN & TAROKO NATIONAL PARK TAROKO NATIONAL PARK

Taroko Gorge

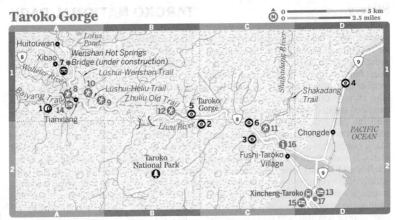

Chinese settlers. In 1896 the Japanese marched in looking to exploit the forestry and mineral resources. After a bloody 18-year struggle, they finally forced the outnumbered and out-weaponed Truku to submit, and most villages were relocated to the foothills or plains of Hualien.

The Japanese built roads and widened existing trails (using Truku labour) to form the 'Old Hehuan Mountain Rd' from the base of the gorge to Wushe in Nantou County. The road facilitated control over mountain tribes and the extraction of the area's natural resources. It also spurred the first wave of tourism in the area, with hiking becoming a popular activity by the mid-1930s.

In the 1950s the KMT extended the road west as part of the first cross-island highway. Many of the road workers later settled in the area, often marrying Truku women and becoming farmers.

As with Yushan National Park, plans to turn the Taroko area into a national park surfaced in the 1930s. WWII initially scuttled that idea and it was not until the 1960s that the KMT government began to draft a national park act. The park was officially established on 28 November 1986.

◎ Sights

Bulowan AREA
(布洛灣, Bùluòwān; ⊙ visitor centre 8.30am-5pm, closed 1st & 3rd Mon of each month) Nearing completion at the time of research, a breathtaking new suspension footbridge at Bulowan will soon cross the gorge, dizzyingly high above the river, for a dazzling new range of views. Bulowan itself is a twin-level shelf of almost flat land high above the main valley where a Truku mountain village once stood. Two exhibition halls tell some of that village's dramatic history; there is a great little nature walk with English explanations, and on the upper level is an upper-market cabin hotel run by Truku and celebrating their culture.

Bulowan is accessed by 1.7km of hairpins starting at Km179. Many but not all Taroko buses detour here en route to and from Tianxiang.

Taroko Gorge   AREA

(太魯閣, Tàilǔgé) This 18km marble-walled gorge is Taroko National Park's crown jewel. It's a must-see attraction whether you're hiking its trails, peering at its geological features or simply driving along the road that runs right through the middle (albeit much of the way in tunnels), wondering just how high are those mountains floating so vertiginously far above.

Xibao Viewpoint   VIEWPOINT

(Km106.5, Hwy 8) Driving beyond Tianxiang, the zigzagging road climbs steadily up through the forested mountainsides, with many appealing vistas. One of the best that also has easy parking is just after Xibao village at Km160.5, where there are a couple of very simple local cafes.

Qingshui Cliffs   AREA

(清水斷崖, Qīngshuǐ Duànyá; Chingshui Cliffs; Km178-157, Hwy 9) Very steep rock-and-forest mountainsides north of Taroko descend directly into the sea from several hundred metres' altitude. That means that roads and railways here are funnelled mostly through tunnels, but where they emerge briefly to cross side valleys or to run along ledges, drivers can catch glimpses of the coastline formations stretching far ahead.

The main 'cliff' zone stretches 21km between Chongde and Heren. Coming from Hualien on Hwy 9, the first cliff-viewing point is right at the Km176.4 lay-by (no coaches). If you continue through the long tunnel and stop at Km174.6, there's a much bigger parking area from which it's a six-minute walk down a section of old road to another series of views. If you're not driving (or on a coach tour), an original alternative offered by Hualien agencies is to join a sea kayaking group or to quad-bike along the beach from Chongde.

Eternal Spring Shrine   MEMORIAL

(長春祠, Chángchūn Cí) Picturesque for its setting, backed by toweringly steep mountainsides, this small shrine sits above a gushing spring that pours out onto the rocks below, creating what some have likened to a hoary old beard.

Most, but not all, southbound buses stop in a car park just off the main Rte8 from which there's a fine view of the shrine and two other associated forest buildings. A 2.2km loop walk takes you from here via a half-tunnel lane to the shrine, climbs up a very steep zigzag stairway to a cave, then cuts back through the forest past the Taroko Tower and Bell Tower (superb views) before crossing a rickety suspension bridge to the Chungchuang Temple. From the latter, a paved road leads back to a point just 150m short of where you started (via a tunnel – beware of traffic).

Swallow Grotto   AREA

(燕子口步道, Yànzi Kǒu Bùdào; Yanzikou; Rte 8, Km178) This half-kilometre slice of gorge-side old road twists and turns between rock-cut pillars and minitunnels, reminding visitors of how the Taroko route once felt for its entire length. Walking allows you to stare over the edge at geological features below, but the road is narrow and passing vehicles make the stroll less than relaxing. Try to visit before 9am or after 5pm to avoid the crush.

Due to the one-way system it's best to visit west-bound. When driving take the right fork at Km178 and beware that there's very limited parking nearby (what there is is at the far end of the access lane). By bus, use the Yanzikou stop.

Baiyang Waterfall   WATERFALL

(白楊瀑布, Báiyáng Pùbù) Falling a total of around 200m, this waterfall is in fact a pair of cascades, only parts of which are visible from the viewing bridge. To get there, you'll need to walk. The trail is 2.2km each way (allow two hours total) starting with a 380m unlit tunnel (bring a torch). That starts around 1km beyond the Tianxiang bus stop, with an opening in the concrete side of a road that is itself a semitunnel.

🏃 Activities

★ Zhuilu Old Trail   HIKING

(錐麓古道, Zhuī Lù Gǔ Dào; https://npm.cpami.gov.tw/en/open.aspx; access from Swallow Grotto, Rte8, Km178; permit NT$200; ⊘ starting time 7-10am, trail closes 6pm) Assuming you can get the gold-dust permit, this 3.5km out-and-back hike is likely to be one of the most spectacular accessible hiking paths you take in Taiwan. It's nicknamed the Vertigo Trail thanks to a section barely 70cm wide, passing along a ledge cut into the cliff face some 500m above the Liwu River.

The bird's-eye view of the gorge is spellbinding.

EASTERN TAIWAN & TAROKO NATIONAL PARK TAROKO NATIONAL PARK

TWO-WHEEL TAROKO

Cycling through the Taroko Gorge grows in popularity each year, but be aware that considerable sections of the main route are in tunnels, others can get narrow, and in holiday periods the road can get pretty busy with coaches. The ascent is fairly steady to Tianxiang (elevation 470m) and many riders make it there and back in a day from Xincheng-Taroko station where bikes can be rented. Alternatively Taroko Lodge (p171) offers various permutations of a drive-up/cycle-back bike experience.

For something far more challenging, masochistic riders can take Hwy8 all the way to Dayuling (75km) and on via Hwy14 to Hehuanshan, crossing the 3275m Wuling Pass, Taiwan's highest section of public road. Rewards, beyond the physical accomplishment, include world-class mountain vistas as your constant companion. At Guanyun (altitude 2374m), around 4km before reaching Dayuling junction, there's a handy hostel.

Numerous, now-classic spots allow walkers to take photos showing themselves in the seemingly most precarious of positions.

To limit numbers, permits are limited to only 96 on any given day. Apply online, ideally at 7am, 30 days before departure, then pay at the reception booth at Km178 if the trail is considered safe to walk that day. Note that, other than a short-stop lay-by opposite the fee window, and a few spots 700m further north, most parking is over 1km away. If no permits are available online for the date you require, you might still find a Hualien agency who can take you as part of a package.

Lüshui-Wenshan Trail   HIKING

(綠水文山步道, Lǜshuǐ Wénshān Bùdào) After the Zhuilu Old Trail (p169), this is Taroko's best day hike, a superb four- to five-hour tramp through subtropical forests with grand sweeping views down the peak-studded gorge. With few hikers about, you stand a good chance of seeing wildlife, including shy monkeys, barking deer, squirrels and various pheasants.

At the time of research, the bridge that connects Rte8 (at Km166) across the river to Wenshan Hot Springs (at the upper/western end of the trail) was being rebuilt, so check the route's status before assuming that it's open. At the east end, the trailhead is the same as for the Lüshui-Heliu (p171) walk. You need a mountain permit for this hike: apply on the same day at Tianxiang.

Baiyang Trail   HIKING

(白楊步道, Báiyáng Bùdào) This 2.1km trail, to a viewpoint surveying sections of the Baiyang Waterfall (p169), is one of the most popular short walks in Taroko National Park so start early. However, it's not ideal for claustrophobes as the walk starts with a 380m pedestrian tunnel which is unlit. Bringing a torch as well as an umbrella and raincoat is wise if you take the extra detour near the end to the Water Curtain Cave (水濂洞; Shuǐ Lián Dòng), where water gushes out of faults in a man-made tunnel, creating a scene that makes for popular selfies.

The Baiyang Trail's entry tunnel starts within a car semitunnel around 700m up the main road from Tianxiang.

Shakadang Trail   HIKING

(砂卡礑步道, Shākǎdāng Bùdào) This easy and well-maintained trail follows the deep-cut side valley of the crystal-clear Shakadang River. Watch egrets fishing in turquoise pools while cicadas and frogs compete to outsing stretches of gurgling rapids. The route is attractive right from the start, but it's worth going to at least Km2.4 to get a full sense of its beauty. Start very early to avoid the crowds.

The Wujianwu snack-shack at Km1.5 sells mochi (rice-based cakes) and particularly good sausages made with mountain pepper. At Km2 many visitors ignore the no-swimming signs and cool off in the turquoise waters. At a cabin known as Sānjiānwū (4.4km), the main trail ends but a branch climbs out of the valley towards the high, isolated hamlet of Datong (one homestay). It's also possible to do a very long loop back to Taroko National Park HQ via the somewhat bigger village of Dali. Though marked 'closed' on older maps, the Datong-Dali trail has in fact been open since 2019.

The start of any of these hikes is beneath the east end of the Shakadang road bridge on Hwy 8. Coming from the direction of the National Park Headquarters, that's on the right immediately after emerging from the first tunnel, but the bus stop and parking area are across the bridge. Traffic is eastbound only here.

If you're walking from the National Park HQ, you can avoid most of the road tunnel (except the easternmost end) by using the well-marked 1.1km Xiaozhuilu Trail to get to the bottom of Shakadang Bridge. Follow the metal steps down from the bridge to the river to access the path. There's a parking lot just past the trailhead.

Lüshui-Heliu Trail   HIKING
(綠水-合流步道, Lǜshuǐ-Héliú Bùdào) Part of the Old Hehuan Mountain Rd, this 2km trail runs above the highway along a cliff, with fantastic views of the Liwu River.

It starts behind a building at Km170.7 of Hwy 8. Although the route was damaged in the April 2019 earthquake with rockfalls burying and severely injuring two walkers, it was slated for rapid reopening at the time of research.

✹✹ Festivals & Events

Taroko International
Marathon   SPORTS
(太魯閣國際馬拉松, Tàilǔgé Guójì Mǎlāsōng; ☎03-856 0952; www.taroko-marathon.com.tw; ☉Nov or Dec) The gorge is one of the most beautiful settings for any major marathon. It attracts runners from all over the world, often selling out within a week of enrolment opening (generally late June).

🛏 Sleeping

Liwu Inn   HOTEL $
(立霧客棧, Liwù Kèzhàn; ☎hostel 0937-011 637, hotel 03-861 0660; www.liwu.hoseo.tw; 242-2 Fushi village; 富世村富世242之2號; dm/d incl breakfast NT$600/1400; ⊛🛜) This older hotel has a foyer of large rock-and-wood art and 19 large bedrooms with sashes on comfortable new beds and partly updated bathrooms. Separately managed within the same building, the LiWu Hostel (https://liwuhostel.wixsite.com/liwuhostel) has both bunk and mat-on-floor dorms with coin lockers outside to deposit your luggage if you arrive before check-in (3pm).

Kuan Yun Youth Activity Centre   HOSTEL $
(觀雲山莊, Guānyún Shānzhuāng; ☎04-2599 1173; http://kwan.cyh.org.tw; 22 Guanyuan; 觀雲 22號; dm/d incl breakfast from NT$500/2200) A remote but very handy overnight break for cyclists crossing Taiwan via Rte 8, this hostel sits at an altitude of 2374m, offering mattress-on-floor dorms or decent ensuite rooms, but (at least officially) guests should

be under 40 years old. It's 400m off the main road (Rte 8), some 60km west of Tianxiang.

Taroko Lodge   GUESTHOUSE $$
(嵐天小築民宿, Lántiān Xiǎozhú Mínsù; ☎0922-938 743; https://rihang.wordpress.com; 35-5 Minzhi, Xiulin township; 秀林村民治路35-5號; s/d incl breakfast NT$2000/2500; ⊛🛜) This hard-to-find place is very much a homestay in the old sense: three very ordinary rooms in a family home whose charm lies in the garden, tree-lined approach and wrap-around balcony that gives something of a Deep South US vibe.

The main draw is their drive-up, bike-back bicycle-rent service, a great way to visit the Taroko National Park on two wheels.

Though it is only around 600m west of Xincheng train station as the crow flies, the convoluted actual route is 2.1km via a double-back beside the big cement works, so you'll be pleased to be picked up by the hosts if you don't have your own wheels.

Liiko Hotel   BOUTIQUE HOTEL $$$
(立閣人文旅店, Lìgé Rénwén Lǚdiàn; ☎03-861 1969; www.liikohotels.com.tw/en; 63 Xinxing Road, Xincheng; 新城鄉新興路63號; d NT$3510-4300) One of the Taroko region's best options, Liiko Hotel offers top-quality rooms, English-speaking staff, an artistically contemporary foyer and unstuffy fine dining that combines international, Chinese and local flavours.

As you exit Xincheng train station, turn left (east) and walk 400m to Rte 8, and the hotel is the eight-storey tower on your left.

RIVER TRACING AT SANJHAN

The Sanjhan North River (三棧北溪; Sānzhàn Běi Xī) flows through a southern part of Taroko National Park that's disconnected from the main gorge area. Unlike the Liwu River Valley it remains almost entirely undeveloped as a visitor attraction. So to reach the waterfalls and deep, blue-tinted pools of its **Golden Canyon** (黃金峽谷, Huángjīn Xiágu; www.sanjhan.com/goldengrotto_en.shtml; Pratan Scenic Area, Sanjhan, 布拉旦風景區, 三棧溪), you'll need to be fit, agile and prepared to join a guided canyoning tour. Some Hualien agencies can help, but indigenous villagers are keen that you engage their own guides through the Pratan Visitor Centre in the village of Sanjhan.

Taroko Village Hotel CABIN $$$
(太魯閣山月村, Tàilǔgé Shānyuè Cūn; ☑03-861 0111; www.tarokovillage.com; 231-1 Fushi Village; 富世村231-1號; s/d incl half board from NT$4150/4900; 🅿❄🛜) Run by members of the Taroko tribe, in part as a way to illustrate their culture and history, this comfortable, low-rise resort consists of 18 two-room cabin-style buildings ranged around grassy lawns in the upper level of Bulowan (p168). The experience includes a full indigenous-cuisine dinner and dance show, and all around there are forests, wildlife and postcard-perfect mountain views.

🍴 Eating

HuHu's Restaurant TAIWANESE INDIGENOUS $$
(赫赫斯, Hèhèsī; ☑0905-136 071; https://huhus-restaurant.webnode.tw; 5 Minle, Fushi 9; 富世村9鄰民樂5號; set mains NT$250-290, wild boar NT$390; ⏱11am-1pm & 5.30-8pm; ❄🛜) This unpretentious but contemporary place in Fushi/Taroko village serves set meals with plenty of fresh local ingredients, giving an accessible introduction to regional cuisine.

The Mei Yuan $$$
(☑03-869 1155; https://taroko.silksplace.com/en/dining; 18 Tianxiang Rd; set lunch NT$550; ⏱noon-2pm) At the Silks Place Hotel (太魯閣晶英酒店, Tàilǔgé Jīngyīng Jiǔdiàn; ☑03-869 1155; https://taroko.silksplace.com/en/index; 18 Tianxiang Rd; 天祥路18號; d with half board from NT$8140; ❄🛜🏊), only guests can enjoy the dinner buffets but at lunchtime, when business is slow, the low-voltage Mei Yuan accepts all comers for artistically presented meal sets that combine local and international cuisines and give them a Japanese twist.

ℹ️ Information

Earthquakes, typhoons and landslides regularly affect which trails are open and a small number of visitors have been injured or killed in recent years from falling rocks.

TRUKU COOKING

Pork and especially wild boar is fundamental to Truku culture. Other key elements of local Truku cuisine include millet wine, bird's nest fern leaves (山蘇花; shān sūhuā), sticky rice cooked in bamboo tubes, and sausages spiced with maqaw (litsea cubeba; 山雞椒 shān jījiāo) – peppercorn-sized seeds with a citrussy tang of lemongrass.

Taroko National Park HQ (太魯閣遊客中心, Tàilǔgé Yóukè Zhōngxīn; www.taroko.gov.tw/en; ⏱8.45am-4.45pm, closed 2nd Mon of month) This centre has a busy cafe and bookshop but is most useful for information (in English) concerning the status of trails and condition of roads in the park. Grab free maps, hiking brochures and bus timetable leaflets.

ℹ️ Getting There & Away

Tours mostly start from Hualien, as do roughly hourly **Taroko Tourist Shuttle buses** (☑03-833 8146, 03-862 1100; www.taroko.gov.tw/en/Tourism/Timetable; NT$161 one way). If you're planning to return the same day, buy a one-day, hop-on/hop-off, multi-use ticket (NT$250) at the bus station window before boarding.

A good alternative is to head first by train to **Xincheng-Taroko station** (新城站, Xīnchéng zhàn; 4km south of the national park gate) where you can rent bicycles, scooters or motorbikes from a **shop** (車頭前機車行; 車頭前機車行, Chētóu Qián Jīchēxíng; ☑03-861 0215; 91 Xinxing, Xincheng; 新城鄉新興路91號; bicycle/scooter per 24hrs NT$250/400; ⏱7am-7pm) on the square out front that's happy to accept international licences. Taroko buses start from the same square, and Taroko Tourist Shuttle buses pick up here too.

TRAIN

Trains stopping at Xincheng-Taroko station (新城站, Xīnchéng zhàn) are mostly only the slower local Hualien-Yilan services running once or twice an hour, but there are a couple of daily direct trains to Taipei and beyond.

ℹ️ Getting Around

Even if you're happy to do long road walks, visiting Taroko on foot is not a great idea as there are long tunnels between some trailheads and distances are considerable. It's better to use buses to hop between them: if you keep the timetables to hand, getting around the park's key sights by bus is perfectly feasible.

Having your own wheels adds flexibility and the chance to continue into beautiful but little visited areas well beyond Tianxiang, where most tourists turn around.

Due to the one-way tunnel system, you should plan to see Swallow Grotto (p169) while heading northbound and the Eternal Spring Shrine (p169) southbound.

Reaching Taroko from western Taiwan is possible by a tortuously long, winding but very scenic road via Puli.

BUS

There are two main bus providers running through the park between Xincheng-Taroko station and Tianxiang (NT$84, 40 to 45 minutes):

> ### ℹ SCOOTER TO THE PARK
>
> If you want to see the gorge by scooter, renting from the square outside Xincheng train station makes more sense than from Hualien as the shop (p172) here is less fussy over foreign licences, rates are good and Xincheng is far nearer the national park.

Taroko Bus (302) Departs from Xincheng-Taroko every 50 minutes from 7.10am to 11.20am and 1pm to 5.10pm. The last return from Tianxiang is at 6.50pm.

Taroko Tourist Shuttle Bus (1133A) Starts from Hualien train station roughly hourly from 7am to 3.10pm, picks up passengers at Qixingtan then Xincheng-Taroko station (35 minutes after Hualien), then takes a further 45 minutes to reach Tianxiang. Last return is 5pm from Tianxiang.

Each service includes stops in both directions at the National Park HQ, Swallow Grotto approach and at Lushui, plus westbound-only at the Shakadang trailhead and eastbound-only at Changchun (the viewpoint for Eternal Spring Shrine). Only the Tourist Shuttle detours to Bulowan (westbound only).

In addition there are four further Hualien Bus (p180) services including the once-daily Hualien-Lishan bus (1141). East of Tianxiang, these accept passengers using the NT$250 Taroko Tourist Shuttle day pass, but Taroko buses require separate payment.

HUALIEN

📞 03 / POP 187,300

Hualien (花蓮; Huālián), together with its suburban twin Ji'an, forms the east coast's largest population centre. With a vast range of great dining, bargain-value lodging and transport possibilities, it's commonly used as a base for visiting the upper east coast, including Taroko Gorge.

The central grid of streets can feel rather formless, but is full of colour and life. Meanwhile, around Meilunshan Park (美崙山公園; Měilúnshān Gōngyuán) and the harbour area, you'll find landscaped parks and a riverside bike route leading to an oceanfront area with several boutique hotels. East, beyond an industrial district of marble cutters and cement factories, there's a more peaceful bay front area at Qixingtan.

⊙ Sights

★ Jing Si Hall
CULTURAL CENTRE

(靜思堂, Jìngsītáng; ☎ 03-856 1825; www.facebook.com/HualienJingSiHall; 703 Zhngyang Rd, Sec 3; 中央路3段703號; ⊙ 8.30am-5pm) FREE Built in 2000, this gigantic temple-cum-performance venue has a simple yet striking, white-and-grey exterior. At its tallest point, the building is equivalent to 11 storeys high. The main chapel-hall is enormous too, but what makes a visit worthwhile is the extensive and engrossing exhibition floor showcasing the remarkable range of charitable works undertaken by the Tzu Chi Buddhist organisation. Founded by the remarkable Buddhist nun Cheng Yen (p177), the organisation's efforts are underpinned by a combination of corporate professionalism with a belief that anyone can become a living bodhisattva (enlightened being) through good works. The hall is 1.2km northwest of the train station between Tzu Chi's equally huge hospital and its university.

Gangtiangong
TEMPLE

(花蓮港天宮; ☎ 03-856 0031; www.50015.com.tw; 15, Lane 500, Zhongshan Rd, Sec 1; 中山路一段500巷15號; ⊙ 5am-8pm; 🅿) Climb through a dragon's mouth into one of two spiral staircases that front this gigantic Matsu temple – the biggest in Hualien. There is particularly lavish ornamentation in the central shrine rooms.

It's nearly 3km north of the train station via Zhongshan Road, eventually turning east through a gateway opposite the Hualien Baseball Stadium.

Martyr's Shrine
SHRINE

(忠烈祠, Zhōngliè Cí; ☎ 03-832 1501; Linsen Rd; 林森路) Designed like an antique Chinese palace, this colourfully gabled 1980s complex is set amid lush foliage on a small rise overlooking Hualien's single most attractive scene.

It honours Kuomintang soldiers who died during the Chinese Civil War, but before WWII the site had been home to the 1915 Japanese-style Karenko Shrine (花蓮港神社; Huālián Gǎng Shénshè).

The access stairway climbs up through a *paifeng* (ornamental gateway) where Linsen Rd reaches a T-junction at its northeastern end after crossing the river.

Qixingtan
WATERFRONT

(七星潭, Qīxīng Tán) FREE Qixingtan (Chihsingtan) is a former fishing hamlet whose

Hualien

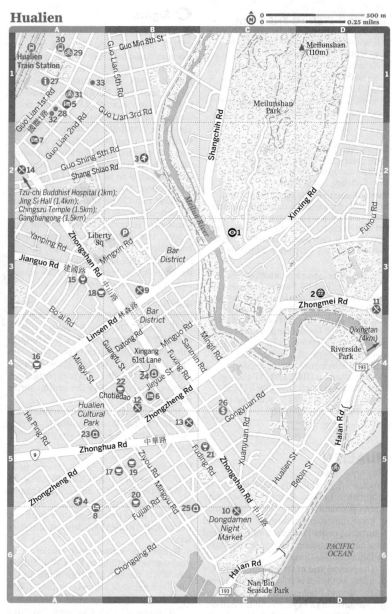

few remaining, old, tin-roofed shacks are outnumbered by a gaggle of small but fanciful hotels. The promenade is a popular place to stroll, cycle or picnic while admiring a very extensive curl of grey-shingle beach, though the strong currents make swimming here unwise.

Pine Garden

HISTORIC BUILDING

(松園別館, Sōngyuán Biéguǎn; ☑ 03-835 6510; http://pinegarden.com.tw; 65 Songyuan St; 松園街65號; adult/child NT$60/30; ☺ 9am-5.30pm) Set in a graceful garden that's all a-twitter with birdsong, this 1940s concrete building

Hualien

was used by the Japanese military to wine and pleasure their kamikaze pilots the night before their suicide missions. Such history is more interesting than the relatively limited gallery inside, but even if you don't go in, the attractive site is worth cycling past.

🏃 Activities

Hualien Outdoors WATER SPORTS
(☎0989-512 380; www.hualienoutdoors.org; 2-14 Guolian 5th St; 國聯五路2-14號) Canadian-run Hualien Outdoors offers customised river-tracing trips to Taroko Gorge and the Golden Canyon, as well as less challenging venues for those who just want a swim in crystal-clear waters surrounded by lush scenery. It also does trips to remote and wild hot springs.

Peace Diving WATER SPORTS
(和平潛水, Hépíng Qiánshuǐ; ☎03-832 6444, Kim Chang 0917-928433; www.facebook.com/peace.adventure; 341 Heping Rd; 和平路341號; ⊙8am-9pm) Organises scuba, river-tracing and snorkelling adventures, and also sells equipment.

👉 Tours

UniqueFun TOURS
(☎0966-780 607; https://uniquefuntw.com/?lang=en) Multi-activity provider used by several hotels and hostels.

IslandLife TOURS
(☎0978-045 868; www.islandlifetaiwan.com) English-speaking agency with a wide range of activity tours and an informative online guide to Hualien and the region.

🛌 Sleeping

Meci Hotel HOTEL $
(回然慢時旅居, Huírán Mànshílûjū; ☎03-836 1116; www.mecihotel201.com; 201 Guolian 1st Rd; 國聯一路201號; d NT$1400; ✲) With the youthful vibe of a hostel but the quality fittings of an upper midrange hotel, Meci is a great choice in the station area, with good beds, excellent showers and a pleasing bevvy of extras.

Bird House Hostel HOSTEL $
(花蓮鳥窩青年旅舍, Huālián Niǎowō Qīngnián Lûshè; ☎0906-970 166; www.facebook.com/birdhousehostel; 5 Guomin 5th St; 國民五街5號; dm/s/d from NT$350/580/820) Peaceful and less flashy than many competitors, this clean, pleasant station area hostel wins on its friendly family management, its bright, naturally lit dorms and its free-to-use bicycles that are alone worth the very reasonable rent.

Peace Prison Cafe Inn DESIGN HOTEL $
(和平公獄, Hépíng Gōngyù; ☎03-835 1009; 306 Heping St; 和平路306號; s/q from NT$700/1400; ⊙bar 4pm-1am; ✲ 🛜) Steel rebar, manacles

and taps fashioned from old petrol pumps give a striking image to the ground-floor pub which plays high-volume rap music. Upstairs, the prison theme continues, but rooms are remarkably comfortable at prices that are astoundingly reasonable for quality beds and good ensuite bathrooms.

★ **Leaf Inn** DESIGN HOTEL **$$**
(葉宿, Yè Sù; ☑ 03-822 2899; www.theleafinn.com/about-2; 55 Minsheng Rd; 民生路55號; d/q from NT$1998/2076; ⓟ❄☏) The Leaf absolutely nails it with a jazzy, artistic take on industrial chic that has miraculously transformed a seemingly hopeless monstrosity of 1960s concrete into an oasis of design-book cool.

Check in at the droolingly hip cafe which also serves beers and single-malt Nantou whiskey at a bar fronted by a collage of discarded piping...plus a half-size racing car. There's easy parking and bicycles are provided since the port area location is a tad out of the centre, beside the contrastingly grandiose Fullon Hotel, whose twin domes do a colour-changing turn at night. Prices change daily according to demand.

Cheese Bon BOUTIQUE HOTEL **$$**
(☑ 03-831 2092; www.cheesebon.com.tw; 74 Guangfu St; 光復街74號; d NT$1980-2480; ⓣcafe 11.30am-2.30pm & 5.30-8pm; ❄☏) As though tumbling out of a Tim Burton film set, Cheese Bon goes overboard with shutters and suitcases, upside-down lampstands and a giant metal clock face to create an enthralling yet adorably mellow architectural statement.

Hotel Bayview CASA PARTICULAR **$$**
(七星潭渡假飯店, Qīxīngtán Dùjiǎ Fàndiàn; ☑ 03-823 2443; www.hotelbayview.com.tw; 10 Mingtan St, Qixingtan; 大漢村明潭街10號; d NT$2480-3300; ❄@☏) While Qixingtan now has several suave new alternatives, Bayview remains hard to beat, especially if you score a seaview balcony room. There are blue shutters, model boats and tile-pattern floors, but the

Greek island theme isn't taken too far. Bed and cleaning standards are exemplary and staff speak fluent English.

✖ Eating

★ **Ba'le #1** TAIWANESE **$**
(芭樂一號, Bālè yīhào; ☑ 03-832 0862; 1 Zhunguo Rd; 建國路1號; meals NT$90-100; ⓣ11am-2pm & 5-7.30pm Mon-Sat; ☏) Vinyl, enamel advertising signs and ethnographic ornaments add even further to the character of this authentic yet unpretentious, century-old cottage where beautifully balanced bargain meals are a Hualien dining highlight.

Wang's Tea Lounge TAIWANESE **$**
(王記茶舖, Wángjì Chápù; ☑ 03-833 9388; www.wangs.com.tw; 565 Zhongshan Rd; 中山路565號; mains from NT$73; ⓣ8.30am-11pm; ❄) Open till late, Wang's serves delicious yet inexpensive meals in an enticing environment full of water features and glimpsed timbers. Design is a contemporary take on an old Japanese pavilion, staff speak English and the menu ranges from hotpots to ooling tea tofu to peanut butter toast. The red snapper rice bowl with sesame dressing is especially excellent.

Dongdamen Night Market MARKET **$**
(東大門夜市, Dōngdàmén Yèshì; www.dongdamen.com.tw; Bo'ai Rd;; ⓣ6pm-midnight; 🚌301, 301區) This extensive array of children's entertainments, live music and food stalls fills the pedestrianised lower ends of Bo'ai and Fuding roads south of Chongqing Rd, and is liveliest in the cross-street with its indigenous music stage area.

From the train station, catch bus 301 or use the 301區 electric tour bus which runs four times a night (6.05pm, 6.45pm, 7.45pm and 8.35pm).

Laozhou Dumplings DUMPLINGS **$**
(老周蒸餃小籠包, Lǎozhōu Zhēngjiǎo Xiǎolóngbāo; ☑ 03-835 0006; 4-20 Gongzheng St, Hualien;

EAST COAST CYCLING

The 180km route from Hualien to Taitung (p194) is the most popular long-distance bicycle ride in Taiwan, typically taking sport-cyclists at least three days. Using the coastal route, you're essentially forced to follow Hwy 11, which is scenic and has only one major climb (around Baci Viewpoint), but the road is becoming increasingly busy with trucks and speeding coaches so some riders prefer the quieter Rift Valley (p186) route. That offers several variants but the core choice is between fairly busy Hwy 9, which is wide and (mostly) equipped with a cycle-scooter lane, or more convoluted but far more peaceful route 193, adding in some sections of cycle-only trail along former railway tracks.

THE MAVERICK: CHENG YEN

Octogenarian Buddhist nun Cheng Yen (證嚴法師; Zhèngyán Fǎshī) is an iconoclastic made-in-Taiwan special. Her followers call her Shangren ('the exalted person') and consider her a living bodhisattva. But she's also a powerful and effective CEO, head of the worldwide Tzu Chi organisation (http://tw.tzuchi.org/en), the largest formal Buddhist charity in Taiwan, if not the Chinese-speaking world. With hundreds of thousands of lay volunteers, Tzu Chi has also been a leader in the development of hospice care in Taiwan, a major force in disaster relief, campaigner for recycling and the founder of a medical university that places a unique stress on the moral cultivation of physicians. The organisation believes in 'Living Buddhism', emphasising the joys of doing good to others rather than expounding on scriptures, as you'll learn if you visit their impressive Jing Si Hall (p173) in Hualien.

Born to a wealthy family in 1937, Cheng Yen sought comfort with local Buddhist nuns after the death of her businessman father. Aged 24, she made the extraordinary move of running away with another nun and spent the following years wandering the island, living in huts and caves, and studying scripture as a lay Buddhist. Cheng Yen's devotion and spirit caught the attention of the Venerable Yinshun, a major advocate of reformist humanitarian Buddhism. Yinshun took Cheng Yen on as his last student and helped her to become ordained. For the next year, the nun meditated, endured hardship and, according to her small number of disciples, performed 'miracles'. Two chance events set the stage for the formation of Tzu Chi. First Cheng Yen witnessed a poor indigenous woman die of a miscarriage. Then, soon after, in 1966, three Catholic nuns challenged her as to why Buddhist monks did not do charity work despite their concept of universal love. Spurred into action, Cheng Yen started a charitable society to help impoverished locals, initially funded by 30 housewives each pledging 50 cents a day, which they deposited in bamboo piggy banks.

By 1979, her group had grown large enough to attempt a ten-year project to build a hospital in then poor and mostly indigenous Hualien. With the lifting of martial law in the late 1980s, a new sense of freedom saw Taiwanese rapidly forming civil associations. Membership in by then well respected Tzu Chi expanded rapidly as the middle class began looking for a faith that didn't smack of superstition and perceived backwardness. Though hit in 2015 with a whiff of scandal over financial opacity and attempts to build on environmentally sensitive land (ironically to create a recycling centre), Tzu Chi remains highly regarded, an international organisation with millions of worldwide members, chapters in 57 countries, and assets worth billions of US dollars. For more information, read Julia Huang's 2009 book *Charisma and Compassion: Cheng Yen and the Buddhist Tzu Chi Movement*, available as a pdf on www.academia.edu

公正街4之20號; dumplings per portion NT$30-50; ⊙24hr) This modest shop has been whipping up delicious dumplings of all sorts, as well as noodles and soups, since 1975.

★ **Flower Space**　　　　VEGETARIAN $$
(花草空間, Huācǎo Kōngjiān; ☑03-831 4959; 140 Bo'ai St; 博愛街140號; meal sets NT$250; ⊙noon-2pm & 5-8.30pm Tue-Thu, noon-8.30pm Fri-Sun; 🅿🖋) Delicious vegetarian meal sets contain such a multiplicity of ingredients and subtle flavours that the menu can't keep up, but whatever you pick is likely to be superb. The setting is relaxingly calm amid dangling pot plants, fresh flowers and owl statuettes, with semiprivate dining spaces ranged around a centrepiece featuring the owner's extraordinary collection of handmade doll's house furniture.

Dou Sang　　　　TAIWANESE $$
(多桑, Duō Sāng; ☑03-832 9492; 2 Jungmei Rd; 中美路2號; dishes NT$180-300; ⊙6pm-midnight, closed Tue) Seemingly unchanged for decades, timber-walled Dou Sang is an unrestored time warp of a place full of old pop pin-ups, fading collages of business cards and benchseats perched at vinyl-covered wooden tables. Food is old-school Taiwanese, with local families coming to savour the nostalgic flavours their grandparents grew up with, but it's not set up for single diners or couples.

★ **Mu-Ming**　　　TAIWANESE INDIGENOUS $$$
(慕名; ☑03-823-9336; http://muming.tw; 23 Lane 10, Mingtan St, Qixingtan; 明潭街10巷23號; lunch NT$350-650, dinner NT$650-850; ⊙11am, 1pm, 5.30pm & 7.30pm) With a hearty 'Nga'ayho' ('hello' in Amis), Mu-Ming presents diners with a 90-minute, multicourse dining

STEEL PIPE TEA

A curious Hualien classic is steel pipe tea (鋼管紅茶; *gāngguǎn hóngchá*), served by pipes from upstairs, where it has been pre-made in bulk and rested for what is perceived to be extra flavour. There are three classic outlets: **Gangguan Heicha** (钢管黑茶, 201 Zongshan Rd, ⊙24 hr), **Liming** (黎明紅茶, 185 Nanjing St) and Miaokou.

experience full of flavour-packed indigenous creativity. Offerings change daily, the lack of a menu making ordering easy without language, but even the basic lunch is inventive and generous. Note that there are limited dining slots and you must usually reserve at least 30 minutes ahead. It's 5km east of Hualien station, set just back from the promgarden in the middle of Qixingtan.

Drinking & Nightlife

★ Caffe Fiore
CAFE
(咖啡花, Kāfēi Huā; ☑03-832 5172; 78 Zhongxiao St; 忠孝街78號; ⊙1.30-9pm Thu-Tue) This minuscule, triangular cafe lies half-hidden by foliage in a little wooden house so picturesque that they sell postcards of it. Beneath dangling bunches of drying flowers, sip excellent matcha lattes in the company of friendly felines.

★ Springfield Coffee House
CAFE
(春田咖啡屋, Chūntián Kāfēiwū; ☑0922-552 138; 209 Bo'ai Street; 博愛街209號; ⊙11.30am-6pm) The age-blackened timbers of this 70-year-old building complement mellow jazz and excellent barista coffee to create one of central Hualien's most restful cafe retreats.

Salt Lick
PUB
(Chicago; 火車頭 道地美式烤肉屋, Huǒchētóu Dàodìměishì Kǎoròuwū; ☑03-833 2592; www.facebook.com/lickbbq; 151 Zhongshan Rd; 中山路151號; ⊙11.30am-2.30pm & 5-9.30pm Sat-Thu, to 10pm Fri) Cowboy hats, lassos, Buffalo Bill portraits and framed lengths of 19th-century barbed wire give this diner-pub a Wild West theme, set to a soundtrack ranging from Bowie to Guns N' Roses. They serve barbecue ribs, deep-pan pizzas and Louisiana gumbo, but the big attraction is the blackboard listing of Taiwanese craft beers (usually five on tap).

Aboriginal Bistro
COCKTAIL BAR
(原醉酒餐館, Yuán Zuìjiǔ Cānguǎn; ☑03-832 3676; www.facebook.com/AboriginalBistro; 73 Jianguo Rd; 建國路73號; ⊙11.30am-1.30pm & 5.30pm-1am) The pasta and steak are excellent, but what makes this bar-restaurant stand out is its range of imaginative cocktails based around house-made 'makau wine' (local lemony pepper steeped in vodka) and cloudily viscous rice wine.

Maytreecoffee
COFFEE
(五月樹, Wǔyuèshù; 220 Shanghai St; 上海街220號; ⊙1-6pm) A veritable shrine for serious coffee lovers, this intimate place has several dozen fresh roasts (NT$150 to $500), which are listed on a board with detailed tasting notes. All are in Chinese but owner Lin, or enthusiastic fellow guests, delight in explaining. Opening days vary somewhat.

Black Whale Coffee
CAFE
(黑鯨咖啡, Hēijīng Kāfēi; ☑0953-428 861; 255-1 Linsen Rd; 林森路255-1 號; ⊙9am-7pm Mon-Sat, 2-6pm Sun) This small, two-floored cafe serves coffee from NT$80, with a good-value Baileys latte (NT$140) plus a small range of local ales, notably osmanthus-flavoured beer from Lanyu (NT$200).

Miaokou Black Tea
TEAHOUSE
(廟口紅茶, Miàokǒu Hóngchá; ☑03-832 3846; 218 Chenggong St; 成功街218號; ⊙6am-11pm Thu-Tue) This corner shop is famed for its 'steel pipe tea' (鋼管紅茶; gāngguǎn hóngchá; from NT$25), which is sent down to the serving counter via a system of tubes.

There are three variants: black, milk or caffeine-free almond tea (杏仁茶; xìngrén chá) with no real sign of tea in it whatever. To nibble, try one of three flavours of sponge finger 'macaroons' (NT$18) or perhaps a leaf-wrapped sticky rice parcel.

King Tang Cafe
COFFEE
(Golden Drip Cafe, 金湯達人咖啡館, Jīntáng Dárén Kāfēiguǎn; ☑03-832 2263; 431 Jung Shan Rd; 中山路431號; ⊙9am-6pm; ☎) In this relaxing cafe, you can watch the coffee beans being roasted as you sip drip-, syphon- or espresso-based brews sourced from a dozen different countries. Behind it lies a surprisingly extensive garden with a WWII-era air raid bunker.

Shopping

Da-Ai Technology
CLOTHING
(大愛感恩科技, Dà-ài Gǎn'ēn Kējì; www.daait.com/index.php/en/storesen; Jing Si Hall; ⊙9am-5.30pm) Da-Ai (meaning 'Big Love')

specialises in turning recycled PET plastic bottles into fabrics from which it creates lightweight garments, blankets, suitcases and even sunglasses.

A-Zone
GIFTS & SOUVENIRS

(www.a-zone.com.tw; 144 Zhonghua Rd; 中華路144號; ⊘ 11am-9pm Mon-Fri, from 10am Sat & Sun) It's not cheap, but spacious A-Zone presents a handy one-stop opportunity to browse a vast range of regional and Taiwanese products from leatherwork to millet wine, rice bran soap to origami figures of the country's 17 tribal costumes.

Stone Carvers Square
ARTS & CRAFTS

(石藝大街, Shíyì Dàjiē; cnr Bo'ai St & Chongqing Rd; ⊘ 3-10pm) Semiprecious stones, made into anything from tiny brooches to 500kg jade dragons, are sold from this photogenic series of stalls set in a small garden around a 1936 railway cottage.

Chihsing Tan Katsuo Museum
FOOD

(七星柴魚博物館; www.katsuo.com.tw; 148 Qixing St; 七星街148號; ⊘ 9am-6pm Thu-Tue) This modern showroom sells souvenir packs of various dried fish products, most notably *katsuo* (柴魚; dried bonito) flakes, which are an important condiment in regional cuisine. The shop's museum section is a preserved fish-drying building giving a passingly interesting, all-in-Chinese overview of the bonito industry in former times.

Hualien Daily
HOMEWARES

(花蓮日日, Huālián Rìrì; ☑ 03-831 1770; 37 Jieyue St; 節約街37號; ⊘ 11.30am-8.30pm) Stocks an appealing selection of ceramics, hand-sculpted wooden animal figures and distinctive art postcards.

Upstairs is an eight-room B&B (per person NT$1200 year-round). If you're attracted by 1960s nostalgia, the use of period furniture and pre-Beatles design styles might appeal, though if you're in your 50s or older, the feelings evoked might be more those of a secondary school classroom.

Adic Driftwood Workshop
HOMEWARES

(阿迪克工作室, Ā Díkè Gōngzuòshì; ☑ 0937-079 115; 360 Hai'an Rd, Ji'an township; 吉安鄉海岸路360號; ⊘ phone ahead) This Ji'an workshop is where celebrity sculptor Adic Chun Kuan Wang and his apprentices turn driftwood and other waste timber into unusual furniture, spoons, smartphone cases and especially artistic light fittings. DIY chopstick-making experiences take around two hours (NT$200+). The shop and workshop is an outwardly uninteresting metal box unit beside Rte 11, around 5km southwest of central Hualien.

Alternatively, it's 3km southeast from Ji'an train station. Adic (literally 'earthworm') is an honorific name in the Amis language.

❶ Information

Visitor Information Centre (花蓮觀光資訊中心, Huālián Guānguāng Zīxùn Zhōngxīn; ☑ 03-836 0634; http://tour-hualien.hl.gov.tw/en/TravelInformation/Visitor.aspx; 106 Guolian 1st Rd, Hualien; 國聯一路106號; ⊘ 8am-8pm) Professional tourist office with multilingual brochures and a left-luggage service (same-day only, NT$50). It's on the right as you leave the train station using the 'front' (east) exit. For tour packages, compare with other commercial operations.

Bank of Taiwan (台灣銀行, Táiwān Yínháng; ☑ 03-832 2151; www.bot.com.tw; 3 Gung Yuan Rd; 公園路3號; ⊘ 9am-3.30pm Mon-Fri) Changes money. Compare the rates with Mega Bank across the street.

Tzu-chi Buddhist Hospital (慈濟醫院, Cíjì Yīyuàn; ☑ 03-856 1825; http://hlm.tzuchi.com.tw; 707 Zhongyang Rd, Sec 3; 中央路3段707號; ⊘ 8am-5.30pm; 🚌 202) A hospital known for its excellent facilities, part of the greater Tzu-chi complex, 1km northwest of the train station.

❶ Getting There & Away

AIR

Hualien Airport is 500m east of Hwy 9 in Jiali, around 6km north of the city centre. Mandarin

EASTERN TAIWAN & TAROKO NATIONAL PARK HUALIEN

WATER SPORTS

River tracing (canyoning) is a popular option, with many beautiful rivers in the greater Hualien and Taroko areas. In summer, sea kayaking, stand-up paddleboarding (SUP) and whale-watching trips (per person NT$800) are all typically available at relatively short notice through various agencies. Peace Diving (p175) offers scuba training and sells masks and snorkels: a potentially useful purchase if you're heading to Green Island. While Hualien has beaches, for swimming you'll need to head around an hour's drive down the coast to Jici (p182). There are surf spots just south of Yanliao, but the scene is generally much further down the coast at Donghe and Dulan (p185).

Airlines flies to Kaohsiung (daily) and Taichung (three weekly). UniAir flies to Taipei twice daily, but the train is likely to be faster once you've added check-in and transfer times.

Hourly buses loop from the train station to Hualien airport in 40 minutes (NT$38), returning via Tzu-chi Hospital in just 20 minutes.

BOAT

TourKing (天海旅行社, Tiānhǎi Lǘxíngshè; 02-2515 6565; http://rera.tourking.com.tw; Wharf 23, Hualien Port, 66 Haian Rd; 海岸路66 號) catamaran ferries that link to Suao (adult/ bicycle NT$700/100, two hours) are more pleasure rides than practical transportation. Departures each way are at 10am and 4pm on Friday, Saturday and Sunday.

BUS

Buses depart from around the square that lies directly east of Hualien train station. Most **Hualien Bus Company** (花蓮客運, Huālián Kèyùn; 03-833 8146; www.hualienbus.com. tw) routes start from the northern side, including approximately hourly buses along Hwy 11 to Chenggong (routes 1127 & 1145) and the 9.30am service to Taitung (NT$520, 3½ hours) via Shihtiping and Dulan. However, the 2.10pm Diingdong (p199) bus 8119 to Taitung (NT$547, four hours) departs from the south side near the Visitor Information Centre, as do Tourist Shuttle buses and city bus 301.

TRAIN

Taipei Around 40 trains run daily from 6am to 10pm. Most take two to 2½ hours and cost NT$440. Six slower Chu-Kuang expresses (NT$340) take three to 3½ hours. Booking well ahead is wise, especially at weekends and other busy times.

Taitung NT$264 to NT$343, taking 1½ to 3½ hours. Departures are at 6.08am and 6.36am, then once or twice hourly from 8.23am to 10.20pm. Fastest services at 9.43am and 3pm.

For Kaohsiung, you'll often need to change in Taitung.

ⓘ Getting Around

Hualien is a little too big for walking but a little too small to have an extensive public transport system, so getting a bicycle or scooter makes a lot of sense while you're here.

BICYCLE

Some hotels and hostels lend bicycles to their guests. **Giant** (捷安特, Jiéāntè; 03-833 6761; giant.d21134@msa.hinet.net; 35 Guoxing 1st St; 國聯里國興一街35號; 9am-6pm Fri-Wed), one block from the train station's front exit, rents bicycles from NT$300 per 24 hours; more for advanced sports bikes. If you don't need the bike at night, you can save NT$100 on city bicycles by renting from **Lime** (单车柠檬, Dānchē Níngméng; 0911-928 385; 95 Guolian 1st Rd; 國聯一路95號; 8am-9pm) which offers eight-hour hires for NT$200.

BUS

Taroko Bus routes 301 and 302 cross the city (adult/child NT$23/12). Timetables are available on www.ropobus.com/route?area=6

CAR & MOTORCYCLE

There's a plethora of car hire agencies on either side of the train station, though even with an international driver's permit, some agents will not rent to foreigners. Although official rates typically start at NT$2400 per day, discount offers are rife, so NT$1800 is a better target price for short rents, or NT$1200 if you're planning several days' hire. Friendly agency **UB Car Rental** (聯邦租車, Liánbāng Zūchē; 03-8342333; www.uflc.com.tw; 37 Guoxing 2nd St; 國興二 街37號; 8.30am-8.30pm) offers better rates than many, especially for longer hires (10-day rentals from just NT$10,800 if you stick to the east coast region). Prices at **Pony** (小馬租車集 團; 03-835 4888; www.ponyrent.com.tw; 21 Guolian 4th Rd; 國聯四路21號; 8am-8pm) and **CarPlus** (0800-222 568, 03-831 6688; www.car-plus.com.tw; 117 Guolian 1st Rd; 國聯 一路117號; 8am-8pm) are generally a little higher, but they have more staff that speak fluent English.

Almost none of the major companies will rent a scooter to foreigners without a Taiwanese licence, but some hostels will, including **Rhino** (03-835 7333, Ophelia - Whatsapp 0988-709 389; www.rhinorentalcar.com; 129 Guolian 1st Rd, 國聯一路129號; call), or you can get electric scooters from many agents.

TAXI

There's a taxi rank slightly hidden to the left as you exit the train station's east ('front') exit. A 24-hour taxi service can be called on 0800-255 255.

BREEZY RIDES IN HUALIEN

A great way to see the city's gentler side is to take an easy cycle ride from the train station area along the riverside bike path down to the Nan Bin Seaside Park then along the waterfront to the night market area. Riding around Qix-ingtan (p173) is appealing, but getting there from central Hualien means a couple of kilometres through far less pleasant industrial areas.

CENTRAL EAST COAST

Between Hualien and Taitung, the coastline rarely has more than a narrow strip of flat land fronting countless layers of plunging mountainsides, painted deep green with thick forests and interspersed with minor patches of orchard and rice terrace.

Much of the appeal is stopping at assorted viewpoints, beaches and headlands to gaze out over the Pacific. Heavy seas make swimming unwise in most places, but there are fine surf spots between Chenggong and Dulan, most notably off Jinzun harbour near Donghe. Artists' retreat Dulan is by far the most western-oriented village, though you might not notice that at first glance.

⊙ Sights

Farglory Ocean Park   AMUSEMENT PARK
(遠雄海洋公園, Yuǎnxióng Hǎiyáng Gōngyuán; ☑03-812 3100; www.farglory-oceanpark.com.tw; 189 Yanliao village, Hwy 11; 花蓮縣壽豐鄉鹽寮村福德189號; adult/child/toddler NT$890/790/free; ☺9.30am-5pm Thu-Tue; ℙ) This family-oriented theme park combines Disney-style 'castle', cable car, Ferris wheel, log flume, rollercoaster and pirate ship along with some ocean-based educational elements. While hardly state of the art, queues for rides are modest (outside major holidays periods) and there are sweeping sea views.

It's around half-an-hour's drive south of Hualien. Exact timings can vary by season.

Amis Folk Centre   CULTURAL CENTRE
(阿美族民俗中心, Āměizú Mínsú Zhōngxīn; Duli Park, Km124.7, Hwy 11; ☺9am-5pm Thu-Tue, performances 11am & 2pm; ℙ) FREE On a convex grassy hillside amid trees both young and wizened, a series of contemporary outdoor sculptures add to wide sweeps of sea view. Down a stairway from the car park, beyond a large stone-stepped amphitheatre is a 'hamlet' of half a dozen reconstructed bamboo-and-thatch buildings giving a sense of Amis traditional living conditions.

Baxian Caves   CAVE
(Caves of the Eight Immortals, 八仙洞, Bāxiān Dòng; ☑089-881 418; Hwy 11, Km76.8; ☺8.30am-5pm; ℙ) Backing a pretty landscaped garden right beside Hwy 11 are a series of rocky cliffs cut into which are at least 30 natural caves and crevices. Within, archaeologists have found signs of human habitation from around 30,000 years ago: the oldest yet known in Taiwan. Learn more in the small visitors cen-

tre then climb stairs to the main caves, which are on two different levels.

Niushan Huting   ARTS CENTRE
(牛山呼庭, Niúshān Hūtíng; ☑03-860 1400; https://8898go.com/huting/; 39-5 Niushan, Shuilian Village; 水璉村牛山39-5號; entry NT$50, meal sets NT$200-350; ☺10am-5.30pm) This eccentric if unpolished beachfront complex attracts visitors with its comically naive collection of driftwood art formed into gruesome faces beneath a little avenue of broadleaf trees. You can recoup the NT$50 entry fee against drinks or surprisingly impressive meal sets that include Amis salt pork or decent vegetarian options.

The steep 1.5km access lane from Hwy 11 (Km26.6) is marked by a rough wooden gateway with a cow head signed 'The Forgotten Hometown'. It's possible to stay overnight whether camping (simple plots per person NT$150) or sleeping in driftwood cabins (d with shared shower from NT$1980/1200 weekend/weekday) but dine early: the restaurant's last order is at 5.30pm.

Tropic of Cancer Monolith   MONUMENT
(Km69.8, Hwy 11) Busloads of visitors stop at Km69.8, where a tall, white monolith marks the Tropic of Cancer, though probably, before seeing it, few had ever stopped to wonder much about that line's geographical significance. In fact it marks the line of latitude, 23°26'N, at which the sun is directly overhead at noon on the summer solstice (the year's longest day, 21 or 22 June).

🛏 Sleeping & Eating

Coconut Beach B&B   BOUTIQUE HOTEL $$$
(椰子海岸民宿, Yēzi Hǎi'àn Mínsù; ☑0952-404 521, 089-281 022; www.coconutbeach.com.tw; No 150 Hwy 11, Beinan, at Km150.5; 卑南鄉杉原150號(台11線150.5公里處); d/q/apt NT$4500/6000/7000; ℙ❋@☎) All nine rooms of this relaxed, upper-market guesthouse look out across flower-edged lawns (and the main road) to a palm-fronted stretch of coast. There's plenty of outdoor decking on which to relax and stargaze, and an expansive breakfast-bar room decorated with pebbles, elements of repurposed old wood and lamps like stylised insects. Having your own transport is essential.

Hadila   TAIWANESE $
(哈地喇小吃, Hādělǎ Xiǎochī; ☑089-831 085; 長濱鄉五鄰21號; 21 5th St, Changbin; mains NT$50-160; ☺11.30am-2pm & 5.30-7pm) It's the

roughest-looking old shack, with open sides painted green and red, but this utterly simple place run by an older couple in central Changbin is hard to beat as a budget lunch stop if you're passing by, especially for their excellent steamed gyoza dumplings.

🍷 Drinking & Nightlife

Moonlit Sea Cafe
CAFE

(月光海咖啡屋, Yuèguāng Hǎi Kāfēiwū; ☑089-841 005; Duli Park, Km124.7, Hwy 11; ☉10am-5pm Fri-Wed) With a lawn-fronted sweep of sea view, this serene cafe serves top-quality, handmade ice cream and brownies as well as great coffee and craft beers from the Route 11 microbrewery in Dulan. It's in the large park of the Duli Visitor Centre and Amis Folk Village (p181) and also sells a small but tasteful selection of souvenir items.

ℹ️ Getting There & Away

Access is by road from Taitung or Hualien.

BUS

From Guangfu Hualien Bus (p180) 1125 runs five times daily to Fengbin via Rte 11甲 (NT$67, 35 minutes)

From Hualien Roughly hourly Hualien Bus (p180) services run to Jingpu, some continuing to Chenggong.

From Taitung Diingdong Bus (p199) routes operate roughly hourly to Taiyuan, Chenggong or Jingpu, all driving via Dulan and Donghe. These are also stops on the Taiwan Tourist Shuttle bus linking Taitung to Sanxiantai via Chenggong.

Fengbin

☑03 / POP 4700

The little town of Fengbin (豐濱; Fēngbīn) sits on one of the most unspoilt stretches of Hwy 11, where layer upon layer of steep, green mountain plunges towards the Pacific surf. Traffic is relatively light and there are several places to pull over and admire the scenery. Much that's of interest is actually around 5km north in Xinshe (新社), aka Patarongen village, home to an artistically minded community of the Kbalan (Kavalan) indigenous community.

👁 Sights

Fengbin Skywalk
VIEWPOINT

(豐濱天空步道, Fēngbīn Tiānkōngbùdào; Km40.9, Hwy 11; adult NT$40; ☉9am-4.40pm; [P]) This short but memorable seascape experience includes a cliff-ledge walk where a 40m sec-

tion is along a glass-floored protruding shelf above the Pacific. The glass is now misting so you don't really see beneath your feet, but the gentle exhilaration of the walk is well worth the entry fee and warrants a 20-minute stop if you're driving by.

Return to your car or bike through a former road tunnel that now houses a coffee shop, snack-cafe and two unexpectedly upmarket souvenir shops. Access is from the slip road right beside the south end of the Xinfeng Tunnel (新豐隧道): look for 'Qinbuzhizi Maritime Ancient Road' signs.

Baci Viewpoint
VIEWPOINT

(芭崎眺望台, Bāqí Tiàowàngtái; Km31.55, Hwy 11) On a bend of Hwy 11, this small roadside rest stop has what is arguably the most beautiful panorama of the whole east coast. Leafy branches frame the perfect view down across Jici Bay, with the curving beach backed by further mountains and bays that melt into a misty infinity.

Patarongen Rice Terraces
SCULPTURE

(新社梯田, Xīnshè Tītián; Km42.8, Hwy 11, Xinshe village) The indigenous Kavalan people migrated to Patarongen (新社) from Yilan, settling on a nearly flat headland which they converted into terraced rice fields overlooking the ocean. Adding to the beauty of the scene is a curious group of bamboo creations by local artists, including a huddle of huts and straw figures.

🏃 Activities

Jici Beach
BEACH

(磯崎海濱遊憩區, Jīqí Hǎibīn Yóuqìqū; ☑03-871 1381; 6-1 Fengbin township, Hualien; 磯崎村6-1號; adult/child NT$100/50; ☉9am-6pm Jun-Oct) At the southern end of a long, attractive bay is a grey-sand pay-beach, one of only two considered safe for swimming between Hualien and Taitung.

🛏 Sleeping & Eating

★ Ocean Skyline
GUESTHOUSE $$

(☑0936-578 096, 03-879 1758; www.oceanskyline.tw; Km47.9, Hwy 11; d NT$3200-4000; q NT$4500-5000) Gaze across Pacific swells from the well-tended lawns of this high-quality family guesthouse where each of the five comfortable rooms has direct sea views. The decor favours primary colours softened with modern art and cuddly elephants. It's run by English-speaking classical musicians and is not listed on most booking sites, so you'll need to contact them directly.

Gamalan
SEAFOOD $$

(噶瑪蘭海產店, Gámálán Hǎichǎndiàn; ☐0955-085 151; Km43.1, Hwy 11; 42 Xinshe village; 新社42號; mains NT$200-550; ☺11.30am-1pm & 5-6.30pm Wed-Mon) Widely reckoned to be the Fengbin area's best restaurant, this seafood specialist is famed for its lobster. Less extravagant diners will find plenty of alternative seafood options, while the huge mixed vegetable plate (NT$200) is excellent and could feed two. A little English is understood but the menu is a blackboard with nothing but Chinese script.

🍷 Drinking & Nightlife

Laichu Haibien
COFFEE

(☐0937-167 966; www.goto-sea.com.tw; Km47.1, Hwy 11; ☺8am-5pm) Sip a cinnamon-dusted cappuccino or robust espresso on a semi-open terrace perched high above a stretch of rocky beach. Coastal views sweep north to a full-on soundtrack of crashing waves.

❶ Getting There & Away

Hualien-Fengbin and Hualien-Chenggong buses use Hwy 11, passing Baci Viewpoint, Jici Beach and the gateway for Niushan Huting (p181), though for the latter that would still leave a 1.5km walk down a very steep, dead-end road.

Bus 1125 (NT$67, 35 minutes) links Fengbin and Guangfu five times daily via Rte 11甲.

Shihtiping

☑03 / POP 200

The Kuroshio Current runs closest to Taiwan at Shihtiping (石梯坪; Shítīpíng; Shiti fishing village) and misty conditions along the coast make the vegetation greener and denser than elsewhere. The volcanic coastline has also eroded to form the beautiful natural formations that the place is named after (*shihtiping* means 'stone steps').

Shihtiping is divided into a rough-hewn village, a fishing harbour below this, and a nicely landscaped park south of the harbour. Further south are a number of tiny Ami settlements where fishermen cast nets at the mouths of rivers, and wood craftsmen transform driftwood into furniture and sculptures.

Tour bus crowds can overload the entrance to the landscaped park, but if you head down toward Shihtiping Campground, you'll find a quieter area of limestone rocks with beautiful lookouts down the coast.

◉ Sights

Shihtiping Geopark
PARK

(石梯坪遊憩風景區, Shítīpíng Yóuqì Fēngjǐngqū; Km63.4 Hwy 11; ☺24hr; ℗) One of Taiwan's most beautiful areas of unspoilt coastline runs south from Fengbin, culminating at a headland beyond Shitigang fishing harbour, known as Shihtiping. Here, a reserve area offers pathways and viewing platforms from which to appreciate a series of wave-battered geological formations, including deep rock pools and a white-coloured cuesta (sloping scarp) onto which you can clamber.

The site somewhat immodestly touts itself as a 'world-class outdoor geological classroom', but anyone can appreciate the splendid views looking north at layer upon layer of steep green slopes rising from the frothing Pacific. Or, on a calm day, watch fish darting in the shallows. The park's spine is a 1.1km toll road starting from Km63.4 on Highway 11. Come at dawn for the sunrise or after 6pm to enjoy the scene with few other tourists. At weekends and especially during Chinese holiday periods, the site can become a contrastingly crowded traffic jam thanks to limited parking and passing places.

🛏 Sleeping

Shihtiping Campground
CAMPGROUND $

(石梯坪露營區, Shítīpíng Lùyíngqū; ☐0922-211 336; http://camping33.pgo.tw; 52 Shihtiping; 石梯坪52號; sites Sun-Thu NT$1000, Fri & Sat NT$1200) In a lovely sea-facing spot at the far end of Shihtiping's geopark area is a small but well-laid-out campsite with raised tent platforms beneath sturdy wooden covers. There are hot-water showers (evenings only) and toilets.

You'll need to prebook online (which is hard if you don't speak Chinese) or call on the morning of arrival and check in at the visitor information centre at the end of the road. Using the site without advance booking can render you liable to a fine of five times the daily rate.

Adagio
BOUTIQUE HOTEL $$$

(緩慢民宿, Huǎnmàn Mínsù; ☐03-878 1789, 0916-552 230; www.theadagio.com.tw; 123 Shihtiwan; 石梯灣123號; d incl breakfast weekends from NT$6100, weekdays NT$5500; ☐1127, 1140, 1145, 8119) The plushest of the three guesthouses to lie right within the Shihtiping Geopark area, Adagio offers a thoughtful sense of modernist designer style that contrasts with the natural wilderness setting. Though set back from the ocean, the sea is visible from the vast plate-glass windows in most of the rooms.

The sign is so subtle that it's hard to spot: continue 300m beyond the Shihtiping car ticket barrier and the hotel is just after the turn where the park road swings south.

✗ Eating

Yina Feiyu   CAFE $$
(伊娜飛魚, Yīnà Fēiyú; ☑ 0927-850 136, 0927-850 126; Km64 Hwy 11; mains NT$150-250; ⊙ 11am-7pm) Fronted by eccentric concrete art swirls and fish-smoking racks, this cafe draws crowds for its flying fish dishes. But if you don't like a mouthful of bones, there's plenty of easier-to-eat seafood plus a few offbeat, indigenous vegetable dishes (rattan heart soup, fried reed pulp). It's beside Hwy 11 around 300m south of the Shihtiping park turn.

ℹ Getting There & Away

From Hualien, several Hualien Bus (p180) routes, including those bound for Jingpu and Chenggong, stop on request at Shihtiping (NT$221, 90 minutes). For Taitung, change in Chenggong or flag down one of two direct services, Hualien Bus 1127 around 11.10am (NT$316, 2¼ hours) or Diingdong Bus (p199) 8119 (NT$345, 2½ hours) around 3.40pm.

Chenggong

☑ 089 / POP 14,200

Squeezed between forest-fuzzed mountains and crashing Pacific swells, Chenggong (成功; Chénggōng; Chengkung), is a centre for summer whale watching, and a growingly popular alternative to Dulan as a base for surfers. Though it's the biggest coastal town between Hualien and Taitung, don't expect a city: it's small and a little unrefined, but there's plenty of good dining, especially if you love fresh fish. Beware that when using auto-translation apps, 成功 (Chenggong) often appears rather cryptically as 'success'.

◉ Sights & Activities

Sanxiantai   ISLAND
(Platform of the Three Immortals, 三仙台, Sānxiāntái; ☑ 089-854 097; Km2, Rte 東15-1; Ⓟ) FREE The best-known icon of the whole east coast is the eight-humped pedestrian bridge that leads from a windswept headland to this craggy little offshore island. Ringed by wave-pummelled rocks and grey beaches, the scene is especially photogenic at sunrise

or sunset, but expect plenty of company from tour-bus crowds.

Whale Watching   WHALE WATCHING
(賞鯨豚, Shǎng Jīngtún; ☑ 089-851 408; www.dolphin-wan.com.tw; 港边路1-5号2楼; 2nd fl, 1-5 Gangbian Rd; adult/child/infant NT$800/600/300; ⊙ late-May-Sep) Whale- and dolphin-watching boats set out at 9.30am and 2.30pm when weather is fair and assuming at least ten passengers. It's worth checking the website and calling ahead.

Boats leave from the new (northeast) section of the harbour with tickets sold upstairs in the Marine Environment College building.

🛌 Sleeping

Zhen Wang Zi Hotel   GUESTHOUSE $
(Prince Hotel, 真王子大旅社, Zhēnwángzǐ Dàlǚshè; ☑ 089-851 612; 56 Zhongshan Rd, Chenggong; 中山路56號; d from NT$750) It's dated and simple, with rucked carpets, chipped tiles and ageing furniture, but the place is friendly and has about the cheapest ensuite beds you'll find in Chenggong town.

Happiness House   GUESTHOUSE $$
(台東幸福小築民宿; ☑ 0912-198 577; http://happinesshouse.tdbnb.net; 1-68 Zhitan Rd; 成功鎮芝田路1-68號; d/q NT$2000/3500) With friendly English-speaking management, this new family guesthouse is set amid pretty rice paddies just far enough from town to be quiet, but close enough for convenience.

The upper four-person rooms have sunrise views across fields and the ocean horizon. It's 1.5km from the bus station: take narrow Rte 東16 to the northwest just after leaving Chenggong on northbound Hwy 11.

✗ Eating

★ Meet Marlin   CAFE $$
(旗遇海味, Qíyù Hǎiwèi; ☑ 0932-396 089, 089-852 889; www.meetmarlin.com; 19-8 Ggngbian Rd, Chenggong; 成功鎮港邊路19-8號; meals NT$200-300; ⊙ 10am-8pm) Sit overlooking the fishing port, a bossanova beat enlivening this designer-sparse concrete-floored cafe which serves sashimi (from NT$250) and a small, well-chosen menu of other fresh fish meals.

Or just come for a drink. There are excellent barista coffees, fruit wines and a range of beers from standard Taiwan lager to hoppy, Belgian Chouffe Houblon IPA.

Makaira Coffee   SEAFOOD $$$
(旗鱼咖啡, Qíyú Kāfēi; ☑ 089-854 899; 65-1 Datong Rd, Chenggong township; 大同路65號之1;

fish dishes NT$350-900; ⊘ 11am-2.30pm & 5-8pm) This misleadingly named seafood restaurant specialises in top-quality swordfish served in a multitude of ways, including raw as excellent sashimi. There's a menu in English, but the Chinese version is far more extensive, including generous two-person meal sets from NT$890.

ℹ Getting There & Away

Buses run along Hwy 11 to Hualien (routes 1127 & 1145) approximately hourly. To Taitung train station, four daily Diingdong services (routes 8120 & 8119, NT$167, 1¼ hours), leaving at 6.20am, 505pm, 7.50pm and 8.50pm, supplement five daily Tourist Shuttle buses (NT$173, 80 minutes) that continue to Taitung bus station. The latter start at Sanxiantai. All make useful stops at Donghe and Dulan.

Bus 8181 runs cross-country to Yuli station (NT$129, one hour) at 6am, 10.30am and 2.40pm.

Dulan

🎧 089 / POP 800

Driving Hwy 11 through little Dulan (都蘭; Dūlán) you might not think it much different from any other standard roadside village. But look again. In fact, the strip's shophouses include two surf shops and around a dozen restaurants serving an array of international cuisines. There's also a wide range of art-and-craft workshops, especially around the disused Sugar Factory, where Saturday nights see live music. A web of tiny country lanes lead steadily up into foothills behind and hide a surprising wealth of hidden guesthouses and little-heralded cafes, plus a couple of small archaeological sites from the millennia-old Beinan culture.

Today, Dulan has a large Amis population whose presence in the arts scene is strong, and few villages in Taiwan are as accustomed to westerners: many visitors stay here far longer than planned.

◉ Sights

★ Moonlight Inn   VIEWPOINT

(月光小棧, Yuèguāng Xiǎo Zhàn; ☎ 089-530 012; Rte 42東, Km3.0; coffee NT$80-150; ⊘ 11am-5pm Thu-Mon) FREE For spectacular views looking down across Dulan towards the ocean and horizon-silhouette of Green Island, you can't beat the upper balcony of this little gallery-cafe 3km above town. It's in a Japanese-era building which was renovated

as the set for the 2005 movie *The Moon Also Rises*, with some props from the production still on display.

The beautiful if rather narrow 3km route from central Dulan follows Rte 42東, starting almost beside the Family Mart. It's well signposted in English, but has steep sections that are a little testing for cyclists.

Dulan Sugar Factory   ARTS CENTRE

(都蘭糖廠, Dūlán Tángchǎng; 61 Dulan village; 都蘭村61號) FREE One of the east coast's most appealing concentrations of craft shops, artists' workshops and quirky cafes is clustered around the former sugar refinery towards the southern end of Dulan's main strip (Km44.3).

On weekdays, the art scene is pretty quiet, but on holidays and at weekends you can usually watch carvers at work, and there's typically a concert outside the factory's Highway 11 Cafe on Saturday nights.

Water Running Up   LANDMARK

(水往上流, Shuǐ Wǎng Shàng Liú; Hwy 11, Km146; ⊘ 24hr) FREE Is the anti-gravity stream-flow an optical illusion or a hydrological oddity? Decide for yourself while strolling this attractively landscaped park 1km south of central Dulan.

It's well worth a five-minute stop if you're driving by, though on holiday weekends it can get pretty packed with tour groups shopping for tribal trinkets at the gift shop.

If alighting from the Tourist Shuttle bus, walk 100m south from the stop then 50m west.

🏃 Activities

WaGaLiGong   SURFING

(哇軋力共, Wa Yà Lì Gòng; 🎧 089-530 373; www.facebook.com/wagaligong; 89 Dulan village; 都蘭村89號; ⊘ 8am-midnight) Combining an English-speaking surf shop with a popular bar and one of Dulan's cheapest hostels (mat-on-floor bed spaces from NT$300), WaGaLiGong is a perennial favourite hangout with the foreigner crowd. Surfing/ stand-up paddleboarding (SUP) lessons cost from NT$1500/1800, board rental from NT$600/1500 per day.

🛏 Sleeping

The Travel Bug   HOSTEL $

(🎧 089-531 668, 0989-484 009; 134 Dulan village; 都蘭村134號; dm/d NT$450/1400; ⊘ 8am-10pm) Plum in the middle of the main drag (at Km45.1), Dulan's best hostel sits above a vegetarian bistro-bar with a trancey vibe and instruments available for impromptu jam sessions. The rooftop doubles as yoga space, there's a fair-sized rear garden and owner Nick makes hummus and fresh coffee for the included breakfast.

Jailhouse Hostel
HOSTEL $

(背包監獄, Bèibāo Jiānyù; ☑ 0910-111 412; 225-6 Dulan; 都蘭225-6號; dm NT$500-600, s/tw/d without bath NT$750/1400/1450; ☎) The only jailbirds in this friendly three-room hostel are painted on the wall murals. It's a quiet, laid-back place with guests encouraged to fraternise through welcome-board sign-ups and cook-your-own-egg breakfasts. The dorms are unsophisticated but there's a rooftop, kitchen-lounge and attractive yard seating. A couple of bicycles are free to use.

Piao Yang Dulan
B&B $$

(飄洋都蘭, Piāoyáng Dōulán; ☑ 089-531 310; www.piaoyangdulan.com.tw; Neighbourhood 27, No 196-2 Dulan; 都蘭村27鄰都蘭196之2號; d from NT$2500) Upper market guesthouse Piao Yang stylishly incorporates elements of indigenous art into spacious contemporary rooms that are bright and comfortably well equipped.

The Amis owners are a warm-hearted couple, but they don't live on site so you'll need to arrange arrival times carefully. The property is one block inland from Hwy 11 on the lane leading to Moonlight Inn (p185).

✗ Eating

Dulan Sugar 61
TAIWANESE INDIGENOUS $$

(都蘭糖廠61號, Dōulán Tángchǎng 61; ☑ 089-530 330; 61 Dulan village; 都蘭村61號; mains NT$110-240; ☑ 9am-6pm; ☎) In a spacious Japanese-style wood-and-glass building at the entrance to the Dulan Sugar Factory (p185) complex, this is a fine place to try regional delicacies incorporating sailfish, burdock, taro and salted pork.

♟ Drinking & Nightlife

Cape Cafe
CAFE

(海角咖啡, Hǎijiǎo Kāfēi; ☑ 0903-262 923; www.capecafe.tw; 14-10 Jupu Rd; 舊部路10之14號; ☑ 11am-6pm) Order a craft beer, organic tea or Spanish meal at this outwardly unpretentious cafe and you gain the right to swim in their open-air pool. That's across a former golf course on a clifftop with superb views across Dulan Beach. It's a little hard to find, 2km northeast of the Sugar Factory (p185).

To get there, take the tiny rural lane that starts from the concourse of Dulan's northern petrol station (Hwy 11, Km144). That runs east then swings north after the Coffee Box 'train' cafe. After another 500m, turn right where there's a sign written in Chinese on an old surf board. In summer, Cape Cafe organises sailing and kayaking trips.

Highway 11 Craft Beer
BAR

(台11手工啤酒, Tái 11 Shǒugōng Píjiǔ; ☑ 0978-092 087; ☑ 6pm-midnight Wed-Fri, noon-midnight Sat, noon-5pm Sun) Built into the structure of the original sugar mill, this funky gift shop and artisan brewer is a great place for simple cocktails, mead made from local honey, and their own microbrewed beer.

CoffeeBox
COFFEE

(☑ 1-6pm) In an achievement of wonderfully comic absurdity, CoffeeBox has somehow transplanted a railway carriage, rails and all to a field outside Dulan and turned it into a barista cafe. Extra seating on the roof affords wonderful 360-degree views.

To find it, take the lane that starts from the courtyard of Dulan's more northerly petrol station (Hwy 11, Km144), then go 250m towards the sea.

ⓘ Getting There & Away

Taitung-bound buses from various starting points pass through roughly hourly. Diingdong services (NT$60, 50 minutes) use different Dulan stopping points from the Tourist Shuttle bus (www.taiwantrip.com.tw, five daily, NT$75), which halts on request outside the Sugar Factory (p185) plus around 700m further south close to Water Running Up (p185).

Northbound, the Tourist Shuttle continues to Sanxiantai (NT$83, one hour) via Chenggong. For Hualien, bus 8119 passes through Dulan at 6.41am (NT$463, 3¾ hours), and bus 1127 (NT$487) at 3.30pm.

ⓘ Getting Around

Some hostels lend or rent basic bicycles, but for scooter rental the nearest place is Taitung.

EAST RIFT VALLEY

Endlessly beautiful agricultural landscapes are backed on either side by soaring green slopes throughout the East Rift Valley (花東縱谷; Huādōngzòng Gǔ), a long alluvial plain separating Taiwan's two main mountain ranges. Geologically, it forms the collision point between the Philippine and Eurasian tectonic plates. For cyclists and motorists, however, it's a delightfully bucolic way to meander between Hualien and Taitung through some of Taiwan's best farming country and its prettiest rice paddies.

Sights

Sixty Stone Mountain   MOUNTAIN
(六十石山, Liùshí Shí Shān) At 952m, Sixty Stone Mountain offers one of the east coast's most mesmerising landscapes. Zigzag up eight kilometres through subtropical foliage to the first of nearly a dozen viewing pavilions which survey a surreal upland area of steeply undulating farmland hillocks. Many have been planted with day lilies. When blooming in early summer, these turn the already glorious landscape into an unforgettable golden carpet, counterpointed with a backdrop of darkly brooding mountain forests plunging back into the Rift Valley.

In summer, several farms on the uplands open B&Bs and sell a variety of lily-based comestibles, including ice creams. However, outside midsummer, one of the only places to stay open is **Wang You Yuen** (www.60stoneday lily.hlbnb.tw, ☎ 0972-837 928), combining a fairly basic motel with a decent little coffee shop.

You'll need a vehicle to get here: turn east off Hwy 9 at Km308.6, around 12km south of Yuli. Less than two kilometres up the winding access road, consider a short diversion to Dongfu Buddhist Nunnery. It's a new structure set in a lovely manicured garden and has a curious set of giant figurines in the temple. This is a fine place to spot the Taiwan Blue Magpie (台灣藍鵲; Táiwān Lánquè) as a few pairs breed here in April.

Lintianshan   VILLAGE
(林田山, Líntiánshān; ☎ 03-875 2100, 03-875 2378; www.forest.gov.tw/EN/0000221; Hwy 16; ⊙exhibition hall 9am-5pm Tue-Sun) FREE An attractively set 'cultural village' and tour bus magnet, Lintianshan was founded in 1918 as a Japanese-era logging village. At its 1960 peak, it housed over 2000 workers in well over 100 wooden buildings. Many of these have been preserved, even though the industry stopped in 1988 and the village became something of a ghost town.

A couple of exhibition halls highlight logging, firefighting and woodcarving; there's a Japanese-style coffee shop and preserved section of logging railway infrastructure.

The village is around 2.5km east of Wanrong (萬榮) via Hwy 16. Although Wanrong has a train station, public transport access is easier from either Guangfu or Fenglin stations between which Lintianshan is a stop on the Tourist Shuttle bus (NT$27, eight to 15 minutes, seven daily).

Activities

Walami Trail   HIKING
(瓦拉米古道, Wǎlāmǐ Gǔdào; www.ysnp.gov.tw/css_en/page.aspx?path=473) One of Taiwan's 'must-do' hikes, this beautiful trail climbs steadily up through subtropical jungle that's all a-flutter with butterflies and occasional monkeys chattering and crashing through the foliage. For many visitors, the first 2km gives a sufficient taster, with plunging drops below the first suspension bridge, a waterfall beneath the second and some fine valley views just beyond that.

Without a permit you can walk on through essentially similar terrain to Jianshin – around two hours each way from the trailhead. To get there from Yuli (12km), rent a scooter or bicycle, or pay around NT$500 for a taxi. Around halfway is the helpful, English-speaking **Nanan Visitor Centre** (南安遊客中心, Nán'ān Yóukè Zhōngxīn; ☎ 03-888 7560; www.ysnp.gov.tw; Km6, Hwy 30; ⊙9am-4.30pm, closed 2nd Tue of month, permits 7-9am) and 2km beyond, consider a quick stop at Km4.1 for a view of Nanan Waterfall (南安瀑布; Nánān Pùbù).

> ### EDIBLE DAY LILIES
> Over the last two decades, some of the Rift Valley's mid-altitude rice- and tea-growing areas have switched to cultivating day (tiger) lilies (金針; jīnzhēn). Taiwanese consumers eat the pre-blooming shoots in soup and use the flowers to flavour a variety of teas and other products. The result is areas of mountain upland that are beautifully carpeted with orange blossoms. While you might see a little of this colour from May, the peak blooming season is August. The most dramatic spread is on the upper slopes of Sixty Stone Mountain, but an alternative is around the 5km loop road that starts 11km up the narrow hairpins of Chike Mountain (northeast of Yuli). There's even a small patch beside Hwy 30 at Km 24-25.

Note that the trail continues right across the Yushan National Park for around ten days' trek but to go beyond Jianshin, you'll need permits. If you're returning the same day, you can get a one-day pass at the Nanan Visitor Centre as long as you arrive there before 9am. If you plan to stay overnight in the park, you'll need to apply online, at least a week (but no more than two months) in advance. Depending on your itinerary, you might be required to give proof of hiking/ camping experience (photos might suffice). The most popular permit option is a two-day return, overnighting at Walami Cabin (14km, around six hours each way). That is free and your permit will include a numbered sleeping space, but there is neither bedding nor provisions available, so you'll need to be self-sufficient with sleeping bag and food.

⭐ Festivals & Events

Bunun Ear
Shooting Festival   CULTURAL
(布農打耳祭, Bùnóng Dǎ'ěrjì, Malahodaigian; www. tipp.org.tw/ceremony.asp?CD_ID=135; 永康多功能文化廣場; ☺April/May) Based on timeless, coming-of-age ceremonies, this is the most important festival of the Bunun people. It's held in the tribe's villages throughout the East Rift – dates vary according to the moon.

The festival's main focus was originally teaching boys to hunt deer (the name refers to the challenge of shooting a deer through the ear), though these days the archery targets are cut-outs. Other physical tests include millet pounding and sumo-like wrestling contests, and there's still a sacrifice and a pig-catching game that might upset some visitors.

A list of participating villages is typically posted in March on the website www.face book.com/uninang.taluhan. The best known venue is Yongkang (永康) as it's easy to reach, barely a kilometre north of the Luye Highland area. Look for their schedule (in Chinese) on www.ttypg.gov.tw. In 2019, Yongkang celebrated what was officially classified as its 108th Ear Shooting Festival.

🛏 Sleeping & Eating

Hualien Sugar Factory
Guesthouses   GUESTHOUSE $$$
(台糖花蓮旅館, Táitáng Huālián Lǚguǎn; ☑886-3870 2881, 886-3870 5881; www.hualiensugar. com.tw; 19 Tangchang St; 大進村糖廠街19號; d hard-floor/tatami from NT$2520/2880, weekend NT$4200/4800, q/ste NT$6600/8400; ℗) The

48 rebuilt wood-cabin rooms, originally workers' residences for the Hualien Sugar Factory, now offer comfortable visitor accommodation. Interiors have two different styles: the slightly pricier ones are Japanese-style with tatami-mat flooring and futons in the cupboards, ready for you to make your own bed.

Cafe Lovely   CAFE $$
(拉芙里咖啡店, Lāfúlǐ Kāfēidiàn; ☑03-870 0098; 186 Zhonghua Rd, Guangfu; 光復鄉大華村中華路186號; mains NT$100-250; ☺1-8pm Mon-Sat; ❄🐾🛜) This refreshingly air-conditioned coffee shop and afternoon eatery doubles as a showroom for the owner's handmade leatherwork. Home-cooked meals are full of flavour and come with a delicious soup and plate of fresh vegetables.

From Guangfu train station, walk a short block east then 30m north to find it.

🛍 Shopping

Hualien Sugar Factory   LANDMARK
(光復糖廠, Guāngfù Tángchǎng; ☑03-870 5881; www.hualiensugar.com.tw/index.asp; Tangchang St, Guangfu; 大進村糖廠街; ☺museum section 9am-5pm, shops 8am-8pm) FREE For 80 years before its 2002 closure, this plant was one of Taiwan's biggest sugar refineries. Today, the main factory building is essentially derelict but forms the focus of an extremely popular shopping experience, with a variety of outlets selling snacks, souvenirs and overrated ice cream. Shops are interspersed by fountain pools, old processing equipment and the odd sugar-pulling rail car and steam loco.

The site is just south of Guangfu: turn off Hwy 9 at Km251.5. Seven daily Tourist Shuttle buses (www.taiwantrip.com.tw) come here from Hualien (NT$205, 1¾ hours) via Liyu Lake; last return 5.50pm.

ℹ Getting There & Away

Eastern Taiwan's only railway follows the valley between Hualien and Taitung, paralleled by Hwy 9. That's pretty busy with trucks and much less scenic than lovely, far quieter alternatives Rte 193 (Guangfu to Yuli), 花55 (Fuyuan to Ruisui Hot Springs) and 花75 (Yuli to Chishang). Rte 197 is a little-used option between Chishang and Taitung, but it is extremely long, winding and hilly, especially south of Guanshan. It's possible to cut across the Coastal Mountain Range via four different minor routes (over Guangfeng Hwy 11, Ruigang Hwy 64, Walami Hwy 30 and Hwy 23). At the southern end of the valley, Luye is easy to visit as a part-day return trip from Taitung.

ⓘ Getting Around

Trains connect Hualien and Taitung via Guangfu, Ruisui, Yuli, Chishang and Luye, but having your own transport is very useful as much of what is interesting here is getting off the beaten track. Of the valley stations, Yuli is convenient for renting bicycles and scooters and Chishang has a car rental agency and countless quadricycle rental places for touring the rice fields.

Hualien Bus (p180) route 1122 links Hualien and Ruisui, while routes 1137 and 1142 include Guangfu-Ruisui-Yuli legs.

Ruisui

✔ 03 / POP 11,600

Ruisui (瑞穗; Ruìsuì) is best known as a little hot springs town, though that's actually centred on Hongye sub-village, 3.5km west of the train station. Well-spaced spring hotels here range from very simple to a giant new fairy-tale resort in the form of a pseudo-Loire-Valley chateau.

Within a few kilometres' drive, you'll find plenty of very scenic countryside. There are farm visits and a tea plantation at Wuhu, a winding river gorge cutting east of Ruisui is popular for rafting, and there's an accessible nature experience 10km north at Fuyuan Forest Recreation Area. The latter is perhaps a more appealing place than Ruisui itself to take a hot-spring dip if you're not staying in an upper-market hotel.

◉ Sights

Fuyuan Forest Recreational Area   PARK

(富源國家森林遊樂區, Fùyuán Guójiā Sēnlín Yóulè Qū; ✆03-881 2377; www.bvr.com.tw; adult/child NT$100/50, hot springs NT$250; ⊙park 6am-5pm, info centre 10am-5pm, hot springs 10am-10pm) Fuyuan takes an area of serene natural beauty and tames it just enough to make accessible the abundant birdlife and multitudinous butterflies that flit between lush woodlands, mossy rocks and an attractive riverside. There's also a more manicured garden and butterfly houses for both living and pinned specimens. Several forest trails link up into a 3.5km loop, with shortcut options.

Near the car park is a small area of rare surviving camphor trees, festooned with epiphytes. In the late 19th and early 20th century, Taiwan dominated the world market of camphor production that was used in everything from embalming fluid to medicine to insect repellent.

Inside the park, Butterfly Valley Resort is an upper market hotel whose excellent rooms come with walk-in hot-spring bathtubs (from NT$6300 half board). Non-guests can dine at the restaurant (mains NT$260–320). The reserve is 3.5km west of Fuyuan train station. From the Ruisui hot-spring area, a scenic and delightfully quiet route uses Rte 花55.

☆ Activities

Fuyuan Hot Spring   HOT SPRINGS

(富源溫泉, Fùyuán Wēnquán; Guangdong Rd, Fuyuan; adult/child NT$150/120, incl admission to Forest Recreational Area NT$250/180; ⊙10am-10pm Mon-Fri, to 11pm Sat & Sun) Within the lovely Fuyuan Forest Recreational Area, this small but attractive series of open-air, hot-spring pools is considerably more appealing than the public options in Ruisui. Wear bathing costume/swimming shorts, and if you don't have your own, you'll need to buy a swimming cap (NT$80) and towel (small/large NT$50/200).

Ruisui Rafting Service Centre   RAFTING

(瑞穗泛舟服務中心, Ruìsuì Fànzhōu Fúwù Zhōngxīn; ✆03-887 5400; www.erv-nsa.gov.tw/en/attractions/detail/83; Km89.8 Rte 193; 215 Zhongshan Rd, Sec 3; 中山路3段215號; per person from NT$700; ⊙6am-3pm Jun-Aug, 7am-4pm May & Nov, 8am-5pm Oct & Dec-Apr) Essentially similar 3½-hour rafting trips run by a series of different operators, with most departures leaving before noon. The starting point is across the car park from the Xiuguluan Visitor Centre (秀姑巒溪遊客中心, Xiùgūluán Xīyóukè Zhōngxīn; Km89.8, Rte 193; ⊙9am-5pm), around 4km southeast of Ruisui train station. That's easy to spot thanks to a three-storey face statue that's visible from afar.

🛏 Sleeping & Eating

Sunshine Hot Spring B&B   BOUTIQUE HOTEL $$

(瑞穗山下的厝溫泉民宿, Ruìsuì Shānxià Decuò Wēnquán Mínsù; ✆03-887 0203; www.sunshine hotspring.com; 137 Wenquan Rd Sec 3; 溫泉路三段137號; d/q incl breakfast from NT$3600/4850; ℗ ❄ 🛜) Low-key but contemporary hot-spring hotel where the 'golden' mineral water is piped to your private walk-in tub, or you can use the small communal pool in the garden.

★ Grand Cosmos Resort   RESORT $$$

(瑞穗春天國際观光酒店, Ruìsuì Chūntiān Guójì Guānguāng Jiǔdiàn; ✆03-887 6000; www.grand cosmos.com.tw; 368 Wenshan Rd Sec 2, Ruisui; 瑞

RUISUI RAFTING

The Ruisui Rafting Service Centre (p189), 4km east of Ruisui train station, is the put-in point for popular, relatively leisurely rafting trips (泛舟; fànzhōu) on a 24km-long route down the Xiuguluan River to Dagangkou near Jingpu. This generally takes about 3½ hours to complete, with almost all departures before 11am. During peak season (May to September), you can usually just show up in the morning and join a trip (per person from NT$700). If you're coming from Hualien, you might prefer a package deal that includes return transport (around NT$1400 per person).

穗鄉溫泉路二段368號; d with half board from NT$9900; P❄🛜🏊) Especially at night when its chateau-like turrets are lit up, this unforgettable resort has a Las Vegas fantasy feel, with a hot-springs water park, spa and swimming pool. Luxurious rooms, each with its own mineral-spring bath, are spread over a whole series of fanciful buildings.

Qiancao Yuan   CAFE $$
(千草園, Qiāncǎo Yuán; 📞03-887 2817; 210 Zhongshan Rd, Sec 2; 中山路二段210號; mains NT$280-380; ⏰11am-8pm; ❄🛜) Whether for coffee and cake (NT$120), pasta or risotto with a cheesy gratin-style topping, this cafe is appealing, with its array of foliage, pet cats and cutesy art. It's around 1km east of Ruisui train station along Rte 193.

Orchid Ramen   JAPANESE $$
(蘭花町日本拉麵, Lánhuātīng Nihon Ramen; 📞03-887 6355; 42 Zhongzheng Rd; 中正北路一段42號; meal sets NT$170-260; ⏰11.30am-2.30pm & 5-8.30pm Tue-Sun; 🛜) Far more appealing than most of the other boxy shopcafes in central Ruisui, this recently modernised ramen specialist also serves a typical range of simple, Japanese dishes (oyakodon, katsu curry rice), plus extra sides like kimchee and burdock. From Ruisui train station, turn left on the main road and walk one block north. The shop is easy to miss, three doors beyond the Yang Homestay.

ℹ️ Getting There & Away

Ruisui is a stop on the Hualien-Taitung line between Guangfu and Yuli. From Hualien, fast/slow trains (NT$143/110) take one/1½ hours.

ℹ️ Getting Around

Attractions are spread very widely so having your own wheels is useful. Bike and scooter rental is available from **Xiao Yan** (小燕租車, Xiǎo yàn zūchē; 📞0972-157 518; 86 Zhongzheng Rd; 中正北路一段86號; bicycle/scooter/electric-scooter per 24hrs NT$100/400/600; ⏰8am-7pm or call), a small shop two blocks north of the train station on the main road. Ask for a free visitor map showing local attractions.

Alternatively, city bikes can be rented for free at the tourist office so long as you return them by 5pm: however, as that's 4km east of the station – beside the Ruisui Rafting Service Centre (p189) – it's not ideal as a starting point for those using public transport.

Yuli

📅 03 / POP 23,960

With the Central Mountains looking over its shoulder, and the Rift Valley under its nose, Yuli (玉里; Yùlǐ) is a launching point for day trips to hot springs, mountains covered with day lilies, the organic rice-growing valley at Loshan, and the eastern section of Yushan National Park. The town itself is a likeable, low-key place with lots of modest eateries. It was one of the earliest nonindigenous settlements on the east coast, established in the mid-19th century by Hakka immigrants from Guǎngzhōu.

🏃 Activities

WM Hotsprings   HOT SPRINGS
(山灣水月景觀溫泉會館, Shānwān Shuǐyuè Jǐngguān Wēnquán Huìguǎn; 📞03-888 3299; www.wmhotspring.com.tw; Leheli 41-8 樂合里41之8號; day-use NT$300; ⏰8.30am-10pm; 🚗) To enjoy the village of Antong's mildly sulphurous mineral baths in an environment that's more attractive and inviting than at the concrete-block riverside hotels, wind 1km up valley-side hairpins to this classy midrange hotel where your NT$300 fee includes use of two small infinity-style hot-spring pools with views down across the valley.

Lockers, drinking water and a small towel are provided, there are good little private bathing rooms and the wearing of swimming caps is not enforced. The hotel rooms with comfortable beds, balconies and hot-spring baths cost from NT$3600 (NT$4200 on Saturdays). Note that while receptionists speak good English, signage is only in Chinese: follow signs to New Life Hot Springs, but stop 100m before getting there.

Antong Hot Springs
HOT SPRINGS

(安通溫泉, Āntōng Wēnquán; www.an-tong.com. tw; Antong Hot Springs Hotel, Km21.5 Hwy 30; adult/ child Mon-Fri NT$300/200, Sat & Sun NT$350/250; ☺8am-10pm) At Antong's original hotel, the day-entry fee gives you access to private and sex-segregated indoor pools where you bathe naked, plus various outdoor pools for which you need swimming wear plus a cap (NT$50 if you don't have your own). Conditions aren't luxurious and the outdoor area, while not unpleasant, is overlooked by rather drab hotel buildings and lacks views.

🛏 Sleeping

Bliss Inn 1719
HOSTEL $

(一斉一宿, Yīqíyī Sùkè; ☏0960-369 434; 4th fl, 17 Chengsi 6th St; 城西六街17號4樓; dm/tw NT$500/1260) It's well worth the three flights of stairs to discover central Yuli's best back-packer hideaway, with bright, well-spaced dorms, small lockers, a pleasant twin room and wide-ranging views from the open rooftop. There's a bicycle parking area too.

From Yuli train station, walk south down Datong Rd, which then curves east. Turn right on Chensi 5th St (beside 87 Datong Rd), then first right again and the hostel is in the tallest building in the short street ahead.

★ Wisdom Garden
HOMESTAY $$

(智嵐雅居民宿, Zhìlán YǎJū Mínsù; ☏0921-986 461; www.wisdom-garden.com; 玉里鎮大禹里5 鄰酸甘98-1號; 98-1 Suangan, 5 Dayuli; d NT$2200-3000, q NT$3200-4000; [P][⊛][@][🛜]) Set amid lawns, views, palms and dangling orchids, this magical homestay is filled with Chinese art, Buddhist mandalas, antique furniture and calligraphic art. Much of the latter is by the spiritually minded owner, who speaks English and is unendingly obliging. Gourmet breakfasts are included, but you'll need your own wheels to make the most of the wonderfully peaceful rural location.

The Wisdom Garden is 5km north of Yuli. Turn west off Hwy 9 at Km289.4 and follow the signed, narrow lanes for 800m. Book ahead and arrange arrival times as the hosts aren't always home.

New Life Hot Springs Resort
GUESTHOUSE $$

(紐澳華溫泉山莊, Niǔàohuá Wēnquán Shānzhuāng; ☏03-888 7373; www.twspa.com.tw; 41-5 Antong Wenchan; 安通溫泉41-5號; d/tr/q/villa incl breakfast from NT$3000/4600/5400/6200, dm NT$680-900) This friendly, woodland lodge-style resort high above Antong has airy rooms with lashings of varnished pine panel-ling and villas with their own stone-surround private bathing space. It's up four hairpins, directly east of Antong Hot Springs (p191).

🍴 Eating

★ Bistro 103
CAFE $

(巧遇103, Qiǎoyù 103; ☏03-888 6103; https://103-bistro.business.site; 174 Zhongshan Rd, Sec 2; 中山路二段174號; mains NT$100-220; ☺11.30am-2pm & 5-8pm Mon-Sat) In an 1898 wooden building that was originally a police station, this utterly charming cafe is classically Japanese in both its wood-framed interior and its attractively presented lunches (ramen, donburi, curry rice etc). Alternatively, just soak up the atmosphere over barista coffee brewed on a Faema machine (NT$90). Minimal English is spoken. It's less than 15 minutes' walk from the train station: head east to the central roundabout then turn left (Zhongshan Rd) and it's at the northernmost end.

Asen Noodles
NOODLES $

(阿森麵店, Āsēn Miàndiàn; ☏03-888 1613; 94 Zhongshan St, Sec 2; 中山路二段94號; meals NT$50-60; ☺8am-5pm Tue-Sun) This bland-looking diner with its stainless-steel tables has been serving filling bowls of classic Yuli noodles since 1971 and still has the locals clamouring. From the train station, walk east along Guangfu Rd to the traffic circle then 200m north. The shop is between a 7-Eleven and a juice bar.

Jowu
ASIAN $$

(雞九屋, Jījiǔwū; G九屋; ☏03-886 1928; Km302.1, Hwy 9; mains NT$180-320; ☺11am-1.15pm & 5-7pm) If you're driving or cycling Hwy 9, consider stopping to eat one of the imaginative multidish meals at this outwardly inauspicious roadside diner 7km south from Yuli.

Highlights include *matsusaka* pork (thin strips of slow-cooked fatty pork layered on a salad combining dressed lettuce and fresh fruit), fried garlic kale with bacon, and the soup which, in season, is made with day lily shoots. It's very close to the Dongli cycling station where the former railway-track cycle path from Yuli ends.

ℹ Getting There & Away

Trains run roughly hourly to Yuli from Hualien (fast/slow train NT$189/145, 1¼/two hours) and Taitung (NT$154/118, 50/70 minutes). Buses 1137 and 1142 link to Guangfu via Ruisui. Cross-country bus 8181 leaves the station at 8am, 12.40pm and 6.50pm for Chenggong (NT$129, one hour) travelling via Rte 30.

EASTERN TAIWAN & TAROKO NATIONAL PARK YULI

ⓘ Getting Around

TR9 (☑ 0938-105 559; Yuli train station; ⊙ 8.30am-6pm) at the train station rents various qualities of city bicycle (per 3hrs/day from NT$150/250) and, for those with international driving permits, scooters (NT$300/500, deposit NT$1000) and cars (per day from NT$1800, deposit NT$3000). If you rent for three hours, you can leave bags in their lockers/storeroom for no extra charge.

For cheaper city bikes and for touring bicycles with 20+ gears, walk two blocks east then 50m north to find **Giant** (捷安特, Jié Ān Tè; ☑ 03-888 5669; 47 Heping Rd; 和平路47號; ⊙ 8am-9.30pm) bike store.

Chishang

☑ 089 / POP 8300

The merrily buzzing little town of Chishang (池上; Chíshàng) is surrounded by beautiful rice paddies, overlooked by viewing platforms and interlinked by a web of cycleways that are ideal for charming, low-energy ambles. Domestic tourists rush to a stretch known as Mr Brown Boulevard, but there are many alternative pathways that are far more idyllic and less touristed. If you speak Chinese, you'll be able to appreciate Chishang's several museums which celebrate rice processing, Hakka culture and – across the river in Haiduan – the Bunun tribe. If you're driving, Chishang also makes a good base from which to visit Sixty Stone Mountain (p187).

◎ Sights

Xiangyang   NATURE CENTRE
(向陽森林遊樂區, Xiàngyáng Sēnlín Yóulè Qū; ☑ 0912-103 376; https://tour.taitung.gov.tw/zh-tw/attraction/details/214; Km 154.5 Hwy 20; ⊙ permits 5am-5pm, visitor centre 8.30am-4.30pm) FREE This remote forest experience centre at 2320m, around 60km west of Chishang, introduces regional wildlife and doubles as the application point for permits to hike towards Jiaming Lake. If you want a much shorter stroll, you can peruse the mountainside woodlands on five different loops ranging from 500m to around 3km, some with sections of stepped wooden walkways.

🏃 Activities

★ **Chishang Waterway
Circle Cyclepath**   CYCLING
The quintessential Chishang experience is taking a bicycle or quadricycle and gliding around a web of cycleways through a magnificent array of mountain-hemmed rice paddies. There are several variants, but given 90 minutes, you have plenty of time to pass a waterwheel, climb the Daguan view pavilion and return past a lily-edged lake.

The experience varies by season and is best when the rice is young and emerald green (typically April), and when the organic fields are re-fertilised by planting swathes of flowers.

Jiaming Lake   HIKING
(嘉明湖, Jiāmíng Hú; https://recreation.forest.gov.tw/EN/Trail/RT?typ=3&tr_id=139; Xiangyang Forest Recreation Area; 向陽森林遊樂區) Sunny days give this elliptical alpine lake a gemlike quality. It's above the main treeline at 3310m, and offers good chances of spotting endemic yellow-throated martens and sambar deer. Humans are rarer as the place is only accessible by driving nearly 60km from Chishang then trekking a strenuous 13km each-way, mountain-ridge trail for which you'll need permits and prebooked accommodation in at least one of the two cabins and campsites en route.

As supply is limited, you'll need to apply at least eight days ahead and be lucky in the lottery that picks among the applicants. Start the hike from Xiangyang. Organising the trip through an agency can simplify the bureaucracy.

Chief Spa Hot Spring   HOT SPRINGS
(天龍溫泉, Tiānlóng Wēnquán; ☑ 089-935075; www.chiefspa.com.tw; 1-1 Wulu village, Km180.5, Hwy 20; 霧鹿村1-1號; spring-use/cap NT$250/50; ⊙ 6am-9am & 4-10pm) Surrounded by the Wulu Gorge's steep, forested ridge-sides, this small outdoor hot spring has a pair of linked pools, one fed by an artificial stream trickling prettily through rocks. It's tucked behind the Chief Spa Hotel.

That's a boxy building 30km from Chishang where you can also stay in similarly boxy rooms with hot-spring baths (from NT$2310 weekdays, NT$2920 Saturdays). The site would be worth a stop if driving the 200km cross-Taiwan Hwy 20, but that has been closed since 2009 and reopening dates have not yet been confirmed. Two daily buses on the Taitung-Lidao route stop outside the springs hotel (NT$79, 1¾ hours), arriving at 8.07am and 2.57pm, but as they return at 8.56 and 3.46pm, the timings don't mesh well with taking a leisurely long dip, given that the springs are mostly closed during the daytime. There is no Chishang-Lidao bus.

Lisong Hot Spring   HOT SPRINGS

(栗松溫泉, Lìsōng Wēnquán; Haiduan township, Taitung; only attempt Nov-May) **FREE** Lisong is a totally uncommercialised natural hot spring set amid colourful mineral deposits in a deep river valley. But getting here requires at least a 3km hike with sections that descend almost vertical slopes using ropes and rope ladders. Ask advice before going in case these have deteriorated beyond repair. Better still, take a guide.

Access to the trailhead is from Km168.5 of Rte 20, the Southern Cross-Island Hwy (ie about 9km north of Litao). A sign to the trailhead points you down a degraded farm road for 1km or so (sometimes too rough to drive). Thereafter, the path descends 400 vertical metres on roots and mudslides between twisted branches and trees dripping with epiphytes. If you manage to reach the riverside in the valley far below, the springs are to the left. A couple of river crossings are required so bring suitable footwear and don't attempt this after rain or in the wet season, when water levels will be dangerously high.

Sleeping & Eating

★ Dao Hua Siang   BOUTIQUE HOTEL $$

(DSB Guesthouse, 稻花香民宿, Dàohuāxiāng Mínsù; 089-865 565; www.dhsbnb.com.tw; 76-3 Xinxing Rd, Chishang; 池上鄉新興村新興76之3號; d from NT$2800) Suave, spacious rooms all look across the valley with its rice paddies laid out before you. Views are especially impressive from the upper-floor rooms – there's even a view from your bathtub. Rates include a breakfast of filled croissant and fruit.

It's around 2km south of central Chishang. Follow Rte 東1 to Km7 then turn southeast for 100m and the hotel is on the right.

Original House   B&B $$

(原來宿B&B, Yuánláisù B&B; 0928-814 320; 59 Zhonghua Rd, Chishang; 池上鄉中華路59號; d NT$2000-2400; ❄ ❋) The name doesn't lie. This small guesthouse really does ooze originality, fronted by a bar-bookshop and with offbeat curiosities giving character to the small but well equipped rooms.

It's across the rail tracks from the town centre, less than five-minutes' walk from Doremi Story Museum. Its vegan food is also worth a trip, but you might need to book ahead as the dining area is very small and stocks run out rapidly.

Doremi Story Museum   TAIWANESE $$

(089-864 283; www.drr.com.tw; 193-1 Zhongshan Rd, Chishang; 池上鄉中山路193號1樓; mains NT$110-220, set meals NT$200-270; 11am-7.30pm) Excellent set meals – one of them featuring utterly delicious chilli chicken with mountain pepper – come with miso soup, fruit salad and as much rice as you want. And that rice is superb, as you'd hope from a venue which doubles as a rice shop and features a huge wooden rice-processing contraption as a museum-like centrepiece.

Shopping

Since 1939 Ricebag Museum   FOOD

(池上飯包文化故事館, Chíshàng Fànbāo Wénhuà Gùshìguǎn; 089-862 326; 259 Zhongxiao Rd, Chishang; 池上鄉忠孝路259號; 8am-8pm) Originally founded in 1939 as a tiny vendor of rice dumplings and sweet potatoes, this store has morphed into a large and appealingly chaotic showcase for Chishang's ever-expanding range of rice-based comestibles. It's fronted by historic railway carriages in which you can picnic on the store's wares, including wildly popular lunch boxes.

Getting There & Away

Chishang is a stop on the Hualien-Taitung train line.

Getting Around

Numerous shops and most guesthouses rent bicycles and four-person quadricycles with which to cruise through the flat, pretty scenery on traffic-free cycleways.

Luye

089 / POP 7860

The East Rift Valley closes its attractive southern end around Luye (鹿野; Lùyě), a name meaning 'wild deer' for the herds that were once hunted by Amis and Puyuma peoples. Today, the area around Luye train station is a forgettable strip town but Gaotai – a large, flat-topped hill that rises steeply to the east – comes alive in July and early August with dozens of hot-air balloons. Outside the balloon season, it's still possible to do tandem paragliding jumps here, but otherwise the Luye Plateau (p194) becomes a rather over-touristed viewpoint from which to overlook a lovely valleyscape.

EASTERN TAIWAN & TAROKO NATIONAL PARK LUYE

SLIDING & GLIDING IN LUYE

Outside balloon season, the best viewpoint at Luye Plateau is at the southern end of the plateau, where two steep triangles of astroturf are the launch points for tandem paragliding experiences (NT$2500 for 20 minutes). There are also a few amusements for children and a large gift shop. Behind that, a grassy field stretches back around 500m. At the northern edge a short, steep bank is used for 'grass skiing' (10-second sledge ride NT$100).

⊙ Sights

Luye Plateau AREA

(鹿野高台, Lùyě Gāotái; ☑ Luye Visitor Centre 089-551 637) The area known as the Gaotai is a hill which rises fairly abruptly above Luye, surveying the surrounding green mountain ridges in all directions. For most of the year, a 15-minute visit is ample to enjoy the panoramas and shop for locally grown tea and dried pineapple in the souvenir stores. But in July and early August, if the weather is fine, don't miss coming to see the numerous hot-air balloons which gather here for what's dubbed the International Balloon Festival.

✱✱ Festivals & Events

Taiwan International
Balloon Festival AIR SHOW

(台灣國際熱氣球嘉年華, Táiwān Guójì Rèqìqiú Jiā'niánhuá; http://balloontaiwan.taitung.gov.tw/en; Luye Plateau; 鹿野高台; tethered balloon ride NT$500, free-float balloon ride NT$9000; ⊙ Jul-mid-Aug) More a season than a festival, this annual gathering brings dozens of international and Taiwanese hot-air balloons to Luye Plateau, creating a colourful midsummer spectacle. Many are in fanciful shapes.

On days when weather permits, you can take brief 'tethered ascents' in a balloon that simply bobs up then returns while attached to a fixed point, but queues can be considerable and most of the thousands of visitors are content to simply photograph the scene. On 'Night Glow' Saturday evenings, balloons 'perform' as part of big outdoor concerts held at different venues around Taitung County.

⊨ Sleeping

Lutai Guesthouse GUESTHOUSE $$

(鹿台民宿, Lùtái Mínsù; ☑ 089-550 528; www.lutai.com.tw; 5-89-42 Gaotai Rd; 高台路42巷89弄 5號; d/q NT$2900/3900) While there are classier places on the surrounding lowlands and slopes, if you want to be right at the highest point of Luye Plateau, with the best sweeping views, you can't beat Lutai. Seven rooms are tucked above a perfectly located souvenir shop and winebar-restaurant, which is at the top of Gaotai's grass ski slope.

Frog & Pheasant B&B GUESTHOUSE $$

(青蛙與雉雞民宿, Qīngwā Yǔ Zhìjī Mínsù; ☑ 886 9738 29665; http://fp.taitungbnb.tw; Lane 21, No 16, Pingding Rd, Ruilong village, Luye; 瑞隆村坪頂路21巷16號; d/q NT$2000/2800; ✳🔊🐾) For a middle-of-nowhere, agricultural vibe, head 6km north of Luye where this neat if simply adorned Spanish-style villa is set amid fields around 400m east of Ruiyan train station, one stop north of Luye.

ⓘ Getting There & Away

The Taiwan Tourist Shuttle bus (www.taiwantrip.com.tw/line/17?x=4&y=2) runs six times daily from Taitung bus station, taking an hour to Luye train station (NT$95), or 80 minutes to the Gaotai terminus stop on the plateau (NT$120). Last returns are at 4.10pm or 5.10pm.

ⓘ Getting Around

The plateau has several bus stops, with the shuttle bus service looping around from the visitor centre to Gaotai (alight for paragliding) and Gaotai East (at the bottom of the grass ski slope).

TAITUNG

☑ 089 / POP 105,500

The relaxed coastal city of Taitung (台東 or 臺東; Táidōng) is a highly likeable transportation hub from which travellers access Green Island, Lanyu and Taiwan's southern east coast.

A former spur-line station once brought trains into the centre, the former station is now part of a vibrant urban renewal project, the 'Railway Art Village'. That's a fine area in which to base yourself while in town. Citywide, there are plentiful Taoist temples and shrines amid the otherwise modern street grid, which is softened at the edges with large seaside and forest parks and backed in the near distance with lush green mountains. You don't need to scratch too hard beneath the surface to discover the city's cultural diversity, with its strong indigenous presence and a growing inflow of Taiwan's more bohemian set, some of whom have settled here to open cafes.

⊙ Sights

Taitung Railway Art Village ARTS CENTRE
(台東鐵道藝術村, Táidōng Tiědào Yìshùcūn; ☑089-320 378; 369 Tiehua Rd; 鐵花路369號) A spur line once brought trains to the centre of Taitung. That line was decommissioned in 2001 and has since been turned into an excellent cycle path. The old station building now hosts an information centre, exhibition room, bus station and graphic design gallery. The area all around has been gentrified into a park-like cultural space with a range of enticing bars and eateries.

National Museum of Prehistory MUSEUM
(國立臺灣史前文化博物館, Guólì Táiwān Shǐqiáng Wénhuà Bówùguǎn; ☑089-381 166; https://en.nmp.gov.tw; 1 Museum Rd; 博物館路1號; adult/child NT$80/50; ⊙9am-5pm Tue-Sun) This hi-tech and engaging if occasionally disorientating museum charts Taiwan's geological birth and human prehistory as well as introducing the island's indigenous Austronesian peoples.

There's a cafe serving indigenous food (closed Tuesdays) and the vast building is set in attractively manicured parkland. It's 8km west of central Taitung. The only sensible bus services leave Taitung bus station (NT$25, 20 minutes) at 11.30am and 3.50pm, plus 8.30am on public holidays, returning at 4.31pm and 5.11pm

Beinan Site Park PARK
(卑南遺址公園, Pēinán Yízhǐ Gōngyuán; ☑089-233 466; www.nmp.gov.tw; 200 Wenhua Gongyuan Rd; 文化公園路200號; exhibition centre adult/child NT$30/15; ⊙park 24hr, buildings 9am-5pm Tue-Sun) If you've got an hour to wait for a train, a fine way to spend it is strolling through this landscaped park. It features a significant Neolithic site, but is more visually interesting for the reconstructed straw and bamboo prehistoric houses designed on the evidence of the archaeological findings.

An exhibition centre gives more context. From the train station, it's only 400m away: exit past the taxi rank then turn right and walk under the rail-bridge. At the T-junction, climb the steps and turn left to find the dig site. Walk through or around that to find the main park sections.

Seashore Park PARK
(Paposogan, 海濱公園, Hǎibīn Gōngyuán; Datong Rd; 大同路; ⊙light show 8pm & 9pm.) FREE A pleasant place to smell the sea air, this park's signature feature is known immodestly as the Taitung International Landmark (台東國際地標; Táidōng Guójì Dìbiāo). That's a snaking arc of artistically pointless pedestrian ramp with rattan-weave shading that puts on a ten-minute light show at night and a central pavilion that looks like a partly deflated soufflé. Inside that hides a curious tree-like structure.

Tianhou Temple TEMPLE
(天后宮, Tiānhòu Gōng; www.taitungmazu.org.tw; 222 Zhonghua Rd, Sec 1; 中華路一段222號; ⊙6am-10pm) Set on a big courtyard of ornate gateways lit with massed clusters of lanterns, this is Taitung's largest temple. It's a beautifully proportioned, intensely colourful landmark, dedicated to Mazu, the goddess of the sea.

Liyushan Park PARK
(鯉魚山公園, Lǐyúshān Gōngyuán; Bo'ai Rd; 博愛路) For sweeping views across Taitung to the ocean and, on clear days Green Island, climb to the viewing platform in this steep, wooded park. It's just ten minutes' walk from the bus station. The park has other walks and an eight-storey concrete pagoda that looks much more authentic at night.

MID-JULY HARVEST FESTIVAL

A photogenic highlight of the **Rukai Harvest Festival** (Tsatsapipianu, 魯凱族豐收祭, Lǔkǎizú Fēngshōují; Dongxing village, Beinan township; 卑南鄉東興村; ⊙mid-Jul) sees colourfully dressed Rukai women standing, one after another, on a *tiyuma* (a swing hung from tall bamboo crosspieces), each being pushed ever higher by a male tribe member (traditionally her beau). Dancing and singing enfold the scene.

Another feature is the baking of millet cake whose moistness (or lack thereof) is thought to foretell the amount of rainfall that will be received in the coming year. By far the best-known version is held at the far end of Taromak (達魯瑪克), as locals call interesting Dongxing village. The giant swing stand and several thatched festival huts can be seen year-round and are worth a quick visit if you're driving by. The site is 1.2km off Hwy 9: turn west at Km384 and follow the river.

Xiaoyeliu
PARK

(小野柳, Xiǎo Yěliǔ; ☑ 089-281 136; No 500, Sec 1, Songjiang Rd; 松江路一段500號; ☺ visitor centre 8.30am-5pm; Ⓟ) FREE The seafront rocks within this coastal park are geological curiosities, many forming cuesta structures: angled geological sandwiches with alternating soft and hard layers where differential erosion creates a range of picturesque shapes, often evoking culinary names, notably mushrooms and tofu.

🏃 Activities

Taitung Shanhai Bicycle Trail
CYCLING

(台東山海鐵馬道, Táidōng Shānhǎi Tiěmǎdào; ☺ 24hr) FREE This 21km mostly flat loop around Taitung follows a clearly signposted, tree-shaded path, starting from the Railway Art Village (p195) and initially following the old railway spur line. It passes canals and paddy fields and loops back to the oceanfront via the delightful **Forest Park** (臺東森林公園; Táidōng Sēnlín Gōngyuán; 300 Huatai Rd; 華泰路300号; adult/child NT$30/20; ☺ 6am-7pm).

🛏 Sleeping

Rococo Blue
HOSTEL $

(洛可可藍的櫥窗裡, Luòkěkě Lánde Chúchuānglǐ; https://154587658100.web.fullinn.tw; 5th fl, 490 Boai Rd; 博愛路490號 5樓; dm $660-800; ☺ reception 3-8pm; ❀ 🛜) An unlikely blue metal door and four flights of stairs lead to this flashpacker marvel where dorms have top-quality mattresses and linens, shared showers use organic herbal shampoo, hairdryers are in velvet bags and you can make yourself fine coffee on a De'Longhi machine.

Traveller Inn
HOTEL $

(TieHua Cultural and Creative Hotel, 旅人驛站 - 鐵花文創館, Lǚrén Yìzhàn – Tiěhuā Wénchuàng Guǎn; ☑ 089-352 200; www.traveler-inn.com; 402 Zhonshan Rd; 中山路402號; dm/d from NT$700/2200; ☺ reception 24hr; ❀ 🛜) Perfectly located, this sparkling new place offers comfy, unfussy contemporary rooms along with high-quality, curtain-bunked dorms with good lockers.

Hostel Who Knows
HOSTEL $

(遊民公社, Yóumín Gōngshè; ☑ 08-936 1279; www.facebook.com/who.knows.hostel; 265 Fujian Rd; 福建路265號; dm NT$500; ☺ reception 3-9pm) Of Taitung's cheaper, downtown minihostels, Who Knows wins on its low-key, jazz/bohemian vibe, its unusually bright and airy layout and the great spoken English of owner Jackson. The two dorm areas are pretty spacious and bunks have personal lamps, but the lack of lockers might worry security-conscious guests.

⭐ The Gaya Hotel
LUXURY HOTEL $$$

(度假酒店, Dùjiǎ Jiǔdiàn; ☑ 08-961 1888; www.gaya-hotels.com; 169 Xinsheng Rd; 新生路169號; d from NT$4279) In a brilliantly located, guacamole-coloured tower, Gaya's upmarket lobby creates a distinctive, brooding mood with its acres of black bamboo. Hallways are artistic, with lamp-box room numbers, and beds are swoon-worthily comfortable. But the killer feature is the 11th-floor rooftop infinity pool with almost 360-degree views.

🍴 Eating

Hefei Seafood
SEAFOOD $

(合發漁食, Héfā Yúshí; ☑ 0952-043 020; http://picdeer.com/hefaseafood; 305 Fugang St; 富岡街305號; mains from NT$90; ☺ 8.30am-4.30pm) A whole row of ultrasimple eateries at Fugang Port offer superb fish at very reasonable prices, cooking up a catch that's just been landed from boats that dock behind. Choose whichever restaurant takes your fancy, or pick Hefei for its English-language menu and extraordinarily generous portions of top-quality swordfish sashimi.

Red Quinoa
HEALTH FOOD $

(七里坡, Qīlǐpō; ☑ 08-932 5777; 203 Zhongzheng St; 中正路203號; mains NT$60-180; ☺ 11am-8.15pm Thu-Tue; ❀) While by no means meat-free, this semi-fast-food, counter-order place has plenty of vegetarian options, some vegan, and most incorporating at least some locally produced quinoa. Don't miss adding one or two of the small, imaginative side dishes like palate-baffling lotus root in grapefruit.

Ming Long Vegetarian Restaurant
TAIWANESE $

(明隆春捲專賣店, Mínglóng Chūnjuǎn Zhuānmàidiàn; 453 Zhengqi Rd; 正氣路453號; wraps NT$40; ☺ 8am-8pm) The interior is blandly neutral but Ming Long's wholewheat vegan wraps are the draw here, not the decor.

⭐ Uncle Pete's
PIZZA $$

(披薩阿伯, Pīsà Ābó; ☑ 0952-179 165; 167 Linhai Rd Sec 1; 臨海路一段167號; half/full pizza NT$195/360; ☺ 5-9pm Wed-Mon & 11.30am-2.30pm Wed-Fri; ❀) The pizza is excellent, with a thin, crispy, melt-in-the-mouth crust (half is ideal for one person). But the idiosyncratic decor is a big part of the attraction

BOMBING MASTER HANDAN

Taitung's most popular Lantern Festival activity only began in 1954, and is intimately tied to the gangsterism that has long plagued small-town life in Taiwan. Called Bombing Master Handan (炸寒單; Zhà Hándān), the festival is, depending on which legend you believe, a celebration of a former Shang dynasty general (and god of wealth and war) who hates the cold, or a more recent thuggish leader who asked for his followers to blast him to death in payment for his crimes.

Either way, 'warming' him with firecrackers and bottle rockets as he passes by is considered a good way to win this god's favour.

The twist in the Taitung festival is that volunteers accompanying the Handan god statue on his procession across town wear nothing but red shorts and a few protective items (goggles, gloves, scarf, amulet). So dressed, they willingly subject themselves to the same treatment Handan is getting. Few can stand this for more than ten minutes. That's one reason why this strange tradition has been seen as linked to organised crime: volunteers might be current or ex-gangsters looking to display their courage, or to atone for past sins.

Though banned for years because of its connection with mobsterism, the festival, which takes place on the 15th day of the Lunar New Year, has regained popularity and is now one of Taiwan's top folk events.

For a behind-the-scenes look at the festival, check out Ho Chao-ti's *The Gangster's God: A Film of the Taiwanese Underworld* (炸神明).

too, with surfboards out front, swing table in the middle, and piano, violin and guitars awaiting spontaneous musical outbursts.

MiBaNai TAIWANESE INDIGENOUS $$$
(米巴奈山地美食坊, Mǐbānài Shāndì Měishífāng; ☑089-220 336; 470 Chuanguang Road; 傳廣路470號; meals NT$330-550; ⊗11am-1.30pm & 5-7.30pm; ⊛) Popular with tour groups, MiBaNai is Taitung's classic address for local indigenous cuisine, including stir-fried venison, roast salt fish, betel-flower salad (summer only) and their signature baby corns wrapped in bacon. The distinctive green-roofed building is 2km north of the Railway Art Village, 3km southeast of the train station. Reservations are advisable.

🍷 Drinking & Nightlife

⭐ **Taimali Cafe** COFFEE
(太麻里文創咖啡館, Tàimálǐ Wénchuàng Kāfēiguǎn; 307 Fujian Rd; 福建路307號; ⊗10am-6pm Wed-Mon, to 7pm in summer; ⓐ) In a garden of poinsettia, one of Taitung's finest Japanese-style wooden houses acts as showcase for local floral teas (NT$120) and single-estate organic coffees (NT$250) grown in Huayuan village. A small but excellent range of snacks includes French toast served with tangy custard-apple sauce. Even the music is local.

Liang Ge Beer CRAFT BEER
(喨哥Beer, Liàng Gē Beer; 241 Fujian Road; 福建路241號; ⊗7.30pm-late Mon-Sat) This unassuming little box of a bar is a veritable treasure trove for beer lovers, stocking dozens of mostly Belgian brews, including a wide range of Trappists.

Mese Coffee CAFE
(草月咖啡館, Cǎo yuè kāfēi guǎn; ☑089-362 168; 54 Rende St; 仁德街54號; ⊗2-10pm Fri-Tue; ⓐ) Passionate coffee enthusiast Rory Lee lovingly roasts his own beans, producing edgy espressos (from NT$70) and a range of single-origin brews (NT$150-200) including a local Taiwanese 'Wild Lilly'. This relaxed cafe is in the lane directly behind (ie north of) Tianhou Temple (p195).

☆ Entertainment

Tiehua Music Village LIVE MUSIC
(鐵花村音樂聚落, Tiěhuācūn Yīnyuè Jùluò; ☑08-934 3393; www.tiehua.com.tw; 26 Lane 153, Xinsheng Rd; 新生街135巷26號; ⊗2-10pm Wed-Sun) An old railway repair facility has been artistically repurposed with the help of Taitung's independent musicians and artists, into a magical bar and performance space which hosts an open-mic night on Wednesdays, local bands Thursdays and bigger names on some weekends.

LOCAL KNOWLEDGE

FUGANG HARBOUR

This fishing **port** (富岡漁港, Fùgǎng Yúgǎng), 6km northeast of central Taitung, is an interesting place to wait for a ferry. There's a whole row of fishmonger-cafes along the wharf where you can get utterly stupendous fresh sashimi at prices that seem absurdly reasonable (15 slices of tuna and swordfish NT$150). If you walk 10 minutes north, you'll reach the interesting visitor centre of Xiaoyeliu (p196), a sizeable park that features sea-eroded rock formations and banyan trees. To find the pedestrian shortcut, look for the grey-green gate where the port's sea-mosaic wall ends. If that's locked, the walk takes a few minutes longer.

City buses and the East Coast Tourist Shuttle both stop right outside the ticket office. Diingdong public buses to/from Dulan, Chenggong etc pass by on the main road, stopping outside the Xiaoyeliu main entrance.

Shopping

Bolton FASHION & ACCESSORIES
(Bolton 皮革工房, Bolton Pígé Gōngfáng; ☑089-341 136; www.boltontw.com; 15 Lane 586, Chonghua Rd Sec 1; 中華路一段586巷15號; ⊘10am-9pm) For handmade leather craft and bags fashioned from repurposed sacking, visit this workshop/boutique in a quirky little neighbourhood of graffiti-muralled houses tucked behind the old train station.

Kintuka Coffee Plantation COFFEE
(金土咖莊園, Jīntǔkǎ Zhuāngyuán; ☑089-513 682; 132 Taikeng Lane, 8th Commercial Rd, Taimali; 太麻里鄉八鄰產業道路大坑道路132號; ⊘8am-6pm) One of Taiwan's niche coffee growers, little family-run Kintuka also bakes homemade, stick-shaped coffee biscuits, creates turmeric-yellowed tea and produces August-ripening 'golden fruit' (*abiu*, originally from Amazonia). Assuming you plan to buy something, tastings are free on a small shaded terrace overlooking an amphitheatre of green ridges and Huayuan Bay beach, some 400m vertically below.

Coffee beans cost NT$800 for 225g, tea NT$900 for 30 bags, cookies NT$250 per pack. Access is up 3km of very narrow lane starting from the traffic lights at Km396.5 of Hwy 9, around 6km north of central Taimali.

Information

Taitung Visitor Information Centre (遊客服務中心, Lǚyóu Fúwù Zhōngxīn; ☑089-357 131; https://tour.taitung.gov.tw; 369 Tiehua Rd; 鐵花路369號; ⊘8.30am-5.30pm Mon-Fri, 8am-6pm Sat & Sun) English-speaking help and free, if slightly confusing, maps right beside the bus station, with another branch outside the train station.

Bank of Taiwan (373 Zhonghua Rd; 中華路373號; ⊘9am-3.30pm Mon-Fri) Money exchange and 24-hour international ATM

Taitung Hospital (臺東醫院, Táidōng Yīyuàn; ☑089-324 112; www.tait.mohw.gov.tw; 1 Wuquan St; 五權街1號) This government hospital has a 24-hour emergency department.

Getting There & Away

AIR

The civilian **airport** (臺東航空站; Táidōng Hángkōngzhàn (TTT); www.tta.gov.tw) is 5km northwest of the city centre. There are flights to Taipei-Songshan with Uni Air (www.uniair.com.tw) and Mandarin Airlines (www.mandarin-airlines.com). For Lanyu and Green Island, you'll need **Daily Air Corporation** (☑089-362 675; www.dailyair.com.tw; Taitung Airport; ⊘7am-4pm) which uses 19-seater prop-planes and suffers regular cancellations on windy days. They have an all-in-Chinese website but to book you need to phone – the Visitor Information Centre can help – then pay on the day of departure once the flight's operation has been confirmed.

From the bus station there are currently eight daily airport-bound #8128 services (NT$25, 20 minutes, first 7.50am, platform 7). Three much slower TTB minibuses (NT$25, first 6.30am, platform 8) take 40 minutes. From the airport, last services back to town are at 6.40pm and 9pm.

There are also 13 daily buses from the airport to the train station and four daily to Fugang Harbour (departing at 7.10am, 10.30am, 3.40pm and 5.20pm).

BOAT

Boats to Lanyu and Green Island (Ludao) depart from Fugang Harbour.

Website ferry.tw gives an idea of potential sailings, but actual departures on all routes will be dependent both on weather and the number of passengers so cancellations are common, especially in winter. Ask a Chinese-speaking friend (or tourist office) to book on the phone, but verify on the day of travel. Arrive at least 40 minutes ahead of departure to pay for the ticket: you'll need a passport or Taiwanese ID to do this. Prepaying a return is wise and can later be changed. Boarding starts half an hour before departure.

If you want to visit both islands, then it's possible from approximately May to August to buy a triangular ticket (三角航線船票), but you must go to Lanyu first as usually it doesn't work in reverse.

BUS

Some buses start from the helpfully central **bus station** (台東轉運站, Táidōng zhuǎnyùn zhàn; ☑ 089-357 131; https://taitung.biz; 369 Tiehua Rd; 鐵花路369號) beside the Railway Art Village (p195). Others start opposite the train station. Some call at both.

Useful services include:

Coastal Towns Tourist Shuttle East Coast Line (8101, www.taiwantrip.com.tw/line/40?x=4&y=2) has five daily buses from Taitung bus station via the train station to Sanxiantai (NT$202, 1¾ hours) with useful stops at Fugang Harbour (for boats to Green Island and Lanyu), Xiaoyeliu, Shanyuan Beach, Dulan, Jinzun and Chenggong. **Diingdong buses** (鼎東汽車客運公司, Dǐngdōng Qìchē Kèyùn Gōngsī; ☑ 089-325 106; http://diingdong.myweb.hinet.net) to various other coastal destinations, notably Chenggong, leave Taitung around hourly, some from the bus station, others from the train station. These go via Dulan but for Fugang Harbour you'll need to hop off at Xiaoyeliu and walk (less than 10 minutes).

Hualien Bus 8119 and 1127, each once daily, are the only through services. Otherwise change in Chenggong.

Luye Plateau The Tourist Shuttle East Rift Valley service (route 8168, NT$120, 80 minutes) departs Taitung bus station at 8.30am, 9.30am, 11.30am, 1.30pm, 2.30pm and 3.30pm, collecting passengers at the train station 15 minutes later. Last return is at 5.10pm.

Zhiben Bus 8129 (NT$50, 20 minutes) runs 16 times daily from the bus station platform 1. Last return at 10pm.

Other There are a few daily buses to Kaohsiung, but trains are faster and cheaper. There is no direct bus to Kenting.

TRAIN

The train station (臺鐵臺東站) is around 5km north of the city centre. From here trains serve:

Hualien (fast/Chu-Kuang/local NT$343/264/220), two to 3½ hours, over 20 per day

Kaohsiung (fast/Chu-Kuang train NT$351/279), 2¼ to 3½ hours, at least 12 daily

ⓘ Getting Around

BICYCLE

Taitung is built for cycling, with several great trails. Most hotels rent basic bicycles, and you can find others at the Seashore Park (p195), but for something higher quality, go to the **Giant store** (捷安特台東店, Jié'āntè Táidōngzhàn; ☑ 0980-014 283; 255 Xinzhan Rd, Yanwanli; 岩灣里新站路255號; ⊙ 8am-6pm) one block east of the main train station, or get a racer from **TR9** (☑ 0958-883 188; Taitung train station; scooters per day NT$450-500; ⊙ 8am-6pm).

BUS

From the train station to the bus station (NT$25, 25 to 35 minutes), there are three or four buses per hour, the last at 9.25pm, 10pm and 10.45pm. The tourist info office in the station (open till 5.30pm) has a full timetable. They depart from the southeast side of the station car park – across the east-west station access road from what appears to be the lost nose cone of a space shuttle.

The land-sea-air express line route (陸海空快線去; lùhǎikōng kuài xiànqù) has buses roughly hourly from the train station to Fugang Port for boats to Green Island and Lanyu. Others link the airport, train station and bus station about as often.

CAR & MOTORCYCLE

Most of Taitung's scooter-rental places refuse foreigners unless they have a Taiwanese licence. However, TR9 is an exception and will rent if you have an international driving permit and possibly even with your national licence. As you exit from the main train station it's well signed, immediately on your right within the OK convenience store.

TAXI

Yellow taxis congregate at the train station and opposite Traveller Inn (p196) near the bus station.

CHIHPEN

☑ 089 / POP 3000

Chihpen (Jhiben; Zhiben; 知本; Zhīběn) lies about 15km southwest of Taitung in a narrowing valley cutting into the Dawu Mountains. Regularly attracting over 70,000 visitors a month, it's one of Taiwan's most popular hot-spring areas, with rows of multistar hotels, garish karaoke parlours and clogged traffic at weekends. At the far end of the canyon, however, there's respite in the lush jungle park with its beautiful banyan forest.

⊙ Sights

Chihpen Forest Recreation Area PARK (知本森林遊樂區, Zhīběn Sēnlín Yóulè Qū; ☑ 886-8951 0961; www.forest.gov.tw; Km0, Rte 194; adult weekday/weekend NT$80/100, child NT$50; ⊙ 8am-4.30pm, to 5.30pm Jul & Aug) The core of this forest park is a 45-minute walk to a bamboo grove past a botanic garden, herb

ⓘ WHERE TO STAY?

Visiting from Taitung makes sense, but if you want to stay there's a huge array of options. Many of the hotels are large, rather unattractive buildings but there are also smaller guesthouses and if driving in, you might see roadside touts waving signs at you offering deals.

garden and a 'forest fun' area for children. Longer trails wind through an area of giant 'weeping fig' (banyan) trees with hanging, aerial roots that form a complex spider-web-like design. However, at the time of research this route was temporarily closed.

In the deeper forest areas, it's common to see Formosan macaques, and you might also catch a glimpse of barking deer. The recreation area is across the bright-red bridge at the end of Rte 194, around 5km west of the start of the hot-spring area.

🏃 Activities

Toyugi Hot Spring Resort & Spa
HOT SPRINGS
(東遊季溫泉度假村, Dōngyóujì Wēnquán Dùjiàcūn; ☑089-516 111; www.toyugi.com.tw; 18 Lane 376, Wenquan Rd; 溫泉路376巷18號; per person NT$300; ☺8am-11pm) If you've come to Chihpen for a few hours' soak rather than to sleep in a resort hotel, Toyugi is a good choice as you get not only a choice of covered and outdoor hot-spring pools, but also a fair-sized swimming pool in a pleasant garden area.

Bring swimwear, cap and towel or purchase them in the spa shop. The complex is in a relatively open site near the far (eastern end) of Chihpen. Turn north at Km4 of Rte 194, just before the big 7-Eleven store and it's around 300m. Should you choose to stay, their hotel rooms start at NT$2500/2750 weekdays/weekends.

ⓘ Getting There & Away

From Taitung bus station platform 1, bus 8129 (NT$50, 20 minutes) runs 16 times daily, with the last return bus at 10pm. The final stop is around 600m short of the Forest Park (p199).

GREEN ISLAND

☑089 / POP 4070
Green Island (綠島; Lǜdǎo) is a popular resort destination for Taiwanese seeking rest and recreation, particularly snorkelling

and diving. But in the not-too-distant past, the phrase 'off to Green Island' conjured up entirely different images in the Taiwanese psyche: until its closure in the 1990s, the island was synonymous with its notorious prison camp to which the regime's political opponents were sent to languish during the martial law period.

Lying 30km east of Taitung, the island is ringed by a 19km road that you can get around on a scooter in 40 minutes. The northwest corner is blandly urbanised, but the rest of the coast is delightfully underpopulated, with thick woodlands and some dramatically wild ocean landscapes along the east edge.

◉ Sights

★ National Human Rights Museum
HISTORIC SITE
(白色恐怖綠島紀念園區, Báisè Kǒngbù Lǜdǎo Jìniàn Yuánqū; Green Island White Terror Memorial Park; ☑089-671 095; https://en.nhrm.gov.tw; 20 Jiangjunyan; 將軍岩20號; ☺9am-5pm) FREE Green Island's windswept northeast corner was completely out of bounds for much of the 20th century, occupied by a large prison camp. Here, political opponents of the regime were incarcerated and 're-educated' during Taiwan's White Terror and Martial Law periods (1949–87). Most of the watchtowers and chillingly banal buildings still stand, now forming a sprawling memorial museum. It's well worth a visit, but pick up the free explanatory leaflets as little else is in English.

Directly east of Gongguan harbour, the first related site is a beautifully manicured lawn containing an excavated trench in which is the National Human Rights Monument. Fronted by photogenic, wave-lashed rocky spires, views from the park are memorable. Around 200m beyond, the most obviously prison-like structure was sardonically referred to as Oasis Villa (綠洲山莊; Shānzhuāng). Here you can peep into the forlorn, mostly featureless jail cells. However, rather more interesting (if less visited, 300m further east), is the New Life re-education camp, where two of the timber-walled halls demonstrate living conditions of the time using waxwork mannequins.

If you continue 800m further along the coast, the road soon degenerates into a rough stoney track, passing razor-wired old walls and a 'water torture' pillbox before dead-ending at a lonely little graveyard for some of the '13th Squadron' (ie the prisoners who succumbed). It's a sombre but scenically memorable spot. Walk another 400m along the beach past scuttling crabs, then climb a short rise to reach a large cave full of swooping swallows. This was once used as theatre in which inmates rehearsed and performed re-education plays to demonstrate their new-found faith in the regime. Some say it was also used as an execution ground and mortuary, and consider it haunted.

Little Great Wall   VIEWPOINT
(小長城, Xiǎo chángchéng; Rte 90東, Km8) One of the most beautiful viewpoints on Green Island is reached by walking a 300m path along a precipitous high promontory called Little Great Wall. This was formed as the northern crater lip of the volcano that produced Green Island. From a pair of pavilions, gaze down across the crater bay, Haishen-ping (海參坪; Hǎishēnpíng), to a natural rock arch called Sleeping Beauty (睡美人; Shuì Měirén).

Youzihu   GHOST TOWN
(柚子湖, Yòuzǐhú) Signposted down paved switchbacks off the east coast road, Youzi-hu is a ghost village whose overgrown ruins sit on a cove set behind a dramatic array of stone formations and a rock-pool waterfront lashed by pounding waves. For a bracing walk (low tide only), head north to a large sea-eroded cave.

Guanyin Cave   TAOIST SHRINE
(觀音洞, Guānyīn Dòng) Worth a one-minute stop when driving the lovely east coast route, this little cave-shrine features a stalagmite wrapped with a red cape. The stalagmite is thought to resemble the form of the goddess Guanyin, who is renowned for saving distressed seamen.

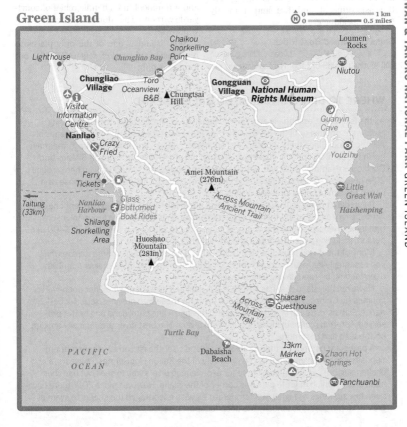

🏃 Activities

⭐ Zhaori Hot Springs   HOT SPRINGS

(朝日溫泉, Zhāorì Wēnquán; ☑089-671 133; 167 Wenquan Rd; 溫泉路167號; adult/child NT$200/100; ⊘6am-11pm or later) Planet Earth is only known to have three seawater hot springs, and Zhaori (Chaorih) is one of them. The lonely complex encloses an area of rock-pool beach with a trio of simple, circular dip pools close to the waves and a more enticing set of modern outdoor pools near the entrance. There are also a couple of shaft wells used for proving that the water is naturally hot enough to cook an egg: it takes 12 minutes and costs NT$50 per egg.

Blue Safari
Diving Centre   DIVING, SNORKELLING

(藍莎潛水中心, Lánshā Qiánshuǐ Zhōngxīn; ☑089-671 888; www.blue-safari.com.tw; 72 Gong-guan village; 公館村72號; ⊘8am-6pm) Reputable and professional, this PADI dive club in the centre of Gongguan is run by enthusiasts Vincent and Eva and a mostly English-speaking crew.

Glass Bottomed Boat Rides   BOATING

(綠島鄉公所玻璃遊艇, Lǜdǎo Xiānggōngsuǒ Bōlí Yóutǐng; ☑089-672 180; Nanliao Harbour; per person NT$300; ⊘9am & 3pm) To see colourful fish and remnant corals without getting in the water, these brief boat trips give you a glimpse of the Shilang reef. The ticket office opens 20 minutes before each departure, but it's easier (and the same price) to book through your hotel.

Taiwan Dive   DIVING

(☑0916-130 288; www.taiwandive.com) Advanced divers wanting to observe the hammerhead shark migration off Green Island's southeast point might consider organising a specialist tour with this highly experienced outfit.

🛏 Sleeping

Slow Island Hostel   HOSTEL $

(綠島緩島旅宿, Lǜdǎo Huǎndǎo Lǚsù; ☑0928-035 826; Nanliao 110-1; 南寮110-1號; dm/tw NT$800/1800; ❄🛜🖳) Making up for somewhat cramped living spaces, this new, sociable midstrip hostel has hammocks and a minipool in its handkerchief of courtyard garden. The dorms are comfy but windowless.

Slow Island is one of the only places to rent mask-and-snorkel sets (NT$100), but for guests only.

WHERE TO DIVE & SNORKEL ON GREEN ISLAND

As the island was essentially an off-limits penal colony for decades, the surrounding reefs were pristine until the 1990s, with over 200 coral types and up to 600 varieties of fish recorded. Since then, thousands of snorkellers, divers and fishermen each year have given the coral a pounding. In season, the popular shore-dive sites just off Shilang and Chaikou are jammed solid with wetsuit-sporting groups, yet somehow even here around 20% of the corals cling to life and the plethora of colourful fish will impress those who haven't swum at better-preserved sites.

If you didn't bring your own snorkel, mask and flippers, it's very tough to rent one as almost every agency (and there are dozens) demands that you join a group to ensure that inexperienced swimmers don't get carried out to sea. Group trips cost NT$400 per person, including wetsuit, booties and life jacket, but no flippers.

Many of the diving trips offered (NT$2500, two hours) are beginner tasters in which you essentially learn just enough not to kill yourself, then float in water less than 10m deep feeding fish and having selfies taken.

However, the island also has several PADI-qualified dive shops who offer open-water courses (in Chinese) and more ambitious dives for those with previous scuba experience. Dabaisha Beach (大白沙; Dà Báishā) has fine white coral sand and better preserved, fish-rich reefs which are popular with divers. The best dives are, logically enough, boat-based and cost more.

A particular hotspot for marine life is the island's southeast corner, where nutrient deposits have been enriched by the proximity of the Zhaori Hot Springs. For years, a challenging but satisfying quest here for experienced divers was to seek out hammerhead sharks which migrate past this corner of the island. However, since 2017, there have been few sightings as higher sea temperatures have encouraged the sharks to swim at greater depth that is essentially too deep for sport divers.

Blue Safari Diving
Centre Hostel
HOSTEL **$**

(藍莎潛水中心, Lánshā Qiánshuǐ Zhōngxīn; ☑089-671 888; www.blue-safari.com.tw; 72 Gongguan village; 公館村72號; dm/d incl breakfast NT$860/1800; ❄️🛜) Next door to its dive shop, Blue Safari has a well-maintained 10-bed mixed dorm above a communal sitting room. There are no lockers, but the timber bunks are curtained and come with power points, personal lamps and small windows.

Good Viewing Spot
GUESTHOUSE **$$**

(好望角無敵海景民宿, Hǎowàngjiǎo Wúdí Hǎijǐng Mínsù; ☑0934-082 252, 089-672241; http://h-w-j.okgo.tw; 33 Gongguan; 公館村33號; r without/with balcony NT$3500/4500; ❄️🛜) Immaculately maintained contemporary rooms are softened with picture detailing in this Mediterranean-flavoured guesthouse, which is enviably placed on the peaceful harbourfront lane that parallels Gongguan's main drag.

Shiacare Guesthouse
B&B **$$**

(Chagall B&B, 夏卡爾民宿, Xiàkǎ'ěr Mínsù; ☑0928-438 018, 089-672 800; www.ith.idv.tw; 48 Wenquan; 溫泉路48號; d from NT$2500-4000; ❄️🛜) This welcoming, 11-room B&B is an excellent choice for families, with ample play space and a large sunrise view lounge. It's a rare east-coast option, just 1.5km north of the hot springs.

★ Toro Oceanview B&B
BOUTIQUE HOTEL **$$$**

(Toro 觀海民宿, Toro Guānhǎi Mínsù; ☑0955-737 555; www.torovilla.com.tw/en; 33-2 Chaikou; 柴口33-2號; d NT$6000-7000; ❄️🛜) Pure class. This beachfront villa has just three guest rooms but each has large ocean-view terraces and a pampered sense of relaxed-yet-sophisticated style. There's also a kitchen and wooden, floor-seated lounge area in classic Japanese style. Eran speaks good English.

It's 300m west of the Chaikou snorkelling point.

✖ Eating

Seaside
FUSION **$**

(海邊坐坐, Hǎibiān Zuòzuò; ☑0983-724 268; 67 Gongguan; 公館村67號; meal sets NT$160-190; ⏱11.30am-2pm & 6-10pm Wed-Mon) Choose from four beautifully presented sticky-rice meal sets that come artistically arranged on wooden plank-plates with well-chosen garnish dishes. The standouts are the scrumptious peeled baby tomatoes steeped in honey-lemon-plum liquor.

There's an interesting range of Taiwan Head fruit ales, and the young owners are delightful. It's the last house as you drive north through Gongguan before the vista of the triple rock suddenly appears.

Crazy Fried
SEAFOOD **$$**

(非炒不可, Fēichǎo Bùkě; ☑0988-384 323, 089-671057; 126 Nanliao village; 南寮126號; dishes from NT$250; ⏱11am-2.30pm & 5-9pm) One of the most reliable main-strip eateries, the specialities here revolve predominantly around fresh seafood, including catch of the day, garlic scallop strips and sashimi sets. You can also get other local cuisine including stir-fried venison with scallions.

🍷 Drinking & Nightlife

★ The Reefs
COFFEE

(石在有人咖啡館, Shízài Yǒurén Kāfēiguǎn; ☑0930-337 636; 60 Gongguan; 公館村60號; ⏱7.30am-6pm) Boasting one of the island's top baristas, The Reefs use locally grown beans for their excellent coffees, including deliciously subtle (if huge) 'sea salt lattes' (海鹽咖啡拿鐵; hǎiyán kāfēi nátiě). Accompany with lemon cheesecake or a cranberry brownie.

Seats are like solid wooden egg cups, and beautifully cut branches are used as ornamental features. Breakfast sets are available before 10am, and lunch options (noon-3pm) include seafood on turmeric rice with curry sauce (NT$230).

Rudi Shisha
BAR

(鹿迪泰式料理, Lùdítài Shīliàolǐ; ☑0963-335 427; www.facebook.com/LudaoLuChuMo; 111-2 Nanliao; 南寮111-2號; ⏱11am-2pm & 5-10pm) Combining Thai restaurant and shisha bar, this inviting little space has an intriguing 'secret' back room with pit seating and a historic-style hanging kettle over a small fireplace.

ℹ Information

The ATM in Nanliao village does not accept international cards, so bring the cash you'll need.

The main **visitor information centre** (遊客中心, Yóukè Zhōngxīn; ☑089-672 026; 298 Nanliao village; 南寮298號; ⏱8.30am-5pm) offers free brochures and a basic introduction to the island's flora, fauna, aquaculture and history. It's barely a minute's walk from the airport, and has a pleasant little garden behind.

CROSS-GREEN ISLAND TRAILS

Two 1.8km trails cross Green Island, starting within a few hundred metres of each other on the mountain road to Huoshao, descending to the east coast. Both traverse tropical forest on wide, clear paths, with informative signs explaining the botany, and you might spot sika (tiny barking deer). The more southerly of the two routes, called the Across Mountain Ancient Trail (過山古道; Guòshān Gǔdào) offers better views than the confusingly similar-sounding Across Mountain Trail (過山步道; Guòshān Bùdào).

Note that the summit of Huoshao (281m), the island's highest point, is out of bounds due to the military presence.

For a much shorter but very rewarding walk, stroll 500m northeast from a signed turn on the Gongguan to Guanyin lane. This brings you to a grassy bowl of meadow called Niutou, which rises to three sharply pointed minipeaks with magnificent sea and sunrise views.

❶ Getting There & Away

AIR

Daily Air Corporation (www.dailyair.com.tw) has three daily flights between Taitung and Green Island (NT$1028, 15 minutes) on small 19-seat propeller planes. During winter, flights are often cancelled due to bad weather. In summer, you might need to book several weeks ahead. The tiny **airport** (綠島機場, Lǜ Dǎo Jīchǎng; ☑ 089-671194; 231 Nanliao Rd) is at the northern end of the Nanliao commercial strip.

BOAT

Boats leave from Taitung's Fugang Harbour (p198), taking 50 minutes to Green Island (NT$460). From May to September, boats run approximately hourly from 7.30am, with the first return from Green Island at 8.30am. Outside summer, there should be three boats a day (9.30am, 11.30am and 1.30pm from Fugang), but that assumes weather conditions are favourable, and cancellations are possible. Pacific swells at any time can make it an uncomfortable ride, and many passengers get seasick.

A passport or Taiwanese ID is required to buy the ticket. The ferry ticket office in Nanliao is just a couple of windows built into the rear wall of the Profond Duty Free Shop on the north side of the port, but ferries actually leave from the south side, docking beside the long harbour arm.

❶ Getting Around

Almost all hotels offer free pickups if you confirm your arrival flight/boat in advance. Renting a scooter makes sense as a way to see more than the nearest snorkelling site.

BICYCLE

Many hotels rent bicycles for around NT$300 per day, but few are really good enough to cope with the steep slopes on the east coast road.

BUS

Buses circle the island eight to 11 times a day depending on the season. They stop at various tourist points, and can be flagged down anywhere. Schedules are posted at each stop.

SCOOTER

Hundreds of scooters await renters at the harbour, and virtually every accommodation will have their own for hire (NT$350 to NT$450 per day). The hotel might ask if you have an international licence, but will rarely demand to actually examine it. The island's **petrol station** (中油站; Zhōngyóu Zhàn; 7 Yugang Rd, 漁港路7號; ⊙7.30am-6pm) is by the port.

LANYU

☑ 089 / POP 5080

History

Tao folklore suggests that the tribe's progenitors came from Batanes in what is now the Philippines. This seems to fit linguistically, but archaeological evidence hints at the opposite – that Batanes was populated by Tao folk. Either way the close connection shouldn't be so surprising: after all Lanyu is closer to Batanes (145km) than it is to Hualien.

For countless generations, the Tao pretty much had the island to themselves. During the early 20th century, the Japanese were fascinated by the Tao's customs but did little to interfere with their way of life. However, things changed drastically in 1950s after the Kuomintang came to power and attempted to introduce Chinese language and culture, sending boatloads of mainland Chinese to the island. The Tao resisted this encroachment and years of fighting with the Mainlanders ensued. In the late 1960s, Soong Mei Ling (wife of Chiang Kai-shek) declared that the traditional underground homes of the Tao were not fit for humans and ordered they be torn down and new cement structures built in their place. The new houses were poorly made and couldn't hold up to the typhoons that lashed the island every year. At about the same time, the island was opened up to tourism and Taiwanese tourists began to arrive in droves. Christian missionaries soon followed. A large percentage of the population were converted and remain, to this day, primarily Christian.

The Tao are doing their best to preserve their culture in the face of various social issues not uncommon in indigenous communities. Alcoholism is a problem on the island, as is the overall brain drain caused by so many young people leaving to find greater economic prosperity in mainland Taiwan. Even so, Tao traditions on Lanyu remain alive, and one of the benefits that tourism has brought to the island has been to support the younger generation to learn more about their heritage before heading off to mainland Taiwan to seek their fortunes.

Languorous Lanyu (蘭嶼; Lányǔ) has a Pacific island vibe which feels more like Tahiti than Taipei. The indigenous Tao people are of Austronesian descent and speak their own language, calling their home 'Pongso No Tao' (Island of the People). The Taiwanese name Lanyu means Orchid Island, for the flowers that were picked to near extinction after WWII.

Around 65km southeast of Taitung, this volcanic island is made up of two steep, jungle-covered mountains surrounded by a thin strip of coastal land, with six villages and a 36km ring road of bumpy concrete.

Be aware that due to high winds and difficult sea conditions, the island essentially shuts down from November to February or longer. Restaurants, hotels and dive shops close for the season, but a few homestays still operate... if you can reach them.

◎ Sights

Five-hole Cave
CAVE

(Jikarahem, 五孔洞; Wǔkǒng Dòng; Km4.8 Rte 80) **FREE** This is a series of large roadside caves. Visitors can walk through one U-shaped interconnected pair with a white cross at one end. Other entrances are gated and reserved for use by the island's Presbyterian congregation for services on special occasions, such as Easter.

Two Lions Rock
NATURAL FEATURE

(雙獅岩, Shuāngshī Yán; Km11.3, Rte 80) This dramatic rock formation resembling two lions lying face to face rises from the coral beach at the northeastern tip of the island. At high tide it becomes an island. From here, continuing down the east coast is a journey full of scenic drama, with offshore islands visible at Km11.5, particularly glorious views of a crag-backed bay at Km12.3 and a minor pass at Km13.8 from which a trail runs down to a natural rock arch.

Virgin Rock
NATURAL FEATURE

(To-jimavonot, 玉女岩, Yùnǚ Yán; Km5.5, Rte 80) This roadside rock formation has gone through various Chinese names over the years – Virgin Rock, Maiden Rock, Couple Rock, Torch Rock – all reflecting the changing taboos of how to sensitively address its perceived resemblance to feminine anatomy. The Tao, however, call it *To-jimavonot*, meaning Reed Bundle.

Weather Station
VIEWPOINT

(蘭嶼氣象站, Lányǔ Qìxiàng Zhàn) If you're taking the cross-island lane it's possible to make a short detour half-way along that leads up

---

WATER SPORT ON LANYU

Lanyu offers some of Taiwan's most unspoiled coral reefs. Most homestays can arrange snorkelling trips for NT$500. If you have your own snorkel kit, a good place to head is the north coast at Km10.3, where there's parking and access to the reef via a path between the tetrapods.

Blue Ocean (p206) and Tec Only (p206) offer scuba diving and PADI open-water courses, but it's wise to reserve well ahead. For novices, a one-to-one taster dive experience costs NT$2500.

Heavy currents and a dearth of sandy beaches mean that Lanyu isn't ideal for casual swimming, but a couple of grey shingle beaches near Hongtou are OK and there's a lovely little 'secret swimming hole' cut into the coral just northeast of Dongqing: take the lane north from a small coffee shop at Km14.4 past the pig farm, walk five minutes across the rough rocks, then climb down gingerly through the crack.

Lanyu

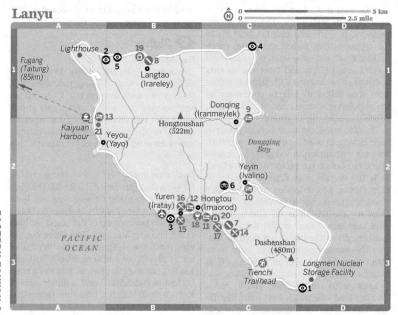

0 ————— 5 km
0 ————— 2.5 mile

Fugang (Taitung) (85km)

Lighthouse
2 5 19 8 Langtao (Irareley) 4
13 21 Yeyou (Yayo) Donqing (Iranmeylek) 9
Kaiyuan Harbour Hongtoushan (522m) Dongqing Bay
Yeyin (Ivalino) 6 10
Yuren 16 12 Hongtou (Iratay) (Imaorod)
3 15 18 11 20 7 14 17
PACIFIC OCEAN
Dashenshan (480m) Longmen Nuclear Storage Facility
Tienchi Trailhead 1

EASTERN TAIWAN & TAROKO NATIONAL PARK LANYU

and up to a weather station at 324m altitude. The station, founded in 1940, is not an attraction in itself but its setting, above the treeline, affords a wide series of views.

Dragon Head Rock NATURAL FEATURE
(龍頭岩, Lóngtóu Yán; Viewpoint Km23.9, Rte 80) Viewed from the south, this rock supposedly resembles the profile of a whiskered Chinese dragon roaring at the sky.

Lan An Cultural Centre CULTURAL CENTRE
(蘭恩文教基金會, Lánēn Wénjiào Jījīn Huì; ☑089-732 073; www.lanan.org.tw; Km31, Rte 80, Yuren; 漁人村147; adult/child NT$100/50; ☺8.30am-noon & 1.30-5pm) This cultural foundation has a museum-like section with costumed mannequins and, in the yard, an example of a Tao underground house. You can generally catch a glimpse without joining a full tour.

🏃 Activities

Blue Ocean House Diving DIVING
(藍海屋潛水, Lánhǎi Wū Qiánshuǐ; ☑0988-331 116; www.boh.com.tw/play; Km28.4, Rte 80; 紅頭村1-8號; ☺7am-10pm Mar-Nov) One of the island's best PADI-certified dive shops.

Tec Only DIVING, SNORKELLING
(TecOnly潛水中心, TecOnly Qiánshuǐ Zhōngxīn; ☑089-732 151; 2nd fl, 3-1 Langtao Village; 朗島

村3-1號2樓; Km6.9, Rte 80; ☺7am-9pm Apr-mid-Oct) Tec Only is a reputable, PADI-certified diving centre with several dive guides who speak English.

The office, facing the harbour in Langtao (Irareley), is upstairs in the yellow three-storey building beside a shop named Among.

🎊 Festivals & Events

Flying Fish Festival CULTURAL
(飛魚季, Fēiyú Jì) A traditional coming-of-age ceremony for young men whose societal standing was traditionally based on how many fish they could catch. The springtime festival is a localised affair and each village celebrates it between March and May on a different day chosen by the elders.

During the festival, the men of the village wear traditional Tao loincloths, bark helmets and breastplates. They smear the blood of a freshly killed chicken on the rocks by the sea and all the while chant 're-turn flying fish' in unison. Then they head out to sea in their *dadala* canoes.

According to custom, women are not allowed to view the festival, but most villages will make exceptions for visitors.

Lanyu

◎ Sights

◎ Activities, Courses & Tours

◎ Sleeping

◎ Eating

◎ Drinking & Nightlife

◎ Shopping

◎ Transport

🛏 Sleeping

Rover Hostel HOSTEL $

(旅人, Lǚrén; ☑ Nick 0933-089 849; https://dearbnb.com/bnb/rover-hostel; 65 Yuren village; 漁人村65號; dm NT$700; ⊙ Apr-mid-Oct; ❋🛜) Lanyu's hippest hostel features a black motorbike as part of the decor in a common room which feels more like a bar than a lounge. The dorms are sex-segregated, with lockers (bring your own padlock), but bunks are small and could prove too short for taller guests. Owner Nick speaks great English.

Fa'ai Homestay HOMESTAY $

(法艾民宿, Fǎài Mínsù; ☑ 0978-641 587; www.facebook.com/lanyufaai; 91 Yeyin village; 野銀村91號; Km16.9, Rte 80; d/q NT$1500/2000; ❋🛜) Eight ensuite rooms in two different properties are relatively simple with older bathrooms at prices that drop to almost dormitory levels outside peak periods (from NT$500).

Owner Hsiao Chiang has an encyclopaedic knowledge of the island and can show you his family's underground houses (NT$250). He speaks no English, but helper Alan does. Look for the bright, mustard-yellow building on the main street of Yeyin (Ivalino), often fronted with wetsuits hung out to dry.

★ DoJimineyLi GUESTHOUSE $$

(原部落精緻民宿, Yuán Bùluò Jīngzhì Mínsù; ☑ 0919-231 100; www.dojimineyli.8898go.com; 142 Dongqing village; 東清村142號; Km14.2, Rte 80; dm/d NT$800/3400) Brand-new, superclean rooms don't have much decor, but their winning feature is the view down onto the azure bay framed by wild, rocky ridges. To get the spectacular full panorama, go up to the open rooftop, though some rooms (notably 308) have partly obscured versions.

It's the three-storey house with canoe-patterned frontage and blue polka-dot sides – one of the last buildings on the seaward side of Rte 80 as you head north out of Dongqing (Iranmeylek). Delightful owner Tai Hui Lan is adept at communicating using Google Translate.

★ Meni's Place HOMESTAY $$

(墨泥家, Mòní Jiā; ☑ 0978-719 003; http://meni.place; 87 Hongtou village; 紅頭村87號; d NT$2000-3200, q NT$3200-4700; ⊙ late-Mar-mid-Oct; ❋🛜) Comfort, views and an artistic take on designer minimalism come together to make Meni's Place so popular that it doesn't even need a sign. The five rooms use an industrial-grey palate enlivened by knick-knacks, distressed furniture and occasional bursts of mural flamboyance. Twin-aspect balconies make the top-floor quad especially superb.

The youthful caretaker speaks English. Meni's Place is not far from the main road but a little hard to find. In Hongtou, take the most northerly of the short lanes that climb inland, then after barely 50m, turn left and walk 40m down the narrow passageway between houses 51 and 83.

Two Fish GUESTHOUSE $$

(兩隻魚, Liǎngzhī Yú; ☑ 0975-190 350; http://twofish.okgo.tw; 296-12 Yeyou village; 椰油村296之12號; d/q NT$3600/4800) Two Fish offers nine clean, comfortable rooms, six of them with balconies overlooking Kaiyuan Harbour where ferries arrive. It's above the west coast's only 7-Eleven, so it's easy to find, though the shop's incessant door chimes, along with noise from the rooftop barbecue restaurant/pub, might disturb early sleepers.

✕ Eating

★ WaWa
FUSION $$

(哇哇, Wāwā; ☑ 0963-165 257, 089-731 615; Km28.9, Rte 80, 7-2 Hongtou village; 紅頭村7-2 號; meals NT$200-300; ⊘ 11.30am-2pm & 5-8pm Mon-Sat Apr-Sep) Driftwood branches, netting and shell-mosaic lamps give a gentle charm to this cosy wooden restaurant, hidden just off the main road in Hongtou (Imaorod) village. The short menu of set meals includes fried flying fish, bacon-taro, Thai chicken and delicious if ill-described 'meat packages', which are actually thin slices of pork in tahini sauce. Delightful staff manage some English.

Driftwood Cafe
CAFE $$

(漂流木, Piāoliúmù; ☑ 089-732 668; 24-2 Yuren village; 漁人村24-2號; Rte 80 Km30.6; meals NT$290-390; ⊘ drinks 10am-10pm, meals 11am-2.30pm & 5.30-9pm, closed Tue) Decorated like a heavily stylised tree, this roadside coffee shop gets wildly busy on holiday lunchtimes for meal sets served on lotus leaves. These include fried flying fish (April to June), but the fatty pork with kimchee on rice is easier to eat.

Blue Fish
SEAFOOD $$

(藍魚海景餐廳, Lányú Hǎijǐng Chāntīng; ☑ 0978-081 089; Km28.1, Rte 80, 1-11 Hongtou; 紅頭村一鄰1-11號; dishes NT$150-450; ⊘ noon-2pm & 4.30-9pm) This is a reliable choice for fresh seafood, though there's minimal atmosphere, with round family tables plonked blandly on a concrete floor.

Epicurean Cafe
TAIWANESE INDIGENOUS $$

(無餓不坐, Wúè Búzuò; ☑ 089-731 623; 77 Yuren village; 漁人村77號; meals NT$200-350; ⊘ 11am-1.30pm & 6-8pm, closed Wed; 🕾) This bright yellow cafe has an attractive open-sided perch for tasting local Tao food or sipping coffee with views across stone-walled lotus ponds towards Lanyu's coral coastline.

HOW THE TAO EAT

Though plagued with bones, fried flying fish (炸飛魚; zhà fēiyú) is a popular seasonal dish, between February and May. Other Tao family favourites include yam, taro and boiled wild vegetables, along with pork and goat meat for special occasions. The Tao traditionally eat with their hands, sometimes using a lotus leaf as a plate.

🍷 Drinking & Nightlife

Rover
COCKTAIL BAR

(旅人, Lūrén; Km29.6, Rte 80; ⊘ 10am-midnight late Mar-early Oct) Lanyu's most happening nightspot, raised just above an attractive bay, serves classic and local cocktails (NT$200-300) – try Lanyu (not Long Island) Ice Tea or lemongrass beer.

🔒 Shopping

Renren Souvenir Shop
GIFTS & SOUVENIRS

(人人特產店, Rénrén Tèchǎn Diàn; ☑ 089-732 583; 47 Hongtou village; 紅頭村47號; ⊘ 8am-9pm) A wonderfully wacky one-stop souvenir stop for all your minicanoe and owl model needs, with a 'museum' in the house next door.

It's in the heart of Hongtou (Imaorod) village, one street back from the coast road and directly behind a shop with the confusingly similar name Wen Wen (km29.2, Rte80). That also has its own decent stock of souvenirs, plus good-value snack meals.

Canaanland
ARTS & CRAFTS

(迦南園工藝坊, Jiānányuán Gōngyìfǎng; ☑ 089-732146; 224 Langtao village 17-1, Km6.5, Rte 80; ⊘ 8am-6pm, restaurant 11am-2pm & 5-7.30pm) This community-run operation occupies an offbeat building with canoe-shaped prow set in its own organic vegetable garden. Partly built with nuclear compensation money, it has a reliable restaurant and sells handmade jewellery and carved wooden relief panels.

It's also the place to come if you want to learn to construct a full-sized Tao canoe by making advance arrangements with master Zong Ja San.

❶ Information

There are no international ATMs on Lanyu.

❶ Getting There & Away

AIR

Daily Air Corporation (德安航空, Déān hángkōng; ☑ 089-732 278; www.dailyair.com. tw) timetables eight to ten flights a day between Taitung and Lanyu (outbound/inbound NT$1428/1360, 30 minutes) but in winter months, bad weather makes cancellations common. Bookings for the 19-seat planes fill up quickly, but as you only pay on the day of departure (once favourable wind conditions are confirmed), last-minute standby seats are often a possibility.

Hotels and homestays provide transport to and from the airport if notified in advance.

LANYU HIKES

The interior of the island has some magnificent hiking, and one of the best leads up to **Tienchi** (Tiānchí, Heaven Lake), an often-dry pond formed inside a volcanic crater on top of Tashenshan (Tashen Mountain). The hike starts easily enough with a stairway at Km26.5, but later gets moderately difficult with one section requiring hikers to navigate their way through a large, rocky ravine. As you climb higher into the jungly elevations, the views open up and there are good opportunities for bird- and butterfly-watching. Allow three to four hours to do the round-trip hike.

For something far easier, park your scooter at Km25.7 where snack vans set up on busy holiday afternoons. Follow the well-worn path towards the sea, turning right at the only junction. This takes you past fine views of an offshore sea stack to a grassy sunset-viewing hillock – lovely but gets crowded at weekends. Allow 20 minutes there and back from the road.

BOAT

Lanyu's port is just north of Yeyou village. There are two access routes, both costing single/return NT$1200/2300 and operated by **Long Honghang** (龍鴻航, Lóng Hónghǎng; ☑ 089-280 108; https://bluebus.com.tw/order), who plan to introduce online ticketing. Although there can be up to four services a day in peak holiday season, this drops to one a day in March and as few as two per week in winter.

From Taitung's Fugang Harbour (p198), boats take around 2½ hours, usually departing at 7.30am year-round, plus additionally at 9.30am and 1pm between April and September, with return trips at 10am, 1pm and 3.30pm. In summer, the 1pm usually stops at Green Island en route to Fugang, but there is no Green Island to Lanyu service whatever. A triangular ticket Fugang-Lanyu-Green Island-Fugang costs NT$2700.

From Houbitou (Kenting), boats depart summertime only at 7.30am and 1pm, returning 10am and 3.30pm.

ⓘ Getting Around

Virtually every guesthouse provides free pickup from the airport or port for prebooked guests. Thereafter, renting your own wheels is pretty much essential.

Kilometre posts for the 36km ring road (Rte 80) start at the petrol station just south of the harbour and are counted clockwise so Langtao (Irareley) is Km7, Dongqing (Iranmeylek) Km15, Yeyin (Ivalino) Km 17, Hongtou (Imaorod) Km29, Yuren (Iratay) Km30.5, the airport Km31.4, and Yeyou (Yayo) Km35

BICYCLE

A few guesthouses rent simple bicycles. For bikes with gears (per day NT$250 to NT$300), call Ganuben (☑ 0905-783 057), which has a storeroom hidden away in the upper back lanes of Yuren village.

CAR & MOTORCYCLE

Any hotel or homestay can arrange rental (car/scooter NT$2000/500 per day). Indeed some will simply assume you need a scooter and will have it waiting when you arrive, leaving you to follow them and your bags back to the property. Nobody seems to think about licences, and few locals bother to wear helmets either (though they are always available and technically compulsory).

If you have arrived by ferry without accommodation reservations, grab a scooter from the **parking lot** (☑ 0975-586 059, 0910-583 277; Rte 80, Km0.1; per 24hrs NT$500; ⊗ 8am-5pm or call) that's raised just out of sight from the harbour opposite the fishery protection office – less than 200m from the ferry disembarkation point.

Western Taiwan

Why Go?

If you're looking for variety in your Taiwan travel experience, go west. The Mazu Pilgrimage, one of the country's biggest and holiest celebrations, is definitely a highlight. This nine-day parade across half of Taiwan is an extravaganza of feasting, prostrating, praying and great acts of generosity.

Keen on the outdoors? Head to Yushan National Park to climb the highest peak in Northeast Asia; if you continue down the back-route trails you'll be in total wilderness for days at a time. Alternatively, feel the breeze in your hair and the mud between your toes at Gaomei Wetlands. For a glimpse of indigenous traditions, spend the night at one of the firefly-lit villages in the Alishan Range.

Fancy a taste of Taiwanese nostalgia? Look no further than the Japanese-era railway legacy in Alishan and Chiayi, or Lukang's quaint red-tiled streets, all of which provide inspiring examples of the Taiwan of yore.

Best Places to Eat

➡ Smart Fish (p228)

➡ JL Studio (p220)

➡ Vegan Project (p219)

➡ Tu Pang (p220)

➡ Do Right (p229)

➡ Fengjia Night Market (p219)

Best Places to Stay

➡ Sun Moon (p246)

➡ Forro Cafe (p218)

➡ South Urban Hotel (p228)

➡ Joy Inn (p238)

➡ Forte Hotel (p234)

When to Go
Taichung

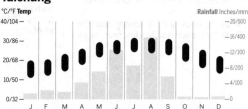

Apr The Mazu Pilgrimage is a nine-day procession for the patron goddess of seafarers and fisherfolk.

Mar–Jun Firefly-watching in Alishan.

Sep–Dec Best time for hiking in Yushan National Park.

Western Taiwan Highlights

1 Lukang (p235) Visiting graceful Longshan Temple, grazing your way through winding streets, and ending your day with a coffee in an old house.

2 Taichung (p215) Enjoying excellent museums, strolling in lovely urban parks, having great ice cream, and partying at hidden dives into the wee hours.

3 Mazu Pilgrimage (p231) Seeking the spiritual at this legendary procession, which starts in Dajia.

4 Chiayi (p225) Exploring historic temples and night markets, and checking out the exciting new cocktail bars.

5 Alishan (p224) Loading up on restorative negative ions and admiring the sun-and-cloud drama as you hike in stunning ancient forests.

6 Yushan National Park (p212) Conquering Northeast Asia's highest mountain and experiencing climate zones: from subtropical to alpine in the same day.

7 Sun Moon Lake (p244) Cycling, boating and strolling at one of Taiwan's best-known scenic spots.

ℹ Getting There & Around

Taichung International Airport (p222) has international and domestic services.

Regular trains run frequently down the coast, connecting all major and minor cities, and there are decent bus services to most smaller towns. The High Speed Rail (HSR) is in service here, but stations are located quite far away from city centres. A narrow-gauge alpine train called Alishan Forest Railway (p223) – still partly out of commission due to typhoons in 2014 – does the route from Chiayi to Alishan.

The domestic Chiayi Airport (p232) has flights to Penghu Island and Kinmen Island.

WESTERN TAIWAN

The only areas where public transport is inconvenient are Yushan National Park, the more remote parts of the Alishan National Scenic Area and on Hwy 14 past Puli.

In most cities you'll find scooter- and car-rental outlets. **U-Bus** (統聯汽車客運; www.ubus.com.tw) can also get you about the region.

YUSHAN NATIONAL PARK

Covering 3% of the landmass of Taiwan, Yushan National Park (玉山國家公園; Yùshān Guójiā Gōngyuán) is in an area that sits on the junction of the colliding Philippine and Eurasian plates. The landscape is strikingly rugged, marked by thick forests, deep valleys, high cliffs and rocky peaks. Among these peaks, 30 are over 3000m, and one, the eponymous Yushan (Jade Mountain), is the

highest mountain in Northeast Asia at 3952m and attracts hikers from all over the world.

Yushan National Park covers areas of Chiayi, Nantou, Kaohsiung and Hualien counties. A 20km drive west will take you to the Alishan Forest Recreation Area (p224). From Yuli in the east, you can reach the Nanan section of the park, with its fantastic Walami Trail. The South Cross-Island Hwy, which skirts the southern borders of the park, is no longer passable.

You can visit the park year-round for hiking or sightseeing.

History

In 1697 Chinese travel writer Yu Yung-ho wrote, 'Yushan stands amidst 10 thousand mountains. It is white like silver, and appears at a distance covered in snow. It can be seen, but not reached. The mountain is like jade.'

Yushan National Park

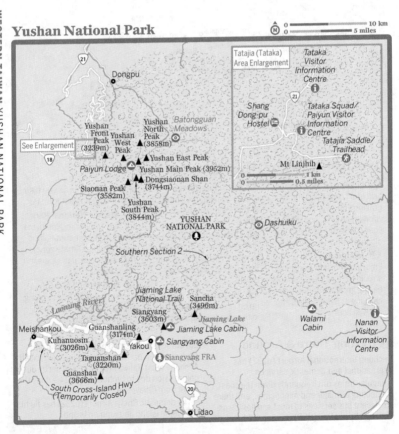

It was the first recorded account of the mountain and its Mandarin name. Around the same time people from the Bunun tribe were starting to emigrate to the central mountains, and they gave the highest peak their own name: Tongku Saveq (the Sanctuary). More renamings were to come.

In 1896 a Japanese officer made the first recorded ascent of Yushan. By the 1920s two hiking routes had opened: one from Alishan and another from Dongpu. High-school kids started to climb the mountain as a graduation trip, much as they do today.

During the Japanese colonial era, Yushan was the highest mountain in the empire, 176m higher than Mt Fuji. In 1897 it was renamed Niitakayama (New High Mountain) – which incidentally was the code name for the attack on Pearl Harbor: 'Climb Niitakayama'.

The Japanese recognised the Yushan area as one of Taiwan's most biodiverse. In the late 1930s they drew up plans for an 1800-sq-km national park. WWII scuttled the plans, but by the late 1970s the Kuomintang (KMT) had revived the idea.

The 1050-sq-km Yushan National Park came into official existence on 10 April 1985. In 2009 the main peak was shortlisted by the New7Wonders foundation in a contest to choose seven modern wonders of nature.

🏃 Activities

Park trails are well maintained and usually clear to follow. Signs are in English and Mandarin. Before beginning a hike to the main peaks make sure your permits (p37) are in order.

The best time to hike in the park is during autumn and early spring (October to December and March to April). May has seasonal monsoon rains, and typhoons are a problem from June to September. In winter the main peaks are usually closed for almost two months to give the environment a rest, though the day hikes around Tatajia are open year-round.

Yushan Peaks   HIKING
(玉山山峰, Yùshān Shānfēng) The trail runs relatively wide and flat most of the way, skirting the northern slopes of the deep, V-shaped Cishan River (旗山溪) valley. Elevation is gained in a couple of short steep sections. Though Yushan National Park covers six forest zones, here you're squarely in a cool-temperate zone. The pure hemlock forests are sublime. The yellowish grass trying to reclaim the trail is actually dwarf bamboo (Yushan cane).

From the Tataka Squad and Paiyun Visitor Centre (a short walk up a side road from Hwy 18), where permits are processed, a shuttle bus transports hikers to Tatajia Saddle, the official start of the trail to the main peak (玉山主峰; Yùshān Zhǔfēng; elevation 3952m).

At Paiyun Lodge (排雲山莊; Páiyún Shānzhuāng; elevation 3402m) hikers rest for the night in preparation for the ascent on the main peak. Be on the lookout for yellow-throated marten at the cabin, and even serow (goat-antelope) on the slopes.

If you arrive early at Paiyun Lodge and still have energy to spare, you can tackle Yushan West Peak (玉山西峰; Yùshān Xifēng; elevation 3518m). The 2.2km trail starts to the left of the cabin.

The next day most hikers get a 3am start in order to reach the summit by daylight. It's switchback after switchback until a loose gravel slope. At the top of the slope hikers enter a steel cage, exit onto a tiny rocky pass, and then make a final scramble up the roughest and most exposed section of the trail to the ingot-shaped peak.

On the way up, watch for the hemlock and spruce forest giving way to fields of rhododendron and stands of juniper, at first tall and straight and then twisted and dwarfed. At the highest elevations, lichens and tenacious alpine flowers clinging to the wind-swept rocks are about all the life you'll find. This is also when the cold starts to chill you to the bone.

After resting on the summit and taking in the views, hikers return to Paiyun Lodge to gather their stuff and hike back to Tataja.

If the weather is clear, consider hiking across to Yushan North Peak (玉山北峰; Yùshān Běifēng; elevation 3858m). The way is obvious and the view from the weather station on the peak shows the sweeping ridgeline of Yushan that's portrayed on the NT$1000 note.

If tackling the southern set of peaks that include Yushan South Peak (玉山南峰; Yùshān Nánfēng; elevation 3844m) and Dongsiaonan Shan (玉山東小南山; Yùshān Dōngxiǎonán Shān; elevation 3744m), hikers stay at the lofty Yuanfong Cabin (圓峰營地; Yuánfēng Yíngdì; elevation 3752m), about 2.5km (1½ hours) south off the main trail. You'll need a couple more days to bag these extras.

Japanese Occupation Era
Batongguan Traversing Route HIKING

(八通關日據越道線, Bātōngguān Rìjù Yuèdào Xiàn) This 90km, seven-day-long trail was hacked across the mountains in 1921 during the Japanese era, following in part an earlier Batongguan route built by the Qing in 1875.

The alternative name of the Japanese trail, 'The Pacifying the Natives Old Rd', gives an idea what purpose it served besides facilitating travel, trade and communication between east and west Taiwan. A small number of old police stations (or forts, really) can be seen abandoned along the trail, and at least half a dozen stelae that commemorate battles between Japanese and indigenous forces.

The trail climbs for three days to reach Dashuiku, a meadow of Yushan cane high above the treeline. It then begins to descend and, by the fifth day, most hikers will be back in mixed temperate forest around Dafen, site of a former trading post. This area is now a Formosan black bear reserve; if you were going to see one of these elusive creatures anywhere, it would be here.

The Batongguan trail starts in Dongpu and ends in Nanan, near Yuli on the east coast.

Southern Section 2 Trail HIKING

(南二段線, Nán Èrduàn Xiàn) This is an eight-day trail running from the South Cross-Island Hwy to Dongpu, or Tatajia via the back route to Yushan. It's one of Taiwan's toughest high-mountain hauls, with almost daily climbs of 1000m, followed by descents of 1000m just to even things out.

The challenges keep the crowds away, but also allows the relationship between altitude and forest cover unfold before your very eyes. By the end of the trip you'll be able to make rough guesses of your altitude just by the surrounding vegetation: 'If this is juniper, we must be above 3500m!'

There are cabins, campgrounds and water sources along the length. The first two days follow the trail up to Jiaming Lake (嘉明湖; Jiāmíng Hú).

🛏 Sleeping

On the trail, cabin quality varies. Paiyun Lodge has bunk bedding, flush toilets, running water, solar lighting and a cafeteria.

Most cabins around the park are sturdy A-frames, with open floors for sleeping on, a loft for extra bedding, solar lights, a water source and ecotoilets. Some cabins also have cleared outdoor space for camping and a deck for cooking and lounging.

Shang Dong-pu Hostel HOSTEL $

(東埔山莊, Dōngpǔ Shānzhuāng; ☑04-9270 2213; http://dongpu.mmweb.tw; 77 Zizhong District, Zhongshan village, 中山村自忠77號; dm NT$300) The only place to stay in the park if you're not on a trail is this hostel at Tatajia. The rustic old wooden building has bunk beds, showers and toilets. Simple meals can be arranged with advance notice; and instant noodles and snacks are sold at the front desk. Book ahead.

ℹ Information

A number of visitor centres provide maps in English, brochures and information on current trail conditions.

Nanan Visitor Information Centre (南安遊客中心; ☑03-888 7560; 83-3 Choching village, 卓清村83-3號; ⊘9am-4.30pm)

Tataka Visitor Information Centre (塔塔加遊客中心; ☑049-270 2212; 118 Taiping Lane, Tongfu village, 同富村太平巷118號; ⊘9am-4.30pm)

Yushan National Park Headquarters (玉山國家公園管理處, Yùshān Guójiā Gōngyuán Guǎnlǐchù; ☑049-277 3121; www.ysnp.gov.tw; 515 Jungshan Rd, Sec 1, 水里鄉中山路一段515號; ⊘8.30am-12.30pm & 1-5pm) Has English brochures and films about Yushan National Park, as well as the latest road and trail information. Usually you'll find someone who speaks English.

ℹ Getting There & Away

The Yushan National Park website (www.ysnp.gov.tw/css_en) has detailed instructions on how to get to the northeastern, southern and eastern sections of the park.

A STANDARD YUSHAN HIKING ITINERARY

➜ Tatajia trailhead to Paiyun Lodge: 8.4km, four to six hours.

➜ Paiyun Lodge to Yushan West Peak: 2.5km each way, three hours return.

➜ Paiyun Lodge to Yushan Main Peak: 2.4km, three hours.

➜ Yushan Main Peak to Yushan North Peak (detour): 3km each way, 2½ hours return.

➜ Yushan Main Peak to Paiyun Lodge: 2.4km, 1½ hours.

➜ Paiyun Lodge to Tatajia trailhead: 8.4km, four hours.

ℹ Getting Around

Public transport is nonexistent in the park. If you don't have your own vehicle or driver, you might be able to hire a taxi in Alishan, or catch the sunrise-tour buses.

TAICHUNG

✔04 / POP 2,746,000

Under Japanese, and later KMT, economic planning, Kaohsiung became the centre of heavy industry, Taipei the centre of colonial administration...and Taichung? The centre of light industry. If your image of 'Made in Taiwan' still conjures up visions of cheap toys, shoes and electrical goods, then you've got old Taichung in mind.

Today the name Taichung (台中; Táizhōng) tends, among locals anyway, to conjure up visions of great weather and unfortunately, increasingly, air pollution. Taipei and Taichung may have similar average temperatures but Taichung is much drier, receiving around 1700mm of rain per year compared with Taipei's 2170mm.

Taichung is a transport hub of western Taiwan and you are likely to stop over or even spend a night or two here, especially if you plan to head inland. The city centre has several attractions and it's a good base to make side trips to the outer area, which has a lot to offer.

◎ Sights

★ Gaomei Wetlands   AREA
(高美濕地, Gāoměi Shīdì; ⊙24hr) FREE Beautiful wetlands teeming with life rendered surreal by the sight of wind turbines on the horizon. It is especially photogenic at sunset and makes for a nice day out for the family. Take a local train to Qingshui (清水), then board bus 178 (NT$20, 30 minutes). There are only five buses a day, so consider taking a taxi (NT$300). Many people go at sunset for phenomenal views.

★ National Museum
of Natural Science   MUSEUM
(國立自然科學博物館, Guólì Zìrán Kēxué Bówùguǎn; ✔04-2322 6940; www.nmns.edu. tw/index_eng.html; 1 Guanqian Rd, 館前路一號; adult/children over 6 NT$100/70; ⊙9am-5pm Tue-Sun; ⚹; ◻300, 302, 303) A fantastic place for kids and botany fans, this massive museum has over 50 exhibit areas covering space, the environment, rainforests, gems and minerals, dinosaurs, and Han and Austronesian cultures. Galleries have fun, interactive displays; there are also theatres and a huge botanical garden. Some zones impose separate admission charges (NT$20 to NT$100). Most exhibit labels are bilingual but detailed explanatory material is in Mandarin only. However, that shouldn't stop you from enjoying the museum.

★ National Taiwan
Museum of Fine Arts   MUSEUM
(台灣美術館, Táiwān Měishùguǎn; ✔04-2372 3552; http://english.ntmofa.gov.tw/English; 2 Wuquan W Rd, Sec 1, 五權西路一段2號; ⊙9am-5pm Tue-Fri, to 6pm Sat & Sun; ⚹; ◻71, 75) FREE Taiwan's top fine-art museum features the works of both established and upcoming Taiwanese artists, as well as famous foreign creators such as Japanese 'Polka Dot Lady' Yayoi Kusama. There's a hands-on play area and storybook centre on the lower floors to keep children entertained.

Audit Village   MARKET
(審計新村市集, Shěnjì Xīncūn Shìjí; Lane 368, Minsheng Rd, 民生路368巷; ⊙1.30-7pm Mon-Fri, 11am-6.30pm Sat & Sun Oct-Feb; 2.30-8pm Mon-Fri; 11.30am-7.30pm Sat & Sun Mar-Sep; ◻5, 51, 23, 71) An attractive example of the old building-turned-artsy-marketplace formula, the handful of old civil-servant dormitories known as Audit Village are now the site of a browse-worthy handicraft market, with some cafes and pastry shops. Some of the ltter were particularly impressive (think delectable custard tarts, light-as-air souffle pancakes, and crumbly Chinese mung-bean cakes).

Taichung Park   PARK
(台中公園, Táizhōng Gōngyuán; 65 Shuangshi Rd, Sec 1, 雙十路一段65號; ◻55) A historical landmark, this beautiful 20-hectare park was designed by the Japanese in the early 1900s. The elegant Japanese pavilion was a later addition – purpose-built for a visit by the Japanese prince to witness the launch of the Taiwan Railway. All around the lake, stately banyans offer shade to people walking their dogs, picnicking or catching a few winks. A boat ride on the lake is NT$300.

Luce Memorial Chapel   ARCHITECTURE
(東海大學路思義教堂, Dōnghǎi Dàxué Lùsìyì Jiàotáng; 1727 Taiwan Blvd, Sec 4, Xitun District, 西屯區臺灣大道四段1727號; ◻300, 323, 324, 307) An early work (1963) of the late IM Pei, the chapel that resembles a tepee is the landmark of Tunghai University. It stands on a

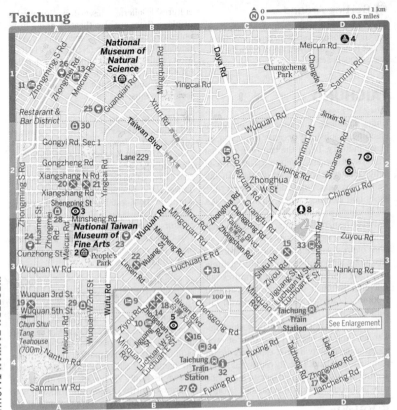

lawn, one of many on the luxuriant campus founded by Methodist missionaries over 60 years ago. The chapel is not usually open when there's no service.

Taichung Baseball Field   NOTABLE BUILDING
(台中棒球場, Táizhōng Bàngqiú Chǎng; 16 Shuangshi Rd, Sec 1, North District, 北區雙十路一段16號; ☐ 500, 700, 159) Adjacent to Taichung Broadcasting Bureau (p217) is a piece of interesting nostalgic sports architecture. This old stadium (1935) was once the home of several Taichung baseball teams, including Taichung Agan (臺中金剛) of the Taiwan Major League. Go in for a peek if it's open. The stands, the arena, the lockers and the corridors look like part of an old movie set.

Rainbow Village   VILLAGE
(彩虹眷村, Cǎihóng Juàncūn; Lane 56, Chun'an Rd, 春安路56巷) To the west of the city, an ageing village has been transformed into an art piece with vibrant colours and drawings on every inch of the walls by Mr Wong, the nona-

genarian 'resident painter' who's a KMT veteran of the Chinese Civil War (1945–49) and originally from Hong Kong.

To get there, take bus 27 (50 minutes) from Taichung train station. Alight at Gancheng 6th Village (干城六村; Gānchéng Liùcūn), cross the road, walk through the archway (Chun'an Rd), pass a primary school, then turn left into an alley and walk to the end.

Paochueh Temple   BUDDHIST TEMPLE
(寶覺寺, Bǎojué Sì; 140 Jianxing Rd, 北屯區健行路140號; ⊙9am-5pm; ☐ 31) This Buddhist columbarium-and-temple complex has a few unusual monuments – a giant golden laughing Buddha with oddly placed windows, and an old temple (c 1920s) enshrined inside a new one built for the purpose of preserving it. Near the main entrance is a small graveyard with a Shinto shrine containing the bones of Japanese who died in Taiwan during WWII. Japanese diplomats come to pay their respects every year. Behind it, a pagoda

Taichung

commemorates 36,000 Japanese soldiers of Taiwanese descent.

Taichung Folk Park PARK
(台中民俗公園, Táizhōng Mínsú Gōngyuán; www.facebook.com/imtfm; 73 Lu Shun Rd, Sec 2, 北屯區旅順路二段73號; ⊙9am-5pm Tue-Sun; 🚌58) **FREE** The park is divided into several sections but most of the interesting material is to the far right as you enter. Don't miss the collections of folk artefacts – everything from ceramic pillows to farming implements.

Taichung Broadcasting Bureau NOTABLE BUILDING
(台中放送局, Táizhōng Fàngsòngjú; 📞04-2220 3108; 1 Diantai St, North District, 北區電台街1號; ⊙10am-6pm; 🚌55, 73, 50, 100, 500, 131) Not far from Taichung Park (p215) is this leafy complex with a quaint western-style building, a small lily pond and some lovely trees. The bureau was built in the 1930s so the Japanese in Taichung could watch a live broadcast of the coronation of Emperor Hirohito. There are mildly interesting exhibitions in the building.

Activities

Houfeng Bicycle Path CYCLING
(后豐自行車道, Hòufēng Zìxíngchē Dào) This visually sumptuous 4.5km path begins under the Fengyuan section of Expressway No. 4 and ends at Houli Horse Farm (后里馬場), or you could go further on to the lovely Pi-Lu Buddhist Monastery (p220). You'll be riding over a picturesque stream, on scenic bridges and through old tunnels.

Festivals & Events

Taichung Jazz Festival MUSIC
(台中爵士音樂節, Táizhōng Juéshì Yīnyuè Jié; www.taichungjazzfestival.com.tw; ⊙Oct) The excellent and much-anticipated Taichung Jazz Festival is a nine-day extravaganza held at the Civic Sq, along Jingguo Blvd Parkway and indoors at art and cultural centres.

Sleeping

Backpacker Hostel HOSTEL **$**
(背包41,BēibāoSìshíyī; 📞0952-612212;www.kaobp41.com; 59 Jiguang St, 中區繼光街59號; dm NT$410; ❀🌐@🛜) A pleasant courtyard set back from the street leads you to this clean, solar-powered hostel offering five floors of single-sex dorms with eight to 10 beds each. You'll find a terrace, atrium, kitchenette and laundry facilities. The rates are among the cheapest in town, given its convenient location. The hostel is popular with round-island cyclists, especially sporty grandpas from Japan.

INSTAGRAM-WORTHY RUINS

Hidden away in tourist-thronged downtown Taichung is the semiderelict former shopping mall known as **Qianyue Building** (千越大樓, Qiānyuè Dàlóu; 113 Luchuan W St, 綠川西街113號; 🔄 75). The 11-storey structure has grungy empty spaces, awesome graffiti, artworks, and a rooftop with sweeping views over the city – in short, everything that appeals to fans of ruins.

Built in 1978, Qianyue housed a skating rink (in the basement), tutorial school, love hotel, banquet restaurant, shops, karaoke bar and residential flats, some of which you can still make out today. In the late 1990s, a fire broke out in a part of the building, killing many, and Qianyue was left to become the stuff of urban legends.

All visitors go to the roof to take pictures with the surreal cylindrical structure that used to be a restaurant and bar. Nicknamed Flying Saucer House (飛碟屋; Fēi Dié Wū), it makes for surreal photos and the views are great.

Afternoon is the best time to visit. Watch your step. Note that there are a few tenants still residing there so be respectful.

An art group is managing (more or less) the place, and visitors may be asked to pay NT$100 entrance fee.

N Joy Bike   HOSTEL $

(☑04-2326 6177; 602 Zhongmei St, West District, 西區中美街602號; s/d from NT$600/1200; ⊕❄📶; 🚌301, 303, 304) A homey hostel with basic rooms (blue for male, violet for female), some spacious and others with only mattresses on the floor. The dressing room in the female showers is a thoughtful touch. There's also a kitchen for communal use, a large bunk bed on the ground floor that guests can use as a couch, self-service laundry (NT$50) and bikes for hire (NT$100/200 for half/full day).

★ Forro Cafe   B&B $$

(☑04-2310 1661; www.facebook.com/forrocafe; 47 Jingcheng 3rd St, West District, 精誠三街47號; s/d from NT$1300/1980; ⊙9am-6pm; ⊕❄📶) Four bright, airy and cheerful rooms – Herb, Cozy, Rock and Lounge – above an attractive cafe (open 1pm to 10pm, Fri to Sun) that has live music most Fridays and Saturdays. See their Facebook page for the programme.

Bus routes 300 to 308 come here. Get off at Zhongming Elementary School (忠明國小). Go down Jingpin Rd (精誠路) and turn left into Jingpin 3rd St (精誠三街). You should see the white low-rise that is Forro after five minutes.

Inhouse Hotel   HOTEL $$

(愛悅酒店, Aìyuè Jiǔdiàn; ☑04-2201 6111; https://taichung.inhousehotel.com/en; 228 Wuquan Rd, 北區五權路228號; d from NT$2500; ⊕@❄📶; 🚌12, 18, 20) A modern hotel offering pristine service and long, narrow but supercomfortable rooms equipped with trendy gadgets and excellent beds. Decor is all about moody ambience, lots of wood and faux marble. The breakfast is quite forgettable, but there are plenty of breakfast options in Taichung so this shouldn't be a problem.

Reloading Hotel   HOTEL $$

(綠柳文旅, Lǜliǔ Wénlǔ; ☑04-2221 7668; www.reloading-hotel.com; 55 Zhongshan Rd, 中區中山路55號; cubicles NT$600-1000, d NT$1680-3600; ⊕❄📶) Forty rooms and 10 backpacker cubicles over several floors across the river from Miyahara (p219). The rooms are neat and compact, with white walls and beddings punctuated by paintings. The five cheapest doubles have no windows, while the most expensive ones overlook the river and come with a bathtub. The hotel is an 800m walk along Zhongshan Road from Taichung train station.

1969 Sky Blue Hotel   HOTEL $$$

(藍天飯店, Lántiān Fàndiàn; ☑04-2223 0577; www.1969blueskyhotel.com; 38 Shifu Rd, 中區市府路38號; d/quad from NT$5600/10,000; ⊕❄📶; 🚌300, 301, 302, 303) Sixty simple, spacious rooms on a quiet street not far from Taichung train station. The '60s building used to house a chamber of commerce and has been done up in a more or less art deco style. The reception staff's service is cavalier by Taiwan standards.

From Taichung Train Station, go straight on Zhongshan Rd then turn left at Shifu Rd.

🍴 Eating

Taichung is coming into its own as a Taiwanese culinary heavyweight, just after Taipei. For fine dining, award-winning and otherwise, there's JL Studio (p220) and Tu Pang (p220), and Vegan Project is an excellent vegan restaurant. For casual eats, a few popular streets are south of the National Taiwan Museum of Fine Art (p215), and the restaurant-and-bar district about 1.2km northwest along Taizhonggang Rd (台中港路).

Fengjia Night Market   MARKET $
(逢甲夜市, Féngjiǎ Yèshì; Wenhua Rd, near Feng Chia University, 西屯區文華路,逢甲大學附近; ⊙6pm-midnight;) A sprawling night market well known for its innovative and cheap street food. Vegetarian nibbles are especially well represented. A taxi from Taichung train station is about NT$260.

Jinzhi Yuan Caodai Fan   TAIWANESE $
(金之園草袋飯, Jīnzhī Yuán Cǎodài Fàn; 04-2220 7388; 174 Chenggong Rd, Central District, 成功路174號; bento NT$130; ⊙11am-7.30pm Fri-Wed) This small shop is famous for its stepped-up bento classics: rice with succulent fried pork chop (香酥排骨飯, xiāngsū páigǔ fàn) or with flavourful fried chicken leg (酥嫩雞腿飯, sū'nèn jītuǐ fàn). Veggies are NT$50. Get takeaway if the line is long. It's very close to Taichung train station.

Miyahara   ICE CREAM $
(宮原眼科, Gōngyuán Yǎnkē; www.miyahara.com.tw; 20 Zhongshan Rd, 中山路20號; per scoop NT$90; ⊙10am-10pm;) The flagship store of pineapple-cake specialist Dawncake (日出鳳梨酥) also sells ice cream in flavours such as Hakka lei cha (擂茶, léi chá) and, of course, pineapple. The high ceilings and faux-vintage card-catalogue cabinets evoke Harry Potter, but the building was actually an eye hospital during Japanese rule.

Yang Qinghua Spring Rolls   TAIWANESE $
(楊清華潤餅, Yángqīnghuá Rùnbǐng; 04-2372 0587; 68 Wulang St, West District, 西區五廊街; spring rolls NT$40; ⊙9am-2pm Mon-Sat; 51, 300, 25) A clean family-run institution that serves your order of spring roll – plain (原味, yuánwèi) or wasabi-flavoured (芥末, jièmò) – with a cup of bonito broth. Its homemade plum juice (酸梅湯, suānméitāng) is equally refreshing.

Weng Ji Restaurant   TAIWANESE $
(翁記剝骨鵝肉, Wēngjì Bōgǔ Éròu; 99-1 Xiangshang Rd, Sec 1, 西區向上路一段99號; dishes NT$20-180; ⊙5pm-1am; 25, 5, 51, 300) The crowd out front should tell you something about this much-loved goose specialist. Try

the smoked (燻鵝, xūn'é) or drunken variety (醉鵝, zuì'é), or the goose liver (鵝肝, é gān). If you're hungry, there are a ton of other dishes to choose from.

★Vegan Project   VEGETARIAN $$
(菜市場, Cài Shìchǎng; 04-2301 6873; www.facebook.com/菜市場-Vegan-Project-2183230818570037; 167 Xiangshang N Rd, 向上北路167號; main course NT$260; ⊙11.30am-2.30pm, 6-9pm; ; 5, 51) A no-frills restaurant where you can see the chef whipping up delicious and beautiful western vegan meals. Kale, quinoa, and fermented beans in all forms figure prominently. The handmade pastas are excellent, including the raw cucumber strands with kale pesto. The tofu burrito is popular with hungry brunchers. Booking is a must – call at least a day ahead.

Fourth Credit Union   DESSERTS $$
(第四信用合作社, Dìsì Xìnyòng Hézuòshè; 04-2227 1966; 72 Zhongshan Rd, Central District, 中區中山路72號; shaved ice for 2-4 NT$550; ⊙10am-10pm;) The owner of Miyahara has transformed an old bank (1966) into a trendy three-storey cafe and restaurant. The old vault doors and standing-height counter are still there looking handsome. The sundaes, waffles and ice-cream puffs here are sumptuous, generously portioned and pricey, and there's always a line. You can also hop in for a peek without eating.

Fourth Credit Union is five minutes on foot from Taichung train station.

Shih Sundry Goods   TAIWANESE $$
(施雜貨, Shī Záhuò; 04-2392 5885; shih.sundrygoods@gmail.com; 261-1 Zhongshan Rd, Sec 2, Taiping District, 太平區中山路二段261-1號; set meal NT$350; ⊙11.30am-3.30pm Wed-Sun) A multitalented family built this graceful rustic restaurant with scraps. The meals they prepare are tasty and honest using only organic ingredients (homegrown or from nearby farms). The six-course lunch comprises soup and salad, home-baked bread, three stir-fries, and dessert. Book two days in advance as they don't usually entertain walk-ins.

However, if there are only a couple of you and you haven't booked, you can try your luck by just showing up. The restaurant also serves pizza, salad and cake. There's also a nook selling children's wear made with used fabrics. Bus 41 from Taichung train station stops at the Taichung Armed Forces General Hospital (國軍台中總醫院) across the road.

WESTERN TAIWAN TAICHUNG

EURO-STYLE BUDDHIST MONASTERY

Built by a devout Taichung family in the 1920s, **Pi-Lu Buddhist Monastery** (毘盧禪寺, Pílú Chánsì; 1000 Shanshang Rd, Houli, 后里鄉山上路1000號; ⊘5am-6pm) looks more like a mansion than a monastery, with its red-bricked facade, Doric columns and portal entrances. Framed by pines in the garden out front, the monastery stands graceful and reverent, though not without a hint of quirkiness, due to the unusual proportions of the western architectural features. This atypical monastery is tucked away in the foothills of Taiping Shan (太平山) in Taichung's northwestern district of Houli.

Inside the building is a lofty hall with large windows and a green ceiling – in Buddhist colour symbolism, green signifies the absence of desire. There are shrines to Avalokitesvara bodhisattva and Gautama Buddha, the resident gods.

To the far left of the monastery is an interesting European-style dome building in white. It's a columbarium; if the door is open, you can see white stone tablets with the names and pictures of the dead stacked like bricks along the curved wall, a shrine to the bodhisattva in the centre, and Buddhist chants playing in the background.

The scenic Houfeng Bicycle Path will take you here. If you're driving, head north on Hwy 13 from Taichung's Fengyuan District (豐原市). You'll see the sign for the Horse Farm (馬場) soon after passing Houfeng Bridge (后豐大橋). Turn right and you'll see the Horse Farm after 3km. In the fork right before the farm, bear right to enter the hill. You'll see the monastery after 2km. The travelling distance from Fengyuan District to the monastery is about 14km.

Old Uncle's Hotpot
TAIWANESE $$

(老舅酸菜白肉鍋, Lǎojiù Suāncài Báiròu Guō; ☑04-2280 2888; 282 Zhongxiao Rd, East District, 東區忠孝路282號; ⊘11.30am-2pm & 5-10pm Tue-Sun, 5-10pm Mon; 🖳12, 100) Fermented cabbage is the star here and it appears in various dishes – the signature hotpot (酸菜鍋, suāncài guō) alongside dried shrimp, celery and whatever meat and veggies you choose to dunk in; in steamed buns with pork (酸菜包子, suāncài bāozi); and a delicious assortment of dumplings and noodles.

Qinyuan Chun
SHANGHAI $$

(沁園春, Qìnyuán Chūn; ☑04-2220 0735; 129 Taiwan Blvd, Sec 1, Central District, 中區臺灣大道一段129號; dishes from NT$200; ⊘11am-2pm & 5-9pm Tue-Sun) Qinyuan Chun offers hearty, old-fashioned Shanghainese cooking. The restaurant opened in 1949, the year Chiang Kai-shek and his forces fled to Taiwan, and in some ways still seems to belong to that era. Among its meagre decorations are an antique Chinese vase, a calligraphic scroll and photos of the then-presidential family. The pastries are excellent.

★ Tu Pang
FRENCH $$$

(地坊餐廳, Dìfāng Cāntīng; ☑04-2375 5098; www.facebook.com/TU-PANG-地坊餐廳-1580999092169474; 13 Lane 96, Wuquan W 6th St, 五權西六街96巷13號; NT$1350 per person; ⊘noon-2pm, 6.30-9pm Wed-Mon; 🖳75) 🍃 The ecoconscious chef of this private kitchen takes great pains to source quality Taiwan ingredients for his skilful French-style meals – line-caught fish, chemical-free shrimp, cheese made locally with milk from Taiwan farms, even the fried cricket for the salad came from Taiwan. Mr Zhang spends a few minutes explaining (with justified pride) how he sources ingredients. Booking a must.

★ JL Studio
SINGAPOREAN $$$

(現代新加坡料理, Xiàndài Xīnjiāpō Liàolǐ; ☑04-2380 3570; www.facebook.com/jlstudiotaiwan; 689 Yifeng Rd, Sec 4, Nantun District, 南屯區益豐路四段689號; tasting menu NT$2800/3800; ⊘6-10.30pm Tue-Sun; 🖳27, 75, 81) Award-winning Jimmy Lim, former head chef at the illustrious Le Mout, reimagines Singaporean street food at his elegant restaurant, and the results are a visual and gastronomical wonder. Lim works his magic on local ingredients with help from European culinary tech: satay comes with ice-cream and *bak kuh teh* (herbal spare-rib broth) is made with mushroom and abalone. JL Studio is one of Taichung's hottest dining spots, so book as early as you can.

🍷 Drinking & Nightlife

★ Goût Bar
COCKTAIL BAR

(好吧, Hǎobā; ☑04-2376 3203; www.facebook.com/好吧-Goût-Bar-1958602227697926; 46 Cunzhong St, West District, 西區存中街46號; per cocktail NT$500; ⊘6pm-1am; 🖳51, 75) At this relaxing speakeasy, mixologists Jacko and

Calvin et al whip up impeccable cocktails behind a circular bar where waiting guests munch on smoked nuts. Goût is ingeniously accessed via stairs behind a bookshelf, located in a space that turns into a noodle bar by day. When you arrive, press the doorbell even if you can't see anyone inside.

★13 Coffee   COFFEE
(十三號咖啡, Shísān Kāfēi; ☎0917-646 373; 200 Huanzhong Rd, Sec 5, Nantun District, 市南屯區環中路五段200號; per person NT$200; ⊗2-8pm) The versatile '13' (Shísān) has turned his family's car-repair shop into this wonderfully eccentric cafe that he spent four years building with old school desks, river stones and other discarded materials. The cafe consists of a dramatic loft-like space with Gaudí-esque furniture and an arena, and an enchanting two-storey cabin. Guests are offered two small cups of the brew of the day.

Bus route 54 departing from near Chaoma bus station (朝馬車站) every 10 to 30 minutes stops near the junction of Liming Rd (黎明路) and Huanzhong Rd (環中路). Walk along Huanzhong Rd until you come to the overhead highway, and turn into a small village path.

★ChangeX Beer   CRAFT BEER
(精釀餐酒館, Jīngniàng Cānjiǔ Guǎn; 234 Zizhi St, 自治街234號; ⊗5pm-midnight; 🚌51, 71) A laid-back taproom offering a hundred craft bottles (NT$145 to $220) and whisky-barrel-aged brews (NT$390 to $1190), plus Asian brands on tap (NT$200 to $300). A flight of four beers is NT$480. During happy hour – weekdays 5pm to 7.30pm – you get 50% off the second draught beer.

Le Cellier des Poètes   WINE BAR
(詩人酒窟, Shīrén Jiǔkū; ☎04-2327 2924; 331 Taiwan Blvd, Sec 2, 台灣大道二段331號; ⊗noon-9pm; 🚌323, 324, 325) Oenophiles, this is one of the best places in Taiwan to buy and sample fine wines. The range is impressive and there are knowledgeable staff to make recommendations should you need them. Take your bottle home or go to the bar at the back and drink it in your glass of choice.

Three Giants Brewery   BREWERY
(巨人啤酒, Jùrén Píjiǔ; ☎0903-093 671; www.facebook.com/3giantsbrewing.com.tw; 569 Fengdong Rd, 豐原區東路569號; ⊗7pm-midnight Tue-Sun; 🚉Fengyuan) A microbrewery with an attached pub in the far-flung district of Fengyuan. It was opened by two South Africans and an Irishman and offers seven selections (and counting) on tap, including ale, lager, IPA and unfiltered wheat. Beers are around NT$150 each. From downtown Taichung, take the train to Fengyuan station (豐原站). Three Giants is about 700m away.

Chun Shui Tang Teahouse   TEAHOUSE
(春水堂, Chūn Shuǐ Táng; ☎04-2327 3647; 9 Dadun 19th St, 大墩19街9號; ⊗8.30am-10.30pm; 🚌5, 81, 290) Taiwan bubble tea has taken the world by storm, and this modern outlet of the multibranch Chun Shui Tang is supposed to have started it all. The bubble tea here certainly lives up to its name. You can also learn to make your own – 50-minute sessions three times a day, Monday to Friday, for under NT$400 per person.

Zhang Men Brewery   CRAFT BEER
(掌門精釀啤酒, Zhǎngmén Jīngniàng Píjiǔ; ☎04-2329 1823; 490 Taiwan Blvd, Sec 2, 台灣大道二段490號; ⊗5pm-midnight Mon-Thu, 3pm-1am Fri & Sat, 3pm-midnight Sun; 🚌301, 302, 303) Zhang Men is a Taipei brewery with nine branches in Taiwan and a couple in Hong Kong. This lively and relaxing branch on Taiwan Boulevard offers 32 taps (NT$200 to $240) ranging from honey ale to stout, and a flight of six for dithering drinkers. Booking is advised for Friday and Saturday nights.

☆ Entertainment

★The Cave   LIVE MUSIC
(洞穴, Dòngxué; ☎04-2224 2606; www.facebook.com/TheCave.tw; Lane 37, Fuxing Rd, Sec 4, 復興路4段37巷左側; ⊗8pm-2am Wed-Mon; 🚌51, 75) Sweet indie spot that has people coming from all over the island for its gigs. Acts featured here include visual-art-and-drummer duo Adrena Adrena, Taipei-based Tsusing, and Punčke, a rock band from Croatia. It's funky and cavernous, with a proper bar and outdoor seating. Performances every weekend but open six days a week. See their Facebook page for updates. The Cave is on the left side of Lane 37.

National Taichung Theater   ARTS CENTRE
(台中國家歌劇院, Táizhōng Guójiā Gējù Yuàn; http://en.npac-ntt.org; 101 Huilai Rd, Sec 2, Xitun, 惠來路二段101號; 🚌300, 301, 302, 303) With three state-of-the-art theatres, a playhouse and a beautiful sky garden, this theatre is one of Taiwan's premier cultural venues. The modern, dramatic-looking structure was designed by Japanese architect Toyo Itō and hosts performances by top international and Taiwanese artists in dance, music and theatre.

🛍 Shopping

Donghai Bookshop
BOOKS

(東海書苑, Dōnghǎi Shūyuàn; ☑04-2378 3613; 104 Wuquan W 2nd St, West District, 西區五權西二街104號; ⊘noon-10.30pm; 🚍158, 99) This hippy indie bookstore specialises in social science and literature, with a small selection of tomes in English. It also has its own cafe decked out with Jim Morrison and Martin Luther King posters and the like.

Chu Jun
DESIGN

(蛆菌, Qū Jūn; ☑0963-175 567; www.facebook.com/tshu.khun; 32 Xinglin Rd, 西屯區杏林路32號; ⊘3-9pm Fri-Mon; 🚍303, 304, 323, 324) Chu Jun ('maggot bacteria') is a cult space that marries Japanese schoolgirl culture with the grotesque. The shop sells '70s Japanese paraphernalia and showcases the installations and designs of its illustrator owner. The gallery is devoted to works by Taiwanese and visiting artists; we saw an ode to '90s Japanese cult and video-game art by a French illustrator.

ArtQpie
BOOKS

(佔空間, Zhàn Kōngjiān; ☑0982-723 359; www.facebook.com/ArtQPie; 135 Zhongmei St, West District, 西區中美街135號; ⊘4-8pm Wed-Fri, 3-8pm Sat & Sun; 🚍79, 159) A lovely shop and gallery inside an old house in a state of romantic crumble – there's skylight in the open kitchen, peeling pillars and hanging succulents. ArtQpie sells photography and art books, plus homeware by Taiwanese designers. They hold monthly art exhibitions.

Fantasy Story
FASHION & ACCESSORIES

(范特喜微創文化, Fàntèxǐ Wēichuàng Wénhuà; www.fantasystory.com.tw; West District, 西區; 🚍83,88) The two-storey dormitories of an old water utility have been taken over by bookstores, fashion boutiques and other creative businesses. The premises have been done up, but old trees and structural features remain. The area covers Lane 117 of Meicun Rd, Sec 1 (美村路一段117巷), Xiangshang North Rd (向上北路) and Zhongxing 1st Lane (中興一巷) in the West District.

ℹ Information

Air pollution in Taichung can be quite serious. There are periods of blue skies, but sometimes the level of PM 2.5 is high for days in a row, resulting in poor visibility and bad air. On such days, the sun resembles a bright smear, and being outdoors can feel like being submerged in gaseous milk. The situation is due largely to a massive coal-fired power plant in the suburbs.

A number of weather apps and Air Matters (https://air-matters.com) give forecasts of air-pollution levels for given cities. Use them to plan your trip and decide if you need to bring a breathing mask.

Taichung Government website (www.taichung.gov.tw) The official website.

Visitor Information Centre (台中車站旅遊服務中心, Táizhōng Chēzhàn Lǚyóu Fúwù Zhōngxīn; ☑04-2221 2126; 172 Jianguo Rd, Central District, 中區建國路172號; ⊘9am-6pm) Located in Taichung train station. Staff speak English and have an abundance of useful information.

Taichung Hospital (台中醫院, Táizhōng Yīyuàn; ☑04-2229 4411; www.taic.mohw.gov.tw; 199 Sanmin Rd, Sec 1, West District, 三民路一段199號)

🚌 Getting There & Away

Taichung has **Ching Chuan Kang Airport** (台中國際機場, Táizhōng Guójì Jīchǎng; www.tca.gov.tw; 128 Zhonghang Rd, Sec 1, 中航路一段168號), but it's unlikely you'll ever use it.

BUS

Near Taichung train station, **Nantou Bus Company** (南投客運; ☑049-298 4031; www.ntbus.com.tw; 35-8 Shuangshi Rd, 雙十路35-8號) has frequent buses to Puli (NT$140, one hour) and Sun Moon Lake (NT$195, 1½ hours), though you can also catch the bus at the HSR station.

U-Bus (p212) has frequent buses to Taipei (NT$300, 2½ hours) and Kaohsiung (NT$350, 3 hours).

Taichung bus station (台中車站; ☑04-2226 3034; 145 Jianguo Rd; 建國路145號) has services to Taipei (NT$260, 2½ hours, hourly) and Chiayi (NT$170, two hours, every two hours) near Taichung train station.

HIGH SPEED RAIL

A commuter train connects the HSR station located in the southern Taichung suburb of Wuri (烏日區) with central Taichung and Taichung train station (NT$15, 10 minutes, every 20 minutes). Shuttle buses also travel to central Taichung from the HSR station (average price NT$20, free if you are using EasyCard, 1 hour, every 15 minutes).

An HSR train travels to/from Taipei (NT$700, 60 minutes, four to five trains hourly). There are also buses from the HSR station to Sun Moon Lake, Puli and Lukang.

TRAIN

There is a train service from Taipei (fast/slow train NT$375/241, 2½/three hours) and Kaohsiung (fast/slow train NT$469/361, 2½/three hours).

ℹ️ Getting Around

The public transport system is improving, but do check with the Visitor Information Centre for the latest on the services and schedules available. An EasyCard entitles you to 10 km of free bus rides anywhere within the greater Taichung area. Four Mass Rapid Transit (MRT) lines are gradually being completed at the time of writing; the Green line will be in service by the end of 2020.

Many buses call at Rainbow Village: six routes run from the train station (NT$30, one hour, every 15 to 30 minutes), three from HSR (NT$20, 30 minutes, hourly).

DASYUESHAN FOREST RECREATION AREA

At the western edge of the Snow Mountain Range, Dasyueshan Forest Recreation Area (大雪山國家森林遊樂區; Dàxuě Shān Guójiā Sēnlín Yóulè Qū; Big Snow Mountain) rises from 1000m to just under the gold standard of 3000m. It offers fantastic hiking opportunities and great wildlife viewing, in particular birdwatching. The climate is humid and cool, with an average temperature of 12°C, making it a popular summer retreat.

If you want to stay in the area **Dasyueshan Cabins** (大雪山客房, Dàxuěshān Kèfáng; ☑ 04-252 2 9696; https://tsfs. forest.gov.tw/cht/index.php?; d Mon-Fri NT$2700, Sat & Sun NT$3600) offer pleasant wood cabins in a village at the Km43 mark. You can book online but do call afterwards to confirm. Set meals (NT$150) are also available, but you're better off bringing your own supplies.

ℹ️ Information

The **visitor information centre** (遊客中心, Yóukè Zhōngxīn; ☑ 04-2587 7901; 18 Xueshan Rd, 雪山路18號; ☉ 9am-5pm) in the village at the Km43 mark has simple maps of the recreation area.

ℹ️ Getting There & Around

You will need your own transport.

ALISHAN NATIONAL SCENIC AREA

If you want to see Taiwan's natural environment raw, visit a national park. If you want to see how humans have tried to make a go of settling on landslide-prone mountains and battered escarpments (as spectacular as they are merely gaze upon), come to 1400-hectare Alishan Forest Recreation Area (p224), part of the Alishan National Scenic Area (www.ali-nsa.net).

From a starting altitude of 300m in the west at Chukou, the 327-sq-km recreation area quickly rises to heights of more than 2600m. The great diversity of climate, soils and landscapes allows for the growing of everything from wasabi and plums to high-mountain oolong tea.

Tourists have been finding their way to this region since the early days of the Japanese period. They come for the local specialities, the natural and human-designed landscapes and, more recently, the legacy of the colonial period, which includes a very rare narrow-gauge forest train.

WESTERN TAIWAN DASYUESHAN FOREST RECREATION AREA

SCENIC ALISHAN RAILWAY

The famous **Alishan Forest Train** (阿里山火車, Ālǐshān Huǒchē; www.ali-nsa.net) runs on narrow-gauge track (762mm), ascending to 2216m from a starting altitude of 30m. The total length of track is 86km, spanning three climatic zones.

The Fenqihu–Alishan section of the railway was damaged by typhoons in 2014. At the time of research you could only ride from Chiayi to Fenqihu, not all the way to Alishan. Services between Chiayi and Fenqihu usually run once daily on weekdays (9am) and twice on weekends (9am and 10am). The trip takes two hours and 30 minutes; tickets are NT$384 each.

From Alishan station, you can take the Zhaoping Line (every 30 minutes from 9am to 3.345pm, NT$100), Senmu Line (every 15 minutes from 10.15am to 4.30pm, NT$100) and Zhushan Line (aka Sunrise Viewing Train, departure time announced the day before, NT$150).

As you ride up it may feel like the train is going backwards. It is! The track arrangement employs a unique system of switchbacks that allow it to traverse slopes ordinarily too steep for trains.

You can now book tickets online (https://afr.forest.gov.tw/tra-afr-web/index), although the site is only in Mandarin.

Alishan Forest Recreation Area

The high-mountain resort of **Alishan** (阿里山森林遊樂區, Ālǐshān Sēnlín Yóulèqu; ☎ 05-267 9971; www.ali-nsa.net/user/main.aspx?lang=2; 59 Zhongzheng village, 中正村59號; NT$200) has been one of Taiwan's top tourist draws since the 1920s. Today, it's most popular with senior Chinese tour groups, who arrive by the busload virtually every day of the year. True, there may be similar – and less-visited – beauty elsewhere in Taiwan, but do not let the crowds at Alishan spoil your visit, as they usually only stay for a couple of hours in the morning.

In spring the cherry trees in Alishan are in bloom, while summer is busy with city folk looking for a cool retreat. Any time between March and early June is a good time to see fireflies. Summer temperatures average from 13°C to 24°C, while those in winter are 5°C to 16°C. You should bring a sweater and a raincoat no matter what time of year you visit.

History

In former times the recreation area was probably home to Tsou hunting grounds rather than the site of permanent settlements. Modern development began with the Japanese, who became aware of the abundant stands of *hinoki* (cypress) growing in the misty mountains. In 1906 the first railway into the mountain was established, and by 1913 the tracks had reached Alishan at Chaoping station.

Logging was the mainstay of activity in Alishan, but the area attracted hikers and sightseers early on. In 1926 the Japanese opened a 43km trail from Chaoping to the summit of Yushan, later shortening it by extending the railway to Tatajia.

Logging continued into the 1970s, when the first steps towards creating a forest park were taken. In the 1980s Hwy 18 opened, and the fast connection between Alishan and Chiayi caused an explosion in tourism.

In 2001, the Alishan National Scenic Area (which covers far more than just this recreation area) opened with the mandate to regulate and limit development. These days the administration's hands are filled repairing typhoon damage and getting things back to how they were.

 **Festivals & Events**

Cherry Blossom Festival CULTURAL
(櫻花季, Yīnghuā Jì; ⊙Mar/Apr) The Cherry Blossom Festival runs for two weeks while the trees are in bloom. This is an extremely busy time for the park.

Sleeping

Ying Shan Hotel HOTEL $$
(櫻山大飯店, Yīngshān Dàfàndiàn; ☎ 05-267 9803; www.ying-shan.com.tw; 39 Zhongzheng village, 中正村39號; d NT$4000; ☒✿🛜) Ying Shan has three floors and 40 large, comfortable rooms with tree views and dated decor. The staff are patient and polite.

Alishan House HOTEL $$$
(阿里山賓館, Ālǐshān Bīnguǎn; ☎ 05-267 9811; www.alishanhouse.com.tw; 16 Xianglin village, 香林村16號; r from NT$9800; ☒✿🛜) The old-world charm from this Japanese-era hotel is a bit faded, but it's still Alishan's top hotel. The food in the restaurant is so-so, but the outdoor cafe has a lovely setting among the cherry trees. Make sure to get the hotel to pick you up, as it's a bit of a walk from the village car park or train station.

❶ Information

Both the village post office (郵局) and the 7-Eleven have ATMs but we advise that you bring cash with you.

Alishan National Scenic Area's website (www.ali-nsa.net) has information about travel here.

There is also a **visitor centre** (旅客服務中心, Lǚkè Fùwù Zhōngxīn; ☎ 05-267 9971; 59 Zhongzheng village, 中正村59號; ⊙8.30am-5.30pm) located below the entrance to Alishan House, where you can pick up an excellent English-language map.

The local **public health clinic** (香林村衛生室, Xiānglíncūn Wèishēngshì; ☎ 05-267 9806; 58 Zhongshan village, 中山村58號) keeps irregular hours, but is always open in the mornings and often afternoons. It's just down the road from the Catholic Hostel, near the entrance gate to the park.

❶ Getting There & Away

Buses to Chiayi Train Station (Route 7322, NT$250, 2½ hours, hourly) run from 9.10am to 5.10pm and leave from in front of the 7-Eleven. There are four buses to Chiayi HSR station (Route 7329, NT$278, three hours) leaving at 10.10am, 1.30pm, 2.40pm and 4.40pm.

TOUGH TRAIL, EASY TRAIL
....

Taiwan's official forest recreation website (https://recreation.forest.gov.tw/EN/Trail) has details of the trails, but here are two popular ones requiring drastically different strength and endurance levels. Bringing your own food is always advisable when hiking in the forest.

Yuanzui–Shaolai–Xiaoshue National Trail

Though the total length of the Yuanzui–Shaolai–Xiaoshue National Trail (鳶嘴稍來小雪山 國家步道; Yuānzuǐ Shāolái Xiǎoxuěshān Guójiā Bùdào) is only 15.5km, it takes two days to complete. You are required to register at the Dadong police station (at the Km15 mark of the trail) before you hit the road.

Most hikers just do a small portion starting at the Km27 mark. It's about one to 1½ hours uphill on a great path to Yuanzui Shan (鳶嘴山; elevation 2130m), where an observation tower gives you views of Yushan.

From here another two to three hours along steep rocky ledges takes you to Shaolai Shan (稍來山; elevation 2307m). Another hour takes you back to the main road at the Km35 mark. It's possible to continue walking to Anmashan (鞍馬山; Ānmǎshān) and down to the village at the Km43 mark, but that would take another day.

No matter which route you take, be prepared. In 2010 a group of foreign hikers wandered off the (clear) trail and spent a bitterly cold night in the mountains before being rescued in the morning.

Xueshan Sacred Tree Trail

Xueshan (or Syueshan) Sacred Tree Trail (雪山神木步道; Xuěshān Shénmù Bùdào) provides an easy 2km hike that runs from the car park at the Km49.5 mark to Tianchih, a pond filled with water year-round at 2600m, and onwards to the 1400-year-old Formosan red cypress. The walk takes around two hours return.

Chiayi

♪ 05 / POP 524,783

While Chiayi (嘉義; Jiāyì) is not part of the Alishan National Scenic Area (p223), almost every traveller will have to pass through here to get there. The narrow-gauge train to Alishan (p223) leaves from Chiayi Train Station, as do buses and taxis. There are a few sights worth checking out in and around Chiayi, so plan to spend a day or so before moving on.

Central Chiayi is small enough to walk across in 30 minutes.

History

Chiayi is the capital of Chiayi county and was once the home of plains indigenous peoples. During the Dutch occupation of Taiwan, however, Fujian farmers began to settle in numbers. The name Chiayi was given by the emperor Chien-lung, intended as a reward for Chiayi citizens taking the 'right' side in an 18th-century islandwide rebellion. The city prospered under Qing and later Japanese rule, when it was the capital of the sugar industry and one of the most modern cities in Taiwan. Today, sadly, there is too little of this prosperity remaining.

◉ Sights

★ **National Palace Museum Southern Branch**   MUSEUM

(國立故宮博物院南部院區, Guólì Gùgōng Bówùyuàn Nánbù Yuànqū; ♪ 05-310 1588; http:// south.npm.gov.tw; 888 Gugong Blvd, Taibao, 太保 市故宮大道888號; NT$150; ⊙9am-5pm Tue-Fri, to 6pm Sat & Sun; 🚌7211) Fans of historical art and antiques will have a field day here: there is exquisite Buddhist art from Asia's oldest civilisations, excellent displays on Chinese and Japanese tea culture, Asian jade and textiles, and other artefacts of Chinese, Taiwanese or Asian heritage. The museum's architecture is sleek and modern, a stark contrast to the Chinese palace–style mothermuseum (p78) in Taipei.

Buses depart regularly from Chiayi HSR Station for the museum; it takes 15 minutes.

★ **City God Temple**   TAOIST TEMPLE

(城隍廟, Chénghuáng Miào; www.cycht.org.tw; 168 Wufeng N Rd, East District, 吳鳳北路168號; ⊙9am-5pm; 🚌7320) This is the spiritual centre of Chiayi and is dedicated to the City God. First constructed in 1715, many of the best parts of the temple hail from a 1941 reconstruction. Look for the gorgeous spiderweb

Chiayi

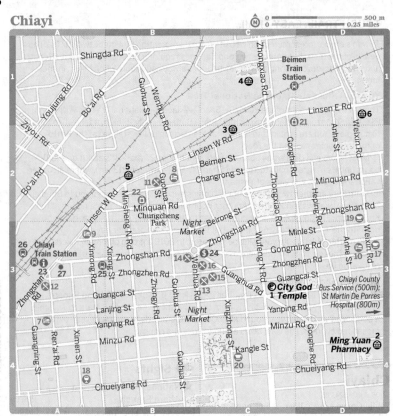

WESTERN TAIWAN

Chiayi

plafond (decorative) ceiling and two rows of lively cochin (brightly coloured, glazed ceramic) figures on the walls of the main hall.

Beigang Old Street
AREA

(北港老街, Běigǎng Lǎojiē; Zhongshan Rd, Beigang, 中山路; ☑7201) Beigang Old St is the long strip of Zhongshan Rd in front of Chaotian Temple. It's been a hub of commercial activity since the Qing dynasty, its prosperity inseparable from how brightly the incense burns at the temple. Flanking the wide, very walkable street are traditional shops and stalls selling Beigang specialities such as sesame oil, goose eggs and peanut candy, as well as daily necessities such as farming implements and miniature deities.

Museum of Old Taiwan Tiles
MUSEUM

(台灣花磚博物館, Táiwān Huāzhuān Bówùguǎn; ☑0979-060 750; www.facebook.com/taiwan. tiles; 282 Linsen W Rd, 林森西路282號; NT$50; ☉10am-noon, 2-5pm Wed-Sun; ☻) An old timber house is the lovely setting for this museum that throws light on the history and preservation of Taiwan's old tiles. The gorgeous patterns are turned into objects that make wonderful souvenirs, like stickers, coasters, fridge magnets and shopping bags. Children can also learn to paint their own tiles. The entrance fee is deducted from spending you make here.

Chaotian Temple
TEMPLE

(朝天宮, Cháotiān Gōng; www.matsu.org.tw; 178 Zhongshan Rd, Beigang township, Yunlin, 中山路178 號; ☑7201) This temple was founded in 1694 when a monk brought a Mazu statue to the area. Like its neighbour, Fengtian Temple, Chaotian was at one time or another razed by fire, flood and earthquake. It was even occupied by Japanese troops in 1895. What you see today is what has been here since 1908 (except for the neon tigers). Note that its grand, open stone design is quite unlike most other temples in Taiwan.

Take Beigang-bound buses from Chiayi County Bus Service station. (p232)

Fengtian Temple
TEMPLE

(奉天宮, Fèngtiān Gōng; ☑05-374 2034; 53 Xinmin Rd, Xingang, 新民路53號; ☉6am-10pm; ☑7202) This temple, founded in 1622, claims to be the first Mazu temple on mainland Taiwan. The original temple is said to have collapsed, been rebuilt, collapsed again and then been destroyed by flood. It was relocated, but the new temple was ruined by successive earthquakes. The present structure was built in 1922 and has survived to this day.

The temple is on the route of the annual nine-day Mazu Pilgrimage (p231).

Alishan Forest Railway Chiayi Garage
MUSEUM

(阿里山森林鐵路嘉義車庫, Ālǐshān Sēnlín Tiělù Jiāyì Chēkù; 2-1 Linsen W Rd, 林森西路2-1 號; ☉8am-6pm; ☑7320) FREE The tree-lined garage is actually a park with an assortment of old steam locomotives. Train buffs and kids alike will love it. Look for the SL13 (built in 1910), the oldest in the collection.

Prison Museum
MUSEUM

(獄政博物館, Yùzhèng Bówùguǎn; ☑05-278 9242; 140 Weixin Rd, 維新路140號; ☉9.30-11.30am & 1.30-3.30pm Tue-Sun; ☑7320) FREE Offering a taste of life behind bars, free admission to this museum includes an hour-long guided tour, which is repeated four times per day Tuesday to Sunday (9.30am, 10.30am, 1.30pm and 2.30pm). The museum is on the site of the old Chiayi Prison, built in the 1920s and the only wooden prison structure in Taiwan that has survived from the Japanese era. Check out the fan-shaped cell complex and the Japanese shrine atop the central control room.

Aogu Wetlands and Forest Park
NATURE RESERVE

(鰲鼓溼地生態展示館, Áogǔ Shīdì Shēngtài Zhǎnshì Guǎn; ☑05-360 1801; 54 Aogu village, Sec 4, 鰲鼓村四股54號; ☉9am-4.30pm Tue-Sun) FREE The sprawling 15-sq-km wetland park includes mud beaches, marshes, lagoons, fish farms, beefwood forests and tracts of thick shrub. Dozens of bird species can be spotted here with nothing more than the naked eye. These include drongos, egrets, cranes, ducks, cormorants, hawks and eagles. In total, 245 species have been recorded in the wetlands, with the majority being migratory.

Aogu is easily reached off Hwy 17 if you have your own vehicle, but be aware that the reserve is a maze of dirt roads.

Wude Temple
TEMPLE

(武德宮, Wǔdé Gōng; 330 Huasheng Rd, Beigang township, Yunlin, 華勝路330號; ☉9am-5pm; ☑7325, 7202) Wude Temple is one of Taiwan's earliest and largest temples dedicated to the God of Wealth (財神), the folk deity whose bearded image graces doors and red packets during Lunar New Year. It's a very busy and prosperous-looking temple with its own cafe.

WESTERN TAIWAN CHIAYI

CHIAYI'S DRUG STORE ARBORIST

Ming Yuan was a **pharmacy** (明原藥局, Míngyuán Yàojú; ☎ 05-227 7067; 75 Zhaoyang St, East District, 朝陽街75號i; ⏱ 9.30am-8pm; 🖨 7211); now it's a shrine to Taiwan's indigenous flora. Owner Mr Tsai has managed to cram every corner of the tiny shop with unusual seeds, suspended above, stuffed into boxes stacked ceiling-high, or poking out from behind a mirror.

The intense and sociable 60-year-old will show you single-seed red beans (單子紅豆, *dānzi hóngdòu*) and sandbox-tree capsules (沙盤樹, *shāpán shù*), which he collects and turns into lovely ornaments (NT$20 to $300).

Mr Tsai has written extensively about Taiwan's trees. He speaks little English but can rattle off 'Ormosia monosperma' faster than you can say, 'What?' The shop is closed when he's out in the hills. Ming Yuan is 1.7km from Chiayi Train Station via Zhongzheng Road.

Behind Wude is a shiny new Taoist temple with a soaring ceiling and golden interiors.

🛏 Sleeping

An Lan Jie Hostel HOSTEL $
(安蘭居, Ānlán Jū; ☎ 05-229 0102; www.anlanjie hostel.com/?page_id=3821&lang=en; 14th fl, 465 Lanjing St, 蘭井街465號14樓; dm/d/quad from NT$500/$1500/$2500; ⊝✳🛜) Occupying two floors of a building, this youth hostel offers clean and welcoming dorms (mixed and women's), doubles and suites. Our favourite is the 'Kano' dorm with 180 degree views of the sunset and Alishan. The friendly hostel also organises a plethora of activities for guests that include tours to Alishan, Guanziling and Ruili, and walking tours of old Chiayi. The hostel is a five-minute walk from Chiayi train station.

Petite Hostel HOSTEL $
(小青旅, Xiǎo Qīnglǚ; ☎ 0966-725 905; 460 Linsen W Rd, West District, 林森西路460號; dm/d from NT$500/1200; ⊝✳🛜) Cool, understated place with no signage (it's next to a tattoo parlour) where you'll find four dormitory-type rooms and two doubles, all with shared bathrooms. The top floor is a laundry room and the basement a former air-raid shelter where the owner now lives. Staff are friendly and speak English. It's a five-minute walk from Chiayi train station.

★Hodua B&B HOSTEL $$
(好住民宿, Hǎozhù Mínsù; ☎ 05-782 6727; www.0932587227.com.tw; 37 Gongmin Rd, Beigang, 公民路37號; d from NT$2800; ⊝✳🛜) 🍴 A historic bank building has been converted into a hostel run by the amicable Ms Liu. The 10 rooms are furnished with Taiwan cypress and natural fabrics, and are very homey. And great news for allergy sufferers: towels are

homespun and beddings are washed with organic detergent and sun-dried.

Hodua also supplies tea-tree-oil-infused body wash and shampoo, but encourages guests to bring their own toothbrush and toothpaste. The restaurant (open for lunch and dinner) serves very good pasta made by the owner's son, who trained as a chef in Taipei.

★South Urban Hotel BOUTIQUE HOTEL $$$
(南院旅墅, Nányuàn Lǚshù; ☎ 05-271 6565; www.southurban-hotel.com.tw/zh-TW; 65 Gongming Rd, 公明路65號; d NT$4800; ⊝✳🛜🅿; 🖨7203) A hip upmarket hotel with bright, clean, medium-sized rooms and stellar service by young, English-speaking staff. Decor features a soothing palette with light grey and pine, and restrained accents. A small gym and an outdoor lap pool complete the hotel. South Urban is named after the Southern Branch of the National Palace Museum (p225) but is nowhere close to it.

🍴 Eating

Chiayi is most famous for turkey rice (雞飯, *jī fàn*) and you'll find plenty at and around the Wenhua Road Night Market (p229). If you head east on Minzu Rd for 1-2km, you'll hit the business area of town, where you'll find nice cafes and restaurants. The district of Minxiong also has a few culinary gems.

★Smart Fish TAIWANESE $
(林聰明沙鍋魚頭, Lín Cōngmíng Shāguō Yútóu; ☎ 05-227 0661; www.smartfish.com.tw; 361 Zhongzheng Rd, East District, 中正路361號; per person from NT$150; ⏱ noon-10pm Wed-Mon) At this hugely popular restaurant featured on Netflix's *Street Food*, silver carp heads are deep-fried and simmered in a milky pork broth with vegetables, fungus and tofu. The end

product is the most delicious of land and sea distilled into a bowl. The wait for a table can be over an hour on weekends. Go with friends and go early.

Wenhua Road Night Market MARKET $

(文化路夜市, Wénhuà Lù Yèshì; Wenhua Rd, 文化路; ⏱5pm-11pm) This food bazaar that starts at a roundabout with a fountain is one of Taiwan's neater and less crowded night markets. Chiayi, Changhua and southern Taiwan specialities are well represented here, such as turkey rice (雞肉飯), beef soup (牛肉湯), pork-belly rice (爌肉飯), and milkfish (虱目魚). For dessert, there's sweet bean curd (甜豆花) and a plethora of fruity concoctions.

Fengzha Egg Pancake BREAKFAST $

(峰炸蛋餅, Fēngzhà Dàn Bǐng; 252-1 Changrong St, 長榮街252-1號; porkchop roll NT$55; ⏱6am-11.30am) There's always a crowd in front of this fabulous breakfast place in a small street next to **Maison de Chine** (兆品酒店, Zhàopǐn Jiǔdiàn; ☑05-229 3998; 257 Wenhua Rd, 文化路257號; r from NT$2800; ⊖❋🗐). They whip up five dozen varieties of sandwiches and pancake rolls, but the star by far is the delectable egg pancake with tonkatsu or Japanese fried pork cutlet (峰炸蛋餅, fēngzhà dàn bǐng).

You can eat there at one of the many makeshift tables or get takeout. Either way, the wait is likely to be long (45 minutes at peak times). The restaurant closes on the second and fourth Tuesday of the month.

Pen Shui Turkey Rice TAIWANESE $

(噴水火雞飯, Pēnshuǐ Huǒjīfàn; 325 Zhongshan Rd, 中山路325號; bowl NT$60; ⏱9.30am-9.30pm; 🗐7319) Everyone in Taiwan knows that Chiayi is famous for its turkey-rice dish (火雞肉飯, huǒjīròu fàn). This is the place that started it all 60-odd years ago. It's very busy so expect to wait for a table.

Guo's TAIWANESE $

(郭家, Guō Jiā; 148 Wenhua Rd, 文化路148號; NT$20-100) A no-frills family-run shop in the Wenhua Road Night Market specialising in turkey rice (雞肉飯) and savoury rice pudding in soup (粿仔湯), with an assortment of side dishes laid out near the entrance such as sliced octopus, blanched veggies and cold tofu.

Gongbing Vegetarian Restaurant VEGETARIAN $

(宮賓素食館, Gōngbīn Sùshí Guǎn; ☑05-227 3461; 457 Ren'ai Rd, 仁愛路457號; meals from NT$100; ⏱6.15am-7pm; 🖉; 🗐7318, 7319) A modest veg-

etarian restaurant with buffet and a la carte options, and vegan foodstuff for sale.

Huihuang Beef Shop TAIWANESE $

(輝煌牛肉店, Huīhuáng Niúròu Diàn; 136-4 Bo'ai Rd, Beigang, 北港鎮博愛路136之4號; ⏱8.30am-5pm Tue-Sun) Behind Chaotian Temple (p227), where Bo'ai Rd (博愛路) meets Datong Rd (大同路), a green awning and open frontage mark this old shop specialising in local beef (牛肉, niúròu), which is served lightly blanched, in soup, or braised. The meat is lean, chewy, flavourful and cheap, excellent with a bowl of luscious Taiwanese rice.

★ Do Right TAIWANESE $$

(渡對, Dù Duì; ☑05-226 2300; 21 Dongrong Rd, Minxiong, 東榮路21號; mains from NT$200; ⏱noon-9.30pm Wed-Sun; 🕿) Do Right sure does it right. Students, professionals and expats come to this cafe for its hearty yet refined Taiwanese home cooking and delectable cakes and pastries. The restaurant occupies the premises of an old rice mill that used to process grains from Minxiong before they were transported up the railroad to Northern Taiwan. Take the train from Chiayi to Minxiong (adult/child NT$15/8) and the restaurant is a one-minute walk from the east exit.

Minxiong Goose TAIWANESE $$

(民雄鵝肉町, Mínxióng Eròu Tīng; ☑05-226 5987; 1-1 Zhongle Rd, Minxiong, 中樂路1-1號; quarter/half/whole goose NT$350/700/1400; ⏱7.30am-8.30pm; 🚃Minxiong) Zhongle Rd, just across from Minxiong Train Station, is lined with shops selling a Minxiong speciality – goose! But this shop has the most customers. The birds are braised till flavourful and juicy, then thinly sliced and eaten plain or with condiments. Get takeout if the line is long.

🍷 Drinking & Nightlife

★ Casa Lounge COCKTAIL BAR

(☑0922-882 673; www.facebook.com/Chiayi.Casa; 512 Daya Rd, Sec 2, 大雅路二段512號; cocktails NT$200-350; ⏱7pm-1am Mon-Sat; 🗐7211) A cosy cocktail den with a cute resident pup. Both belong to a prize-winning mixologist known for his passion for animal rights and his creativity. The story of how he was once presented soy milk by a customer and what he did with it is the stuff of urban legend. There are only a dozen seats here; go early.

★ Saint Tower Coffee CAFE

(聖塔咖啡, Shèngtǎ Kāfēi; ☑05-228 2025; 10 Xingzhong St, 興中街10號; coffee NT$60-300;

noon-9pm Thu-Tue; 🐾; 🖥 66, 7211) One of the best places in Chiayi for a cup of joe, Saint Tower is where you're likely to find the owner working the Fuji Royal bean-roasting machine for his impeccable pour-overs and espressos. On cool evenings, the glass doors of the brick-walled corner shop are opened so guests can enjoy their Geisha coffee on the street.

Akana
CAFE
(赤名咖啡, Chìmíng Kāfēi; www.facebook.com/赤名咖啡-あかなAkana-2041516425891708; 616 Zhongshan Rd, 中山路616號; coffee NT$60-300; noon-6pm Thu-Tue; 🐾; 🖥 7314) This breezy cafe occupying part of the premises of an old liquor factory serves very good coffee that comes with wacky names like 'Young Man', 'Uncle Blue' and 'Goddess', as well as Taiwanese craft beer, and pastries. They also make their own fruit-infused liquor.

Akana is inside the not-too-exciting Chiayi Cultural & Creative Industries Park.

Cocktails of Pioneers
COCKTAIL BAR
(COP; www.facebook.com/copbartw; 54-1 Ximen St, 西門街54-1號; NT$250-400; 7pm-2am Mon-Sat; 🖥 7301, 7311) Stylish COP with its green walls and cool industrial lights is known for tea-infused cocktails, and the more floral and fruity side of drinks. But if this is not your thing, they do a spicy and heady Blanco Negroni as well. The space is long and narrow, with a small room for groups at the end.

Azulejo Coffee
CAFE
(花磚咖啡, Huāzhuān Kāfēi; 0527 77363; www.facebook.com/花磚咖啡淺嚐館-402596480174755; 59-1 Gongming Rd, 公明路59-1號; coffee NT$100-250; 10am-6pm Tue-Sun; 🐾; 🖥 7211) A cool and relaxing cafe with Mediterranean floor tiles that serves only coffee – but very good coffee. It's located at a busy junction, which makes street watching from its plush colour-coordinated banquettes or old-school iron stools all the more enjoyable.

Daisy's Grocery Store
COFFEE
(Daisy的雜貨店, Daisy de Záhuò Diàn; 05-277 0893; www.facebook.com/wowwpie; 73 Weixin Rd, East District, 維新路73號; 2-9pm; 🖥 7211, 7327) An artsy cafe in an old Japanese house with the original beams and rafters, and sliding doors. The small space is tastefully crammed with books and art. You can browse as you wait for your excellent tea or coffee should you manage to find a seat at the counter, in the alcove with velvet chairs, or on the tatami mat.

☆ Entertainment

Fake Qoo
LIVE MUSIC
(廢窟, Fèikū; www.facebook.com/FAKEQOO/?ref=br_rs; No.27-3 Dapiantian Wei (番路鄉新福村 大片田尾27-3), Xinfu Cun, Fanlu township; 8pm-2am Fri & Sat; 🖥 7314) This alternative, laid-back space feels like someone's home and is rented by 12 young music-and-art lovers to host live gigs and movie screenings. See their Facebook page for the monthly music performances. If nothing's on, you can go Friday or Saturday night to drink and chill.

Take bus 7314 at Chiayi Station and ride 25 stops to Wuhuliao (五虎寮; Wǔhǔliáo). Disembark and walk 1.4km to your destination. Fake Qoo is on Dapianwei Road, in a village called Xinfu Cun in Fanlu township. A taxi from central Chiayi takes 30 minutes.

🛍 Shopping

Moor Room
MUSIC
(荒屋, Huāngwū; 0977-550 130; www.facebook.com/moor.vintage/?epa=SEARCH_BOX; 1 Lane 197, Zhongyi St, 忠義街197巷1號; 2-8pm Wed, Thu & Sun, to 10pm Fri & Sat; 🖥 7320A, 7325) An old timber house in an alley is the location of this vintage shop, selling clothes, wooden handicrafts, and music by indie bands from Taiwan and the rest of Asia. The owner Su (蘇) is a musician, and unplugged performances take place here one or two Saturdays a month. See details on their Facebook page.

Hinoki Village
ARTS & CRAFTS
(檜意森活村, Guìyì Sēnhuó Cūn; 05-276 1601; www.facebook.com/hinokivillage; 1 Linsen E Rd, East District, 林森路1號; 10am-6pm; 🖥 7202, 7304) A nicely landscaped site where you'll find lily ponds and a crafts and coffee 'village' converted from Japanese-style dormitories of the Alishan Forest Railway. The shopping is not mind-blowing, though you may be able to find souvenirs, but the village is certainly lovely enough for a visit.

ℹ Information

There are numerous banks and ATMs on Ren'ai Rd near Chiayi Train Station. **First Commercial Bank** (第一商業銀行, Dìyī Shāngyè Yínháng; 05-227 2111; 307 Zhongshan Rd, 中山路307號; 9am-3.30pm Mon-Fri) has ATMs and currency exchange. Many convenience stores have ATMs as well.

St Martin De Porres Hospital (天主教聖馬爾定醫院, Tiānzhǔjiào Shèng Mǎ'ěr Dìng Yīyuàn; 05-275 6000; www.stm.org.tw; 565 Daya Rd, Sec 2, 大雅路二段565號) offers basic medical services.

THE MAZU PILGRIMAGE

The Goddess Mazu

The unquestioned patron deity of Taiwan, Mazu, although often referred to as the Goddess of the Sea, is officially Tianhou (Empress of Heaven). Her divine jurisdiction extends from protecting fisherfolk and helping women in childbirth to restoring social order.

Mazu was once Lin Mo-niang (林默娘; b AD 960) from Meizhou, Fujian. As a young girl Mo-niang was noted for her quickness to master magical arts and soon began to be regarded as a female shaman. Her particular forte was helping fishermen survive at sea: one of her most famous exploits was rescuing her own father.

Mo-niang died young, aged 28, but almost immediately people in Meizhou began to worship her. As word of her divine effectiveness spread, so did her cult. Her highest title, Empress of Heaven, was conferred after she reportedly assisted in overthrowing Dutch rule in Taiwan – by stemming the tides, as legend has it.

Mazu worship came to Taiwan with the earliest settlers and her oldest temples date back to the 16th century. Today there are more than 500 Mazu temples around the island. Statues of the goddess usually depict her with black skin, a beaded veil and a red cape. Standing next to her are her loyal attendants, General See-all and General Hear-all, two demons that she subjugated and rescued from hell.

The Pilgrimage

The Mazu pilgrimage is the largest and most celebrated religious and folk activity in the country. Hundreds of thousands of pilgrims and spectators from all over the island and abroad escort a palanquin graced by a statue of Mazu, from Dajia to Hsinkang in Southern Taiwan, then back again, covering a distance of over 350km. The goddess is carried through 50 towns; over a million people see her pass their homes.

Many devotees will follow Mazu for the full nine days. They'll jostle each other to touch the sedan chair, while the most devout will jump to the front and actually kneel down on the road to allow the goddess to be carried over them. According to legend, touching the palanquin will confer good luck for a whole year.

The dates for the pilgrimage are announced every year in March. *Bwah bwey* (casting moon blocks) are used to determine the starting dates, though the goddess is only given weekends as a choice. The first, fourth – when the palanquin reaches Fengtian Temple (p227) – and last days are the most spectacular, but now many subordinate temples are starting to let their own statues and palanquins arrive early to avoid overcrowding and the frequent gang fights that erupt on the last day.

If you decide to join the pilgrimage, note that temples and volunteers along the way provide water, basic meals and accommodation. The schedule is usually as follows:

➡ Day 1: Pilgrims leave Chenlan Temple (鎮瀾宮) in Dajia around midnight and end their walk at Nanyao Temple (p234) (南瑤宮), Changhua city.

➡ Day 2: Fuxing Temple (福興宮) in Siluo township, Yunlin county.

➡ Day 3: Fengtian Temple (p227) (奉天宮) in Hsingang township, Chiayi county.

➡ Day 4: Main blessing ceremony and a second night at Fengtian Temple.

➡ Day 5: Fuxing Temple (福興宮) in Siluo township, Yunlin county.

➡ Day 6: Cheng'an Temple (奠安宮) in Beidou township, Changhua county.

➡ Day 7: Tianhou Temple (天后宮) in Changhua city.

➡ Day 8: Chaohsing Temple (朝興宮) in Qingshuei township, Taichung county.

➡ Day 9: Pilgrims return to Chenlan Temple in Daija.

For information on the dates and events of each year's pilgrimage, check the website www.dajiamazu.org.tw.

To reach Dajia take a train from Taipei. Chenlan Temple is a few blocks straight ahead as you exit from the front of the train station.

WESTERN TAIWAN

⊙ Getting There & Away

Chiayi is the gateway to Alishan National Scenic Area (p223).

AIR

The two-runway **Chiayi Airport** (嘉義航空站; ☑ 05-286 7886; www.cya.gov.tw/web/index. asp; 1 Rongdian Rd, Shuishang, 水上鄉榮典路1號) in the town of Shuishang (水上鄉) has flights to Penghu and Kinmen Islands.

BOAT

All Star (滿天星航運, Mǎntiān Xīng Hángyùn; ☑ 05-347 0948; www.aaaaa.com.tw; one-way/return NT$1000/1950) runs in the summer months between Budai Port (near Chiayi) and Makung on Penghu (NT$1000, 1½ hours). There are four sailings a day between 8am and 2.30pm.

BUS

Chiayi Bus Company (嘉義客運; ☑ 05-222 3194; www.cibus.com.tw/; 503 Zhongshan Rd, 中山路503號) Has buses to Guanziling (Route 7214, NT$90, one hour, hourly, 7am to 5.40pm).

Chiayi County Bus Service (嘉義縣公車管理; https://bus.cyhg.gov.tw; 635 Daya Rd, Sec 2, 大雅路二段635號) Buses to Fenqihu (7302, NT$163-185, 3-4 daily, 6.55am-2.55pm) and Alishan (7322A/7322D, NT$221-251, 5-10 daily, 5.55am to 1.55pm)

Kuo Kuang Hao Bus Company (國光客運公司, Guóguāng Kèyùn Gōngsī; www.kingbus.com. tw; 1 Zhongxing Rd, 中興路1號) Offers buses to Taipei (NT$440, 3½ hours, every 30 minutes) and other cities on the west coast. Buses leave from the company's bus station at the back of the train station. Other intercity bus companies also leave from here.

Taiwan Tour (台灣好行; www.taiwantrip.com. tw) Runs buses from 6.05am to 2.05pm to Alishan (NT$240, 2½ hours, hourly). There is also frequent service to Beigang (NT$70, 45 minutes, every 30 minutes) and Budai Port (NT$124, 1½ hours, hourly), and less frequent service to Rueili and Fenqihu – see the **visitor information centre** (遊客服務中心, Yóukè Fùwù Zhōngxīn; ☑ 05-225 6649; 528 Zhongshan Rd, West District, 中山路528號; ⊙ 8.30am-5pm) for the schedule.

HIGH SPEED RAIL

A bus connects the HSR station with Chiayi train station (NT$48, 30 minutes, every 20 minutes). The shuttle-bus stop is at the back of the train station, near the intercity bus companies. Trains travel frequently to Taipei (NT$1080, 80 minutes, three to four trains hourly).

TRAIN

At the time of writing, Alishan Forest Railway (p223) only reaches Fenqihu station (NT$384,

2½ hours, weekdays at 9am, one more train on weekends and holidays at 10am). Trains travel to/from Taipei (fast/slow train NT$598/385, 3½/4½ hours) and Kaohsiung (fast/slow train NT$245/158, 1½/two hours).

⊙ Getting Around

Scooter rentals (機車出租; ☑ 05-228 9135; 396 Linsen W Rd, 林森西路396號; per day NT$350-500) are available from shops across from Chiayi Train Station. An international driving permit (IDP) and ID are required.

Taxis are not as prevalent as in Taipei and Kaohsiung, but all hotels, bars and restaurants will call a cab for you upon request. 7-Eleven convenience stores also have machines that you can use to call taxis – if you find that hard to use, ask the staff to do so for you.

Chiayi County Bus Service has buses going to different places within Chiayi.

CHANGHUA

☑ 04 / POP 1,291,000

Changhua city (彰化市; Zhānghuà Shì), the capital and political heart of Changhua county, has usually been thought of as a gateway to the old town of Lukang, but there are some treats in the town itself, including stately old temples, a giant hilltop Buddha, an old sugar factory, and a rare fan-shaped train garage that contains a half-dozen old steam engines.

Birdwatchers should note that Changhua is on the migratory route of the grey-faced buzzard and that the hilltop with the Great Buddha Statue affords a 360-degree panoramic view.

Changhua is not a compact city, but you needn't wander too far from the train station during your stay. Even the Great Buddha Statue is only a couple of kilometres to the east.

⊙ Sights

Baguashan AREA
(八卦山, Bāguàshān; ⊙ 24hr; 🚌 6900, 6912) The Baguashan slopes were for centuries a military observation zone. The area affords views over the whole city and far out to sea. It's a pleasant place to stroll, especially in the spring, when the snow-white flowers of the Youtong trees are in bloom. At the top of the staircase leading from the entrance, you'll find a 22m-high **Great Buddha Statue** (八卦山大佛像, Bāguàshān Dàfóxiàng; 31 Wenquan Rd, 溫泉路31號; ⊙ 8.30am-5.30pm) to your right up some more steps, and, to your left, a large

Changhua

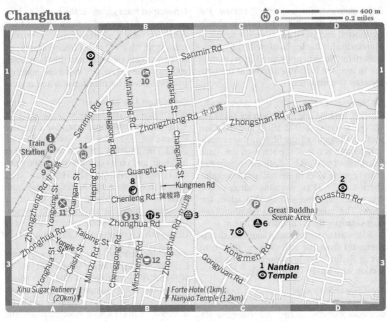

Changhua

semicircular viewing deck with a wooden walkway. You can see the sunset from there.

The large black Buddha sitting on a golden lotus was built in 1962. You can go inside the 22m-tall structure, which has five floors of fantastical sculptures of phoenixes and elephants, and life-sized exhibits depicting the life and teachings of the Buddha.

The Nine Dragons Pond (九龍池, Jiǔlóng Chí) is really a fountain, and it's situated in a semicircular plaza under the viewing deck. There are nine golden dragons with jaws gaping skyward.

In the southern foothills of Baguashan is the bizarre **Nantian Temple** (南天宮, Nántiān

Gōng; 12 Lane 187, Gongyuan Rd, Sec 1, 公園路一段 187巷12號; adult/child NT$50/30; ☺8am-5.30pm) and haunted gallery, where Taiwanese parents used to take their kids to scare them into obedience. You'll see gory scenes from a Buddhist inferno enacted by mechanised animatronic dioramas. On the 3rd floor is a temple dedicated to the Monkey King that looks like it belongs to a '70s period movie, like those of director Li Han-hsiang. The top floor houses a new section of the haunted house that's darker, louder and more theme-park-like, but less interesting than the first one.

Look for the green sign that says Nantian Temple (南天宮) directly opposite

Baguashan's main entrance. Follow the narrow path downhill. The path is clearly signposted and you'll see advertisements, in Mandarin, for '18 levels of hell fully mechanised' or 'No expense spared in recreating the 18 levels of hell'. You'll arrive at the temple after five minutes.

★Nanyao Temple   TAOIST TEMPLE
(南瑤宮, Nányáo Gōng; 43 Nanyao Rd, 南瑤路43號; ◷6am-8pm; ☐6900, 6912) Located 2km south of Changhua Train Station, this remarkable temple is one of the stops on the Mazu Pilgrimage (p231). The distinctive character of the complex lies in the hall in the middle: check out the Doric columns, baroque-style decor and Japanese shrines that adorn the space. The sanctum, a 1920s addition, honours Guanyin, the bodhisattva of mercy.

To get to the temple, head south on Zhongzheng Rd from the train station, then turn left to Ren'ai Rd. When you reach the intersection with Nayao Rd, turn right.

Xihu Sugar Refinery   LANDMARK
(溪湖糖廠, Xīhú Tángchǎng; ☑04-885 5868; www.facebook.com/tscl4.taisugar; 762 Zhangshui Rd, Sec 2, 溪湖鎮彰水路二段762號, Xihu; ◷8am-5.30pm) The heavy roller mills, boiling vats and centrifuges you see in this large and photogenic refinery once produced the largest volume of sugar per day in Taiwan. The refinery, in operation from 1921 to 2002, also has a lovely park, an ice-cream production facility with an attached supermarket, and vintage locomotives you can ride on for NT$100. They depart on the hour (except noon) from 10am to 4pm on weekends.

From Changhua train station, take a Xihu-bound train and disembark at Xihua station, then follow the signs.

Confucius Temple   CONFUCIAN TEMPLE
(孔廟, Kǒng Miào; 30 Kungmen Rd, 永福里孔門路30號; ◷8am-5.30pm, closed national holidays) This 1726 beauty ranks as one of the oldest Confucian temples in Taiwan and as a first-class historical relic. Inside the ancestral hall, there's an inscribed plaque donated by the Qing-dynasty emperor Chien Long. Every year on Confucius' birthday (28 September) there is a colourful ceremony at dawn. The temple is 10 minutes on foot from the train station.

Changhua Roundhouse   NOTABLE BUILDING
(扇形車庫, Shànxíng Chēkù; 1 Changmei Rd, 彰美路1段1號; ◷10am-4pm Sat & Sun, 1-4pm Tue-Fri) FREE Great for families with children, the fan-shaped train garage is the last of its kind in Taiwan. In essence, a single line of track connects with a short section of rotating track from which 12 radial tracks branch out. A train engine rides up onto the short track, rotates in the direction of its garage, and then proceeds inside for maintenance and repairs.

Changhua Arts Museum   MUSEUM
(彰化藝術館, Zhuānghuà Yìshù Guǎn; ☑04-728 7243; http://art.changhua.gov.tw; 542 Zhongshan Rd, Sec 2, 中山路2段542號; ◷9am-5pm Tue-Sun) FREE The museum sits in a lovely heritage building, and on its grounds is the 300-year-old Hongmao Well (紅毛井; Hóngmáo Jǐng). This is the last of the original Dutch-built wells in central Taiwan (hence the name Hongmao, meaning 'red hair'). The exhibitions feature Taiwanese artists, primarily those with a connection to Changhua.

Yuanching Temple   TAOIST TEMPLE
(元清觀, Yuánqīng Guān; 207 Minsheng Rd, 光華里民生路207號; ◷8am-6pm; ☐6912) This splendid southern-style temple, founded in 1763, boasts elegant, swallowtail rooftop eaves and a wealth of fine interior woodcarvings. The resident deity is the supreme Jade Emperor.

🛏 Sleeping

Soul Map   HOTEL $
(心旅地圖, Xīnlǚ Dìtú; ☑0985-680 812 (10am-10pm); http://soulmaphostel.com/accommodation; 2nd fl, 230 Sanmin Rd, 三民路230號2樓; dm/d from NT$500/1200; ❀✳🎧) This hostel has colourfully decorated en-suite rooms and dormitory-type rooms (mixed and women-only). Bathrooms have separate showering and toilet facilities, but living quarters may be small by some standards. Soul Map is a seven-minute walk from the train station.

★Forte Hotel   BUSINESS HOTEL $$
(福泰商務飯店, Fútài Shāngwù Fàndiàn; ☑04-712 5228; www.fortehotels.com.tw/changhua; 20 Jianbao St, 建寶街20號; r from NT$3000; ❀✳🎧; ☐6912) Modern hotel with 100 rooms on the property of a hospital (with a postpartum care centre on the 5th floor). The rooms are spacious; suites come with massage chairs and bathtubs. The 10th floor has laundry facilities and a business centre. The English-speaking staff are very well trained. The breakfast buffet is quite a treat.

Hotel Taiwan   HOTEL $$
(台灣大飯店, Táiwān Dàfàndiàn; ☑04-722 4681; www.hoteltaiwan.com.tw; 48 Zhongzheng Rd, Sec 2, 中正路二段 48 號; d from NT$2100; ✳@🎧)

The refurbished Hotel Taiwan is one of the best midrange options in Changhua. Rooms are decently sized and modern. Its location, right next to the train station, is an additional convenience.

✗ Eating

Changhua is famous for its *ròu yuán* (肉圓, meatballs) and you'll find many places to try them on Chenling Rd.

For cheap eats and cafes, there are plenty of places around the train station and on Guangfu St.

Cat Mouse Noodle   NOODLES $
(貓鼠麵, Māoshǔmiàn; ☑ 04-726 8376; 223 Chenleng Rd, 陳稜路223號; noodles from NT$40; ⊙9am-8pm) The Changhua tourist website claims that this shop's special noodle dish is one of the three culinary treasures of the city. It's a stretch, but the tangy noodles are pretty tasty. The shop has its odd name because the owner's nickname sounds like 'cat mouse' in Taiwanese – not because of anything you'll find in the food.

♟ Drinking & Entertainment

Stable Fly   CAFE
(穩定飛行模式, Wěndìng Fēixíng Móshì; ☑ 04-722 0663; 2 Lane 44, Yongle St, 永樂街44巷2號; coffee from NT$100; ⊙10am-8pm Wed, Thu, Sun, to 10pm Fri & Sat; ☎; ➲6900, 6912) This place is like walking into someone's pretty livingroom. There are communal tables, a vintage dental light in one corner, a glass skull on a table, jars of fruit-infused liquor, and lots of reading materials and handicrafts. They serve good craft beer, coffees and teas, and passable meals.

No. 9 Workshop   COCKTAIL BAR
(酒號工作室, Jiǔhào Gōngzuò Shì; 55 Chenggong Rd, 成功路55號; cocktails NT$300-$350; ⊙7pm-midnight; ➲6900, 6912) This moody bar plays lots of '80s Japanese pop and makes very good cocktails. The fruity ones come with lots of fresh seasonal fruit. They don't serve food, but you're welcome to get takeout from stalls and shops outside and eat here.

FDLC Livehouse   LIVE MUSIC
(福大祿昌展演空間, Fúdà Lùchǎng; ☑ 04-727 2062; www.facebook.com/FDLClivehouse; 266-1 Zhonghua Rd, 中華路266-1號; ⊠Changhua) Changhua's underground music spot hosts performances by indie bands from Taiwan and other parts of Asia on some weekends. See its Facebook page for announcements.

Shows usually start around 8pm and tickets cost upwards of NT$250. FDLC is 500m from Changhua train station.

❶ Information

Bank of Taiwan (台灣銀行; ☑ 04-722 5191; www.bot.com.tw; 130 Chenggong Rd, 成功路130號; ⊙9am-3.30pm Mon-Fri) Offers a currency-exchange service.

The Changhua county website (http://tourism.chcg.gov.tw) is a valuable source of travel information in the area. The city's website (www.changhua.gov.tw) also has helpful information for visitors. There is a **visitor centre** (火車站旅遊服務中心; ☑ 04-728 5750; 1 Sanmin Rd, 三民路1號; ⊙9am-5pm) inside the train station, where you can pick up English-language maps of the surrounding area.

❶ Getting There & Away

Buses to Lukang (NT$51, 40 minutes, every 30 minutes) depart from the **Changhua Bus Company** (彰化客運; ☑ 04-722 5111; www.changhuabus.com.tw; 563 Zhongzheng Rd, 中正路563號) station, near the main station.

Trains travel from Taipei (fast/slow train NT$415/256, 2½/3½ hours) and Kaohsiung (fast/slow train NT$429/276, two/three hours) to Changhua.

LUKANG

☑04 / POP 86,112

Ninety percent of Lukang (鹿港; Lùgǎng) is as nondescript as most small towns in Taiwan...but then there is that other 10%. Containing some of the most gorgeous temples in the country, and featuring curiously curved streets, heritage buildings and dusty old shops, it is this small part of Lukang – coverable on foot within one long day – that justifiably brings in the crowds.

People call Lukang a 'living museum' and this is true as much for the food as it is for the buildings and streets. Traditional dishes are cheap and readily available near all major sights. Look for the enticingly named phoenix-eye cake, dragon whiskers and shrimp monkeys, among many other dishes.

Lukang is just half an hour from Changhua by bus, and is easily reached from anywhere on the west coast.

⊙ Sights

★**Longshan Temple**   BUDDHIST TEMPLE
(龍山寺, Lóngshān Sì; 100 Longshan St, 龍山街100號; ⊙9am-5pm) Built in the late 18th

Lukang

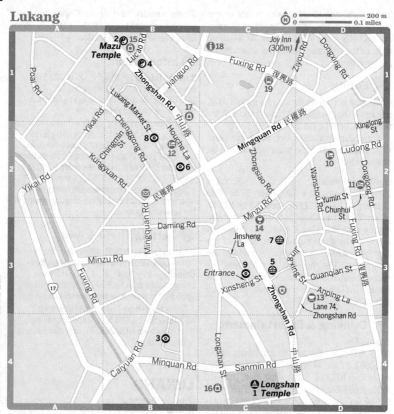

century, Longshan Temple remains a show-case of southern temple design. The temple is expansive, covering over 10,000 sq metres within its gated walls, so give yourself a few hours to take in the grandeur and admire the

minutiae. Some highlights include the front mountain gate, with its elegant *dǒugǒng* (special bracketing system for Chinese architecture) and sweeping eaves. Before the front of the Hall of Five Gates you'll find the most famous carved dragons in Taiwan: note that the head of one runs up the column while its twin runs down.

Also check out the hall's window lattice for two fish that curl around each other in the shape of the yin and yang symbol. Inside the hall you'll find one of the most stunning plafonds in Taiwan, as well as brackets and beams carved into a veritable smorgasbord of traditional symbols: there are clouds, dragons, bats, lions, melons, elephants, phoenixes, fish and more.

The resident deity at Longshan Temple is the bodhisattva Guanyin. You'll find her shrine at the back worship hall.

★ Mazu Temple   TAOIST TEMPLE
(天后宮, Tiānhòu Gōng; ☑ 04-777 9899; www. lugangmazu.org; 430 Zhongshan Rd, 中山路430號; ☻ 6am-10pm) This holy structure was renovated in 1936, a high period in Taiwan's temple arts. The woodcarvings are particularly fine in the front hall, and the high plafond is gorgeous. The Mazu statue in this temple is now called the Black-Faced Mazu, as centuries of incense smoke have discoloured her original complexion.

The area around the Mazu Temple is pedestrian-only and great crowds gather here on weekends, though the atmosphere feels festive and not touristy. Vendors and the surrounding stores sell a variety of traditional snacks, sweets and drinks.

Lukang Old Street   AREA
(鹿港老街, Lùgǎng Lǎojiē; Yaolin & Butou Sts, 瑤林街, 埔頭街) Lukang's old commercial hub, Yaolin and Butou Sts, is now a protected heritage zone. The narrow, century-old lanes are worth checking out for their red-tiled flair and for the arty boutiques, crafts shops and old residences, as well as vendors and stores offering sweet tofu pudding, oyster croquettes or a warm pork bun. But keep in mind that the area is heavy with tourists on holidays, so set aside more time if you want to go.

Lukang Folk Arts Museum   MUSEUM
(民俗文物館, Mínsú Wénwùguǎn; www.lukangarts. org.tw; 152 Zhongshan Rd, 中山路152號; NT$130; ☻ 9am-5pm Tue-Sun, no entry after 4.30pm) The handsome building of this museum was designed by a Japanese architect (who also designed the Presidential Office Building in Taipei) and built in 1919 for an affluent local family. You'll get to walk through sumptuous rooms housing the museum's huge collection of ordinary household items dating from the Qing dynasty to the turn of the 20th century.

Din Family Old House   HISTORIC BUILDING
(丁家進士古厝, Dīngjiā Jìnshì Gǔcuò; ☑ 04-778 3488; 132 Zhongshan Rd, 中山路132號; ☻ 9am-4.30pm Tue-Sun) FREE This beautifully restored Fujian-style house, founded in the Qing dynasty, is the last remaining imperial scholar's home in Lukang. The Dins were descendants of Arab traders from Quanzhou in Fujian. They played an important role in the commercial development of Lukang.

Glass Mazu Temple   TAOIST TEMPLE
(玻璃媽祖廟, Bōlí Māzǔ Miào; 30 Lugongnansi Rd, 鹿工南四路30號) A remarkable structure standing inside the coastal park 8km west of the old town, this Lukang attraction is built with 70,000 pieces of glass, while the mountain behind the Mazu statue is made with 1400 glass pieces layered one on top of the other. Visit at night when the LED lights are on.

City God Temple   TAOIST TEMPLE
(城隍廟, Chénghuáng Miào; ☑ 04-778 8545; www. cheng-huang.com; 366 Zhongshan Rd, 中山路366號) Lukang's City God Temple has roots in Fujian's Quanzhou and was probably built in the mid-18th century. Paying your respects here is believed to be effective in helping to solve problems, in particular theft. The temple is traditionally favoured by merchants and shop owners.

Half-Sided Well   LANDMARK
(半邊井, Bànbiān Jǐng; 12 Yaolin St, 瑤林街12號) This now-filled well sits half inside the wall of a residence and half outside. The arrangement is a remnant of humbler days when not everyone could afford to have their own well, and those who could would share their water with their neighbours.

Nine Turns Lane   AREA
(九曲巷, Jiǔqū Xiàng; Jinsheng Lane btwn Minzu Rd & Sanmin Rd, 金盛巷, 民族路和三民路中間) Don't bother counting the turns as you wend your way past some of the oldest and most charming residences in Lukang on Nine Turns Lane. The number nine refers to the ninth month – cold winds blow down from Mongolia at this time of year and the turns function as a natural windbreak.

Breast Touching Lane   AREA
(摸乳巷, Mōrǔ Xiàng, Mo-lu Lane; alley off 38 Caiyuan Rd, 菜園路38號旁的巷子) The narrowest alley in Lukang gets its comical label from

DEER HARBOUR

Lukang translates as 'deer harbour': large herds of deer once gathered here in the lush meadows adjacent to one of the best natural harbours on the west coast. In the 17th century the Dutch came to hunt and trade venison and pelts (which they sold to the Japanese to make samurai armour). In the 18th century, trade grew and diversified to include rice, cloth, sugar, timber and pottery, and Lukang became one of the most thriving commercial cities and ports in Taiwan. Over the years settlers from different provinces and ethnic groups in China made their home here and left a legacy of temples and buildings in varying regional styles.

In the 19th century, silt deposits began to block the harbour, and the city began to decline. To make matters worse, in the early 20th century conservative elements in Lukang refused to allow trains and modern highways to be built near their city. Lukang became a backwater, only to be reborn decades later when modern Taiwanese began to search for a living connection with the past.

the fact that a man could not pass a woman down the narrow inner passageway without her breasts brushing against him. A true gentleman would always wait for a lady to pass first.

✦ Festivals & Events

Mazu's Birthday   RELIGIOUS
(媽祖聖誕, Māzǔ Shèngdàn; ⊙ Apr) The birthday of Mazu, held on the 23rd day of the third lunar month, is cause for intense celebration at both the Mazu Temple (p237) and the Glass Mazu Temple (p237).

Lukang Dragon Boat Festival   CULTURAL
(鹿港慶端陽, Lùgǎng Qìng Duānyáng; https://eng.taiwan.net.tw/m1.aspx?sNo=0002019&lid=080042; ⊙ May-Jun) The Lukang Dragon Boat Festival consists of dragon boat races and feasts held on select days between mid-May and mid-June. It usually ends with a three-day folk arts festival in June. This is a crowded but rewarding time to visit Lukang. See website for the latest schedule.

🛏 Sleeping

Back Inn   HOSTEL $
(鹿港鉑鉚民宿, Lùgǎng Bókě Mínsù; 18 Lane 21, Minzu Rd, 民族路21巷18號; d from NT$1580-1780; ❀❋🛜) A narrow building with six en-suite doubles. The grey-walled rooms feature a bed on a raised pine platform, separate toilet and showering facilities, a desk and a balcony. Reception is on the ground floor, as is the communal fridge. The walls are thin on the top floor so let them know if you need a quiet room.

Smalleye Backpacker   HOSTEL $
(小艾人文工房, Xiǎoai Rénwén Gōngfáng; ☎ 0973-365 274; www.facebook.com/smalleyeback

packer; 46 Houche Lane, 後車巷46號; dm/d from NT$500/1200; ❀🛜) Mixed and all-female dorms in a 100-year-old house that also runs photography exhibitions and tours. The metallic beds are creaky but comfortable and you'll get to meet friends and ask knowledgeable locals about Lukang's history and culture. There are coin-operated laundry facilities and a communal fridge. Note that the stairs are steep as this is a very old house.

★ Joy Inn   HOTEL $$
(澄悦商旅, Chéngyuè Shānglǔ; ☎ 04-778 1313; www.joy-inn.com.tw/?lang=en; 1 Lane 510, Zhongzheng Rd, 中正路510巷1號; d/q/ste from NT$2880/4080/6000; ❀❋🛜) Joy Inn is essentially a business hotel but families may also appreciate the warm service of the staff, the sofa bed and private balcony, the sumptuous buffet breakfast, and the provision of soft water. Rooms, in greys and tans, are clean and bright, with comfortable beds. The 8th-floor bar has a terrace with great views.

Lukang B&B   B&B $$
(二鹿行館, Èrlù Xíngguǎn; ☎ 04-777 4446; www.lkbnb.com.tw; 46 Chunhui St, 46春暉街; d/tr/q from NT$2450/2800/3800; ❀❋🛜) The four-storey home of a wealthy family has had its spacious rooms – still in a groovy '70s style – turned into guestrooms. You can see the attractive living room on the 1st floor with its original '70s furniture, minibar and mini-wine bottles. The staff are attentive and thoughtful.

🍴 Eating & Drinking

There's hardly a street in Lukang that doesn't offer wall-to-wall eating, and the pedestrian-only zone around Mazu Temple (p237) is a market of food stalls. Famous local dishes include oyster fritters (蚵嗲, é diǎ) – the best ones are just outside the temple – and sweet treats such as phoenix-eye cake (鳳眼糕), cow-tongue crackers (牛舌餅, *niúshé bǐng*) and dragon whiskers (龍鬚糖, *lóngxū táng*).

★ Fang Kofi
CAFE

(凡咖啡, Fán Kāfēi; www.facebook.com/fangkofi; 38 Lane 74, Zhongshan Rd, 中山路74巷38號; coffee from NT$130; ⊙10am-6pm Sun, Mon, Wed-Fri, 10am-8pm Sat; 🐾) Stylish, LGBTQ-friendly Fang Kofi comprises an airy, industrial-style cafe connected by a spiral staircase to a shabby-chic 2nd-floor space where the walls and beams of the original building are left exposed. They make great coffee and coffee-laced cocktails; there's cake and savoury dishes, too, if you're hungry. It's the kind of place where you can sit for hours.

It sometimes closes on Monday, too. Enquire via Facebook before you go.

Home Bar
BAR

(勝豐, Shèng Fēng; ☑04-778 5232; 131 Minzu Rd, 民族路131號; ⊙4pm-midnight Mon-Wed & Fri, 2pm-midnight Sat & Sun; 🐾) Opened by an engaging Lukang native in a charming old building, Home Bar offers dozens of craft beers, a handful of whiskies and the occasional fried canapé to go with your booze. It's very relaxing in the evening after all the day trippers have left.

🛍 Shopping

Wu Tun-Hou Lantern Shop
ARTS & CRAFTS

(吳敦厚燈舖, Wúdūnhòu Dēngpù; ☑04-777 6680; http://linker.tw/folklanterns; 310 Zhongshan Rd, 中山路310號; ⊙9am-noon & 2-10pm) Founded in the 1940s by master Wu Dunhou, this shop attracts collectors from all over the world. These days you're likely to see Wu's sons (highly skilled themselves) and grandsons at work outside.

Mr Chen's Fan Shop
ARTS & CRAFTS

(陳朝宗手工扇, Chéncháozōng Shǒugōngshàn; ☑04-777 5629; 400 Zhongshan Rd, 中山路400號; ⊙10am-6pm) The shop is on the right just before you enter the pedestrian-only area near Mazu Temple. Fans range from a few hundred dollars to many thousands for the larger creations. Mr Chen has been making fans since the 1950s; he began when he was 16.

Wan Neng Tinware
ARTS & CRAFTS

(萬能錫舖, Wànnéng Xīpù; ☑04-777 7847; www.tinart.com.tw; 81 Longshan St, 龍山街81號; ⊙9am-9pm) The master here is a fourth-generation tinsmith. His elaborate dragon boats and ex-

pressive masks cost thousands but are worth the price for their beauty and craftsmanship.

ℹ Information

Lukang's website (www.lukang.gov.tw) is an informative introduction to the town's history and sights. The **visitor centre** (遊客中心, Yóukè Zhōngxīn; ☑04-784 1263; 488 Fuxing Rd, 復興路488號; ⊙9am-5.30 Mon-Fri, to 6pm Sat & Sun) is easy to spot, located in a large field/car park across from the Changhua Bus Company Station. Pick up a brochure in English covering many of Lukang's sights.

ℹ Getting There & Away

There are direct buses from Taipei's main bus station to Lukang (NT$400, three hours, every two hours) with U-Bus (p212). Buses to Changhua (NT$51, 40 minutes, every 30 minutes) leave from the **Changhua Bus Company Station** (彰化客運鹿港乘車處; ☑04-722 5111; cnr Fuxing & Zhengxing Rds, 復興路與正興路交叉口). The last bus returns at 8.35pm.

Taiwan Tour Bus (p240) runs buses from Changhua to Glass Mazu Temple (NT$73, 40 minutes) via Lukang six/11 times a day on weekdays/weekends, with the last bus back at 7pm.

NANTOU COUNTY

Taiwan's second-largest county is a vacationer's heaven, with beautiful rolling hills, dozens of soaring mountains over 3000m high, and gorgeous lakes. From these natural gifts have sprouted relaxing lakeside resorts such as Sun Moon Lake, sublime mountain retreats like Cingjing, and quaint towns with scenic railroads such as Jiji and Checheng. Nantou offers plenty of breathtaking forests of various climes in which to hike, or simply to enjoy cherry blossoms in spring or maple in cooler months; Shanlinxi and Hehuanshan are examples. Indigenous tribes were the earliest settlers in the mountainous areas here, and you can still get a taste of their culture in Nantou, such as at the Aowanda Forest Recreation Area. Tea grows extremely well in Nantou, and if you love tea, the flavours of fine, high-altitude oolong will likely infuse your memories of your travels here for a long time to come.

⦿ Sights

Shanlinxi
FOREST

(杉林溪, Shānlínxī; Zhushan township) The forest-Resort area known as Shanlinxi Forest Recreation Area (literally, Sun Link Sea FRA) has waterfalls, cherry blossoms in spring, and maple in autumn. It is less developed and has fewer tourists than the more popular Sitou to its north, and offers long hikes away from the crowds. There are few eating options here, but the restaurants at the couple of hotels serve set meals for NT$200 to $350 per head.

Nantou Bus Company (p222) has five buses (Route 6871) daily from Taichung to Shanlinxi (NT$281, 4 hours, 6.45am to 4.25pm). **Taiwan Tour** (台灣觀巴; www.taiwantrip.com.tw) runs frequent buses from Taichung to Sitou (NT$167, 1½ hours, from 6.40am to 3pm), via Taichung train station and Taichung HSR station. The bus departs at 10am daily and goes to Shanlinxi after it stops at Sitou. From Sitou one bus departs daily at 7.30am for Shanlinxi (NT$57, 45mins).

Aowanda National Forest Recreation Area

NATIONAL PARK

(奧萬大國家森林遊樂區, Àowàndà; ☑ visitor centre 049-297 4511; https://recreation.forest.gov.tw/EN/Index; NT$200; ⊙ visitor centre 8.30am-5pm) Located along the scenic Hwy 14 near Wushe, this national park is famous for its maples. The park ranges in altitude from 1100m to 2600m, making it a cool retreat in summer. You can walk from one end of the reserve to the other in about two hours, on well-developed trails with bilingual signs.

You can stay overnight in the quaint wooden cabins surrounded by plum and maple trees. Aowanda has a visitor centre offering maps and brochures in English. From Taichung, Nantou Bus Company (p222) usually runs buses on the weekends from autumn to spring. Call for the schedule.

🛏 Sleeping

Aowanda National Forest Recreation Area Cabins

CABIN $

(奧萬大國家森林遊樂區住宿, Àowàndà Guójiā Sēnlín Yóulè Qu Zhùsù; ☑ 049-297 4519; 2-6 people NT$1500-5200; ⊙ ❀) Cabins – some wooden, some concrete – in three different styles, which accommodate a total of 90 guests inside the forest recreation area. Rooms are basic, but cabins made of Formosan cypress have a nice fragrance. You can also stay in the main lodge where the rooms are cheaper.

ℹ Information

Taiwan Tour Bus connects Taichung train station, Taichung HSR station and Puli with Sun Moon Lake (NT$265, two hours whole journey, every 30 minutes).

Nantou Bus Company (p222) operates six buses daily from Taichung to Puli via Cingjing Farm (NT$251, two hours).

ℹ Getting There & Away

Buses to Sun Moon Lake (NT$54, 30 minutes, hourly) are available with **Green Transit Bus Company** (Fengrong Bus Company, 豐榮客運; ☑ 0800-280 008; www.gbus.com.tw), and Nantou Bus Company has six buses going from Sun Moon Lake to Shuili station (NT$56, 25 minutes, every 80 minutes).

Yuanlin Bus Company (員林客運; ☑ 049-277 0041; www.ylbus.com.tw) has buses from Shuili to Dongpu (NT$112, 80 minutes, six daily). Note that buses to these places run during daylight hours only (6am to 5pm or so). To reach the bus station, exit Shuili train station and turn left on Mingquan Rd. The bus station is just opposite a 7-Eleven.

The **Fengrong Bus Company** (豐榮客運), with vehicles going to Sun Moon Lake, is further down the road on the same side.

Cingjing

☑ 049 / POP 1000

Between Wushe and Hehuanshan, Cingjing (清境; Qīngjìng) was once a cattle ranch of the Seediq; it wasn't until the 1960s that this place was turned into farmland, providing livelihood to KMT veterans from the Chinese Civil War. Today, Cingjing covers more than 700 hectares of rolling meadow, and is a hill station especially popular among Taiwanese, Singaporean and Chinese visitors. Most visitors come here for the Evergreen Grasslands, a quasi-agricultural attraction near the Km10 mark.

If Cingjing is on your itinerary, try to visit during the week to avoid the huge weekend crowds.

◎ Sights

Evergreen Grasslands

FARM

(青青草原, Qīngqīng Cǎoyuán; ☑ 049-280 2748; www.cingjing.gov.tw; 170 Renhe Rd, Datong village, 大同村仁和路170號; weekday/weekend NT$160/200; ⊙ 8am-5pm) Cingjing Farm is Cingjing's number-one attraction for Asian families, and Evergreen Grasslands is its highlight. This is Taiwan's Heidi country, with rolling greens dotted with sheep, and it's picture perfect. Children will enjoy feeding the animals and watching the outdoor show, which gives a jazzed-up taste of how things work on the farm with the help of some dogs, a couple of joke-cracking cowboys, and more sheep.

ECCENTRIC EARTH GOD TEMPLE

If you enjoy quirky folk temples, the strange and carnivalesque **Zinan Temple** (紫南宮, Zǐnángōng; 40 Dagong St, Zhushan District, 竹山鎮社寮里大公街40號) might fit the bill.

Dedicated to the Earth God, the Taoist-folk temple celebrates entrepreneurship and is perpetually busy, as is the marketplace that has grown around it. The temple teems with fortune-tellers and vendors of charms and votive offerings. There's a bizarre chicken statue with a hole that believers are supposed to pass through (front to end) for good fortune. There's another (bronze) chicken you can pet for luck – beak for wealth, breast for peace and prosperity, wings for a good spouse.

Devotees come to Zinan Temple not only to pray for prosperity, but to borrow money – the temple is a famed moneylender. Taiwanese with proper ID can take out a loan of up to NT$600 that is supposed to bring luck if invested in business. You don't need to pay it back, but apparently many borrowers do, and locals will tell you stories of those who struck gold with the loan returning astronomical amounts as a show of gratitude.

The other highlight at the temple is the public toilet. It's shaped like silver bamboo shoots and features a skylight, fake flower arrangements and stalls lined up like VIP dining rooms in Chinese restaurants.

If you're driving, exit Expressway No. 3 to the Zhushan Interchange (竹山交流道) near the Km243 mark, then turn left passing a hospital (竹山秀傳醫院). You'll soon see a sign for the temple. Turn right and after passing a 7-Eleven store, go on for 3km. You'll soon see Sheliao Police Station (社寮警察局) on your left. Turn left and drive for 200ft and you're there. From 8.40am to 4.40pm daily, there's a free hourly shuttle bus that takes passengers to the temple from Zhushan Interchange (竹山交流道). Wait for the shuttle at the guard station inside Chelungpu Fault Preservation Education Park (車籠埔斷層教育園區內). The same bus takes you back from near the stage (戲臺旁) of the temple.

Bowang New Village   VILLAGE
(博望新村, Bówàng Xīncūn; Ren'ai township) Bowang New Village was one of several villages used to settle Shan ethnic soldiers from Burma (Myanmar) and Yunnan who fought for the KMT during the Chinese Civil War. At over 2000m, it's the highest veterans' village in Taiwan. Life was hard for the veterans, who had to build roads, farms and houses to make their new mountainous home habitable. You can still see simple, one-storey residences and a run-down hall that gives a brief overview of the history of this place.

🛏 Sleeping

★ Julie's Garden   GUESTHOUSE $
(情境峰情, Qíngjìng Fēngqíng; ☑049-280 1123; www.taomt.com.tw; 46 Rongguang Lane, Datong village, 大同村榮光巷46號; ⊖❄🛜) Julie is the mother of the current owner Mr Liao, and if this homey compound is anything to go by, she's hospitable, has a green thumb and loves animals – they have four dogs, three cats, a swan and a pig. The 11 rooms are relaxing, with some offering views of the mountains and tea fields. Julie's Garden has free shuttle-bus service to sights nearby and back (before the dinner service).

They can arrange tours to tea farms and other experiences if guests request ahead of time.

Tianxiang Tea   GUESTHOUSE $$
(天祥觀景民宿, Tiānxiáng Guānjǐng Mínsù; ☑049-280 2029; www.tstea.com.tw; 36-1 Xinyi Lane, Ren'ai township, 仁愛鄉信義巷36之1號; s/d from NT$900/1600; ⊖❄🛜) This is a solid non-touristy option with huge Japanese-style rooms, adequate modern comforts, and pretty mountain views. The singles are cheap but without private bathrooms. Tianxiang is part of a family-run teashop that's open from 11.30am to 9pm. Go in the direction of Qingjing and Hehuan Mountain after passing Wushe. The guesthouse is on your right, near the Km4.5 mark.

Cingjing Veterans
Farm Guest House   HOTEL $$
(清境國民賓館, Qīngjìng Guómín Bīnguǎn; ☑049-280 2748; http://hotel.chingjing.com.tw; 25 Dingyuan New Village, 定遠新村25號; d incl breakfast from NT$3000; ⊖❄🛜) The run-of-the-mill rooms at this hotel won't wow you but they are very comfortable. The rates include admission to Evergreen Grasslands and the Small Swiss Garden. The hotel is 7.5km north of the 14A provincial route.

Eating

Cingjing has the highest concentration of restaurants and cafes along Hwy 14甲. Bai cuisine from Yunnan, China, is a speciality here, thanks to the KMT veterans and their indigenous wives from Yunnan who settled here. Urn-baked chicken (甕仔雞) is served in every single restaurant in the area. Most homestays also serve meals, some requiring advance booking.

Lu Mama Yunnan Restaurant CHINESE $$
(魯媽媽雲南擺夷料理, Lǔmāmā Yúnnán Bǎiyí Liàolǐ; ☑ 049-280 3876; http://lumama.tw; 210-2 Renhe Rd, 大同村仁和路210-2號; dishes NT$200-980; ☺ 11am-8.30pm) A remnant of Cingjing's Yunnan and Southeast Asia connection, this restaurant was started by a woman of the Bayi tribe who set up house in Cingjing with her KMT-veteran husband. A range of tasty Yunnan classics are available, including hotpot (汽锅, qìguō), tossed pig skin (涼拌薄片, liángbàn bópiàn) and preserved-papaya-and-chicken soup (酸木瓜雞湯, suān mùguā jītāng).

❶ Getting There & Away

Nantou Bus Company (南投客運; ☑ 049-299 6147; www.ntbus.com.tw; 338 Zhongzheng Rd, 中正路338號) runs 12 buses daily to Cingjing (NT$127, one hour, hourly) from Puli.

Hehuanshan Forest Recreation Area

At over 3000m, this recreation area sits mostly above the treeline, and the bright, grassy green hills of the Mt Hehuan Range roll on and on, often disappearing into a spectacular sea of clouds. Driving up from the western plains of Taiwan, the change in a few hours from urban sprawl to emerald hills is miraculous.

The last interesting stop on Hwy 14甲 before the descent into Taroko Gorge (p169) is Wuling Pass (not to be confused with the forest recreation area called Wuling). At 3275m, it sees Hwy 14甲 reaching the highest elevation of any road in East Asia. It snows up here in winter, and when it does the road becomes a skating rink, parking lot and playground for the Taiwanese.

Summer is delightfully cool and highly scenic as different alpine flowers bloom from May to September. Autumn and spring are excellent times for hiking.

🛏 Sleeping

Camping is possible in the car park at the information centre.

HIKING HEHUANSHAN

There are a number of short hikes starting close to the former Hehuan Cabin, which now houses a visitor information centre. You are advised to get a proper map of the area, and be aware that fog or rain can come in suddenly in the mountains, so always be prepared with warm clothing and rain protection. Be aware, also, that if you have driven straight up from lower altitudes, your body may need some time to get used to exercising at 3000m-plus elevation. For overnight hikes, check the Hehuanshan website (https://tsfs. forest.gov.tw/cht/index.php?code=list&ids=31).

No permits are needed to tackle the following hikes:

➡ The trail to Hehuanshan East Peak (合歡山東峰; Héhuān Shān Dōngfēng; elevation 3421m) starts next to the Ski Villa (p243). It's a two-to-three-hour return hike to the top.

➡ The marked trailhead to Hehuanshan North Peak (合歡山北峰; Héhuān Shān Běifēng; elevation 3422m) starts 200m north of Taroko National Park Hehuanshan Station at Km37. It's a three-to-four-hour return hike.

➡ The trailhead for Shimenshan (石門山; Shímén Shān; elevation 3237m) is just north of the visitor information centre on the east (left) side of the road. It's a short walk to the top. People often come here to watch the sunrise.

➡ The paved path up to Hehuanshan Main Peak (合歡山主峰; Héhuān Shān Zhǔfēng; elevation 3416m) starts at the Km30.5 mark (just before Wuling) and is about a two-hour return hike.

➡ The trail up to Hehuan Jian Shan (合歡尖山; Héhuānjiān Shān; elevation 3217m) starts just behind the former Hehuan Cabin. It takes about 15 minutes to reach the top.

Ski Villa   HOTEL **$$**
(滑雪山莊, Huáxuě Shānzhuāng; ☎04-2522
9696; http://tsfs.forest.gov.tw/cht/index.php?
code=list&ids=35&#d1; dm/d incl breakfast & dinner
NT$1200/2900; ❋) You can stay overnight at
Ski Villa, down the lower lane from a toilet
block opposite the visitor information centre.
The upper lane leads to the overpriced Song
Syue Lodge (松雪樓; Sōngxuě Lóu).

Take Hwy 14 from Puli to Mushe, and then
14甲 to Hehuanshan.

❶ Getting There & Away

Nantou Bus Company (南投客運; Nántóu
Kèyùn; ☎049-298 4031; 18-1 Zhongzheng 4th
Rd, Puli, 中正路四段18-1號) operates three
buses daily from Puli Cingjing Farm to Hehu-
anshan (NT$83, 70mins) at 8.30am, 11am and
2.20pm; return times from Hehuanshan are
9.40am, 12.20pm and 3.50pm. Tickets can be
reserved online (https://ntbus.welcometw.
com/tour/listAll?category=030).

From Puli/Cingjing, you can take a taxi to
Lishan, where you can connect to bus 6508 at
5pm for Wuling Forest Recreation Area, and the
next day continue by bus down to Yilan or Taroko
Gorge.

Jiji

☑049 / POP 12,035

Jiji (集集; Jíjí), the fifth stop down the Jiji
Small Rail Line (p244), has a real country
charm, with banana fields, betel-nut trees,
grapevines and cosmos flowers lining the
roads. The small town lies at the feet of Great
Jiji Mountain. You'll see the old cypress
train station, a reproduction of the original
Japanese-era station, which was levelled in
an earthquake in 1999.

The visitor centre is just 100m north of the
train station.

⊙ Sights

Taichi Gorge   CANYON
(太極峽谷, Tàijí Xiágǔ; NT$50; ⊙7.30am-5pm)
It's not hard to see why a 1986 rockslide that
killed 28 visitors closed Taichi Gorge to the
public for over two decades. The precipitous-
ly high, narrow and rocky terrain just doesn't
allow for easy trail development. Kudos to
the forestry bureau for the wall-hugging
wooden steps and the thrilling 136m Ladder
to Heaven (天梯; Tiāntī) – it's one of Taiwan's
longest suspension bridges, and certainly the
only one with built-in steps (to help you de-
scend faster).

You'll need a few hours in Taichi Gorge if
you want to explore some of the narrower
chasms, as well as the waterfall pools at the
bottom of the gorge.

Taichi Gorge is 15km south of the town
of Zhushan (竹山; Zhúshān) – itself about
20km southwest of Jiji – on Township Rd 49.
It's best to have your own vehicle to get there
but public transport is also possible. Yuanlin
Bus Company (p244) has three buses daily
from Zhushan to the entrance of Taichi Gorge
(NT$75, 50 minutes) at 8.20am, 12.50pm
and 4.20pm. Buses back from the gorge
to Zhushan depart at 9.10am, 1.40pm and
5.10pm. Zhushan itself is connected by buses
to and from Jiji, Sitou, Douliu and Taichung.

Wuchang Temple   TAOIST TEMPLE
(武昌宮, Wǔchāng Gōng; 89-34 Minsheng Rd, 民
生路34巷89號) Wuchang Temple became
famous after the 1999 earthquake collapsed
its lower floors, leaving the roof to stand in
ruin. It now lies photogenically crumpled like
a dishevelled king beside a newly built twin
that has taken over the functions of the fallen
temple. To reach the temple, turn right as you
leave the Jiji Train Station and walk roughly
900m to Ba Zhang St (八張街). Turn left and
walk another 900m.

🛏 Sleeping & Eating

★**Backpacker Young House**   HOSTEL **$**
(旅安背包客驛站, Lǚ'ān Bèibāokè Yìzhàn; ☎0987-
389 429; 9 Fomiao Lane, 佛廟巷9號; dm NT$600-
1000; ❸❋☞) A residence offering bright and
spotless dorm rooms in Jiji town. The owner
makes spring-onion pancakes in the spacious
open kitchen on the ground floor. From Hwy
139, turn right into Jiji St, then into Minsheng
Rd where you'll find the hostel.

★**Footprint Inn**   INN **$$**
(兩腳詩集, Liǎngjiǎo Shījí; ☎049-276 2198; www.
footprint-inn.com.tw; 326 Mingquan Rd, 民權路326
號; s/d NT$1600/2280; ❸❋☞) Opened by a
schoolteacher, Footprint has 19 immaculate
and sizeable rooms with balconies. Staff go
out of their way to be helpful, and the tasty

❶ EAT LIKE A LOCAL

You'll find places to eat around the train
station and at various stops along the
bike routes. Every Tuesday and Saturday, a night market materialises along
Yucai St (育才街) near No. 188, offering
local foods and drinks.

JIJI SMALL RAIL LINE

Branching off the west-coast trunk line in flat, rural Changhua, the train on this 29km narrow-gauge railway (集集小火車線; Jíjí Xiǎohuǒchē Xiàn) chugs past some lovely stretches of rural Taiwan before coming to a halt in Checheng, a vehicle yard and former logging village in the foothills of Nantou county.

While the ride takes just 45 minutes, the list of things to see and do at the seven stops is long: you can cycle, hike and monkey-watch, as well as visit temples, museums, kilns, dams and historical buildings. The most visited stations are Ershui, Jiji (p243), Shuili and Checheng. You can sometimes get a map at the train stations, but they're only in Mandarin.

Most of the towns have 7-Elevens with ATMs.

homemade breakfast (served in a dining room with school desks) is a welcome treat. The owner loves tea – feel free to ask him for recommendations on where to buy the best. It's about 550m away from train station in the direction of Shuili.

Mountain Fish Water Boutique Hotel HOTEL $$
(山魚水渡假飯店, Shān Yú Shuǐ Dùjià Fàndiàn; ☑049-276 1000; www.mfwhotel.com.tw; 205 Chenggong Rd, 成功路205號; d incl breakfast NT$2400-4800; ❋@❋) Off a quiet leafy road with views of the hills, this hotel offers cosy good-value rooms, use of a swimming pool fed with mountain spring water, and, in summer, a steam room and spa facilities. To reach the hotel, go north from the train station to Chenggong Rd (成功路) and turn right.

⊙ Getting There & Away

Nantou Bus Company (p247) has six buses daily from Sun Moon Lake to Jiji station (NT$90, 35 minutes, every two hours).

Yuanlin Bus Company (員林客運, Yuánlín Kèyùn; ☑049-264 2005; www.ylbus.com.tw) has two buses daily to Dongpu via Shuili (NT$118, 1½ hours, 10.50am and 3.45pm).

Sun Moon Lake

Sun Moon Lake (日月潭; Rìyuè Tán), so-called because it comprises a round eastern section and a crescent western section, with a tiny island roughly in the middle, is on the itinerary of every Chinese group tour to Taiwan year-round. But do not be deterred by the crowds – at an altitude of 762m, the largest body of freshwater in Taiwan is one of the island's most lovely natural vistas. Boating is popular and hiking and biking allow you to get off the beaten path while staying on the tourist trail.

Sun Moon Lake is part of the 90-sq-km Sun Moon Lake National Scenic Area. Accommodation is plentiful, with the majority of hotels centred in Shueishe village (水社村) and Ita Thao (伊達邵). Ita Thao, with its strong indigenous Thao presence, is a obvious contrast to the predominantly Taiwanese atmosphere at Shueishe.

⊙ Sights

★**Antique Assam Tea Farm** FARM
(日月老茶廠, Rìyuè Lǎochá Chǎng; ☑049-289 5508; 38 Youshui Ln, Yuchi township, 魚池鄉中明村有水巷38號; ☺8am-5pm) An operating tea farm that's also a showcase for the reinstatement of tea shrubs to Sun Moon Lake. The speciality here is Assam black tea, introduced by the Japanese from India. In its heyday, this factory had over 200 workers, but it was forced to close down in the early 2000s due to farmers' preference for cultivating the more lucrative betel nut. A handful of veteran workers persisted and began growing organic Assam; they also turned the factory into a tourist attraction.The tea farm lies to the West of Hwy 21.

Shueishe Village VILLAGE
(水社村, Shuǐshè Cūn) FREE The area by Shueishe Pier is a great place to kick back or go for a leisurely stroll. Lakeside walking paths extend from Shueishe village (often referred to as Sun Moon Lake Village) in either direction. Going east would take you all the way to Wenwu Temple (p245).

Xuanzang Temple BUDDHIST TEMPLE
(玄奘寺, Xuánzàng Sì; ☑049-285 0220; 389 Zhongzheng Rd, 中正路389號; ☺6am-5.30pm) Serene and charming, Xuanzang Temple keeps a tiny piece of the skull of Monk Xuanzang or Tripitaka (AD 600–664), who is fictionalised in the novel *Journey to the West* as the India-bound, backpacking companion of the Monkey King and Pigsy. The bone fragment is in a small cauldron on the 2nd floor, watched over by CCTV.

Sun Moon Lake

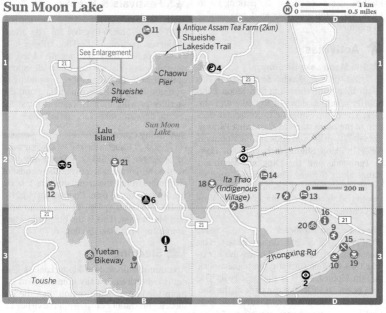

Sun Moon Lake

WESTERN TAIWAN SUN MOON LAKE

Wenwu Temple TAOIST TEMPLE
(文武廟, Wénwǔ Miào; 63 Zhongshan Rd, 中山路 63號; ◷24hr) The imposing temple by Sun Moon Lake has superb natural lookouts and faux northern Chinese–style temple architecture. It's extremely popular with tour groups. Go early in the morning if you want to experience its arresting beauty in silence.

Sun Moon Lake Ropeway CABLE CAR
(日月潭纜車, Rìyuètán Lǎnchē; ☎049-285 0666; www.ropeway.com.tw; 102 Zhongzheng Rd, Yuchi, 魚池鄉日月村中正路102號; return NT$300; ◷10.30am-3.30pm weekdays, 10-4pm weekends) The seven-minute, 1.9km ride offers an unparalleled bird's-eye view of the lake as you rise into the nearby hills. The gondola terminates at the Formosan Aboriginal Cultural Village (九族文化村; Jiǔzú Wénhuà Cūn), an amusement park–like venue. The ropeway is closed on the first Wednesday of the month.

Ci'en Pagoda MONUMENT
(慈恩塔, Cíēn Tǎ; ◷9am-4.30pm) The stately Pagoda of Kindness and Grace (1969) was built by Chiang Kai-shek in honour of his

mother. The ascent from the parking lot to the tower, 960m above sea level, takes under 10 minutes.

🏃 Activities

⭐ Sun Moon Lake Bikeway   CYCLING
(日月潭自行車道, Rìyuètán Zìxíngchē Dào) The 29km bike path encircling Sun Moon Lake affords uplifting views of the lake and the hills. The 5.7km Shueishe to Xiangshan section of the route starts at Zhongxing Parking Lot (中興停車場) and ends at Boji Mountain (薄觀山; Báojí Shān), with vistas of Hanbi Peninsula and the Qinglong Mountain Range along the way. The section is suitable for all ages and offers abundant opportunities to rest, including at the Xiangshan Visitor Centre. (p248)

Shueisheshan Trailhead   HIKING
(水社大山步道, Shuǐshè Dàshān Bùdào) The most clearly signposted and hence most popular trail to Shueisheshan, the highest peak on Sun Moon Lake, is at the West Peak. The trail begins next to the car park at the Sun Moon Lake Youth Activity Centre. The 6km trail has an altitude variation of over 305m, which means you will encounter a rich assortment of flora and fauna during your seven-hour saunter.

Maolanshan Trailhead   HIKING
(猫囒山步道, Māolánshān Bùdào) This 2km trail offers the best sunrise views in all of Sun Moon Lake, but even if you go later in the day, the 2km walk, accompanied by birdsong, soaring cedars and views of tea plantations and the lake, will still charm. On a clear day you can see the hills of Jiufen from the peak. Entrance to the trail is at Hwy 21 next to a middle school.

SUN MOON LAKE BOAT TOURS

Boat tours (NT$100 between two piers, NT$300 round the lake) are a popular way to take in the scenery and sights; they leave every 30 minutes between 9am and 6pm. You can get on or off at any of the four piers – Shueishe (p248), Ita Thao (p248), Chaowu (p248), and Syuanguang Temple (p248) – wander round and catch the next boat out. You can also take bikes on the boats.

Most hotels will sell you a ticket without commission. Otherwise, pick one up at any pier.

🎉 Festivals & Events

Thao Harvest Festival   CULTURAL
(邵族豐收節, Shàozú Fēngshōu Jié) The annual Harvest Festival of the Thao tribe is held every summer (the eighth month of the lunar calendar). Visitors can watch all aspects of the festival, including mortar pounding to summon the people, fortune-telling and the sacrifice of wild animals. Festivities last for several days and take place in Ita Thao.

Swimming Carnival   SWIMMING
(日月潭泳渡, Rìyuètán Yǒngdù; www.pulifourswim. tw; application fee NT$1000; ⊘ Sep) Every year at the Midautumn Festival, thousands of swimmers from Taiwan and overseas take on the 3000m course from Chaowu Pier (p248) to Ita Thao Pier (p248) at the picturesque Sun Moon Lake. This is the only time when swimming in the lake is allowed.

🛏️ Sleeping

Accommodation in Sun Moon Lake is generally overpriced. Usually homestays on the main road are a better option than the hotels. As you wander down from the visitor information centre (p248) towards the village, there are a dozen small homestays. But there are exceptions. The boutique-y Sun Moon and the pragmatic Bamboo Rock Garden are worth their dollars.

⭐ Sun Moon   INN $$
(山慕民宿, Shānmù Mínsù; ☑ 0921-010 335; www.sunmooninn.com; 216 Zhongshan Rd, 中山路216號; d/quad from NT$3680/5580) Not your run-of-the-mill Sun Moon Lake lodging despite the name. Sun Moon stands out with industrial-chic decor, great attention to detail and stellar service; even the breakfast is healthy and delicious, with a mix of Taiwanese and western goodies. The rooms are elegant, comfortable and blessed with lots of natural light. The staff will answer any questions you may have.

⭐ Bamboo Rock Garden   HOTEL $$
(竹石園, Zhúshí Yuán; ☑ 049-285 6679; www. bamboorock.com.tw; 8 Zhongshan Rd, 中山路8號; d from NT$3200; ❄ ❂ ☎) Gleaming glass panes, pristine bed linen and large rooms are on offer inside this repurposed botanical research facility with a bamboo grove in its backyard. The staff are patient and thoughtful; the cafe serves passable meals.

The hotel is about 2km northeast of Shueishe Visitor Information Centre (p248). Follow the Shueishe Lakeside Trail northwards

WEIRD & WONDERFUL CHAN TEMPLE

The staggering **Chung Tai Chan Temple** (中台禪寺, Zhōngtáichán Sì; ☏ 049-293 0215; www.chungtai.org; 2 Zhongtai Rd, 中台路2號; ◑8am-5pm) and its excellent museum in Puli are worth a visit if you like Buddhist art and architecture.

This 43-storey temple is more than just one of the quirkiest buildings in Taiwan (think tiled mosque meets Macau's Grand Lisboa) – it's a global centre of Buddhist academic research, culture and the arts. Opened in 2001, it represents an international branch of Buddhism founded by the Venerable Master Wei Chueh (1928–2016), who is said to have revived the Chan (Zen) tradition in Taiwan.

From the entrance doors with their giant guardians to the 18 lohan reliefs, only top-quality materials and artists, both Taiwanese and foreign, were used to build this awe-inspiring contemporary edifice. Another highlight is the seven-storey indoor pagoda, which was created without any metal nails or screws. Designed by Taipei 101 architect CY Lee, Chung Tai Temple, with its colossal icons and massive halls, almost brings to mind a totalitarian aesthetic.

Several resident nuns speak good English, and it is their responsibility to give guided tours to any visitors. Reservations must be made three days in advance.

There are also weekly meditation classes held in English, and week-long retreats during Lunar New Year and summer. Other retreats, lasting three days, are held on an irregular basis. During retreats, guests stay at the temple.

Adjacent to the temple is the superb **Chung Tai World Museum** (中台世界博物館, Zhōngtái Shìjiè Bówùguǎn; ☏ 049-293 2999; www.ctwm.org.tw; 8 Chung Tai Rd, 中台路6號; NT$200; ◑9am-5pm Tue-Sun), a fabulous showcase of Buddhist artefacts dating from as early as AD 386.

If you wonder why one Buddha has a medicine ball in his hand while another is holding a lotus, look for the answers on the touchscreen panels. These tools will also help you understand the history of Buddhism, the statues, motifs and iconography, as well as the 22 physical markings of the Buddha.

How to Get There

Nantou Bus Company (南投客運; www.ntbus.com.tw) runs hourly buses between Puli and Sun Moon Lake (NT$62, 40 minutes). You can get to the temple in a taxi from Puli (NT$350). If you are driving, head north on Zhongzheng Rd out of Puli and then follow the signs. The temple is about 6km away.

until you see a slope branching off Zhongzheng Rd, just past the petrol station (p248). Cross Zhongzheng Rd and follow the slope for 300m. You should see the hotel.

Youth Activity Center HOSTEL $$
(日月潭青年活動中心, Rìyuètán Qīngnián Huódòng Zhōngxīn; ☏ 049-285 0070; http://sun.cyh.org.tw; 101 Zhongzheng Rd, 中正路101號; with IYH card tr/quad from NT$3800/4500, villa NT$12000) This centre is a 20-minute bus ride from Shueishe village (the round-the-lake bus stops here). It has its own restaurant, a store and bikes for hire. You'll need an International Youth Hostel card or to be under 45 years of age to stay here.

Lalu Hotel LUXURY HOTEL $$$
(日月潭碧涵樓; ☏ 049-285 5313; www.thelalu.com.tw/en; 142 Zhongshan Rd, Yuchi, 魚池鄉水社

村中興路142號; d from NT$14,000; ❄❁❀❁) Once the residence of the Japanese Crown Prince and the holiday home of Chiang Kai-shek, Lalu is still zen-like and elegant, despite slightly tired furniture and facilities. Viewing spots abound to maximise your enjoyment of the surroundings; and the lap pool overlooks the lake. Service is fit for a prince or a president.

✖ Eating

If you are on a budget there's a 7-Eleven in Shueishe, and stir-fries and set meals are available from the nearby restaurants (set meals from NT$320). Minghu Restaurant (p248) is a reliable option. Most of the hotel restaurants don't serve anything too different from the street shops.

SUN MOONING ON TWO WHEELS

While circling the 29km round-the-lake road is the most popular option, many cyclists are now riding down to towns along the Jiji Small Rail Line (p244) via County Rd 131. The 18km from the lake to Checheng (the end of the Jiji line) passes quiet villages, thickly forested hills and a final stretch following the downstream flow of the Shuili River, dammed in several places to store water released from Sun Moon Lake for the generation of hydroelectric power.

You can also ride on the path that joins Shueishe village with the 8km Yuetan Bikeway (月潭自行車道; Yuètán Zìxíngchē Dào) and a circular route through Toushe (頭社; Tóushè), a scenic peat-soil basin south of the lake.

The Giant bicycle shop has a variety of bikes for rent. It's beneath the visitor information centre.

Minghu Restaurant
TAIWANESE $$

(明湖老餐廳, Mínghú Lǎocāntīng; ☑049-285 5228; 15 Mingsheng St, 名勝街15號; mains NT$200-600; ⊙11.30am-2pm & 5-8pm) This old restaurant near Shueishe Pier is one of very few at Sun Moon Lake that serves more-than-reasonable-quality food at reasonable prices. The NT$600 set meals come with three dishes and a soup; it's NT$350 more for four dishes. Portions are generous, too.

❶ Information

There are no banks here, but the 7-Eleven on the main road up from the village has an ATM.

Sun Moon Lake National Scenic Area's official website (www.sunmoonlake.gov.tw) is an excellent online resource, with bus information for getting there and around.

Xiangshan Visitor Information Centre (向山遊客中心, Xiàngshān Yóukè Zhōngxīn; www.sunmoonlake.gov.tw; 599 Zhongshan Rd, Yuchi, 中山路599號; ⊙9am-5pm Mon-Fri, 9am-5.30pm Sat & Sun) and the **Shueishe visitor centre** (遊客服務中心, Yóukè Fùwù Zhōngxīn; ☑049-285 5668; 163 Zhongshan Rd, Shueishe village, 水社村中山路163號; ⊙9am-5pm) have English-speaking staff on hand.

❶ Getting There & Away

Purchase bus tickets at the kiosk outside the visitor information centre. On the kiosk side of the road, Nantou Bus Company (p247) has hourly buses to Puli (NT$58, 30 minutes), Taichung HSR (NT$195, 1½ hours) and Taichung city (NT$195, two hours).

Across the street from the kiosk, Nantou Bus Company has buses to Sitou (NT$188, 90 minutes, every two hours) via Jiji (NT$84, 40 minutes). **Green Transit Bus Company** (豐榮客運, Fengrong Bus Company; ☑0800-280-008; www.gbus.com.tw/sys/index.php) has buses to Shuili Snake Kiln (NT$56, 20 minutes, six daily between 6.10am and 4.30pm).

❶ Getting Around

BICYCLE

Songmeng Bikes (松鎰組車, Sōngměng Zǔchē; ☑049-285 6691; 12-8 Zhongxing Rd, Shueishe village, 水社村中興路12巷8號; 3hr from NT$180; ⊙8am-5pm) is a helpful husband-and-wife store with tons of bikes for hire, including electric vehicles and three-seaters.

BOAT

Boats dock at four piers – **Chaowu Pier** (朝霧碼頭, Cháowù Mǎtóu), **Shueishe Pier** (水社碼頭, Shǔishè Mǎtóu), **Ita Thao Pier** (伊達邵碼頭, Yīdáshào Mǎtóu) and **Syuanguang Temple Pier** (玄光碼頭, Xuánguāng Mǎtóu). There are several operators and the different fleets have slightly different times. Seasonal and other variations aside, there are sailings roughly every 30 to 60 minutes from around 8am to 5pm, from each of the piers. The Sun Moon Lake website (www.sunmoonlake.gov.tw) has the latest schedules.

You can buy tickets at booths at Shueishe Pier, Chaowu Pier and Ita Thao Pier, or at authorised ticket booths brandishing the shuttle-boat icon; Syuanguang Pier is where visitors to Xuanzang Temple disembark. Prices are NT$300 for a cruise of the entire lake and NT$100 per section of the journey. The website has details.

BUS

The round-the-lake bus (all-day pass NT$80, roughly hourly from 8.10am to 5.20pm) leaves from in front of the visitor information centre and turns back at Xuanguang Temple. An English schedule is available at the visitor information centre.

CAR & MOTORCYCLE

Good-quality scooters (NT$500 per day) can be hired from shops on the main street of Shueishe. An international driver's permit is needed. There's a **petrol station** (台灣中油加油站; ☑049-285 5160; 20 Zhongshan Rd, 中山路20號; ⊙9am-9pm) at 20 Zhongshan Rd.

Southern Taiwan

Best Places to Eat

➡ House of Crab (p264)

➡ One Bar (p264)

➡ Zhuxin Residence (p286)

➡ Shumin Kitchen (p264)

➡ Ruifeng Night Market (p263)

➡ Wang's Fish Shop (p285)

➡ Three Generations Spring Roll (p263)

Best Places to Stay

➡ Hok House (p262)

➡ UIJ Hotel & Hostel (p283)

➡ Casa Aperta (p297)

➡ Casa Ostia (p298)

➡ Wabi Sabi (p285)

➡ Hsieh's Old House Inn (p285)

➡ Caoji Book Inn (p283)

➡ Your Fun Apartment (p283)

Why Go?

Southern Taiwan is a land of timeless rituals and vibrant folk culture. The yearly calendar is chock-full of some of Taiwan's most unforgettable festivals: when they're not burning boats to ask for peace, southerners let off fierce fireworks to seek supernatural protection against disease.

To many, Tainan – the island's former capital – is Taiwan's most Taiwanese city. Expect a feast of original street snacks, flamboyant temples and enduring relics at every turn. In Kaohsiung, southern traditions are given a charismatic 21st-century spin as art greets industry by the harbour and chefs reinvent century-old dishes. Outside the cities, wonderful biking routes and beaches offer a world of possibilities for action travellers. From the limestone drama of Little Liuchiu Island (p299) to the oddity of mud volcanoes outside Kaohsiung (p251), this is Formosa at its most formidable. No wonder millions of purple and yellow butterflies return yearly to overwinter in Maolin (p381) and Meinong (p269). They've chosen well.

When to Go
Tainan

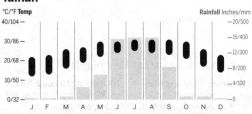

| Mar–Apr Two music festivals turn up the heat: Megaport in March and Spring Scream in April. | Sep–Oct The heat abates and it's harvest time at Pingtung's cocoa plantations. | Oct–Dec The triennial Burning of the Wang Yeh Boats lights up the coast. |

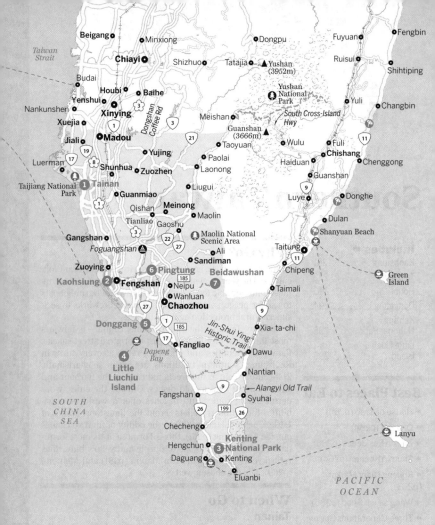

Southern Taiwan Highlights

1 Tainan (p272) Experiencing ancient temples and relics of a maritime era by day, then sleeping in a charming old house by night.

2 Kaohsiung (p251) Enjoying art, jazz and craft beer by the harbour; visiting vibrant markets and feasting on seafood.

3 Kenting National Park (p295) Swimming, surfing and cycling year-round.

4 Little Liuchiu Island (p299) Snorkelling at Taiwan's only coral island, or finding out for yourself if those limestone formations are aptly named.

5 Donggang (p294) Partaking in a festive procession

then watching a ceremonial boat erupt into flames.

6 Pingtung (p291) Making your own chocolate at a cacao plantation.

7 Beidawushan (p301) Taking in cloud-tinged views from the most southerly of the 3000m-plus peaks in Taiwan.

SOUTHWEST COAST

The stars of the southwest coast are Tainan (p272) and Kaohsiung. Tainan offers elegant manifestations of a long and varied history, from brooding temples through canalside cafes to art deco. Kaohsiung is a hub of modern southern sophistication, with its exciting culinary landscape and a vibrant art-and-music scene; it's a city of intense blue skies where the sea and a riveting industrial past are never far away.

Not far from Tainan, Togo village (p290) in Houbi exemplifies the partnership between grass-roots and intellectual Taiwan, while the footsteps of German missionaries can be retraced in Jingliao village (p291).

The southwest coast also lays claim to a beautiful national park that is habitat for the endangered black-faced spoonbill. It's a land of possibilities, some as different as fire and water, which, miraculously, in the mud hot springs of Guanziling (p288), can coexist.

Kaohsiung

♫ 07 / POP 2,779,000

The southern city of Kaohsiung (高雄; Gāoxióng), Taiwan's largest port and its second-largest city, has reinvented itself and undergone a cultural renaissance. Today's Kaohsiung is a modern metropolis of airy cafes, wide streets, waterside parks, cycling lanes and cultural spots. It is a home to excellent museums, one of Taiwan's top arts venues, the finest jazz bars, and a hot-blooded music festival – a far cry from its days as a centre of heavy industry. There are also two swimming beaches within the city area, and 1000 hectares of almost-pristine forest right on its doorstep.

History

The Chinese settled on Cijin Island (p253) in the late Ming dynasty, and throughout the Qing period Kaohsiung was an administrative centre for the Taiwan territory. The Japanese were responsible for its modern character. 'Rice in the north and sugar in the south' was the colonialist policy, and under it Kaohsiung became a major port for the export of raw materials. During this time the grid pattern of streets was laid out, the harbour was expanded and rail lines were built.

The Japanese called the harbour area 'Hamasen', a name still used by older residents and the tourism bureau. The area

lay in ruins after Allied bombing at the end of WWII, but was slowly rebuilt under the Kuomintang (KMT). Once again, with central planning, Kaohsiung became the heavy-industry centre.

Under mayor Frank Hsieh (1998–2005) the city started to clean up and to shift its industrial base towards tourism, high technology, automation and other capital-intensive industries. He was followed by the popular mayor Chen Ju (2006–18) who propelled the city's cultural development forward. Some of her initiatives included building libraries, major cultural venues such as the National Kaohsiung Centre for the Arts (Weiwuying) (p265) and a top-notch concert hall due to open in the early 2020s; and bringing troupes to the countryside to perform and conduct art education. Ju's successor, Han Guo-yu, won the 2019 election on vows that he would make Kaohsiung rich. He has begun talks with China to export Taiwanese fruit and has plans to attract more tourists from Asia.

⊙ Sights

★ **Neiwei Flea Market**   MARKET
(內惟跳蚤市場, Nèiwéi Tiàozǎo Shìchǎng; Map p256; 1488 Jiuru 4th Rd, 鼓山九如4路1488號; ⊙8am-5pm Sat & Sun; 🚌219A) This sprawling flea market in Neiwei may possibly offer one of the most authentic and fabulous experiences of Taiwan. You'll find everything under the sun here and then some. Cut-and-paste shard figurines, Japanese swords, marionettes, dehumidifiers – you name it – and of course, clothes, jewellery and furniture. The best thing about this place, however, is the snapshots of ordinary Kaohsiung life it offers, like chess players with a puppy tucked under one arm or an impromptu Sunday-morning jam session.

★ **Museum 50**   CULTURAL CENTRE
(50 美術館, Wǔshí Měishù Guǎn; ♫0987-738 168; www.facebook.com/museum50kaohsiung; 1st fl, 80 Minzu Rd, 民族一路80號1樓; ⊙by appt only; 🚌72A) **FREE** A true hidden gem, this private museum has a small but exceptional collection of sculpture and antiques by mid-19th-to 20th-century Japanese artists who were inspired by Taiwan or who had taught early Taiwanese masters. There's mind-blowing *jizai okimono* (articulated animal figures), such as iron snakes that move like real ones and a metallic pheasant comprising 700 parts; *netsuke* (small carved ornaments) of outstanding artistry; and beautiful paintings

Central Kaohsiung

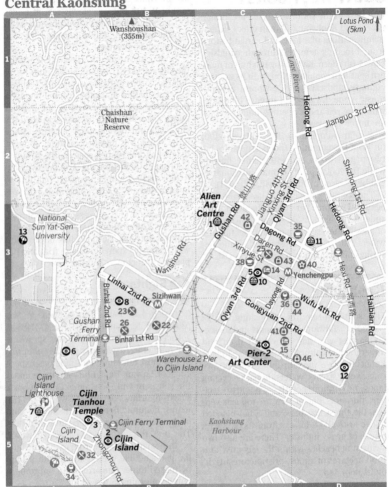

SOUTHERN TAIWAN KAOHSIUNG

and vases. Most are unique or one of under a handful ever made.

To visit make contact via Facebook messaging or by calling English-speaking owner Mr Guo, a month in advance. There needs to be at least eight of you to visit, but he can also let you join other visitors. Mr Guo is an excellent guide. The museum is located in a commercial building called 50樓 (50 Building).

★ **Alien Art Centre**　　　MUSEUM
(金馬賓館, Jīnmǎ Bīnguǎn; Map p252; ☑ 07-972 1685; www.alien.com.tw/en; 111 Gushan Rd, 鼓山區鼓山路111號; adult/student NT$250/150; ☺ 3-6pm Wed-Sun (last entry 5pm); Ⓜ Yanchengpu) A

remarkable museum in a unique location. From the '50s to the '70s this white building was a hostel for young men departing for compulsory military service on the islands. Now this site of tears and goodbyes houses strong contemporary art from Taiwan and overseas. We saw photography by Taiwanese Juan I-jong, works playing with light and space by American James Turrell; installations by two Hong Kong artists; and abstract jewellery designed by a German.

The museum's Mandarin name 'Jinma Binguan' translates as Kinma Hostel; 'Kinma' being an elision of 'Kinmen' and 'Matsu', the islands where the young men were stationed.

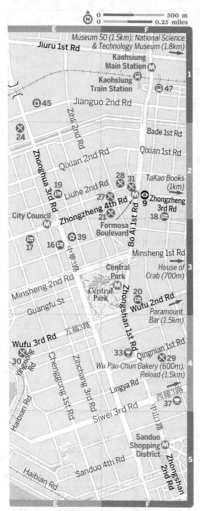

afternoon when the weather's not too hot. There are also lawns strewn with installation art and old railway tracks, where people enjoy picnics and fly kites at sunset; there are rides for children. And no matter what you do in Pier-2, Taiwan's most gorgeous harbour sights are always within reach.

The NT$99 pass includes admission to a contemporary art gallery and some other exhibitions. But honestly, there's plenty to see and do for free. Do note, however, that many of the shops don't open until at least 1pm.

★ **Cijin Island** ISLAND

(旗津, Qíjīn; Map p252; 🚢 Cijin) This narrow island that acts as a buffer to the harbour and extends down the city coastline makes for a lovely day trip from the mainland. The main attractions are Tianhou Temple (p253), **Cihou Fort** (旗後炮臺, Qíhòu Páotái; Map p252), a **lighthouse** (旗津燈塔, Qíjīn Dēngtǎ; Map p252; ⊙ 9am-4.30pm) FREE and a frenetic seafood street (Hǎichǎn Jiē) where you can get dishes for NT$60 to NT$250. There's also a tunnel through a mountain that opens onto boulders and the harbour, Cijin Beach and a picturesque coastal park with wind turbines.

The beach on Cijin Island is just a five-minute walk from the Cijin Ferry Terminal (p267). When going in the water, be aware that there are serious rip tides along the more-open parts of the beach.

Cycling around the island is about 15km and takes four hours. The bicycle rental shops near the ferry terminal will let you have a vehicle for NT$100 a day.

You can also take your own bike over on the ferry (NT$20 to NT$40), which runs from 5am to 2am between the Gushan Ferry Terminal (p267) and the Cijin Ferry Terminal. On weekends, holidays and daily in July and August, a new ferry service runs from Warehouse 2 (p267) in Pier-2 Art Center to Cijin.

★ **Cijin Tianhou Temple** TEMPLE

(旗津天后宮, Qíjīn Tiānhòu Gōng; Map p252; 93 Miaoqian Rd, 廟前路93號; ⊙ 5am-10pm) One of Kaohsiung's few temples that made the national protected relics list is also its oldest Mazu temple – constructed in 1673 and restored in the 1920s. There's a sense of graceful antiquity in its interiors, particularly in the relief sculptures, mosaics and decorative paintings by master of folk art, Chen Yu-feng (1900–64), which time and smoke have made hauntingly beautiful. The temple also has fanciful Fujian-style swallowtail eaves and two exquisite stone lions guarding its door.

There is a display on the building's unusual history, which explains and documents this once-transitional space with old photographs and the oral histories of veterans.

The museum is a five-minute walk from Shoushan Light Rail Station.

★ **Pier-2 Art Center** AREA

(駁二藝術特區, Bóèr Yìshù Tèqū; Map p252; http://pier-2.khcc.gov.tw; exhibitions NT$99; ⊙ 10am-6pm Mon-Thu, to 8pm Fri-Sun & national holidays; 👶; Ⓜ Yanchengpu) An attractive sprawl of old warehouses by the port is separated by tree-lined boulevards, and hosts shops, galleries and cafes. It's a wonderful place to spend an

Central Kaohsiung

'Big Gutter Cover' Old Street HISTORIC
(鹽埕大溝頂老街, Yánchéng Dàgōudǐng Lǎojiē; Map p252; Ⓜ Yanchengpu, Exit 2) Dàgōudǐng (literally 'Big Gutter Cover') Old Street is a shopping arcade from the 1950s. It's located between Wufu 4th Rd (五福四路) in the south and Dagong Rd (大公路) in the north, and cut off briefly by Xinyue St (新樂街) and Daren Rd (大仁路). Enter next to a lottery stall two shops from 3080s Local Style (p262) and step into history. You'll see an old noodle factory, wet market, button shop, sundries store, *qipao* (cheongsam) tailors and Dagouding Milkfish Noodles (p263).

Neiwei Afternoon Market MARKET
(內惟黃昏市場, Nèiwéi Huánghūn Shìchǎng; Map p256; 1450 Jiuru 4th Rd, 鼓山區九如四路1450號; ⊘ 3-7pm Mon-Sat, to 5pm Sun; 🚍 219A) After checking out the wondrous Neiwei Flea Market (p251), hop over to this food bazaar for cheap, satisfying grilled chicken, stuffed buns and sushi, and buy some fruit for evening.

Lotus Pond AREA
(蓮池潭, Liánchí Tán; Map p256; Ⓜ Zuoying, Exit 2, then bus R51 or 301) The scenic pond in the north of the city has been a popular destination since the Qing dynasty and is well known for the 20 or so temples dotting the shoreline and nearby alleys. The majority of these structures are garishly kitsch, which can be fun for some. At night they're illuminated, creating multicoloured reflections in the water.

Starting from the southern end and heading clockwise around the lake, you'll first encounter sections of the Old Wall of Fengshan (Fèngshān Jiùchéng), built in 1826. The intact north gate wall runs along Shengli Rd.

On the southern edge of Lotus Pond are the red-and-yellow seven-storey **Dragon & Tiger Pagodas** (龍虎塔, Lónghǔ Tǎ; Map p256; 9 Liantan Rd, Zuoying, 蓮潭路9號; ⊘ 8am-5pm; Ⓜ Xinzuoying), built in full-blown '70s flamboyance. They're connected to a temple by a zigzag bridge. Leading to the twin towers are corridors built in the likeness of the epony-

FOGUANGSHAN

Considered the centre of Buddhism in southern Taiwan, **Foguangshan** (佛光山, Fóguāngshān; ☑ Buddha Museum 07-656 3033, ☑ Pilgrim's Lodge 07-656 1921; www.fgs.org.tw; Xingtian Rd, Dashu District, 大樹區興田路; ⊙ Buddha Museum 9am-7pm Mon-Fri, to 8pm Sat & Sun) a good place to learn more about Buddhism as the staff and some of the monks and nuns speak English. The temple complex covering five hills and 30 hectares consists of older Buddhist temples and other religious (as well as educational and burial) facilities, and the newer Buddha Museum.

The Buddha Museum (http://www.fgsbmc.org.tw/en) consists of eight pagodas symmetrically arranged along a boulevard at the end of which is a main hall and a giant Shakyamuni Buddha. There are exhibits, interactive activities and even a Buddhist wedding room in the pagodas. The main hall has multiple shrines and several galleries of Buddhist relics and artefacts, some quite fascinating.

If you want to spend the night here, the sizeable Pilgrim's Lodge offers clean family rooms and dormitories. Food wise, take your pick among a buffet-style vegetarian canteen (it's for volunteers so make a donation), an all-you-can-eat vegetarian eatery, a classy Hong Kong–owned vegetarian restaurant, food stalls, and Starbucks (vegetarian too!).

If you're interested in guided tours and short Buddhism courses, make contact with the temple.

There are 11 buses a day between Foguangshan and Kaohsiung (NT$85, 1 hour); 15 buses run between Zuoying HSR station and Buddha Memorial Centre (NT$70, 40 minutes). The old and new parts of Foguangshan are within walking distance of each other, or hop on the shuttle buses (NT$20, every 20 minutes) that link the two places.

mous creatures. Be sure to enter through the dragon's mouth and exit through the tiger's jaws. To do otherwise would bring terrible luck. To their left are the fun and gaudy **Spring & Autumn Pavilions** (春秋閣, Chūnqiū Gé; Map p256). The two octagonal towers in green and yellow are dedicated to Guandi, the God of War, and feature Guanyin riding a dragon that you can walk through like you do the dragon and tiger at the pagodas.

Standing right across the road, the **Temple of Enlightenment** (天府宮, Tiānfǔ Gōng; Map p256; 158 Liantan Rd, Zuoying, 蓮潭路158號) is the largest temple in the area. It's guarded by two giant temple lions hugging equally giant stone balls.

Most structures around the lake are modern and gaudy, with the exception of the **City God Temple** (城隍廟, Chénghuáng Miào; Map p256; 1 Dianzaiding Rd, Zuoying, 左營區店仔頂路1號). In the entrance hall, look up to admire the detailed *plafond* (decorative ceiling); the traditional woodcarvings are filled with symbolism, such as the fish representing yin and yang, and the crabs representing official promotion. The roof has some fine examples of dragons and phoenixes in *jiànnián* (mosaic-like temple decoration).

Back at the pond, follow the pier to the walkway out to the imposing 24m statue of **Xuantian Shang-di** (玄天上帝, Xúantiān Shàngdì; Map p256; Liantan Rd, Zuoying, 左營區蓮潭路),

the Supreme Emperor of the Dark Heaven and guardian of the north. This Taoist deity is also known as Xuan Wu (玄武; Mysterious Warrior) and in Hong Kong as Emperor of the North (北帝; Pak Tai), and is usually presented barefoot with one foot on a serpent and the other on a tortoise – two monsters wreaking havoc on Earth that the deity, originally a prince, is believed to have subdued.

The final temple of note is the **Confucius Temple** (孔廟, Kǒng Miào; Map p256; 400 Liantan Rd, Zuoying, 蓮潭路400號; ⊙ 9am-5pm Tue-Sun; Ⓜ Xinzuoying) on the pond's northern end. Completed in 1976, it's the largest Confucius temple complex in Taiwan (167 sq metres), and a stately 1970s replica of a Song-dynasty temple and the famous Qufu Confucius Temple in Shandong. It sits on the northwestern corner of Lotus Pond.

Daitian Temple   TEMPLE
(代天宮, Dàitiān Gōng; Map p252; www.daitiankung.org.tw; 27 Gubo St, Gushan, 鼓波街27號; ☑ 1, 31, 50, 99) A temple with a Taoist hall at the front and a Buddhist hall (青雲寺) at the back, both richly decorated with folk art. In fact Daitian Temple has the largest collection of works by master painter Pan Lishui (潘麗水) of any such structure in Taiwan, and includes a massive landscape mural. The square in front is full of vendors selling traditional eats like flying-fish balls and Shantou noodles.

Lotus Pond

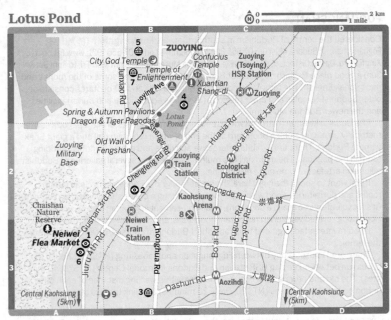

Lotus Pond

There's a small museum in the complex showing more of Pan Lishui's work. It's open Tuesday to Sunday from 9am to noon and 1.30pm to 5pm.

Kaohsiung Museum of History MUSEUM
(高雄市立歷史博物館; Gāoxióng Shìlì Lìshǐ Bówùguǎn; Map p252; http://khm.org.tw; 272 Zhongzheng 4th Rd, 中正四路272號; ⊙9am-5pm Tue-Sun; ⓜYanchengpu) FREE This lovely museum is housed in what was the city-government building during Japanese times. The building of the museum was one of the important historical sites of the 2-28 Incident (p352) and it's said that the first gunshot in Kaohsiung was fired here in March 1947. Tucked into neat rooms down the blonde-wood and marble hallways are photographic displays, a semipermanent 2-28 memorial, and exhibits that change quarterly.

Guomao Community LANDMARK
(果貿社區, Guǒmào Shèqū; Map p256; 9 Zhonghua 1st Rd, Zuoying, 中華一路9號; ⓡ218) Dramatic residential blocks with curved facades encircle a diaspora community in the Guomao area. The dozen-or-so 12-storey buildings were constructed for the mainland Chinese soldiers of the ROC navy and their families when an old military dependants' village had to be torn down. A self-sufficient community frozen in time, you'll find here barbershops, clinics, a market, a basketball court in red, white and blue (the colours of the ROC flag) and, most famously, shops selling delicious mainland Chinese delicacies.

For ordinary Kaohsiung citizens, the main draw of the Guomao Community is the authentic Peking-style dumplings, Shanghainese pastries, Sichuan cold dishes and Shanxi noodles served at its many ground-floor stalls. You'll also hear more Mandarin than Taiwanese spoken in the area, and some older people may be eager to strike up a conversation in Mandarin with Chinese-looking tourists. The community, sometimes also known as Guomao Military Dependants' Village (果貿海軍眷村; Guǒmào Hǎijūn Juàncūn), is in Zuoying District.

'Guomao Community' (果貿社區; Guǒmào Shèqū) is the 15th stop on the bus route from Kaohsiung Main Station.

Former Japanese Navy
Fongshan Radio Station HISTORIC SITE
(原日本海軍鳳山無線電信所, Yuán Rìběn Hǎijūn Fèngshān Wúxiàn Diànxìn Suǒ; ☎07-222 5136; Lane 10, Shengli Rd, Fengshan, 勝利路10號; ⊙9am-5pm Tue-Sun; Ⓜ Fongshan Junior High School) This mysterious national relic in Fengshan was a Japanese naval radio station that later became an interrogation facility under the Republic of China, then a disciplinary camp during the White Terror. The grassy complex full of mango trees has nine sites of interest, including a cross-shaped communication facility with steel vault doors and the original telegraph equipment, unnerving solitary-confinement blockhouses, a fort with blast-resistant windows, and a cavernous interior that used to house cages for disobedient servicemen.

Kaohsiung Museum
of Fine Arts MUSEUM
(高雄美術館, Gāoxióng Měishùguǎn; Map p256; ☎07-555 0331; www.kmfa.gov.tw/Exhibition.aspx; 80 Meishuguan Rd, Gushan, 鼓山區美術館路 80號; ⊙9.30am-5.30pm Tue-Sun; ☒57, 73, 205) FREE Set in a large park, this wonderful museum specialises in the works of Taiwanese artists, in particular, painters, sculptors, and installation and digital artists from the south. The museum is also a world-renowned authority on research on Austronesian art.

National Science &
Technology Museum MUSEUM
(科學工藝博物館, Kēxué Gōngyì Bówùguǎn; ☎07-387 8748; www.nstm.gov.tw; 720 Jiouru 1st Rd, 九如一路720號; NT$100; ⊙9am-5pm Tue-Sun; ☒; ☒60) Features an hourly IMAX show and high-quality, hands-on science exhibits designed for children. The exhibit on the industrial history of Taiwan, one of the few in English, is so informative that it alone is worth the price of admission, plus visitors over the age of 65 or under six can visit for free on weekdays.

Gangshan Eye VIEWPOINT
(崗山之眼, Gǎngshān Zhīyǎn; https://khskywalk park.com; Xiao Gangshan, 小崗山; adult/child NT$60/30; ⊙9am-5pm Tue-Fri, Sat & Sun to 6pm;

☒ Gangshan South, Exit 1) A music-themed viewing bridge atop a hill between the districts of Gangshan and Yanchao. The attractive 88m-long structure is suspended 40m high by cables issuing from pylons shaped like the scroll of a violin, and easy jazz emits from speakers. On a clear day, you can see beyond the fields to the North Dawu Mountain, Kaohsiung's 85 Sky Tower, and even the Taiwan Strait. From Exit 1 of Gangshan South Station (train not KMRT), bus 68 takes you to Gangshan Eye, or share a taxi with other visitors at the exit.

Story House of Naval
Base Zuoying MUSEUM
(左營軍區故事館, Zuǒyíng Jūnqū Gùshì Guǎn; Map p256; ☎07-587 5877; www.cna.edu.tw/navyStory; 211 Shijian Rd, 市左營區實踐路211號; ⊙9am-noon & 2-5pm Tue-Thu, 9am-noon & 2-8pm Fri, to 8pm Sat & Sun; ☒301A) In a compound next to Taiwan's largest naval base, this small museum pays tribute to Zuoying's strong military heritage. By means of relics, photos, warship models and replicas of old living quarters, a narrative is presented of the development of the navy and the navy veterans' village, from the 17th century through Japanese rule and the American presence to more recent times. The museum is staffed by smartly dressed students from the naval academy nearby.

The compound where the museum is located is called Sihai Yijia (四海一家, sìhǎi yī-jiā), literally 'Four Seas One Family', that also includes a guesthouse and a restaurant. It was built in 1950 as an entertainment venue for KMT naval officers and their families who had fled to Taiwan from China. The site now occupied by the museum used to be a library.

The guesthouse is a little old but offers some of the cheapest double rooms (under NT$2000) in Kaohsiung, though (ostensibly at least) only those with connections to the Taiwanese navy can stay there.

Military Dependants'
Village Museum MUSEUM
(眷村文化區, Juàncūn Wénhuà Qū; Map p256; ☎07-581 2886; www.facebook.com/Mingdexinchun; Mingde village, junction Haigong Rd & Haijing St, 左營區海功路海景街交叉, 明德新村; ⊙11am-5pm Tue-Fri, 10am-6pm Sat & Sun; ☒R51A, R55) Four houses of a military dependants' village have been restored and turned into a quaint museum. Besides exhibits on the KMT retreat from China and the US presence in Taiwan, there are replicas of former living quarters, a bar frequented by US servicemen, a movie

SOUTHERN TAIWAN KAOHSIUNG

theatre and even a small gallery devoted to famous poets from Zuoying.

Ginza Shopping
Arcade
HISTORIC BUILDING

(國際商場, Guójì Shāngchǎng; Map p252; Lane 260, Wufu 4th Rd, Yancheng, 五福四路260巷; Ⓜ Yanchengpu, Exit 2) Known locally as 'Ginza' (銀座), this crumbling arcade was Kaohsiung's first shopping mall when it opened in 1937, although the current structure harks back to the '60s. Western fashion and other luxury goods smuggled by sailors in to Kaohsiung Port were sold here. It was the poshest hang-out, and every Sunday its shops and bars were thronged with shoppers. Old Ginza is currently receiving a blood transfusion – a B&B is moving into the premises and old businesses are being revived.

The arcade is right next to a tea shop near the junction between Wufu 4th and Qixian 3rd Rds. You'll spot its old, three-storey facade between much-newer buildings. There's a 7-Eleven convenience store across the road.

British Consulate
Residence at Takou
HISTORIC SITE

(打狗英國領事館, Dǎgǒu Yīnguó Lǐngshìguǎn; Map p252; http://britishconsulate.khcc.gov.tw/home01.aspx?ID=1; 20 Lianhai Rd, 蓮海路20號; adult/student/child NT$99/49/39; ⊙ 9am-7pm Mon-Fri, to 9pm Sat & Sun) Built in 1865, this handsome red-brick consulate residence sits 70m above the mouth of Kaohsiung Harbour, a perfect location for watching giant container ships sail through the tiny mouth of the harbour. There's also an interesting clash of cultures to observe here, as Chinese tourists react in bewilderment to the open presence of Falun Gong posters decrying the Beijing government.

While in the area, check out a tiny temple to the left of the larger temple beside the consulate. It's the only shrine in Taiwan to deify 17th-century Dutch naval commanders, much in the way old Chinese generals have been deified over the centuries.

The consulate is a five-minute walk from Shihzuwan Beach.

Shihzuwan Beach
BEACH

(西子灣海灘, Xīzǐwān Hǎitān; Map p252; adult/child under 120cm NT$70/30; ⊙ 10am-6pm; Ⓜ Sizihwan) Shihzuwan Beach is smaller than Cijin Beach (p253), but it's a calmer swimming beach and is an excellent place for hanging out and watching the sunset.

Formosa Boulevard
KMRT Station
NOTABLE BUILDING

(美麗島站, Měilìdǎo Zhàn; Map p252; Ⓜ Formosa Boulevard) Stop to see the resplendent Dome of Light (光之穹頂; Guāngzhī Qióngdǐng) by Italian glass-artist Narcissus Quagliata. Formosa Blvd is south of the main train station.

Ciaotou Sugar Factory
NOTABLE BUILDING

(橋頭糖廠, Qiáotóu Tángchǎng; www.tscleisure.com.tw/museum; 24 Tangchang Rd, 糖廠路24號; ⊙ 9am-5pm; Ⓡ Ciaotou Sugar Factory) Taiwan's first modern sugar factory (c 1901) is no longer in use, but you can still see the old mechanisms and the vats. There's also a village here that retains most of its early-20th-century flavour, some handsome mid-century-style offices and a couple of air-raid shelters. Ciaotou is by no means Taiwan's most colourful sugar-making facility to visit, but it's quaint and adorably landscaped with sunflowers and whimsical art.

The sugar factory and village grounds begin as soon as you exit Ciaotou Sugar Factory KMRT station. There are good English interpretation signs around.

🏃 Activities & Tours

i-Ride
AMUSEMENT PARK

(i-Ride 體驗中心, i-Ride Tǐyàn Zhōngxīn; ☑ 07-537 2858; www.irideexperiencecenter.com; 9 Fuxing 4th Rd, 復興四路9號; NT$480; ⊙ 9.30am-noon & 1.30-5pm Mon, Wed-Fri, 9.30am-5pm Sat & Sun; Ⓜ Shihjia) Cutting-edge virtual-reality theatre that takes you soaring, plunging and whizzing past some of Kaohsiung's best-known sights, with sound, wind and smell special effects to enhance the experience. There's also an i-Ride in Taipei (p111).

Taroko Park
AMUSEMENT PARK

(大魯閣草衙道, Dàlǔgé Cǎoyádào; www.tarokopark.com.tw; 100 Zhongshan 4th Rd, 前鎮區中山四路100號; ⊙ 11am-10pm Mon-Thur, to 10.30pm Fri, 10.30am-10.30pm Sat, to 10pm Sun; Ⓜ Caoyadao) Taroko is a mini-amusement park that's part of a shopping mall. The park features a mini–Suzuka circuit, go-karts, Ferris wheel, carousel and mechanical rides that young children will enjoy. For older kids and adults, the mall has an indoor games centre where you can play laser tag, throw hoops, play baseball, and do flips on a trampoline.

C-bike
CYCLING

(www.c-bike.com.tw) Kaohsiung's public bicycle-rental system has rental sites near most KMRT and train stations. It's free for

FANTASTICAL STONE TEMPLE

Stone Temple (田寮石頭廟, Tiánliáo Shítóu Miào; ☑ 07-636 1154; 2-7 Xinxing Rd, Tianliao, 田寮區新興里新興路2-7號; ⓧ 8am-5pm) is a fantastical, Gaudí-esque interpretation of a Taoist temple by Southeast Asian migrant workers. The 500 men had been hired to build a highway in the area, but the contractor went out of business and they were stranded with no means. A temple took them in, after trying in vain to negotiate with the labour authorities. In return for free food and lodging, the men were asked to build a temple, which they did in the early 1990s with seashells, corals, stones and loads of imagination.

Stone Temple worships a number of Taoist gods, but the main deity here is the Cundi bodhisattva (準提菩薩). You'll see her and a plethora of other gold-faced deities lined up along colonnaded corridors.

The temple puts out a delicious vegetarian buffet daily for devotees. Make a donation, grab a bowl and chopsticks, and join in.

Take bus 8013 from Gangshan (岡山) to Tianliao (田寮) and get off 30 minutes later at the 20th stop, Niulu Wan (牛路灣), which is the road outside the temple compound. There are only three buses a day, departing from Gangshan at 5.40am (7.35am on weekends and holidays), 11.05am and 5.20pm. Buses leave Tianliao daily at 6.15am (8.20am on weekends and public holidays), 11.50am and 6.05pm.

You could also consider taking a cab from Kaohsiung (40 minutes, one way NT$700 to NT$800). It's best to negotiate with the driver to wait for you while you explore, as there are no taxis at the temple and few will drive out to pick you up.

The temple is also known as Cíxuán Shèngtiān Gōng (慈玄聖天宮).

---

the first 30 minutes, then the per-minute rate is NT$5 from the 31st minute, NT$10 from the 61st minute, and NT$20 from the 91st. See their excellent website for details.

★**3080s Local Style**   WALKING
(叁捌地方生活, Sānbā Dìfāng Shēnghuó; Map p252; ☑ 07-521 5938; www.facebook.com/3080s; 226 Wufu 4th Rd, 鹽埕區五福四路226號; ⓧ 2-9pm Sat & Sun; Ⓜ Yanchengpu, Exit 2) 3080s is run by young Kaohsiungers who are passionate about preserving the culture of Yancheng District. Weekly two-hour walking tours in English are NT$500 per head for a group of 10 (or NT$5000 per group); tours in Mandarin are NT$400 per head (or NT$4000 per group). There are also architectural tours. Book two weeks in advance by emailing or calling.

🎊 Festivals & Events

★**Megaport Music Festival**   MUSIC
(大港開唱, Dàgǎng Kāichàng; Pier-2 Art Center, 1 Dayong Rd, 駁二藝術特區,大勇路一號; ⓧ Mar; Ⓜ Yanchengpu, Exit 1) If you want to experience a music festival with a strong southern Taiwan vibe, this is it! Hip, wild and raucous, Megaport features some of Taiwan's best-loved indie-rock bands as well as foreign acts from Japan and Europe. Every set begins with the blast of a ship horn. Held over one March weekend.

Spring Scream   MUSIC
(春天吶喊, Chūntiān Nàhǎn; www.springscream. com; Cijin Beach, Cijin Island, 旗津島海灘) Indie-music fans should try to time their visit in April or May for Spring Scream, Taiwan's longest-running music festival. The event brings together names in Asia's indie scene, along with American and European acts. While for years it had taken place in Pingtung, Spring Scream moved to Cijin Beach in Kaohsiung for the three-day 2019 edition.

Neimen Song Jiang Battle Array   CARNIVAL
(內門宋江陣, Nèimén Sòngjiāng Zhèn; www. who-ha.com.tw; Neimen District, 內門; ⓧ Mar/Apr; 🚌 8032) An annual folk festival combining martial arts and religion, it's believed to have roots in rural self-defence militia in the Qing dynasty. Details differ yearly, but the mainstays are martial-arts rituals and contests by various Song Jiang Battle Array troupes, roadside banqueting (辦桌, bànzhuō), and much singing and dancing. It's a very southern Taiwanese event where the sun is hot, the music rocking, the people loud, and the temples bright and bold.

Song Jiang Battle Array (SJBA) takes place in Kaohsiung's Neimen District and three temples take turns being the organiser: Nanhai Zizhu Temple (南海紫竹寺; Nánhǎi Zǐzhú Sì), Neimen Shunxian Temple (內門順賢宮; Nèimén Shùnxián Gōng) and Neimen Zizhu Temple (內門紫竹寺; Nèimén Zǐzhú Sì).

SHOP HISTORY & BUTTONS AT BIG GUTTER COVER

Turn-of-the-Century Malls

Dàgōudǐng or 'Big Gutter Cover' (p254) is an area in Yancheng District in the southwestern tip of Kaohsiung, that got its very local and literal name from a handful of shopping lanes parallel to Qixian Rd (七賢路), namely Dagouding Old Street (p254) and the three Juejiang Shopping Arcades (堀江商場; Jūjiāng Shāngchǎng). They were built in the 1950s (although some businesses have been around for longer) and are great for getting a feel for old Kaohsiung. But not only that – you can still shop and eat here, and the area is undergoing a revival. From classy fabric-covered buttons echoing your herringbone overcoat to pipes, absinthe, dumplings or mochi, there's a pleasant array of vendors in Big Gutter Cover.

Japanese Development of Yancheng

Before the 19th century, what is now Yancheng District was a sprawl of salt fields; in fact 'Yancheng' means 'open space for salt harvesting'. Running through here was a tributary of Love River (p262) that started near Hexi Rd (河西路) in the north and emptied into Kaohsiung Harbour in the south. After the Japanese colonised Taiwan, they began to develop the area. Over the course of half a century, they deepened the port, made roads out of salt fields by filling them with dredged mud from the harbour, and built a railway to transport sugar and bananas to the coast, from which they were shipped to Japan. It was during this time that the tributary was turned into a huge gutter.

The Path to Prosperity Post-WWII

After WWII, people from towns and villages in southern Taiwan flocked to this portside neighbourhood in Kaohsiung in search of employment. Young people from Penghu Island, Tainan and Chiayi set up stalls along the clean gutter, selling tea, sundries and Japanese food; they operated billiard rooms. As the population grew, concerns over shortage of space, pollution and safety led the government to install a cover over the gutter in the 1950s. This was reinforced with wooden planks and concrete to form lanes with shop spaces that were rented out to vendors, and existing operators were relocated inside.

These shopping arcades materialised in phases. The last to finish were Juejiang Shopping Arcades 1, 2 and 3. They're still around on Wufu 4th Rd (五福四路): Arcade 1 at Lane 229 and Arcades 2 and 3 at Lane 239, opposite 3080s (p262). These shops, offering clothes, antiques, tobacco and liquor, were considered very fancy back in the day, more so than Dagouding Old Street with its bakeries, sundries store, button shop, noodle factory and disused wet market (where parties and cultural events are today held by a heritage group).

Layout of the Shops

All the shops have an attic accessible via wooden or iron stairs that was used for storage and sleeping quarters for apprentices and assistants. In some cases, the owner's entire family slept there and part of the shop downstairs was used for cooking and washing in the evening. Some families put out beds in the corridors to sleep after everyone had closed for the day.

The Golden Era

The 1950s to the 1970s were Yancheng's heyday. The imposition of martial law and trade restrictions meant that imported products, much coveted by Taiwanese consumers, were

Originating in the plains south of Jiayi, SJBA is still celebrated in many places in Tainan, but the Neimen edition in Kaohsiung is most famous and arguably the most spectacular.

In the Qing dynasty, villagers in southwestern Taiwan took the job of protecting their homes into their own hands because government support was inadequate. They practised martial arts and formed 'block watch' groups. These are sometimes believed to be the origin of the Song Jiang Battle Array.

As temples were the centre of spiritual and social life in agricultural communities, such activities soon extended to the protection of palanquins carrying gods at processions, and evolved into a cultural performance.

SJBA is purportedly also inspired by one of the four great classical novels of Chinese literature – *Water Margin* by Song dynasty writer Shi Nai'an, which revolves around the adventures of the patriotic bandit Song Jiang and his 108 companions. Folk tales and legends

hard to come by on the island. This and the close proximity to Kaohsiung Port created a huge black market for foreign goods in Yancheng. Sailors, American soldiers on shore leave, and basically anyone with the privilege of foreign travel smuggled goods from abroad. There are stories of people wearing multiple layers of clothes with pockets stuffed to the brim offloading their spoils in the shops. Yancheng became southern Taiwan's hub of foreign products and a flamboyant trendsetter.

Americans and the Vietnam War

During the Vietnam war when Kaohsiung was used as an American support base, navy personnel from the 7th Fleet on R&R spent a lot of time in Yancheng. This led to a proliferation of bars on Qixian Rd (七賢路). Soldiers would take the bar girls out to movies and western-style restaurants; gift them jewellery bought from Xinyue St (新樂街) with the red-and-yellow signage you still see; and buy fabric with them to make *qipao* (cheongsam) at tailors nearby. And Americans were not the only consumers. Middle-class Taiwanese from all over the island would come here seeking all kinds of rare and high-quality products – clothes and handkerchiefs from Hong Kong, soap from Thailand, watches and sweets from Japan and wine from Portugal. When hungry, they would stop for a bowl of milkfish noodles (p263) or a few slivers of braised offal, and pick up a few things from the wet market before heading home. Yancheng was essentially one giant shopping mall.

Good Old Ginza

Ginza Shopping Arcade (p258), crumbling but being revived as we speak, was just a wooden structure in the Japanese era. During the boom, the owners of the two dozen shops went on a field trip to Japan, and upon return built a brand-new earthquake-proof arcade fashioned after the glamorous and sturdy malls of Ginza. When unveiled in 1964, it was Kaohsiung's most luxurious shopping centre. There are still residents on the upper floors, while a liquor store, hair salons and an old tailoring shop occupy the ground floor, with new tenants expected.

Revival

Yancheng lost its shine after the Vietnam War and as development moved east to the district known as Xinxing or 'New Prosperity'. However, recent years have seen renewed interest among young, cultured Kaohsiungers in Yancheng, and new hostels and cafes have appeared, alongside efforts to restore old businesses. In 1965 there were over 60,000 people living in Yancheng, making it the most populous district in Kaohsiung; today it's the least populous but one of the most interesting, especially with the development of Pier-2 Art Center (p253) close by. You can combine your visit to Pier-2 with a walk and some shopping in Yancheng. Preceding or ending your ramblings with an aromatic siphon coffee at Hsiao Ti Cafe (p265) is an excellent idea.

Keep in mind that most eateries are open for breakfast and lunch, but many shops don't open till around midday. The area is served by Yancheng Pu KMRT station. Exit 2 is good for most sights listed here.

spawned by the famous work made their way into traditional Taiwanese opera (歌仔戲, *gēzǎi xì*), which was (and sometimes still is) performed at the birthday celebrations of deities. An ancient array may easily comprise upwards of a hundred performers, but over the centuries, the numbers have gone down. Today they usually consist of 36. However many of the weapons used still hark back to the novel and performers' faces are painted to represent the original heroes.

Take bus 8032 (Kaohsiung Express C) to Cishan bus station, then change to bus 8035 to Neimen. On event days, there is a free shuttle-bus service between Cishan bus station and Neimen. See website for details.

Art Kaohsiung   ART
(高雄藝術博覽會, Gāoxióng Yìshù Bólǎnhuì; www.art-kaohsiung.com; Pier-2 Art Center, 駁二藝術特區; ⊙Dec) Southern Taiwan's premier international art fair, the three-day event

RIVER OF LOVE

Love River (愛河, Ài Hé; Map p252; M Yanchengpu) was once an open sewer that has seen a remarkable transformation in recent years. The waters flow clean and the bankside promenades with shady trees and outdoor cafes are attractive. You can cruise along the river on boat rides (25-minute rides are NT$150, and run from 3pm to 10pm on weekdays, and 9am to 10pm on Saturday and Sunday). There are two piers: Ren'ai Pier (p268) and Guobin Pier (p268).

showcases works by over a hundred art galleries from China, Japan, the Philippines, Hong Kong, Malaysia, Singapore, Vietnam and the USA. The fair has been steadily expanding the scope of its featured collections every year since it opened in 2013.

International Lion Dance Festival & Competition
DANCE

(高雄戲獅甲藝術節, Gāoxióng Xìshījiǎ Yìshùjié; 07-222 5136; 757 Bo'ai 2nd Road, Zuoying, 左營,博愛二路757號; ☉ Oct, Nov or Dec, biennial; M Kaohsiung Arena, Exit 5) The International Lion Dance Festival & Competition, held in the Kaohsiung Arena (高雄巨蛋體育館) every two years, is a raucous folk extravaganza. The two-day event draws tens of thousands of visitors from all over Asia.

🛏 Sleeping

With Inn
HOSTEL $

(同居, Tóngjū; Map p252; 07-241 0321; www.withinnhostel.com; 28 Lane 5, Wenheng 1st Rd, Xinxing District, 新興區文橫一路5巷28號; dm/d from NT$500/1600; ⊜❄❀; M Central Park, Exit 2) Five nifty dormitories and two doubles in an utterly charming '60s residence. Owned by a family in the construction business, apparently no expense was spared in its building and restoration was painstakingly carried out. Most of the original layout has been kept, and so have the tiles, banisters and beautiful patterned glass.

Legend Hotel
HOTEL $$

(秝芯旅店, Lìxīn Lüdiàn; Map p252; 07-287 7766; www.legendhotel.com.tw; 55 Xinsheng 1st St, 新盛一街55號; s/d incl breakfast NT$1100/1800; ❄@❀; M City Council) Just a short walk from the KMRT station, this good-value choice is the best gateway to the market action, but

is also far enough away not to be disturbed by it. The 49 rooms are reasonably sized and bright. The cartoonish decor won't wow you (though it might wow your kids), but you'll get a good night's sleep.

★ Hók House
B&B $$

(鶴宮寓, Hè Gōng Yù; Map p252; 07-201 1988; https://hokhouse.com; 2nd fl, 41 Zhongzheng 4th Rd, 中正四路41號2樓; dm NT$660, d/ste from NT$2580/3080; ⊜❄❀; M Formosa Boulevard) At Hók House, you can enjoy history and style without sacrificing comfort and your wallet. The 1950s building was the old Grand Crane Palace Hotel (鶴宮大旅社) – see the original lettering above the entrance. Interiors were rebuilt from scratch in a restrained Japanese art deco style. The 15 rooms, shared living room and communal kitchen are impeccably designed and presented.

Hotel Dùa
HOTEL $$

(Map p252; 07-272 2990; www.hoteldua.com; 165 Linsen 1st Rd, 林森一路165號; d from NT$3400; ❄@❀) This hotel has 158 ultramodern and sleek rooms with enormous beds inside a completely renovated building. The dark-hued furniture blends well with the wooden-planked walls and muted contemporary decor. There's also a beautiful rooftop lounge where you can enjoy breakfast or cocktails.

FX Inn
HOTEL $$

(富驛商旅, Fùyì Shānglǚ; Map p252; 07-970 8777; www.fxinn.com.tw; 81 Zhonghua 3rd Rd, 前金區中華三路81號; r from NT$3200; ❄@❀; M City Council) This clean, comfortable hotel offers spacious, light rooms and a tasty, if creative, buffet breakfast – shepherd's pie in the morning, anyone?! The 'fitness centre' is tiny, but regular bikes are available to borrow free of charge. Conveniently located by the MRT station and in walking distance to shops and restaurants on Zhonghua Rd and the Liuhe night market (p264).

3080s Local Style
HOSTEL $$$

(叁捌地方生活, Sānbā Dìfāng Shēnghuó; Map p252; 07-521 5938; www.facebook.com/3080s; 226 Wufu 4th Rd, 鹽埕區五福四路226號; per month NT$15,000; ❄❀) A once-flourishing wedding shop has been turned by the owners' grandson into a quirky hostel that won an architectural award for its restoration. The fitting room, tailoring shop and living quarters are now guest rooms. The deluxe suite, called 'Grandma's Home', features the bar where the owners used to entertain their guests and the matrimonial bed.

City Suites HOTEL $$$
(城市商旅, Chéngshì Shānglǚ; Map p252; ☑ 07-521 5116; www.citysuites.com.tw; 83 Gongyuan 2nd Rd, 公園二路83號; r from NT$5500; 😊❄🛜; 🚇Dayi Pier-2) Quiet, comfortable rooms right next to the southeastern end of Pier-2 Art Center (p253). Rates include a sumptuous breakfast buffet. There are always plenty of taxis just out the door.

🍴 Eating

★ Ruifeng Night Market MARKET $
(瑞豐夜市, Ruìfēng Yèshì; Map p256; junction btwn Yucheng & Nanping Rds, 裕誠路和南屏路交叉口; ⏰6pm-midnight Tue, Thu-Sun; Ⓜ Kaohsiung Arena) Kaohsiung's largest and arguably best night market. Stalls cater to locals rather than big tour groups, and they're concentrated in one area, which makes it easy to cover many of them (if you're hungry).

Chou's Angelica Duck TAIWANESE $
(周記當歸鴨, Zhōujì Dāngguī Yā; Map p252; 148 Sanmin St, 三民街148號; mains NT$50-60; ⏰8am-8pm; Ⓜ Kaohsiung Main Station) Sanmin St heaves with cheap and cheery stalls brandishing all kinds of deliciousness. One of the most famous is Chou's, for its duck cooked in angelica broth (當歸鴨, dāngguī yā), a Chinese herb that improves blood circulation. It shouldn't be hard to find someone to translate the menu for you – Chou's attracts eaters from all over.

Ju Tang TAIWANESE $
(聚堂, Jù Táng; Map p252; ☑ 0958-733 139; www.facebook.com/聚堂-蔥抓餅-鍋燒麵-海鮮粥-535754873196785; 58 Haibin 1st Rd, 濱海一路58號; ⏰12.30-11pm; ❄; Ⓜ Sizihwan, Exit 1) A casual 1km stroll from Pier-2 Art Center (p253) through a charming neighbourhood brings you to this neat little place that serves up tasty and affordable soup noodles (鍋燒麵, guōshāo miàn), seafood congee (海鮮粥, hǎixiān zhōu), and fluffy spring-onion pancakes (蔥抓餅, cōng zhuābǐng). The last is made fresh in a myriad of flavours just outside the restaurant.

**Three Generations
Spring Roll** TAIWANESE $
(三代春捲, Sāndài Chūnjuǎn; Map p252; ☑ 07-285 8490; 1 Zhongshanheng Rd, Xinxing District, 中山橫路1號; spring roll NT$40; ⏰10am-7pm; Ⓜ Formosa Boulevard, Exit 1) At this small, 60-year-old stall, place your order and watch the lady assemble the rolls, her hands darting over huge plates of Chinese cabbage, sprouts, egg shreds,

spring onions, pork and powdered peanut, like an orchestra conductor. Her rolls (春捲, chūnjuǎn) are crunchy, light and delicious.

Laojiang Black Tea TEAHOUSE $
(老江红茶, Lǎojiāng Hóngchá; Map p252; 51 Nantai Rd, 新興區南台路51號; ⏰24hr; Ⓜ Formosa Boulevard) Great place for breakfast or a late-night snack – it's open all the time. At a glance it's just a regular street shop that specialises in milk tea, but the flavour is stronger and there's a hint of smokiness. It goes swimmingly with the sumptuous egg pancakes and toast, which may explain why this place is crazy busy.

**Dagouding Milkfish
Noodles** TAIWANESE $
(大溝頂虱目魚米粉, Dàgōudǐng Shīmùyú Mǐfěn; Map p252; 198-38 Xinyue St, 鹽埕區新樂街198之38; milkfish noodles from NT$60; ⏰5.30am-1.30pm; Ⓜ Yanchengpu, Exit 2) Milkfish is associated with Tainan, but Kaohsiung has its own version, too. Instead of serving the meat as is, slivers of meat are wrapped in fish cake processed from the cruder bits of the animal to make sure nothing goes to waste. It's the food of workers and is tasty when fried or with noodles, as it is at this stall.

Milkfish is 虱目魚 (shīmùyú) in Mandarin and most people like to have it in soup with rice noodles (米粉, mǐfěn). This place in an alley only opens for breakfast and lunch, and is always busy. Just see what other customers are having and let the vendor know what you want.

**Behind-the-Temple
Seafood Congee** SEAFOOD $
(廟后海產粥, Miàohòu Hǎichǎn Zhōu; Map p252; ☑ 0986-343 155; 33-1 Jie Sing 2nd St, Gushan, 捷興二街33-1號; seafood congee NT$120; ⏰11am-2pm & 4.30-9pm; Ⓜ Sizihwan) This wonderful street-corner shop with an iron roof whips up delicious soups and congee with fresh local seafood. The signature seafood congee (招牌海產粥, zhāopái hǎichǎn zhōu) is excellent with the oyster omelette (蚵仔蛋, hézǐ dàn, NT$100). Tick your selections on the order form, hand it over, pay, get your condiments of choice, and you're set. It's closed every other Monday.

Cafe Hifumi CAFE $
(一二三亭, Yīèrsān Tíng; Map p252; ☑ 07-531 0330; www.facebook.com/cafehifumi; 2nd fl, 4 Guyuan St, 鼓山區鼓元街四號二樓; coffee/meals from NT$120/250; ⏰10am-6pm; ❄🛜; Ⓜ Xiziwan, Exit 2) A chilled cafe in an old Japanese-

Taiwanese house (c 1900s) that's nostalgic and elegant without trying too hard. You can spend a relaxing hour here under beams and rafters enjoying good iced coffee and checking emails. In its previous incarnations, this place was a high-class restaurant with geisha performances.

Liuhe Night Market
MARKET $

(六合夜市, Liùhé Yèshì; Map p252; Liuhe Rd, 六合路; ☺6pm-midnight; Ⓜ Formosa Boulevard) This market is famous islandwide for its 100-plus food stalls offering everything from squid on a stick to fresh chicken wraps. You'll see a convoy of buses bringing tour groups in the evening.

★One Bar
TAIWANESE $$

(萬吧, Wànbā; Map p252; ☑07-331 3322; 1 Lane 261, Qingnian 1st Rd, 苓雅區青年一路261巷1號; set meals NT$330; ☺restaurant 11am-8pm; ☒ ☎; Ⓜ Formosa Boulevard, Central Park) A hip restaurant with Eames-inspired, futuristic paraphernalia, plus an oldies playlist, beaming you to the late-Japanese-colonial era. The set meals here are expertly prepared with top-notch ingredients. Choose among chicken or mushroom stew, braised pork and grilled fish. Dessert is NT$100 more. There's a bar on the 3rd floor, accessible via a spiral staircase outside the restaurant.

★Shumin Kitchen
TAIWANESE $$

(庶民廚房, Shùmín Chúfáng; Map p252; ☑07-215 5660; 7 Yingxiong Rd, 苓雅區英雄路七號; mains NT$200-700; ☺11am-midnight; ☒; Ⓜ Central Park) A laid-back restaurant known for well-executed Taiwanese dishes and above-average pricing. At lunch, it's full of middle-class families and couples. At night it morphs into an izakaya (Japanese gastropub), attracting drinkers with its good booze selection and dishes to go with your tipple, like blanched squid (白切透抽, báiqiē tòuchōu) and handmade fish cake (手工黑輪片, shǒugōng hēilúnpiàn). Picture menu available.

Wu Pao Chun Bakery
BAKERY $$

(吳寶春麥方店, Wúbǎo Chūnmài Fāngdiàn; ☑07-335 9593; www.wupaochun.com; 19 Siwei 3rd Rd, Lingya District, 四維三路 19號; loaf NT$350; ☺10am-8.30pm; ☒; Ⓜ Sanduo Shopping District) The flagship store of the Taiwanese baker who won top prize (bread category) in the Bakery World Cup in Paris. And he did it with a wheat loaf that he embedded with millet wine, rose petals and dried lychees. Since then Wu has continued to impress flocking customers with both European-style breads and soft Asian pastries.

Ban Jiushi
TAIWANESE $$

(半九十, Bàn Jiǔshí; Map p252; ☑07-281 5195; 71 Zhongheng 4th Rd, Xinxing District, 中正四路71號; mains from NT$200, minimum charge NT$150; ☺11am-10.30pm; ☒ ☎) An elegant teahouse that makes refined versions of classics such as braised pork and panfried milkfish. Pore over a book or watch the world go by as you await your tea-infused soup noodles or homemade black-date cake. It's just below Marsalis Jazz Bar (p266) and, like the bar, is closed the last Tuesday of every month.

Ya Jiao Seafood Restaurant
SEAFOOD $$

(鴨角活海產店, Yājiǎo Huóhǎichǎn Diàn; Map p252; 22 Miaoqian Rd, Cijin Island, 旗津廟前路22號; per person from NT$80; ☺10.30am-9.30pm; ☒) For fresh seafood, locals recommend Ya Jiao on Cijin Island. It's the kind of place for eating sautéed clams or local fish sashimi, drinking cheap beer, and being loud. Tell the staff how much you want to spend and they will arrange dishes for you. Try the stir-fried clams with basil (塔香海瓜子, tǎ xiāng hǎi guāzǐ) and blanched shrimp (白灼蝦, báizhuóxiā).

★House of Crab
SEAFOOD $$$

(蟳之屋, Xún Zhī Wū; ☑07-226 6127; 93 Minsheng 1st Rd, 新興區民生一路93號; ☺11.30am-2pm & 5.30-9pm; ☒; Ⓜ Sinyi Elementary School) This upmarket restaurant where locals and expats bring their guests offers some of the best seafood dishes anywhere in Taiwan. The menu has no prices, but rest assured it's an honest establishment. You can ask for a quote before ordering or request the much briefer 'tourists' menu' which comes with the prices.

The name Xun Zhi Wu (蟳之屋) means 'House of the Giant Mud Crab' and the English-speaking owner hails from Penghu Island. This means you can't go too wrong ordering crab dishes and Penghu specialities like stir-fried rice noodles with pumpkin rice (炒南瓜米線, chǎo nánguā mǐxiàn) and squid balls (花支丸, huāzhīwán).

🍸 Drinking & Nightlife

One Bar
COCKTAIL BAR

(萬吧, Wànbā; Map p252; ☑07-331 3322; 1 Lane 261, Qingnian 1st Rd, 苓雅區青年一路261巷1號; minimum charge NT$300 Mon, Wed & Thu, NT$600 Sat & Sun; ☺bar 8pm-2am Wed-Mon) Similar to the restaurant downstairs, this bar features retro Japanese decor and music. Cocktails are carefully prepared by mixologist Neil.

Hang around long enough and he may let you sample vintage liquors from the owner's collection. The dozen seats fill up quickly on weekends, after which customers are asked to wait downstairs.

Reload   CRAFT BEER

(精釀啤酒, Jīngniáng Píjiǔ; ☑0908-625 739; www.facebook.com/ReloadCraftBeer; 55 Lingquan St, 苓雅區林泉街55號; ⊙3pm-midnight Fri-Wed; Ⓜ Cultural Centre, Exit 3) Young beer connoisseurs from Kaohsiung like to hang out at this spacious taproom and discuss local politics over a strong ale or a light Belgian brew. Reload has beers from all over the world, including refreshing seasonal selections from Taiwan. The owner is ready to explain the features of each and let you sample before ordering.

★ Hsiao Ti Cafe   CAFE

(小堤咖啡, Xiǎodī Kāfēi; Map p252; ☑07-551 4703; 10 Lane 40, Yancheng St, Yancheng District, 鹽埕街40巷10號; coffee NT$100; ⊙8.30am-8.30pm; Ⓜ Yanchengpu, Exit 2) One of Kaohsiung's oldest cafes, Hsiao Ti was started by a Japanese-speaking Taiwanese woman 40 years ago and it seems nothing has changed since then – neither the aromatic siphon coffee nor the artificial flowers and the leather chairs. All you'll be asked is 'Hot or cold?' before being given a glass of water (iced in summer) and a rolled towel.

Hsiao Ti is now run by the owner's younger sister. It's closed the 2nd and 4th Sundays of each month.

Cijin Sunset Bar   BAR

(旗津沙灘吧, Qíjīn Shātān Bā; Map p252; ☑07-571 6120; www.facebook.com/cijinsunset; 1050 Qijin 3rd Rd, Qijin District, 旗津三路1050號; ⊙noon-9pm Sun-Fri, to 10pm Sat) A laid-back bar right on Cijin Beach offering an assortment of craft beers and fresh fruit smoothies. It's great for watching the sunset, especially during happy hour (5pm to 7pm). There are beach parties every Saturday. Details on its Facebook page.

Little Green   WINE BAR

(小綠, Xiǎolǜ; Map p256; ☑07-550 3722; 2 Meishu S 5th St, 鼓山區美術南五街2號; ⊙6pm-1.30am Wed-Mon; Ⓡ Museum of Fine Arts) This classy European-style restaurant is one of the few places in southern Taiwan that sells fine European wine by the glass, with a decent Belgian beer selection to boot. It's a five-minute walk from the Museum of Fine Arts Train Station (not KMRT).

Old Trick   BAR

(老掉牙商行, Lǎodiàoyá Shānghángs; Map p252; ☑07-551 9555; 68 Dayong Rd, 鹽埕區大勇路68號; ⊙7pm-2am Mon-Fri, to 3am Sat & Sun) A warm, jovial place offering good cocktails, craft beer and open frontage. Decor is a light nod to old Kaohsiung with wooden shutters and a calligraphic plaque at the entrance. It's nice to sit out on the pavement when it's not hot. You're welcome to bring your own food.

Shan Ming Teashop   TEAHOUSE

(香茗茶行, Xiāngmíng Cháhángs; Map p252; ☑07-551 4374; 264 Wufu 4th Rd, 鹽埕區五福四路264號; ⊙9am-9pm Mon, Tue & Thu-Sat, 10am-9pm Sun; Ⓜ Yanchengpu, Exit 2) A fragrant teashop offering an assortment of quality loose-leaf teas from Taiwan. If you want to buy, the English-speaking owner can explain their features to you. If you're just thirsty it can sell all kinds of tea drinks (from NT$40) take away, as well as tea-flavoured soft swirl (NT$70).

Ruh Cafe   COFFEE

(路人咖啡, Lùrén Kāfēi; Map p252; ☑07-537 0673; 217 Siwei 3rd Rd, Lingya, 四維三路217號; ⊙10am-8pm Tue-Thu, to 10pm Fri-Sun; Ⓜ Sanduo Shopping District) A laid-back roadside cafe run by musicians. You can sit on the bench outside and play with the cat or ascend a narrow staircase to a quiet apple-green room with tatami mats to read under a whirling fan. The espresso is excellent.

Brickyard   CLUB

(紅磚地窖, Hóngzhuān Dìjiào; Map p252; ☑07-215 0024; www.facebook.com/brickyardclub; 507 Zhongshan 2nd Rd, Qianjin District, 中山二路507號; ⊙9pm-4.30am Wed-Fri, to midnight Sat; Ⓜ Central Park, Exit 2) *The* place for clubbing in Kaohsiung, with a DJ and themed parties almost every night of the week and an international clientele. At the time of research, Thursday was LGBT Night and Friday was Latin Night. See their Facebook page for the latest.

☆ Entertainment

★ National Kaohsiung Centre for the Arts (Weiwuying)   ARTS CENTRE

(衛武營國家藝術文化中心, Wèiwǔyíng Guójiā Yìshù Wénhuà Zhōngxīn; ☑07-262 6666; www.npac-weiwuying.org/?lang=en; 1 Sanduo 1st Rd, Fengshan District, 鳳山區三多一路1號; ⊙11am-9pm; Ⓜ Weiwuying, Exit 6) This 9.9-hectare, Dutch-designed building resembling a giant stingray is the premier centre for art and culture in southern Taiwan. It has a state-of-the-art opera house, a play house, concert

SOUTHERN TAIWAN KAOHSIUNG

and recital halls, and an outdoor theatre. Besides hosting performances by international and Asian troupes, Weiwuying organises activities for the community on a regular basis, like film screenings and workshops.

★ Marsalis Jazz Bar
JAZZ

(馬沙里斯爵士酒館, Mǎshā Lǐsī Juéshì Jiǔguǎn; Map p252; ☏ 07-281 4078; 71 Zhongzheng 4th Rd, 中正四路71號; ⊙ 7pm-2am; ⓜ Formosa Boulevard, Exit 2) A classy jazz bar hosting accomplished musicians from Taiwan and Asia most Fridays and Saturdays, from 8pm to 10pm. Tickets range from NT$400 to NT$800, with a minimum charge of NT$300 on show nights. Marsalis has a branch in Taipei, but this is the original. It's closed on the last Tuesday of every month.

Rocks
LIVE MUSIC

(岩石音樂, Yánshí Yīnyuè; Map p252; www.facebook. com/Rocks-岩石音樂-299848316725349; basement, 219 Juguang St, 鹽埕區莒光街219號B1; ⓜ Yanchengpu) Live-music venue and production studio that sees local and international indie bands performing a few times a month. See their Facebook page for announcements. If nothing special is on, Friday is open jam night.

Paramount Bar
LIVE MUSIC

(百樂門酒館, Bǎilèmén Jiǔ Guǎn; ☏ 07-389 0501; www.facebook.com/paramount.bar; 70 Sanmin 1st Rd, 三民區民族一路70號; tickets NT$300-400; ⊙ 8pm-2am Tue-Sun; 🚌 29, 30, 33) Kaohsiung's premier live-music venue hosts indie acts from Taiwan and Asia several times a week. See monthly schedules on Facebook. Shows usually start at 7.30pm. If nothing's on, go for a drink at the bar – it's open six days a week, very laid-back and offers discounted beer Saturday to Monday.

If taking the bus, disembark at Fruit and Vegetable Market station (果菜公司站; Guǒcài Gōngsī Zhàn) and walk to the bar. If taking the KMRT, the nearest station is Houyi (後驛站). Paramount Bar is roughly 1.7km from Exit 2 of the station.

Mountain Music Station
LIVE MUSIC

(山寨音樂餐廳, Shānzhài Yīnyuè Cāntīng; Map p252; ☏ 07-272 2418; 75 Xinsheng 2nd St, Qianjin District, 新崛二街75號; ⊙ 8pm-4am Wed-Sun; ⓜ City Council, Exit 3) A chill venue where music-industry types hang, and everyone seems to know everyone else. There are performances by indie acts and singer-songwriters from Taiwan and Asia every month; on oth-

er nights indigenous musicians may take to the stage. After leaving the KMRT, walk along Zhongzheng 4th Rd until you pass Zhonghua 3rd Rd. Turn right into Xinsheng 2nd St. Shanzai is near the junction with Ziliheng Rd.

🔒 Shopping

Nan Gua
VINTAGE

(南瓜, Nánguā; Map p252; ☏ 0912-046 397; www. facebook.com/nanguavintage; 3-2 Lane 99, Wufu 4th Rd, 鹽埕區五福四路99巷3-2號; ⊙ 3-9pm Sat & Sun, also by appt; ⓜ Yancheng, Exit 4) A funky vintage shop selling interesting pre-1990s garments, watches and earrings from all over the globe. What we also love is the colourful glass art by the owner and his friends that is for sale.

In Blooom
FASHION & ACCESSORIES

(印花樂, Yìnhuālè; Map p252; ☏ 07-531 3176; www. inblooom.com; 23 Lane 36, Yancheng St, 鹽埕區鹽埕街36巷23號; ⊙ 11am-7pm Mon-Thu, to 8pm Fri-Sun; ⓜ Yanchengpu, Exit 2) A small fabric-art boutique selling lovely bags, garments and souvenir items printed with images native to Taiwan; in particular, the island's flora and fauna. You can also try your hand at printing your own bag or T-shirt in the workshop upstairs, with a variety of patterns and colours to choose from.

TaKao Books
BOOKS

(三餘書店, Sānyú Shūdiàn; ☏ 07-225 3080; www. facebook.com/takaobooks214; 214 Zhongzheng 2nd Rd, 中正二路214號; ⊙ 1.30-9pm Wed-Mon; ⓜ Cultural Centre, Exit 3) A delightful bookshop strong in the arts and humanities. Most books are in Mandarin, but there are photography titles in English as well as CDs of music and poetry by Taiwan singer-songwriters. Literary and music events are held in the cafe upstairs. The site used to be a guava plantation and this building was one of the earliest on Zhongzheng Rd.

Bandon Stationery Store
STATIONERY

(本東倉庫商店, Běndōng Cāngkù Shāngdiàn; Map p252; ☏ 07-521 9587; 14-1 Guangrong St, Yancheng, 光榮街14-1號; ⊙ 10am-7pm) Who says pens and erasers are obsolete? All the kinds of stationery that a kid has ever dreamed of owning – you'll find them here, including retro items. The shop is perpetually crammed with excited children and tired parents. In between bouts of browsing, there's reasonably priced beer, ice cream and quick meals (sold near the entrance) to keep everyone happy.

He Tai
FOOD & DRINKS

(合泰, Hétài; Map p252; 211-1 Jianguo 4th Rd, 鹽埕區建國四路211-1號; ⊙9am-6pm Mon-Fri, to 5pm Sat, to noon Sun; Ⓜ Yanchengpu, Exit 2) This old shop makes unbleached winter-melon sugar (冬瓜糖, dōngguā táng) and snacks. The sugar can be consumed as sweets, added to tea, or melted in hot water with a splash of lemon juice or milk for a refreshing drink. Winter melon purifies the body in Chinese medicine. Take care you don't trip on the giant gourds near the entrance.

Wuguan Books
BOOKS

(無關實驗店, Wúguān Shíyàn Shūdiàn; Map p252; ☑07-531 8813; 2-1 Dayi St, 鹽埕區大義街2-1號; ⊙2-8pm Tue-Fri, 11am-8pm Sat & Sun; Ⓜ Yenchangpu) You'd think you've stumbled into a bar or a mysterious Buddhist cave, but no, this is a bookshop. Save for dots of light on individual tomes, this quirky place is pitch black. The 500 titles and handful of lifestyle products focus loosely on erotica, which apparently also means textbooks for learning Mandarin, alongside *Madame Bovary*, strapless bras and sex toys.

Entry limited to those 18 and over.

Sanfong Central Street
MARKET

(三鳳中街, Sānfèng Zhōngjiē; Map p252; Sanfong Central St, 三鳳中街; ⊙8.30am-10pm; Ⓜ Kaohsiung Main Station) Kaohsiung's largest grocery wholesale market, the southern equivalent of Taipei's Dihua St, is here in Sanmin District, near Kaohsiung Main Station. The youngest shop in this atmospheric arcade has been here for over two decades; the oldest, two generations. You can buy all manner of cheap traditional goods here, from incense sticks to dried cuttlefish.

ⓘ Getting There & Away

AIR
Kaohsiung airport (高雄國際機場; www.kia.gov.tw; 2 Zhongshan 4th Rd, 中山四路2號), sometimes known as Siaogang airport, is 9kms south of the city and connects seamlessly to the city centre by KMRT (Kaohsiung Mass Rapid Transit). Domestic and international terminals are joined and you can quickly walk from one to the other.

Kaohsiung airport has domestic flights to Kinmen and Penghu. Uni Air (www.uniair.com.tw) and Daily Air Corporation (www.dailyair.com.tw) fly from here. Internationally, there are flights to most Southeast Asian countries, Japan, Korea and China. EVA (www.evaair.com) and China Airlines (www.china-airlines.com) fly from here.

There are visitor information centres in the domestic and international terminals. Staff speak passable English and can help with hotels, tours, MRT travel, car rentals etc.

BOAT
Taiwan Navigation Company (台灣航業; www.tnc-kao.com.tw/about.aspx) runs year-round boats from Kaohsiung to Makung, Penghu Island (NT$860, 4½ hours). The schedule changes every three months and is unreliable in winter. It's best to go directly to the ticketing office to check the schedule and buy tickets on the spot. Boats depart from Gushan Ferry Terminal.

BUS
Kaohsiung Ke Yuan (高雄客運; Map p252; ☑07-237 1230; www.ksbus.com.tw; 245 Nanhua Rd, 南華路245號) has buses to Donggang (NT$141, 50 to 70 minutes, every 30 minutes, 8.30am to 5.45pm), Foguangshan (NT$80, 40 minutes, eight per day), Kenting (every 30 minutes from 9am to 7pm) by Kenting Express (NT$392, two hours) or regular bus (NT$352, three hours), and to Meinong (NT$136, 1½ hours, hourly).

Kuo Kuang Bus Company near Kaohsiung Train Station has buses to Taipei (NT$590, five hours, every half-hour, 24 hours) and Taitung (NT$540, 3½ hours, 3am, 7am, 12.30pm and 5.30pm).

TRAIN
Kaohsiung is the terminus for most west-coast trains. Trains run frequently from early morning until midnight to Taipei (fast/slow NT$843/650, five/seven hours) and Taichung (NT$469/301, 2½/4½ hours).

There is a High Speed Rail (HSR) line from Zuoying station to Taipei every 15 minutes (NT$1490, 1½ to two hours).

ⓘ Getting Around

TO/FROM THE AIRPORT
Taking the KMRT Red Line to the airport and Zuoying HSR costs NT$35. Taxis to the airport or Zuoying HSR cost NT$320 from the city centre.

BOAT
Ferries run from 5am to 2am between the **Gushan Ferry Terminal** (鼓山渡船站，西子灣渡輪站, Gǔshān Mǎtóu; Map p252; 109 Binhai Rd, 濱海路109號) and the **Cijin Ferry Terminal** (旗津碼頭; Map p252; ☑07-571 7442; 10 Hai'an Rd, Cijin Island, 海岸路10號); the trip takes 10 minutes and tickets cost NT$40.

There is also a new ferry route to Cijin Island from **Warehouse 2** (棧貳庫旗津碼頭; Map p252; 17 Penglai Rd, 蓬萊路17號) of Pier-2 Art Center, running every half-hour between 11am and 8pm on weekends and holidays, daily in July and August.

TEMPLE TOURING ON THE SOUTHWEST COAST

The southwest coast contains some of the most ancient temples in Taiwan. In most cases these centre on the stars of southern folk faith: Mazu and Wang Yeh (the Royal Lords, general protectors).

Two of Taiwan's most historically important temples are at Luermen. It is well worth listening to the detailed English audio guides at both if you want to understand the history and know who's who. The massive Luermen Mazu Temple (鹿耳門天后宮; Lùěrmén Tiānhòugōng), is close to Koxinga's alleged landing spot during his campaign against the Dutch. The large Mazu statue in the main worship hall is one of Taiwan's oldest and was reportedly brought to Taiwan by Koxinga himself on his battleship in 1661. The roof of the temple is crammed with gorgeous examples of glue-and-paste shard art and cornice decorations. Ascend to the upper floor of the galleries flanking the main courtyard for a closer look.

Close by the Mazu Temple is the Orthodox Luermen Mazu Temple (聖母廟; Shèngmǔ Miào), which, unusually for a Taiwanese temple, is modelled after the Forbidden City in Beijing. The highlight here is an ancient boat on the left of the main hall, said to have drifted from Fujian in China to Tainan in 1913. Both temples are located near the Sihcao Dazhong Temple (四草大眾廟; Sìcǎo Dàzhòng Miào) and can be reached by bike.

Two temples off Provincial Hwy 19 are worth the effort to find if you have any interest in traditional temple arts. The Zhenxing Temple (振興宮; Zhènxīng Gōng) in Jiali (佳里), just past the Km119 mark, contains some fantastic tableaux of figures in *jiǎnnián* (mosaic-like temple decoration). However, these figures are not on the roof, as is usual, but on the sides of the entrance portico.

At the front of the temple, check out the unique cochin (brightly coloured, glazed ceramic) figures of an old man and woman crouching as if to support crossbeams. They were created by **Master Yeh Wang** (交趾陶館, Jiāozhǐtáo Guǎn; Map p226; 275 Zhongxiao Rd, 忠孝路275號; ⊙9am-noon & 1.30-5pm Wed-Sun; ☎7320) **FREE** and are called *The Fool Crouching to Raise the House*.

About 5km north of Jiali, in the town of Xuejia (學甲), the Ciji Temple (p276) protects more of the remaining works of Master Yeh Wang. The beautiful works are collected in a four-storey museum beside the temple. Ciji itself is a lovely southern-style temple, with a graceful swallowtail roof, and stonework and woodcarvings from the 19th century.

From Xuejia, head coastwards for Provincial Hwy 17 and you'll reach Nankunshen Temple (南鯤鯓代天府; Nánkūnshēn Dàitiān Fǔ) within 15 minutes. Established in 1662, this massive temple is the centre of Wang Yeh worship (don't confuse these gods with Master Yeh Wang). Don't miss the ornate caisson ceilings and the 6.6m-high golden tablet in the main hall.

On most Sundays the temple explodes with exuberant displays of ritual devotion: there are fireworks, parades and chanting. If possible, try to visit during the Welcoming Festival for Wang Yeh (end of the third lunar month).

Eccentric Madou Temple (麻豆代天府; Mádòu Dàitiānfǔ) is in Madou (麻豆), 15km southeast of Xuejia. What you see today comes from after 1956 (the original temple dates back to the Ming dynasty) and many Tainanese can claim a common childhood memory of receiving an unorthodox moral education inside the garish, gigantic dragon behind the main temple. To re-create what they went through, pay NT$50 to go to hell from the dragon's tail, or to ascend to heaven from its mouth. This hell is the last of two such Infernos remaining in Taiwan, the other being the bizarre Nantian Temple (p233) in Changhua.

You can also cruise along Love River on boat rides (25-minute rides are NT$150, and run from 3pm to 10pm on weekdays, and 9am to 10pm on Saturday and Sunday). There are two piers: **Ren'ai Pier** (愛河仁愛站, Aihé Rénài Zhàn; Map p252; 150 Hexi Rd, 河西路150號) and **Guobin**

Pier (愛河國賓站, Aihé Guóbīn Zhàn; Map p252; 178 Hedong Rd, 河東路178號).

BUS

The city has a decent bus system that ties in with the KMRT. The bus hub is directly in front of the train station, and buses have English signage at the front and electronic English displays inside indicating the next stop.

Routes are clearly mapped in English at every KMRT station, and a one-zone fare is NT$12.

LIGHT-RAIL

The first phase of Kaohsiung's Spanish-designed light-rail system (LRT) is now in operation, running from Hamasen, and connecting with the MRT at Sizihwan and Kaisyuan stations, in a residential area north east of the port. This first section runs along the waterfront, through the Pier-2 Art Center (p253), and is a good way to see the southeastern end of the harbour and the major construction projects under way there.

Once complete, the light-rail system will form a circular route connecting areas not currently serviced by the MRT. Tickets are NT$30 per trip.

TAXI

In Kaohsiung, the taxi hotline is ☑ 0800 087 778 or ☑ 07-315 6666. If you have safety concerns, call for a cab – all calls are recorded and saved for one month.

TRAINS

Kaohsiung's public-transit network, the MRT (www.krtco.com.tw), is handy for visitors, going to all of the main spots that travellers want to visit. Trains generally run 6am to midnight and abundant English signs and maps make the system easy to use.

Individual fares start at NT$20 and can be purchased at every station. A day pass costs NT$180 – buy directly from any staffed station booth. A MRT/ferry (Gushan–Cijin) combo ticket is NT$90.

Meinong

☑ 07 / POP 40,776

In 1736 the intrepid Lin brothers led the first Hakka immigrants to settle the plains of Meinong (美濃; Měinóng). While the Hakka make up about 15% of the population of Taiwan, in Meinong the percentage today is around 95%. The Hakka of Meinong can count a disproportionate number of PhDs (and in the past, imperial scholars) among their population; the vestiges of their glory are manifested in the elegant courtyard houses and temples, and on display in the Hakka museum (p270).

Thoroughly rural in character, and once the centre of a well-protected tobacco industry, Meinong was hit hard by Taiwan's entry into the World Trade Organization (WTO) in 2002. With the monopoly system abolished, the town refashioned itself into a country retreat. Hakka culture, historic sites, local

cuisine and butterfly-watching became the cornerstones of the new economy.

Winter is a great time to visit, as it is warm and dry and tourists are few. Summer is the season of the yellow butterflies.

◉ Sights

Guangshan Temple   TAOIST TEMPLE

(廣善堂, Guǎngshàn Táng; ☑ 07-681 2124; 281 Fumei Rd, 福美路281號) This showpiece of a southern temple, complete with beautiful swallowtail roof, was constructed by Gu A-jhen and 12 other local worthies in 1918. If you walk past the front halls to the back, you'll see the oldest hall built 100 years ago with four large characters in calligraphic script on its walls – 忠 (loyalty), 孝 (filial piety), 廉 (integrity) and 節 (perseverance).

Qishan Old Street   AREA

(旗山老街, Qíshān Lǎojiē; Zhongshan Rd, Sec 11, 中山路一段11號) This charming old street has tonnes of snack and dessert shops tucked into faux-baroque facades and crumbling Fujian-style courtyard houses, as well as newer structures. A highlight is the old Qishan Train Station, in a quaint Tudor style. Qishan Old Street was once a lively marketplace for bananas. Plenty are sold here still – the valley is full of banana plantations.

Qishan Living Cultural Park   HISTORIC SITE

(旗山生活文化園區, Qíshān Shēnghuó Wénhuà Yuánqū; 7 Wenzhong Rd, Qishan, 旗山區文中路7號; ◔9am-6pm; ☑) This Japanese western-style complex was a primary school for Japanese children built in 1912. The nicely restored classrooms and offices now house child-friendly exhibitions such as the one we saw on the area's banana farmers of yesteryear. There is also a lovely cafe that sells sumptuous banana pastries and fresh-fruit popsicles.

Old Meinong Police Station   HISTORIC BUILDING

(舊美濃警察分駐所, Jiù Měinóng Jǐngchá Fēnzhù Suǒ; 212 Yong'an Rd, 永安路212號; ◔9am-5pm; ☑) This handsome western-style building (1933) across from the old bridge (美濃舊橋, Měinóng Jiùqiáo; 213 Yong'an Rd, 永安路213號) used to be Meinong's political and financial centre. It's now run by Meinong Hakka Culture Museum (p270). The low Japanese-style dormitory at the back is a children's reading hall.

Meinong Hakka Culture Museum   MUSEUM

(美濃客家文物館, Měinóng Kèjiā Wénwù Guǎn; 49-3 Minzu Rd, 民族路49-3號; adult/concession

SOUTHERN TAIWAN MEINONG

Meinong

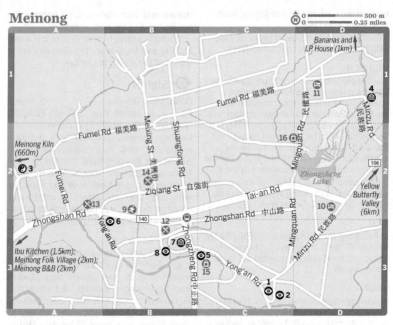

0 ————— 500 m
0 ————— 0.25 miles

Bananas and
LP House (1km)

Fumei Rd 福美路

Meinong Kiln
(660m)

Fumei Rd 福美路

Zhongzheng
Lake

106

Yellow
Butterfly
Valley
(6km)

Ziqiang St 自強街

Tai-an Rd

Zhongshan Rd

Zhongshan Rd 中山路

Ibu Kitchen (1.5km);
Meinong Folk Village (2km);
Meinong B&B (2km)

Yong'an Rd

Meinong

◎ Sights
1	Earth God Shrine	C3
2	East Gate	C3
3	Guangshan Temple	A2
4	Meinong Hakka Culture Museum	D1
5	Meinong Old Bridge	C3
6	Minongzhuang Oblation Furnace	B3
7	Old Meinong Police Station	B3
8	Yong'an Road	B3

❸ Activities, Courses & Tours
9	A Lin Bicycle Shop	B2

⊜ Sleeping
	Guangshan Temple	(see 3)
10	Lin Home	D2
11	Renzi Shanzhuang	D1

⊗ Eating
12	A Hai Bantiao Dian	B3
13	Meinong Traditional Hakka Restaurant	A2
14	Meixing Street	B2

⊜ Shopping
15	Jing Shing Blue Shirts Shop	C3
16	Kuang Chin Sheng Paper Umbrella	C2

NT$40/20; ☺9am-5pm Tue-Sun) Using videos and displays of tools used by the Hakka, this museum helps you to understand the Hakka's migration from mainland China to Taiwan, and how they made a living. There's a small section on the upper floor devoted to artists and musicians of Hakka descent such as singer-songwriter Lin Sheng-xiang (林生祥).

Yong'an Road
STREET

(永安路, Yŏngān Lù) This was the first street in Meinong, and some of the oldest family residences can still be found in the narrow back alleys.

Just behind the **East Gate** (東門, Dōng-mén; junction btwn Dongmen St & Minzu Rd, 東門街和民族路口) at the end of the street is a famous **Bogong shrine** (伯公神壇, Bógōng Shéntán; 496-6 Fumei Rd, 美濃富美路496巷6號旁), dedicated to the Earth God and especially popular among the Hakka. In old Hakka style no statue is used, just a stone tablet and incense. There are over 400 Bogong shrines around Meinong, but this is the most valued. Bow three times to this or any other shrine to bring peace to your life.

Meinong residents have long placed a high premium on book learning. Oblation furnaces such as the 18th-century **Minong-zhuang Oblation Furnace** (瀰濃庄敬字亭, Mínnóngzhuāng Jìngzìtíng; junction btwn Zhong-shan Rd & Yong'an Rd, 中山路與永安路交叉口) at the start of Yong'an Rd were designed to dispose of paper that contained written text, thus signifying the paper's exalted status.

Yellow Butterfly Valley

AREA

(黃蝶翠谷, Huángdié Cuìgǔ) Late spring and summer are the best time to visit the valley. Over 100 butterfly species can be found here, and the chances of having a dozen species flittering about you at any moment are high. In late July you may see half a million individuals within a couple of hectares of open riverbed and the surrounding forest.

The valley is 7km northeast of central Meinong. Head north from Minzu Rd and follow the English signs to the valley.

Activities

A Lin Bicycle Shop

CYCLING

(阿麟的店, Ā Lín De Diàn; ☎07-681 0096; 166 Zhongshan Rd, Sec 1, 美濃區中山路一段166號; 3/5hr NT$100/150) Meinong's most-popular bicycle shop. Boss Lin also likes art, as you'll see from his shop. Call before you go as he keeps irregular opening hours.

Sleeping

Renzi Shanzhuang

HOMESTAY $

(人子山莊, Rénzǐ Shānzhuāng; ☎07-682 2159; www.5658.com.tw/range2; 66-5 Mingquan Rd, 民權路66-5號; r NT$2500; ⊕❋🕏🐾) The rooms here won't blow you away, but you may enjoy the house and the decor designed by the hosts – an art teacher and her photographer partner. The couple give art classes and tours, or you can explore on your own using their beautiful hand-drawn map. You can bring your dog for an extra $200 cleaning fee; let them know ahead of time.

Remember to bring your own soap and shampoo.

Guangshan Temple

HOSTEL $

(廣善堂, Guǎngshàn Táng; ☎07-681 2124; 281 Fumei Rd, 福美路281號; s/d NT$800/1000; ⊕❋) This pretty temple has a small and basic pilgrim's house where you can stay if you reserve in advance.

★ Bananas and LP House

B&B $$

(香蕉與黑膠民宿, Xiāngjiāo yǔ Hēijiāo Mínsù; ☎0912-823 556; www.facebook.com/美濃山下-香蕉與黑膠三合院-1440393262869551; 34 Lane 112, Xinglong 1st St, 興隆一街112巷34號; d NT$3600; ⊕❋🕏) A elegant courtyard house with simple, tasteful rooms, and a remarkable collection of 5000 vinyl records. It is sandwiched photogenically between low hills and rice paddies, and the scenery is best before mid-May when the rice is harvested. The house, a former tobacco factory, was remodelled by the Zhongs, a warm and lovely family whom you'll meet during your stay.

The rate includes a delectable breakfast prepared by the owners.

Lin Home

HOMESTAY $$

(林家民宿陶坊, Línjiā Mínsù Táofang; ☎0921-245 800; www.facebook.com/LinHouseMeiNong; 53-7 Minzu Rd, 民族路53-7號; d incl breakfast from NT$1800; ⊕❋🕏) This B&B with a pottery workshop has four modern rooms inside an elegant replica of a Hakka courtyard complex. Bikes are free for guests. There is no English signage, but the entrance is lined with pottery. Advance booking a must.

Meinong B&B

B&B $$

(戀戀美濃民宿, Liànliàn Měinóng Mínsù; ☎07-681 3737; www.facebook.com/Meinongbnb; 679 Zhongshan 2nd Rd, 中山路679號; d from NT$2000; ⊕❋🕏) Five spacious and relaxing rooms featuring luxurious stone bathtubs ('spa') and views of rice paddies or flower fields. Rates dip below NT$2000 on weekdays off-season. Complimentary breakfast is served include in the attractive cafe on the ground floor.

Eating

Meixing Street

HAKKA $

(美興街, Měixìng Jiē; noodles from NT$40) This street in central Meinong is lined up with *bantiao* (flat-rice noodles, 炒粄條, chǎo bǎntiáo) joints and each has a different recipe. A Hai Bantiao Dian is a local favourite.

A Hai Bantiao Dian

TAIWANESE $

(阿海粄條店, Ā Hǎi Bǎntiáo Diàn; ☎07-681 6689; 43 Meixing St, 美興街43號; noodles NT$50, dishes from NT$100; ◷10am-8pm Thu-Mon) Locals say this is the best *bantiao* shop on Meixing St. The noodles, made the traditional way, are indeed delicious. There's also an assortment of other dishes such as Hakka stir-fry (客家小炒, kèjiā xiǎochǎo), and a rather unusual savoury peanut-tofu pudding called 花生豆腐 (huāshēng dòufu).

Meinong Traditional Hakka Restaurant

HAKKA $

(美濃古老客家菜, Měinóng Gǔlǎo Kèjiā Cài; ☎07-681 1156; 362-5 Zhongshan Rd, Sec 1, 中山路一段362-5號; dishes NT$130-300; ◷9am-2pm & 5-9pm) A proper sit-down restaurant favoured by families, this busy place dishes out simple bowls of stirfried *bantiao* noodles (flat-rice noodles, 炒粄條, chǎo bǎntiáo) and other

STOPPING BY THE MOON

If you are on the way to Meinong from Tainan, the geopark **Tianliao Moon World** (田寮月世界, Tiánliáo Yuèshìjiè; 36 Yueqiu Rd, Chongde village, 崇德里月球路36號; ⊙10am-5pm), off Hwy 28 in Tianliao, will give you a taste of a very different landscape. The strange-looking badlands reminiscent of the moon's surface may make you wish you'd paid attention in geography class.

It's especially worth a visit if you're breaking for lunch – there are many local chicken restaurants nearby.

famous Hakka treats, such as the mouthwatering but artery-clogging *méigān kòuròu* (梅干扣肉), succulent fatty pork on dried leaf mustard).

Ibu Kitchen TAIWANESE INDIGENOUS $$
(阿香的厨房, Axiàng dí Chúfáng; ☑07-681 7212; www.facebook.com/ibu.kitchen; 635 Zhongshan Rd, Sec 2, 中山路二段635號; set meals for 2 NT$800; ⊙11am-1.30pm & 5.30-8.30pm Wed-Mon) 🍴 Rustic Ibu is a specialist in indigenous cuisine and a worthy one at that. Ingredients are sourced from surrounding hills – fresh mushrooms for soup, tart plums sweetened into plum sauce and eaten with tofu, and zesty mountain pepper (馬告, *mǎgào*) to add to steamed mullet. It's insanely busy at lunch so make a reservation or be there at 11am.

🔒 Shopping

★ Kuang Chin Sheng Paper Umbrella ARTS & CRAFTS
(廣進勝紙傘, Guǎngjìn Shèng Zhǐsǎn; ☑07-681 3247; 47 Mingquan Rd, 民權路47號; paper umbrellas NT$600-3500; ⊙9am-5pm; 🚗) This shop in a courtyard house is the Louis Vuitton of Taiwanese oil-paper umbrellas. It was founded during Japanese rule and appeared on the cover of an American magazine in 1976. The umbrellas feature intricate paintings of Meinong, cherry blossoms, and water fowl in bright but balanced palettes. It's real craftsmanship at work here.

The most expensive parasols take two days to make and have a drying time of seven days. Prior to that the bamboo is soaked in water for over a month to remove the sugar content. Persimmon oil is brushed onto paper to make it waterproof. Children can paint their

own umbrellas on the spot – it's NT$100 for a plain mini-umbrella and paints.

Jing Shing Blue Shirts Shop CLOTHING
(錦興行藍衫店, Jǐnxīngxíng Lánshāndiàn; ☑07-681 1191; 177 Yong'an Rd, 永安路177號; ⊙9am-5pm) This little family-run shop opened in the 1930s making traditional Hakka-style indigo clothing and accessories. A loose-fitting shirt costs NT$3000.

Meinong Kiln HOMEWARES
(美濃窯, Měinóng Yáo; ☑07-681 7873; www.meinung.com.tw; 496-6 Fumei Rd, 福美路496巷6號; ⊙9am-5pm) A large compound with a tile-making factory, a cafe, and a shop selling ceramic sculptures, tableware, crockery and vases for NT$50 to NT$2 million. Some of the larger pieces were made by artist Chu Pan-hsiung (朱邦雄), who's known for his public murals, including the one gracing Kaohsiung's Qiaotou station.

Meinong Folk Village ARTS & CRAFTS
(美濃民俗村, Měinóng Mínsú Cūn; ☑07-681 7508; 80 Lane 421, Zhongshan Rd, Sec 2, 中山路二段421巷80號; ⊙8.30am-5pm, to 6pm Sat & Sun) FREE This artificial re-creation of an old-fashioned neighbourhood is definitely touristy, but you can still watch traditional crafts being made, sample Hakka *lei cha* (擂茶, *léi chá*, pounded tea), and purchase well-made paper umbrellas, fans and bamboo baskets.

❶ Getting There & Around

Buses on route E28, between Meinong (美濃車站, Měinóng Chēzhàn; 11 Zhongshan Rd, Sec 1, 中山路一段11號) and Kaohsiung (NT$136, 1½ hours), run hourly.

If you're driving from Kaohsiung, get on National Hwy 1; after 4.5km, exit and from Yanping Rd (延平路) in Qishan District (旗山區), follow Provincial Hwy 184 (甲) until you reach Zhongshan Rd in Meinong.

Meinong is small but the surrounding countryside is expansive and you'll need a vehicle or bicycle to get around. B&B owners may be able to help you hire a scooter.

Tainan

☑06 / POP 1,886,000

You'll almost certainly receive looks of jealousy from any Taiwanese person if you mention you're going to Tainan (台南), and it's not hard to see why. Traditional culture continues to thrive here, in the oldest city in

Taiwan. The name 'Taiwan' was once used to refer to Dayuan (大員), the former name of Anping where the Dutch fort is located. Inside temples, *bwah bwey* (moon blocks, 搏杯) are cast to determine the best course of action, as it was done hundreds of years ago. Outside, young Tainanese show off their art and make coffee in former canalside houses. Tainanese are fastidious about their food, and a number of dishes are exclusive to the region (but renowned all over the island).

Tainan is best visited in winter: it's warm (in the high-20°Cs) and dry, but there are few tourists. Traditional festival days are, of course, a great time to come, as are the local birthdays of temple gods.

History

Before the Dutch, the majority of inhabitants in the Tainan area were indigenous peoples. After being booted off Penghu by the Ming dynasty, the Dutch established Tainan as an operational base from which the Dutch East India Company (VOC) engaged in trade with Japan and China. However, unable to persuade the Taiwanese to grow rice and sugar for export, and unable to persuade Dutch rulers to allow immigration, the VOC looked to China for cheap labour and began encouraging Fujianese to migrate to the Tainan area.

When the Ming loyalist Zheng Chenggong aka Koxinga defeated the Dutch, he established a central government in Tainan and started building up the city (a project later continued by his sons). Koxinga's son constructed Taiwan's first Confucian temple (p277), helping to establish Tainan as a cultural and educational centre.

In 1683, when the Qing dynasty gained control of Taiwan, Tainan was chosen as the capital. The city remained the political, cultural and economic centre under the Qing, but lost this status in 1919 when the Japanese moved their colonial capital to Taipei, which meant Tainan managed to dodge the fate of being overdeveloped by the new government. To the discerning eye, Tainan's pedigree is apparent from the stately quality of the city's temples and historic sites.

Modern Tainan has industries producing metals, textiles and machinery, and old masters working on traditional crafts, as well as a science park (in former Tainan county) that promises to bring the region into the avant-garde of Taiwan's high-tech revolution. Tainan city and county merged into one municipal area in 2009.

◉ Sights

Most of the sights in Tainan are concentrated around the city centre west of the train station and in the Anping district. Both areas are compact enough to get around on foot, though you may want a taxi or bus to take you from one area to the other.

★ Grand Mazu Temple   TAOIST TEMPLE
(大天后宮, Dà Tiānhòu Gōng; 18 Lane 227, Yongfu Rd, Sec 2, 永福路二段227巷18號; ⊙ 5.30am-9pm; 🚌 2, 5, 7, 11, 14) This lively temple once served as the palace of Ning Jin, the last king of the Ming dynasty. If you wish to confirm visually that a king's status is lower than an emperor's, count the steps to the shrine. There are only seven; an emperor would get nine.

Right before the king's death, the palace was converted to a Mazu temple according to his last wish. Some features to note include the 300-year-old Mazu statue and, in the back, the shrine to Mazu's parents in an area that used to be the king's bedroom. Look up and you'll see the roof beam from which the king's concubines hanged themselves so many years ago; those women are honoured in the Wufei Temple (p281).

★ Thousand Fields Seed Museum   MUSEUM
(千畦種子博物館, Qiānqí Zhǒngzǐ Bówùguǎn; ☑ 06-236 0035; www.facebook.com/QianQiZhong ZiGuan; 29-1 Lane 451, Dongfeng Rd; 東豐路451巷29-1號; NT$100; ⊙ 10am-noon & 1.30-5.30pm, by appt only) This horticultural Eden is a home with a fantastical garden overrun with plants, and seeds, seeds, seeds – some 500 species, most endemic to southern Taiwan, stuffed in jars, strewn all over shelves and tables, and hanging from wooden beams. You'll see the electric blue of traveller's palm seeds, and get to dab annatto seeds on your cheeks for rouge as women in the past had done. Visit is strictly by appointment only.

Call a couple of days in advance. The admission fee includes a half-tour tour in Mandarin by the owner Mr Liang. For tours led by Mr Liang's English-speaking son, make contact at least 10 days in advance; it's NT$6000 for a group of five.

The beautiful gift shop on the premises carries jewellery made with seeds, soaps, hydrosols (flower waters) and teas.

★ National Museum of Taiwan Literature   MUSEUM
(國家台灣文學館, Guójiā Táiwān Wénxué Guǎn; ☑ 06-221 7201; www.nmtl.gov.tw; 1 Zhongzheng Rd,

Central Tainan

SOUTHERN TAIWAN

0 ——— 500 m
0 ——— 0.25 miles

Thousand Fields
Seed Museum
(650m)

Hsiao Rd

Lin'an Rd

Minsheng Rd

Tainan River

Fuqian Rd

Yunghua Rd

Jinhua Rd

Jiankang Rd

Ximen Rd

Xialin Rd

Zhongzheng Rd

Zhengxing St

You Ai St

Minsheng Rd

Minguan Rd

Yongfu Rd

Shennong Street

Grand Mazu Temple

Guohua St

Hai'an Rd

Minzu Rd

Chenggong Rd

Gongyuan Rd

Zhongshan Rd

Minzu Rd

Chenggong Rd

CPC Gas
Station

National Cheng Kung
University Hospital (1km)

Cyanfeng Rd

Tainan
Train Station

Linsen Rd

Dongning Rd

Changrong Rd

Linsen Rd

Siaodong Rd

Dasyue Rd

Sheng Li Rd

Sheng Li Rd

Chingtung St

Qingnian Rd

Dongmen Rd

Beimen Rd

Fuqian Rd

Kaishan Rd

Datong Rd

Wufei Rd

Chingzhong St

Shulin St – Sec 2

Jianye St

Nanmen Rd

Zhongyi Rd

Zhongyi Rd

National
Museum of
Taiwan
Literature

City God
Temple

Lane 79,
Zhongshan Rd

182

20

National Cheng Kung

Central Tainan

中正路1號; ⊙9am-6pm Tue-Sun) **FREE** This serious and excellent museum details the development of Taiwanese literature from the time of the pre-Han indigenous peoples to the modern era. Textual explanations are supplemented by original manuscripts, readings, video footage and literary relics. There's a large hall showcasing 'mother-tongue literary works', which includes works in Hakka, Taiwanese and indigenous dialects. The museum is housed in a gorgeous piece of Japanese-colonial architecture that was once the Tainan District Hall, which goes to show the importance the Taiwanese give their literature.

There are free audio tours for visitors in English. Enquire at the service counter. The museum is a 1.3km walk along Zhongshan Rd from Tainan Train Station.

★ **City God Temple**   TAOIST TEMPLE
(城隍廟, Chénghuáng Miào; 133 Qingnian Rd, 青年路133號; 🚌2, 5, 6, 7, 15) When you enter the temple, look up for the two large abacuses used to calculate whether you have done more good than bad in life; check out the most famous words ever written on a temple plaque in Taiwan: '爾來了' or 'You're here at last'. Nonchalant words in a wild and

formidable script that may evoke fear, unease, relief or joy, depending on how you've lived your life.

The City God (Chenghuang), officially the protector of towns, also tallies this life's good and bad deeds after we die. It is therefore not unusual that his image appears in the last chamber of Dongyue Temple (p281), which is dedicated to the underworld, nor that these two temples sit near each other.

In the worship hall, look for pink slips of paper on the altar. They're from students asking for help to pass an exam. Yep, school is hell everywhere.

★ **Shennong Street** AREA

(神農街, Shénnóng Jiē) Cafes, art galleries, fashion boutiques and B&Bs have flowered in the hub of Tainan's former Five Canals (p280) area, taking full advantage of the long, narrow, loft-like spaces in the former canalside shophouses. Wedged among them are small shop-sized temples, traditional workshops and crumbling homes. The 90m Shennong St is book-ended by the King of Medicine Temple (p281) to the west and the Water Fairy Temple (p281) inside a market to the east.

★ **Ciji Temple Museum** MUSEUM

(慈濟宮葉王交趾陶文化館, Cíjì Gōng Yèwáng Jiāozhǐ Táo Wénhuàguǎn; ☑06-783 6110; www.tcgs. org.tw/treasure_koji.html; 170 Jisheng Rd, Xuejia, 濟生路170號; ⊙8.30am-noon & 2-5pm Tue-Sun) FREE In focus here is Koji pottery that is used to embellish roof ridges and walls by sculptor Ye Wang (1826–87). The first such artist to be born in Taiwan (in Chiayi), Ye took inspiration from history, classical novels and folktales, and this is the largest collection of his works in Taiwan. You'll also see the intricate glass and ceramic appliqué works of southern Chinese master He Jinlong (1878–1945), as well as temple plaques and doors, and ancient garments. The museum is part of Xuejia Ciji Temple.

Xuejia Ciji Temple TEMPLE

(學甲慈濟宮, Xuéjiǎ Cíjì Gōng; www.tcgs.org. tw; 170 Jisheng Rd, Xuejia, 濟生路170號; ⊙6am-9.30pm) The magnificent Ciji Temple in the town centre of Xuejia worships the God of Doctors (保生大帝; Bosheng Dadi), a deified medical practitioner from Fujian who was well versed in acupuncture and herbal remedies. The temple was originally raised in 1701 and subsequent restorations resulted in the addition of exquisite artwork by Taiwanese and Chinese masters. You can see wonderful examples of Koji pottery, ceramic appliqué and wild cursive script both inside and at the Ciji Temple Museum.

Chuan Mei Theatre THEATRE

(全美戲院, Quánměi Xìyuàn; 187 Yongfu Rd, Sec 2, 永福路二段187號; ☑14) This old second-run theatre (1950) is worth a look for the movie posters created by Master Yan Jhen-fa, the last such painter in Taiwan. You can see Hollywood's superheroes in their 2D glory above the entrance. Master Yan's workshop is just across the road and he is often spotted working on the footpath. The half-blind artist (b 1962) was invited by Gucci to paint a wall for the luxury brand in Taipei.

Chuan Mei Theatre was mentioned by award-winning Taiwanese director Ang Lee (*Crouching Tiger, Hidden Dragon*; *Brokeback Mountain*) as the place that nurtured his interest in filmmaking as a young man.

Tainan Art Museum Bldg 2 MUSEUM

(台南美術館2館, Táinán Měishùguǎn Èrguǎn; www.tnam.museum; 1 Zhongyi Rd, Sec 2, 中西區忠義路二段1號; ⊙9am-5pm Sun-Tue & Thu, to 9pm Fri & Sat) Created by Japanese architect and Pritzker Prize–winner Ban Shigeru, Building 2 of the Tainan Art Museum has a dozen galleries spread over five floors. The white, eye-catching structure atop flights of steps, has a pentagon-shaped roof and stacked spaces offering different touring routes. It hosts shows by Taiwanese and overseas artists, with an emphasis on southern Taiwanese masters. At the time of research, the exhibition 'Taiwan Panegyric' was on.

Tainan Art Museum MUSEUM

(台南市美術館, Táinán Shì Měishùguǎn; www. tnam.museum; 37 Nanmen Rd, 中西區南門路37號; ⊙9am-5pm Sun-Tue & Thu, to 9pm Fri & Sat; ☑1, 2, 6) Both buildings of the Tainan Art Museum are now open – this one (Building 1), the former Tainan City Police Station raised in the Japanese era; and the sleek Ban Shigeru–designed Building 2. At the time of research, Building 1 of the museum was hosting the exhibition 'The Glory of Tainan', which traces the development of cultural and aesthetic identity in this southern city.

Ten Drum Rende Creative Village ARTS CENTRE

(十鼓仁德文創區, Shígǔ Réndé Wénchuàng Qū; ☑06-266 2225; www.facebook.com/tendrum. cultrue; 326 Wenhua Rd, Sec 2, Rende, 仁德區

文華路二段326號; adult/child NT$399/350; ⏱9am-5pm Mon, to 9pm Tue-Thu, to 9.30pm Fri-Sun; 📷) Tainan's largest art village is this awesome 7.5-hectare Japanese-era sugar refinery run by award-winning native percussion group, Ten Drum (十鼓). You can see old vats and machines, a museum converted from molasses storage tanks, and a children's playground with a long tube slide. What's more, you can now release sky lanterns inside the 100-year-old chimney of the sugar-cane bagasse incinerator. It's NT$200 for a large lantern, and NT$100 for a small one (1.10pm to 8.50pm Tuesday to Sunday, 1.10pm to 4.50pm Monday).

Take the train to Bao An Station (保安站). Walk along Wenxian Rd (文賢路), turn into Wenhua Rd (文華路) and cross the tracks.

Hayashi Department Store   NOTABLE BUILDING

(林百貨, Lín Bǎihuò; www.hayashi.com.tw; 63 Zhongyi Rd, Sec 2, West Central District, 忠義路二段63號; ⏱11am-10pm) This art deco department store from the 1930s has been so beautifully restored that it's worth going in just to ascend the sweeping staircase, peer through the geometrical window openings, and have a ride on the grandma lift with the dial floor indicator. There's even a viewing deck on the top floor where you'll find a Shinto shrine and evidence of the damage it suffered during WWII.

Known locally as Lin's Department Store (林百貨) or Five Stories (五層樓), Hayashi was Tainan's first department store and Taiwan's second when it opened in 1932, and is therefore close to the hearts of older Tainaners. Everyone wanted to ride on its lift even if they couldn't afford the goods. Earnings made by the store were delivered just across the road to the neoclassical Nippon Kangyo Bank, predecessor of the Land Bank. In the 1930s Hayashi was doing so well that locals joked that to bring the money somewhere further away would be too risky. The duo were the cornerstones of Tainan's most affluent area.

Being the tallest building in Tainan brought trouble during WWII. Hayashi was seriously damaged by air raids and the top floor was subsequently used to conduct anti-aircraft warfare. Today the roof is a vantage point for taking good pictures of Land Bank across the road.

Take the Red Line bus heading towards Anping Industrial Park from Tainan Train Station, and get off at Hayashi Department stop.

Land Bank   ARCHITECTURE

(土地銀行, Tǔdì Yínháng; 28 Zhongzheng Rd, West Central District, 中正路28號; 🚌1, 19, 7, R2) The neoclassical-style Land Bank dates from 1928. Japanese architects were heavily influenced by western ideas at the time and neoclassical revival was a dominant style for public monuments in the USA and Europe. The bank was built with features of a Grecian temple, yet not without taking local practices into consideration. Land Bank lies at a busy intersection; instead of having the pedestrian pathway run in front of it, it runs through it, behind the Doric columns, as footpaths do through Taiwanese shophouses.

Confucius Temple   CONFUCIAN TEMPLE

(孔廟, Kǒng Miào; 2 Nanmen Rd, 南門路2號; grounds free, temple NT$25; ⏱8.30am-5pm; 🚌1, 3, 16, 17) Built in 1666 by the son of Ming loyalist Zheng Chenggong (Koxinga), Taiwan's first Confucian temple and official school is quiet, dignified and coloured red, signifying nobility. The most important among the halls, pagodas and courtyards here is the elegant Dacheng Hall with its unusually tall double-eave roof and minipagoda. The temple gardens are lovely, a community hangout where you'll find people exercising, feeding the squirrels and sketching.

Entry to the temple grounds is free, but you must pay to enter the palace area. Look out for the stone tablet on the right as you enter the Edification Hall. It explains the school rules (the site was once a centre for Confucian studies), such as prohibitions of gambling, drinking and cheating.

A solemn Confucius Memorial Ceremony takes place outside Dacheng Hall on 28 September every year and a smaller one on the spring equinox (春分), around 21 March. Dancers in rows perform choreographed moves that supposedly originate from the ceremonial dances of the imperial court.

Across the street from the temple entrance is a **stone arch** (泮宮石坊, Pàngōng Shífang; western end of Fuzhong St, 府中街西側) that was crafted by masons in Quanzhou, Fujian, in 1777. It's now the gateway to a pedestrianised street filled with cafes and small eateries.

Anping Fort   HISTORIC SITE

(安平古堡, Ānpíng Gǔbǎo, Fort Zeelandia; 82 Guosheng Rd, 國勝路82號; NT$50; ⏱8.30am-5.30pm; 🚌2, 88, 99) Behind the Mazu Temple (p278), the fort was a stronghold of Dutch power until its 1661 capture by Koxinga after a nine-month battle. Most of it has been reconstructed, but it's still an impressive site. A small museum on the grounds highlights the history of the Dutch occupation of Taiwan. Buses come from Tainan train station; the stations you want are respectively Post Office (郵局) and Anping Fort (安平古堡).

Anping Old Streets   AREA
(安平老街, Ānpíng Lǎojiē; 🚍 2, 88, 99) To the right of the Anping Fort entrance (p277) (with your back to the fort), you'll find some of the oldest streets in Taiwan. As you wander about, look for stone lion masks (劍獅, jiànshī) with swords across the mouth. They were once used to protect a house against evil, but today there are only a few dozen left.

Siaozhong St (效忠街; Xiàozhōngjiē) is an interesting street that leads to a number of back alleys with restored brick buildings. Yenping St (延平街; Yánpíngjiē) is the site of the first market in Taiwan. it now teems with shops and stalls offering traditional Tainan foods.

Anping Mazu Temple   TAOIST TEMPLE
(安平天后宮, Ānpíng Tiānhòu Gōng; 33 Guosheng Rd, 國勝路33號; ⊙ 8am-6pm; 🚍 2, 88, 99) This temple is one of many claiming status as the oldest in Taiwan. Its interior is more elaborately decorated than most in central Tainan, and features a splendidly ornate and deep plafond (decorative ceiling) above the main shrine. Near the altar, little packets of 'safe rice' are available free of charge to help keep you and your family safe.

National Museum of Taiwan History   MUSEUM
(國立臺灣歷史博物館, Guólì Táiwān Lìshǐ Bówùguǎn; www.nmth.gov.tw; 250 Changhe Rd, Sec 1, 長和路一段250號; NT$100; ⊙ 9am-4pm Tue-Sun) Eight kilometres north of the city centre of Tainan, this three-storey museum is a good introduction to the ethnocultural history of Taiwan. The visually appealing exhibits and multimedia installations give an overview of Taiwan's history, covering the early settlement of the indigenous groups, the Dutch occupation, the Japanese era, the KMT takeover and today's democracy.

The museum also has a well-designed park that includes lakes, an ecological education centre, walking paths and birdwatching areas. The combined treat is certainly worth the time it takes to get there.

Bus 18 (NT$18) leaves from the hub opposite Tainan train station for the museum every 30 minutes on weekends. On weekdays, there are six buses going in each direction between 7am and 7.55pm.

182 Art Space   GALLERY
(么八二空間, Mebā'èr Kōngjiān; www.facebook.com/182artspace; 182 Xinmei St, 新美街182號; ⊙ 2pm-midnight Wed-Mon) FREE A fabulous gallery inside an attractive 50-year-old building. The three-and-a-half floors of space hosts well-curated exhibitions of works – paintings, photography and installation – by young Taiwanese and Asian artists. See their Facebook page for the latest. If nothing's on, you can head to the cosy, yellow-walled cafe on the 1st floor for a beer.

Old Japanese Martial Arts Academy   NOTABLE BUILDING
(台南武德殿, Táinán Wǔdé Diàn; 2 Zhongyi Rd, Sec 2, 忠義路二段2號; ⊙ 8am-6pm Sat & Sun) This sleek and poised Japanese building next to the Confucius Temple was a butokuden, a place where the Japanese taught and promoted martial arts such as kendo in Tainan. It's one of Taiwan's largest buildings of its type and now belongs to a primary school. It opens weekends when there are no activities in the school.

Koxinga's Shrine   HISTORIC SITE
(延平郡王祠, Yánpíng Jùnwáng Cí; 152 Kaishan Rd, 開山路152號; ⊙ 8am-6pm; 🚍 18) FREE This shrine was built in the Qing dynasty, but its roots date back to a shrine commemorating Ming loyalist Koxinga (Zheng Chenggong) in the 1660s. The Japanese paid their respects here, too, as Koxinga's mother was Japanese, but it was still renamed Kaizan Shinto Shrine. The southern-style temple was rebuilt in a northern style by the KMT government in the 1960s. Many of the artefacts are historical, however, including boxes holding the original imperial edict from 1874 that permitted the current shrine's construction.

Chihkan Towers   HISTORIC SITE
(Fort Proventia, 赤崁樓, Chìkǎn Lóu; 212 Minzu Rd, 民族路212號; NT$50; ⊙ 8.30am-9.30pm; 🚍 17, 88) This old fort is a splendid place to roam around, or to enjoy an outdoor concert on weekends. However, only the foundation is the original. Chihkan has gone through many masters – Ming, Qing and Japanese, and the Kuomintang (KMT) – since the foundations were first laid by the Dutch in 1653. At that time the seashore reached the fort's outer walls.

Taijiang National Park PARK
(台江國家公園; Táijiāng Guójiā Gōngyuán; ☑ 06-284 1610; www.tjnp.gov.tw; ⊙ 8.30am-5pm) Taiwan's eighth national park, Taijiang covers a patchwork of coastal lands north of Anping Harbour. The 50 sq km of land and 340 sq km of sea include tidal flats, lagoons, mangrove swamps and wetlands that are critical habitats for rare fish, crustaceans and mammal and bird species, including the endangered black-faced spoonbill.

Taijiang covers an area dear to the hearts of Taiwanese, as it was here that their ancestors first landed after the dangerous crossing of the Black Ditch (the Taiwan Strait).

Once a giant inland sea, Taijiang silted up during the 18th century, facilitating the development of local salt and fish-farming industries. These days only the fish farms remain active.

Cycling is possible in Taijiang, as the land is flat, the climate is sunny year-round and parts of the new bike trail have been completed. You can boat through the mangrove swamps and further out to the estuary of the Yenshui River from a pier close to the Sihcao Dazhong Temple (四草大眾廟; Sìcǎo Dàzhòng Miào). A 30-minute ride through the Mangrove Green Tunnel (紅樹林綠色隧道; Hóng Shùlín Lǜsè Sùidào) is NT$200/100 per adult/child, while the 70-minute ride that goes out to larger channels and into the mouth of the Yenshui River is NT$200/150. Boats leave when full, so on most weekdays you will be waiting a long time.

Bus 10 (NT$30, every hour) from Tainan runs out to the temple daily, while the tourist bus 99 (NT$36, every 30 minutes) runs from 9am to 5.15pm on weekends. You can take bikes on the buses.

Taiwan Ecotours (p282) offers kayaking through the mangroves.

Former Tait & Co
Merchant House and
Anping Tree House HISTORIC BUILDING
(德記洋行暨安平樹屋, Déjì Yánghángng Jì Ānpíng Shùwū; Gubao St, 古堡街; NT$50; ⊙ 8.30am-5.30pm; ☐ 88) The merchant house was built in 1867 and holds a permanent exhibit of household artefacts from the 17th century. Through a series of decorated rooms, the exhibit highlights the lifestyle of Dutch, Chinese and indigenous families.

But nobody comes for that. Instead, it's the Anping Tree House (Ānpíng Shùwū) that draws in the curious with its massive banyan strangling the gutted roofless walls of the back quarters.

Both houses are up Gubao St and behind the primary-school grounds.

Official God of
War Temple TAOIST TEMPLE
(祀典武廟, Sì Diǎn Wǔmiào, Sacrificial Rites Temple; 229 Yongfu Rd, Sec 2, 永福路二段229號; ⊙ 5am-9pm; ☐ 17) This is the oldest and most impressive temple in Taiwan dedicated to Guandi (Guan Gong), a Han-dynasty general deified as the God of War. He is the patron of warriors and those who live by a code of honour. Unlike most temple plaques, which remind believers to pay tribute to the gods, the very famous one here – '大丈夫' – means an 'upright and honourable man' and describes the essence of the deity enshrined.

The temple's overall structure was established in 1690, although much splendid artwork and many historically valuable objects have been added over the years. The long, deep-rose-coloured walls of this temple have always been one of its highlights. Other interesting features include the beggar seats around the doorframe that the poor used to beg alms from every visitor, and the high threshold at the entrance (originally designed to keep women out!).

Black-Faced Spoonbill
Reserve & Exhibition Hall WILDLIFE RESERVE
(黑面琵鷺生態保護區和展示館, Hēimiàn Pílù Shēngtài Bǎohùqū hé Zhǎnshì Guǎn; ☑ 06-788 1180 ext 204; www.facebook.com/blackfacedspoonbillhall; 47 Haipu, Shifen Li, Qigu District, 十份里海埔47號; ⊙ 9am-4.30pm Tue-Sun) FREE The exhibition hall at the Black-Faced Spoonbill Reserve on Tainan's west coast explains the ecology of the Tseng Wen River (曾文溪) and the creatures that live there, which includes the extremely rare black-faced spoonbill. The reserve, open 24 hours, is a small section of wetlands that's dedicated to protecting the water bird, which spends the summer (May to September) in Korea and northern China, and migrates to Tainan for the winter.

If you visit the reserve you won't be able to see the birds up close, but there are high-powered binoculars you can use for free. The reserve is part of Taijiang National Park.

To get to the reserve, head north up Hwy 17 from Tainan and look for the English signs around the Km162 mark after crossing the Zengwen River. You could also contact Taiwan Ecotours (p282) for private tours.

SOUTHERN TAIWAN TAINAN

STROLLING THE FIVE CANALS

Tainan's most mesmerising sites are in the old river port area known as Five Channels Harbour. The canals leading to Anping Harbour were developed by the Qing authorities to facilitate sea trade with Fujian. They spawned homes, businesses and places of worship, and became Tainan's most prosperous area.

Geographically, the five artificial canals were sprawled like the fingers of a hand from north to south. Near Mingquan Rd, Sec 3 and Linan Rd, they merged into a single canal that made its way west to the sea between Anping Fort (p277) and **Eternal Golden Castle** (億載金城, Yìzài Jīnchéng; 3 Guangzhou Rd, Anping, 光州路3號; NT$50; ⊙8.30am-5.30pm; 🚌2, 4, 88).

Shennong Street

The waterways are long gone – urbanisation under the Japanese wiped out the last traces of them. But some of the commercial activities and the institutions they produced remain. The cornerstone of the Five Channels zone is the 300-year-old Shennong Street (p276), built parallel to the canal. Now an attractive art village, it was a bustling working-class neighbourhood where goods were transferred, stored and traded.

Shennong Street is flanked by shophouses shaped like modern-day containers – long with narrow facades. In the past, boats would go right up to the back doors of the houses, where workers would offload the goods and haul them by rope and pulley to the spacious upper floor for storage. You can still see small gates on the upper-floor facades of some houses. The ground floor was the shop and living quarters. Go into any cafe, gallery or boutique on Shennong Street to check out the structure.

Sometimes several shops would share the same cross-beam as they were built concurrently. This means that anyone wishing to tear down their shop would need the approval of the other owners – a reason why Shennong Street has managed to retain a rather impressive number of old houses.

Wind God Temple

Around the corner from Shennong St is **Wind God Temple** (風神廟, Fēngshén Miào; 8 Lane 143, Mingquan Rd, Sec 3, 民權路三段143巷8號; ⊙7am-9pm), one of Taiwan's few temples for nature worship. Boats carrying Qing court officials would steer through the canal to its doorsteps. You can see the old Official Reception Stone Arch (接官亭石坊) in the courtyard for receiving Qing representatives in Tainan. The officials would give thanks to the God of Wind before reporting for duty. And rightly so – what's more important than having a favourable wind in your travels and career?

Altar of Heaven — TAOIST TEMPLE

(天壇, Tiāntán; 16 Lane 84, Zhongyi Rd, Sec 2, 忠義路二段84巷16號) Tainan families have been coming here for generations on the 1st and 15th of every lunar month to pray to the supreme Taoist entity, the Jade Emperor. The temple has no statue of the god as the supreme deity is supposed to be shapeless and formless like the sky. There's a famous *Yī* (One) inscription over the altar. This single-stroke character embodies both the beginning and the end, signifying that all the world's truths are here and nothing goes unseen by heaven.

Fahua Temple — BUDDHIST TEMPLE

(法華寺, Fǎhuá Sì; 100 Fahua St, 法華街100號; ⊙8am-5pm; 🚌88) One of Tainan's two most ancient Buddhist temples, Fahua has clean lines and understated aesthetics. A simple gourd, exorcist of evil spirits, sits on the roof

ridge of the main hall. On the wing walls of the front halls, you'll see the works of master of colour painting Pan Lishui (潘麗水). They're in black and white like traditional ink and brush paintings.

Duiyue Gate — GATE

(兌悅門, Duìyuè Mén; junction Wenxian Rd & Xinyi St, 中西區文賢路、信義街口; 🚌7, 14) This gate (1835) was part of Tainan's outer city walls in the Qing dynasty. You can see the coral stones in the base and the red bricks making up the low arch. Although eclipsed by taller neighbours, this Grade II national relic is still very much a part of the daily life of pedestrians and scooter drivers.

Dongyue Temple — TAOIST TEMPLE

(東嶽殿, Dōngyuè Diàn; 110 Mingquan Rd, Sec 1, 民權路一段110號; ⊙7am-9pm; 🚌1, 7, 17) People come to this temple to communicate with

King of Medicine Temple

At the end of Shennong St is the formidable **Yaowang Temple** (藥王廟, Yàowáng Miào; Yaowang Temple; 86 Jinhua Rd, Sec 4, 金華路四段86號; ☺6am-6pm), Taiwan's first temple to the King of Medicine who offers protection against illness. The banyan tree in front of it is said to be 300 years old. During festivities, when Mazu's icon visits Tainan from her temple in Beigang, she spends a night at Yaowang Temple before leaving for the Grand Mazu Temple (p273). Yaowang temple has ornate carvings on every inch of its facade. It faces the east, towards the Water Fairy Temple in a feng-shui arrangement that is beneficial for the Five Canal area.

Water Fairy Temple

At the head of Shennong St, tucked away in a sleepy market, is the **Water Fairy Temple** (水仙宮, Shuǐxiān Gōng, Shuixian Temple; 1 Shennong St, 神農街1號; ☺7am-5pm). Enshrined here is a deified king famed for his flood-taming skills and worshipped by merchants, sailors and fishermen. The other deities here include Qu Yuan, the patriotic Chinese poet associated with the Dragon Boat Festival, who killed himself by jumping into the river; and Xiang Yu, a warlord who also killed himself by jumping into the river.

This temple was founded by three powerful trade unions who, together with five clan-based worker organisations, were responsible for the digging and the daily operation of the canals. The unions used the temple as their religious and administrative headquarters from which they ran the show around these parts.

Coming-of-Age Temple

In old Tainan, religion and commerce were inseparable in more ways than one. Gambling dens and brothels mushroomed around the dockyards, and child labour was rife. **Kailung Temple** (開隆宮, Kāilóng Gōng; Coming-of-Age Temple; Lane 79, 56 Zhongshan Rd, 中山路79巷56號; ☺6.30am-8.30pm; 🚌2, 5, 7, 15, 19) was founded to ask for protection for the Oliver Twists of the Five Canals and to celebrate the ascendance into adulthood of those turning 16. The latter was more than a rite of passage – it marked the time at which a child was eligible to receive full adult wages. The resident deity here is Princess Seven Stars or Chiniangma (七娘媽), protector of children. The temple comes alive on the seventh day of the seventh lunar month, for the 'coming of age' ritual (七夕節十六歲成年).

the dead through spirit mediums. It's a fascinating place to catch a glimpse of Taiwanese folk culture. It's said that you can hear the screams of tortured spirits at night.

The first chamber of the temple holds the God of Mount Tai, the Taoist king of the underworld; the second, Ksitigarbha bodhisattva, who vowed to not attain Buddhahood as long as there was still one suffering soul in hell; the last, a number of demon gods who rule the underworld.

The grim murals on the walls of the second chamber are as graphic as the depictions of hell by Hieronymus Bosch, including depictions of disembowelment, eye gouging, stabbing and boiling.

Great South Gate
HISTORIC SITE

(大南門城, Dà Nánmén Chéng; Lane 24, Nanmen Rd, 南門路24巷; ☺8.30am-5pm) FREE There used to be 14 city gates in Tainan and a city

wall spreading several kilometres. This old gate is the only one of the four remaining gates that still has its defensive wall intact. The inner grounds feature several cannons and a section of the old wall that is marvellously overgrown with thick roots. At the far end of the park a collection of handsome stelae commemorate centuries of battles, bridge constructions and official promotions.

Wufei Temple
TAOIST TEMPLE

(五妃廟, Wǔfēi Miào; 201 Wufei Rd, 五妃街201號; ☺8.30am-5.30pm; 🚌5, 88) Dainty Wufei Temple was built in honour of the concubines of the Prince of Ningjing, Zhu Shugui, the last contender for the Ming throne. When Koxinga's grandson surrendered to the Manchus in 1683, all hope of restoring the Ming ended. The prince committed suicide and his concubines hanged themselves on a beam in the bedroom of his palace. The palace is now the shrine to Mazu's parents at the Grand Mazu Temple (p273) and the beam is still in place.

Lady Linshui's Temple TAOIST TEMPLE

(臨水夫人媽廟, Línshǔi Fūrén Mǎ Miào, Chen Ching Gu Temple; 16 Jianye St, 建業街16號; ⊙6am-8.30pm) For generations, women have come to this temple to ask Lady Linshui to protect their children. This is demanding work and the goddess employs 36 assistants (three for each month), whose statuettes can be seen in little glass vaults around the inside walls of the temple. In addition to incense offerings, you'll often see flowers, face powder and make-up left here. If you are extremely lucky you might see the unique southern-temple spectacle associated with Lady Linshui called the Twelve Grannies Parade (十二婆姐陣; Shíèr Pójiě Zhèn), which consists of older men wearing women's clothing and old ladies' masks.

Room A LIBRARY

(計時圖書館, Jìshí Túshū Guǎn; ☑06-220 9797; www.facebook.com/on.RoomA; 3rd fl, 21 Kangle St, 中西區康樂街21號3樓; 1st hour NT$60, then NT$1/min, half-day/full-day NT$180/300; ⊙10am-10.30pm Sat-Mon, 1-10pm Wed-Fri; 🚌2, 5) You pay by the hour at this unusual library-cafe stocked with magazines, comics and visual arts books. It's a great place to chill – there's free coffee, tea and cold drinks, and pastries for sale; you can also buy food (but not drinks) from outside for consumption on the premises. The sunny corner flat feels like someone's home, with windows all around and a terrace full of potted plants. Take the stairs next to the sushi restaurant.

 ## Activities & Tours

Anping has lots of flat, open areas and footpaths, so walking or cycling are good ways to get around.

A riverside bike path runs westcoastwards, where you can continue north through Taijiang National Park (p279) or south along the Taiwan Strait and into the harbour area. Bikes can be rented from the Tainan City program at Anping Fort (p278), Eternal Golden Castle (p280) and Anping Tree House (p279).

Anping Canal Cruise CRUISE

(安平運河遊, Anpíng Yùnhé Yóu; ☑0903-232 168; https://anpingcanal.com; 50min cruise Sat & Sun NT$300-500; ⊙10am-6pm; 🚌77) The artificial Tainan Canal connecting central Tainan with Anping straddles three bodies of water

and passes 12 bridges and a great number of sights. Canal cruises allow visitors to experience Tainan from the water. Boats depart from Anping Bridge Fisherman's Pier (安億橋漁人碼頭; Anyì Qiáo Yúrén Mǎtóu). Schedules change monthly. Call or see the website for the latest.

HG Barbershop MASSAGE

(華谷理容院, Huágǔ Lǐróng Yuàn; ☑06-298 8178; http://comevisitbarbershop.blogspot.hk; Lane 410, 37 Yiping Rd, 怡平路410巷37號; ⊙massage 2pm-1am, other services by appt) A sputtering 40-year-old beauty parlour revitalised through a crowdfunding initiative, HG offers haircuts (from NT$500), shaving (from NT$200), facials (from NT$650), manicures (from NT$250) and massage (from NT$700). All services, except manicure and massage, are available only to male customers.

Taiwan Ecotours ECOTOUR

(https://sites.google.com/site/taiwanbirdinfo; 1-4 days per person US$180-500) Richard, a Tainan-based guide, offers custom-made tours outside the city, with a focus on hiking, flora and fauna.

⭐ Festivals & Events

Yanshui Fireworks Festival FIREWORKS

(鹽水蜂炮, Yánshuǐ Fēngbāo; ⊙Feb/Mar) There may be nothing stranger in this land than this annual fireworks festival – or battle, or blowout – in which thousands of people place themselves willingly in a melee of exploding fireworks. The festival takes place every year during the Lantern Festival, two weeks after Lunar New Year.

Officially the festival re-enacts the Yenshui people's supplication to Guandi (the God of War and Righteousness) to save them from a terrible epidemic. It was 1875, and cholera was killing off the town; no known remedies were helping. In desperation, people began to parade their gods through the town and set off noisy and smoky firecrackers to scare away evil disease-spreading spirits.

For the older generation, the current Yanshui festival still honours the old event, but for the younger crowd it's an opportunity to live life on the edge. Crowds of 100,000 or more can gather. It's hot, smoky and tense, very tense. When a nearby 'beehive' is set off, thousands of bottle rockets fly at you and over you (though hopefully not through you). The noise deafens, the smoke blinds and the rockets sting.

Some people travel from overseas every year to be part of the excitement. Tens of thousands more come in from all parts of Taiwan. Accidents and burns are common, though the vast majority of people wear protective clothing resembling hazmat suits from afar. A motorcycle helmet is considered mandatory, as are thick, nonflammable clothing, swimming goggles and earplugs. Many people also wrap a towel around their neck to prevent fireworks from flying up under their helmet. There are garments for hire by the roadside on the day of the festival, ranging from NT$400 to NT$800. There's little leeway for bargaining.

If you're injured you should be able to find medical help nearby, but don't expect any sympathy, and certainly don't expect any compensation. You participate at your own risk.

Yanshui is in the north of Tainan county. You can reach the town by taking an express train to nearby Sinying, then a taxi. Be prepared to be out all night, and take care of your valuables.

🛏 Sleeping

★Caoji Book Inn   B&B $

(艸祭, Cǎojì; ☑0935-686 854; www.caoji.com.tw; 71 Nanmen Rd, 中西區南門路71號; dm NT$750-850; ➡✽🛜; 🖵1) You can sleep among tomes here – part of the premises used to be a bookshop – and there are two blocks of dormitories, women's and mixed. But what we like best about Caoji is the attention to detail. It has beds of (fragrant) recycled cypress; eco-friendly, made-in-Taiwan toiletries; and herbal packets in cubicles to keep mosquitoes away.

Catch Phoenix   HOSTEL $

(捉鳳凰, Zhuō Fènghuáng; ☑0980-716 478; www.facebook.com/catchphoenix; 296-11 Haian Rd, Sec 2, 海安路二段296巷11號; r from NT$2300; ➡✽🛜; 🖵88) Inviting hostel converted from a 100-year-old house with beautiful octagonal windows. The bright, spacious rooms accommodate two-to-four and two-to-six people respectively. They're rented out to parties of two or more on weekdays, and four or more on weekends. The weekend rate is NT$4200. The same owner has three other locations in town, two within walking distance of Catch Phoenix.

The hostel holds regular parties and cook-ins where you'll get to meet all the super-friendly staff and ask them about Tainan. It also has an exchange program whereby students from Taiwan or abroad can trade labour for lodging. The hostel is a five-minute walk from Shennong St (p276) and around NT$100 from Tainan Train Station by cab.

158 Hostel   HOSTEL $

(158 棧, Yīwǔbā Zhàn; ☑06-220 1700; www.facebook.com/158[]-1976381415759204; 5 Lane 158, Zhongyi Rd, Sec 2, 中西區忠義路二段158巷5號; dm NT$600; ➡✽🛜; 🖵88) A smartly restored 1940s residence with three clean dormitories (of four bunk beds each), communal bathrooms, and laundry facilities arranged around an airy courtyard where guests can mingle after their day's adventures The all-women dorm is on the 2nd floor. Beds are NT$100 more on Friday and Saturday.

★UIJ Hotel
& Hostel   ACCOMMODATION SERVICES $$

(友愛街旅館, Yǒuàijiē Lǚguǎn; www.uij.com.tw; 5 Lane 115, You Ai St, 友愛街5號115巷; dm NT$700, d NT$3500-4000; ➡✽@🛜; 🖵5, 18) A cheerful block housing a hotel with 87 rooms plus a 110-bed hostel. The agreeable rooms come with industrial-chic interiors that are echoed by the steel and canvas of the well-appointed dormitories. The amenities floor has a bright living room with cushion-strewn floor seating, a well-stocked kitchen, and a leafy terrace overlooking a market.

★Xiangqi Guesthouse   B&B $$

(想起民宿, Xiǎngqǐ Mínsù; ☑0968-527 567; www.facebook.com/old.houselive; 1 & 2 Gonghou St, 宮後街1, 2號; s/d from NT$800/2750; ➡✽🛜; 🖵14) A meticulously restored 50-year-old house with three large rooms and two singles, all furnished with period pieces and the owner's collection of Japanese-era paraphernalia. Our favourite is the chic top-floor suite. Rates include detailed information on Tainan attractions, plus a shopping tour to Shuixian (p281) market nearby then cooking up the ingredients for breakfast.

★Your Fun Apartment   B&B $$

(有方公寓, Yǒufāng Gōngyù; ☑06-223 1208; www.trip235.com; 9 Lane 269, Haian 2nd Rd, 海安路二段269巷9號; r from NT$2300; ✽🛜) With a mix of vintage and designer furniture in the communal areas, and rooms that combine old-world charm with minimalism, this B&B has stolen the hearts of many visitors. Exhibitions and talks are held from time to time in the engaging 60-year-old building.

Rates are NT$500 or NT$600 more on weekends. Your Fun Apartment is one

SOUTHERN TAIWAN TAINAN

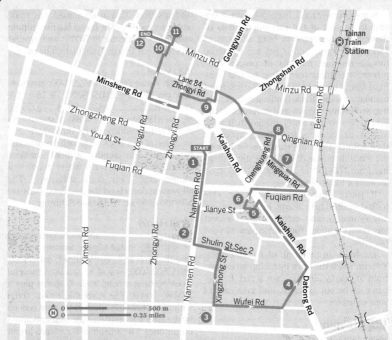

Town Walk
Tainan Temples

START CONFUCIUS TEMPLE
END GRAND MAZU TEMPLE
LENGTH 6KM; FOUR HOURS

Explore the elegant classical layout of the ❶**Confucius Temple** (p277), then head south. You'll pass the ❷**Great South Gate** (p281) with its defensive wall. Turn left on Shulin St and take the first right. At Wufei Rd, you'll see ❸**Wufei Temple** (p281), shrine to the concubines of the last contender for the Ming empire. Head east down Wufei Rd and turn left just past building No 76. You'll soon see the grounds hosting the simple outlines of the 300-year-old ❹**Fahua Temple** (p280).

Continue up the alley to a large intersection, then head north up Kaishan Rd until you see the stately ❺**Koxinga's Shrine** (p278) on the left. When you leave the compound, take the back-right gate to visit ❻**Lady Linshui's Temple** (p282). It's mostly visited by women seeking protection for their children.

Return to Kaishan Rd and turn right at the intersection. Head east down Fuqian Rd, turning left at the big intersection onto Mingquan Rd. At ❼**Dongyue Temple** (p280) check out

the terrifying paintings of hell and listen for the screams of tortured spirits.

Continue up Mingquan to Chenghuang Rd and turn right. At the end of this short street you'll see ❽**City God Temple** (p275), which welcomes visitors with the most famous words ever written on a temple plaque in Taiwan: 'You're here at last'. Now head west down Qingnian and turn right up Mingquan. Cross Gongyuan and turn left. You'll see a bank then a small alley. Turn right into the alley to get to ❾**Altar of Heaven** (p280). Say a prayer for protection from bad luck.

When you leave the alley and Lane 84, Zhongyi Rd, it's a quick left then a right onto Minsheng Rd. A block later, turn right up Yongfu Rd. Two blocks ahead you'll see the beautiful rose-coloured walls of the ❿**Official God of War Temple** (p279).

Now continue to the end of Yongfu Rd to ⓫**Chihkan Towers** (p278), whose foundations were laid by the Dutch in the 17th century. On the opposite side of the street, a tiny alley leads to the ⓬**Grand Mazu Temple** (p273). Don't forget to check out the door gods and roof beams.

minute away from Shennong St (p276). The best way to get there is to enter from Lane 259; its blue entrance is to your right.

★ Wabi Sabi
B&B $$

(和寂, Héjì Mínsù; ☑ 0968-527 567; www.facebook. com/Wabi-Sabi-和寂-食泊-435841176592710; 1 Gonghou St, 宮後街1號; r from NT$2750; ➌❄🛜; ☐14) Right next to Xiangqi Guesthouse (p283) is this graceful 100-year-old building run by the same folks. There's a large room with three beds, and a single; the latter is small, but quiet and tastefully furnished and the occupant has the use of the entire floor. Wabi Sabi is suitable for history-loving travellers who are not in a rush.

★ Hsieh's Old House Inn
GUESTHOUSE $$$

(謝宅, Xiè Zhái; ☑ 0953-852 280; www.facebook. com/TainanOldHouseInn; 141 Daren St, 大仁街141 號; r NT$3280-4280; ➌❄🛜; ☐2) This 140-year darling has a beautiful Chinese maple growing indoors through three floors, as well as terrazzo stairs, '60s furniture, and contemporary architectural touches for added comfort. The three rooms come with mosquito nets and tatami mattresses by old Tainanese masters. The top one has a Japanese-style chamber with wooden beams, and an outdoor *onsen* for soaking under the moonlight.

🍴 Eating

As the birthplace of many Taiwanese street snacks, Tainan's streets are chock-a-block with eateries. The neighbourhood of Guohua St and Yongle Market is a foodie's paradise. The reputed 'golden triangle' here are pudding-in-a-bowl (碗粿, *wǎnguǒ*), spring rolls (春卷, *chūnjuàn*) and pork belly buns (割包, *gēbāo*). In Anping, the areas around Chihkan Towers (p278) and Anping Fort (p278) are known for their traditional snacks.

★ Wang's Fish Shop
TAIWANESE $

(王氏魚皮店, Wángshì Yúpí Diàn; ☑ 06-228 8095; 612 Anping Rd, 安平路612號; per person from NT$70; ⏰ 4am-Mon-Fri, to 3pm Sat & Sun; ☐2, 19, 77) This white-tiled roadside shop, operated by a milkfish (虱目魚, *shīmùyú*) farmer, slaughters the fish in the wee hours to prepare the popular breakfast of fish-meat broth (魚肉湯, *yúròu tāng*). Fish belly (魚肚, *yúdù*) also comes braised (魯, *lǔ*) or panfried (煎, *jiān*). Fresh milkfish is rich and unctuous, utterly delicious but also filling – the cold dishes laid out near the entrance will help to cleanse your palate.

Da Dong Night Market
MARKET $

(大東夜市, Dàdōng Yèshì; 276 Linsen Rd, Sec 1, 東 區林森路一段276號; ⏰ 6pm-midnight Mon, Tue & Fri) Da Dong hasn't yet caught the attention of mass tourism despite the high number of delicious stalls. Vendors here have clearly delineated boundaries: if you're seen gobbling yummy fried sweet-potato balls (地瓜球, *dìguā qiú*) in space belonging to the oyster griller (烤蚵仔, *kǎo ézai*), you'll get yelled at. The way out is to try his succulent molluscs as well.

Fusheng Hao Rice Cake
TAIWANESE $

(富盛號碗粿, Fùshèng Hào Wǎnguǒ; ☑ 06-227 4101; 11 Minzu Rd, Sec 3, 中西區民族路3段11 號; bowls NT$35; ⏰ 7am-5.30pm Fri-Wed; ☐77, 5, 3) Fusheng is famous for *wǎnguǒ*, a Tainan speciality that translates into 'pudding in a bowl'. Essentially steamed rice gruel embedded with sliced pork, dried shrimp and crunchy radish, it's served slathered with thick soy sauce and eaten with a soup spoon. Business is roaring at this market stall; expect to wait for a table.

Uguisu Ryori
DESSERTS $

(鶯料理, Yīng Liàolǐ; ☑ 06-221 0595; www.face book.com/eaglehill14tainan; 18 Lane 84, Zhongyi Rd, Sec 2, 中西區忠義路2段84巷18號; snacks from NT$60; ⏰ 1.30-9pm Tue-Sun; ☐1) Possibly the world's most elegant place to suck on a popsicle. This beautiful Japanese house with koi pond and pruned bushes was built in 1925 as an entertainment venue for politicians and the glitterati. Today this lovely place is overrun with plebs drawn here by treats like all-natural fruit popsicles and ice cream on Tainan brown-sugar bun (椪餅冰 淇淋, *pèngbǐng bīngqílín*).

Ho Hsin Fish Soup
TAINAN $

(和興號鮮魚湯, Héxīng Hào Xiānyú Tāng; ☑ 06-221 5257; 49 Zhongyi Rd, Sec 2, 中西區忠義路二 段49號; fish soup NT$180; ⏰ 11am-2pm & 5-8pm) This modern milkfish joint sells the usual suspects – fish broth, panfried milkfish and braised pork rice, plus innovations like soy milk- or miso-based broth, and multigrain rice. Flavours are clean, fresh and delicate. One soup comes with pickled green watermelon (西瓜綿, *xīguā mián*), a traditional Tainanese pickle of underripe melons that lends acidity to the taste of seafood.

A Cun Beef Soup
TAIWANESE $

(阿村第二代牛肉湯, Ācūn Dì'èrdài Niúròu Tāng; 7 Lane 41, Baoan Rd, 保安路41-7號; per person NT$120-200; ⏰ 4am-midday & 6pm-midnight)

Beef soup (牛肉湯, *niúròu tāng*), a Tainan speciality, is served as early as 4am for breakfast, right after the cattle are slaughtered. One of the best places to savour the soup and the meat at its freshest is A Cun, a street-side stall that has been feeding late-night revellers and early risers for more than four decades.

From Tainan Train Station, take bus 6 (bound for Longgang Elementary School, 龍岡國小) and get off at Baoan Temple (保安宮). Walk towards where you came from and turn right at Guohua St, Section 2 (國華街二段). The shop is at the junction of Baoan Rd (保安路) and Guohua St (國華街).

Chi Kin Danzaimian
TAIWANESE $

(赤崁擔仔麵, Chì Kǎn Dànzǐmiàn; 180 Minzu Rd, Sec 2, 民族路二段180號; dànzǎimiàn bowl NT$60; ⊙11am-9pm; 🚌1, 3, 5) Set in a Japanese-era merchant's house, this is a fun place to try traditional *dànzǐmiàn* (擔仔麵), a simple dish that mixes noodles with a tangy meat sauce. *Dànzǐ*, literally 'two baskets and a stick', refers to the baskets used to carry the noodles around for sale. This shop uses no MSG.

Anping Bean Jelly
TAIWANESE, DESSERT $

(同記安平豆花, Tóngjì Ānpíng Dòuhuā; 433 Anbei Rd, 安北路433號; desserts from NT$35; ⊙9am-11pm; 🚌2) There are a dozen items on the menu in this celebrated eatery, and its claim to fame is the bean jelly (or bean curd; 豆花, *dòuhuā*), made with organic soybeans and dressed with tapioca or red beans. There are a few branches in town, but this flagship is the locals' all-time favourite.

An-Ping Gui Ji Local Cuisine Cultural Restaurant
TAIWANESE $

(安平貴記美食文化館, Ānpíng Guìjì Měishí Wénhuàguǎn; ☑06-222 9794; 93 Yenping St, 延平街93號; set meals from NT$159; ⊙11am-7pm; 🚌2, 77) If you want to try an assortment of Tainan snacks in one plac, head here rather than hopping all over town in search of the 'best' place for each. This is a solid choice in terms of price, deliciousness and environment. Try Chou's shrimp rolls, oyster omelette and steamed dumplings.

★Zhuxin Residence
TAIWANESE $$

(筑馨居, Zhùxīn Jū; ☑06-221 8890; www.facebook.com/筑馨居-408529669303867; 96 Xinyi St, 中西區信義街96號; per person from NT$500; ⊙11.30am-2pm & 5.30-9pm; 🚌7, 14) This restaurant serves traditional Tainanese dishes inside a rustic 100-year-old house. There's no menu, but the generously portioned

seven-course meals may include braised pork, chicken, fish and stir-fry. Call or message a few days in advance to book. Look around the house before your meal – there are interesting relics on display.

★L'Esprit Cafe
CAFE $$

(初衷咖啡, Chūzhōng Kāfēi; ☑06-221 8822; 401 Minsheng Rd, Sec 2, 中西區民生路二段401號; coffee from NT$160; ⊙8.30am-6pm; 🐾; 🚌2) This gem with glass frontage, blue-and-brown palette and white floor tiles offers great respite from the busy street beyond its door, not to mention that the coffee, salads and sandwiches are excellent. A delightful place for breakfast or a light meal any time of day, or just to unwind and watch the world go by.

Guli Restaurant
VEGAN $$

(穀粒蔬食自然風味料理, Gǔlì Shūshí Zìrán Fēngwèi Liàolǐ; ☑06-293 9797; 15 Lane 148, Yonghua 1st St, 中西區永華一街148巷15號; mains from NT$280-550; ⊙12.30-8.30pm Fri-Mon, Tue-Thu by appt only; 🥢; 🚌19) 🌿 A haven for the health and environmentally conscious, this restaurant uses naturally farmed local produce. The Asian fusion food is light and lightly flavoured, but tasty and presented elegantly. Rice comes with nuts and fruits; the hotpot is a treat if you crave fresh veggies. It also serves vegan stinky tofu, which has been fermented with fruits.

Zyuu Tsubo
JAPANESE $$

(十平, Shípíng; www.facebook.com/zyuutsubo; 22 Lane 158, Zhongyi Rd, Sec 2, 忠義路二段158巷22號; meals from NT$400; ⊙usually noon-2pm & 6-8pm; 🐾; 🚌88) A narrow corner space that whips up a mean *donburi* (Japanese rice bowl), and other goodies like fried chicken and beer (served in frosty mugs). There are only 10 counter seats, which allows you to chat with the owner but also means you may have to wait for a table. Go 30 minutes before opening to register. See their Facebook and Instagram for the latest opening hours, announced at the end of each month.

A Xia Restaurant
SEAFOOD $$$

(阿霞飯店, Āxiá Fàndiàn; ☑06-221 9873; 7 Lane 84, Zhongyi Rd, Sec 2, 忠義路2段84巷7號; dishes NT$500-1300; ⊙11am-2.30pm & 5-8.30pm Tue-Sun; 🚌2) This worthy modern restaurant is a popular venue for weddings. It's a good place to try more elaborate restaurant-type dishes such as the delectable steamed sticky rice with mud crab (紅蟳米糕, *hóngxún mǐgāo*; NT$1300), which you can't find in small restaurants.

🍷 Drinking & Nightlife

★ Narrow Door Cafe
CAFE

(窄門咖啡, Zhǎimén Kāfēi; ☎ 06-211 0508; www. facebook.com/narrowdoor99; 2nd fl, 67 Nanmen Rd, 南門路67號二樓; coffee from NT$150; ⏰ 11am-8.30pm; 🛜; 🚇 1) A 38cm-wide alley leads to this charmer where the colours are bold, the ceilings high, and on a fine day, there's always a breeze dancing. The patterns and ambience may transport you to living rooms by 20th-century European artists like Matisse or Kandinsky. Settle by one of the large windows overlooking the Confucius Temple and enjoy the coffee.

Narrow Door is a favourite haunt of the literati – you'll see on the wall autographs of celebrated writers and painters including Nobel Prize winner Gao Xingjian. The owner Jessica is a proponent of wearing *qipao* or cheongsam, a traditional body-hugging dress for Chinese women. She has a selection of the garments for rent, from NT$300 (wearing for photos inside the cafe) to NT$900 (taking it outside and returning before closing).

★ Lola
BAR

(蘿拉冷飲店, Luólā Lěngyǐn Diàn; ☎ 06-222 8376; www.facebook.com/Lola蘿拉冷飲店-229480470 793019; 110 Xinyi St, 中西區信義街110號; beer from NT$120; ⏰ 6pm-1am, Tue-Thu & Sun, to 2am Fri & Sat; 🚇 7, 14) A moody venue in an old village residence that has retained much of its original look, down to the creaky wooden doors. The bar is at the back, dimly lit with an embellished mezzanine. The music playing could be anything from Korean rock to Pink Floyd. See their Facebook page for live acts on the weekend.

TCRC Bar
BAR

(☎ 06-222 8716; 117 Xinmei St, 新美街117號; cocktails from NT$300; ⏰ 8pm-3am; 🚇 3, 5) Directly opposite Mazu Temple, TCRC (The Checkered Record Club) is cool in all the right places – a speakeasy vibe, indie sounds, colourful cocktails and a hip low-key following. TCRC has a small underground live-music dive (p288) nearby that hosts weekly concerts, and a new upmarket sister bar, Bar Home, that attracts a slightly older crowd.

The wait for a seat on weekends can be frustrating. Arrive at the door before 7.30pm to register with the staff then come back at the time you've been assigned.

Pari Pari Apartment
CAFE

(☎ 06-221 3266; www.facebook.com/paripariapt; 2nd fl, 9 Lane 158, Zhongyi Rd, Sec 2, 忠義路2段 158巷9號二樓; coffee from NT$150; ⏰ 10am-6pm; 🚇 88) A elegant cafe serving good single-origin coffees, homemade cakes and thirst-quenching drinks. You can relax at the communal table and read their books on design under milk-glass globe lights; or take a seat next to the large windows with the sheer '60s curtains and watch the goings-on in the quiet street below.

If you like the '60s decor, Pari Pari has two guestrooms in a similar style a floor above, for two and four sharing respectively. Price for a room is NT$2850 on weekdays and NT$3180 on Saturday, Sunday and public holidays. You can request to add up to two extra beds, at NT$500 each, to one of the rooms. Message them or enquire at the cafe.

Bar Home
COCKTAIL BAR

(☎ 06-223 2869; 1 Lane 23, Zhongshan Rd, 中西區 中山路23巷1號; minimum charge 2hr NT$350, cigar room NT$600; ⏰ 7pm-1am Mon-Sat, cigar room 9.30pm-1am; 🚇 2) The glamorous younger sister of TCRC Bar, Bar Home is all red velvet curtains, green walls and chandeliers, like a cross between old Tainan and Cluedo. Decent cocktails are mixed and served by staff who are eager to please, and an appetising selection of miniburgers and kebabs is also available. Those who'd like a puff can retire to the cigar room behind the bar. Minors accompanied by adults are allowed in from 7pm to 11pm.

Gandan Café
CAFE

(甘單咖啡, Gāndān Kāfēi; ☎ 06-222 5919; 13 Lane 4, Mingquan Rd, Sec 2, 民權路二段4巷13號; coffee from NT$100; ⏰ 1-9.30pm; 🚇 1, 2, 6, 7) The owner here has built a lush cafe from a rubbish heap by filling it only with recycled materials. The hip spot is wedged into an old building facing Kailung Temple, down a hidden alley, and is more accessible via Lane 79, Zhongshan Rd.

The cafe is closed Monday to Thursday in the last week of the month.

Dai Ran Po
PUB

(大乱步, Dàluàn Bù; 5 Lane 116, Zhongxiao St, 中西 區忠孝街116巷5號; ⏰ 7pm-1am Wed-Mon; 🚇 3, 77) A cosy pub cluttered with quirky Japanese toys and other kidult bait. They have a good assortment of Asian and European craft beers; most young locals also come for their tasty 'taco rice' (NT$180) and banter with the friendly owner.

Pista Alcohol
BAR

(畢氏酒精, Bìshì Jiǔjīng; ☎ 06-221 3850; 138 Zhongyi Rd, Sec 2, 中西區忠義路二段138號;

HOT SPRINGS & COFFEE IN GUANZILING

Mountainous Guanziling (關子嶺; Kuanziling; Guānzǐlǐng) is a hot spring and coffee-growing area in northern Tainan. Only three places in the world can lay claim to having mud hot springs and Guanziling is one of them.

The area is essentially one long dip off County Rd 172 on leafy Township Rd 96. The village, on the eastern end of the dip, is divided into lower (the older part of town) and upper sections that are joined by a series of stone steps for walking. You'll find many hot-spring resorts here.

Guanziling's mountain roads offer some fine road cycling. A particularly scenic route is County Rd 175, aka Dongshan Coffee Rd. From the roadside you won't see much sign of coffee growing, but you will get expansive views over the alluvial plains of rural Tainan and the choppy foothills of the Central Mountains.

Many plantations have cafes where you can enjoy an exceptional cup of Dongshan coffee and buy some beans, such as **Ta Chu Hua Chien** (大鋤花間, Dàchú Huājiàn; ☑ 06-686 4350; 109-17 Gaoyuan village, Gaoyuan, 高原村高原109-17號; ⊙ 10am-6pm Mon & Wed-Fri, to 9pm Sat & Sun) and **Hua Xiang Cafe** (樺香咖啡, Huàxiāng Kāfēi; ☑ 05-590 1113; 1-5 Taoyuan, Gukeng, 古坑鄉 桃源1-5號; ⊙ 10am-6pm Thu-Mon; ⏺).

You can catch a train from Tainan to Xinying, and then a bus (NT$80, 60 minutes) to Guanziling. Another bus runs from Xinying bus station via Chiayi HSR station to Guanziling on weekends and public holidays (NT$232, two hours, 9.30am, 11.30am, 1.30pm and 3.30pm).

beer from NT$100; ⊙ 2pm-midnight Mon-Thu, to 1am Fri, 1pm-1am Sat & Sun; ☐ 88) A shipping container wedged into an alley and converted into a bar and gelateria. Buy your craft beer and salami platter from the counter and proceed upstairs to the indoor sitting area. if it's too early to drink, have a gin- or whisky-laced gelato.

Daybreak 18
Teahouse TEAHOUSE
(十八卯茶屋, Shíbāmǎo Cháwū; ☑ 06-221 1218; 30 Mingquan 2nd Rd, 民權路二段30號; tea from NT$120; ⊙ 10am-6pm Tue-Fri & Sun, to 9.30pm Sat; ☐ 1, 2, 6, 7) Tucked away in the garden of the historic Tainan Public Hall (公會堂, Gōnghuì Táng), this elegant teahouse takes the form of a 1930s Japanese wooden structure. Settle in and taste the wide tea selection – black, white, green, oolong, fruit and herbal brews – complemented by ice cream and waffles, or buy beautiful pots and boxes of healing leaves.

Lily Fruit Shop JUICE
(莉莉水果店, Lìlì Shuǐguǒ Diàn; 199 Fuqian Rd, Sec 1, 府前路一段199號; fruit drinks NT$50; ⊙ 11am-11pm; ☐ 2, 6) Across from the Confucius Temple is this famous shop serving delicious *bàobīng* (刨冰, shaved ice and fruit) and fruit drinks. There's always a crowd waiting for a seat at one of the crammed tables on the pavement.

☆ Entertainment

Eirakucho Drum Tea House THEATRE
(永樂町鼓茶樓, Yǒnglè Dīng Gǔchá Lóu; ☑ 06-223 6722; 15 Gonghou St, 中西區宮後街15號; show with meal NT$500/800; ☐ 14) A handsome 140-year-old street house has been turned into a venue for tea and theatre, with daily performances of Taiwanese comedic dialogue. A tasty traditional meal is served during the shows, which are followed by a tour that takes you to the gallery and tearoom on the upper floors.

The shows, at 5.30pm or 7.30pm on Saturday and Sunday, and 12.30pm Monday to Friday, feature two characters in period costume drumming and relating the history and attractions of Tainan in a snappy modern stand-up of sorts. Dialogue is in Taiwanese; English subtitles are provided most of the time though the quality has room for improvement.

★ TCRC Live House LIVE MUSIC
(前科累累俱樂部, Qiánkē Lěilěi Jùlèbù; ☑ bar 06-222 8716; www.facebook.com/TCRClivehouse; basement, 314 Ximen Rd, Sec 2, 西門路二段314號 B1, 西門圓環上; from NT$300; ☐ 3, 5) This intimate dive at Ximen Roundabout is *the* place for live indie music in Tainan and a top one in southern Taiwan. There are weekly gigs by local, Asian and international artists. Shows start from 6pm or 9pm. Its Facebook page has the weekly line-ups or ask the bartender at TCRC Bar (p287) or Bar Home (p287).

🛍 Shopping

⭐ Ubuntu
BOOKS

(烏邦圖書店, Wūbāngtú Shūdiàn; ☑06-222 6919; www.facebook.com/Ubuntu烏邦圖_書店-1810180462608887; 2nd fl, 27 Lane 129, Huanhe St, 環河街129巷27號2樓; drinks from NT$85; ☉8.30am-8.30pm Wed-Mon; 📷; 🚃2) An airy bookshop-cafe with large windows framing the sky, trees and canal outside. The books are mostly in Chinese, and lean towards the arts and humanities. Buy a drink and stay put all day, or follow the sun and change seats every hour – the cafe is drenched in light in the morning and afternoon. Literary pickings may be slimmer for non-Mandarin readers, but there are high tables if you wish to use your laptop.

⭐ Hayashi
Department Store
DEPARTMENT STORE

(林百貨, Lín Bǎihuò; www.hayashi.com.tw; 63 Zhongyi Rd, Sec 2, West Central District, 忠義路二段63號; ☉11am-10pm) The elegant Hayashi Department Store sells attractive homewares and fashion created by Taiwanese designers, as well as gorgeously packaged Taiwanese cakes and sweets. They make excellent gifts. The top floor offers aerial views of neighbouring Land Bank. Take the Red Line bus heading towards Anping Industrial Park from Tainan Train Station, and get off at Hayashi Department stop.

Wu Wan Cun Incense Shop
HOMEWARES

(吳萬春香舖, Wúwànchūn Xiāngpu; ☑06-225 6842; www.wuwanchun1895.com.tw/wuwanchun 1895; 253 Mingquan Rd, Sec 2, 中西區民權路二段253號; ☉9am-6pm & Wed-Mon) This family-run incense business started 120 years ago in the Qing dynasty. Today the fragrant sticks and cones are still handmade from all-natural materials and categorised by material, longevity and usage. There are also tonnes of incense burners and gadgets, in modern or traditional designs, that you could buy as souvenirs.

Maru Yang Betel Nut Stall
GIFTS & SOUVENIRS

(馬路楊檳榔會社, Mǎlù Yáng Bīnláng Huishè; ☑06-224 3092; 136 Minzu Rd, Sec 3, 中西區民族路3段136號; ☉6am-midnight; 🚃2) Not 'just' a roadside stall, this one is run by the gregarious armchair historian Maru Yang. Mr Yang likes to share recommendations with travellers, some of whom visit his shop at night to shoot the breeze and drink. The booze is cheap and it's open till late. He also sells betel-nut keychains that make unusual souvenirs.

Song Leng
FOOD

(松稜, Sōngléng; ☑06-223 2376; http://songling.com.tw/songling; 405 Minzu Rd, Sec 2, 中西區民族路二段405號; ☉11am-8pm Wed-Mon; 🚃18) All kinds of fragrant sugar-cane smoked and braised deliciousness, such as tofu and eggs for immediate consumption, or hock and an entire chicken, vacuum-packed and chilled for your trip to your lodgings.

Tainan Kuang Tsai
Embroidery Shop
ARTS & CRAFTS

(府城光彩繡莊, Fǔchéng Guāngcǎi Xiù Zhuāng; ☑06-227 1253; 186-3 Yongfu Rd, Sec 2, 永福路2段186-3號; ☉8am-10pm; 🚃3,5) Mr Lin, one of the last remaining embroidery masters in Tainan, has been working at his craft for more than 50 years and now he and his daughter have taken the craft to a new, modern level. All his pieces have the light touch and expressiveness of a craftsman truly at the peak of his skills.

ℹ Information

After Taipei, Tainan is probably the most English-friendly city in Taiwan. The government is on a mission to make the city even more so. Nearly every sight worth seeing has English interpretive signs around it; important temples provide English audio tours and translations of fortunes told; and popular restaurants have English menus.

Tainan City Government's website (http://tour.tainan.gov.tw) has a wealth of information on everything to see, do and consume in the city. There is also a **visitor information centre** (遊客服務中心; ☑06-229 0082; 4 Beimen Rd, Sec 2, 北門路二段4號; ☉7.30am-7pm) in the train station with English-speaking staff and maps.

ℹ Getting There & Away

AIR

Tainan airport (台南機場; www.tna.gov.tw; 775 Jichang Rd, 機場路775號) is in South District of Tainan City. It has flights via China Airlines to Hong Kong and Osaka; via Uni Air to Kinmen and Magong; and via VietJet Air to Ho Chi Minh City.

Bus 5 connects the airport with Tainan Train Station (NT$18, 20 minutes). HSR shuttle buses (route H31) connect the HSR station at the airport with Tainan City Government Station (free, 40 minutes, every 30 minutes).

BUS

Ho-Hsin Bus Company (和欣客運; www.ebus.com.tw; 23 Beimen Rd, 北門路23號) offers services to Taipei (small/large seat NT$460/630, five to six hours, every 30 minutes).

UBus (www.ubus.com.tw) offers services to Taipei (NT$480, 4½ hours, every 30 minutes)

QING DYNASTY TRAIL

This foggy 18km Qing-dynasty **road** (浸水營古道, Jìnshuǐ Yíng Gǔdào; Chunri township, 枋寮鄉) once started at Fangliao and crossed the entire southern part of the island. Today it still covers half the island and takes six hours of downhill walking to reach the end of the trail, near Dawu on the east coast. Along the way you pass the remains of a Qing-dynasty army camp and a nature reserve.

The trail begins in the mountains east of Fangliao and runs along a jungle that receives the second-highest rainfall in Taiwan. You have a good chance of spotting local wildlife en route, including the Formosan rock macaque, the Reeves' muntjac, wild boar, wild pangolin and over 80 species of birds.

The last section of trail after the suspension bridge is washed out and it's a bit tricky to navigate the new paths over the ridge and onto the back roads to Dawu. Only during the winter months you can walk the last 5km stretch along the dry bed of the Dawu River, almost 1km across at this point.

To hike the trail you need a police permit and your own transport.

and Taichung (NT$270, three hours, every 30 minutes).

TRAIN

Tainan is a major stop on the Western Line with fast/slow trains to Taipei (NT$738/569, four/six hours) and Kaohsiung (NT$106/68, 30 minutes/one hour).

The High Speed Rail (HSR) station is a 30- to 40-minute drive or bus ride south of the city centre. High-speed trains to Taipei (NT$1350, two hours) leave every half-hour.

ⓘ Getting Around

BICYCLE

The city has a government bicycle-rental program called **T-Bike** (https://tbike.tainan.gov.tw; NT$10 per 30 minutes). Rental sites include Chihkan Towers (p278), Koxinga's Shrine (p278), Eternal Golden Castle (p280) snd Anping Parking Lot (near Anping Fort and Anping Tree House). You can return bikes to any station.

BUS

Tainan Bus (http://tainanbus.info) covers most of the city. Basic fares are NT$18, and buses run every 30 to 60 minutes. The hub across from the train station is **Tainan Bus Station** (台南公車站; Tainan Train Station, 台南火車站). Most city buses stop here, as do the tourist buses.

Tour bus 88 runs daily (NT$18, hourly from 10am to 8pm) to all major historic sites. Tour bus 99 runs to Sihcao Dazhong Temple in Taijiang National Park, or Taiwan Salt Museum (NT$18 to NT$36, every 30 minutes from 8.45am to 5.15pm, more frequently on weekends). The visitor information centre (p289) has a map of all routes and stops.

Sinan Bus Company (興南客運; ☏ 06-265 3132; www.snbus.com.tw; 72 Xinyue Rd, 新樂路72號) offers services throughout Tainan and the suburbs.

SCOOTER

Scooter rentals (機車出租) cost NT$300 to NT$400 per day and are available at **shops** (上好機車出租行, Shànghǎo Jīchē Chūzū Xíng; ☏ 06-274 4775; 176 Qianfeng Rd, East District, 東區前鋒路176號; per day from NT$300; ⏰ 7am-10pm) behind the train station. You only need an international driving permit (IDP) and ID.

TRAIN

Shalun train station is a five-minute jaunt from HSR station, and Tainan train station is only four stops away (NT$25, 25 minutes).

Houbi

 06 / POP 23,495

Houbi (後壁; Hòubì), 50km north of Tainan, has been regarded as the 'granary of Taiwan' because of the excellent quality of grains it produces. To visitors, the miles of farmland mean there are easy cycling opportunities and it makes a good day-trip option from Tainan or Chiayi.

Jingliao (菁寮; Jīngliáo) is another charming village on County Rd 82, 2km northwest of Houbi Train Station. It's undergoing rural revitalisation so guided tours and handicraft workshops for visitors are on the rise.

◉ Sights

Saint Cross Church   CHURCH
(菁寮天主堂, Jīngliáo Tiānzhǔtáng; ☏ 06-662 2975; www.jingliaochurch.org.tw; 294-1 Molin Lane, Jingliao, 菁寮墨林里294之1號) The unmissable Saint Cross Church, a Roman Catholic church designed by German architect Gottfried Boehm in the 1950s, is the highlight of a walk around atmospheric Jingliao village. If you want to see the interior, make con-

tact via email or by completing the bilingual application form on their website at least a week before your intended visit.

Jingliao Old Street LANDMARK
(菁寮老街, Jīngliáo Lǎojiē; Jingliao Lane, 後壁菁寮巷) The brief but charming Jingliao Old Street has an old clock shop, wooden houses, vintage hair salons and a handsome pharmacy, all built in a rural style between the 1900s and the 1950s. Many close before 6pm and some only open on weekends, so it's best to go on Saturday or Sunday.

**Togo Rural Village
Art Museum** AREA
(土溝農村美術館, Tǔgōu Nóngcūn Měishùguǎn; ☑06-687 4505; www.facebook.com/土溝-179826279340537; 56-1 Tugou, 土溝里56-1號; ⊙10am-5pm) This museum comprises two-dozen galleries and workshops housed in courtyard homes in Tugou village. Most are free to visit, but during special exhibitions a fee of NT$280 may apply. There are a lot of alleys, but getting lost is part of the fun and every turn can be a surprise when you see paddy fields adorned with artworks. The village is 3km northeast of Houbi Train Station.

🛏 Sleeping

Dutch Well Guesthouse GUESTHOUSE $
(荷蘭井湧泉民宿, Hélán Jǐngyǒngquán Mínsù; ☑0931-033 700; cnlceramists@yahoo.com.tw; 129 Jingliao Old St, 菁寮老街荷蘭井129號; r from NT$600; ❋⊜) With paddy fields just beyond the door and heart-warming hospitality, the rural atmosphere is unbeatable at this guesthouse inside a century-old courtyard home. Rooms are clean and simple, and decked out in jovial colours. The rice here is famous. You can taste it freshly harvested or even try your hand at gathering crops.

❶ Getting There & Away

To get there, take a local train from either Tainan or Chiayi to Houbi. There are bike rentals (NT$150 per three hours) right outside Houbi train station.

PINGTUNG COUNTY

☑08 / POP 847,917
Taiwan's poorest county has some of the country's best beaches, most fertile farmland, richest fish stocks and balmiest weather. Pingtung county (屏東; Píngdōng) also

boasts one of the most exuberant festivals in Taiwan, the Burning of the Wang Yeh Boats (p292), and there are outdoor pursuits aplenty – swimming, snorkelling and birding at Kenting National Park (p295), and cycling along the quiet county roads that roll slowly past calming fields and foothills.

👁 Sights

Choose Chius FARM
(邱氏咖啡巧克力, Qiūshì Kāfēi Qiǎokèlì; ☑0930-475 009; www.facebook.com/taiwancocoa; 328 Fufeng Rd, Neipu township, 內埔鄉富豐路328號; ⊙10am-8pm Tue-Sun; ▣) This is where Taiwan's first cacao grower, Mr Chiu, and his son run their restaurant and chocolate-making facility. They're the only Taiwanese chocolate maker using 100% Taiwan-grown beans and their pesticide-free products are delectable. Some things to try: rich drinking chocolate, Japanese-style ganache (生巧克力, *shēng qiǎokèlì*) squares, 80% dark chocolate, and juice of the cacao fruit (creatively named 'Tears of the Moon'). You can also buy coffee beans – the Chius have been growing coffee for over 20 years.

The young Mr Chiu runs 2½hr tours that include an orchard tour and making your own bonbons. It's NT$400 per person for a group of five. Book by phone or email at least a week in advance. The closest train stations are Xishi (西勢) station, and the old, Japanese-style Zhutian (竹田) station, but taxis are extremely hard to come by in these parts. If you've booked a tour, the Chius will pick you up from the station. Alternatively you can travel to the much-busier Chaozhou station and from there it's a 20-minute taxi ride to Choose Chius.

Cocosun FARM
(巧克力工廠, Qiǎokèlì Gōngchǎng; ☑08-781 0569; www.facebook.com/Cocosun巧克力工廠-481826391909927; 2-55 Fuxing Rd, Wan Luan township, 萬巒鄉萬和村復興路2之55號; ⊙9am-6pm; ▣Chaozhou) This no-frills cacao farm and ice-cream maker has a shop, cafe and orchard where you can sample ice cream made from the sweet pulp of the cacao fruit, or hot chocolate made with 100% local beans, and buy sweets to take home. It offers 40-minute guided tours of its well-equipped factory in English. Book one to two weeks prior to your arrival by phone or Facebook message. Cocosun is a five-minute cab ride from Chaozhou Train Station in Pingtung.

THE SPECTACULAR BOAT BURNING FESTIVAL

One of Taiwan's top folk festivals, the **Burning of the Wang Yeh Boats** (燒王船, Shāo Wángchuán; www.dbnsa.gov.tw) comprises a series of powerful spectacles over eight days. They include ceremonies performed to invite the gods to earth, feasting them, parading a boat all over town, then burning the vessel on a beach just before sunrise. The festival takes place every three years, and will next be held in the years of the Ox (2021), Dragon (2024), Goat (2027) and Dog (2030).

The festival is celebrated in fishermen's settlements along the southwestern coast of Taiwan. Even Cijin Island (p253) and Penghu Islands (p326) have their own versions, the frequency of which depends on tradition and availability of funds. The largest and most colourful celebrations by far take place in Pingtung – at Donglong Temple (p294; 東隆宮; Dōnglóng Gōng) in Donggang, Sanlong Temple (p299; 三隆宮; Sānlóng Gōng) on Little Liuchiu Island, and Datian Temple (代天府; Dài Tiānfǔ) in Nanzhou. In Donggang, what makes the festival so highly enjoyable is that everyone, the faithful and the spectators, are so taken in by it. Sublime, dignified, bizarre, entertaining and stirring: the boat burning is all that, and for most people, usually all at once.

The festival is sponsored by the resplendent Donglong Temple, established in 1706 and long one of the centres of folk faith in southern Taiwan. The exact dates vary, but the festival always starts after National Day on 10 October, on a Saturday, and ends on a Friday night (into Saturday morning). The next boat burning will happen in autumn 2021.

History

The origins of boat-burning festivals go back over 1000 years to the Song dynasty and are connected with the Wang Yeh, deities once worshipped for their ability to prevent disease.

The festivals were brought to Taiwan by Fujian immigrants in the 18th and 19th centuries, and have continued into modern times. Many southern temples still hold their own small boat burnings, but a greater number have simply merged their traditions with Donglong Temple.

The meaning of boat burnings has changed considerably today, and they are now held as prayers for peace and stability. But the dark and solemn plague-expulsion rituals remain central to the festival. There are also variations among the three versions of the event. For example, on Little Liuchiu, the temple casts 5000 cattys of candies and cookies at the crowds and the boat is paraded around the island to worship its four 'corners'.

Known officially as the Sacrifice of Peace and Tranquillity for Welcoming the Lords (東港迎王平安祭典; Dōnggǎng Yíngwáng Píng'ān Jìdiǎn), the festival runs for eight consecutive days. Most visitors (and you can expect tens of thousands of them) attend the first and last days.

The Ceremony

Day One

On Day One, a Saturday, the gods are formally invited. Around noon a procession leaves Donglong Temple for the beach, where it meets five Wang Yeh who are returning to earth for this year's festival. At the beach, spirit mediums (乩童, jītóng) write the names of the quintet in the sand when they sense their arrival. When the leader of the five Wang Yeh arrives, his surname is written on a large yellow banner. Usually the procession doesn't get back to the temple till late afternoon.

Shimen Historical Battlefield   HISTORIC SITE (石門古戰場, Shímén Gǔzhànchǎng; Checheng township; ⊙8am-5pm) This historic battlefield site is worth the steep 45-minute ascent more for its excellent views than for its historical remains. These include a memorial and an old military building. The mountains Shimen (石門山) and Wuzhongxi (五重溪山) form a natural entrance here, hence the

name, 'Shimen' or 'stone gate'. The battlefield trail is located along County Rd 199 near the 29.5Km mark.

Shimen is the site of Mudan Incident (牡丹社事件) in 1871 in which shipwrecked sailors from the then Ryukyu Kingdom accidentally wandered into the autonomous community of Mudan (牡丹社), inhabited by Paiwan tribes. For reasons that vary among

At around 7pm, local Donggang leaders carry the Wang Yeh (on sedan chairs) over live coals before they enter Donglong Temple.

Things to watch for on this day include people with paper yokes around their necks. Square yokes indicate that a wish has been asked. A fish or round yoke means a wish has been fulfilled.

Down at the beach there will be hundreds of other temple representatives with their gods and sedan chairs. Many will take the chairs into the ocean for a rough watery blessing. Painted troupes representing the Song Jiang Battle Array will also be around, though they usually perform earlier.

Days Two to Six
A number of rites and ceremonies take place in the days between the first and last days of the festival. The Passing over Fire Ceremony sees the palanquins of the Wang Yeh and the statues of other deities being passed over bonfires to cleanse them. This event is followed by a pilgrimage lasting several days during which different temples in the vicinity send representatives to accompany the Wang Yeh.

Days Seven & Eight
On the day before the burning, the Wang Yeh are carried around town on an inspection and are then feasted. The boat is also blessed. Volunteers parade the boat through town to allow it to collect every bit of misfortune and evil that it can. The boat returns to Donglong Temple around 7pm and is loaded with all manner of goods, as if truly going on a voyage.

Between 10pm and 11pm, Taoist priests burn pieces of paper spells and chant in the courtyard. This ritual relieves hundreds of gods and their thousands of foot soldiers from the duties they have performed this past week. After 11pm, watch (and have your camera ready) a priest with a wok, bagua symbols (Chinese religious motifs), broom, rice sifter and sword as he leads a large group of priests to dance and perform rituals to direct the demons onto the boat.

Around midnight the leaders of the temple offer the Wang Yeh one last special feast of 108 dishes, which include famous traditional palace foods, local snacks, fruit and wine. This is one of the most solemn and beautiful rites of the festival, but it's hard to get near enough as there is an ocean of people. Instead, you may want to wander around town a bit as many of the temples also hold interesting celebrations and rituals.

Around 2am the boat is dragged on wheels out of the temple grounds through a famous gold foil arch (it's a sight you'll never forget) and down to the beach. Expect a lot of exploding fireworks.

At the beach hundreds of tonnes of ghost paper is packed around the ship to help it burn, and the anchors, mast, sails (made of real cloth), windsock and lanterns are hoisted into place.

Finally the five Wang Yeh are invited onto the boat and firecrackers are used to start a fire, which slowly engulfs the entire ship. The burning takes place between 5am and 6am and it's proper to flee as soon as the boat is lit, to avoid having your soul taken away. These days only older locals follow this custom; most people actually go nearer to the fire, cameras in hand.

Paiwan, Japanese and Chinese versions of the story, dozens of the sailors were killed. This eventually evolved into Japan annexing the Ryukyu Islands. The Ryukyu Kingdom had been paying tribute to China for centuries up until then.

The incident was pivotal in shaping the political landscape in the Asia-Pacific region and Taiwan's fate.

🛏 Sleeping & Eating

Hua Yuan Guesthouse & Campground
GUESTHOUSE, CAMPSITE $
(華園休閒度假園地, Huáyuán Xiūxián Dùjiǎ Yuándì; ☑08-882 4208, 0938-771 758; http://hyhg.uukt.tw; 1-7 Damei Rd, Shimen village, Mudan county, 1-7大梅路，石門村，牡丹鄉; campsite NT$800, d from NT$1300) This modest guesthouse with Paiwan ethnic touches has four neat and simple rooms, and a campground

where you can pitch your own tent. The Damei Community has its own hot-spring source and is right next to the old Sichongsi Hot Springs area where *onsen* options abound.

Between the Km33 and Km32 markers of County Rd 199, turn into the conspicuous gates of the Damei Coummunity (大梅社區). Go straight and you'll see signs for the guesthouse.

Nanfang Buluo   TAIWANESE INDIGENOUS **$$**
(南方部落, Nánfāng Bùluò; ☑0975-260 277; Lin 2, 1-16 Shimen Rd, Shimen village, 石門村2鄰, 石門路1-16; dishes NT$100-700; ⊙9am-8pm) A rustic indigenous restaurant that whips out great Amis and Paiwan dishes. Signature items include chicken soup (雞湯, *jītāng*) with local cinnamon, and fish cooked with *magaw* (馬告魚, *mǎgàoyú*). 'Maqaw' is the name used by the indigenous Atayal for mountain pepper. There's also Lover's Tears (雨來菇), a healthy dish containing an algae similar to Chinese black-ear fungus. Portions are generous, too.

❶ Getting There & Away

Kaohsiung Bus Company operates services (routes 9188 and 9189) between Zuoying High Speed Rail (HSR) Station and Checheng. Some guesthouse owners in mountain areas can provide transportation to and from Zuoying HSR Station or help you arrange a taxi.

❶ Getting Around

Pingtung Bus routes 8205 and 8239 run between Pingtung and Checheng from Pingtung Main Station. It is best to have your own transportation if you plan to travel in mountain areas within Pingtung. County Rd 199 cuts through most of Checheng township and can be reached from Provincial Hwy 26 or Provincial Hwy 9.

Donggang

☑08 / POP 48,233
During the Qing dynasty, Donggang (東港; Dōnggǎng) was one of three main commercial ports in Taiwan, the landing site for the ancestors of millions of modern Taiwanese (in particular the Hakka), and a rather prosperous little town. Today the town of about 50,000 people remains an important centre for fishing, especially the prized bluefin tuna and mullet, but its heyday is long gone. Donggang is perhaps best known for its spectacular Burning of the Wang Yeh Boats

Festival (p292), which happens in October once every three years.

◉ Sights

★**Fu Wan Chocolate**   FARM
(福灣巧克力, Fúwān Qiǎokèlì; ☑08-835 1555; www.fuwanshop.com; 100 Dapeng Rd, 東港大鵬路100號; ⊙9am-6pm; ⚑) Cacao orchard, boutique, and hotel in one, Fu Wan makes fabulous, (mostly) tree-to-bar chocolate that's bagged multiple laurels at the International Chocolate Awards. You can buy bars, ice cream and drinks at their lovely boutique. Flavoured chocolate includes Thai curry shrimp in white chocolate and 70% dark with lychee. You can see the manufacturing process, from the trees and pods to drying and fermentation. If that wasn't enough, the upstairs gallery explains everything with bilingual infographics and samples to smell and taste. Fu Wan also runs child-friendly chocolate-making workshops at NT$250 per person – cheaper for guests at their hotel and groups of eight. Email to book or for enquiries.

To get here from New Zuoying High Speed Rail (HSR) Station in Kaohsiung, take the Kenting Express to Dapeng Station at Zuoying. Travel time is 50 minutes. From there, it's a 1.3km walk to Fu Wan. Alternatively you can book a ride online with Fu Wan; it's NT$1000 to NT$2000 per person for a trip to or from Zuoying HSR station.

Donglong Temple   TAOIST TEMPLE
(東隆宮, Dōnglónggōng; 21-1 Donglong St, 東隆街21-1號; ⊙5am-10pm) A resplendent monument impossible to miss, Donglong is the centre of Wang Yeh worship in these parts. The original temple was built over a hundred years ago in the Qing dynasty. The imposing four-storey archway you see today is covered with gold foil and gleams even at night. During the triennial Burning of the Wang Yeh Boat festival (p292), it is in the courtyard here that the ceremonial vessel is kept and that many of the rituals take place.

⌖ Sleeping

★**Fu Wan Villa**   VILLA **$$$**
(福灣莊園, Fúwān Zhuāngyuán; ☑08-832 0888; www.facebook.com/villafuwan; 100 Dapeng Rd, 東港大鵬路100號; villa NT$2800-16,800, ste NT$2500-7000; 🅿❄☀🛜🏊; 🐾) A few steps from the chocolate boutique are relaxing resort-type suites and villas. Four of the villas

come with a small lap pool and kitchenette. You can buy fresh seafood (for which Donggang is famous) from the market and cook it yourself while your kids run around in the outdoor living room. Rates include breakfast, and are slighter higher on weekends.

The hotel has a restaurant specialising in seafood dishes; mains are NT$150 to NT$1380.

To get here from New Zuoying High Speed Rail (HSR) Station in Kaohsiung, take the Kenting Express to Dapeng Station at Zuoying. Travel time is 50 minutes. From there, it's a 1.3km walk to Fu Wan. Alternatively you can book a ride online with Fu Wan; it's NT$1000 to 2000 per person for a trip to or from Zuoying HSR Station.

✗ Eating & Drinking

Kao Wei Xian BARBECUE $
(烤味鮮; 113 Yanping Rd, 延平路113號; skewers NT$20-50; ⊘5pm-1.30am) At this semi-outdoor barbecue joint, mark your selections on a slip of paper and hand it to waitstaff or, if you can't read Chinese, just point; have a beer as you wait. Everything from chicken wings and pork belly to rice cakes and asparagus is skewered and grilled – as good for a snack for one, as a feast for many. There's a stall out the front for takeaway orders.

Baiwago Plus CAFE
(百瓦哥咖啡, Bǎiwǎgē Kāfēi; ✆08-833 9568; 192 Zhongzheng Rd, 中正路192號; ⊘7am-9pm) Bai-

wago is a tiny cafe that whips out excellent coffee and bags of Pingtung beans for sale. It's the one with open frontage and white tiled walls, and just a couple of tables by the side of busy Zhongzheng Rd.

❶ Getting There & Away

Buses from Kaohsiung (NT$141, 50 to 70 minutes, every 30 minutes) and Pingtung (NT$82, 50 minutes, every 20 minutes) drop you off near the McDonald's in central Donggang. Facing McDonald's, turn left and left again at the first intersection. Donglong Temple is about 500m down the road on the left.

If you're here for the Wang Yeh boat burning festival (p292), consider taking a bus or taxi down to Kenting afterwards. You'll need some rest.

Kenting National Park
⏲08

Kenting National Park (墾丁國家公園; Kěndīng Guójiā Gōngyuán) drew lots of attention first as a setting for Taiwanese director Wei Te-sheng's blockbuster *Cape No. 7*, and later for Ang Lee's *Life of Pi* in 2012. But long before this cinema-fuelled tourism spike, the park, which occupies the entire southern tip of Taiwan, was drawing in flocks of visitors who came to swim, surf, snorkel, dive, hike and enjoy a little nightlife – all year round. The average January temperature is 21°C and it's usually warm enough for you to swim. In July it can get to

---

WHERE TO SWIM, SURF & SNORKEL IN SOUTHERN TAIWAN

Taiwan's waters have treacherous currents and undertows not far offshore. Some sound advice is to go no deeper than where your feet can still touch the sand.

Kenting Beach is the longest swimming beach in the area. The beach across from the Caesar Hotel is smaller but set in picture-perfect Little Bay (小灣; Xiǎowān). It has a beach bar and showers (free for Caesar Hotel guests, a nominal fee for others). This beach is very family-oriented.

The vibe at Nanwan (南灣; Nánwān; South Bay) is young and brash. The beach has been cleaned up a lot but expect tractors on the beach, and jet-ski heroes making runs at the sand with complete disregard for whoever might be in their way.

The sweet little crescent beach at Baisha Bay (白砂灣; Báishā Wān) is a little further afield but has been in the limelight after Ang Lee shot parts of *Life of Pi* here. Still, it's the least crowded beach around.

Jumping off the chin (and other protuberances) of Sail Rock (船帆石; Chuánfán Shí), aka Nixon Rock, and swimming round the landmark is also a popular swimming option.

The waters around Jialeshui and the nuclear power plant at Nanwan have the best surfing waves. Jialeshui is by far the more laid-back and less crowded of the two. You can hire surfboards (NT$800 per day) almost everywhere.

For snorkelling, check out the coral formations near Sail Rock. You can hire gear across the road.

a scorching 38°C. Low mountains and hilly terraces prevail over much of the land in the park, along with rugged high cliffs and sandy deserts. The swimming beaches with yellow sands and turquoise waters are wonderfully suited to recreation, and sightseeing on a scooter or bicycle is highly enjoyable.

◉ Sights & Activities

Sheding Nature Park
WILDLIFE RESERVE

(社頂自然公園, Shèdǐng Zìrán Gōngyuán; 186-1 Shexing Rd, Hengchun, 社興路186-1號; ⊙8am-5pm) **FREE** This well-protected expanse of scrubby hills and open grasslands is a favourite with picnickers, hiking families and ecotourists. A pathway runs through creaking bamboo groves and crevices between huge coral rocks. The reintroduced sika deer is often spotted in the brush, as are endemic bird species, dozens of butterfly species, macaques and even wild boar.

Kenting Forest Recreation Area
FOREST

(墾丁森林遊樂區, Kěndīng Sēnlín Yóulèqū; 201 Gongyuan Rd, 公園路201號; adult NT$100-150/ student NT$75; ⊙8am-5pm) Once an undersea coral reef, this forest area is now a quirky landscape of limestone caves, narrow canyons and cliff walls strangled with the roots of banyan trees inhabited by wild macaques. There are stellar views to be had from some of the paths, as well as a viewing tower in the middle of the park. It's one of the most visited places in Kenting National Park, so try to arrive early. Tickets are sold at the entrance.

CYCLING KENTING

Hengchun Peninsula is one of Taiwan's best cycling destinations.The 100km-long Kenting coastal loop is a popular and scenic cycling route. From Checheng, take County Rd 153 along the coast down to Nanwan; from there, switch to Hwy 26 and head east to Jialeshui. The roads are usually not busy and run through a beautiful landscape of beaches and coastal bluffs. From Jialeshui, the 200 takes you back to Hengchun via beautiful Manzhou. At Checheng, another good alternative is to head east on the County Rd 199, one of the sweetest rural roads in the south.

Eluanbi Lighthouse
LIGHTHOUSE

(鵝鑾鼻燈塔, Éluánbí Dēngtǎ; 90 Dengta Rd, Hengchun, 燈塔路90號; adult/child NT$60/30; ⊙7am-5.30pm Jan-Mar & Oct-Dec, 6.30am-6.30pm Apr-Sep) Kenting's best-known landmark – a still-functioning lighthouse built in the 1880s – is at Eluanbi Cape, the southernmost end of Taiwan's Central Mountain Range and inside Eluanbi Park. The park, open 24 hours, is a part of Kenting Forest Recreation Area and is served by a separate entrance. Eluanbi Park has hiking trails running through vines and past huge coral rocks, as well as a coastal walkway and lookout points.

Jialeshui
AREA

(佳樂水, Jiālèshuǐ; adult/child NT$80/40; ⊙7.30am-5.30pm) The admission fee buys you a half-hour tour-bus ride (and back) along a 2.5km-long stretch of coral coastline, as the driver explains to you the monikers of rocks that have been eroded into interesting shapes. After buying the ticket at the entrance, wait in line for the tour bus.

★Eyai Sailing Club
BOATING

(伊亞帆船俱樂部, Yīyà Fānchuán Jùlèbù; ☑0905-656 228; http://eyaiboat.okgo.tw; 79-5 Daguangli Rd, Hengchun, 恆春鎮大光里路79-5號; ⊙9am-5pm) The club takes passengers on excursions on its Lagoon 380 catamaran and Yamaha 242 jet. For the catamaran, it's NT$2000 per person for 90 minutes, and the rate includes a boatman and 30 minutes of snorkelling, with gear provided; or NT$25,000 for the whole boat for two hours. The jet is NT$10,000 an hour for up to five people.

Sailings are usually 10am, 2pm and 4pm daily, but times and frequency vary by season.

The captain, Mr Kai Chen, is a flamboyant character who brings his golden retriever on board with him. The canine, named Mijiang (米漿; Rice Milk), has been trained for lifeguard duty. Call at least a day in advance to make reservations. The university students working at the club in exchange for free accommodation speak English.

🛏 Sleeping

★Rainbow Wave
HOSTEL $

(彩虹波浪, Cǎihóng Bōlàng; ☑08-888 3421; http://rainbowwavecrew.blogspot.com; 92 Zhongzheng Rd, Hengchun, 中正路92號; dm NT$400-500, d NT$1200; ❀❅🛜) This hostel, opened by a photographer and a surfing instructor, has doubles, triples and large dormitory rooms, and an awesome vibe. The spacious

Kenting National Park

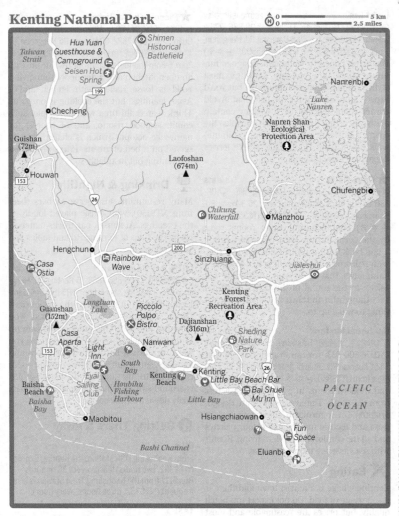

communal areas, including the rooftop where you can do laundry or watch the stars, are decked out with ecofriendly furniture. The hostel also holds impromptu jamming and hotpot sessions, and arranges surfing lessons and tours upon request.

⭐**Casa Aperta**　　　　　　　　B&B **$$**
(迷路爲了看花, Mílù Wéile Kànhuā; www.casa
aperta.com; 58 Shulin Rd, Hengchun, 恆春鎭樹
林路58號; d NT$2220-4200; ⊕❋🛜🏊) This
casa is remotely located, but in exchange for
convenience, you get (seven) gorgeous rooms
that call to mind villas in the Aegean, a pool
overlooking the ocean, lounge chairs and a

lawn for relaxation, and a sumptuous breakfast. There are no restaurants around so it's well worth having dinner here, too – the cooking is remarkable.

Casa Aperta is a 15-minute drive from Kenting village.

Fun Space　　　　　　　　HOSTEL **$$**
(放空間, Fàng Kōngjiān; 📞08-885 1685; www.fun-
space-inn.com; 208 Shadao Rd, Hengchun, 恆春砂
島路208號; d NT$2000-3000; ❋🛜) Nine dou-
bles are pristine and light-flooded, including
six with balconies overlooking the beach.
Rates include breakfast, and are NT$400 to
NT$800 more on weekends.

Light Inn
BOUTIQUE HOTEL $$

(光現旅舍, Guāngxiàn Lǚshě; ☎08-886 7768; www.the-light.com.tw; 78-6 Daguang Rd, Hengchun, 恆春大光路78-6號; r NT$3000-5500; ❄❀🛜) Featuring concrete walls and designer furniture, these are possibly Kenting's most stylish rooms. They're comfortable but you'd expect more service for the price tag. Avoid corner rooms ending in '1' as they contain a disconcerting lightwell that shrinks the room. Light Inn is a 1.2km (or 20-minute) walk uphill from Houbi Lake where ferries depart for Lanyu Island.

★ Casa Ostia
B&B $$$

(聽著海聲迷路, Tīngzhuó Hǎishēng Mílù; ☎08-886 9866; https://casa-ostia.com; 25-3 Wanli Rd, Hengchun, 萬里路 25-3號; NT$3500-4900; ❄❀🛜) Four beautiful, quiet rooms right by the ocean on the west coast of Kenting – laid-back with a refined but lived-in vibe, with balconies, floor-to-ceiling windows, and hammocks that allow you to literally fall asleep to the sound of the waves. Staff are very thoughtful and their breakfast is a great thing to wake up to.

Bai Shuei Mu Inn
BOUTIQUE HOTEL $$$

(白水木水漾會館, Báishuǐmù Shuǐyàng Huìguǎn; ☎0976-600 333; www.wwwhouse16.com; 16 Lane 852, Chuanfan Rd, Erluanbi, 鵝鑾里船帆路852巷16號; d from NT$3880; ❄❀🛜) Eight bright, clean and modern rooms in a low-rise just across from Sail Rock. The living spaces are design-oriented (in a furniture showroom sort of way) and feature understated colour palettes and all the comforts of modern living. Rooms with sea views are more expensive.

🍴 Eating

Kenting village is a tourist town and there is no shortage of food. Do not expect top-notch quality, but prices are reasonable and most places are open late. Hengchun and the strip in Nanwan are also loaded with restaurants. Houbi Lake has a few good seafood venues that are only open during the high season.

Kenting Night Market
MARKET $

(墾丁大街夜市, Kěndīng Dàjiē Yèshì; Kenting Main St, 墾丁大街; ⏱7pm-late) Kenting's night market is renowned as being one of the best in Taiwan, and that's saying something. Every evening as the sun goes down, the vendors stalls begin to set up along about a 1km strip of the town's main street, Kenting Dajie. Stalls run the gamut from freshly grilled scallops and squid to fried noodles, stinky tofu, deep-fried milk and heaps of fruity cocktails.

★ Piccolo Polpo Bistro
ITALIAN $$$

(迷路小章魚餐酒館, Mílù Xiǎozhāngyú Cānjiǔ Guǎn; ☎08-888 2822; 60 Nanwan Rd, Hengchun, 恆春鎮南灣路60號; mains NT$480-2000; ⏱noon-3pm, 6-8pm Thu-Tue) Charming restaurant with an open kitchen and a decidedly young vibe. Food is loose Italian with French and/or Asian leanings, but the cooking is on point. Think seared ahi tuna with pineapple, duck confit, seafood risotto, and of course, the namesake octopus which is chargrilled and served on a bed of greens. Prices are higher for Kenting but justifiably so.

🍷 Drinking & Nightlife

Many restaurants also serve as bars (beer from NT$150), with music played loudly in the evenings. At sunset, bar trucks materialize by the sides of Kenting Rd and tables and stools are set up.

Little Bay Beach Bar
BAR

(小灣酒吧; ☎08-886 1888; 6 Kenting Rd, Hengchun, 墾丁路6號; beer from NT$150; ⏱11am-10pm) Though it's run by the mega-sized Caesar Park Resort across the road, you wouldn't know it. This outdoor bar-cafe on Little Bay Beach (小灣海灘) is everything you want in a beach bar: chilled-out tables and loungers, sunny tunes and free-flowing booze right next to the sand. The best time of day is around sunset, when the golden orb floats lazily down over the coast.

ℹ Getting There & Away

BUS

From Kaohsiung HSR station, the Kenting Express (NT$392, two hours) leaves every 30 minutes. Bus 9117 from the Kaohsiung Train Station is less frequent (NT$352, three hours, every hour).

TAXI

Taxis take groups of passengers from the main train station in Kaohsiung to Kenting village for NT$350 per person (two hours). Single travellers can wait until the taxi fills, which usually doesn't take long. However, it's difficult for a single traveller to take a shared taxi from the HSR (NT$400 per person) unless your hotel has arranged this.

ℹ Getting Around

Kenting Shuttle Bus (墾丁街車; Kěndīng Jiēchē) has four routes; it runs roughly every 30 minutes and stops at almost all major sights in the park. A day pass costs NT$150. Hotels can arrange car, 4WD or scooter rental. Scooter-rental shops (NT$400 to NT$500 per day) are to the right as you enter Kenting village from the north. Some shops now refuse to rent to travellers unless they have a Taiwanese driving licence.

Little Liuchiu Island

📮08 / POP 12,675

The pretty, coral Little Liuchiu Island (小琉球; Xiǎo Liúqiú) offers sea vistas, convoluted caves, sandy beaches, odd rock formations and temples to keep you happy for a long, long day. Best of all, it's simple to get to and to get around. Going green has never looked better on the island: in 2013 the destructive practice of gill-net fishing was banned to protect the corals and the 200 endangered green sea-turtles inhabiting the coasts. During the turtles' nesting season (May to July), residents and visitors alike are not allowed access to certain parts of the coast after dusk.

You can visit Liuchiu all year round, but winters are lovely: warm and dry, with temperatures averaging in the mid-20°C range. The island is part of the Dapeng Bay National Scenic Area.

👁 Sights & Activities

You can ride around Little Liuchiu on a scooter in about 30 minutes, but give yourself at least a day. This island was made for exploring. The main attractions are Vase Rock, a giant eroded coral with a thin base and large head, and the less impressive Black Dwarf and Beauty Caves. Some sites require an entrance ticket; one ticket for NT$120 is good for all of them, and are sold near sight entrances, and at hostels and the pier.

You can also check out the narrow, twisting, root-strangled coral passageways at Shanzhu Ditch (山豬溝; Mountain Pig Ditch; Shānzhū Gōu) and Lingshan Temple (靈山寺; Língshān Sì), just up from the pier. The tem-

MORE THINGS TO DO

The best place for a swim is at Zhong Ao Beach (中澳沙灘; Zhōng Ào Shātān). The beach at Vase Rock is nice for wading or snorkelling, while the tiny but picturesque stretch of shell-sand beach at Geban Bay (蛤板灣; Gébǎnwān) makes for a sweet picnic spot.

To learn about the island's marine life, evening guided tours to Shanfu Ecological Corridor (杉福生態廊道; Shānfú Shēngtài Lángdào) can be arranged at all homestays. It's the only intertidal zone on the island open to the public.

ple offers fine, clear views across the Taiwan Strait. For off-the-beaten-path scenery, head to the southeastern coast, where wind and waves have created fantastic rock sculptures.

⭐**Vase Rock**   BEACH

(花瓶岩, Huāpíng Yán; included in island-wide sights NT$120) One of Taiwan's most iconic landmarks, Vase Rock, close to the pier, is a 9m-tall block of coral-limestone with a large head and a tapering body. It's called Vase Rock because vegetation covers its top, but it also looks like a windblown mushroom. The shallows leading to Vase Rock teem with tiny marine life that children can spend hours observing.

Sanlong Temple   TEMPLE

(三隆宮, Sānlóng Gōng; 45 Zhongshan Rd, 中山路45號; ⏰6am-9pm) Located on a hillside 1.6km from the pier, the immense Sanlong Temple, aka 'Wang Yeh Temple', is Little Liuchiu's religious heart. The island's Wang Yeh boat is built in a dedicated shed (廟王船閣; Miàowáng Chuán Gé) on the temple's left for the boat-burning festival (p292), held every three years. The spacious courtyard is where crowds gather to partake in the peace praying ritual. On non-festival days the temple is quiet, with two illuminated miniature boats blinking in its side halls.

Houshi Fringing Reef   BEACH

(厚石裙礁, Hòushí Qúnjiāo) Several kilometres of rock platform are distributed along the island's southeastern coast – erosion has sculpted it into fantastic formations that the locals have named. The beaches in this area are arguably the most beautiful in all of Little Liuchiu Island.

🛏 Sleeping

Backpacker Inn   HOSTEL $

(背包棧, Bèibāo Zhàn; 📞08-861 2302; www.facebook.com/棧背包-1427852854175063/timeline; 186-1 Zhongzheng Rd, 大福村中正路186-1號; dm NT$600; ❄✳📶) Possibly the cheapest beds on the island belong to this hostel with three dorms for six or eight persons. Service is minimal so it's good for guests who like to be left alone. The preferred mode of reservation is via the chat app, Line (ID: backpack186) or the hostel's Facebook page. If calling, do so between 9am and 9.30pm.

⭐**Secret Path B&B**   B&B $$

(小琉球朵小路北歐民宿, Xiǎoliúqiú Duǒxiǎolù Běiōu Mínsù; 📞0988-598 592; 63-2 Fuxing Rd, 復興路163之2號; d NT$2400-3200; ❄✳📶) Secret Path is popular among young families

Little Liuchiu Island

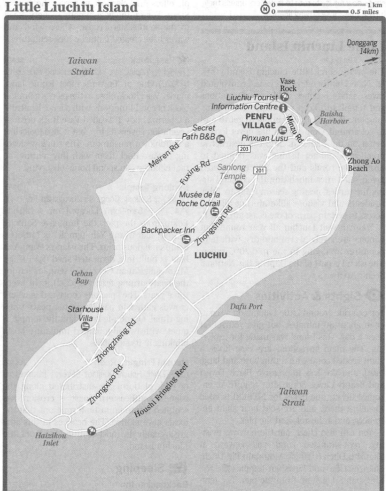

with children. And it's not surprisingly: rooms are large, fresh and modern, their cool-tones accented by cute, toy-like ornaments. All rooms have a decent-sized balcony. Breakfast is prepared to order and will likely fill you for the rest of the morning.

★ **Musée de la
Roche Corail**   BOUTIQUE HOTEL **$$**
(瑚岩藝術館, Húyán Yìshù Guǎn; ☑ 0928-707 585, 0933-620 438; www.corail23.com; 23 Zhongshan Rd; 中山路23號; d from NT$2400; ❀❄☎) A Tainan sculptor and his friend have created a hotel on an outlying island so cool it was featured in an architecture magazine. This

grey concrete structure punctuated by hole-like windows rises out of the ground like coral limestone and houses a living room, an art gallery and nine discreet rooms arranged around an atrium.

Pinxuan Lusu   B&B **$$**
(品軒旅宿, Pǐnxuān Lǚsù; ☑ 0921-288 406; www.facebook.com/品軒旅宿-199520623945143; 7 Lane 1, Zhongshan Rd, 本福村中山路一巷七號; d NT$3000; ❀❄☎) Three cosy doubles above a sushi joint also owned by the amicable Chens. Artistic driftwood pieces and ink-and-brush calligraphy embellish the rooms. The beds with silver-grey bedding

HIKING BEIDAWUSHAN

Sandimen (三地門; Sāndìmén) is a stronghold of the Rukai and Paiwan tribes, 30km east of Pingtung. A side route off County Rd 185 south of Sandimen takes you to the trailhead to Beidawushan (北大武山; Běidàwǔshān). The most southerly mountain in Taiwan, it rises to over 3000m. A holy peak, home to spirits of the Rukai and the Paiwan, it now requires a tough two-day hike to reach it. From the summit you can observe both the Pacific Ocean and the Taiwan Strait, and look down upon a reserve that might be the last refuge of the clouded leopard.

The trail to the summit is about 12km in length. Signposts are in both English and Mandarin.

The trailhead begins at an elevation of 1160m. After an hour or two of steep climbing (370m up), the trail widens and it's a 3km hike to Kuaigu Inn (aka Cedar Valley Lodge; altitude 2150m), which has running water, toilets and a campground. Note that you need to reserve online with a Taiwanese ID should you want to stay in the inn (but not the campground). Allow yourself five to six hours to go from the new trailhead to the camp-ground. Formosan macaques and flying squirrels can be spotted en route.

The next day you need to be on the trail by 6am. Expect a lot of switchbacks, with some tricky rope sections before the ridge. Highlights include a 1000-year-old red cedar (with a 25m circumference), a Japanese-era shrine and forests of rare hemlock spruce.

The last couple of hours to the summit run along a wooded ridgeline.

You need your own vehicle to get to the trailhead and expect to get lost a few times getting here. As you ride along County Rd 185 heading south, turn left just past the Km40 mark, heading towards the hills and Jiaping village (佳平村; Jiāpíng Cūn), also known as Taiwu village.

One kilometre up the hill, stop at the police station to apply for mountain permits. From then on, consult a good map.

---

are low and plush. The Chens are happy to share their experience of driftwood scavenging if you're game. The rate includes a western-style breakfast.

This B&B is conveniently located close to the port and Vase Rock (p299).

Starhouse Villa HOTEL $$$
(琉星嶼, Liúxīng Yǔ; ☑ 08-861 3808; www.starhouse.tw/villa-room-2.html; 7-6 Zhongzheng Rd, 天福村中興路7-6號; d/villa for 2 from NT$3500/4200; ◉❋🌐📶) This place overlooking the sea has large colourful gues-trooms, some with a balcony, and a host of open-layout luxury villas that each come with a small outdoor pool. Weekend rates are NT$1000 more.

ⓘ Information

There's an ATM in the 7-Eleven in Penfu village.
Liuchiu Tourist Information Centre (遊客服務中心; ☑ 08-861 4615; www.dbnsa.gov.tw; 20-1 Minzu Rd, 民族路20~1號; ☺9am-5pm) is just above Lingshan Temple on the cliff. Very little English is spoken but the view up here is good.

ⓘ Getting There & Away

BOAT

Boats to Baisha Harbour leave Donggang hourly in the morning from 7am, and every 1½ hours in the afternoon until 5pm (NT$410 return, 30 minutes). The last return boat to Donggang leaves at 5.30pm.

BUS

Buses stop in central Donggang diagonally opposite McDonald's. From here catch a quick taxi (NT$100) to the harbour ferry terminals. Use the first terminal on the right before the fish market.

To Donggang, buses leave from Pingtung every 20 minutes (NT$82, 50 minutes), and from Kaohsiung (NT$141, 50 to 70 minutes) every 30 minutes.

ⓘ Getting Around

The island is only 9km around so you could theoretically walk it in a day, though that could give you heat stroke in the summer months. Electric-bike (NT$300 per day) and scooter hire (NT$250/300 per half-/full day) are available at the harbour – you don't need ID or a licence.

Taiwan Strait Islands

Includes ➡

Best Places to Eat

➡ Cauliflower Old Memory (p335)

➡ La Table de Moz (p335)

➡ Jingwo Xiaochi (p320)

➡ Furen Cafe (p323)

➡ Jin Shui (p316)

➡ Beichen Market (p335)

Best Places to Stay

➡ Piano Piano B&B (p307)

➡ Grace Homestay (p316)

➡ So Lohas (p319)

➡ PH Hostel (p334)

➡ Flowerhouse51 (p338)

➡ Hostel 55 (p323)

➡ Yun-Jin Villa Matsu (p323)

Why Go?

The very existence of Taiwan's outlying islands comes as a surprise to many foreign visitors, although the three main archipelagos are rapidly growing as domestic tourist destinations. Attractions include traditional villages, beaches, birdwatching, marine life and, in Kinmen and Matsu, a plethora of intriguing ex-military sights. Both Kinmen and Matsu lie far closer to mainland China than they do to Taiwan itself, and for decades – until relations thawed between Taipei and Beijing – both island groups were effectively strings of defensive strongholds. Ironically, despite suffering years of bombardment, much traditional domestic architecture survived as the non-military economy was stagnant and many Fujianese-style houses were simply left while their owners sought safety elsewhere.

Penghu has some perfect sand beaches, pristine waters and diveable coral reefs, while reliable breezes make the ocean here one of Asia's top spots for windsurfing.

When to Go
Makung (Penghu Island)

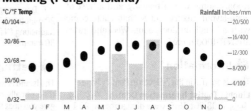

Apr–mid-Sep High season; pleasant and warm weather, usually several degrees cooler than Taipei.

Mar & Apr Thick fogs possible in Kinmen and Matsu causing flight delays.

Oct–Mar Windy season in Penghu, which reduces boat transport, but good news for kitesurfers.

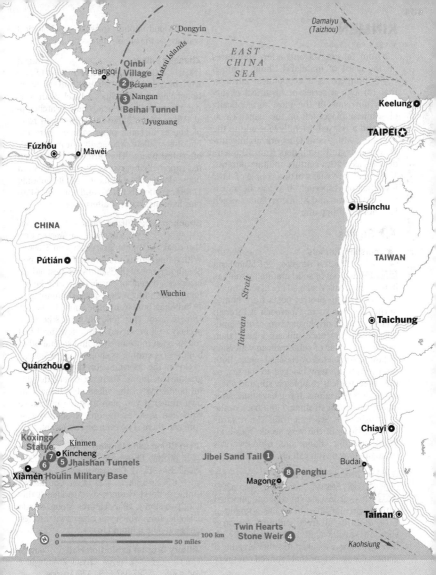

Taiwan Strait Islands Highlights

1 **Jibei Sand Tail** (p337) Posing for desert island photos on this often empty stretch of paradisaical beach.

2 **Qinbi Village** (p318) Pottering about the stairway-alleys of Taiwan's best preserved historical village.

3 **Beihai Tunnel** (p321) Taking a night-time boat ride

through naval sea tunnels to observe the twinkling algae.

4 **Twin Hearts Stone Weir** (p337) Finding romance in a fish trap.

5 **Jhaishan Tunnels** (p304) Exploring an underground canal big enough to hide a small navy.

6 **Houlin Military Base** (p314) Dressing up in combat fatigues to shoot laser-simulation rifles.

7 **Koxinga Statue** (p309) Crossing a low-tide causeway to reach this 9m-tall statue.

8 **Penghu** (p329) Windsurfing with the champions.

KINMEN

082 / POP 127,800

Far from Taiwan, yet only a few kilometres off the coast of mainland China, Kinmen (金門; Jīnmén) is a geopolitical curiosity that through a series of historical chances, is now one of the most authentically old-Chinese places left on the planet. Great food and a relaxed, friendly vibe add to the appealing Ming- and Qing-era architectural remnants and reminders from Kinmen's decades as a 20th-century military outpost. The islands are well worth a couple of days' investigation, especially if you're in transit between Taiwan and Xiamen (China), which is a short boat hop away.

◉ Sights

★ Jhaishan Tunnels HISTORIC SITE

(翟山坑道, Zháishān Kēngdào; ⊙8.30am-5pm) FREE Blasted out of solid granite by soldiers in the 1960s, this V-shaped arc of sea tunnels was designed to protect boats from bombs during the war years. Approach it through a large garden displaying two of the landing vessels that once unloaded here, then descend to a pair of subterranean waterside walkways serenaded by classical music. Both tunnel ends are now blocked to the sea, so the water inside is completely still and offers mirror-like reflections. If you have time, after exiting it's worth strolling 250m back to the coast using the 'Seasight Trail'. The rewards are fine views of the very scenic rock-and-forest coastline. Some bus 6/6A services come this way or you can use Tourist Bus A.

Beishan Broadcasting Wall HISTORIC SITE

(北山播音牆, Běishān Bòyīn Qiáng; Map p306) FREE This vertical slab of concrete punched with 48 circular holes looks like a forgotten work of 1970s abstract sculpture set on a very low seaside 'cliff'. In fact, behind each hole was once a speaker, together creating a giant noise generator that cranked out prop-

aganda loud enough to wage psychological warfare on the enemy across the strait.

Zhushan Village VILLAGE

(珠山村, Zhūshān Cūn; ☒3, 6, 6A, 8) All a-twitter with birdsong, Zhushan is Kinmen's traditional village core, chock-a-block with low-rise, tile-roofed homesteads built in archetypal Fujian style. Unlike the regimented rows of houses in some other villages, here the buildings radiate organically out from a pair of central ponds. The shrine at building 60 has superb door carvings. Virtually every old house doubles as a homestay, while building 17 serves coffee (NT$100) and wine (NT$150) plus light meals in the afternoons.

Shanhou Folk Culture Village VILLAGE

(山后民俗文化村, Shānhòu Mínsú Wénhuà Cūn; Map p306; ☒31 from Shamei, 25 from Shanwai) With a fine setting in a bowl of green slopes, Shanhou is one of the island's prettiest old villages with dozens of classic tile-roofed Fujian homes, including a close-packed grouping of 18 buildings built by a single family in the late Qing dynasty. This 'folk village' has been especially well preserved with a few furnished rooms open museum-style and several other buildings operating as shops (8am to 5pm).

Go in the morning for the best photographic conditions. There are several delightful homestays in the village. but bring your own dinner if you plan to stay (or arrange with your host) as the only shops close by 5pm and there is no evening restaurant.

Chen Ching Lan Mansion MUSEUM

(陳景蘭洋樓, Chénjǐnglán Yánglóu; Map p306; ☑082-334 915; 1 Chenggong village; 成功村1 號; ⊙8.30am-5.30pm; ☒3) FREE Considered Kinmen's finest 'western-style' residence, this 1921 two-storey villa features stone arcade balconies from which you gaze down through parkland onto a limpid bay.

Military Brothel Exhibition Hall MUSEUM

(特約茶室展示館, Tèyuē Cháshì Zhǎnshìguǎn; Map p306; ☑082-337 839; 126 Xiaojing, Jinhu; 金湖鎮小徑126號; ⊙8.30am-5pm; ☒藍 Blue 1) FREE This museum examines the rarely mentioned subject of officially-sanctioned prostitution to entertain military personnel. Euphemistically known as a 'Special Tea-house', the brothel was in operation between 1951 and 1990.

Guningtou War Museum MUSEUM

(古寧頭戰史館, Gǔníngtóu Zhànshǐ Guǎn; Map p306; ☑082-313 274; ⊙8.30am-7pm) FREE For

---

ℹ **WHERE TO HOMESTAY**

If you plan to tour the island using the tourist bus services, it makes sense to stay in Kincheng or Shanwai within walking distance of the start points. If you have wheels, consider a less central homestay. For an extensive list (in Chinese), see http://guesthouse.kmnp.gov.tw.

domestic tourists, this is one of Kinmen's top sights due to the pivotal nature of a battle fought here over 56 hours in October 1949. For outsiders, the main attraction is often discovering the war-era subterranean fort that backs the museum and climbing through it to a viewpoint over the beach, the sands still viciously prickled with an array of sea-facing spikes to prevent enemy boats from landing.

Around 1km west are the attractive twin villages of Beishan and Nanshan. A couple of brick houses here have been preserved in a partly unrestored state to remind visitors of the damage caused in the battle. Tourist Shuttle bus route B stops at Guningtou and Beishan. Alternatively, you can get here using bus 9 from Kincheng (five times daily); it returns at 11.15am, 2.30pm and 3.45pm.

Ou Cuo Beach   BEACH
(歐厝沙灘, Ōu Cuò Shātān; Map p306; 🚌3, 8) From the attractive old town area of Ou Cuo, a concrete road leads 800m south to a superb, yet little frequented, sandy beach with small rocky islands visible in the distance. The only facilities are toilets and a tap.

Mt Lion Howitzer Station   HISTORIC SITE
(獅山砲陣地, Shīshān Pàozhèndì; Map p306; ⊙8.30am-5.30pm) FREE Walk through a wide, 200m rock-hewn tunnel to reach the emplacement of a howitzer canon surveying a wide view towards distant China. Nothing is in English, but the displays of artillery pieces are self-explanatory.

A mock military drill is performed by volunteer residents and students daily except Thursdays at 10am, 11am, 1.30pm, 2.30pm, 3.30pm and 4.30pm. The entrance is just 600m east of Shanhou Folk Culture Village.

Mt Taiwu   MOUNTAIN
(太武山, Tàiwǔ Shān; Map p306; https://kinmen. travel/file/248) Peaking at 253m, Taiwu is less a mountain than an attractive hill ridge that forms Kinmen's east–west backbone. Knobbly patches of beige rock show through gaps in its mostly wooded flanks, which are traversed by footpaths linking viewpoints and assorted military remnants.

From the west, a road takes you up to a shrine and a 1952 soldiers' cemetery (gōng mù) from which the summit is another hour's stroll. Alternatively, from Caicuo Tourist Centre to the north is a longer, steeper hike that's been recently restored with signs and new steps. This Caicuo Ancient Path (蔡厝古道) is also known as the Tofu Trail, as walking

food salesmen once used the route between Shanwai and Shamei.

Near the top of Mt Taiwu is a much photographed large boulder inscribed with one of Chiang Kai-shek's favourite one-liners, 'Wú Wàng Zài Jǔ' (勿忘在莒; Don't forget the days in Ju). Referencing a legend from the Warring States period in ancient China, this is a reminder not to forget the humiliation of losing the mainland, and an implied vow to 'recover' it.

August 23 Artillery War Museum   MUSEUM
(八二三戰史館, Bā'èrsān Zhànshǐ Guǎn; Map p306; 460 Boyu Rd, Jinling township, Sec 2; 金寧鄉伯玉路二段460號; ⊙8.30am-5pm Wed-Mon; 🚌23) FREE Set in a beautifully peaceful garden of banyan trees, this engrossing bilingual museum documents the horrific 44-day bombardment in 1958 during which communist China put Kinmen under siege and pummelled the islands with nearly 500,000 shells. Outside you'll find fighter planes, tanks, cannons and one of the crucial landing crafts that helped Kinmen survive the siege.

It's about 1km east of Shanwai near the northeast corner of attractive Tai Lake,; a body of water that was hand dug in the 1960s. From Shanwai bus station (山外車站) you can take bus 23 (alight at Jinmen Gaoji; 金門高職), join tourist bus D, or simply walk.

Beishan   VILLAGE
(北山; Běishān; Map p306) Along with equally antique Nanshan (南山; Nánshān), a few hundred metres across Shuangli Lake,

---

WIND LIONS

Dotted all over Kinmen are Wind Lions (風獅爺; Fēngshīyé), traditional totems said to have the power to control the winds and keep the land fertile. These totems began appearing after Kinmen was deforested to build Koxinga's navy around the early Qing era (early 17th century). The locals, forced to turn to supernatural aid as the denuded soil of their island ceased bearing crops, began placing the lions around the island. They can still be found in almost every village around the island, some wizened stone figures, other tackily cartoonesque. Many stand upright and are draped in flowing capes. The most famous are shown at https://kinmen.travel/en/ discover/shisa.

TAIWAN STRAIT ISLANDS

Kinmen

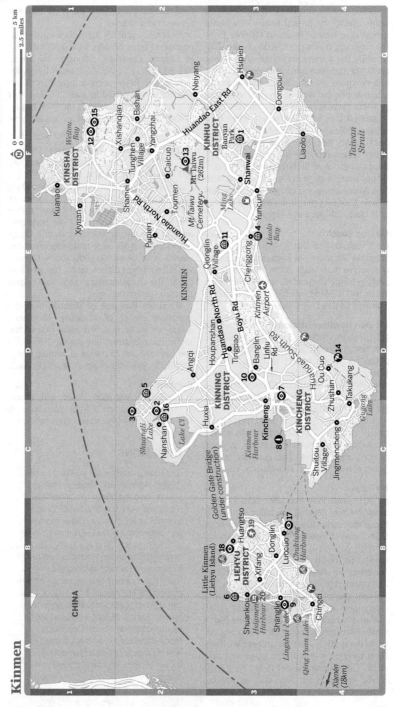

CHINA

Xiàmén
(18km)

KINSHA DISTRICT

Weitou Bay

Kuanao
Xiyuan
Shamei
Tunghei
Village
Xishanqian
Bishan
Yangzhai

⊙12 ⊙15

Pupien
Huandao North Rd
Caicuo
Toumen

⊙13
Mt Taiwu
(262m)

Neiyang

Huandao East Rd

KINHU DISTRICT

Banyan
Park

☆1

Hsipien

Dongcun

Liaolo

Taiwan
Strait

Shanwai

Mt Taiwu
Cemetery

Ming
Lake

Yuncun

⊙4

Liaolo
Bay

🏛11

Qionglin
Village

KINMEN

Chenggong

Kinmen
Airport

Angqi

Houpanshan
Huandao North Rd
Tingpao
Boyu Rd

Banglin

Linhu
Rd

Huandao South Rd

Ou Cuo

Takukang

KINNING
DISTRICT

10
⊙

Huxia

⊙7

Hua
Rd

Zhushan

☆14

🏛5
2🏛
⊙3
Nanshan
16

Lake Ci

Shuangli
Lake

Kincheng

8⊙

Kinmen
Harbour

KINCHENG
DISTRICT

Shutou
Village

Jingmencheng

Ougang
Lake

Golden Gate Bridge
(under construction)

Huangtso

☆19

⊙17

Chingci

Chuktung
Harbour

Donglin

LIEHYU
DISTRICT

Xifang

Luocuo

⊙18

Shuankou
Hsiamen
Harbour

6⊙

🏛20

Shanglin

Chingci

Little Kinmen
(Liehyu Island)

9⊙

Lingshui Lake

Qing Yuan Lake

0 5 km
0 2.5 miles

N

Kinmen

Beishan (北山; Běishān) is a settlement that retains a high proportion of old-style houses. Tourist Shuttle bus B stops outside one that has been preserved with all its bullet holes to commemorate the 1949 battle of Guningtou.

Shuangli Wetlands Area Centre GALLERY
(雙鯉溼地自然中心, Shuānglǐ Shīdì Zìrán Zhōngxīn; Map p306; ☑ 082-313 271; 1-6 Nanshan village, Guling; 古寧村南山村1-6號; ⊙ 8.30am-5pm; ▣ 9, 10, 11) FREE This professional centre, across little Shuangli Lake from Beihai, has bilingual introductions to the region's flora and fauna, notably the cormorants, egrets and other birds that you can see by walking the trail directly south between a series of shallow dyke-divided ponds.

🛏 Sleeping & Eating

★ **Piano Piano** B&B $$
(慢漫民宿, Mànmàn Mínsù; ☑ 0988-182 832, 082-372 866; www.pianopiano.com.tw/pipi2x/index.php; 75 Zhushan village; 珠山75號; s/d from NT$1600/2000; ❄ 🛜) Arguably the loveliest B&B in attractive Zhushan, this traditional house is full of elegant Chinoiserie and quirky touches like bird-cage lamps. A shared veranda, with loungers and dining table, overlooks the village pond. Similarly historic houses at Nos 20 and 24 are co-managed by the same widely travelled owner.

Lexis Inn HOMESTAY $$
(來喜樓, Láixǐlóu; ☑ 082-325 493, 0966-517 665; www.facebook.com/zhushan.lexisinn; 82 Zhushan village; 珠山82號民宿; d from NT$1800; ❄ 🛜; ▣ 3) This historic mansion in Zhushan was built in a fusion east–west style by emigrants who made their fortune in the Philippines. Rooms are neatly renovated, there's an attractive if unfussy common area and views look out across the pretty village

from the brick-arched balcony. Breakfast is included.

Visit Kinmen Guesthouse HOMESTAY $$
(忘了飛民宿, Wànglefēi Mínsù; Map p306; ☑ 082-352 058; www.visit-kinmen.com; 84 Shanhou village; 山后84號; d/q incl breakfast NT$2200/3200) Overflowing with character, this old house, with comfortable rooms themed by season, lies on the rise directly above the main Shanhou Folk Culture Village (p304). The English-speaking hosts – who are knowledgeable birdwatchers – don't live on-site so call ahead.

Booking two nights saves around 30% off-peak. Two minutes' walk away, larger rooms at their similarly historic second property, Bird Lodge, cost NT$2800 to $3800 per night. That's at the top of the village (more easily reached by road), past the Mt Lion Howitzer car park. Turn right by the first of two new houses – it's tucked behind the second one.

Cheng Gong Dumplings TAIWANESE $
(成功鍋貼館, Chénggōng Guōtiēguǎn; ☑ 082-333 979; 99-5 Chenggong village; 正義里成功99-5號; minimum order NT$100; ⊙ 11am-2pm & 5.30-8pm Wed-Mon) This nondescript eatery in Chenggong village is famous for its guōtiē (鍋貼, pot stickers) and oyster omelettes. Entering Chenggong from the north, it's on the right just after the first sharp bend.

ℹ Information

There are tourist information centres at the airport, ports, some museums and at the bus stations in Kincheng and Shanwei. Pick up the detailed Tour Introduction map (free) and the latest bus timetables, but (other than at the airport) don't assume that these places will have English-speaking staff. Website https://kinmen.travel/en is superbly helpful.

ℹ ISLAND EATING

You'll generally need a Chinese speaker to help your culinary adventures as English menus are virtually non-existent. Exceptions are the cafe-restaurants at the airport and Shuitou Port: the former serves several Kinmen specialities including *yùtóu páigǔ* (芋頭排骨; a stew of taro and pork spareribs). Dining choices abound in Kincheng and aren't bad in Shanwai, but they're very limited elsewhere. Smaller villages don't necessarily even have a convenience store.

At Shuitou Pier (p317), the ferry terminal ticket hall has several bank windows that will exchange Chinese yuan with NT$. To change other currencies, head to Mega Bank (p313) in Kincheng, open only during standard weekday working hours. Two ATMs in Kincheng accept international credit cards: the Bank of Taiwan ATM (p313) is the more central.

ℹ Getting There & Away

AIR

In spring, **Kinmen airport** (金門尚義機場, Jīnmén Shàngyì Jīchǎng; Map p306; www.kma. gov.tw) often gets fogged in, even when nearby Kincheng is sunny and clear. If your flight is cancelled, the fare is refunded leaving you to rebook your own alternative, which can mess up plans significantly when all other flights are full. Fog permitting, flights operate to/from Taipei-Songshan (one way NT$1400 to NT$2220), Kaohsiung (NT$2000) and other west coast cities with Mandarin Airlines (www.mandarin -airlines.com) and Uni Air (www.uniair.com.tw). Uni Air also links to Magong in Penghu (N$1580) three times a week, but if that's cancelled, you'll have a very long detour.

BOAT

Passenger ferries run almost every half-hour to Xiamen (China), but there's no boat service to Taiwan's main island. From Shuitou Pier (p317), nearly 20 daily high-speed passenger boats zip across to Xiamen's Wutong Port (NT$750, 30 to 40 minutes) between 8am and 5.30pm. See http://info.quemoybus.net for exact timings. Buy tickets at the port. Travellers who need a visa for China should be aware that these are not available in Kinmen. Five more boats depart daily for Quanzhou, but only Chinese and Taiwanese citizens may use them.

ℹ Getting Around

Kinmen Airport is 8km east of Kincheng city. Buses 3 and Blue 1 (NT$12) call at the terminal

between Kincheng and Shanwei (hourly, both ways). Getting to Kincheng by taxi costs a flat NT$250.

BICYCLE

Cycling is a great way to see the islands. K-Bike, a system of card-release automated rental stations, has been established, but was not operational at the time of research.

BOAT

Ferries link Shuitou Pier (p317) and Little Kinmen (NT$60, 12 minutes), every half-hour from 7am to 7pm, plus there are a couple of later evening services.

BUS

Local buses (金門公車; http://bus.kinmen. gov.tw) operate on both Kinmen and Little Kinmen with schedules posted at hub stations in Kincheng, Shanwai and Shamei. Routes are mapped at http://ebus.kinmen.gov.tw/driving-map. Download the app through https://play. google.com/store/apps/details?id=com. maxwin.itravel_km. Tourist Shuttle buses (www.kinmendiway.com/en/) operate morning and afternoon routes from both Kincheng and Shanwai.

Tourist Bus

Four tourist bus routes give a pretty exhaustive coverage of the main island's major sights. Each takes around 3½ hours to complete and includes a tour guide (Chinese only) and limited time to explore many of the key attractions. Buy tickets (NT$250/400/700 per half-day/full day/two days) at the bus stations or online via www. kinmendiway.com/en/ which has more detailed route information.

From Kincheng

Route A (starting 8.25am) includes Jugang Tower (half-hour stop), Shuitou (45 minutes), the Jhaishan Tunnels (40 minutes) and Jhushan village (stops but doesn't wait). Route B (starting 1.25pm) starts by walking you 1.2km through the cramped, dark civil defence tunnels (p309) before heading to an oyster-farming museum, Guningtou (50 minutes), Beishan (10 minutes) and the Shuangli Wetlands Centre (25 minutes).

From Shanwai

Route C (8.25am) links the Shanhou Folk Culture Village, the Mt Lion site and outlook point and a cultural museum. Route D includes the August 23 site (one hour), the Military Brothel Museum (15 minutes), Qionglin village (one hour) and two other sites. At weekends and peak holiday periods, there's also a pair of route E options.

CAR & MOTORCYCLE

Kinmen's traffic is calm and the easiest way to see the island is by car or scooter. Vehicles can be rented from **KM FunCar** (KmFun金豐租車;

082-371 888; www.kmfun.tw; Kinmen Airport; scooter/car per day from NT$400/1600; 8am-6.30pm) at the airport and from SanDe (p317) at Shuitou Port for similar rates. An international driving permit is required and will be carefully examined.

TAXI

Taxis have meters but drivers prefer to ask for flat fares, notably NT$250 from the airport to Kincheng and NT$300 from the airport to Shuitou port. Taxi tours cost NT$3000 a day; you can assume that your driver won't speak English.

Kincheng

082 / POP 35,200

Kincheng (金城; Jīnchéng) is Kinmen's busiest town, but it remains a charmingly laid-back place with plenty of winding alleys, ornate temples, brick-paved shopping streets and a scattering of old civic architecture.

⊙ Sights

Houpo 16 Art Zone HISTORIC BUILDING
(後浦16藝文特區, Hòupǔ 16 Yìwén Tèqū; 082-327 139; 106 Juguang Rd; 莒光路106號) FREE By day it looks a little over-gentrified, but at night the junction of Juguang and Zhongxing roads is one of Kincheng's most atmospheric corners. The so-called Art Zone here includes a small row of handicraft shops in the century-old courtyard buildings, which flank an historic ancestral hall (陳氏宗祠; Chénshì Zōngcí).

Koxinga Statue STATUE
(鄭成功石雕像, Zhèngchénggōng Shí Diāoxiàng; Map p306; Jiangongyu; 7B) This stern, 9m statue of Koxinga (鄭成; Zheng Cheng) gazes towards China from a tiny islet connected to the rest of Kinmen by a pedestrian causeway, which becomes submerged as the tide rises. It's flanked by silhouetted oyster fishermen figures: modern art installations that seem to walk on water at high tide. But the scene is at its most beautiful when sunset and low tide coincide.

Koxinga, the Ming-loyalist Chinese general who ousted the Dutch from Taiwan in 1661–62, is also celebrated in a nearby faux-ancient shrine that sits in well-tended gardens across the road from the causeway access path.

Juguang Tower HISTORIC SITE
(莒光樓, Jǔguāng Lóu; Map p306; 082-325 632; 1 Xiancheng Rd; 賢城路1號; 8am-10pm; 3, 6) FREE This three-storey tower, built in classical Chinese form, is an iconic local landmark

that has often featured on Taiwanese stamps. Yet it only dates from 1952, erected as a memorial to fallen soldiers. Set in attractive parkland just south of Kincheng, the tower looks best when floodlit at dusk. Climb for distant views of the skyscrapers of Xiamen (China), which become much more visible on the horizon at night. Inside, the ground floor gives a helpful introduction to Kinmen's food, architecture and wind lions. Upper floors aren't in English but feature photos of the Welcoming the City God (p311) festival plus the history of the tower itself.

Memorial Arch to
Qiu Liang-Kung's Mother HISTORIC SITE
(邱良功母節孝坊, Qiū Liánggōng Mǔ Jiéxiào Fǎng; Juguang Rd, Sec 1; 莒光路一段) Kinmen's only national-level heritage site, this 1812 carved arch across Juguang Rd was built from Fujian granite and bluestone by a Kinmen native who had risen to become governor of China's Zhejiang province.

Maestro Wu Factory-Store FACTORY
(金合利鋼刀, Jīnhélì Gāngdāo; Map p306; 082-323 999; http://maestrowu.8898.tw; 236 Bóyù Rd, Sec 1; 伯玉路一段236號; knives NT$600-14,000; 8.30am-noon & 1.30-6pm) FREE Kinmen's famous super-sharp knives (p312) are still fashioned from bomb casings at a display workshop at the back of this stylish Banglin boutique. Each shell yields up to 60 blades and there are stacks of them still awaiting use.

Kincheng Civil Defence Tunnels TUNNEL
(金城民防坑道, Jīnchéng Mínfáng Kēngdào; Kincheng Bus Station; 1.30pm & 8.30pm, museum 10am-10pm) FREE Claustrophobes beware: Kincheng has 2.6km of wartime tunnels and you can walk 1.2km of them, but they're not much wider or taller than a large man. What makes the experience especially memorable is that two sections are pitch black: feel your way forward while bomb and gun noises blare.

Before starting, peruse the bilingual info boards in the museum room above the bus station. That's accessed via the camouflage-painted stairs on Minsheng Rd. For groups, there are several daily time slots for the walk-through, but if you're alone come at 1.30pm or 8.30pm, which are the only guaranteed departure times.

Kinmen Qing Dynasty
Military HQ HISTORIC SITE
(清金門鎮總兵署, Qīng Jīnménzhèn Zǒngbīngshǔ; 53 Wujiang St; 浯江街53號; 9am-10pm)

Kincheng

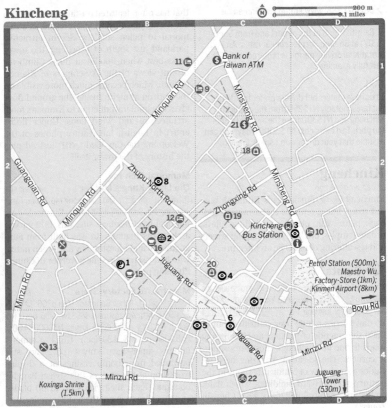

Kincheng

FREE The oldest surviving Qing government building in Taiwan, this three-courtyard structure doubles as a passably interesting museum explaining Kinmen's place in Ming and Qing history through bilingual displays, models of military junks, military pennants and wax figures in period costume.

Mofan Street
HISTORIC SITE

(模範街, Mófàn Jiē) This charming little street is lined with attractive shops behind brick-arched facades dating back to 1924.

City God Temple
TAOIST TEMPLE

(浯島城隍廟, Wúdǎo Chénghuáng Miào; 40 Guangqian Rd; 光前路40號; ⊙8am-5pm) Originally raised in the Qing dynasty, this Taoist delight is all you'd hope for in a fanciful Chinese temple, complete with ornate roof embellishments, ancient plaques and an atmospheric interior, plus a couple of stone memorial steles in the courtyard.

Kuei Pavilion
HISTORIC SITE

(奎閣, Kuí Gé, 魁星樓, Kuíxīng Lóu; 43 Zhupu East Rd; 珠浦東路43號; ⊙9am-5pm) Backed by a couple of classic, if crumbling, western-style 1930s buildings, this 1836 pavilion-shrine to the god of literature is a dinky, hexagonal structure that looks like a mini pagoda.

Wu River Academy
HISTORIC SITE

(吳江書院, Wújiāng Shūyuàn; 35 Zhupu North Rd; 珠浦北路35號; ⊙9am-5pm) **FREE** This handsomely restored walled complex was originally built as a centre of learning in 1780. The two main shrine-like study rooms honour Chu Hsi, a scholar who sought a revival of Confucian values during the Sung dynasty (AD 960–1279).

✸ Festivals & Events

Welcoming the City God
CULTURAL

(城隍祭, Chénghuáng Jì) On the 12th day of the fourth lunar month the City God Temple in Kincheng is the epicentre of this mass festival. A parade runs down the western side of the island and you'll find traditional opera and dancing, fireworks and costumed troupes en route.

One intersting part of the festival involves children dressed as characters from history and mythology. Depending on the village, the kids ride on tricycles or rickshaws.

🛏 Sleeping

If you don't have your own wheels, staying in central Kincheng makes sense: you'll be near the bus station for Tourist Shuttle tours and within a stone's throw of a wide range of great dining.

Backpack 497
HOSTEL $

(背包客棧497; ☎0905-134 369; www.facebook.com/backpack497; 6 Lane, 7-1 Minsheng Rd; dm/d NT$550/1300; ❂❉🛜) Tucked down a side lane in the centre of Jincheng, this stylish mini hostel has sturdy bunks in key-carded, sex-segregated dorms. Bathrooms are small but fresh and basic, and free snacks are provided in the communal kitchen. The two en-suite double rooms are great value.

Ru Yi Jia
HOMESTAY $

(如一家民宿, Rúyìjiā Mínsù; ☎082-322 167; www.facebook.com/如一家民宿-476591435744025/; 35-1 Zhupu North Rd; 珠浦北路35-1號; d from NT$1580; ❉🛜) This friendly, well-appointed guesthouse has a reception and breakfast room on one side of Zhupu Road, but many of its most appealing rooms are in a historic structure opposite, set artistically off a tiny courtyard garden. It's in the heart of old Kincheng, between the Wu River Academy and the 1924 Kinmen Church.

Quemoy Hotel
HOTEL $$

(金瑞旅店, Jīnruì Lǚdiàn; ☎082-323 777; www.quemoyhotel.com.tw; 166 Minquan Rd; 金城 民權路166號; s/d from NT$1600/1800; ❉🛜; 🚌3, 7, 9, 10) With helpful English-speaking staff on reception and very fair pricing, the Quemoy's 100 neat and unpretentious rooms sell out fast. They come with a good walk-in shower, kettle and desk. Breakfast is included.

La Place House
HOTEL $$

(那個地方, Nàgè Dìfang; ☎082-328 337; www.laplace-kinmen.com; 2nd fl, 6 Minsheng Lu; 民生路6號; d/tr from NT$1800/2400) Despite minor signs of wear, La Place's 20 rooms retain a sense of designer-casual style with intentionally off-beam mirrors and semi-spiritual aphorisms on the walls. Also signposted as 'Urban Farmhouse', it's easy to find, above the 7-Eleven shop opposite the bus station.

The high-ceilinged common room has a big meet-up table, magazines to read (in Chinese) and postcards pegged to a washing line. Some English is understood. Prices rise NT$200 per room at weekends.

🍴 Eating

Kinmen sleeps early with relatively few options open after 9pm. In contrast, early morning and lunchtime sees queues forming for steamed dumplings and filled Kinmen pastries (燒餅, shāobǐng) straight from the baker. Countless small eateries serve Fujianstyle soups and others specialise in locally popular congee (廣東粥, guǎngdōng zhōu), a meat-and-egg rice soup served with a doughnut baton (油條, yóutiáo). Look along Guangqian and Juguang Roads, especially towards Minzu road market.

LOCAL KNOWLEDGE

MAESTRO WU'S BOMBSHELL KNIVES

Living under bombardment has taught the people of Kinmen to make the best of things. A great example is Maestro Wu's knife-making business. A steel-working outfit since 1937, the firm made the best of a WWII shortage of metal by re-using the bomb casings dropped by allied airforces on the then-Japanese-controlled island. The same trick was repeated in the 1950s using shell casings fired over by the Communists, who later turned to sending 'propaganda shells'. These proved especially good for making one-of-a-kind sharp knives. Unlike regular shells, which are designed to shatter into killing fragments, propaganda shells split neatly open with the aim of demoralising the enemy. The result was quite the opposite for Maestro Wu, providing instead a regular supply of free, high-grade metal to work with. The company has several showrooms including an elegant one in central Kincheng. However, if you want to see the knives being made, head for their Banglin Factory-Store (p309), avoiding the lunch break.

Shin Damiaokou SEAFOOD $$

(新大廟口, Xīn Dàmiàokǒu; ☑ 082-320 753; 86 Guangqian Rd, cnr Minquan Rd; 光前路86號; dishes NT$90-450; ⊙ 5-11pm) By day it's just a no-frills kitchen. But by early evening, Damaiokou serves top-quality seafood to eager diners, packed around open-air tables beside the ornate Waiwu Temple (外武廟; Wàiwǔ Miào).

The day's catches are displayed or you can choose from the faded picture menu posted on the wall. This includes great prawns, oyster omelettes (蚵仔煎, oah-jiān) and the house speciality 'black snail' (黑螺肉, Hēiluóròu). The dish that looks like asparagus is actually sandworm (沙蟲, shāchóng), a chewy Fujianese delicacy that's stir-fried in ginger and served on a bed of bean sprouts. If weather is bad, get a takeaway or frequent the snazzier indoor seafood restaurant across the square.

Niu Jiazhuang CHINESE $$

(牛家莊, Niújiāzhuāng; ☑ 082-320 099; 5 Lane 318, Minzu Rd; 民族路318巷5 號; mains NT$180-350, beef noodles NT$100; ⊙ 11am-1pm & 5.30-8pm Wed-Mon) As you might guess from the carved granite bullock outside, this unpretentious but highly regarded family restaurant specialises in beef, along with virtually any other body part of those specially pampered Kinmen cows.

Try the very special dragon-phoenix (龍鳳雙拼, lóngfèng shuāng pīn), beef and tripe chunks in a flavour-packed onion and herb mix, or play it safe with top-quality beef noodles (牛肉麵, niúròu miàn).

Drinking & Nightlife

Kinmen's signature liquor is sorghum-based Kaoliang (Gāoliáng jiǔ). It tastes far better when infused with lemon, coffee or tea, or mixed in cocktails, as you'll find at Kincheng's excellent White Lion Pub. The town also has several cosy, modern coffee houses.

★ **White Lion Pub** BAR

(白獅子酒吧, Bái Shīzi Jiǔbā; 7 Lane 110, Juguang Rd; 莒光路110巷7號; ⊙ 7pm-last customer Tue & Thu-Sun) Tiny but sparklingly imaginative, this Aussie-run pub serves a range of foreign beers (NT$160), three IPA-style craft ales from Taiwan and remarkably well-mixed cocktails (NT$190), some based on home-infused Kaoliang.

Try the *Caprioska* (lemon Kaoliang, Cointreau, brown sugar and muddled lime) or the elegantly subtle Alishan Tea. The small upstairs-downstairs pair of box rooms spills seats onto the attractive Houpu 16 (p309) courtyard.

Local Teahouse CAFE

(後浦泡茶間, Hòupǔpào Chájiān; 2nd fl, 122 Juguang Rd; 莒光路122號2F; ⊙ 1-11pm Fri-Mon) Choose from two dozen Taiwanese craft beers (NT$160) or sip from mini pots of rare Taiwanese teas (NT$160) in this upstairs cafe's 1940s retro interior. You can also sit on the rooftop beside colourful temple-roof gables.

Corner Cafe COFFEE

(轉角 咖啡, Hézí hézǐ jiān; www.facebook.com/cornercafe.com.tw; Guangqian Rd; ⊙ 11am-8pm) There are cheaper cafes, but this lovable place serves deep-roast, chocolatey-flavoured espressos and its comfy upstairs lounge is a great perch for watching people queueing for steamed dumplings at the archetypal tiled shops opposite.

🔒 Shopping

Cute, arty shops huddle on Mofan St and around Houpo 16 (p309). Many shops, notably on Minsheng Rd, sell signature Kaoliang sorghum liquor, often in fanciful bottles.

Maestro Wu   ARTS & CRAFTS

(金合利鋼刀, Jīnhélì Gāngdāo; ☑ 082-373 977; www.maestrowu.com.tw; 51 Wujiang St; 浯江街51 號; ◷ 9.30am-9pm) The most famous of Kinmen's knife-makers has an elegant central shop displaying rusty bomb casings as well as selling the knives (NT$560 to NT$15,000) that are made from them. If you want to see them being created, go instead to their factory (p309) in Banglin, around 2km northeast.

Kinmen Folk Curios   GIFTS & SOUVENIRS

(金門民俗文物之家, Jīnmén Mínsú Wénwù Zhījiā; ☑ 082-325 716; 1 Lane 124, Zhongxing Rd; 中興路124巷1號; ◷ 11.30am-9pm) Ceramic bric-a-brac, crockery and wind lion statuettes are arrayed around the photogenic courtyard of what initially appears to be a typical traditional house.

Enter through the first stone doorway to the left down a lane off Zhongxing Rd.

Joan Ranch   FOOD & DRINKS

(喬安牧場, Qiáoān Mùchǎng; ☑ 0800-566 899; www.shengzu.com.tw; 33-2 Minsheng Rd; 民生路 33-2號; ◷ 9.30am-9pm) Taste before you buy at this elegant shop that specialises in delicious local beef jerky (NT$150 for 180g); the black pepper version is superb.

They also sell wind lion souvenir snacks and have an out-of-town meat fondue restaurant and factory towards Banglin.

ℹ Information

Bank of Taiwan ATM (台灣銀行, Táiwān Yín-háng; Minsheng Rd; 民生路) The more central of only two international ATMs in Kincheng, it's on the west side of Minsheng Rd, just before Minquan Rd.

Mega Bank (兆豐銀行, Zhàofēng Yínháng; https://wwwfile.megabank.com.tw/about/about04_Branch_info.asp?c=1&s=689; 37-5 Minsheng Rd; 民生路37之5號; ◷ 9am-3.30pm Mon-Fri) Has foreign money exchange facilities, but only during normal banking hours.

> ℹ **AUDIO WALK**
>
> At Houpo 16 Art Zone (p309), there's a tiny visitor centre (open 2pm to 10pm) from which you can borrow an audio guide that talks you around Kincheng in around 90 minutes. It's free but you must leave a NT$1000 deposit.

Kinmen County's website (www.kinmen.gov.tw) is an excellent online resource for background on sights and general cultural information.

Visitor Information Centre (遊客服務中心, Yóukè Fùwù Zhōngxīn; ☑ 082-325 548; 7 Minsheng Rd; 民生路7號; ◷ 9am-9.30pm) At the bus station; has brochures and bus timetables, but don't expect much (if any) spoken English.

ℹ Getting There & Away

Morning (A) and afternoon (B) Tourist Shuttle buses start from **Kincheng bus station** (金城車站, Jīnchéng Chēzhàn; http://ebus.kinmen.gov.tw/driving-map; 7 Minsheng Rd; 民生路7號), which also has public bus services to much of the island. Change in Shanwai for destinations in northeast Kinmen or for Tourist Shuttle loops C and D.

PUBLIC BUSES

Useful services from Kincheng:

No 藍1 (blue1) Airport–Xiaojing–Mt Taiwu Park-Shanwai (NT$24). Runs hourly 7.30am to 5.30pm.

No 2 Banglin–Qionglin–Guoxiao–Chenggong NE–Xiaxing–Shanwai (NT$24)

No 3 Kincheng–Jhushan–airport–Chenggong–Shanwai (NT$12)

Nos 7, 7A & 7B Kincheng–Shuitou–Shuitou Pier (NT$12)

Nos 9, 10 & 11 varying loop routes to the Beishan area (NT$12)

TOURIST SHUTTLE

Two Tourist Shuttle routes operate from Kincheng (www.kinmendiway.com/en; 3½ hours), each accompanied by a Chinese-speaking guide. Pay NT$250/400 for one/both.

Route A (starting 8.25am) is an easy option for visiting Kinmen's top attractions, Juguang Tower, Shuitou and the Jhaishan Tunnels. It is possible to hop off near the end of the loop and visit Zhushan village if don't mind paying your own way back by public bus.

Route B (starting 1.25pm) concentrates firmly on military sights. Be aware that the experience starts with a 1.2km walk through the somewhat claustrophobic defence tunnels (p309).

ℹ Getting Around

Central Kincheng is walkably small. Taxis wait on Minsheng Rd 50m northwest of the bus station. Another 150m northwest is the Kymco scooter-hire outfit (Taiwanese licences only) and the main station for the currently out-of-action stands for the K-bike automatic bicycle-hire system. Until that's fixed, you can rent bicycles from **DaHua-Giant** (大华-捷安特; ☑ 082-326 626; 31 Minzu Rd; 民族路31號; per day NT$300; ◷ 8.30am-6.30pm).

Little Kinmen

📶 082 / POP 12,820

Green, windswept and remarkably quiet, Little Kinmen (小金門; Xiǎo Jīnmén) is the popular nickname for Kinmen's baby sister, Liehyu (烈嶼). As the former front line of the 1958 war, the island's main attractions are primarily military-related. Naval tunnels and a free shoot-out simulation experience are the top draws, but there are also small 20th-century forts to be visited every couple of kilometres around the bicycle-friendly lane that loops 18km around the island.

◉ Sights

★ Siwei Tunnel   HISTORIC SITE

(四維坑道, Sìwéi Kēngdào; Map p306; 📶 082-364 411; ⊙8.30am-5pm) FREE Also known as Jiugong Tunnel (九宮坑道), this four-entrance network of wide sea tunnels was blasted out of the gneiss in the 1960s to provide bomb shelters for as many as 50 small boats.

A few mannequins show the labour-intensive drilling processes, while a water-free former hospital section contains a visitor centre with exhibits on Little Kinmen's geology and other attractions. To find it from the ferry dock, simply walk left along the promenade. There are alternative tunnel access points near the bike-hire sheds and from Luocuo fishing village.

Yongshi Fort   HISTORIC SITE

(勇士堡, Yǒngshìbǎo; Map p306; ⊙8am-5pm) FREE Yongshi (Warriors') Fort is one of a pair of 1970s military bunkers in Huangtso. Descend through a 200m-long tunnel that now contains a museum about landmines.

In one section, you must tiptoe gingerly to avoid setting off an explosion (simulated, fortunately). Then exit via Yongshi's twin brother, the immodestly named Iron Men's Fort (鐵漢堡; Tiěhànbǎo).

Facing Yongshi Fort, the unassuming yet top-quality restaurant San Ceng Lou (三層樓, literally '3 Floors') is famed for its local taro-based dishes, including huge servings of taro and bean ice (芋泥冰, yùní bīng).

Lingshui Lake   LAKE

(陵水湖, Língshuǐ Hú; Map p306) Divided by dykes, this array of channels and reed-fringed artificial lakes is a popular place for birdwatching, especially in winter when dozens of migratory species stop by.

As well as cormorants, look for redshanks (赤足鷸, chìzúyù) and African stonechats (黑喉鴝, hēihóuqú). A good access point is the walkway from the small, new temple at Km9.1 of the round-island cycleway (west of Shanglin village on the island's western side). The short path between here and the sea has two twitchers' hides and signs to help identify local flora.

Hujingtou War Museum   MUSEUM

(湖井頭戰史館, Hújǐngtóu Zhànshǐ Guǎn; Map p306; 📶082-364 403; www.kmnp.gov.tw; Hujingtou village; 湖井頭村; ⊙8.30am-5pm Tue-Sun) FREE This small coastal fort has display boards and a looping video that give a sense of how young men were toughened into soldiers to endure life here during times of conflict. Big binoculars make Xiamen's towering skyline look even closer.

From Jiugong Pier, where ferries from Kinmen arrive, most (but not all) buses serve Hujingtou bus stop (湖井頭站; Hújǐngtóu Zhàn).

🏃 Activities & Tours

Houlin Military Base Laser Shooting Simulation   SAFARI

(后麟步槍模擬射擊館, Hòulín bùqiāng mónǐ shèjì guǎn; Map p306; https://lieyut91.business. site; ⊙slots 8.20am to 4.20pm) FREE Dress up in army camouflage fatigues then spend half an hour firing at simulator targets using a convincingly heavy assault rifle with air-powered recoil. Keep the souvenir certificate with your score and photo.

Pre-booking is wise during busy periods as only 12 places are available for each slot (eight on weekdays, 10 at weekends). The experience takes place in a decommissioned military hospital block, 2.5km north of the ferry dock and 250m west of the Houtou 1 (后頭一) bus stop. Eventually, they plan to introduce a NT$350 fee for foreigners, but for now it's free.

Dadan Island   BOATING

(大膽島, Dàdàn Dǎo; https://goo.gl/H9F3N7; tour NT$1500) Since March 2019, it has been possible (unless you have a Chinese passport) to go on a boat tour to the military look-out island of Dadan, which stares down the estuary towards Xiamen. There are arcs of beach, an old propaganda broadcast station and hundreds of concrete lions lining the traffic-free central road. You'll need to apply at least 10 days in advance for a permit, using all-in-Chinese application forms available on www.lieyudadan-tour.com. The tourist authorities hope this process will get easier in future years.

🛏 Sleeping & Eating

Most visitors are day trippers, but there is a small scattering of guesthouses including an excellent, hotel-standard 'homestay' set back from the beach at Shankou.

West Frontier
Guesthouse & Cafe   HOTEL $$
(國境之西民宿, Guójìng Zhīxī Mínsù; Map p306; ☑082-363 522, 0932-757 818; 10-6 Shankou, Xikou village; 西口村雙口10-6號; d/q NT$2200/2600; ⊙10am-10pm; P🛜) Six immaculately clean new rooms provide fine linens on super-comfy beds and balconies facing the sea (and China), four of them with dangling basket seats. Across the car park is a sandy beach that's photogenically prickled with defensive spikes, but softened with a 'Love' arch. The pleasant cafe (at Km7.2) makes a good stopping place if you're riding the round-island cycleway. All room prices rise NT$400 at weekends.

ℹ Information

There's a tourist information point at the ferry jetty and another, the Lieyu Visitor Centre, within the 'hospital cave' of the Siwei Tunnel. The latter has museum-style panels and a 15-minute video introducing the island. Visit https://lieyu.kinmen.gov.tw for more information.

ℹ Getting There & Away

Under construction since 2012, the 4.8km Golden Gate Bridge (金門大橋; Jīnmén Dàqiáo) between Kinmen and Little Kinmen has been plagued by delays and overspend. Claims that it should be operational by 2021 still seem optimistic. Till then at least, ferries link Shuitou Pier (p317) on the main island to Jiugong Pier in Little Kinmen (passenger/scooter NT$60/100, 12 minutes). They depart half-hourly between 7am and 7pm, plus at 8pm and 9pm. Last return boats leave Jiugong at 6.30pm, 7.30pm and 8.30pm (plus 9pm in summer).

ℹ Getting Around

Siwei Tunnel, the island's top sight, is just a short stroll from the arrival pier and the free bicycles make it easy to reach Houlin without too much sweat. Going much further takes more puff as the island is rather hilly. Little Kinmen's public minibus routes (NT$12 per hop) are divided into north (北線) and south (南線) small loops plus longer north–south and south–north variants that essentially combine the two.

Bringing a scooter on the ferry from Kinmen adds NT$100 to the fare each way. Taiwanese licence holders can rent scooters on arrival at Jiugong Port (NT$500 per day), but foreigners might struggle even with an international licence.

BICYCLE

Hiring a bicycle is free once you find the poorly signed **rental shed** (⊙8.30am-noon & 12.30-4.30pm) that is on the rise directly above Siwei Tunnel. From the ferry, turn left and walk along the promenade then climb the second stairway to the right (just after passing the tunnel exit turnstile). Bring your passport.

Shuitou Village

☑082 / POP 1350

Inhabited for over 700 years, Shuitou village (水頭村; Shuǐtóu Cūn) features one of the best collections of old houses in Taiwan. Many are archetypally Minnan (Fujian-Chinese), but overlooking the village green is a group of architectural hybrids, known as *yanglou* (洋樓, *yáng lóu*), which were inspired by the western architecture that had impressed Kinmen emigrants in Southeast Asia. During the late 19th and especially the early 20th century, many of these folk returned from work in Indonesia and Malaysia, or sent large remittances, which helped Shuitou become wealthy. Its advantage was proximity to the island's main port, 1km further west, which is still where ferries arrive frequently from Xiamen (mainland China) and Little Kinmen.

👁 Sights

★ **Deyue Mansion**   ARCHITECTURE
(得月樓, Déyuè Lóu; ⊙8.30am-5pm) Built in 1931, this is Kinmen's most famous 'western' building thanks to the 11m-tall gun tower in its yard, erected to ward off (or at least spot) pirates. The tower itself is closed, but the beautifully maintained house is furnished and, along with the mansion next door, contains interesting bilingual panels shedding light on the Chinese diaspora to Southeast Asia and how their tastes (and money) came to affect architecture on Kinmen. The exhibition continues in a former school across a grassy area to the south.

🛏 Sleeping

Around 30 of Shuitou's old-Fujian houses now operate as homestays. Prebook and arrange arrival times as relatively few are staffed. Possible exceptions include houses 54 and 63-63 whose owners are usually on-site.

YuYuan B&B   BOUTIQUE HOTEL
(裕園民宿, YùYuán Mínsù; ☑0963-000 062, 082-324 546; https://yuyuan.ego.tw; 75 Shuitou; 水頭

GABLES & THEIR MEANINGS

A key feature of the surviving old villages in Kinmen (and to a lesser extent in Penghu) are the low-rise, traditional Fujian-Chinese houses. These have distinctively shaped gables (山牆, shānqiáng) that divide into two main categories. Some homes that were originally built for village dignitaries employ 'swallowtails' (燕尾, yànwěi) – upturned masonry spikes protruding from the roof ends. However, such features are more frequently associated with ancestral halls and temples where you'll see them abundantly decorated with colourful dragon motifs. More common for the houses of the non-elite are flat-ended 'saddle' (馬背, mǎbèi) gables. In original Chinese design, these are sub-divided into five types, each representing one of the five elements: 'gold' for affluence, 'water' for social relations, 'earth' for abundance, 'fire' for protection and 'wood' for growth. You'll generally find only the first three styles. Most ubiquitous is the simple hump shape (gold, 金形, jīnxíng), sometimes with the rounded section pinched into three parts (water; 水形, shuǐxíng). In Kinmen you'll also see tall, flat-topped 'earth' (土形, tǔxíng) gables, though these are far less common as they are thought to bear an unlucky resemblance to tombstones. One place to spot the otherwise vanishingly rare 'fire' shape (火形, huǒxíng) gable is on the temples of Qiaozi village on Beigan (Matsu).

75號; s/d NT$2000/2500; **P** **✳** **🛜**) Incorporating an exclusive whisky boutique, this brand new three-storey building is built in a style that apes Kinmen's classic *yanglou* 'western houses' while oozing modern comforts behind its dazzlingly white balcony arcades.

It's the only hotel in Shuitou with a reception desk, but don't expect spoken English.

⭐ **Grace Homestay**   HOMESTAY **$$**
(水調歌頭民宿, Shuǐdiào Gētóu Mínsù; ☑ 082-322 389, 0932-517 669; www.familyinn.idv.tw/a01. asp; 40 Shuitou; 水頭40號; d incl breakfast from NT$1800; **✳** **🛜**) Three of the loveliest traditional Fujian-style houses in the village centre are co-managed under one name (though not signposted in English). Each features exotically decorated interiors with authentic wood, red brick and antique touches.

Directly north of Deyue Mansion (p315), No 40 is particularly glorious, but if you arrive unannounced, there's a better chance of finding someone home at No 54, around 100m west.

🍴 Eating & Drinking

By night, unless you have reserved at the Jin Shui, the only place to eat in the village is the uninspired little cafe at building No 84, in the Minnan Inn courtyard diagonally opposite YuYuan B&B (p315).

At the ferry dock, there's an international-style coffee shop/restaurant (8am to 6pm) with a wide range of filling, if somewhat generic, counter-ordered meals (mains NT$60 to NT$180) and a helpful English menu.

Jindaodi Snack Shop   TAIWANESE **$**
(金道地小吃店, Jìndàodì Xiǎochī Diàn; ☑ 082-327 969; 15 Shuitou; 水頭15號; dishes NT$70-100; ⏰ 9.30am-5.30pm) It's rough and ready, but this little eatery is a great place to try hand-harvested baby rock oysters (金門石蚵). A Kinmen speciality, they're available as omelettes (蚵仔煎), in soup (蚵仔汤) or with noodles – tossed (蚵仔麵) or in broth (蚵仔麵線).

Fried rice (炒飯) and taro-meat spring rolls (芋香肉捲) are served here too. To help you mark your selection on the printed all-Chinese order paper, there's a small picture menu with translations (into English and Japanese) stuck to one of the fridges. The snack shop is inside a group of old Fujian-style courtyard houses known collectively as the 18 Roof Ridges (頂界十八支樑; Dǐngjiè Shíbā Zhīliáng).

⭐ **Jin Shui Restaurant**   TAIWANESE **$$**
(金水食堂, Jīnshuǐ Shítáng; ☑ 0937-228768, 082-373919; 48 Shuitou; 水頭48號; per head NT$350; ⏰ by reservation only, closed Tue) Occupying the historic building and garden yard beside the Deyue Mansion (p315), Jin Shui serves some truly excellent local cuisine including 'nyonya' (娘惹) dishes – spicy mixed Chinese-Malay recipes brought back to Kinmen by the trader elites. Be aware that a reservation is essential and the only option is the multi-dish meal of the day.

Wind Lion Cafe   TAVERNA
(☑ 082-321 600; www.wuzhou.tw; 42 Shuitou; 水頭42號; ⏰ 8.30am-5.30pm) Easy to spot from the big stylised Mao portrait, this historic

'western' house in Shuitou's main central ensemble is primarily a souvenir shop selling mini ceramic Wind Lions. However, you can also get iced milk tea (NT$80) in Mao-themed takeaway cups or drink shots of Kaoliang (NT$50) while seated at parasol tables in the appealing courtyard.

ⓘ Information

At the Deyue Mansion (p315) information desk, ask for the free Shuitou village map that has detailed house-by-house information (though only partly in English).

Bank windows in the port's ticket office building exchange Chinese yuan for NT$ and vice versa, but for any other currencies you'll need to continue to Kincheng.

ⓘ Getting There & Away

Shuitou Pier (水頭碼頭, Shuǐtóu Mǎtóu; 90-1 Huanghai Rd; 金湖鎮黃海路90-1號; ☏7, 7A, 7B), Kinmen's main passenger port for both China (p308) and Little Kinmen (p315), is around 1km west of Shuitou village.

Buses 7, 7A and 7B link Shuitou Pier to Kincheng via Shuitou village. Bus 6 makes a bigger loop that includes Kincheng and Shuitou village but not the port. At the pier, **SanDe** (金門三德租車, Jīnmén SānDé Zūchē; ☏082-328 610; www.3car.com.tw; Shuitou Port; ⊙9am-5.30pm; ☏7) offers car, scooter and electric scooter hire.

MATSU

☑0836 / POP 13,060

The Matsu (馬祖; Mǎzǔ) group of islands is an overnight boat ride from Taiwan, yet visible from the coast of mainland China. Like similarly located Kinmen, it spent most of the last 70 years as a military outpost. Many of the sights here are defensive tunnels and forts with superb ocean views. A few of these 'strongholds' are being converted into hostels and cafes. Meanwhile a scattering of older traditional houses have survived and a couple of pretty coastal villages present scenes more reminiscent of the Adriatic or southern France.

Note that the term 'Matsu' can refer to the whole archipelago, but is also used in some cases to mean specifically Nangan, the busiest island. And, for good measure, Matsu has temples to Matsu, goddess of the sea, with the world's biggest Matsu statue in Matsu village, as Magang (馬港) is alternatively known. It's not that confusing really.

History

Recent archaeology has shown that people with genetic similarities to Austronesian Pacific islanders were living in Matsu at least 8000 years ago, with a culture based around skin-diving and shellfish collecting. However, more recent human development began in the 1400s with the arrival of Fujianese mainlanders escaping political turmoil in their homeland. Migrant waves increased in the 1600s, the Fujianese fishermen bringing with them the language, food, architecture and religious beliefs of their ancestors, much of which is still around today.

Matsu was largely politically insignificant until the Nationalists fled to Taiwan in 1949 and established Matsu, along with Kinmen, as a front-line defence against the communists. The quiet islands were transformed into battlefields and the mainland bombed Matsu intermittently for a decade. The deployment of the US 7th Fleet in 1958 prevented any further military escalation, but the islands remained on high alert until the late 1970s.

Martial law was lifted from Matsu in 1992, several years after the rest of Taiwan, but in 2001 Matsu (along with Kinmen) became an early stepping stone in cross-Strait travel, with the islands reframing their identities from military to tourist-centric.

ⓘ Information

While the military presence is much reduced in recent years, Nangan still holds live-firing exercises on occasion: warning signs should be obeyed and straying too far off marked roads is a bad idea.

Although some better hotels accept plastic, it's worth bringing ample cash with you from Taiwan. There are ATMs at the ferry ports in Fu'ao (Nangan) and Baisha (Beigan), but not all foreign cards work there so you might need to head to the Bank of Taiwan (p325) in Nangan, which is also the only place that changes money.

ℹ️ Getting There & Away

AIR

Uni Air (www.uniair.com.tw) and only Uni Air flies from Taipei-Songshan to both of Matsu's airports: Nangan (six daily) and Beigan (three daily) .

They also operate a Nangan–Taichung link (NT$2338) that runs on Monday, Wednesday, Friday and Sunday in winter, rising to daily or more in summer.

BOAT

Nangan's **Fu'ao Harbour** (福澳港, Fúaò Gǎng) is Matsu's main ferry hub with services to Keelung (Taiwan) six times weekly and Mawei (马尾港) near Fuzhou (China) daily. There are two boats a day from Beigan to Huangqi (黄岐镇) in China.

ℹ️ Getting Around

From Fu'ao (Nangan) boats leave for the following:
Beigan (adult/child NT$160/80, 15 minutes) Hourly from 7am to 5pm, returning 20 minutes later.
Dongju (adult/child NT$200/100, 50 minutes) and **Xiju** (70 minutes) at 7am, 11am and 2.30pm.
Dongyin (adult/child NT$350/175, two hours) At 9am on even-numbered dates, returning from Dongyin at 7am on odd-numbered dates. No service either way on Wednesdays.

Beigan

Beigan (北竿; Běigān) is a great little getaway for tranquillity, coastal scenery and close encounters with deer (on Daqiu). There are memorable views from former military lookout points and some of the seven villages retain historic Fujian-style stone houses, including the wonderfully preserved examples in Qinbi. There's not a great deal else by way of sights, and most visitors come on day trips from Nangan, but appealing homestays in Qinbi and Qiaozi make overnighting a laid-back pleasure.

◎ Sights

★ Qinbi Village   VILLAGE

(芹壁村, Qínbì Cūn) Qinbi is by far Beigan's most complete traditional village, with its array of interconnected stone homes built on a steep slope, facing the curved bay and small handkerchief of sandy beach. Most homes are now little guesthouses and/or cafes, but despite the fairly regular arrivals of tour buses, the place still feels comparatively uncommercial.

Built from slabs of granite, typical houses feature high, narrow windows to protect the inhabitants from howling winds. House No 14 is said to have belonged to a once-ruthless pirate named Chen. Also seek out the tiny Wild West–style miniature bank building and walk just past the old temple to see its spring pool full of carved frogs.

★ Peace Memorial Park   HISTORIC SITE

(和平紀念公園, Hépíng Jìniàn Gōngyuán; ⊙exhibition centre 8.30am-12.30pm & 1.30-5pm) FREE Until the start of this century, Beigan's steep eastern peninsula housed a slew of defensive military emplacements. Many have been preserved as part of this intriguing and extensive park, combining superb viewpoints with insights into the island's military history. Plenty of artillery pieces still point their barrels out to sea. A scooter is useful both to get here and to shuttle between the site's three main focal points.

Start at the Exhibition Centre, a museum explaining Matsu's geopolitical significance in the 1950s and the battles fought here. There's a great viewpoint upstairs and an even better one at Stronghold 8, 600m east on a lane passing an outdoor display of tanks and anti-aircraft cannons. Much less visited is Stronghold 6, nearly 1km northeast of the Exhibition Centre on a narrow lane that ends with a very steep descent. Continue down on steps, through foxhole tunnels and return to your scooter by a different stairway.

Daqiu Island   ISLAND

(大坵島, Dàqiū Dǎo; ⊙9am-3pm, last return 5pm) Barely five minutes by boat from Qiaozi harbour, a two-hour visit to this windswept, uninhabited island is one of Matsu's great joys – but only when the sea is calm. The small, deserted hamlet near its jetty is being tastefully restored and a concrete footpath makes it easy to stroll the island in around 90 minutes, watched by dozens of remarkably tame Formosan sika deer.

In calm weather several boats shuttle across from Qiaozi. There's no fixed timetable, but most homestays will fix you up with a boatman for NT$300 return per person, or you could call 📱0981-373 840 (in Chinese) to arrange your own. Before boarding you'll need to show your passport (or Taiwanese

LOCAL KNOWLEDGE

BLUE TEARS

Every year from April to September, some of the night-time waters along the Matsu coastline will scintillate when disturbed in an effect that's nicknamed 'blue tears' (藍眼淚, *lán yǎnlèi*). On warm, calm evenings between June and August, lapping wavelets seem to glitter with light, hough when photographed, this looks more like a single, spooky glow. Even when conditions are ideal, you'll need a moonless evening and to get well away from artificial light. Or join a blue tears boat tour into Nangan's Behai Tunnel. In April and September, you might still get to experience it by splashing late at night in low-tide sand pools, with your footprints creating a faint-but-fascinating sparkle caused by the bioluminescent phytoplankton (called dinoflagellates). You'll probably need a guide to find such places, but some better hotels on Beigan will take their guests as part of the service.

If you come out of season, you can still get a basic sense of the phenomenon by visiting the Blue Tears Museum (p322) on Nangan: most information is in Chinese, but you can see the algae through a microscope, stir a bowlful to observe a gentle shimmer then sup on blue-coloured drinks and buy blue tears–themed souvenirs.

ID) to a security officer beside the Star Yang Hotel, which faces the harbour.

Qiaozi Village VILLAGE
(橋仔村, Qiáozǐ Cūn) Though lacking Qinbi's architectural integrity, Qiaozi (Ciaozai) gains a great deal of charm from its setting, nestled around a rocky harbour with interlinked passageways and stairways, plus a pretty little stone footbridge crossing a side gulley.

Qiaozi is the starting point for short boat trips to Daqiu Island and is famed for its clutch of small, rebuilt temples sporting bright red 'fire wall' gables (p316), sharply pointed to form conspicuous M-shapes.

Some of the hamlet's older stone buildings are derelict and partly overgrown, but there are also half a dozen new mini hotels that rate among the island's best. Beside the Musi Seaview Hostel is a small, free museum displaying local fishing equipment.

Hou'ao Village VILLAGE
(后澳, Hòuào, Houwo) Worth a five-minute stop en route to the Peace Memorial Park (p318), this village looks unpromising when you pass on the main street, but if you delve into the small web of back alleys there are quite a few older houses whose varying states of decay create a desolate atmosphere.

The causeway that links Hou'ao to the rest of Beigan crosses a golden sandy beach that is, on dark summer nights, a prime spot for observing blue tears.

Banli Mansion ARCHITECTURE
(坂里大宅, Bǎnlǐ Dàzhái; ☏083-655 663; http://banli.8898.tw; 49-52 Banli village; 坂里村49-52 號; ☺9am-4.30pm) FREE Beside the 7-Eleven shop in Banli is a very short row of four restored Qing dynasty stone-and-timber mansions. One of them is open to visitors as an unstaffed museum, and is worth a quick look if you're passing. Just across the road, take the passageway beside the tourist office to reach an arc of sandy beach that's pretty but unsafe for swimming most of the year.

Beside the museum, a trio of old buildings operates as a 13-room **guesthouse** (d/q from NT$1400/2000, without bath). Conditions are somewhat basic, but there's a reasonable sense of historical authenticity. Make advance arrangements as there's no reception.

🛏 Sleeping

Qinbi Backpacker Hostel HOSTEL $
(芹壁背包客棧, Qínbì Bèibāo Kèzhàn; ☏083-555 007; http://home.chinbeno2.url.tw; 3 Qinbi village; 芹壁村3號; dm NT$500-680, tr/q NT$2400/3000) A couple of homestay rooms plus a dormitory full of slightly claustrophobic capsule-style beds (and another of double capsules) are set in a pair of historic houses at the northern corner of Qinbi village. They share a lovely terrace set around a time-sculpted red-fig tree.

★So Lohas BOUTIQUE HOTEL $$
(漫活海景旅宿, Mànhuó Hǎijǐng Lǚsù; ☏083-655 685; www.lohaslife.tw; 85 Qiaozi village; 橋仔村85 號; d/q NT$3200/5600; P❄🛜) ☝ Perched just above Qiaozi village (p319), this superhospitable family hotel has four floors of luxurious modern rooms, all large with great beds, little balconies and marvellous sea views.

Most views encompass the little port, temples and offshore islands, with the Chinese mainland floating mistily on the horizon.

Beigan

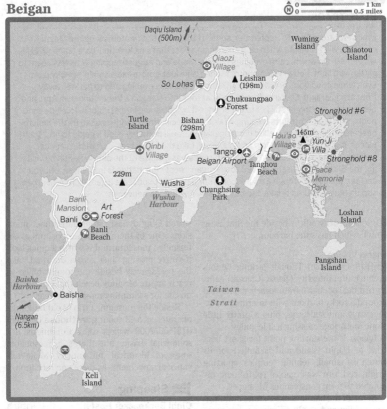

The sunny rooftop has even better views. Breakfast, including real coffee, is included. Upon advance request, you can order one of four dinner options (NT$260) to eat in.

Yun-Ji Villa B&B $$
(☑083-655 380; http://bnb.matsu.idv.tw/yunjivilla; 1-5 Hou'ou village; 后沃村1之5號; s/tw NT$1800/3000; ❋⊛) For total serenity and wonderful views across a hilltop lawn, it's hard to beat this well-equipped B&B that sits high above Hou'ao within the Peace Memorial Park (p318), near the junction of the park's three main lanes. You'll value having your own scooter with no shops or services around.

Chinbe No. 25
Guesthouse HOMESTAY $$
(芹壁村25號民宿, Qínbìcūn Èrshíwǔhào Mínsù; ☑083-655 628; www.chinbe.com.tw; 24 Qinbi village; 芹壁村24號; tw/q NT$1800/3300, with sea view NT$2300/4000; ⊙closed mid-Nov–Mar; ❋⊛) 🅿 One of few Qinbi stone-house

homestays with fluent English-speaking management (Sammy), this place has five hotel-style rooms with enlarged windows, stripped-pine rafters and relatively sleek en-suite bathrooms. It's set in a private garden at Qinbi 24, raised above the main road facing the steps to the beach.

✗ Eating

Tucked away in the pedestrian lanes of Qinbi are half a dozen dining choices, several with pretty terraces. There's more choice in architecturally dreary Tangqi village where shop 142 is a reliable budget eatery. Qiaozi has three snack stands and two restaurants, one of them characterfully ramshackle, but neither is especially recommended. By 7pm almost everything is closed apart from the convenience stores in Banli and Tangqi.

★ Jingwo Xiaochi NOODLES $
(镜沃小吃, Jingwò Xiǎochī; ☑0910-603 577; Qinbi 75; 芹壁村75號; noodles NT$120; ⊙10am-1.30pm

& 4-6.30pm) Delicious Matsu old wine noodles (馬祖老酒 麵線, *Māzǔ lǎojiǔ miàn xiàn*) are served in beautiful ceramic bowls and eaten at an unpretentious bench looking out towards the bay.

Run by a friendly older couple, the place is hidden up a stairway behind the more obvious but less recommended Chinbe Kitchen. If you reach Just Coffee Hostel, double back 20m to the southeast.

Drinking & Nightlife

A couple of shops in Tangqi sell extensive selections of Matsu 'old wine'. There are coffee places in Qinbi and Banli, and a couple of the Qinbi cafes also serve craft beers – notably Chinbe Aegean Sea (Qinbi 54) which has lovely lawn seating with sea views. In Beigan, nightlife essentially means listening to the waves since almost everything closes down by sunset.

Art Forest   CAFE
(亞特森林咖啡, Yàtè Sēnlín Kāfēi; ☑083-656 085; 47 Banli village; 坂里村47號; ⊘9am-5pm; ☎) Beigan's best coffee shop overlooks an attractive sweep of sandy beach from upstairs in the tourist office building in Banli.

ℹ️ Information

There's a large visitor centre opposite the old 'mansion' (p319) in Banli (open 8am to 5.30pm). It doesn't have English-speaking staff, but does give away copies of a very informative map/guide.

ℹ️ Getting There & Away

AIR

The terminal of **Beigan airport** (馬祖北竿機場, Māzǔ Běigān Jīchǎng; ☑083-656 606; www.tsa.gov.tw/tsaMFK/en/home.aspx; 261-2 Tangqi Village; 塘岐村 261-2 號) is right in the middle of Tangqi village. Uni Air (www.uniair.com.tw) has three flights daily from Taipei (full fare/advance purchase NT$1911/1731, 50 minutes).

BOAT

Beigan's main passenger port is at Baisha, with hourly services to Fu'ao on Nangan (NT$160, 15 minutes, 7.20am to 4.20pm). Boats to/from Huangqi (China) leave at 9.30am and 2.30pm in both directions (adult/child NT$650/375).

ℹ️ Getting Around

Beigan is relatively small, but with all the steep hills, renting a scooter makes sense, especially if you want to see the whole place in a day.

BUS

Fourteen times daily a small bus runs from Tangqi to Baisha then back again by a different route (NT$15). The order of stops varies and some runs include side trips to Wusha or Hou'ai. Pick up a copy of the *Beigan Guide Map* for a full timetable (in Chinese).

MOTORCYCLE

Scooter rentals at Baisha harbour cost NT$300/500 per four/24 hours. If nobody's there when you arrive, call 0919-004 154 or ask your homestay to organise for you. When renting, be sure to test the brakes as many of Beigan's roads are frighteningly steep.

Nangan

Nangan (南竿; Nángān; Nankan) is Matsu's transport hub and biggest, most militarised island, but it's nonetheless a peaceful haven with steep, flower-edged lanes and cacophonous birdsong. The biggest settlement, Jieshou (介壽村; also spelled Chiehshou), has a morning market and the island's only bank, but Magang (馬港; Matsu) village has a better selection of dining and Jinsha is prettier than both. Fuxing has a range of old houses and a fine temple, but the overall effect there is spoilt by banal recent buildings.

⊙ Sights

★ Giant Matsu Statue   STATUE
(媽祖巨神像, māzǔ jùshén xiàng; Magang village; 馬港村) At a towering 28.8m, this serene 2009 statue is said to be the world's tallest image of the sea goddess Matsu (Mazu). As well as facilitating many a 'See Matsu in Matsu' tour book slogan, it's a genuinely impressive icon, fronted by a huge wooden viewing deck shaped like a ship's prow. Beneath it runs a curious Y-shaped web of pedestrian tunnels.

★ Beihai Tunnel   TUNNEL
(北海坑道, Běihǎi Kēngdào; Renai village; per person on foot/by boat/by kayak free/NT$150/250, night tour NT$300; ⊘8am-4.30pm, night tours half-hourly 6-8.30pm) This 700m of sea tunnel took three laborious years to carve out with many soldiers losing their lives in the process. Completed in 1971, it was used as a hiding place for up to 120 small boats, protecting them from potential aerial attack. Visits are free on foot (low tide only), or you can pay to float or kayak through the four surprisingly wide, criss-crossed channels.

Across a small, pebble beach is the entrance to the smaller, hand-cut tunnels of the Dahan Stronghold. There's nothing inside, but forking right at the first bifurcation allows you to loop back to the Nangan Visitor Centre via a path that climbs the rocks then descends through pretty woodland.

From April to September, there are evening boat rides six times nightly in the Beihai tunnels giving a fair chance of seeing blue tears (p319): the tunnel lighting is briefly extinguished and, when the waters are stirred with the oars, you'll hopefully see a faint blue glow. Demand is high so it's worth pre-booking: call ☑083-622 177 before 4.30pm or, better, prepay at the tunnel counter.

Matsu Temple
TAOIST TEMPLE

(馬祖天后宮, Mǎzǔ Tiānhòu Gōng; ☑083-622 913; http://tianhou-temple.matsu.idv.tw/; 4-1 Magang village; 馬港村4-1號) This colourful temple is considered one of the most sacred spots in Taiwan, featuring as it does the purported grave of Lin Mo-niang (林默娘; b 960) who later became deified as Matsu (Mazu). Legend claims that she was washed ashore here having drowned in a fateful attempt to save her father (or brothers in some versions) after a shipwreck.

The temple is in Magang (aka Matsu) village and linked by a long stairway to the Giant Matsu Statue (p321), which dominates it from the hill to the north. The path passes the village beach on which there's a collection of military landing craft. Just inland is a pair of pedestrianised streets offering the best selection of dining options anywhere on the island. Matsu's birthday (the 23rd day of the third lunar month – ie in March or April) sees a lavish festival in her honour at the temple, although it's not part of western Taiwan's better-known Matsu Pilgrimage route.

Jinsha Village
VILLAGE

(金沙村, Jīnshā Cūn) Jinsha is Nangan's most attractive old village. Its central core is a series of tile-roofed stone buildings – many now B&Bs – forming a tight-knit unit cut by narrow passages. Several other old cottages, mostly derelict, climb the steep valley sides.

Matsu Folklore Culture Museum
MUSEUM

(馬祖民俗文物館, Mǎzǔ Mínsú Wénwùguǎn; ☑083-622 167; http://folklore.dbodm.com; 135 Qingshui village; 清水村135號; adult/child NT$40/20; ◷9am-5pm Tue-Sun) This large, professional yet little-heralded museum uses many old photos, artefacts and films to introduce the culture and lifestyle of the Matsu islands.

The ground-floor section on the archaeology of an 8000-year old Liangdao Austrone-

sian culture is well explained in English. The 2nd and 3rd floors look at agriculture, fishing and living spaces with visually appealing, mostly self-explanatory displays, but only the titles are translated. The 4th floor hosts a gallery of changing artwork.

Blue Tears Museum
MUSEUM

(藍眼淚生態館, Yǎnlèi Shēng Tàiguǎn; ☑083-623 338; 24 Siwei village; 四維村24號; adult/child NT$350/250; ◷9.40-11.40am, 1.30-5.40pm & 6.40-8.40pm) Most of the information is in Chinese, but if you're visiting Matsu outside the summer season, this three-room interactive museum is the only place you'll see the blue tears (p319) phenomenon. The phytoplankton responsible are cultivated in situ and part of the visitor experience is stirring a bowlful of water containing the critters.

The museum is at Furong'ao, a sandy cove around 1km north of Magang (Matsu) village. Its little cafe, overlooking the oyster beds, serves blue-coloured drinks and great if pricey coffee. Scooter on another 400m to visit the partly preserved old village of Siwei.

Iron Fort
FORT

(鐵堡, Tiě Bǎo; ◷24hr) This dinky little fortified islet, linked by a footbridge to the main island, is a pretty strip of coral topped by a cactus-lined walkway, but cut into the rock beneath is a narrow tunnel linking to a handful of sniper slots. Access is from the attractive, almost traffic-free land that links Renai and Jinsha villages.

Gruesome stories are told by Matsu residents of how frogmen from mainland China would sneak inside the fort at night, slit the throats of the Taiwanese guards on duty and carry back an ear to show their comrades.

🛏 Sleeping

Jinsha is the cutest village to have a selection of homestays in old stone-and-timber houses, but there are more in Fuxing and Qingshui. Staying in Magang (Matsu) village has the advantage of a better range of dining choices. Jieshou has far less charm. Book ahead during holiday seasons as Taiwanese tourists like to stay overnight on Nangan on their way to and from Fujian.

LANGUAGE

The people of Matsu speak a dialect derived from Fuzhou in mainland China, which is mostly unintelligible to speakers of Taiwanese.

★**Hostel 55**   HOSTEL $
(55據點; ☑083-623 426; Jinsha 150; 津沙村150
號; dm/d from NT$780/2200) From the camou-
flage paintwork, you might think this place
was still an army lookout station. However, it has been stylishly repurposed with
top-quality curtained bunk dorms, three private rooms with panoramic seascapes and
even better coastline views from the rooftop
terrace. A kitchen area plus bar with craft
beers add further to the mix. It's around 1km
from Jinsha.

Jinsha Old Street   GUESTHOUSE $
(津沙古街客居, Jīnshā Gǔjiē Kèjū; ☑0928-812
879, 083-626 190; 70 Jinsha Village; 津沙村70號;
d/q without bath NT$1800/2800; ✳☎) Two of
central Jinsha's most charming older homes
now form this attractive guesthouse run by a
caring host who can manage just a few words
of spoken English. Only one room is en suite
(NT$2100). Four cheaper twins are bright-
er with comfortable beds and access to two
large communal sitting areas, but they share
one bathroom/toilet.

Matsu 1st Hostel   HOSTEL $
(馬祖1青年民宿, Mǎzǔ Qīngnián Mínsù; ☑083-
656 698, 083-623 353; www.matsuhostel.com; 71
Jinsha village; 津沙村71號; per person NT$1000;
✳☎) This backpacker hostel occupies a fine
old Fujian-style stone house with a mixture
of capsule-style sleeping spaces and rather cramped dorms. Bathrooms are outside
across the alley and, while very friendly, the
place has a slightly musty air.

It's in the heart of old Jinsha village.

★**Yun-Jin Villa Matsu**   BOUTIQUE HOTEL $$
(雲津客棧, Yúnjīn Kèzhàn; ☑0905-505 811, 083-
626 228; www.yunjin-inn.com.tw; 103-2 Mazu village;
馬祖村103-2號; d/q NT$3200/5600) Combin-
ing character and comfort, each of the nine
rooms is differently designed using elements
of found wood and rock, and all have super-
comfy beds and balconies that provide mem-
orable sunset views across a poetic seascape.

It's on a quiet lane just around the corner
from the Giant Matsu Statue (p321) and an
easy walk to Magang (Matsu) village for a rel-
atively wide selection of dining options.

Dayspring Hotel;   DESIGN HOTEL $$$
(Coast of the Dawn, 日光春和, Rìguāngchūnhé;
☑083-626 666; www.dayspringmatsu.com; 1-1
Renai village; 仁愛村 1-1號; d/ste incl breakfast
NT$5800/8800; ✳☎) One of Nangan's most
stylish properties, Dayspring uses arty, recti-
linear minimalism to contrast with the nat-

ural setting surveyed by its large sweep of
picture windows. Yet, despite the cool design
book looks, staff give the place a delightfully
friendly feel.

✖ Eating

Busy Jieshou has a morning market (7am
to 10am), but Magang (Matsu) village offers
a more appealing lunch and evening choice,
with many decent options concentrated
along a pedestrianised V-shaped strip, hung
with lanterns. Try No 93 for 'Matsu Burgers',
No 82 for pasta, Nos 80 or 78 for seafood and
deep-fried sweet potato dumplings (地瓜餃,
dìguājiǎo), No 54 for hotpot and No 42 for
semi-international meal plates.

Jinsha Xiaoguan   SEAFOOD $
(津沙小館, Jīnshā Xiǎoguǎn; 61 Jinsha village; 津沙
村61號; mains from NT$80, seafood plates NT$250-
450; ☺10am-8pm) Handy for those sleeping
in Jinsha, this visually forgettable restaurant
serves excellent, archetypally local cuisine,
including rice fried in Matsu red yeast, clam
noodles and a whole variety of fresh seafood
plates.

★**Furen Cafe**   CAFE $$
(夫人咖啡館, Fūrén Kāfēiguǎn; ☑083-625 138;
www.furen.com.tw; 40-1 Furen village; 夫人村 40-1
號; mains NT$260-400; ☺10am-10pm) This
marvellously quirky old stone house has a
sheltered patio looking back across the bay
towards Fu'ao (p318), yet is about as rural as
you can get on Nangan. It's a treasure trove
of knickknacks, with lampshades, framed
costumes and century-old beams set amid
flowering shrubs and potted cacti. They sell
NT$150 entry tickets to dissuade time wast-
ers. but you'll get that refunded against pur-
chases of food and drink.

There's a romping rock and blues
soundtrack, and a good selection of typ-
ical local dishes supplemented by some
pseudo-European choices.

Yima's Kitchen   SEAFOOD $$
(依嬤的店, Yīmā de Diàn; ☑083-626 125; 72-1
Fuxing village; 復興村72-1號; set meals NT$330-
380; ☺11am-2.30pm & 5-8.30pm; ☎) This stone
house. with big glass windows and a decor
of signatures grafittied by guests, is a popular choice for in-season seafood and serves a
multi-dish set plate that allows individuals to
sample a range of local flavours.

It's one of two restaurants tucked into the
village of Fuxing. There's subtle signage in
English.

Nangan

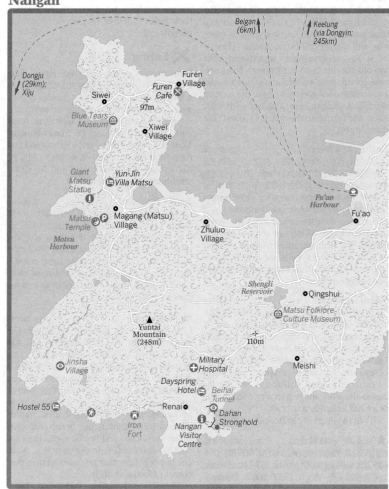

TAIWAN STRAIT ISLANDS NANGAN

🍷 Drinking & Nightlife

★ **Thornbirds Coffee-Book Cafe** CAFE
(刺鳥咖啡書店, Cìniǎo Kāfēi Shūdiàn; ☑ 0933-008 125; Military Stronghold 12, Fuxing-Fu'ao Rd; 復興村222號; ⏰ 10.30am-6pm) For NT$150, you get not only a coffee but also the chance to explore a 'secret' tunnel, then relax in an artistic mishmash of paintings, fresh flowers, books, driftwood furniture and assorted viewpoints.

It's overlooking a beautiful cove with locals fishing on the rocks beneath.

🛍 Shopping

Popular souvenirs include military-style clothing, dried seafood, Matsu alcohol and tubs of the red yeast that is so integral to local cuisine. Everything from mugs to flip-flops can be found adorned with blue tears (p319) images.

Matsu Distillery WINE
(馬祖酒廠, Mǎzǔ Jiǔchǎng; ☑ 083-622 820; www.matsuwine.com.tw; 208 Fuxing village; 復興村208號; ⏰ 8.40-11.30am & 1.40-5pm) FREE The museum-like showroom of Matsu's distillery sells many variants of its sorghum-based Kaoliang liquor (高粱酒, Gāoliáng jiǔ) and

medicinal rice wine (老酒, *làojiǔ*). The most famous is branded Tunnel 88 for the former military tunnel in which it is now aged in sealed ceramic amphorae.

ⓘ Information

The only place in Matsu to change money is the **Bank of Taiwan** (台灣銀行, Táiwān Yínháng; ☎ 083-626 046; Jieshou Village; 南竿鄉介壽村257號; ⊙ 9am-3.30pm Mon-Fri) on a slope above the post office, at the western edge of Jieshou (Nangan). It also has a 24-hour ATM. You'd be smart to take with you what you expect to spend on Matsu. And a little more in case of cancelled transport connections.

Of several Visitor Information Centres, the one at the airport (☎ 083-626 402) is the only one that reliably has English speakers. However, all of them, including the big Nangan Visitor Center at Beihai Tunnel (p321), usually stock the informative English language map-brochure *Let's Backpack in Matsu*. The multilingual Matsu Scenic Area website (www.matsu-nsa.gov.tw) is also handy.

ⓘ Getting There & Away

AIR

Uni Air (www.uniair.com.tw) has six flights daily between **Nangan airport** (LZN, 馬祖南竿機場, Mǎzǔ Nángān Jīchǎng) and Taipei-Songshan (around NT$2000, 50 minutes) plus several weekly flights to/from Taichung (NT$2500, 55 minutes).

The airport is usually, but not always, a stop on both of the Nangan bus routes linking Matsu and Jieshou. Many hotels offer airport pick-up. Taxi fares are unlikely to be over NT$200 to anywhere on the island.

BOAT

All Nangan ferry services start from Fu'ao Harbour (p318).

To Taiwan

The large **Taima Star** (臺馬之星, Táimǎ Zhīxīng; ☎ Keelung 02-2424 6868, Nangan 083-626 655, sailing updates 02-2425 2166; www.shinhwa.com.tw) car ferry to Nangan starts from Keelung's West Terminal, which is a short stroll from the north exit of Keelung train station. The ferry leaves Keelung at 9.50pm and travels overnight. Departures on odd-numbered dates sail direct to Nangan (nine hours). Even-date departures add a stop in Dongyin in both directions so the trip takes up to 11 hours. Returning from Matsu, the boat to Keelung travels by day, offering a chance of seeing dolphins en route. There's no service from Keelung on Tuesdays or back from Matsu on Wednesdays. Fares start at NT$800 seat-only. Economy bunks, with 16 beds to a lower-deck room, cost NT$1200. 'Business class' is much the same but in smaller, more claustrophobic six-bunk cabins, one floor higher (NT$1575). For something vastly more luxurious, take an en-suite VIP cabin with private lounge and double bed (NT$5250 for two people).

Short-notice cancellations due to bad weather (or ship repairs) are fairly common, so check the website and/or call around 10 hours before departure to confirm. Online booking is in Chinese only so get local help. Outside peak periods, the ship is rarely full: for same-day departures, go to the ferry port two hours before scheduled departure. Boarding starts an hour before sailing.

To China

A daily passenger ferry to mainland China departs at 2pm (NT$1300, 1¾ hours), arriving at the largely industrial Mawei Port (福州港马尾客运站) on the outskirts of Fuzhou. Assuming you clear immigration in time, there are onward shuttle buses from Mawei to Fuzhou's Rende bus station at 4pm and 4.30pm (timetable https://fuzhou.8684.cn/x_70b7ef31). From Mawei to Nangan, the boat departs at 9am.

Matsu Inter-Island Ferries

Baisha (Beigan; adult/child NT$160/80, 15 minutes) Hourly from 7am to 5pm, returning 20 minutes later.

Dongyin (NT$350/175, two hours) 9am on even-numbered dates, returning from Dongyin at 7am on odd-numbered dates. No service either way on Wednesdays.

Xiju (adult/child NT$200/100, 70 minutes) via Dongju (50 minutes) 7am, 11am and 2.30pm.

ⓘ Getting Around

BUS

Public buses (NT$15 per ride) link Jieshou to Magang (Matsu) via two possible routes. The 'coast' route (blue) departs Jieshou on the half-hour and drives via Fu'ao (p318) and Zhuluo. The 'mountain' (red) route leaves on the hour and has several variants, some making side trips to Jinsha (p322) or Renai. Outbound 'coast' buses become 'mountain' buses on return and vice versa.

CAR & MOTORCYCLE

Motorcycle rental costs NT$500 per day, including petrol. Arrange through your accommodation, the information counter at the airport or (more awkwardly), try at one of the two souvenir shops outside the Fu'ao (p318) ferry terminals.

TAXI

There are metered taxis (NT$100 for the first 1.25km, NT$5 for every additional 0.25km). For longer journeys, such as to the airport to Jinsha (p322), a flat NT$200 fare might be charged.

PENGHU ISLANDS

☑ 06 / POP 104,700

Penghu (澎湖; Pénghú), once known as the Pescadores, is an archipelago of islands known for surf, sea, sand and sunshine. It's not so hot on must-see sights, though a preponderance of colourful temples feature preposterously ornate dragon-topped roofs with swallowtail eaves.

In the balmy summer months, Penghu attracts sun-worshippers and island-hoppers. However, in winter and spring this is one of the windiest places in the northern hemisphere, becoming a magnet for international wind- and kite-surfers.

History

Archaeological finds on Chimei suggest that Penghu was inhabited around 5000 years ago, possibly exporting stone tools to neolithic cultures elsewhere. However, for reasons unknown, signs of human settlement seem to disappear around 2000 BC, returning only in the 9th century AD, initially with transient Chinese fishermen. The Dutch, who called the archipelago the Pescadori ('Fishing') Islands, arrived in 1622 but soon moved to the Taiwanese mainland when they learned that the Ming imperial court had plans to remove them by force. A stele in Magong's Tienhou Temple inscribes this threat. In 1662 the Ming loyalist Koxinga was sent to oust the Dutch from Taiwan for good and Penghu proved a convenient staging post as he drew up battle plans. Some troops stayed in Penghu after the Dutch were gone and set up their own regime, but this proved short-lived as the Qing court threw them out in 1683. The French were the next to arrive, in 1884, followed by the Japanese, in 1895, who settled in for the next 50 years. Magong developed into a neat, very Japanese town, but was bombed by the allies from October 1944, and in 1945 the Chinese Nationalists arrived.

⊙ Sights

★**Penghu Aquarium**   AQUARIUM
(☑ 06-993 3006; www.penghu-aquarium.com; 58 Qitou village; 岐頭村58號; adult/student NT$300/210; ⊙9am-5pm; 🅿 👪) 🖉 This large, family-friendly experience is home to an engrossing collection of living sea life, from a rescued three-legged turtle and magical family of jellyfish to three types of ray that glide above as you walk through a glass tunnel.

The use of corals in huge display tanks along with the low-intensity blue lighting gives a real sense of being underwater. Don't miss feeding time (11am and 3pm) and do bring the kids to the touch pool (10am to 11am, 1.30pm to 2pm and 3.30pm to 4pm) to learn how to interact respectfully with starfish, urchins and sea cucumbers.

The aquarium is on Baisha Island around half an hour's drive from Magong. Where you turn off the main road, notice the multi-trunked banyon fronting a temple at the junction: it's somewhat smaller than the

Tongliang version, but entirely without the tourist hordes.

Fengkuei Cave & Youfu Pavilion   CAVE
(風櫃洞和幽浮涼亭, Fēngguìdòng Hé Yōufú Liángtíng) At the southernmost tip of Fengkuei is Fengkuei Cave, where strong waves create long rectangular spaces under the coastal basalt. When the tide rises, seawater rushes into the hollow, compressing the air and blasting water out noisily from the crevices in the rocks: hence the Chinese name Fenggui (風櫃) meaning 'bellows'. An attraction in itself is the viewing platform, the white Youfu Pavilion (幽浮涼亭), which appears to be built out of two giant mushrooms – or, perhaps, retro-futuristic champagne glasses.

Erkan Old Residences   VILLAGE
(二崁古厝, Èrkǎn Gǔ Cuò; Erkan village, Xiyu, 二崁村) Penghu's only really 'complete' traditional village, low-slung Erkan oozes charm and is appealingly set on a grassy plateau raised above the sea. Virtually all of the 50 or so homes have round-ridged, red-tile roofs and coral stone walls that look polka-dotted where irregularities peep through the whitewash.

Catering for the regular flow of tourists, almost all homes double as shops or cafes, each with their own speciality: #40 for prickly pear juice, #3 for mini pumpkin cakes, #23 for cactus sorbet. Behind a notable braincoral wall, #38 serves bowls of tofu tea with peanut and bean (NT$40).

Suogang Pagodas   TAOIST SITE
(鎮港子午寶塔, Sǔogǎng Zǐwǔ Bǎotǎ; 69 Tongan St, Sanchong; 三重區同安街69號) The little town of Suogang is dominated by the extraordinary Ziwugong, a gigantic temple topped by a three-storey statue of the Jade Emperor (玉皇太帝; Yù Huáng Dàidì). But what's historic here is a much more modest pair of conical pyramids. Made in seven concentric sections of unpainted basalt, they are reputed to hold supernatural powers that ward off evil and protect residents from natural disasters.

Easiest to find is the 'male' (north) tower (塔公, tǎgōng) beside County Rd 25 on the way to Shanshui. The slightly smaller female version (塔婆, tǎpó) is 200m south then 100m east in a residential district.

Tongliang Banyan Tree   TAOIST TEMPLE
(通梁古榕, Tōngliáng Gǔróng; Tongliang village, Baisha; 通梁村) The 300-year-old Tongliang Banyan Tree covers a remarkable 600 sq metres, sending down roots that essentially form the pillars of a natural hallway that leads into a colourful temple. However, it's partly held up by unsightly brick and concrete frames and the endless tour groups can get noisy.

With little else to do during the 20-minute stop here, most visitors hit the next door 'Cactus Ice' shop for ice creams in fanciful flavours including peanut, aloe and signature prickly pear (one scoop NT$25). This and other boxy buildings face a small fishing dock.

Xiaomen Geology Gallery   MUSEUM
(小門地質館; Xiǎomén Dìzhì Guǎn; ☑069-982 988; 11-12 Xiaomen village; ◷8am-5.30pm) **FREE** This attractively laid-out museum gives a good introduction to the volcanic and sedimentary rocks that make up the archipelago. It sits on the slope that leads from Xiamen village past coral-stone walled gardens to the clifftop path. From here, it's less than five minutes to a rocky erosion arch known, somewhat perplexingly, as Whale Cave.

It's worth walking on around the island for more fine views. Xiamen village has a minor charm too and a handful of restaurants catering for tour groups that often have lunch here.

Yuwongdao Lighthouse   LIGHTHOUSE
(漁翁島燈塔, Yúwēngdǎo Dēngtǎ; ☑886-6998 1766; ◷9am-5pm) **FREE** Almost comically small, this cast-iron lighthouse was built in 1878 by Brits who initially staffed the place on 10-year shifts. The main attractions are the moorland landscapes and bracing sea views.

TURTLES OF PENGHU

The turtle, along with the dragon, chimera and phoenix, is one of the four sacred beasts of ancient Chinese mythology. Representing longevity and fortune, it was said that the future could be divined by examining the marks on turtle shells. Though now endangered, sea turtles still migrate through Penghu's coastal waters and lay eggs on local beaches, notably in southern Wang'an where there's a Green Turtle Tourist Conservation Centre (p337). So it's not surprising that turtle imagery remains especially strong here. Most notably, during the Lantern Festival (p334), Penghu residents offer sacrificial turtle-themed rice cake offerings in temples and parade through the streets with giant turtle effigies accompanying local deities on large palanquins.

TAIWAN STRAIT ISLANDS PENGHU ISLANDS

Penghu

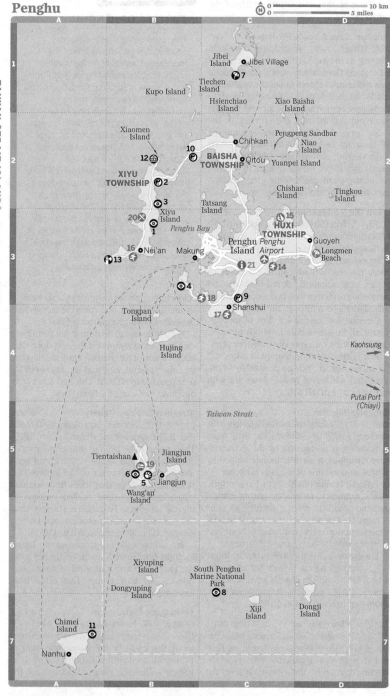

Penghu

About a minute's drive east, a 'bridge to nowhere' is actually the viewing platform to look down onto the Wai'an Decoy Cannon (外垵餌砲; Wài'ǎn Ěrpào), a two-bore 6m gun made in concrete as a cunning ruse by the Japanese to fool reconnaissance that the island was heavily fortified.

Da-yi Temple   TAOIST TEMPLE
(大義宮; Dàyì Gōng; 76 Zhuwan village, Xiyu; 西嶼鄉竹灣村76號; ⊙ 5am-8pm) The 200-year-old Da-yi Temple is dedicated to Guandi, the god of war, with 4m bronze statues guarding the entry stairs. Some say that when the French tried to attack Penghu, mysterious forces kept them away from the temple. In late 2018, environmentalists relaunched a campaign to free the turtles who have been living and breeding for decades in an underground coral pool beneath the temple.

Daguoyeh Prismatic Basalt   AREA
(大菓葉柱狀玄武岩, Dàguǒyè Zhùzhuàn Xuánwǔyán) This minor geological curiosity is a vertically contoured wall of basalt forming a

small outcrop in the grass-and-scrub landscape. There's a glass-box coffee shop along with pleasant views across the bay to receding headlands beyond.

🏃 Activities

★ Shanshui Beach   BEACH
(山水沙灘, Shānshuǐ Shātān) Shanshui is popular with surfers but also with tour groups who delight in photographing not just the lovely golden sands but also the village's ever-growing collection of architecturally curious B&Bs: several Greek-Mediterranean, one pseudo-Middle Eastern and a big hotel with castle-style battlements on its turret.

Buses from Magong (NT$29) leave at 6.45am, 7.50am, 9am and 5.55pm, returning half an hour later.

★ Penghu Windsurf   WINDSURFING
(Guoyeh Sunrise, 菓葉觀日樓, Guǒyè Guānrìlóu; ☑ 06-992 0818; www.penghuwindsurf.idv.tw; 129-3 Guoyeh village; 菓葉村129-3號; ⊙ book ahead; 🖱) Run by champion kitesurfers, this outfit can arrange windsurfing and sea-kayaking opportunities as well as scooter and bicycle rental from their B&B, the blue-and-white building right beside the grandiose port-facing temple in Guoyeh village.

Poseidon   WATER SPORTS
(波賽頓海洋運動俱樂部, Bōsàidùn Hǎiyáng Yùndòng Jùlèbù; ☑ 06-995 0178; www.facebook.com/Poseidon.Wakeboarding.Club; 52-7 Shihli village; 時裡里52-7號; ⊙ Apr-early Oct; 🖱 Fenggui) Poseidon on Shihli Beach is a very professional outfit, teaching high-skill water sports to beginners. Two-hour surfing and stand-up paddleboarding (SUP) courses (NT$800) both run at 9am and 2pm. There are wakeboard classes hourly, and some staff speak good English.

Mahalo Surfing   SURFING
(☑ 06-995 2893, Karen 093-549 7450; www.mahalosurfing.com; 8-6 Shanshui village; 山水里珠江8-6號; surfboards per day NT$500-800, boogie boards NT$250; ⊙ call) Shanshui's surf specialist rents out boards, offers lessons and runs a pizza cafe in the summer season. They also have a great B&B in the multicoloured cubes above the shop.

Nei'an Beach   BEACH
(內垵沙灘, Nèi'ǎn Shātān) The sands of beautiful Nei'an Beach huddle under a cliff beneath the road to Yuwongdao Lighthouse (p327). It offers memorable sunset vistas and relatively

shallow waters, but can get very windy and it's a comparatively long ride from Magong. Waian buses pass close by.

Shihli Beach   BEACH
(蒔裡沙灘, Zhílǐ Shātān; Fenggui) Much of the 1km-long sand-shell beach at Shihli is in front of a small, unspoilt townscape, but at the western end it's just for swimmers and water sports folk, backed by a cafe-viewing platform with shell-shaped roof.

The English-speaking, water sports group Poseidon (p329) offers regular wakeboard, stand-up paddleboarding (SUP) and surfing courses.

Liquid Sport   WINDSURFING
(愛玩水, Àiwánshuǐ; 0911-267 321; www.liquid-sportpenghu.com; 22-3 Qinglo, Huxi; 湖西鄉青螺 22-3號; call) Liquid Sports is set up as a full-service one-stop outfit for windsurfers, kiteboarders and stand-up paddleboarding (SUP) enthusiasts, with equipment rental and a luxurious guesthouse.

It's in a rather obscure village set back from a wetlands area. Contact well ahead to make arrangements.

Aimen Beach   BEACH
(隘門沙灘, Àimén Shātān; Aimen village, Huxi; 湖西隘門村) Aimen Beach is a long, attractive, golden arc that's only slightly spoilt by a trio of chimneys in the distance. The south end of the bay has a small safe-swimming zone, picnic tables, the odd hammock and a summer cafe. The rest of the beach has sharp coral in the shallows and is for jet-skis, banana-boat rides and other water sports.

Sleeping

Bayhouse Hostel Penghu   HOSTEL $
(澎湖北吉光背包客民宿, Pénghú Běijíguāng Bèibāokè Mínsù; 06-995 3005, 0934-263 005; www.bayhouse.tw; 17-26 Shanshui village; 山水里山17-26號; dm/tw NT$750/1400;) Compared to the many more fanciful guesthouse buildings along the Shanshui strip, Bayhouse has a certain homey modesty. Helpful staff speak English, there's a sociable common area and you're just a stone's throw from the beach. It's one block inland from the eastern (fishing port) end of the beach.

Eating

Magong is a seafood-lover's paradise offering simple takeaways such as fried cuttlefish balls (炸花枝丸, zhàhuā zhīwán) to up-market options like raw lobster (龍蝦, lóng xiā) and 'five-flavour' balloonfish (五香刺河豚, wǔ xiāng cìhétún). A classic is braised pork ribs (鮕鮕燉排骨, tuochu dunpaigu) cooked with a sun-dried local octopus.

Also look out for pumpkin noodles (金瓜米粉, jīnguā mǐfěn) and cabbage fried with peanuts (高麗菜炒土豆麩, gāolícài chǎo tǔdòufū).

Outside Magong, choice is relatively limited. Shanshui has four non-hotel restaurants, one open year-round, plus a surfers' pub. There are several lunch options in both Erkan and Xiaomen. Ice creams and snacks are available beside the great banyan tree in Tongliang.

Ching-Shin Seafood   SEAFOOD $$$
(清心飲食店, Qīngxīn Yǐnshí Diàn; 06-998 1128; https://page.line.me/qor5251q; 77-2 Cidong village, Xiyu; 西嶼鄉池東村77號之2; mains NT$160-450; 11.30am-3pm & 5-7pm) It's very humble-looking and way out of Magong, but if you're touring Xiyu, this place is well known for its seafood.

The fish sashimi and fresh Penghu oysters (from NT$260) are specialities, but more basic dishes like pumpkin noodles are also available. In peak season it can get very busy and at any time the big table layout can make it feel a little uncomfortable for individuals wanting anything less than a feast. The restaurant is around 1km from Erkan, west of Rte 203 towards Chixi fishing harbour.

Information

Website https://tour.penghu.gov.tw/en/index.aspx is a very useful resource and the Chinese version is even better. During office hours (8am to 5.30pm) the tourist hotline 06-921 6445 can answer questions in fluent English.

Getting There & Away

AIR
Uni Air (https://www.uniair.com.tw) and Mandarin Airlines (https://www.mandarin-airlines.com) connect Penghu with Taipei and Kaohsiung several times daily. Daily Air (https://www.dailyair.com.tw) links Kaohsiung with Chimei and Wang'an, both once daily. And Uni Air has a Thursday flight to Kinmen. All are strictly weather permitting.

BOAT
All services from Taiwan-proper arrive at Magong. **Tai Hua Shipping** (台華輪船, Táihuá

Lúnchuán; 🖂 enquiries 069-264 087, ticketing 07-561 5313 ext 6; www.tnc-kao.com.tw; ⊘ ticket office 8.30-11.30am & 1.30-4.30pm or two hours before sailing) operates a year-round car ferry from Kaohsiung (from NT$860, 4½ to six hours, one or two boats daily, some overnight). In summer, other companies including **All Star** (滿天星航運, Mǎntiān Xīng Hángyùn; 🖂 06-922 9721, Budai 05-347 0948; adult/child NT$1000/500) operate from Butai Port near Chayi (NT$1000, 1½ hours, one to five boats daily depending on demand). Since 2019, the fastest and steadiest service on that route is the **Pescadores-Brave Line** (百麗航運, Bǎilì Hángyùn; 🖂 06-926 8199; www.pescadores ferry.com.tw; 36-1 Linhai Road; 臨海路36-1號) catamaran, taking just one hour. That company has mooted additional options to Kaohsiung and Taichung in just two hours.

ⓘ Getting Around

For public transport information, the all-in-Chinese website www.phpto.gov.tw is helpful.

BOAT

Public ferries serve most inhabited islands starting from three different ports: Magong Number 3 Port for southern islands, Chikhan for Jibei and Qitou for the eastern isles. In summer, joining a tour to visit several islands in the same group can make a lot of sense and usually doesn't end up costing much more than the ferry fares.

Boats from Magong

Chimei (NT$437, two hours) Via **Wang'an** (NT$269, 40 minutes) at 9.30am.

Tongpan (NT$120, 20 minutes) At 8.30am and 3.30pm (plus 11am on Wednesdays) returning an hour later. Timings might change in summer.

Hujing (NT$120, 30 minutes) Two or three daily, typically 9.30am and 3.30pm.

Wang'an via **Jiangjun** (NT$280, 45 minutes) At 2.30pm but call 06-999 1201 to confirm sailing. Returns next day at 7am.

Multi-island boat tours are often more convenient and the Chimei-Wang'an day trip sometimes runs outside the main summer season.

Boats from Chikhan

Jibei (Chipei, return NT$300 to NT$400, 20 minutes each way) Departures are roughly twice an hour in summer but at 11.15am and 5pm only November to March. Tickets are sold from the **North Sea Tourist Service Centre** (北海遊客 服務中心, Běihǎi Yóukè Fúwù Zhōngxīn; 🖂 06-993 3082; Chikhan Harbour, Baisha Island; 白 沙鄉赤崁村37之4號; ⊘ info desk 8am-5.30pm) in Chikhan. To reach the port from Magong, take a bus bound for Tongliang or Waian, get off outside the Chikhan post office and walk 700m northeast (slightly complex).

Boats from Qitou

Niao (one way NT$50, 12 minutes) Departs 11.30am and returns 2pm.

Pengpeng Sandbar Summer-only boat tours include Pengpeng along with various other islands. Departures are tide-dependent. Enquire at **Citou Visitor Centre** (岐頭遊客中心, Qítóu Yóukè Zhōngxīn; 🖂 06-993 1527; 16-5 Qitou Village; 岐頭村16-5號; ⊘ 8am-5.30pm).

TAIWAN STRAIT ISLANDS PENGHU ISLANDS

WHERE TO SURF, WINDSURF, DIVE & SNORKEL

Windsurfing

From October to March, almost constant northwesterlies make Penghu one of Asia's premier centres for wind- and kite-surfing. If you're a beginner, September and October are best with warm conditions and relatively gentle breezes. For professionals, come in winter when wind speeds can reach 50 knots. A popular spot is Longmen Bay – at other beaches, even the experienced risk being blown out to sea. .

Diving & Snorkelling

The best coral tends to be around small islets, especially in South Penghu. Dive access is usually by boat, notably with Island 77 (p338) based at Jiangjun, the small island across the bay from Wang'an. There's also a Scuba Centre (p334) in central Magong. However, without a grasp of Chinese, you might struggle to make the most of the opportunities.

Surfing

The main surf centre is Shanshui, where English-speaking Mahalo (p329) has a combined surf shop, pizza cafe and B&B right in the heart of the resort. Poseidon (p329) at Shihli Beach, where Amelia speaks excellent English, runs hourly wakeboarding lessons plus two-hour surfing and stand-up paddleboarding (SUP) lessons for beginners at 9am and 2pm (NT$800).

BUS

The islands' bus service is confusing to use as bus numbers aren't generally displayed and some routes make convoluted loops that won't necessarily suit visitors. Fares range from NT$19 to NT$93 according to distance travelled. Exact cash fares are required; no change given.

The daily **Tourist Shuttle** (http://phshuttlebus. penghu.gov.tw/en, NT$350) departs from the bus station at 8.30am then does hotel pick-ups. Over the next 6½ hours, it visits most of the key sights in the northern arc of the main islands. There's recorded commentary in Chinese, English and Japanese, but it's hard to hear thanks to passenger chatter and driver music.

CAR & MOTORCYCLE

There are numerous vehicle hire places, but most are reluctant to rent scooters to foreigners without Taiwanese licenses. If you have an international driving permit, you have a better chance of getting a scooter through your hotel or hostel (NT$350 per day).

TAXI

Drivers prefer flat rates to using the meter. Tours are available for around NT$3000 per day, but it's unlikely your driver will speak English.

Magong

✔ 06 / POP 62,600

Penghu's rapidly growing hub city, Magong (馬公; Mǎgōng; Makung; Makong) hides its attractive but minuscule old town core within an ever-growing mass of concrete hotels, leaving only the faintest echoes of a 700-year history. But what it lacks in architecture, the city makes up for with deliciously distinctive dining, trendy coffee shops, outlandishly colourful temples and a plentiful array of accommodation. The result is a traveller-friendly base from which to explore the Penghu archipelago.

Summer is prime time in Magong, with streets full of tourists and hotel prices rising like the temperature. From December to February, winds howl through a town that's markedly more subdued. March and November are still windy, but temperatures are pleasant and prices are low – however, most tours won't be running and outer-island homestays will likely be closed.

⊙ Sights

★Tianhou Temple   TAOIST TEMPLE
(馬祖天后宮, Mǎzǔ Tiānhòu Gōng; 1 Zhengyi St; 正義街1號; ⊙6am-8.30pm, back hall to 6.30pm) This celebrated 17th-century Matsu temple

sports high, sweeping swallowtail eaves and a wealth of gorgeous Chaozhou-style woodcarvings, mostly from a 1922 restoration.

A stele found here was inscribed with a 1604 order from General Shen Young demanding that the Dutch get out of Taiwan, a discovery that gives some credence to local claims that this is the oldest Matsu temple in Taiwan.

Guanyinting Park   PARK
(觀音亭海濱公園, Guānyīntíng Hǎibīn Gōngyuán; 7 Jieshou Rd; 介壽路7號) Come to this relaxing park for one of Magong's most quintessential experiences: watching the gilded sunset colours spreading across the sea, framed by the 200ft-long Rainbow Bridge. The indulgently over-engineered bridge loops across the mouth of a small bay to link up two coastal walkways. And yes, it really does turn rainbow colours at night thanks to fancy illumination... At least when the lamps are working.

The park is named for a 300-year-old temple that stands in its southeast corner.

★Central Street   AREA
(Magong Old St, 馬公老街, Mǎgōng Lǎojiē; 中央街; Zhōngyāng Jiē) Magong's cute if minuscule historic heart is a forked alley of old-style shops directly east of the Tianhou (Matsu) Temple.

At the top is a famous 'four-eyed' well that allowed multiple users to draw water at the same time from what was once the main water source for the local market. The well is overlooked by an authentic old shop selling traditional Chinese medicines.

Penghu Living Museum   MUSEUM
(澎湖生活博物館, Pénghú Shēnghuó Bówùguǎn; ☑06-921 0405; www.phlm.nat.gov.tw; 327 Sinsheng Rd; 馬公市新生路327號; NT$80; ⊙9am-4.30pm Fri-Wed) This large modern museum offers an excellent introduction to Penghu's history, culture and changing lifestyles. Memorable features include the explanation of stone weirs, the large 1:30 scale model of Huazhai and the almost full-size junk boat.

Geopark Centre   MUSEUM
(澎湖海洋地质公园中心, Pénghú Hǎiyáng dì Zhìgōngyuán Zhōngxīn; ☑06-926 9737; http://pnmg.npu.edu.tw; 71 Xinming Rd; 新明路71號; ⊙8am-11.30am & 1-4.30pm Tue-Sun) FREE To learn about Penghu basalt in all its forms, don't miss this impressive new geological centre one short block south of the Living Museum.

Magong

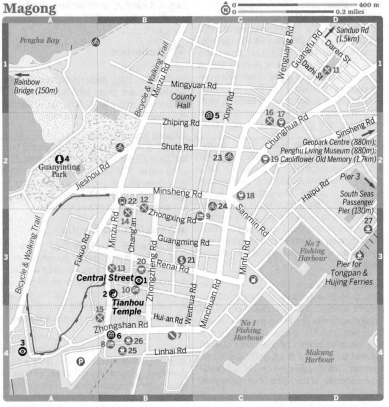

Magong

◎ Top Sights
1	Central Street	B3
2	Tianhou Temple	B3

◎ Sights
3	Duxing 10th Village	A4
4	Guanyinting Park	A2
5	Penghu Reclamation Hall	C2
6	Penghu Underwater Cultural Assets Exhibition	B4

✦ Activities, Courses & Tours
7	Magong Scuba Centre	B4

🛏 Sleeping
8	Calamari Hotel	B4
9	PH Hostel	C3
10	Yimei Guesthouse	B3

🍽 Eating
11	Beichen Market	D1
12	Chaichi	B2
13	Fish Market	B3
14	Guo's Blessed Oysters	B3
15	Jang Jin Restaurant	B4
16	La Table de Moz	C2

🍷 Drinking & Nightlife
17	Bang Bang Banana	C2
18	Freud Pub	C2
19	Grassroots & Fruit	C2
20	Kaffe Katate	B3

ℹ Information
21	Bank of Taiwan	B3

ℹ Transport
	All Star	(see 25)
22	Bus Terminal	B2
23	Giant	C2
24	KHS	C2
25	Magong Passenger Harbour Terminal	B4
26	Pescadores-Brave Line	B4
27	South Service Centre	D3
	Tai Hua Shipping	(see 25)

Penghu Underwater Cultural Assets Exhibition MUSEUM
(澎湖水下文化资产展, Pēnghú shuǐxià Wénhuà Zīchǎnzhǎn; 75 Zhonshan Rd; 中山路75號; ⌚9am-5pm Wed-Mon) FREE This immersive multimedia centre plunges visitors into a deep ocean trench as a way to introduce underwater exploration.

Although only parts are in English, visiting makes for a fun five minutes, if only for getting yourself photographed 'underwater'.

Penghu Reclamation Hall GALLERY
(澎湖開拓館, Pénghú Kāituò Guǎn; ☎06-927 8952; www.phhcc.gov.tw; 30 Zhiping Rd; 治平路30號; adult/child NT$30/free; ⌚10am-noon & 1-4.30pm Wed-Sun) This attractive building from 1933 is fundamentally a Japanese house but with European art deco elements.

Originally the residence of Penghu's county magistrate, it hosts changing exhibitions and has a charming cafe in the tree-shaded front yard.

Duxing 10th Village HISTORIC SITE
(篤行十村, Dǔxíng Shícūn; ☎06-926 9100; 5 Xinfu Rd; 新復路二巷5號) This self-contained 'village' was once the living quarters of military families. The partly derelict area is now being valiantly reworked into a small cultural zone whose main sights are an interesting information centre in a classic Japanese-style house, plus two museums, each celebrating 20th-century Taiwanese pop stars whose families happened to come from here.

STONE WEIRS

Penghu's soils aren't especially rich and the merciless winds make fishing by boat perilous in winter. A clever solution in ancient times was the construction of 'stone weirs'. These are long loops of wall designed so that fish (particularly grouper) find it easy to swim in, but once the tide falls, trap them in a shallow maze. The structures were built by village cooperatives, each family rewarded for its labour by receiving the rights to a certain number of days' claim to whatever they could catch in the 'weir'. By far the most famous is on Chimei (p337), celebrated mainly because its double heart shape makes for iconic photos and can be easily viewed from the cliffs above. However, there are many others, notably on the north coast of Jibei. One day Penghu hopes to have these listed by Unesco.

Activities

Ironman Taiwan SPORTS
(台湾鐵人三項賽, Táiwān Tiěrén Sānxiàng Sài; www.ironman.com; ⌚late Sep) A 3.8km swim, 180km bike ride and 42.2km run along the graciously hill-free Penghu coastline.

Magong Scuba Centre DIVING
(馬公潛水休閒推廣中心, Mǎgōng Qiánshuǐ Xiūxián Tuīguǎng Zhōngxīn; ☎06-926 0357; v9260357@yahoo.com.tw; 2-20 Zhongshan St; 中山路20之2號; ⌚8am-8pm) Diving promotion centre in central Magong. Handily central but no English spoken – at least when we visited.

Festivals & Events

Pengu Ocean Fireworks Festival FIREWORKS
(花火節, Huāhuǒ Jié; www.ezpenghu.com.tw/flower.htm; Kuanyin Pavilion Coastal Seashore Park) During more 20 evenings between mid-April and late June, an extravagant 15-minute display of fireworks bursts forth over the sea, usually launched from beside the Rainbow Bridge.

Lantern Festival LANTERN FESTIVAL
(元宵節, Yuánxiāojié; ⌚15 days after Chinese New Year) Penghu's lantern festival is truly a bacchanalian celebration, including a unique parade carrying gigantic golden turtle effigies through the streets of Magong accompanied by dancers and culminating with fireworks.

In the days before the festival, most bakeries in town devote around half of their oven space to the production of turtle cakes, which are given away and eaten during the course of the festivities.

Sleeping

During summer, rooms can be hard to come by on weekends and holidays. But with hundreds of B&Bs and hotels in all classes, there's likely to be something available at any time. Mid-October to March, prices for hotel rooms often drop by as much as 50%, especially midweek.

★ **PH Hostel** HOSTEL $
(平湖窩行旅, Pínghú Wōxínglǚ; ☎06-927 2151; 22 Zhongxing Rd, 中興路22號; dm NT$450-700; ⌚reception closes 9pm; ❄📶) PH has everything you'd want in a hostel: comfy curtained bunks with international power points, big lockers, a spacious common room and kitchenette with NT$40 beers. English-

speaking receptionist Jacob is endlessly helpful, there's a range of tour options, plus scooter rental is available (NT$70/350 per hour/day).

It's right in the heart of Magong's dining area. The hostel provides towel and slippers, free laundry and (in summer only) a decent breakfast.

Calamari Hotel   HOTEL $$

(凱樂瑪麗, Kǎilè Mǎlì; ☑06-927 1037; www. calamari.com.tw; 75 Zhongshan Rd; 中山路75號; d summer/winter NT$2400/1000; ❋🅟) Right at the harbour, Calamari has sparkling new rooms, the three best presenting triple aspect views of the ferry port area. The hip decor sometimes puts style above function, but you get oodles of extras from toothbrushes and cotton buds to a Mos Burger breakfast voucher.

Yimei Guesthouse   GUESTHOUSE $$

(益美民宿, Yìmeǐ Mínsù; ☑06-927 5223, 097-260 8870; http://ym9275223.myweb.hinet.net; 23 Zhongyang St; 中央街23號; d NT$2000-2800) In the centre of Magong's historic district, this guesthouse has two well-appointed doubles and one quad in an elegant, faux-vintage residence decorated with real antiques collected by the owner.

🍴 Eating

Guo's Blessed Oysters   SEAFOOD $

(福牡蠣屋, Fú Mǔlìwū; ☑06-926 2270; www.blessed oyster.com.tw/restaurant; 73 Zhongxing Rd; 中興路73號; mains NT$60-150; ⊙11am-2pm & 5-9pm) Simple but contemporary, this eat-at-the-counter outlet of a local seafood producer serves their juicy oysters in a range of formats: on the shell (NT$150 for 10, seasonal), in hand-rolls and in fresh-flavoured vermicelli soup. A picture menu makes ordering easy.

★ Beichen Market   MARKET $

(北辰市場, Běichén Shìchǎng; 20 Beichen St; 北辰街20號; ⊙6am-1pm) Penghu's main market bustles with stalls selling everything from fresh veggies and dried fish to shoes and woks. Flanking lanes have a selection of excellent no-fuss eateries.

Try superb meatball-in-mochi dumplings at 30 Daren St, imaginative savoury rice ball creations at 28 Dazhi St, reliable pork rib noodle soup (豬排麵, zhūpái miàn) at 4 Lane 18, Dazhi St and pumpkin noodles (金瓜麵猴, jīnguā miànhóu) at the stall outside 16 Dazhi St. Note that places close when stocks run out – often by 11am.

Fish Market   SEAFOOD $

(漁市場, Yú Shìchǎng; ☑06-926 6098; 26-1 Minzu Rd; meals NT$120-170; ⊙11.30am-2pm & 5-8.30pm, closed mid-Oct-Mar) This place is something of a magnet for western visitors thanks to the tacos, cheap draught beer (NT$80), fried seafood and most of all the owner, Liya, who speaks fluent English having lived in London.

Chaichi   BREAKFAST $

(才記, Cáijì; ☑06-926 7448; 42 Zhongxing Road, 中興路42號; pancakes NT$30-45; ⊙6am-2pm Thu-Tue) Delicious little crispy stuffed pancakes (土司, tǔsī) wash down well with NT$20 iced coffee in this inexpensive cafe decorated with 1940s Japanese-era posters.

★ Cauliflower
Old Memory   TAIWANESE INDIGENOUS $$

(花菜干人文懷舊餐館, Huācài Gānrénwén Huáijiù Cānguǎn; ☑06-921 3695; 4-2 Xindian Rd; 新店路4之2號; mains NT$280-480; ⊙11am-2pm & 5-8.30pm) Gather a group of four or more then make the 25-minute trek to the town's eastern edge for a full range of authentic Penghu specialities, including pumpkin vermicelli, pork-and-octopus soup, wind-dried cauliflower and excellent, lightly fried cabbage in peanuts. The quirky venue has separate little dining rooms each amusingly decorated with bric-a-brac kitsch and 20th-century antique elements. The restaurant is a low-rise brick, stone and red-tile house facing the eastern end of Xinsheng Rd, 1.2km southeast of the very conspicuous Sheraton Hotel.

★ La Table de Moz   FUSION $$$

(莫子嗜物所, Mòzi Shìwù Suǒ; ☑0918-970 270; Bang Bang Banana, 6 Zhiping Rd; 治平路6; 4-course dinner NT$650-800; ⊙6.30pm Wed-Mon, book ahead) Moz, the English-speaking owner of Bang Bang Banana (p336), is an astoundingly talented chef, and before the Bang Bang bar opens, she cooks superb, multi-course, candlelit dinners. Sophisticatedly woven flavours with an emphasis on local ingredients create breathtaking European-fusion cuisine that deserves at least one Michelin star. Book one day or more ahead.

Jang Jin Restaurant   SEAFOOD $$$

(長進餐廳, Zhǎngjìn Cāntīng; ☑06-927 1686; 9 Minzu Rd; 民族路9號; dishes NT$250-490; ⊙11am-2pm & 5-9pm) With over three decades of public acclaim for its top-quality fresh seafood, the owners don't need to worry much about the decor.

Drinking & Nightlife

Bang Bang Banana
BAR

(☑0918-970 270; 6 Zhiping Rd; 治平路6號; ☺8pm-midnight Wed-Mon) A Warhol welcome sets the stage for Magong's quirkiest secret drinking hole: the little yard is intriguing, but pull back the heavy wooden door to find the magical mural-walled main bar.

For fine dining, book ahead for their truly magnificent set dinner (p335).

Kaffe Katate
COFFEE

(肯塔咖啡, Kěntǎ Kāfēi; ☑06-927 6060; 7, Alley 5, Zhongyang St 中央街5巷7號; ☺10am-midnight) Magong has many great cafes, but for a superb barista espresso made in a mad-professor's-laboratory interior, there's no beating local roaster Katate.

Grassroots & Fruit
CRAFT BEER

(草根果子, Cǎogēn Guǒzi; ☑0982-662 194; 1 Shude Rd; 樹德路1號; ☺3pm-midnight) Teas, craft beers and a range of carefully chosen delicacies are served in an intimate one-room cafe with an arty vibe.

Freud Pub
BAR

(弗洛伊得, Fúluòyīdé; ☑06-926 166; 2-I Xinsheng Rd; 新生路2-1號; ☺6.30pm-2.30am) Magong's approximation to a western-style pub.

ℹ Information

The main **tourist information centre** (澎湖遊客服務中心; Pénghú Yóukè Fúwù Zhōngxīn; ☑06-921 6445; http://tour.penghu.gov.tw; 171 Guanghuali; 光華里171號; ☺8am-5.30pm) is not easy to access, but during work hours their telephone helpline can answer questions in fluent English. The **Bank of Taiwan** (台灣銀行; ☑06-927 9935; 24 Renai Rd; 仁愛路24號; ☺9am-3.30pm Mon-Fri) has foreign currency exchange and an international ATM.

ℹ Getting There & Away

AIR

There are over 50 daily flights between **Penghu airport** (澎湖機場, Pénghú Jīchǎng; ☑069-229 123; www.mkport.gov.tw; 126-5 Tuenmen Village; 隘門村126-5號) and Taipei (around NT$2200, 50 minutes), Kaohsiung (NT$1500, 40 minutes), and other west coast cities with Mandarin Airlines (www.mandarin-airlines.com) and Uni Air (www.uniair.com.tw). Uni Air also offers a few flights a week to Kinmen.

BOAT

There are two passenger port areas.

To go to Taiwan mainland embark at the **Passenger Harbour Terminal** (馬公港務大樓, Mǎgōng Gǎngwù Dàlóu; 36-1 Linhai Rd; 臨海路36-1號) beneath the Dreamer Hotel. Tickets are sold on the 2nd floor.

For travel within Penghu boats leave from a line of jetties at Number 3 Fishing Port. Facing these is the **South Service Centre** (南海遊客服務中心, Nánhǎi Yóukè Fúwù Zhōngxīn; ☑06-926 4738; No 3 Fishing Port, 25 Xinying Rd; 新營路25號; ☺6.30am-9.30pm, tourist information 8am-5pm) where you can book multi-island tour packages (mostly April to mid-October only). Year-round public boats for Tongpan (p338) and Hujing usually start from one of the southernmost jetties here (pay on board). The 9.30am ferry to Chimei via Wang'an starts from the South Seas Passenger Pier where tickets are sold before departure.

BUS

Magong's **bus terminal** (馬公公車總站; ☑06-927 2376; 58-1 Minzu Rd, 民族路58-1號) is also the starting point for the Tourist Shuttle.

CAR & MOTORCYCLE

Car rental is available at the airport. Central Magong has dozens of scooter rental places, but most won't accept foreign renters without Taiwanese licences. Fortunately, renting through your hotel or hostel is usually possible. There's a handily central **petrol station** (台灣中油加油站; 18 Minfu Rd; 民福路18號; ☺6am-10pm).

ℹ Getting Around

Both **Giant** (☑06-927 5769; 33-29 Guangfu Rd; 光復路33-29號; per day NT$200; ☺9am-9pm Mon-Sat) and **KHS** (☑06-927 3909; 49-1 Chongqing Lane; 重慶街49之1號; ☺9am-5pm Tue-Sun) rent out bicycles: NT$200/500 per day for standard/racing models.

TO/FROM THE AIRPORT

Buses link the city with Penghu airport once or twice an hour via five different possible routes, with fares and durations varying considerably. From Magong, those bound for Taiwu (太武; first 6.35am), Jianshan (尖山; first 7am) or Wukan (烏崁) are the fastest, taking 20 to 30 minutes (NT$23). Others, notably Longmen (龍門) loop buses, can take up to 50 minutes. From the airport, the buses whose routes originated at Longmen are contrastingly direct, while those from Jianshan are only just starting their outbound circuit so will be very slow. The last fast buses from the airport to Magong are at 6.10pm, 7pm and 8.45pm.

Flat-fare airport taxis called by Magong hotels charge NT$200, but by the meter you'll likely pay between NT$260 and NT$300.

Outer Penghu Islands

A major attraction of visiting Penghu is taking boat rides to the various outlying islands and islets. To the south, Tongpan, Wang'an and more visually dramatic Chimei are popular in part because they are directly accessible from Magong, with multi-island hopper tours available in summer. For beautiful beaches, Jibei is hard to beat with many domestic visitors getting there by bus-and-boat package tours. Several of the smaller islands are reserves for migratory waterfowl and marine life.

◉ Sights

★ Twin Hearts Stone Weir   LANDMARK
(雙心石滬, Shuāng Xīn Shí Hù) Penghu's most photographed icon is a double hoop of stone walls linked to breakwaters in an ocean bay. Built with narrow openings, they were designed to trap fish and leave them floundering as the tide went out. Now, however, the weir's heart shape has made it a symbol of romance, and for visiting couples, taking a selfie from the clifftop high above is often the whole point of a trip to Chimei.

A steep trail leads down the cliffside from near the selfie spot, but if you're doing a typical two-hour package, you might find that getting down and back leaves you rather stretched for time.

★ Huazhai Traditional Dwellings   VILLAGE
(花宅聚落, Huāzhái Jùluò; Zhongshe village, Wang'an island; 中社村) In the west coast fishing village of Zhongshe, over 130 small, traditional houses survive, most tightly packed in two photogenic huddles. Made of local basalt and coral stone, many are in ruins but ongoing restoration has revived a proportion of them and the dwellings are starting to attract small businesses and artists without yet being overly touristed. The village was previously known as Huazhai, a name that was first recorded in a book on Taiwan in 1680.

South Penghu Marine National Park   ISLAND
(澎湖南方四島國家公園, Pēnghú Nánfāng Sìdǎo Guójiā Gōngyuán; www.marine.gov.tw) Comprises a series of small but beautiful islets and sea stacks between Wang'an and Chimei, plus over 35,000 hectares of surrounding waters. The four biggest islands have remnant villages, though they're largely uninhabited these days other than fishermen's shacks and occasionally used temples.

Visits are only possible by tours, which usually stick to diving on the fine reefs and visiting the ocean basalt formations rather than landing on the islands.

Green Turtle Tourism & Conservation Centre   WILDLIFE RESERVE
(綠蠵龜觀光保育中心, Lùxīguī Guānguāng Bǎoyù Zhōngxīn; ☑ 06-999 1368; 1-4 Dong'an village, Wang'an; 望安鄉東安村1-4號; ⊘ 9am-5.30pm Mar-Oct, 10.30am-3.30pm Nov-Feb) **FREE** Exhibits on Wang'an's ecology, flora and fauna are showcased in a large, striking building with modernist, undulating curves. The main focus is sea turtles, which the centre helps to protect by monitoring protected beaches where they breed and releasing hatchlings into the wild.

It's 400m north of Wang'an ferry port, straight up the main road.

DON'T MISS

GORGEOUS JIBEI

The miraculously beautiful Jibei Sand Tail (吉貝沙尾; Jíbèi Shāwěi) is everything you'd hope for in a desert island paradise photo. And that's just the most famous strand on Jibei Island (Chipei, 吉貝; Jíbèi) which is almost totally ringed by sand-shell beaches. From November to March, you're likely to have the sand almost entirely to yourself. In summer, day trippers arrive en masse, mostly as part of coach-boat-activities packages that include playing sport on the beach just northwest of the Sand Tail.

That's around a 20-minute walk southwest of the port, and the only settlement where you'll find a few classic older homes tucked into the back lanes. The tiny family restaurants here operate in summer only, as does the cafe on the main beach. The small assortment of homestays mostly close in winter. Right beside the ferry dock, renting an ageing scooter (NT$150 for two hours) requires no paperwork and allows you to make a full circle of the island, giving you a glimpse of the wind- and rubbish-swept north coast and a series of stone weirs.

A SEAGULL'S VIEW OF THE OUTER ISLANDS

Chimei

The most topographically exhilarating place in Penghu, Chimei (七美; Qīměi) is especially memorable for the grand high cliffs on its east coast, which at times feel more like the Faroe Islands than Taiwan. At the northeastern corner, an ultra-popular selfie point allows love-birds to photograph themselves on the clifftop with Penghu's most 'romantic' icon in the sea far below. That's the Twin Hearts Stone Weir (p337), a double heart-shaped hoop of stone walls whose real purpose was to trap fish and leave them floundering as the tide goes out.

Nearer the port, signs lead to a colourful temple, a mock 'castle' that's actually a walled garden and to Yueli Bay (鮪鯉灣; Wěilǐ Wān), which has a superb basalt outcrop, the strata turned sideways and splaying into a starburst formation.

Nanhu Harbour has several seafood restaurants and homestays, though most are closed from November to October. The two most interesting B&Bs both look as though they've been transplanted from Greek islands.

Tongpan

Tongpan (桶盤; Tǒngpán) is a small U-shaped island that's best known for the 7m-tall cliff of eroded basalt columns on its southwest corner. That's only a 10-minute walk from the port, though beaware that the path is decaying and prone to falling rocks, potentially blocking access to the 'Lotus Seat', a low-tide geological formation.

Although the port area has a large new temple and range of public buildings, Tongpan's permanent population seems to have withered to almost nothing. On the plateau above the port, most of the houses – historic and otherwise – lie in forlorn ruins and cactus growth threatens to overwhelm the few remaining patches of vegetable garden. Most 'residents' commute in from Magong along with fishermen who use rod-and-line, as well as small boats.

Public boats (return NT$240) take 20 minutes each way from Magong, with departures at 8.30am and 3.30pm (plus 11am Wednesdays). Return boats leave Tongpan at 9.30am and 4.30pm (and noon Wednesdays). As 40 minutes is long enough to get a fair sense of the place, you can be back in Magong within just 1½ hours, making the island ideal as a nice little DIY excursion.

Wang'an

Of the many beaches on Wang'an (望安; Wàng'ān), the prettiest are in the southwest corner of the island. From May to October, these are breeding and hatching grounds for rare sea turtles. To protect them, the beaches are off limits after dark, but you can normally swim at

🏃 Activities

Island 77
DIVING

(澎湖島澳七七, Pēnghú Dǎo ào Qīqī; ☑06-990 2303; www.island77.tw; 111-1 Jiangjun village; 將軍村111-1號; ☉mid-Apr–late Sep) Reputable local operator for scuba and snorkelling trips around South Penghu.

They're based in Jiangjun, a small island barely 1km east across the strait from Wang'an. You'll need a Chinese speaker to help make sense of their diary of available activities.

🛌 Sleeping

Chimei, Wang'an and Qibei have homestays, but call ahead especially if you're visiting between October and March when the vast majority will be closed.

Thera Inn
B&B $

(希拉小宿, Xīlā Xiǎosù; ☑06-997 1222; www.thera.com.tw; 11 Nanhuqitou, Nangang village; 南港村南滬崎頭11-1號; d NT$1000-1900) With its blue-domed top-knot and raised, semi-rural location above Nanhu town, Thera Inn is a very distinctive eight-room B&B with owners who can organise snorkelling trips but don't speak English.

⭐Flowerhouse51
B&B $$

(花羨花宅51; ☑098-921 8859; 51 Zhongshe village, 中社村51號; d/q NT$3800/4800; ☉closed Nov–mid-Mar; ❄🛜🍽) In a dazzlingly modern contrast to the surrounding old-world houses of Huazhou, Flowerhouse51 has two super stylish, sea-facing double rooms – one with a vast terrace above the hip kitchen plus quality coffee machine. Jamie speaks decent English and can organise excursions.

them during the day. Double-check the latest details at the Green Turtle Tourism & Conservation Centre (p337), an architecturally striking museum of ecology just 400m north of the ferry jetty.

If you have wheels, it's well worth buzzing around to look at the island's old Fujian-style houses. Most are derelict, but in Zhongshe village the most complete group, known as Huazhai Traditional Dwellings (p337), have been partially restored. The feel here is more authentic and less tourist-centric than at Erkan (p327) with just a couple of trinket shops and one artist-in-residence. A little further, grassy Tientaishan (天台山; Tiāntáishān) is Wang'an's highest clifftop, sitting on Penghu's oldest bit of basalt. It's a fine viewpoint with footpaths leading down towards the waterfront and to a rock imprinted with what's claimed to be the footprint of Lu Tungbin, one of China's 'Eight Immortals'.

Electric scooters await rental at the boat dock where tickets for the return ferry are sold from the Family Mart convenience store. The island has a scattering of B&Bs, but most close between November and mid-March. In summer, guesthouses can organise snorkelling or arrange the short skip across the bay to Jiangjun, where Island 77 is a highly professional snorkelling and scuba outfit.

Hujing

Meaning 'Tiger Well', Hujing Island (虎井島; Hǔjǐng Dǎo) has some imposing basalt walls like neighbouring Tongpan, but the main settlement sits in a lowland saddle so lacks the same sense of desolation, and alleys full of cats add further life. Small restaurants tout a 'unique' version of seafood soup. There's a modern hilltop square with a white Guanyin statue and the 18 arhats lined up in front of her. You can also visit a former Japanese military structure for ocean views and watch mountain goats gambol on the cliff ledge.

South Penghu National Park

Only accessible as part of a tour, Taiwan's South Penghu Marine National Park (p337) comprises a large area of sea and islets between Wang'an and Chimei. Its four biggest islands have remnant villages, but are mostly uninhabited apart from fishermen's shacks and occasionally visited shrines. Tour operators refer to these islands as the New Four Southern Islands (新南方四島). The place most commonly included on a boat tour is Blue Cave (藍洞; Lán dòng), a 'cathedral of rock' where a land bridge of basalt has a hole at the top creating magical lighting effects. It's at the northwest corner of Xiji (西吉) and often combined with summer tours to Chimei.

Jibei Miracle Inn　　　　　　　B&B $$
(吉貝奇蹟旅店, Jíbèi Qíjī Lǚdiàn; ☑0905-008 869; http://ph-miracle.com.tw; 26-7 Jibei village; 吉貝村26-7號; d from NT$3000; ◷closed Nov-Apr; ❉❖) Almost the last house in the village as you circle Jibei Island anticlockwise, Miracle Inn has plenty of low-key style, big terraces and a pleasant location.

It's across the essentially traffic-free main road from a small sand-and-rock bay. A prettier triangle of beach lies 300m further east though it's a place to watch crashing waves, not to swim.

海Go藍　　　　　　　　　　GUESTHOUSE $$
(☑0932-989-990, 06-997 1837; higoland@gmail. com; 35 Nanhu, Chimei Island; 南滬35號; d NT$2100-2700; ❉❖❈) One of two pseudo-Greek houses on Chimei, the unmissable main building looks like a comic book caricature of a Santorini church complete with murals and bell tower. Charming owner Jefferson speaks basic English, rates include breakfast and scooter hire, and there's a little swimming pool.

❶ Getting There & Away

AIR

Using small prop-planes holding around 20 people, Daily Air (www.dailyair.com.tw) flies from Kaohsiung to both Chimei and Wang'an (NT$1754, 35 minutes) and also offers a Chimei–Magong hop (NT$$979, 15 minutes). However, flights are cancelled in medium to strong winds so it's unwise to rely on these routes if you have a tight travel schedule. Book by phone on ☑07-801 4711 then pay on the day if the flight operates. Note that local residents are prioritised.

BOAT

Jibei

In Chihkan, boats for Jibei start from the North Sea Tourist Service Centre (p331), a building with a tower that looks like a brick minaret. Mid-October to March, there are sailings at 11.15am and 5pm, returning from Jibei at 6am and 2pm (NT$150 each way, 20 minutes). April to mid-October, there are many more options, with four companies offering return deals between NT$300 and $400 and departures roughly every 40 minutes between 8am and 5pm. Package deals including water sports are on offer.

Southern Islands

From Magong's South Seas Passenger Pier (p336), a public ferry departs to Chimei at 9.30am, returning at 1.30pm. It takes two hours each way including a stop en route at Wang'an, staying half an hour on the outbound trip and less on the return leg. Twice a month there's also a fast boat direct to Chimei (one hour) at 7am, returning the next day.

For day trippers, a convenient summer option is one of several day-return tour packages sold from the South Service Centre (p336). A popular option sails past the basalt cliffs of Tongan (slowing for photos but not stopping), then gives you two hours in both Chimei and Wang'an. Typically this costs NT$1130 with scooter vouchers for use on both islands. You can otherwise pay a similar price to include bus tours on arrival, or NT$800 for the boat only.

❶ Getting Around

Rental scooters are available on Chimei, Wang'an and Qibei for NT$150 to NT$180 for two or three hours; NT$400 or NT$500 for 24 hours. If you're stopping as part of a one-day island tour, scooter hire is often included in the deal (check). Some homestays provide scooters. Tongpan is small enough to walk around in less than the hour that most tours give you.

Understand
Taiwan

History

Taiwanese believe they have a society distinct from mainland China, and that is largely because of their history. Primarily populated by indigenous peoples until the 17th century, Taiwan later saw centuries of immigration (coupled with colonisation by multiple empires), which resulted in localised arts, cuisine, religious worship patterns and social structures. The country's long road from authoritarianism (which sought to destroy that localisation) to democracy is another key part of the distinction people feel, and understanding this is essential for grasping the issues of the day.

The Dutch Colonial Era

In the 16th century Taiwan was a haven for pirates, who were driven to its isolated ports by Ming dynasty anti-smuggling campaigns. Ironically, these campaigns saw Taiwan become a base for secret trade between Japan and Chinese merchants.

Though Chinese fisherfolk began to settle in Penghu around 1000 years ago, until the 16th century Taiwan was isolated and almost exclusively populated by indigenous peoples. Official Chinese records were even unclear if it was one island or many until the late Ming dynasty. What happened to change the status quo? Trade. This was the era of increasing maritime commercial activity throughout East Asia, and Taiwan quickly became a critical link in the routes between China (mostly Fujian), Japan, Manila and Macau.

Of particular importance were the routes established by the Dutch East India Company (abbreviated VOC). In 1602 the VOC was given a trade monopoly in the east. Unfortunately for the VOC, the company was very late in the game and to become a serious player it had to first break the Spanish and Portuguese monopolies.

In the style of the age, the VOC fleets launched indiscriminate attacks on Portuguese and Spanish ships. By 1622, realising they needed a secure base in the region, the VOC sailed to Penghu (aka the Pescadores), an island group they had explored earlier, and built a small fortress.

From Penghu, the Dutch launched raids off the Fujian coast and disrupted Chinese trade with Manila (under Spanish control). The exasperated Chinese offered the Dutch permission to trade from Taiwan proper. The VOC caught the veiled threat and left Penghu for Tayouan (what is now the Anping area of Tainan), where they established Fort Zeelandia.

TIMELINE	50,000– 10,000 BC	c 10,000 BC	AD 1544
	Human skeletons found in eastern Taiwan and in the Taipei Basin point to prehistoric human habitation of the island during the late Palaeolithic era.	Ancestors of Taiwan's present-day indigenous peoples first come to the island by sea and begin settling around the island.	Passing Portuguese sailors become the first Europeans to lay eyes on Taiwan; they are so enchanted they name the island Ilha Formosa (Beautiful Island).

The Dutch initially considered using Taiwan as an entrepôt but quickly realised they would not be safe from indigenous Taiwanese and Chinese attacks, nor from trade rivals Spain and Japan, unless they could control the island. With this in mind they set out to pacify Plains peoples, import Chinese labour and destroy rival Spain. They also began the first modernisation program of Taiwan, establishing schools, missions (to convert locals) and kilns, as well as issuing licences to Chinese fishers and taxes on the deer-meat trade. Their work was noted, and not always favourably.

The Tao of Lanyu Island are widely believed to be descendants of Austronesians who fled the Spanish occupation of the Philippines two centuries ago.

In the early 17th century, Spain controlled the trade route between Fujian and Manila. The new Dutch presence on Taiwan, an island separated from Fujian by a narrow strait, was perceived as a major threat. In 1626 the Spanish landed and occupied the northern area of Taiwan around what is now Keelung and Tamsui. Over a 10-year period they established four forts, including Fort San Domingo in Tamsui, which remains intact to this day.

Though the Spanish engaged in military actions as far down the coast as Yilan and Hualien, their presence was always small. When the Manila governor, unimpressed with trade, further reduced troops, indigenous groups attacked outposts. The Spanish withdrew to Keelung, where they were then hit by the Dutch. By 1642 they had withdrawn from Taiwan entirely, giving the Dutch control from north to south.

In the 1640s instability in China (the Ming dynasty lost its capital to the Qing in 1644) was causing a wave of immigration from Fujian province into Taiwan. The new settlers chafed at European colonial rule and staged a revolt in 1652. Though the Dutch were successful in quelling that uprising, 10 years later they would be defeated and driven off Taiwan by a Chinese admiral and Ming loyalist called Cheng Cheng-kung.

Cheng Cheng-kung, known in the west as Koxinga, was a colourful character, the son of a pirate turned admiral and his Japanese concubine. When Qing forces began to conquer China in the 1640s, the father capitulated but Koxinga fought on for the Ming's Yongli Emperor.

After a massive defeat in 1659, Koxinga sought refuge with his troops on Kinmen. There, a deputy suggested he invade Taiwan and overthrow the Dutch. Koxinga declined at first, but when both Dutch and Qing policies began to cut into his ability to trade and reprovision his troops, the stage was set.

Koxinga built a new fleet on Kinmen and in April 1661 sailed first to the Penghu Islands, before moving on to Taiwan proper. The outnumbered and outmanoeuvred Dutch surrendered Fort Provenitia, now rebuilt as Chihkan Towers, to him in five days. By February 1662 they had surrendered Fort Zeelandia. The 38-year colonisation of Taiwan by the Dutch was over.

1622–62	1662	1662–83	1683
The Dutch establish colonies on both Taiwan Island and Penghu to facilitate trade with China and Japan. They also encourage the first large migration of Han Chinese to Taiwan.	After a two-year campaign, Dutch forces are driven off Taiwan by Ming loyalist Admiral Koxinga; they surrender to him in Tainan.	Following Koxinga's death in 1662, son Zheng Jing sets up the first Han Chinese government on Taiwan, as a base to try to regain China from the Qing dynasty.	Following Zheng Jing's death in 1681, son Zheng Keshuang rules briefly before being defeated at the Battle of Penghu, resulting in a surrender to Qing forces.

Jonathan Manthorpe's *Forbidden Nation* is a very readable overview of Taiwan's history, with plenty of informed opinions and balanced analyses of the political status of Taiwan.

Around 25,000 to 30,000 Chinese came to Taiwan with Koxinga (adding to a population that was around 100,000 indigenous people and a smaller number of Chinese). With them the admiral set out to create a military base for the retaking of the mainland. As with the Dutch he continued to expand the agricultural system (soldiers had a dual role as farmers), but also introduced Ming-style administration and cultural elements: he built Taiwan's first Confucius Temple and introduced civil service exams. However, his dreams of overthrowing the Manchu were never realised. Koxinga died a year after landing on Taiwan at the age of 37.

After the admiral's death, his son Zheng Jing ruled Taiwan as sovereign of the Tungning kingdom (1661–83). The young ruler encouraged trade, industry and immigration, not just of farmers and soldiers but of also scholars and administrators who did not want to serve the Qing. His death in 1681 led to bloody fights over succession, and in 1683, the Qing, under Admiral Shi Lang, moved in and captured Taiwan.

Afterwards, in one of the pivotal moments of Taiwan's history, Shi Lang convinced the sceptical Kangxi Emperor of the island's strategic importance. The emperor agreed to annexation, and Taiwan became Taiwanfu, a prefecture of Fujian province with a capital in present-day Tainan.

Taiwan in the Qing Dynasty

Taiwan developed rapidly under the Qing. The population grew and Han Chinese became the dominant ethnic group as they spread over the western plains and across the Taipei Basin. Sugar-cane production had dominated the economy under the Dutch, but now rice growing was added. With increased migration to the centre and north of the island, as well as the development of irrigation systems, almost all the arable land became utilised over time.

Immigration from China also increased and the imbalance of men to women led to increasing social problems, including the formation of secret societies. Grievances often led to violence.

During this period almost all immigrants came from the same three areas in China: Zhangzhou and Quanzhou in Fujian, and various locations in Guangdong province. The first two regions are the source of almost all ethnic Taiwanese (Hoklo); the latter the Hakka.

Though Taiwan was becoming Chinese during this era, it was also evolving unique associations and traditions to deal with the unusual immigrant circumstance. For example, lacking family ties, immigrants created social structures based on shared names, village origins and worship of similar folk gods. Even small differences could be a source of

1683–1885	1729	1787	1861–64
Taiwan is governed by the Qing dynasty as a prefecture of Fujian province. Early years are marked by frequent rebellion, riots and civil strife.	The Qing emperor forbids immigration to Taiwan on pain of death. The order is later rescinded, but immigration is officially limited for decades.	The Lin Shuang-wen Rebellion, the largest popular revolt against Qing rule, takes over a year to suppress. The revolt shows the general dissatisfaction in Taiwan with Qing rule.	The Treaty of Tianjin forces open Taiwan ports Anping, Tamsui, Keelung and Kaohsiung to Western trade. Taiwan's camphor and tea exports enter world markets.

conflict: the Zhangzhou–Quanzhou distinction, for example, would be the cause of many small but deadly battles in Taiwan's history.

The latter half of the 19th century was a period of great turmoil for the Qing. Among other crises, they had to contend with the Taiping Rebellion and forced trade with Western powers. Much of this directly and indirectly influenced Taiwan in profound ways.

After the second Opium War ended (1860), for example, Taiwan was opened to trade with the West. Into the now free ports of Tamsui, Keelung, Anping and Kaohsiung flowed Western merchants, missionaries, soldiers, diplomats and scholars. Foreign trade increased rapidly, merchant houses such Jardine, Matheson & Co flourished, and Taiwan's economy became linked to global trade. The island became the largest camphor-supplying region in the world, and its excellent teas were traded widely.

Nearly all the major Western and regional powers also had some kind of skirmish or 'incident' on Taiwan soil in the 19th century. The most

DUTCH & QING COLONISATION AND THE INDIGENOUS TAIWANESE

Controlling a large frontier such as Taiwan was no easy task. As with most colonial governments throughout history, both the Dutch and later Qing administrations had to find a way to maintain law and order without draining the coffers. Both also had to contend with indigenous inhabitants who wouldn't conveniently accept their dominion.

When the Dutch arrived in southern Taiwan in 1622 they found it relatively easy to purchase land for their forts, and also form alliances with the neighbouring tribes. Military force was used when necessary, and Christian missions were vital for keeping the peace once areas had been pacified (by 1643 over 5000 of the locals had been baptised). Elsewhere, the Dutch employed a divide and conquer strategy that resulted in an unstable political landscape of constantly shifting alliances.

Under the Qing *lifan* (indigenous management policy) indigenous people were classified as raw *(shengfan)* or cooked *(shufan)*. The cooked were those already pacified by the Dutch and so subject to taxation, education and military service. The raw were those living free of imperial obligations. To separate the two, the Qing literally drew a line down Taiwan: on one side was the civilised world, on the other the savage. This policy lasted until 1875, at which point the Qing, anxious to show the world they controlled all of Taiwan, reversed direction and attempted to open the interior and east coast by force.

Throughout the Qing era, the cooked were required to participate in the defence of Taiwan. Under a military habitation system *(tuntian)* young healthy indigenous Taiwanese were conscripted to serve in self-supporting garrisons. In their dual role as farmer and soldier they provided an invaluable service shielding Taiwan from both internal and external conflict.

1871	1874	1885	1885–91
Japanese sailors stranded on the southern tip of Taiwan are killed in a conflict with local Paiwan tribespeople. The Japanese government demands compensation from the Qing court.	A Japanese assault on Taiwan is repelled by a combination of locals and Qing troops. Japan withdraws its troops after suffering casualties caused by both battle and disease.	Taiwan is made a separate province of the Qing Empire in response to growing interest in the island's strategic importance and resources by Japan and Western powers.	Under the first provincial governor, Liu Ming-chuan, a railway is built from Keelung to Taipei, the first in all of China. Liu also establishes a telegraph and postal system.

significant was the Mudan Incident (1874) in which Japan sent 3600 troops on a punitive mission to the south over the butchery of 54 Japanese sailors by Paiwan locals in Mudan, Pingtung County, three years earlier.

The incident revealed to the world both the weakness of the Qing government and their limited control over Taiwan (the Japanese had tried to bring their grievances to the Qing court, only to be told that the Paiwan were outside Chinese control). A decade later, French troops invaded and occupied Keelung during the Sino-French War. At last recognising the strategic importance of Taiwan, the Qing began to shore up its defences and spur development. Taiwan was made a province in 1885, with Liu Ming-chuan the first governor.

Liu, a former general who had fought the French in Vietnam, believed in Taiwanese self-reliance. Among his many initiatives were building cross-island roads (the present Hwy 9 from Taipei to Ilan mostly follows his route), pacifying mountain peoples and improving the economy. He implemented land reform, built the first railway from Taipei to Keelung, established a postal system, laid a submarine cable to Fujian, and created bureaux to handle railways, mining, telegraphs and other modern specialities.

Not all of Liu's reforms were successful, but it didn't much matter. Taiwan would not be Chinese territory for very much longer.

The Japanese Colonial Era: 1895–1945

In 1894 war broke out between Japan and China over the Japanese invasion of Korea. China's poorly equipped navy was no match for Japan's modern fleet, and in April of 1895 China signed the Treaty of Shimonoseki that ceded the Ryukyu Islands (Okinawa), Taiwan and the Penghu Archipelago to Japan.

On Taiwan, locals responded to the treaty with alarm. Social and political leaders encouraged Governor Tang Jing-song to issue a statement of self-rule, which led to the declaration of the Taiwan Democratic Republic (also known as the Republic of Formosa) on 23 May. Any hopes that foreign powers would intervene were quickly lost, however, and by 3 June, Japanese forces had taken Keelung. Tang fled and as chaos engulfing the city, elites in Taipei asked Koo Hsien-jung (a businessman whose family is still influential in Taiwanese politics and business) to open the gates to the Japanese.

Resistance continued in the south in the name of the Republic, but when the Japanese army entered Tainan on 21 October, the Republic fell for good. On 18 November the Japanese declared Taiwan 'pacified', though violent, localised resistance would continue for years, especially

In early 18th-century Europe, much of what was known of Taiwan was picked from *An Historical and Geographical Description of Formosa* by George Psalmanazar. The Frenchmen, who claimed to be a native of the island, was later revealed to be a complete fraud.

1895 (April)	1895 (May)	1895 (October)	1921
After being defeated by Japan in the first Sino-Japanese War, China sends a Qing delegation to sign the Treaty of Shimonoseki, ceding Taiwan and the Penghu Islands to Japan in perpetuity.	Unhappy with being incorporated into Japan, local Taiwanese (assisted by disenchanted Manchu officials) establish the Taiwan Republic, the first independent republic in Asia.	After a five-month campaign during which Japanese forces capture towns in a southward march, Republican forces surrender the capital of Tainan, ending the short-lived Taiwan Republic.	Taiwanese elites form the Taiwan Cultural Society to press the Japanese Diet for local representation. Historians consider this the beginning of Taiwan-centred identity.

among indigenous groups, who were treated as savages to be conquered and pacified during the entire colonial era.

In general, though, Japan set out early to turn Taiwan into a model colony, attempting in part to show Western powers that they could match, or outdo, them in every way. They began with thorough studies of Taiwan's land, climate, people, history and natural resources. In 1899 they formed the Bank of Taiwan to facilitate investment; by 1914, Taiwan was not just financially self-sufficient, but contributing taxes.

Over the coming decades, hundreds of kilometres of roads were constructed, and rail lines linked Keelung to Kaohsiung, and Hualien to Taitung. Schools and teaching colleges were established, a relatively fair legal system was implemented based on Western concepts of the rule of law, and cities and towns were redesigned on modern principles of urban planning (which included provisions for sanitation). Advanced agricultural practices saw food production increase over tenfold, and living standards and life expectancy rose rapidly. Taiwan's population surged from 2.6 million in 1896 to 6.6 million by 1943. And this was just the start.

Within Taiwanese society and culture, huge changes were also taking place. Formerly a rural, superstitious and clan-based people, the Taiwanese became increasingly urban and modern. A professional class developed, and while there was still great inequality, it was less entrenched than before. By the 1940s over 200,000 students had studied higher education in Japan and 60,000 had received college degrees.

As early as the 1920s the economy began changing from primarily agricultural to a mix that included light manufacturing and industries such as petrochemicals and machinery. With rising wages and living standards came Western-style leisure activities. People indulged in movies, concerts, sporting events and tourism. Civic associations also began to form among housewives, teachers and youth groups.

The early colonial experience also nurtured a growing sense of a unique Taiwanese (as opposed to Chinese) identity. This identity is sometimes said to have been sparked by the formation of the Formosan Republic in 1895, but it certainly began to take shape during the 1920s as Taiwanese chafed under colonial rule (which still treated them as second-class citizens in their own land), and local leaders pushed for civil rights and self-representation.

One of the most important figures in colonial rule, Gotō Shin-pei, Chief of Civil Affairs from 1898 to 1906, has been called the father of Taiwan's modernisation. Gotō was quick to suppress dissent, but he also believed that Taiwan should not be exploited for the benefit of Japan. As such, he helped lay the foundation for transportation systems, public buildings and urban planning, healthcare and a modern economy.

The five-month Republic of Formosa (1895) adopted a national flag with a yellow tiger on a blue background. Bags with the same design are sold at certain museum shops, including at the National Taiwan Museum (p65) in Taipei.

1927	1930–31	1945	1947
The Taiwan People's Party, the first political party in Taiwan, is formed with the goal of pushing for local rights and representation. The party is suppressed three years later.	In the 'Wushe Rebellion', Japanese authorities and members of the Seediq tribe in Nantou County clash in a series of battles. This is the last large-scale revolt against colonial rule.	After Japan's defeat in WWII, Taiwan is placed under the administrative control of Chiang Kai-shek's Republic of China. Taiwan's social order is thrown into chaos.	A clash between a black-market cigarette vendor and Monopoly Bureau agents leads to an island-wide revolt against KMT rule. This becomes known as the 2-28 Incident.

MARTIAL MADNESS

In 1948, in the closing years of the civil war with the Chinese Communist Party (CCP), Chiang Kai-shek declared martial law on most of China. A year later, Taiwan was also subjected to 'temporary provisions effective during the period of communist rebellion', which would prove anything but temporary. In fact, Taiwan's martial law period was one of the longest in world history, and was a time when there was no right to assembly, protest or free speech, and the Garrison Command had sweeping powers to arrest and detain anyone.

According to government studies, over 140,000 people were arrested during this period (many tortured and shipped off to detention on Green Island), with some 3000 to 4000 executed. This period is known locally as the White Terror (p349).

As a locus of Taiwanese identity, folk culture was also held suspect, and elaborate festivals were banned. (At the same time, statues of Chiang Kai-shek were placed in popular shrines so that people would be forced to worship his image.) The Hoklo, or Taiwanese, language was likewise proscribed in schools and media broadcasts, and many older Taiwanese can still remember being beaten for speaking their native language in the classroom.

After Chiang's death in 1975, enforcements were relaxed, but martial law would stay in effect until 1987.

The Japanese colonial era is usually divided into three periods, which reflect the government's distinct developmental policies. After the first several decades of laying the groundwork for economic development, the colonial government began to assimilate the Taiwanese socially. Education policies began to mimic those in Japan, as did local governance and laws.

In 1937, after the outbreak of the second Sino-Japanese War, the Japanese government initiated the Kominka movement, in which Taiwanese were encouraged to become truly Japanese by changing their names, abandoning Chinese folk worship for Shintoism, speaking Japanese, and pledging allegiance to the emperor. The policy was successful to a degree and many older Taiwanese still living, such as former President Lee Teng-hui (born 1923), have said they believed at the time that they were Japanese. Lee himself went by the name Iwasato Masao.

During the war, Taiwan's economy saw industrial production surpass agriculture. The southern and eastern ports became bases for the imperial navy, as well as training grounds for kamikaze pilots. Around 140,000 Taiwanese would serve in the war, with some 30,000 dying. This, along with the population's widespread adoption of Japanese cultural traits, did not sit well with the Chinese when they gained control of Taiwan following WWII.

1949	1951	1954	1958
The Nationalist army is driven from mainland China by the communists. Chiang Kai-shek moves the ROC government to Taiwan with the intention of using the island as a base to retake the mainland.	Japan signs the Treaty of San Francisco, formally relinquishing all claims to Taiwan and its surrounding islands. However, the treaty does not cede Taiwan to another country.	The First Taiwan Strait Crisis begins when the People's Liberation Army (PLA) shells ROC-occupied Kinmen and Matsu. The conflict leads to the Sino-American Mutual Defense Treaty.	The Second Taiwan Strait Crisis erupts when the PLA again attempts to seize Kinmen and Matsu from the ROC. Despite intense shelling the ROC maintains control of the islands.

Taiwan Under KMT Rule

Taiwan's history after WWII is intimately tied to the Republic of China (ROC), founded in 1911 (in China) after the Qing dynasty was ended by the revolution of Sun Yat-sen (a doctor and Chinese revolutionary considered the father of the modern Chinese nation). Though Taiwan was little discussed in the early decades of the Republic, after the start of the Sino-Japanese War it became part of a rallying call demanding the restoration of territory the Chinese considered stolen by Japan.

That demand was met on 25 October 1945, in a ceremony at Taipei's Zhongshan Hall. There, Chinese General Chen Yi, on behalf of Generalissimo Chiang Kai-shek, leader of the Chinese Nationalist Party (Kuomintang; KMT), accepted the Japanese instrument of surrender on behalf of the Allied Powers. Though mandated only to administer Taiwan, Chen Yi quickly declared the island was once again Chinese territory. Pro-independence Taiwanese sometimes point to this moment as the beginning of what they consider the KMT's illegal occupation of Taiwan.

However, at first, Taiwanese were mostly pleased with being returned to Chinese rule, and local elites hoped that they would finally have a chance at the autonomy they had struggled for under the Japanese. Unfortunately, under Governor Chen Yi, goodwill would be short-lived. Chen Yi refused to share power (he, and many KMT leaders, considered the 'Japanised Taiwanese' as deracinated and degraded beings), and began allowing his ragtag army and civil service to loot, confiscate property and businesses, and monopolise trade. Basic public services, such as rubbish collection, that people had grown used to under the Japanese were also abandoned. The economy went into a tailspin, hyperinflation hit, and in 1947 riots against the government broke out, leading to the deaths of tens of thousands of civilians.

For a descriptive history of Taiwan's transition from colonial holding to vibrant Asian democracy, check out J Bruce Jacob's *Democratizing Taiwan*.

HISTORY TAIWAN UNDER KMT RULE

TAIWAN'S WHITE TERROR

One of the bleakest times in Taiwan's history was the White Terror, when the government started a large-scale campaign to purge the island of political activists during the 1950s. Many who had spoken out against government policies were arrested, charged with attempting to overthrow the government and sentenced to death or life imprisonment. Some who were arrested were indeed political spies but most, it's believed, were unjustly accused. Over 90,000 people were arrested and at least half that number were executed. Taiwanese were not the only targets; a large number of mainland Chinese were arrested or killed. Today Taiwan's White Terror period, though an unpleasant memory, is not forgotten.

1971	1975	1976	1978
UN General Assembly Resolution 2758 transfers the UN seat from the Republic of China to the People's Republic of China. The UN no longer recognises the ROC as a sovereign nation.	Chiang Kai-shek dies aged 87; the government declares a month of mourning and Chiang's body is entombed in his former residence in Taoyuan County.	Taiwanese couple Stan Shih and Carolyn Yeh start a small company called Multitech in Hsinchu with an investment of US$25,000. Later renamed Acer, the company goes on to become a global computer producer.	Chiang Ching-kuo becomes ROC president. While continuing many of his father's autocratic policies, the younger Chiang brings more Taiwanese into government.

THE AUGUST 23RD ARTILLERY WAR

On the morning of 23 August 1958, Beijing, determined to take Kinmen from Chiang Kai-shek's Nationalist army, launched a ferocious bombardment against the island. In just two hours the island was hit with over 42,000 shells. Alarmed, the USA acted to defend Kinmen, realising that if it fell, the security of America's 'unsinkable battleship' (as Harry Truman called Taiwan) would be in severe jeopardy. The USA sent a shipment of jet fighters and anti-aircraft missiles to Taiwan, along with six aircraft carriers.

Communist forces created a tight blockade around Kinmen's beaches and airstrip, preventing any military supplies from getting in. On 7 September the USA sent several warships into the Taiwan Strait to escort a convoy of Republic of China (ROC) military-supply ships; the convoy got within 5km of the blockade and was surprised that the communists refused to fire.

Realising that its navy was outclassed (and no doubt wary of factions in America threatening China with nuclear bombs), Beijing offered the nationalists a very odd cease-fire – it would only fire on Kinmen on odd-numbered days. The deal was agreed to, and the Chinese side continued to shell Kinmen throughout September and October only on odd-numbered days. By November tensions had decreased and the bombing stopped, but not before nearly half a million shells had struck Kinmen, killing and wounding thousands of civilians and soldiers.

Meanwhile, in China, Chiang Kai-shek's Nationalist regime was engaged in a civil war with the Communist Party for control of China, and they were losing badly. On 1 October 1949, Mao Zedong proclaimed the creation of the People's Republic of China (PRC). Two months later on 10 December, Chiang fled to Taiwan, followed by two million refugees comprising soldiers, businesspeople, landowners, monks, artists, gangsters, peasants and intellectuals.

Despite bringing all of China's gold reserve with them, Chiang's regime was broken. Many predicted it would fall soon to the communists, but the Korean War convinced the USA that Taiwan was too strategically valuable to hand over to the Chinese Communist Party (CCP). In 1950 US President Truman ordered the US Navy to protect the Taiwan Strait. US monetary aid followed, and for the next two decades it was vital to keeping the Chiang government afloat and funding in part or in whole nearly every public works project.

Chiang kept alive the hope of retaking the mainland until his death and his rule was quick to crush any political dissent, real or imagined; a period known as the 'White Terror' (p349). However, concurrent with the brutality and paranoia, there were also sound economic reforms that would soon make Taiwan one of the wealthiest countries in Asia. Among the most famous of these were US-guided land reforms, which saw rents

1979	1979	1984	1986
The Taiwan Relations Act is passed by US Congress following the breaking of official relations between the USA and Taiwan. The Act establishes quasi-diplomatic relations between the two countries.	Known as the Kaohsiung Incident, a major gathering for International Human Rights Day in Kaohsiung sees demonstrators clash with military police, and well-known opposition leaders arrested.	Henry Liu, a popular writer and frequent critic of the KMT, is assassinated in his home in California. The assassins, organised-crime members, claim in trial that the ROC government ordered the hit.	The opposition Democratic Progressive Party (DPP) is formed in September; in December, Taiwan holds its first two-party elections.

reduced, leases extended and government land sold off cheaply. Tenant farmers went from 49% of the total in 1949 to 10% in 1960. Agricultural productivity rose, which helped fuel more demand for industrial goods. At the same time, the reforms shifted the huge land capital of Taiwan's gentry class into investment in small- and medium-sized industrial enterprises. By 1960 industry had once again replaced agriculture as the largest share of GDP.

The political changes in this era were no less startling. In 1971 the UN Security Council admitted the PRC. Chiang Kai-shek responded by withdrawing the ROC. The following year US President Nixon travelled to China to normalise relations. In 1979, under President Carter, the USA switched official recognition from the ROC to the PRC. US policy towards Taiwan would now be dictated by the Taiwan Relations Act, which allows the USA to provide defensive arms to Taiwan, and considers any move to settle the status of Taiwan with military force to be a threat to US security. The act also officially ended US recognition of the ROC government.

When Chiang Kai-shek died in 1975, Yen Chia-kan became president for a three-year term and was then replaced by Chiang Ching-kuo (CCK), Chiang Kai-shek's only biological son. CCK had held various positions in the KMT government, including head of the secret police, and later premier. In the latter role, and as president, he initiated a series of major infrastructure projects that helped accelerate Taiwan's economic growth and per capita income.

CCK also began to bring native-born Taiwanese into the highest levels of government. The most important of these was Lee Teng-hui, who had served as agriculture minister and Taipei mayor. Lee was appointed vice president.

The final years of CCK's presidency saw unexpected concessions to a rising democratic spirit within Taiwan. In 1986, with martial law still in effect after 38 years, the president chose not to suppress Taiwan's first opposition party, the Democratic Progressive Party (DPP), after they announced their formation. In 1987 he also declared the end of martial law. The following year he passed away and Lee Teng-hui became the ROC president. For Taiwan, a new era had truly begun.

The Post-Martial-Law Period: 1988–2000

In the late 1980s Taiwan had its first native-born president, but it was still a far cry from a democracy. In the first place, Lee Teng-hui had not been elected by the people, but appointed by Chiang Ching-kuo and voted in by the National Assembly, a body that had last been elected in China in 1947 and was still officially in session over 40 years later – and with largely the same people.

The Park Commemorating Victims of Political Persecution during the Martial Law Period (戒嚴時期政治受難者紀念公園) in Taipei has tombstones honouring some 200 victims of political persecution between 1949 and 1953.

1987	1988	1990	1991
After 38 years, martial law is lifted in Taiwan, setting the stage for the island's eventual shift from authoritarian rule to democracy. Taiwanese citizens are once again allowed to travel to China.	Chiang Ching-kuo dies of heart failure at age 78. He is succeeded by Lee Teng-hui, the first native-born president of Taiwan.	A student demonstration quickly sees 300,000 people gather in Liberty Sq. This eventually helps lead to direct presidential and National Assembly elections six years later.	Lee Teng-hui announces the end of the 'Period of National Mobilization for the Suppression of the Communist Rebellion'. This formally ends the state of war between the ROC and PRC.

THE 2-28 INCIDENT

In the postwar years, the KMT (Kuomintang) government under Chen Yi continued and even expanded the monopoly system begun under the Japanese. However, a combination of graft and mismanagement led to the creation of a large black market of goods, of which tobacco was no small part. On 27 February 1947, agents from the Tobacco Monopoly Bureau in Taipei seized contraband cigarettes and money from a middle-aged widow and pistol-whipped her into unconsciousness. Angry crowds formed and attacked the officers, one of whom responded by shooting into the crowd, killing an innocent bystander.

The next morning businesses closed in protest, and crowds gathered outside the Taipei branch of the Monopoly Bureau, attacking employees and setting the offices on fire. This was followed by an afternoon protest outside the governor-general's office. Here, security forces again fired into the crowds, killing a number of protesters. Violent protests now erupted all over Taiwan and for several days the island was in chaos.

Order was restored by the Taiwanese themselves, and on 2 March local leaders established a Settlement Committee with a list of 32 Demands, which included free elections and an end to government corruption. Chen Yi stalled. He promised to meet and discuss the demands, but in secret he waited for the Nationalist troop reinforcements he had requested from Chiang Kai-shek.

The troops arrived on 8 March and, according to witnesses, began three days of killing civilians. This was followed in the coming weeks by the round-up and summary execution of protest leaders, intellectuals, high-school students and anyone else held suspect by the government. An estimated 18,000 to 28,000 people were killed during this period. Taiwan lost nearly its entire native elite.

Until the lifting of martial law in 1987, there was little open discussion of the event. In 1992 President Lee Teng-hui made a public apology to victims on behalf of the government. Three years later he declared 28 February (2-28) a public holiday, and created a memorial foundation to deal with compensation. Taipei Park was renamed 2-28 Peace Memorial Park, and a 2-28 Memorial Museum was opened in the former radio station that had been taken over following the initial February protests. The museum exhibits were redone in 2010 in response to complaints that under KMT Mayor Ma Ying-jeou (later president) the museum had whitewashed the KMT's, and especially Chiang Kai-shek's, involvement in the incident.

Lee initiated constitutional changes to allow for direct elections of the president and Legislative Yuan (Taiwan's parliament), as well as for the eventual dissolving of the National Assembly. He also ended the provisions that had allowed for martial law and the suspension of civil liberties. In 1991 he officially ended the state of war between the ROC and China.

Lee furthered CCK's policy of bringing more native Taiwanese into government and concurrently began a process of 'localisation' or

1992–93	1996	1999	1999
In the Koo-Wang Talks, representatives from the ROC and PRC meet in Hong Kong to discuss cross-Strait relations. From this arises the '92 Consensus in which each side claims the right to interpret One China in their own way.	Lee Teng-hui is re-elected in Taiwan's first fully democratic presidential election, winning 54% of the vote in a three-way race.	Taiwan is hit by a massive earthquake measuring 7.3 on the Richter scale. Centred on Nantou County, the quake causes massive damage and thousands of deaths throughout the island.	Lee Teng-hui declares to a German reporter that after his government amended the constitution in 1991, Taiwan and China now have a special state-to-state relationship.

'Taiwanisation'. In effect this meant destressing a pan-China (and mostly northern China) focused view of history and culture. Taiwan was now its own centre, with a history and culture worth studying and promoting. In practice this meant emphasising Taiwan's southern Chinese roots, its strong folk religious traditions, its Dutch and Japanese influences, and its multi-ethnic make-up: Hakka, Hoklo, indigenous and mainlander.

The elections in 1996 were a watershed moment in Taiwan's advancement towards democracy. For the first time, Taiwanese would directly elect their leader. Lee ran against democracy advocate Peng Ming-min (and a host of others).

China, outraged that free elections were going to be held in Taiwan, and suspicious that Lee held independence sentiments (which he did, as it turned out), held a series of missile tests from July 1995 to March 1996. The USA responded with a build-up of ships in the region, the largest military display in Asia since the Vietnam War. The people of Taiwan, more angry than scared, responded by giving Lee a clear majority vote (54%).

Lee's second term was marked by deteriorating social order, especially in the first year, which saw three high-profile murder cases involving organised-crime figures terrify the public. Many openly longed for the return of martial law and Lee himself was blamed. More interestingly, critics blamed Lee for using *heidao* (gangsters) himself in order to keep the KMT in power.

However, the infiltration of politics by organised-crime figures both predates the Lee presidency and continues to this day. Even in 1996 intelligence reports showed that 40% of town representatives, 27% of city councillors and 3% of national representatives had organised-crime backgrounds. Criminologist Ko-lin Chin says Taiwan is unique for having such a high level of gangsters in elected office (not even the Italian Mafia, he says, dare to run openly, but try to influence from behind closed doors).

On a more positive note, Lee's second term also saw the continuation of democratic and civil reforms. With respect to cross-Strait relations, the president argued that with the legitimacy of Taiwan's government now solely in the hands of Taiwan voters, the notion that the ROC 'represented' all of China could no longer hold. In 1999 Lee declared that China and Taiwan now held 'special state to state relations'. Neither the Chinese nor the Americans were amused by what they saw as a push towards a formal declaration of independence.

In 2000, Lee, unable to run for a third term, appointed the wooden Lien Chan as his successor. The popular and charismatic James Soong, former provincial governor, believing he should have been chosen to represent the KMT, ran as an independent. This split the KMT's vote, and

2000	2000	2004	2005
Former Taipei Mayor Chen Shui-bian is elected ROC president, winning 39.3% of the popular vote in a three-way race, ending over 50 years of KMT rule in Taiwan.	In an early sign of thawing relations between Taiwan and China, the 'Three Small Links' commence, opening limited trade between China and the Taiwanese-held islands of Kinmen and Matsu.	Chen Shui-bian is re-elected by the slimmest of margins; the day before the election both president and vice president are mildly wounded by the same bullet in a botched assassination attempt.	China enacts an Anti-Secession Law, formalising its commitment to use military force if Taiwan declares independence. Protests against the law draw huge crowds around Taiwan.

THE KAOHSIUNG OR MEILIDAO INCIDENT

For Taiwan, the late 1970s and early '80s was an era of storms: not just internationally, with derecognition from the UN and the USA, but increasingly within its own society. Political dissent, which included calls for democracy and civil rights, was growing. One of the most noteworthy uprisings of the late-martial-law period occurred in December 1979. Called the Kaohsiung Incident, it is still widely regarded as a turning point in Taiwan's shift from authoritarian rule to democracy.

The incident began with the editors of *Meilidao*, a publication often critical of the government, organising a rally to celebrate International Human Rights Day. On the day of the rally, after scuffles broke out between police and protesters, the situation turned into a full-scale riot. The authorities rounded up 50 prominent dissidents and put them on trial. Among these were Taiwan's future vice president Annette Lu and democracy advocate Lin Yi-hsiung. (In February of the following year, Lin's mother and twin daughters were murdered in their Taipei home. It is widely believed the KMT had ordered the killing.)

Though the trial of the activists resulted in long prison terms, it did not quite have the effect the government wanted. In the first place, it gave the voice for independence a wide audience (many foreign reporters were in attendance). It also created the reputation of the next generation of activists. These included two of the lawyers who represented the accused: future Taiwanese president Chen Shui-bian, and future vice president Frank Hsieh.

The majority of people in Taiwan sympathised with the accused and were horrified at the brutal crackdown by their government. The incident brought increased support for democratic reform, which eventually led to the lifting of martial law and the formation of opposition parties.

the DPP's long-shot candidate Chen Shui-bian won with a little over 39% of the vote. Over 50 years of continuous KMT rule came very unexpectedly to an end.

Taiwan in the 21st Century

Chen Shui-bian would serve Taiwan as president for eight years, during which time many long-term trends in politics and society became settled and mainstream. By the end of Chen's second term, for example, both the military and the civil service had generally become neutral bodies, loyal to the country and not just the KMT. Judicial reforms gave people Miranda rights (such as the right to a lawyer), but attempts at education reform, land-use legislation, police reform and streamlining government either failed or stalled.

Lee Teng-hui's localisation and de-Sinicisation policies were kicked up a notch and the names of many public companies and institutions were changed from 'China' to 'Taiwan'. Chiang Kai-shek International

2006	2007	2008	2008
Chiang Kai-shek International Airport is renamed Taoyuan International Airport as part of a general movement to erase homages to the former dictator.	Taiwan's High Speed Rail (HSR) begins operation to much fanfare and publicity. With speeds of up to 350km/h, the HSR cuts rail travel from Taipei to Kaohsiung to 90 minutes.	Former Taipei mayor and long-time KMT favourite Ma Ying-jeou is elected president, regaining control of the executive branch after eight years of DPP rule.	As part of the Ma government's opening to China, regularly scheduled direct flights between the two countries begin. Ma also declares that Taiwan, as the Republic of China, is part of China.

Airport was renamed Taoyuan International Airport, though attempts to rename CKS Memorial Hall resulted in a backlash. Still, Taiwanese of all stripes began to identify with Taiwan more and more; even the children of mainlanders began to call themselves Taiwanese and not Chinese.

To many, though, it sometimes seemed this era was nothing but pure chaos. It began well. Recognising that he had won less than 50% of the vote and lacked a clear mandate (to say nothing of lacking control of the legislature, civil service and military), Chen filled his cabinet with many KMT appointees. He spoke of representing all Taiwanese, including mainlanders, and his message to China was simple: don't attack us and we won't declare formal independence. The president's initial approval rating reached 80%.

Things began to slide when Chen cancelled construction of the fourth nuclear power plant in October 2000, incensing the KMT, whose patronage networks across Taiwan are intimately linked to big construction projects. The following year Taiwan was hit with two economic whammies: the fallout in the agricultural sector from admission to the WTO (Taiwan was forced to open its markets to imported rice) and a recession that resulted from the dot.com bust. As is usual in Taiwan, the president was blamed, and many people openly wondered if the DPP could be trusted to run the economy.

In terms of economic policy, Chen moved away from Lee's slow and careful investment approach to China, and there was an exodus of business, talent and investment across the Strait. Though GDP growth remained reasonably good in Taiwan, stagnating wages and opportunities again left many critical of the president. Among the economic successes of the Chen years, the creation of a tourism industry ranks high. Inbound tourist numbers doubled from 2002 to 2008 and continue to rise today.

Relations with China, which had deteriorated under Lee Teng-hui, went from bad to worse. The nadir was reached in 2005 when China promulgated an Anti-Secession Law that codified China's long-standing threat to attack Taiwan should the island's leaders declare independence. The move was met by mass protest rallies throughout Taiwan.

Chen won re-election in 2004 by a tiny margin. The day before the election, both the president and vice president were mildly wounded in a botched assassination attempt. The KMT immediately cried foul and led weeks of mass, violent protests. To this day, many are convinced (though without evidence) that Chen was behind his own shooting.

Chen's second term was a classic lame duck, as the KMT-dominated legislative assembly blocked his every move. In 2006 Chen's approval rating hit 20% as a series of corruption scandals implicated both his wife and son-in-law.

The Chinese name of Formosa Boulevard Station (美麗島站), Kaohsiung's largest metro station, commemorates the 'Meilidao Incident'.

HISTORY TAIWAN IN THE 21ST CENTURY

2009	2009	2010	2012
Typhoon Morakot causes severe damage to the island, particularly in the southern counties. The storm kills hundreds and causes billions of dollars in damage.	Former president Chen Shui-bian is sentenced to life imprisonment (later reduced to 20 years) on corruption charges; supporters of the former president claim the charges are politically motivated.	President Ma signs the Economic Cooperation Framework Agreement (ECFA), a trade agreement between the PRC and ROC governments, lowering economic barriers between the two sides.	Ma Ying-jeou wins a second term as president, promising to continue policies of opening Taiwan's economy to China. Within months his popularity has sunk to 15%.

After stepping down in 2008, Chen Shui-bian immediately lost presidential immunity; within six months, he was arrested on charges of money laundering, bribery and embezzlement of government funds. Chen was sentenced to life imprisonment in September 2009, which was reduced to 20 years in June 2010 as later trials found him not guilty of embezzling government funds. Taiwan observers claim Chen's conviction did enormous long-term harm to his party and to the cause of Taiwanese independence.

In early 2008 the KMT won a decisive victory in the legislative elections. Two months later former justice minister and Taipei mayor, Ma

ECFA TRADE AGREEMENT OR TROJAN HORSE?

In June 2010, after two years of negotiations that began nearly as soon as Ma Ying-jeou was sworn in as president, Taiwan signed a preferential trade agreement with China called the ECFA (Economic Cooperation Framework Agreement). The pact, similar to those signed between China and Hong Kong and Macau, aims to reduce tariffs and ease trade. Opponents claim it is nothing but a disguise for unification by subsuming Taiwan's economy into China's.

Large-scale protests were held from the time of the first visit by Chinese negotiator Chen Yunlin until 2010. But to no avail. A total of 18 agreements have been signed so far after eight rounds of negotiations.

The Ma government argued that the ECFA would give Taiwan a needed boost in GDP and job growth. More importantly, it would reverse the country's marginalisation as other regional powers connected themselves with free-trade agreements.

The results to date have hardly been spectacular. GDP growth is anaemic, foreign investment near zero, and trade with China appears to be growing less than with other regional economies. In a bad sign, fresh fruit exports (which are growing) are being purchased not by wholesalers but by Chinese officials eager to win the hearts of local farmers.

The ECFA's secondary effects look more promising. In July 2013 Taiwan signed an economic cooperation agreement with New Zealand, its first with a developed country.

When Tsai Ing-wen assumed office in May, she announced intentions to deepen ties with India and the ASEAN countries, and strengthen links with Japan, Europe and the USA. Though she didn't explicitly state whether she would continue the ECFA, Tsai had run on a platform of maintaining the status quo across the Strait and will clearly need to find a way to continue to collaborate with Beijing without alienating those among her supporters who do not believe in collaborating with the mainland.

2012	2013	2016	2019
Taiwan's economy is stalled. Foreign direct investment is the second lowest in the world. With wages stagnated for over a decade, many young people are looking to emigrate.	Taiwan squabbles with Japan over the Senkaku Islands, and with the Philippines over the death of a Taiwanese fisher in disputed waters.	Tsai Ing-wen lands a stunning victory in the presidential elections, making her Taiwan's first female president.	Taiwan's parliament becomes the first in Asia to pass same-sex marriage legislation.

Ying-jeou, won the presidency with 58% of the vote. Ma Ying-jeou's clear victory that year (and again in 2012) signalled yet another new era for Taiwan. The Hong Kong–born Ma began a radical departure from Lee and Chen's policies, especially concerning cross-Strait relations. Once again, under Ma the ROC was declared the legitimate government of all China, and relations between Taiwan and the mainland merely those of special regions within that country. This did not, however, mean accepting PRC rule over Taiwan.

On coming to power, Ma focused on streamlining government (successfully), ending corruption (very unsuccessfully), re-Sinicising society, and bringing economic and cultural relations between China and Taiwan closer. Highlights of the latter include signing an economic agreement, the ECFA (p356), covering trade, finance, services and security; opening Taiwan to direct cross-Strait flights and ferries; encouraging Chinese students and professionals to study and work here; and facilitating the rise of mass Chinese tourism.

Under Ma's leadership, Taiwan's economic performance fell behind that of the other three Asian Tigers – Hong Kong, South Korea and Singapore. Ma also failed to improve cross-Strait relations. If anything, his gestures towards China were seen as part of a grand scheme to unite Taiwan with China, so that he could go down as the Taiwanese president who made history. This struck fear into the hearts of many Taiwanese who saw the fate of Hong Kong as something to be avoided at all costs, and caused more to identify as Taiwanese rather than Chinese. A series of polls showed widespread dissatisfaction with Ma's policies. In late 2015 Ma's efforts culminated in a sudden meeting with Chinese President Xi Jinping and a historic handshake, just before the DPP assumed power.

In May 2016 the pro-independence DPP scored a landslide victory in the presidential elections, making its leader Dr Tsai Ing-wen the island's first female president. Tsai won 56% of the votes, almost double the 31% of her KMT opponent Eric Chu Li-luan. Eight years prior, when Ma took the helm, the KMT was riding high. His policies clearly had a hand in sending the KMT to its demise, from which, it is believed, it can recover only with vigorous reform. After losing the elections, Chu Li-luan resigned as party chair and apologised to supporters.

In her campaign, the charismatic Tsai promised to build consistent and sustainable cross-Strait relations with China and work towards maintaining the status quo for peace and stability. It remains to be seen how this will play out in her policies towards and negotiations with Beijing in the years to come.

2019

Pacific Islands nations Kiribati and the Solomon Islands break diplomatic ties with Taiwan in favour of establishing relations with China.

People of Taiwan

First-time visitors to Taiwan often expect to find a completely homogenised society, with little difference in thinking, customs and attitudes from one generation to the next, from city to countryside, or even from person to person. In fact, the country is a multiethnic melting pot. Customs and traditions go back and forth between groups and evolve over time; these days, family background and life experience are far more indicative of a person's attitudes and beliefs than simple ethnicity.

Taiwan's Modernity

Taiwan has a literacy rate of 98%. The country uses traditional Chinese characters to read and write with, and the average adult must learn to write and recognise thousands.

Taiwan may have some of the world's most colourful traditional festivals and a sizeable population, predominantly in the south, that live by both the lunar and Gregorian calendars, but it's worth keeping in mind that Taiwan is still a very modern country with a strong and charismatic urban culture.

In Taiwan, just as traditional rites are used to celebrate the opening of businesses and honour the passing of lives, pop culture is part and parcel of many religious processions. It's not uncommon to spot pole dancers busting moves on large vehicles at these events, or dance music pumping out of converted cars with gull-wing doors and badass lights, not to mention folk sporting tats and trainers strutting along to the temple dressed as deities. Whatever one's opinion of such modern manifestations of faith, they're not meant to be disrespectful of tradition. If anything, they show how deeply ingrained faith is in the lives of Taiwanese of all ages. And for outsiders, the ease with which the Taiwanese sashay in and out of tradition and modernity is what makes this country so fascinating.

Aside from pop, performance art, literature and a vibrant book-and-lifestyle-shop culture all figure in Taiwan's luxuriant contemporary cultural landscape. It's worth checking out the museums, galleries and performances in the big cities, and the arts festivals. And don't forget the jazz festival and jazz bars, the cool indie dives and the calmly ambitious modern cooking, be it return-to-roots Euro-inspired Taiwanese or chefy Taiwan-inspired French. You'll find these and more in Taipei, Kaohsiung, Taichung and Chiayi, just as you'll find equivalents in any major city in the world.

Ethnicity

About 98% of Taiwan's inhabitants are ethnically Han Chinese, with the other 2% being indigenous. Hoklo and Hakka are often referred to as *běnshěngrén* (本省人; home-province people), while mainlanders, or those who came with Chiang Kai-shek (and their descendants), are *wàishěngrén* (外省人; outside-province people). These titles are gradually falling out of use, however, especially with the younger generation.

Hoklo (Taiwanese)

Accounting for about 70% of the population, the Hoklo (Taiwanese) are the descendants of Chinese immigrants from Fujian province who arrived between the 17th and 19th centuries. While nearly all speak Mandarin, many also speak Hoklo, or Taiwanese, as their native language. Hoklo are found all over Taiwan.

Hakka

About 15% of the population are Hakka, descendants of immigrants from Guangdong Province. Taoyuan, Hsinchu and Miaoli counties are Hakka strongholds, but you'll also find significant populations in Pingtung and Taitung.

Mainlanders

Around 13% of the people are those who emigrated from mainland China following WWII and the defeat of the Nationalist army by the communists in 1949, and their descendants. They tend to be concentrated in urban areas such as Taipei, Taichung and Kaohsiung and are among the most educated, connected and wealthy of citizens, but also among the most poor. Intermarriage and a Taiwan-centred consciousness among the young has made the label somewhat passé, though one still hears the phrase 'high-class *wàishēngrén*' used as a mark of distinction in certain circles.

Indigenous People

The population of Taiwan's 16 officially recognised tribes is over 550,000 (2.3% of the total population). Villages are concentrated along the east coast and the mountainous interior, though many young indigenous Taiwanese work in the major cities. Although indigenous people are by far the least prosperous group in Taiwan, in recent years many villages have seen a rebirth of indigenous practices and pride, and have begun building a sustainable and nonexploitative tourism industry around traditional culture.

Nearly all indigenous people speak Mandarin in addition to their own tribal languages. DNA tests have shown that 88% of ethnic Taiwanese have some indigenous blood in them, likely owing to the lack of Chinese female settlers in the early days of immigration from the mainland.

Indigenous tribes in Taiwan include the following:

Amis (population 177,000) Mostly live on the east coast in Hualien and Taitung counties.
Paiwan (population 86,000) Live in Kaohsiung and Pingtung Counties.
Atayal (population 81,000) Across the central and north mountainous regions, with Wulai (near Taipei) their most northerly extent.
Bunun (population 50,000) Live in the central and southern mountains as well as Taitung County.
Truku (Taroko; population 24,000) Live in Taroko Gorge and other parts of Hualien.
Tao (Yami; population 3500) Live only on Lanyu Island.

Recent Immigrants

Several hundred thousand Southeast Asians and Chinese have immigrated to Taiwan since the 2000s, many as mail-order brides for rural Taiwanese men. There are also a small number of Westerners who have become Republic of China (ROC) citizens and thousands who have become permanent residents.

Taiwanese Women Today

The ROC constitution forbids discrimination on the basis of gender, educational opportunities are equal for boys and girls, and in working life women are found in the upper echelons of many companies, religious organisations and government departments. The president is London School of Economics–educated Tsai Ing-wen. Following the January 2016 elections, a total of 43 women were sworn in as lawmakers in the 113-member legislature, which translates to 38%, the highest in Asia and a historical high for Taiwan.

Epitomising the ideological gap between the generations, Guo Tai-ming, founder of iPhone manufacturer Foxconn, famously remarked that it was beyond him that so many of Taiwan's young today are content simply opening cafes.

Among young women, marriage and childbearing are being delayed longer and longer (the average age now is 29 to 30, higher than most Western countries), with the result that Taiwan has one of the lowest birth rates in the world. What exactly is behind the low rates is multifold. In part it's simply that Taiwanese women have more choices, but economic stagnation also plays a large role: young Taiwanese simply cannot afford their own families.

Boys are still favoured over girls in some families, and it is not uncommon to hear of a mother who is pregnant once again because her first three children were girls. But this is becoming less and less common and comes down to individual family pressure rather than societal pressure.

Lifestyle

Despite the low birth and marriage rate, family still remains central to Taiwanese life. Both young and old are generally deeply committed to each other. Parents dote on and indulge children in a way that seems developmentally harmful to many Westerners, while adult children continue to defer to their parents for major decisions. Male offspring take their role as guardian of the family name with utter seriousness.

Most people in Taiwan live in crowded urban conditions. However, with low taxes, cheap utilities and fresh local foods, to say nothing of excellent low-cost universal medical care, people enjoy a good balance between the cost of living and quality of life. (On the other hand, stagnating wages are a major problem for young people.) Life expectancy is 83 years for women and 77 years for men.

One of the most unfortunate parts of Taiwanese life is education: an emphasis on rote learning means kids are burdened with long hours of homework and evenings spent at cram schools. Primary school is fairly low pressure, but junior and senior high schools are true soul crushers and suicide is common among teens.

Like their peers in the West, young Taiwanese have taken to pop culture, casual dating, sexual experimentation, (limited) drug and alcohol use, and expressing themselves with fashion choices. They have been labelled the Strawberry Generation in that they look perfect but can't bear

TRADITIONAL FESTIVALS

In addition to scores of local cultural holidays and events, Taiwanese celebrate the big traditional Chinese festivals such as Lunar New Year. These are mostly family affairs, but it's good to know a little about them as they are integral parts of local culture, and you might find yourself invited along at some point.

Lunar New Year (農曆新年; Nónglì Xīnnián) Celebrated for two weeks (people get four to nine days of public holidays) in January or February, this is the most cherished holiday of the year. Activities include a thorough clean of the house; decorating doorways with couplets expressing good fortune; and a family reunion dinner on New Year's Eve. On the second day of New Year's, married daughters return to their parents' home. The last days of the public holidays are for visiting friends and travelling. The 15th and final day is the **Lantern Festival** (臺灣燈會; Táiwān Dēnghuì; www.taiwan.net.tw), which in Taiwan is celebrated with a number of exceptional activities.

Tomb Sweeping Day (清明節; Qīngmíng Jié) Ancestor worship is among the most important features of Taiwanese culture, and on this day (Gregorian calendar, 5 April) families return to tend to their ancestral graves (though many now are interned in a columbarium).

Mid-Autumn Festival (中秋節; Zhōngqiū Jié) Originally a harvest celebration, this public holiday falls on the 15th day of the eighth lunar month. Families gather to barbecue, eat moon cakes, gaze at the full moon, and recount the story of the fairy Chang'e and a jade rabbit who lives on the moon and mixes a mean elixir of immortality.

pressure. While often true, many in this generation are also proving to be devoted to social causes and willing to put themselves on the line in protests, as was shown in 2013 when 250,000 mostly under-30s protested in front of the Presidential Palace over the death-by-torture of a young army recruit. Strawberries are also more than willing to drop out of the rat race to pursue a dream. More and more young people favour opening cafes and boutiques over seeking stable employment in a large firm.

In general, relationships are the key to Taiwanese society and this is expressed in the term *guānxi*. To get something done, it's sometimes easier to go through a back door, rather than through official channels. This has serious implications for the rule of law, however, as well-connected people are often able to get away with anything.

The Taiwanese Character

Taiwanese have often been characterised as some of the friendliest people in the world. Reports from Western travellers and officials in Taiwan in the 1930s read like modern accounts, which suggests friendliness is a deep, long-standing quality. Some claim this is likely due to Taiwan's immigrant background in which trust among strangers was paramount.

The important concept of 'face' can seem scary to those prone to social gaffes, but in reality the idea is largely about not causing someone else to lose status or dignity in front of their peers. Locals may often appear humble and polite, but they have a fierce pride. Taiwanese men seem to have an instinctive way of defusing tension, but once things go too far, extreme violence could be the result.

Taiwanese stress harmony in relationships, and if the choice is to be made between maintaining harmony and telling the truth, many people opt for the former. It's best to see this as an expression of different values.

Associated with this is flattery. Travellers are often told how beautiful they are or that their Chinese is terrific. The best response is a smile and a humble reply in the negative, to avoid sounding arrogant. On the other hand people are often shockingly direct once they know you and will tell you directly you have gained weight, gotten ugly, are wearing unflattering clothing, and so on. And between friends and even loved ones a bossy, pushy, insulting tone is often taken. However, one of the best parts of the Taiwanese character is the general capacity for very open, sincere and lifelong friendships.

Sports

Despite their propensity for work and study, Taiwanese are a sports-loving people. Basketball and baseball are the most popular organised spectator sports: both have their own leagues in Taiwan and games are popular with local audiences, especially baseball. In fact, Taiwanese baseball players regularly make it to the big leagues in Japan (which introduced the sport to Taiwan in 1906) and America, with players like Wang Chien-ming now household names around the world. Yani Tseng, the world's youngest player to win five major golf championships, is also Taiwanese.

Taiwanese are also quick to embrace athletes such as probasketball star Jeremy Lin, born in the USA to Taiwanese parents, as one of their own.

When the five-day (more or less) work week was established in 2001, Taiwanese began to take up biking, hiking, surfing and travel in record numbers. Today a sporting and leisure society mentality is well entrenched.

As with most activities, Taiwanese localise some aspects of their sports. Hikers always get up predawn, for example, to watch the sunrise, while cyclists can't bear to be seen outside without the latest flashy gear and clothing.

After giving birth, Taiwanese women partake of the month-long *zuò yuè zi* (坐月子), an ancient custom of post-partum recuperation with specific dietary and movement restrictions. These days *zuò yuè zi* nursing centres provide 24-hour assistance in a hotel-like setting.

PEOPLE OF TAIWAN THE TAIWANESE CHARACTER

Religion & Temples in Taiwan

A funny thing happened to Taiwan on the way to its future. Instead of losing its religion as economic growth, mobility and education brought it into the developed world, the opposite happened. There are more Buddhists today than ever before. Statistics from 2015 show there are 12,106 registered temples, which, in addition to being houses of worship, fill the role of art museum, community centre, pilgrim site and even and a front for money laundering.

A Brief History

Historians generally divide temple development in Taiwan into three periods.

In the early immigrant stage (16th to 17th centuries), settlers, mostly from Fujian province, facing harsh conditions and needing to form new community bonds, established branch temples based upon the gods worshipped in their home villages. These were sometimes little more than a thatched shrine covering a wooden statue brought from China.

In the 18th and 19th centuries, the small shrines were replaced with wood and stone temples. Wages for craftspeople were high and top artisans from China were eager to work here. Most materials were imported. This era also saw the establishment of Hakka temples.

During the late Qing dynasty and into Japanese times, a period of increasing wealth and mobility, many temples began to expand their influence beyond the village level. Famous pilgrim sites arose, and Mazu started her rise to pan-Taiwan deity status.

Three Faiths (Plus One)

When modern Taiwanese are troubled, they're almost as likely as their grandparents to burn incense, toss moon blocks and pray at a temple. But before asking Baosheng Dadi to help rein in their cholesterol, they'll take the medicine the doctor prescribed. But once they're cured, it's the temple that'll get the donation.

The Taiwanese approach to spirituality is eclectic and not particularly dogmatic; many Taiwanese will combine elements from various religions to suit their needs rather than rigidly adhering to one particular spiritual path. Many of the gods, customs and festivals have little to do with any of the three official religions and are sometimes described as part of an amorphous folk faith.

Confucianism

Confucian values and beliefs form the foundation of Chinese culture. The central theme of Confucian doctrine is the conduct of human relationships for the attainment of harmony and overall good of society. Society, Confucius taught, comprises five relationships: ruler and subject, husband and wife, father and son, elder and younger, and friends. Deference to authority and devotion to family are paramount.

The close bonds between family and friends are one of the most admirable attributes of Chinese culture, a lasting legacy of Confucian teachings. But the effects of modernisation have also been pushing society away from a simple adherence to Confucian values, for better or worse.

Taoism

Taoism consists of a vast assembly of philosophical texts, popular folk legends, organised sects, and a panoply of deities numbering in the thousands. Controversial, paradoxical and impossible to pin down, it is a natural complement to rigid Confucian order and responsibility.

Taoism began with Lao-Tzu's *Tao Te Ching*. Its central theme is that of the Tao – the unknowable, indescribable cosmic force of the universe. Organised Taoism came into being in the 2nd century, at which time there was an emphasis on mystical practices to cultivate immortality. Taoism reached a high point during the Tang dynasty when there was a fierce battle with Buddhism and when many branches became increasingly tied to popular religion.

In modern Taiwan, Taoist priests still play a vital role in the worship of deities, the opening of temples, the exorcising of bad luck and illness, and the presiding over of funeral services.

Buddhism

Buddhism came to Taiwan in the 17th century with the Ming loyalist Koxinga, but there were few orthodox associations until Japanese times. Many Japanese were devout Buddhists and supported the growth of the religion during their occupation.

In 1949, thousands of monks, fearing religious persecution in China, fled to Taiwan with the Nationalists. Under martial law, all Buddhist groups were officially organised under the Buddhist Association of the Republic of China (BAROC). By the 1960s, however, independent associations were emerging, and it is these maverick groups that have had the most influence in modern times.

Buddhism in Taiwan is largely Chan (Zen) or Pure Land, though few groups are strictly orthodox. The main Buddhist associations are Foguangshan (the Light of Buddha), Dharma Drum, Tzu Chi (p363) and Chung Tai Chan.

Folk Religion

Beliefs about ancestor worship permeate almost every aspect of Chinese philosophy. Closely tied to ancestor worship is popular or folk religion, which consists of an immense celestial bureaucracy of gods and spirits, from the lowly but important kitchen god *(zào jūn)* to the celestial emperor himself *(tiāndì* or *shàngdì)*. Each god has a particular role to fulfil and can be either promoted or demoted depending on their performance. Offerings to the gods consist not only of food and incense,

---

RÉNJIĀN FÓJIÀO: THIS-WORLDLY BUDDHISM

You won't get far understanding the Buddhist influence on modern Taiwanese society if you simply try to grasp doctrine and schools. In the past 40 years a special form of socially active Buddhism (*Rénjiān Fójiào;* this-worldly Buddhism) has emerged to redefine what that religion means to its practitioners. *Rénjiān Fójiào* draws inspiration from the thoughts of the early-20th-century reformist monk Taixu in China, but has been completely localised by masters such as Chengyan of Tzu Chi.

A central tenet of *Rénjiān Fójiào* is that one finds salvation not by escaping in a monastery but by bringing Buddhist compassion into ordinary life and adapting the dharma to the conditions of modern life. Taiwanese Buddhist groups stress humanitarian work, and teach that traditional beliefs, such as filial piety, should be expanded to encompass respect and consideration for society at large. With a de-emphasis of ritual and a central role for lay followers to take in the organisations, Taiwanese Buddhist groups have made themselves the religion of choice for middle-class urbanites and professionals.

Famous pilgrim sites have a reputation for divine efficacy (靈; *líng*), which is the magical power to answer a worshipper's prayers. Pilgrims visiting such sites expect to have a direct experience of the god's powers, and to return home with both good-luck trinkets and prayers granted.

but also opera performances, birthday parties (to which other gods are invited) and even processions around town.

Other Faiths

Presbyterians are few in number but are politically influential. Indigenous Taiwanese tend to be overwhelmingly Catholic or of other Christian faiths; church steeples are a common fixture in villages.

Pilgrimage

As an integral part of religious life in Taiwan, it's not surprising that pilgrimage fulfils many roles besides worship: it gives people an excuse to travel; it helps reinforce the relations between daughter and mother temples; and it's a major source of funding. Jìnxiāng, the Chinese term for pilgrimage, means to visit a temple and burn incense to the god. The most famous pilgrimage in Taiwan is in honour of Mazu (p231).

Religious Festivals

In all phases of Taiwan's history, the wealthier society got, the bigger the religious festivals became. Good places to catch random celebrations are Lukang and Tainan.

Acts of Worship & Prayer

Worship is known as *baibai* (拜拜). In addition to the following, typical acts of worship include offerings of food, candles and thanks, as well as fasting or refraining from eating meat.

In every temple in Taiwan you will see worshippers holding burning incense in their hands as they do the rounds, bowing first before the main deity and then the host of subdeities. Afterwards the incense is placed in the censer.

Going to a temple to ask gods or ancestors for answers to questions is common. The most typical form of divination is *bwah bwey,* which involves tossing two wooden half-moon divining blocks after a yes-or-no type question has been asked. If the two *bwey* both land curved-side up, the request has been denied. If one is up and one down, the request has

SOME FOLK & TAOIST DEITIES

Those outlined here are just a few of the hundreds of folk and Taoist gods you will come across in temples. Among the most important deities in the south, the Wang Yeh (the Royal Lords), who number in the hundreds, were either once real historical figures or plague demons. Today they are regarded as general protectors.

Mazu (Empress of Heaven) is the closest thing to a pan-deity in Taiwan. She is worshipped as a general protector.

Guandi or Guangong is the so-called God of War, but is better thought of as a patron of warriors and those who live by a righteous code. More generally he is worshipped as a god of wealth and literature. He is easy to recognise by his red face, beard and halberd.

Baosheng Dadi (Great Emperor Who Preserves Life) is the God of Medicine. He played an important role for early immigrants faced with a host of diseases and plagues.

The top god in the Taoist pantheon, the Jade Emperor fulfils the role of emperor of heaven. In Taiwan he is usually represented by a plaque rather than a statue.

The City God (城隍爺; *Chénghuángyé;* protector of cities), also officially the Lord of Walls and Moats, is the moral accountant of the temple, recording people's good and bad deeds for their final reckoning. People pray to him for protection and wealth.

Tudi Gong, the Earth God (and minor god of wealth), has the lowest ranking in the Taoist pantheon. As governor of local areas, he was very important in pre-industrial Taiwan and his shrines can be found everywhere. Look for statues of an old bearded man with a bit of a Santa-like visage.

been granted. If they both land curved-side down, it means you need to try again. There is no limit to how many times you can perform *bwah bwey*, but if you get the same answer three times in a row, you should accept it.

Buddhist, Taoist & Confucius Temples

A Buddhist temple's name will almost always end with the character 寺 (*sì*), while a Taoist temple will end with the character 宮 (*gōng*) or 廟 (*miào*). A Confucius temple is always called a Kǒng Miào (孔廟).

The general architectural features will be the same for all three types, though modern temples may incorporate foreign influences; eg in the design of the Chung Tai Chan Monastery in Puli. Older Buddhist temples, such as the various Longshan temples, are harder to distinguish from Taoist ones, but modern Buddhist temples are usually built in a northern Chinese 'palace style' and adopt a more restrained aesthetic.

Confucius temples are always large red-walled complexes and generally sedate. Taoist temples, on the other hand, will generally be loud, both in noise level and decoration.

Temple Architecture

The basic characteristic of any temple hall or building is a raised platform that forms the base for a wood post-and-beam frame. This frame is held together by interlocking pieces (no nails or glue are used) and supports a curved gabled roof with overhanging eaves.

The layout of most temple complexes follows a similar and comprehensible pattern of alternating halls (front, main, rear) and courtyards, usually arranged on a north–south axis. Corridors or wings often flank the east and west sides, and sometimes the whole complex is surrounded by a wall, or fronted by a large gate called a *páilóu* (牌樓).

Temple Roof

The roof of a traditional Taiwanese temple is usually single or multi-tiered. The roof's ridgeline, slung low like a saddle, will curve upwards at the end, tapering and splitting like the tail of a swallow. This is known as a swallowtail roof, and is a distinctive feature of southern Chinese temples.

The ridgeline is decorated with dragons in mosaic-like *jiǎnnián* (剪粘; cut-and-paste). Sometimes a pearl sits in the centre (which the dragons are reaching for); sometimes three figures (福禄寿; Fu Lu Shou) who represent the gods of good fortune, prosperity and longevity; and sometimes a seven-tier pagoda.

Slopes are covered with tiles (long and rounded like a bamboo tube) and fabulously decorated with vibrant cochin pottery and figures in *jiǎnnián*. Fish and some dragon figures on the ends symbolise protection against fire.

Bracketing & Caisson Ceilings

Wooden brackets help to secure posts and beams, and they are also decorative features. They vary from dragons and phoenixes to flowers and birds, or tableaux of historical scenes unfolding. Complex systems of two- or four-arm brackets found under the eaves of roofs are called *dǒugǒng*. They give builders a high degree of freedom during construction and are one reason why Chinese architecture can be found across a wide region so varying in climate.

Inverted caisson ceilings are called *zaojing* (藻井; *zǎojǐng*) and are constructed with exposed *dǒugǒng* arms that extend up and around in a spiderweb pattern (sometimes swirling like a vortex). Caisson ceilings are probably the most striking of all temple architectural features.

A common sight at religious festivals are the spirit mediums (*jītóng* in Mandarin, *tangki* in Taiwanese). Not sure who these are? Look for wild bare-chested guys lacerating themselves with swords and sticking blades through their cheeks to prove the god is within them.

RELIGION & TEMPLES IN TAIWAN BUDDHIST, TAOIST & CONFUCIUS TEMPLES

Temple Decorative Arts

The training of local talent in temple art began during the Japanese colonisation in the late 19th century. Several highly talented schools of temple artisans developed and much of the fine work you'll see today comes from them.

Traditional Taiwanese temples are constructed in a southern Fujian style (sometimes called Minnan), which essentially follows the Song dynasty aesthetics of playfulness and ornamentation, as opposed to the formal and grandiose expressive of the Ming and Qing periods, best exemplified by Beijing's Forbidden City.

Cut & Paste Shard Art & Cochin Pottery

Jiǎnniàn (剪粘; cut-and-paste) is a method of decorating figurines with coloured shards. True *jiǎnniàn* uses sheared ceramic bowls for raw material. The irregular pieces are then embedded by hand into a clay figurine. These days many artists use premade glass pieces but still embed them by hand. Some temples save money by simply buying prefab figurines. *Jiǎnniàn* is usually found on the rooftops of temples. Figures include humans, dragons, phoenixes, carp, flowers and the eight immortals.

A type of colourful low-fired, lead-glazed ceramic, cochin (also spelled koji) is one of Taiwan's unique decorative arts. The style is related to Chinese tricolour pottery and came to Taiwan in the 18th century. Common themes include human figures, landscapes, flowers and plants, as well as tableaux depicting stories from mythology and history. Cochin pottery is found under eaves, on lintels or on the rooftop.

Carvings & Paintings

Woodcarving is usually found on cross-beams, brackets, hanging pillars (often in the shape of hanging baskets), doors, window lattices and screen walls. Its basic function is decorative, though many parts are integral to the temple structure.

Before the 20th century most stone came from China, and was often used as ballast in the rough ship ride over. Later, locally sourced Guanyin stone became the preferred choice. Stone is most commonly used for dragon columns, lion statues, and relief wall panels showing scenes from history and literature.

Painting is mainly applied to wood beams and walls. Though decorative, painting also helps to preserve wood, and is said to drive away evil, bless and inspire good deeds. Common motifs include stories from literature and history.

Probably the most distinctive paintings at any temple are the guardians on the doors to the front hall. These colourful gods are practically everywhere, not only at temple entrances but also on city gates and house doors, to scare away evil spirits.

Taiwanese Arts

Taiwan has a rich and varied artistic landscape that features top-notch cinema, important literature in the Chinese-speaking world, some of Asia's best modern dance and fascinating visual arts. Local arts are either indigenous or evolved from Chinese genres, carried over by waves of immigrants from mainland China, or a unique mix of both, with Japanese, American and European influences thrown in.

Modern Visual Arts

Western styles of painting were introduced to Taiwan by the Japanese. Ishikawa Kinichiro (1871–1945), now considered the father of modern Taiwanese art, taught local painters to work the tropical landscapes of Taiwan in a French impressionistic style. Ishikawa's students included Li Mei-shu (1902–83) who is best known for his work overseeing the reconstruction of Sansia's masterful Tzushr Temple.

During the 1970s a strong nativist movement, sometimes referred to as 'Taiwan Consciousness', began to develop. Artists found inspiration in Taiwanese folk traditions and the arts and crafts of indigenous tribes. The sculptor Ju Ming (b 1938), whose stone and woodwork can be seen in his personal Juming Museum on the north coast, is the most well-known artist from this period.

The opening of the Taipei Fine Arts Museum and the ending of martial law were two of the most significant events in the 1980s. For the first time, artists could actively criticise the political system without suffering consequences. And they had a public venue in which to do so.

Since then, alternative art spaces have blossomed and Taiwan's participation on the international stage has been well established. Artists regularly exhibit at top venues such as the Venice Biennale, and work in multimedia as much as traditional forms.

The first Taiwanese artist to study in Japan was Huang Tu-shui (1895–1930) whose relief masterwork *Water Buffalo* can be seen in Taipei's Zhongshan Hall.

Indigenous Arts & Crafts

The indigenous peoples of Taiwan have their own distinct art traditions, many of which are alive and well these days.

Woodcarving

The Tao of Lanyu Island are famous for their handmade canoes, constructed without nails or glue. The striking canoes have carved relief designs embellished with human and sun motifs painted in white, red and black.

The Paiwan and Rukai also excel at woodcarving; they build homes and make utensils that feature elaborate carvings of humans, snakes and fantastical creatures. Along the east coast the Amis use driftwood for sculptures of humans and animals, and to create fantastic abstract pieces. You can check out part of the scene at the Dulan Sugar Factory (p185).

The Yingge Ceramics Museum not only covers the history of pottery and ceramics in Taiwan, but also showcases the current leading masters and their efforts to keep expanding the boundaries of their art.

Dance & Music

Vocal music is one way indigenous Taiwanese preserve their history and legends, passing down songs from one generation to the next. This music

The Atayal and
Seediq are well
known for their
weaving, which
uses hand-
prepared ramie
(vegetable fibre).
The bright
'traditional'
colours were
actually intro-
duced in the
1920s.

has become popular in recent years, and music shops in Taiwan's larger cities carry recordings.

Indigenous dances, accompanied by singing and musical instruments, are usually centred on festivals, which may celebrate coming-of-age rituals, harvests or hunting skills. These days, it's relatively easy to watch a genuine performance of traditional dance in the summer along the east coast.

Though rarely performed now, the Bunun *Pasibutbut,* a song with a complex eight-part harmony, was once considered impossible for a 'primitive' hunter-gatherer society to have created.

Music

In addition to indigenous song, Taiwan has a long and rich tradition of classical instrumental music such as Nanguan (southern pipes) and Beiguan, which originated in Fujian Province (the ancestral home of most Taiwanese).

Folk music includes Hakka *shan ge* (山歌; mountain songs), and the Holo music of the Hengchun Peninsula (very southern Taiwan) in which singers are accompanied by the *yuèqín* (月琴; moon lute). In the hit Taiwanese movie *Cape No 7,* the character of Old Mao plays the *yuèqín*.

Taiwanese pop music goes back decades. One of the most popular singers in the 1970s was silky voiced Teresa Teng (1953–95) whose grave in Jinbaoshan Cemetery (just up from the Juming Museum) is still visited by adoring fans to this day. Perhaps even more well known in the Chinese-speaking world is A-mei (阿妹; Ā Mèi; b 1972), a singer-songwriter from Taiwan's Puyuma tribe. Younger stars include Jay Chou and Joline, both huge idols in China.

Since the late 1990s Taiwan has developed a vibrant indie, hip-hop, folk and underground scene, with some bands, like metal Chthonic, becoming near household names. Popular music festivals such as Spring Scream (p259) and Hohaiyan Rock Festival (p151) continue to introduce new bands to a wide audience.

Performing Arts

Taiwanese Opera

The various styles of folk opera commonly seen in Taiwan have their origin in Fujian and Guangdong Provinces, though over the centuries they have been completely localised to the point where they are now recognised as distinct art forms. Initially performed on auspicious occasions such as weddings, birthdays and temple festivals, folk opera later developed into a more public art form, drawing larger audiences. By the 1940s opera was the most popular folk entertainment in Taiwan and remains well received to this day.

Learn more about
native indigenous
arts and crafts at
the Wulai Atayal
Museum, Shung
Ye Museum
of Formosan
Aborigines in
Taipei, Ketagalan
Culture Centre in
Beitou and the
Museum of Art in
Kaohsiung.

Taiwanese opera is complemented by a wide range of musical instruments, including drums, gongs, flutes, lutes and two- and three-stringed mandolins. Common opera styles include Nanguan Xi Opera and Gezai Xi (歌仔戲; sometimes just called Taiwanese opera), which evolved out of a ballad tradition that involved musical accompaniment. It's the most folksy and down-to-earth form of opera, making use of folk stories and sayings and, of course, the Hoklo language. The occasional martial arts display is a result of a merger of Beijing and Taiwanese opera troupes in the 1920s.

Dance

Modern dance in Taiwan has its roots in the 1940s, when it was introduced by the Japanese. In the 1960s and '70s a number of outstanding dancers, trained abroad or influenced by American dancers who had

Top: Chinese opera performance in Kaohsiung

Bottom: Wooden statues at Formosan Aboriginal Cultural Village (p245), Sun Moon Lake

TOPIMAGES / SHUTTERSTOCK ©

toured Taiwan, began to form their own troupes and schools, some of which remain influential today.

The most highly regarded is the Cloud Gate Dance Theatre of Taiwan, founded in the early 1970s by Lin Hwai-min. Lin was a student under Ameriucan Martha Graham and upon his return to Taiwan in 1973 desired to combine modern dance techniques with Chinese opera.

Lin's first works were based on stories and legends from Chinese classical literature. Soon, however, Lin decided to try to explore Taiwanese identity in his work. *Legacy,* one of Lin's most important works, tells the story of the first Taiwanese settlers. Later works are more abstract and meditative as Lin explored Tibetan, Indian and Indonesian influences. No matter what the topic, Cloud Gate performances are breathtaking in their colour and movement.

Cinema

Taiwanese cinema began in 1901 with Japanese-made documentaries and feature films. Many of these show the progress of Taiwan under colonial rule and were clearly meant for a Japanese audience.

In the 1960s the Nationalist government created the Central Motion Picture Corporation (CMPC) and a genuine movie industry took off. During the 1960s and '70s, audiences were treated to a deluge of romantic melodramas and martial arts epics.

In the 1980s a New Wave movement began as directors like arthouse auteur Hou Hsiao-hsien and the Western-educated Edward Yang broke away from escapism to give honest and sympathetic portrayals of Taiwanese life. Hou's *A City of Sadness* (1989) follows the lives of a Taiwanese family living through the KMT takeover of Taiwan and the 2-28 Incident (p352). This movie was the first to break the silence around 2-28 and won the Golden Lion award at the 1989 Venice Film Festival. Other social issues explored by New Taiwanese Cinema included urbanisation, disintegration of the family and the old way of life, and the clash of old and new values (as in Yang's *Taipei Story;* 1985). This cinema is also marked by an unconventional narrative structure that makes use of long takes and minimal camera movement to move the story at a close-to-real-life pace.

In the 1990s directors appeared who came to be known as the Second New Wave. Big names include Ang Lee, known for megahits the *Life of Pi* (2012), *Crouching Tiger, Hidden Dragon* (2000) and *Brokeback Mountain* (2005); and the Taiwan-educated Malaysian art-house guru Tsai Ming-liang for *Vivre L'Amour* (1996) and *What Time Is It There?* (2001) whose bleak, meticulous, slow-moving and sometimes bizarre take on urban life in Taiwan has won him recognition worldwide.

Piracy and competition from Hong Kong and Hollywood films sent the Taiwanese film industry into near collapse by the late '90s. With the release of Wei Te-sheng's *Cape No 7* (2008), a romantic comedy that became a box-office smash, audiences and critics began to feel renewed hope for the industry. Wei's *Seediq Bale* (2011), an epic about an indigenous revolt against the Japanese, as well as Doze Niu's *Monga* (2010), about gangsters in Taipei in the 1980s, and Yeh Tien-lun's *Night Market Hero* (2011), are keeping the dream alive.

Films made in the 21st century generally exhibit greater readiness to embrace market tastes than the unapologetically auteur-oriented titles of the 1990s, often earning both critical and popular acclaim. Silvia Chang's *Murmur of the Hearts* (2015), Yang Ya-che's *The Bold, the Corrupt, and the Beautiful* (2017) and Huang Hsin-yao's excellent *The Great Buddha+* (2017) are cases in point.

At religious festivals and deities' birthdays, it's common to see free performances of opera held on stages outside local temples, sometimes on trucks. Check out Bao'an Temple, Xiahai City God Temple and Dadaocheng Theatre in Taipei.

Literature

Taiwan has a rich and diverse literature. The earliest Taiwanese literature comprises the folk tales of the indigenous peoples, which were passed down by word of mouth. Later, in the Ming dynasty, Koxinga and his sons brought mainland Chinese literature to the island. A great number of literary works were produced in Taiwan during the Qing dynasty, the Japanese colonial era, and later the post-WWII period.

Taiwan spent the first half of the 20th century as a Japanese colony and much of the second half in a close relationship with China. Because of this unique heritage, Taiwan's literature is highly heterogeneous, undermining preconceptions about what constitutes a 'national literature'. There are authors, eg Yang Chichang, who studied Japanese literature in Tokyo in the 1930s and wrote their works in Japanese. There are also writers like Liu Daren, who was born in mainland China, and later, as a young intellectual in Taiwan, engaged in political activism that got him exiled in the 1970s.

Modern Taiwanese literature, like Taiwan's history, is rife with conflicting legacies and sensibilities. It is based on Chinese culture and wears the marks left by Japanese and American influences. Yet it is much more than that.

Taiwan's modern writers, many of whom were serious intellectuals, were keen to fill in the gaps in the Taiwanese cultural narrative that resulted from different political agendas and government-sponsored education. At the same time, they sought to establish a distinctly Taiwanese cultural identity that existed outside the colonising influences of Japan and mainland China. Authors like Lee Min-yung (李敏勇) and Tseng Kuei-hi (曾貴海) strove to gain acceptance for the Taiwanese Hoklo language, the Hakka dialect and indigenous languages – essentially the mother tongues of the majority of the island's people. Serious literature and music were written in these dialects. These writers also turned their focus to Taiwan's folk traditions for inspiration and adopted a largely Taiwanese perspective in their writings. The movement is closely associated with the emergence of Taiwan's democracy in the 1990s.

Translated works of Taiwanese literature include the following:

➡ *Frontier Taiwan: An Anthology of Modern Chinese Poetry* (Modern Chinese Literature from Taiwan), eds Michelle Yeh and N G D Malmqvist

➡ *Indigenous Writers of Taiwan: An Anthology of Stories, Essays, and Poems* (Modern Chinese Literature from Taiwan), eds John Balcom and Yingtsih Balcom

➡ University of California's Taiwan Literature English Translation Series

The National Museum of Taiwan Literature (p275) in Tainan is an excellent resource. The museum's website also has information on its research and translation activities, including a list of publications for sale. The museum has its own translation centre.

Taiwan has a rich puppetry tradition in marionette, glove, rod and shadow styles. Check out Taipei's Taiyuan Asian Puppet Theatre Museum (p86) and the Puppetry Art Centre of Taipei (p83). Hou Hsiao-hsien's *The Puppet Master* (1993), winner of the Cannes Jury Prize, is based on the memoirs of Li Tian-lu, Taiwan's most celebrated puppeteer.

TAIWANESE ARTS LITERATURE

The Landscape of Taiwan

At merely six million years of age, gorgeous Taiwan island is pumping with vigour and potential compared to the 4.6-billion-year-old planet earth. Lying 165km off the coast of mainland China, across the Taiwan Strait, it covers 36,000 sq km (roughly the size of the Netherlands), and is 394km long and 144km at its widest. The country includes 15 offshore islands: most important are the Penghu Archipelago, Matsu and Kinmen Islands in the Taiwan Strait, and, off the east coast, Green Island and Lanyu.

The Beauty

For one of the most unusual geological curiosities in Taiwan – or anywhere – head to Wushanding Mud Volcanoes in Yanchao, 27km north of Kaohsiung. This tiny nature reserve has two volcanoes, where you can get really close to the craters to see the boiling pots of grey goo.

Visitors to Taiwan and the surrounding islands can experience a stunningly broad variety of landscapes, from rugged mountains in the centre of the main island (there's even snow in winter at higher altitudes) to low-lying wetlands teeming with wildlife on the western coast, rice paddies and farmland in the south, and lonely windswept beaches punctuated with basalt rock formations on the outer islands. The east coast, with its towering seaside cliffs and rocky volcanic coastline, is utterly spectacular. The Central Cross-Island Hwy and the Southern Cross-Island Hwy link the island from east to west, cutting through spectacular mountain scenery.

However, Taiwan's colourful – and wild – topography means that the majority of the country's 23 million people are forced to live on the small expanses of plains to the west of the Central Mountain Range, and this is where agriculture and industry concentrate.

Mountains

Mountains are the most dominant feature of Taiwan. The island is divided in half by the Central Mountain Range, a series of jagged peaks that stretches for 170km from Suao in the northeast to Eluanbi at the southern tip. Gorges, precipitous valleys and lush forests characterise this very rugged ridge of high mountains.

Running diagonally down the right half of the island like a sash are the country's four other mountain ranges. The East Coast Mountain Range runs down the east coast of Taiwan from the mouth of the Hualien River in the north to Taitung County in the south. The Xueshan Range lies to the northwest of the Central Mountain Range. Xueshan, the main peak, is 3886m high. Flanking the Central Mountain Range to the southwest is the Yushan Range, home to the eponymous Yushan (Jade Mountain). At 3952m, Yushan is Taiwan's pinnacle and one of the tallest mountains in northeast Asia. The Alishan Range sits west, separated by the Kaoping River valley.

Rivers & Plains

According to the Taiwanese government's Council of Agriculture, the country boasts 118 rivers, all originating in the mountains, and it thus appears rather well watered. However, most of Taiwan's rivers follow short, steep and rapid courses down into the ocean, which causes flooding during typhoon season. During the dry season, on the other hand, the riverbeds are exposed and the reservoirs alone are unable to supply adequate water to the population. An extensive network of canals, ditches and weirs has therefore evolved over time to manage and channel this elusive river flow for irrigation.

The country's longest river is the 186km Zhuoshui, which starts in Nantou County, flows through the counties of Changhua, Yunlin and Chiayi, and serves as the symbolic dividing line between northern and southern Taiwan. It is also the most heavily tapped for hydroelectricity. The Tamsui, which runs through Taipei, is the only navigable stream. Other rivers include the Kaoping, Tsengwen, Tachia and Tatu. Located in the foothills of the Central Mountain Range, Sun Moon Lake is the largest body of freshwater in Taiwan and is one of the country's top tourist destinations.

Fertile plains and basins make up most of western Taiwan, which is criss-crossed with many small rivers that empty into the sea and has the most suitable land for agriculture. Over on the east coast, however, even plains are in short supply. Outside the three cities of Ilan, Hualien and Taitung, the area is among the most sparsely populated on the island.

Wetlands

Taiwan is home to 100 wetlands that have been officially declared 'nationally important', with estuaries being the most common form. There are large wetland concentrations in the southwest and southeast of the island; Tsengwen Estuary and Sihcao Wetland, both in Tainan, are classified 'international class' wetlands.

Besides providing a valuable ecosystem that supports a multitude of life forms including insects, amphibians and fish, Taiwan's wetlands are a precious gift to vast populations of migratory birds. These enamoured, annual visitors stop in Taiwan when migrating from northern areas such as Siberia, Manchuria, Korea and Japan to southern wintering sites in, for instance, the Philippines and Indonesia.

Environmental Issues

When Chiang Kai-shek's Nationalist troops were driven off the mainland, they brought more than just millions of Chinese people fleeing communism with them: they also brought capital, much of which was used to transform a primarily agrarian society into a major industrial powerhouse. Taiwan became wealthy, quickly, but it also became toxic, with urban air quality ranking among the world's worst, and serious pollution in most of its waterways. Indeed, Taiwan's 'economic miracle' came at a serious price, and pollution, urban sprawl and industrial waste have all taken a heavy toll on the island.

Things have improved markedly in the 21st century. Environmental laws, once largely ignored by industry and individuals alike, are now enforced far more rigorously across the board, and the results have been tangible (the Tamsui and Keelung Rivers in Taipei, for example, once horribly befouled, are significantly cleaner in sections). Urban air quality is noticeably better, thanks to a combination of improved public transport, more stringent clean-air laws and a switch to unleaded petrol. The Taiwanese collective unconscious has changed as well: so much of the new 'Taiwanese identity' is tied in with having a clean and green homeland that people are tending to take environmental protection far more seriously.

Lest we paint too rosy a picture, it's possible to counter any perceived step forward with another step back towards the bad old days.

At 3805m, Siouguluan Mountain not only represents the apex of the Central Mountain Range, but it also sits on the busiest tectonic collision zone in the whole of Taiwan. At present, it's rising by approximately 0.5cm a year. Expect more spouting to come.

If you drive along Lanyang River in the dry season, you'll be greeted by a giant cabbage patch instead of flowing waters. To find the impressive, curious sight, follow the highway through the Xueshan and Yushan Mountain Ranges up to Wuling Farm.

One of the bigger issues belying the image that the Taiwanese government hopes to project of an environmentally conscious democracy is that of land expropriation – ie the legal removal of farmers from privately owned lands. Critics said the December 2011 revision of the Land Expropriation Act only served to reinforce the interests of development – which is very loosely defined to cover anything from military construction to projects approved by the executive – over farmers' rights. Government and industrial proponents of expropriation point to the issue of common good, saying that transforming farmland into industrial areas creates jobs, reducing the country's climbing unemployment rate. However, opponents say that the main beneficiaries are a conglomerate of large corporations and real-estate developers. Although Taiwan's High Speed Rail (HSR) has been touted for making travel around the island even more convenient, many feel that placement of the stations – in the far outskirts of Taiwan's westernmost cities as opposed to in the city centres themselves – has actually promoted both increased traffic and urban sprawl. And, of course, the ongoing issue of decaying barrels of nuclear waste buried on the indigenous island of Lanyu has also yet to be resolved to anybody's satisfaction.

Taiwan's environmental issues are a global concern as well. Despite its diminutive size, Taiwan is a major CO_2 producer. A 2009 study contended that the 4130-megawatt coal-burning Taipower was the biggest CO_2 emitter on the planet. To date, it remains one of the most polluting coal power plants globally. That said, the Taichung City Government has negotiated with Taipower to reduce its carbon emissions in central Taiwan and stabilise air quality in the region.

So while it's fair to say that Taiwan has made great strides on the environmental front, it's clear that more remains to be done.

Natural Disasters: Earthquakes, Typhoons & Landslides

Taiwan is in a singular geological and climatic setting. It is highly susceptible to earthquakes and typhoons, while heavy rainfalls exacerbate the risk of landslides.

A fact of life for people living in Taiwan, natural disasters are also something that travellers need to take into account when planning their trip. Aside from the obvious dangers that may arise from being in the vicinity while one is occurring, landslides, typhoons and earthquakes have the potential to actually alter the landscape, rendering once-scenic areas unreachable and roads impassable. Sections of the Central Cross-Island Hwy that once stretched across the middle of the island from Taichung to Hualien remain closed to visitors, while large sections of the Southern Cross-Island Hwy are still impassable after being altered beyond recognition by Typhoon Morakot in 2009.

Earthquakes

Geologically, Taiwan is on one of the most complex and active tectonic collision zones on earth. Sitting atop the ever-colliding (albeit slowly colliding) Eurasian and Philippine plates has given Taiwan the beautiful mountains, scenic gorges and amazing hot springs that keep people coming back. Alas, these same geological forces also put the island smack bang in earthquake central, meaning that nary a week goes by without some form of noticeable seismic activity. Most of these quakes are small tremors, only noticed by folks living in the upper storeys of buildings as a gentle, peculiar rocking sensation. Others can be far more nerve-racking to locals and visitors alike.

ENERGY SOURCES

A lack of energy resources means Taiwan is highly reliant on imports to meet its energy needs. However, the country has a poor record in the use of renewable energy: it is a major exporter of solar panels but there has been almost no domestic use until very recently. Tsai Ing-wen's government has pledged to end nuclear power generation by 2025 and put forward a plan to expand application of wind and solar power. However, the nascent 'energy transition' is drawing scepticism and political controversy, and its future hinges on the presidential election outcome in 2020.

On 4 March 2010 an earthquake measuring 6.4 on the Richter scale with an epicentre 362km south of Taiwan's southernmost city caused buildings to tremble as far north as Taipei, knocking out power and rail service for a short time and causing several injuries. The most devastating earthquake to hit Taiwan is remembered locally simply as '9-21' after the date it occurred, 21 September 1999. Measuring 7.3 on the Richter scale, the earthquake collapsed buildings and killed thousands. In February 2016 an earthquake measuring 6.4 on the Richter scale hit the Meinong district of Kaohsiung, leaving 117 dead and 550 injured. Almost all the deaths were caused by a collapsed residential building.

Damage caused by the catastrophic 9-21 earthquake – especially the dramatic collapse of buildings in commercial and residential neighbourhoods – led to the passage of laws requiring that new buildings be designed to withstand future earthquakes of high magnitude.

Typhoons

Common during the summer months in the western Pacific area and the China seas, typhoons are tropical cyclones that form when warm moist air meets low-pressure conditions. Taiwan experiences yearly tropical storms, some of which reach typhoon level. Having better infrastructure than many of its neighbours, Taiwan tends to weather most typhoons fairly well, with the majority resulting in flooding, property damage, delays and headaches – but little loss of life. In August 2009, however, Taiwan found itself in the direct path of Typhoon Morakot. The island was unable to cope with the massive rainfall brought by the typhoon (it delivered over a long weekend what would be about three years' worth of rain in the UK), which, combined with winds of up to 150km/h, triggered heavy flooding and landslides, especially in the southern counties of Pingtung, Chiayi and Kaohsiung. Nearly 600 people were killed in the disaster.

Although there has been no official consensus on precisely why Morakot was so devastating, many who study local climate and land-use issues in Taiwan factor in poor land management, excessive draining of aquifers and wetlands, and climate change in general as being partially responsible.

Landslides

According to Dave Petley, one of the world's top landslide specialists, Taiwan is the 'landslide capital of the world' because of the high rates of tectonic uplift, weak rocks, steep slopes, frequent earthquakes and extreme rainfall events. But while Taiwan has almost every type of landslide, the number of known ancient rock avalanches remains surprisingly low given the prevailing conditions.

Legendary Japanese engineer Yoichi Hatta (1886–1942) still commands hero status in Taiwan today thanks to the major contributions he made to hydraulic engineering in the country.

Wildlife Guide

To most of the world Taiwan is best known as one of the Asian Tigers, an economic powerhouse critical to the world's IT supply chains. Decades earlier it had a reputation as a manufacturer of cheap toys and electronics. But going back even earlier, Taiwan was the kingdom of the butterfly and an endemic species wonderland where one could find the most astonishing variety of native plants and animals. Is there anything left of this old world? Plenty.

Forests & Climate

Taiwan is 60% forested, with about 20% (and growing) of the land officially protected as national park or forest reserve. One of the absolute highlights of any trip to Ilha Formosa involves getting to know the flora and fauna, much of which you can't find anywhere else on earth.

Taiwan lies across the Tropic of Cancer and most fact books record its climate as subtropical. But with its extremely mountainous terrain (it's almost 4000m high in the centre), Taiwan has a climate ranging from subtropical to subarctic, and its vegetation zones range from coastal to montane to alpine. It's been said that a journey 4km up to the 'roof' of Taiwan reproduces a trip of many thousands of kilometres from Taiwan to the Russian steppes.

Plants

Taiwan has 4000 to 5000 plant species, with an estimated 26% found nowhere else. Travellers will be most interested in the forest zones, which is a good thing because Taiwan has plenty of forest cover.

Foothills (Tropical Zone): 0–500m

Most of Taiwan's original tropical forests have long been cleared to make room for tea fields, orchards and plantations of Japanese cedar, camphor and various bamboos. Intact lowland forests still exist along the east and in parts of Kenting National Park. In other areas you will find dense second-growth forests.

Submontane (Subtropical Zone): 300–1500m

It's in these broadleaved forests that most people get their first taste of just how unspoiled and luxuriant Taiwan's forests can be. It's a jungle-like environment teeming with birds, insects, snakes and so many ferns that you often can't count the number of species in one patch. Though ferns can grow as high as trees (giving forests a distinct *Lost World* feel), common larger plant species include camphor, *Machilus,* crepe myrtle, maple tree, gums and cedar.

You can see submontane plants in Nanao, and near the Pingxi Branch Rail Line, the Walami Trail and Wulai.

Montane (Temperate Zone): 1600–3100m

The montane forests vary greatly because the elevation changes mean there are warm temperate and cool temperate zones. You might start

There are no comprehensive English books on Taiwan's wildlife, but the visitor information centres at the country's national parks sell a wide range of individual books and DVDs that cover butterflies, birds, mammals, reptiles and more.

Springtime waterfall

your journey in a mixed broadleaved forest that soon turns to evergreen oaks. At higher elevations, conifers such as Taiwan red cypress, Taiwania, alder, hemlock and pine start to predominate. In areas that have been disturbed by landslide or fire, you often get large tracts of Taiwan red pine. When its needles fall, the forest floor becomes almost ruby in colour.

Between 2500m and 3100m in elevation, a natural pine–hemlock zone runs down the centre of Taiwan. This is one of the most pristine parts of the country (logging never went this high) and many trees are hundreds and even thousands of years old. A good part of any hike to the high mountains will be spent in this zone.

You can see montane plants along the Alishan Forest Train, Forestry Rd 200, and the hiking trails in Yushan National Park and Snow Mountain.

Subalpine (Cold Temperate Zone): 2800–3700m

You might think that this high-altitude zone is inaccessible unless you hike in, but you can actually reach sections of it by road. Taiwan's highest pass sits at 3275m on Hwy 14, just before Hehuanshan Forest Recreation Area. The rolling meadows of Yushan cane (a type of dwarf bamboo) that you can see from the roadside stand as one of the most beautiful natural sights on the island.

Less accessible are forests of tall, straight Taiwan fir and juniper (a treeline species). To see these you will need to put on your boots and strap on a knapsack.

You can see subalpine plants in the Hehuanshan Forest Recreation Area, Snow Mountain, Tatajia and Wuling Pass.

STOPPING TO SMELL THE FLOWERS

Taiwan is not lacking beautiful flowers to appreciate. The blooming period is long and you can usually see something year-round. Here are a few scented petals to watch out for, besides the sublime day lilies.

Flamegold tree An appropriately named native tree with large yellow and red blooms in autumn. It grows in lowland forests, and is widely planted on city streets as it does well in polluted air.

Youtong The large white flowers of the youtong tree bloom all over the north in April. Around the Sanxia Interchange on Fwy 3, entire mountainsides go near-white in good years.

Rhododendron and azalea These native species bloom from low to high altitudes from April to June.

Formosa lily One of the tallest of lilies, with long trumpetlike flowers. Blooms wild all over Taiwan twice a year in spring and autumn.

Orchid There are many wild species, but large farms around Tainan and Pingtung also grow these delightful flowers. Taiwan is, in fact, the world's largest orchid exporter.

Lotus Baihe in Tainan County has a two-month-long summer festival devoted to this flower.

Cherry blossom Cherry trees bloom in great numbers in February and March in Yangmingshan, Wulai and Alishan Forest Recreation Area.

Calla lily These beautiful long-stemmed white lilies bloom in large fields in Yangmingshan in spring. There's even a festival for them.

Plum blossom The national flower (at least for the Kuomintang) blooms in February in orchards all over the island at midaltitudes. It has an intoxicating scent, too.

Butterfly ginger A hopeless romantic, the white flower of the native butterfly ginger gives off its strongest scent at night. Blooms from spring to autumn all over the island.

Awn grass (silvergrass) A tall, swaying grass, with light, airy blooms. Its blooming signals the end of autumn in the north. The Caoling Historic Trail is one of the best places to see entire hillsides covered in it.

Alpine flowers Taiwan has dozens of petite flowers that splash a bit of colour above the treeline all summer long.

Alpine (Subarctic Zone): 3500+m

If you manage to climb your way to this elevation, you'll be above the treeline. The zone is divided into a lower scrub zone and an upper herb zone where tiny patches of vegetation cling to the exposed rocks. It's a chilly place even in summer, but the views are worth every effort to get here.

You can see alpine plants on the peaks of Snow Mountain and Yushan National Park.

Taiwan has many relic species that survived the last ice age. One of the more intriguing is the Formosan landlocked salmon, which never leaves the mountain streams in which it was born.

Animals

Mammals

There are about 120 species of mammals in Taiwan, and about 70% of those are endemic. Once overhunted and threatened by development, species like the Formosan macaque, wild boar, martin, civet, sambar deer, and the delightful and diminutive barking deer (Reeves' muntjac) have made great comebacks and are relatively easy to spot in national parks and forest reserves. Sika deer, which once roamed the grasslands of the west from Kenting to Yangmingshan, have been reintroduced to Kenting National Park and are doing well. Head out at night in submontane forests with a high-powered torch (flashlight) if you want to catch Taiwan's flying squirrels in action.

Though tropical at lower elevations, Taiwan lacks large species of mammals such as elephant, rhino and tiger. Taiwan's biggest cat, the spotted cloud leopard, is almost certainly extinct, while the Formosan black bear is numbered at fewer than 1000. Your chances of seeing one of these creatures are pretty slim.

You can see mammals in Chihpen Forest Recreation Area, Jiaming Lake National Trail, Kenting National Park, Nanao, Shei-pa National Park and Yushan National Park.

Bird-watching

Birdlife International (www.birdlife.org/asia)

Wild Bird Society of Taipei (www.wbst.org.tw)

Birds of East Asia by Mark Brazil

WILDLIFE GUIDE CONSERVATION

Birds

With its great range of habitats, Taiwan is an ideal place for birds and birdwatchers. Over 650 species have been recorded here: 150 are considered endemic. It's an impressive list and compares very well with larger countries in the region such as Japan.

Bird conservation has been a great success since the start of the 21st century, and it's therefore easy to spot endemics like the comical blue magpie, or multicoloured Muller's barbet, even in the hills surrounding Taipei. For one of the world's truly great shows, however, check out the raptor migration over Kenting National Park. Once threatened by over-hunting, bird numbers have tripled in the 21st century. Several years back, over 50,000 raptors passed over the park in a single day.

You can see birds in Aowanda Forest Recreation Area, Dasyueshan Forest Recreation Area, Kenting National Park, Kinmen, Tatajia, Wulai and Yangmingshan National Park.

Butterflies

In the 1950s and '60s, Taiwan's butterflies were netted and bagged for export in the tens of millions (per year!). Remarkably, only three species became extinct, though numbers plummeted for decades. These days top butterfly areas are well protected, and these delightful creatures can be seen everywhere year-round.

Taiwan has over 370 species of butterflies, of which 56 are endemic. Some standouts include the blue admirals, red-base Jezebels and Magellan's iridescent birdwing, which has one of the largest wingspans in the world. Prominent sites include Yangmingshan National Park's Datunshan, where chestnut tigers swarm in late spring; the overwintering purple butterfly valleys in the south; Fuyuan Forest Recreational Area; and the Yellow Butterfly Valley outside Meinong. You can also see butterflies in Linnei, Maolin and Tatajia.

Other Wildlife

Taiwan has a host of reptiles including a wide variety of beautiful but deadly snakes. Lizards, frogs and a long list of insects including stag beetles, cicadas and stick insects can be found anywhere there's a bit of undisturbed land.

Marine life (whales and dolphins, as well as corals and tropical fish) is abundant on the offshore islands and the east coast where the rich Kuroshio Current passes. You can see corals in Little Liuchiu, Green Island, Lanyu, Penghu and Kenting National Park. Many species of river fish are also making a good comeback, though sports fishers are sadly too quick to catch (and not release) fry.

Conservation

Today, conservation projects all over Taiwan are restoring mangroves and wetlands, replanting forests and protecting the most vulnerable sspecies. A 10-year moratorium on river fishing has succeeded in

WERANUT / SHUTTERSTOCK ©

Top: Formosan macaque

Bottom: Taiwan yuhina

ON WINGS OF GOSSAMER: BUTTERFLY MIGRATION

Butterfly migration is fairly common the world over, but Taiwan's purple crow migration can hold its own. Each year in the autumn, as the weather cools, bands of shimmering purples (four species of *Euploea*, also known as milkweed butterflies) leave their mountain homes in north and central Taiwan and begin to gather in larger and larger bands as they fly south. By November they have travelled several hundred kilometres, and in a series of 12 to 15 warm, sheltered valleys in the Dawu Mountain Range, 10 to 15 million of them settle in for the winter.

This mass overwintering is not common. In fact, Taiwan is one of only two places in the world where it happens: the other is in the monarch butterfly valleys of Mexico. The most famous overwintering site in Taiwan is in Maolin Recreation Area, but according to experts this is actually the least populated valley. It simply had the advantage of being the first to be discovered and written about.

The discovery happened in 1971 when an amateur entomologist was invited into Maolin by local Rukai people. Though not aware of just how significant the find was, the entomologist (and others) continued to study the valley. By the mid-1980s it was obvious that a north–south migration route existed, though it wasn't until 2005 that the 400km route along the west could be roughly mapped out. Since then a second migration path along the east coast and a connecting path joining the two have also been discovered.

The northern migration usually begins around March, and, astonishingly, it involves many of the same individuals who flew down in the autumn (purples have been found to live up to nine months). Some good places to spot the spring migration are Linnei, Dawu (in Taitung County), Pingtung County Rd 199, Taichung's Metropolitan Park, Baguashan and coastal areas of Jhunan (Miaoli County) where the purples stop to breed. In May and June, large numbers of purples appear to take a mysterious detour and are blown back south over the high mountain pass at Tatajia.

If you're curious as to just how the migration occurs in the first place, the answer is relatively simple: seasonal winds. In the autumn they come strong out of Mongolia and China, while in the spring they blow up from the Philippines. Without them the purples would be unlikely to move such great distances and this would mean their death when the temperatures drop during northern winters.

From spring until autumn, purple butterflies are easily spotted all over Taiwan. So give a nod to these brave wayfarers when you encounter them in a park or mountain trail. They may have come a long way.

For a mostly accurate look at the discovery of the western migratory route, check out *The Butterfly Code*, a Discovery Channel DVD.

restocking streams, while a 2013 ban on the destructive practice of gill-net fishing in Little Liuchiu Island should protect the corals and the 200 endangered green sea-turtles inhabiting the coasts.

Further, hundreds of small community projects are bringing back balance to urban neighbourhoods; even in Taipei, the sound of songbirds and the flittering of butterfly wings is common stuff. There are also vast areas now inaccessible to the public because of the closing of old forestry roads (a deliberate policy). In 2012 Pingtung County Government declared the section of coastline along Alangyi Old Trail to be a nature reserve, and the construction of a controversial highway was halted – a victory for the wildlife and ecosystem of the coast (there are 49 protected species, including the endangered sea-turtles).

The National Biodiversity Research Promotion Project

In 2009 a seven-year study by the Biodiversity Research Centre of Academia Sinica reported that Taiwan had 50,164 native species in eight kingdoms, 55 phyla, 126 classes, 610 orders and 2900 families. To cut to

Alishan National Scenic Area (p223)

the chase, this means that Taiwan, with only 0.025% of the world's land mass, holds 2.5% of the world's species. It's a rate of endemism 100 times the world average.

The study, the first since British diplomat and naturalist Robert Swinhoe completed his own in the late 19th century, was a revelation – to put it mildly. Altogether, it was found that 70% of Taiwan's mammals, 17% of its birds, 26% of its plants and 60% of its insects are endemic species.

What accounts for such a high rate of bio-density? It's Taiwan's long isolation from the mainland, as well as a geographic environment that harbours a variety of ecosystems in a small area. About the only ecosystem that Taiwan is missing, scholars have noted, is a desert.

Survival Guide

Directory A–Z

Accessible Travel

While seats and parking for people with disabilities are respected, in general Taiwan is not a very accessible environment. Street footpaths are uneven, kerbs are steep, and public transport, other than the MRT and HSR, is not equipped with wheelchair access. Taipei and other cities are slowly modernising facilities.

Taiwan Access for All Association (www.twaccess 4all.wordpress.com) provides advice and assistance for travellers with disabilities.

Download Lonely Planet's free Accessible Travel guides from http://lptravel.to/AccessibleTravel.

Accommodation

Taiwan provides the full range of lodgings, from basic hostels to world-class resorts, though it's at the midrange level, especially at homestays, that you will get the best value for money. You would be wise to book well in advance during summer,

Lunar New Year and other national holidays.

Homestays Family-run places that often offer a simple breakfast with the room.

Hotels Run the full gamut from world-class international names to budget with threadbare carpets.

Hostels Focus on dorm rooms; pricier than in Southeast Asia.

Booking Services

You can reserve by phone or via Facebook or a dedicated website, but unless you go through a booking site you will likely need to use Chinese. When reserving homestays you may be asked to pay a deposit by PayPal.

Camping

Camping is generally safe and inexpensive, and hot showers (which may be limited to the evenings) and toilets are standard. It is best to bring a freestanding tent, as many sites have raised wooden platforms.

Along the east coast you can set up a tent on pretty much any beach, but it can get very hot if you aren't

under the shade. Public campgrounds tend to have the best facilities.

Homestays

Mínsù (民宿; homestays) are increasingly well run and offer good accommodation at a fair price. In fact, many are far superior to hotels and often offer thoughtfully cooked meals, trips to the market and tours. Tainan and to a lesser extent Kaohsiung have a number of extraordinary *mínsù* operating out of beautiful historic houses. Rates are usually cheaper on weekdays.

Hostels

Taiwan doesn't have the same kind of budget accommodation as many other countries in Asia (although it is still cheaper than Hong Kong, Japan and Singapore).

Basic dorm beds start at NT$500 and vary in quality, from clean berths with curtains and individual potpourri sachets to basic rooms with half a dozen people stacked in. A few hostels provide cubicle-like sleeping spaces that may be claustrophobic for some, but are well maintained nonetheless.

Private rooms, when available, tend to be on the small side and start at NT$1000. You can often arrange weekly or monthly rates.

Taiwanese hostels affiliated with Hostelling International (www.yh.org.tw) offer discounts for cardholders.

BOOK YOUR STAY ONLINE

For more accommodation reviews by Lonely Planet authors, check out http://lonelyplanet.com/hotels/. You'll find independent reviews, as well as recommendations on the best places to stay. Best of all, you can book online.

Almost all genuine hostels are technically illegal, though there is nothing dodgy about them (it's just bizarre regulations, such as the need to have a carpark, that prevent them from getting licences).

Hostels generally have a laundry, simple cooking facilities, computers, wi-fi and a small kitchen or lounge.

Hotels

Budget hotels in the NT$900 to NT$1500 range give you bare-bones accommodation with cheap furniture, a private bathroom and a TV. No English will be spoken.

In the midrange (NT$1600 to NT$4000) you're likely to find a fancy lobby, one or more restaurants on-site, wi-fi, plasma TVs, and these days a laundry room with free DIY washer and dryer (this service is an island-wide trend).

The big cities abound with international-standard, top-end hotels. Typical amenities include business centres, English-speaking staff, concierge services, and a spa, a fitness centre and a swimming pool.

Temple & Church Stays

Many cyclists stay at small temples and Catholic churches, though you'll need to speak Chinese if you want to do this. A small donation is appropriate. **Foguangshan** (佛光山, Fóguāngshān; ☑Buddha Museum 07-656 3033, Pilgrim's Lodge 07-656 1921; www.fgs.org.tw; Xingtian Rd,

Dashu District, 大樹區興田路; ☑Buddha Museum 9am-7pm Mon-Fri, to 8pm Sat & Sun) near Kaohsiung offers accommodation as part of a Buddhist retreat.

Rental Accommodation

If you're looking for somewhere more permanent, the go-to website is www.591.com.tw. Other websites with rentals are TEALIT (www.tealit.com) and Facebook (search for the city and the words 'rentals', 'flats' or 'apartments'). Area is measured in *píng* (坪), which is about 3.3 sq metres.

Basic studio apartments (with no kitchen) in Taipei cost around NT$8000 to NT$15,000 per month depending on location. Small three-bedroom apartments start at NT$20,000 – in good central neighbourhoods, rent is at least double this.

Activities

Taiwan is a wild adventure of mountains, forests and rivers. There's excellent hiking and white-water rafting in the many and marvellous national parks, world-class surfing in Taitung, windsurfing off Penghu Islands, cycling trails that circle the entire country and a scattering of hot springs to soothe tired bodies at the end of it all.

See the Taiwan Outdoors chapter (p34) for more.

Convenience Stores

Convenience stores in Taiwan deserve their name: they are ubiquitous, open 24 hours, and handy for daily food items, fruit and drinks (especially cheap fresh coffee).

Services include bill payment (such as phone, gas and electricity), fax, copy and printing services (take along your USB), ticket purchases (local flights, High Speed Rail and concerts) and calling taxis (useful in cities like Chiayi), while many also have toilets. Taiwan's 7-Elevens also offer cheap shipping of goods across Taiwan to other outlets, and many online purchases can be paid for and picked up at a branch. Most stores also have ATMs that accept international bankcards. What else do you need?

Custom Regulations

Up to US$10,000 in foreign currency (and NT$100,000) may be brought into the country, but there is a limit on goods (clothes, furniture and dried goods) brought in from China. Drug trafficking is punishable by death.

Passengers who are 20 years and older can import the following duty free:

➡ 200 cigarettes, 25 cigars or 1lb of tobacco

➡ one bottle of liquor (up to 1L)

➡ goods valued at up to NT$20,000 (not including personal effects)

Discount Cards

➡ Student discounts are available for buses, museums, parks, and movie and theatre tickets. Student cards issued in Taiwan are always accepted, while foreign-issued cards work in some places.

➡ Children's discounts are available and based on height (rules vary from 90cm to 150cm) or age (usually over six and under 12). Children under six usually get in free. Foreign children are usually eligible for these concessions.

Electricity

Type A
110V/60Hz

Type B
110V/60Hz

➡ Seniors 65 years and older are usually given the same discounts as children. Seniors over 70 often get in free. Foreign seniors are usually eligible for this discount.

Embassies & Consulates

Only a handful of countries and the Holy See have full diplomatic relations with Taiwan. It's likely that your country is represented not by an embassy but by a trade office or cultural institute. These serve the same functions as embassies or consulates would elsewhere: services to their own nationals, visa processing, trade promotion and cultural programs. The following are all located in Taipei.

American Institute in Taiwan (www.ait.org.tw; 100 Jinhu Rd, 金湖路100號; MDa'an Park)

Australian Office Taipei (Map p92;☏02-8725 4100; www.australia.org.tw; The President International Tower, 27th & 28th fl, 9-11 Songgao Rd, 松高路9號27-28樓; ⏰8.45am-12.30pm &

1.30-5.15pm Mon-Fri; MTaipei City Hall)

British Office Taipei (Map p92; ☏02-8758 2088; www.gov. uk/government/world/ organisations/british-office-taipei; The President International Tower, 26th fl, 9-11 Songgao Rd, 松高路9-11號26 樓; ⏰9am-12.30pm & 1.30-5pm Mon-Fri; MTaipei City Hall)

Canadian Trade Office in Taipei (Map p92;☏02-8723 3000; www.canada.org.tw; Hua-Hsin Bldg, 6th fl, 1 Songzhi Rd, 松 智路1號6樓; ⏰9am-11.30am Mon-Fri; MTaipei City Hall)

French Office in Taipei (Bureau Français de Taipei; Map p88;☏02-3518 5151; www. france-taipei.org; 10th fl, 205 Dunhua N Rd, 敦化南路205號 10樓; MSongshan Airport)

German Institute and Trade Office Taipei (Map p92;☏02-7735 7500; www.taiwan.ahk. de; 19th fl, 333 Keelung Rd, Sec 1, 基隆路1段333號19樓之9; ⏰9am-noon & 1-6pm Mon-Fri; MTaipei 101)

Japan–Taiwan Exchange Association (Map p88;☏02-2713 8000; www.koryu.or.jp; 28 Qingcheng St, 慶城街28號; ⏰9-11.30am & 1.30-4pm Mon-Thu, to 11.30am Fri; MNanjing Fuxing)

Korean Mission in Taipei (Map p92;☏02-2758 8320; http:// taiwan.mofa.go.kr; room 1506, 15th fl, 333 Keelung Rd, Sec 1, 基隆路一段333號1506室; ⏰9am-noon & 2-4pm Mon-Fri; MTaipei 101)

Liaison Office of South Africa (Map p88;☏02-2715 2295; www.southafrica.org.tw; Suite 1301, 13th fl, 205 Dunhua N Rd, 敦化北路205號13樓; MSongshan Airport; Zhongshan Junior High School)

Netherlands Trade & Investment Office (Map p92;☏02-8758 7200; www.ntio.org.tw; 13th fl, 1 Songgao Rd, 松高路 1號13樓; ⏰consular services 9am-11am Mon-Wed; MTaipei City Hall)

New Zealand Commerce & Industry Office (Map p92;☏02-2720 5228; www.nzcio.com; 9th fl, 1 Songzhi Rd, 松智路1號9樓; ⊙9am-12.30pm & 1.30-5pm Mon-Fri; MⓂ Taipei City Hall)

Thailand Trade & Economic Office (Map p80; www.tteo.org. tw; 12th fl, 168 Songjiang Rd, 松江路168號12樓; ⊙9am-noon & 2-5pm Mon-Fri; MⓂ Songjiang Nanjing)

Etiquette

Taiwanese are very polite in both the way they speak and how they treat other people.

Transport Be aware of priority seating in buses and the MRT (the seat is usually a different colour). Most Taiwanese would never think of sitting here. They also readily give up their seat to anyone who needs it.

Queues Taiwanese queue for transport and in shops.

Greetings It's fine to shake hands or just smile when meeting someone for the first time. Accept and offer business cards with both hands.

Health

Before You Go
HEALTH INSURANCE

Some insurance policies pay doctors or hospitals directly rather than you having to pay on the spot and claim later. If you have to claim later, make sure you keep all documentation. You may be asked to call (reverse charges) a centre in your home country where an immediate assessment of your problem is made.

Check whether the policy covers ambulances or an emergency flight home.

MEDICATIONS

In Taiwan it may be difficult to find some newer drugs, particularly the latest anti-depressant drugs, blood-pressure medications and contraceptive pills.

If you take any regular medication, bring enough with you.

RECOMMENDED VACCINATIONS

Proof of Yellow Fever vaccination is required if entering Taiwan within six days of visiting an infected country. If you are travelling to Taiwan from Africa or South America, check with a travel-medicine clinic whether you need the vaccine.

Shots for hepatitis A and B are recommended.

RESOURCES

Centers for Disease Control ROC (www.cdc.gov.tw) Latest news on diseases in Taiwan.

Centers for Disease Control & Prevention (www.cdc.gov) Good general information.

Lonely Planet (www.lonely planet.com) A good place to visit for starters.

MD Travel Health (www.md travelhealth.com) Provides complete travel-health recommendations for every country including Taiwan. Revised daily.

In Taiwan
AVAILABILITY & COST OF HEALTH CARE

Taiwan is a developed country with excellent universal medical coverage. Many doctors are trained in Western countries and speak at least some English.

To see a doctor costs around NT$400; medicines and tests such as X-rays are much cheaper than private healthcare in the West.

Most hospitals have a volunteer desk to help foreigners fill in the forms needed to see a doctor.

Taipei has the best medical care, but most major cities will have a decent hospital.

INFECTIOUS DISEASES

Dengue fever This mosquito-borne disease causes sporadic problems in Taiwan in both cities and rural areas. It is more prevalent in the south, particularly Tainan and Kaohsiung. Prevention is by avoiding mosquito bites – there is no vaccine. Mosquitoes that carry dengue bite day and night.

Symptoms include high fever, severe headache and body ache (previously dengue was known as 'breakbone fever'). Use mosquito repellent and take precautions when outdoors, especially in rural areas in southern Taiwan.

Japanese B encephalitis A potentially fatal viral disease transmitted by mosquitoes, but rare in travellers. Transmission season runs from June to October.

Vaccination is recommended for travellers spending more than one month outside of cities.

Rabies Taiwan had its first rabies outbreak in 60 years in 2013. However, it's very rare, and so far only found in ferret-badgers, bats and house shrews.

ENVIRONMENTAL HAZARDS

Air pollution Air pollution, particularly vehicle pollution, is a problem in all urban areas, including many smaller cities. Avoid city centres during busy hours.

Insect bites and stings Insects are not a major issue in Taiwan, though there are some insect-borne diseases such as scrub typhus and dengue fever.

Ticks Ticks can be contracted from walking in rural areas, and are commonly found behind the ears, on the belly and in armpits. If you have had a tick bite and experience symptoms such as a rash at the site of the bite or elsewhere, or fever or muscle aches, see a doctor.

TRADITIONAL & FOLK MEDICINE

Traditional Chinese Medicine (TCM) is very popular in Taiwan. TCM views the human body as an energy system in which the basic substances of chi (qì; vital energy), jing (essence), blood (the body's nourishing fluids) and body fluids (other organic fluids) function. The concept of Yin and Yang is fundamental to the system. Disharmony between Yin and Yang or within the basic substances may be a result of internal causes (emotions), external causes (climatic conditions) or miscellaneous causes (work, exercise, sex etc). Treatment modalities include acupuncture, massage, herbs (usually in powder form in Taiwan),

dietary modification and qijong (the skill of attracting positive energy), and aim to bring these elements back into balance. These therapies are particularly useful for treating chronic diseases and are gaining interest and respect in the Western medical system. Conditions that can be particularly suitable for traditional methods include chronic fatigue, arthritis, irritable bowel syndrome and some chronic skin conditions.

Be aware that 'natural' doesn't always mean 'safe', and there can be drug interactions between herbal medicines and Western medicines. If you are using both systems, inform both practitioners what the other has prescribed.

Insurance

A travel-insurance policy to cover theft, loss and medical problems is a good idea. There is a wide variety of policies available, so check the small print.

Some policies specifically exclude 'dangerous activities', which can include scuba diving, motorcycling and even trekking. A locally acquired motorcycle licence is not valid under some policies.

Worldwide travel insurance is available at www.lonely planet.com/travel-insurance. You can buy, extend and claim online anytime – even if you're already on the road.

Internet Access

➜ Taiwan is internet-savvy; the majority of people own laptops, tablets and smartphones. In urban areas free wi-fi is widely accessible in hotels, hostels, homestays, cafes, restaurants, and in some shopping malls.

➜ The government's free wi-fi, iTaiwan (https://itaiwan. gov.tw), has hotspots at MRT stations, government buildings and major tourist sites. Sign up at any one of the tourism bureau's Travel Information Service Centers. Once you are registered you can also use hotspots offered by TPE-Free, New Taipei, Tainan-Wifi and TT-Free (in Taitung). Service is spotty and slow, but it's better than nothing.

➜ The best option for continuous internet access is to buy a pay as you go SIM card from any one of the major telecom providers (p391), which you can find easily in airports with international flights. A basic package offering unlimited usage for five to 30 days with some call time will cost NT$300 to NT$1000.

➜ If you don't have your own device you can find computers with internet access at libraries, visitor information centres and internet cafes. The latter are not as common as they used to be, though most towns and cities do have them. Ask for a wǎngbā (網吧).

Language Courses

Taiwan is a fantastic place to learn Chinese, and there are many universities and private schools that offer courses. Most offer classes for two to four hours a day, five days a week, as well as private classes for as many hours as you like. Costs vary from NT$500 to NT$700 for a private one-hour class and around

TAP WATER

➜ It is drinkable in Taipei without treatment but still best to boil or filter.

➜ Filtered hot and cold water from dispensers is available in every hotel, guesthouse and visitor information centre, so it's handy to bring your own bottle.

➜ Ice is usually fine at restaurants. Shaved ice (with fruit) is usually fine, but take a look at the conditions in the shop.

PRACTICALITIES

Newspapers, Magazines, Radio & TV

Newspapers The two main English-language newspapers are the *Taipei Times* (www.taipeitimes.com) and the *China Post* (chinapost.nownews.com). You can pick them up in most convenience stores.

International news magazines and newspapers International publications such as the *International Herald Tribune* and the *Economist* are stocked at five-star hotels and larger bookshops as well as many libraries.

Radio Taiwan's only English-language radio station is International Community Radio Taipei (ICRT; www.icrt.com.tw). It broadcasts nationwide in English 24 hours a day at 100MHz (FM) with a mix of music, news and information.

Cable TV Available cheaply throughout Taiwan (and offered in almost all hotels and homestays), with some English movie channels (HBO, AXN), and news channels (CNN). Buddhist groups such as Tzuchi also have their own channels, as do the Hakka and Taiwan's indigenous groups. It's worth watching a Taiwan news show at least once for the craziness of the local coverage, which focuses on domestic disputes and lurid crimes.

Weights & Measures

Taiwan uses the metric system alongside ancient Chinese weights and measures. Fruit and vegetables are likely to be sold by the *catty* (*jīn*; 600g), teas and herbal medicines are sold by the *tael* (*liǎng*; 37.5g), and apartment floor space is measured by *píng* (approximately 3.3 sq metres).

US$4000 per semester at a top university program.

Study in Taiwan (www.studyintaiwan.org) is an excellent resource for finding schools and tips on how to apply for a scholarship and study visa. The Ministry of Education (www.moe.gov.tw) is another good site to get up-to-date information.

Some of the better-known programs include the **International Chinese Language Program** (ICLP; Map p72; ☑02-2363 9123; https://iclp.ntu.edu.tw; National Taiwan University, 4th fl, 170 Xinhai Rd, Sec 2, 辛亥路二段170號四樓, Da'an; Ⓜ Gongguan; Technology Building) and the **Mandarin Training Centre** (MTC; Map p66; ☑02-7734 5130; https://mtc.ntnu.edu.tw; National Taiwan Normal University, 129 Heping E Rd, Sec 1, 和平東路一段129號, Da'an; Ⓜ Guting). Both universities are in Taipei but there are programs around the country.

A decent private school if you are looking for a less rigorous program is the

Taipei Language Institute (TLI; Map p66; ☑02-2367 8228; www.tli.com.tw; 4th fl, 50 Roosevelt Rd, Sec 3, Zhongzheng, 羅斯福路三段50號4樓; Ⓜ Taipower Building).

Legal Matters

Smuggling drugs carries the death penalty; possession is also an arrestable offence. If caught working illegally, you'll get a fine, your visa will be cancelled and you'll be issued an order to leave the country. You may not ever be allowed back.

Oddly, adultery is also a crime.

If you're detained or arrested, contact your country's legation in Taiwan or the Legal Aid Foundation (www.laf.org.tw). You have the right to remain silent and to request a lawyer (your legation can provide a list of English-speaking lawyers), although authorities are under no obligation to provide one. You also have the right to refuse to sign any document. In

most cases, a suspect can't be detained for more than 24 hours without a warrant from a judge – notable exceptions are those with visa violations.

LGBTIQ+ Travellers

Taiwan became the first country in Asia to legalise same-sex marriage in May 2019, when lawmakers passed a bill that would allow gay couples to enter into 'exclusive permanent unions' and apply for marriage registration.

Taipei is an open, vibrant city for gay and lesbian visitors. The Chinese-speaking-world's most vibrant **LGBT Pride Parade** (台灣同志遊行, Táiwān Tóngzhì Yóuxíng; www.facebook.com/Taiwan.LGBT.Pride; ☺ last Sat in Oct; ♿ FREE) has been held in the city every year since 1997. Taipei has also gained a reputation as *the* place for gay nightlife in Asia. Other cities in Taiwan offer less lively options.

Useful resources include Utopia (www.utopia-asia.com/tipstaiw.htm), Taiwan LGBT Hotline Association (www.hotline.org.tw) and Taiwan LGBT Pride (www.facebook.com/taiwan.lgbt.pride).

Money

ATMs

ATMs are widely available at banks and convenience stores. 7-Elevens are on the Plus or Cirrus network and have English-language options. ATMs at banks are also on the Plus and Cirrus networks, and are sometimes on Accel, Interlink and Star networks. There may be limits on the amount of cash you can withdraw per transaction or per day (often NT$20,000 or NT$30,000).

Credit Cards

Credit cards are widely accepted – cheap budget hotels, however, won't take them. If rooms cost more than NT$1000 a night, the hotel usually accepts credit cards, but many homestays do not accept them. Small stalls or night-market food joints never take credit cards. Most midrange and top-end restaurants do, but always check before you decide to eat.

Cash

Taiwan's currency is the New Taiwan dollar (NT$). Bills come in denominations of NT$100, NT$200 (rare), NT$500, NT$1000 and NT$2000 (also rare). Coins come in units of NT$1, NT$5, NT$10, NT$20 (very rare) and NT$50. Taiwan uses the local currency exclusively.

The most widely accepted currency for foreign exchange is US dollars.

Money Changers

The best rates are given by banks. Note that not all banks will change money and many will only change US

dollars. The best options for other currencies are Mega Bank and the Bank of Taiwan or money changers at the airport.

Hotels and some larger shopping malls may also change currency, but the rates are not as competitive.

Apart from at the airport there are few private money changers in Taiwan.

Travellers Cheques

Not widely accepted. It is best if your travellers cheques are in US dollars.

Taxes & Refunds

Prices in Taiwan include 5% value-added tax (VAT). Foreigners can claim back the VAT paid on any item costing NT$2000 and over and bought from a Tax Refund Shopping (TRS) shop (see www.taiwan.net.tw; select Travel Itinerary, Before You Go, then Tax Refund).

CLAIMING TAX REFUNDS

You can claim the refund from Foreign Passenger VAT Refund Service Counters at any of Taiwan's international airports or seaports provided 30 days have not elapsed since you bought the item. You will need to submit an application form, the original receipt and your passport, and show that you are taking the item with you out of the country. They will issue you with a certificate that you can present to a bank to claim the refund.

Photography

In general people in Taiwan are fine with you photographing them.

On Kinmen and Matsu Islands don't photograph military sites. On Lanyu and when attending indigenous festivals, it is polite to ask before taking pictures.

For photography tips check out Lonely Planet's *Travel Photography*.

Post

Taiwan's postal service, Chunghwa Post (www.post.gov.tw), is fast, efficient and inexpensive. A postcard to the UK, for example, costs NT$12 and takes about a week to arrive.

Public Holidays

Founding Day/New Year's Day 1 January

Chinese Lunar New Year January or February, usually four to nine days

Peace Memorial Day/2-28 Day 28 February

Tomb Sweeping Day 5 April

Labour Day 1 May

Dragon Boat Festival 5th day of the 5th lunar month; usually in June

Mid-Autumn Festival 5th day of the 8th lunar month; usually in September

National Day 10 October

Safe Travel

➡ Taiwan is affected by frequent natural disasters, including earthquakes, typhoons, floods and landslides. Stay indoors during typhoons and avoid mountainous areas after earthquakes, typhoons or heavy rains.

➡ Urban streets are very safe, for both men and women, and while pickpocketing occasionally happens, muggings or violent assaults are uncommon. If you forget a bag somewhere, the chances are good it will still be there when you go back.

➡ Pollution in Taichung can be serious. When planning your trip there, use weather apps to check projected pollution indices and bring a couple of medical masks with you.

Smoking

Smoking is not allowed in public facilities, public transport, shopping malls, restaurants or hotels and this is strictly enforced. Even some parks are marked smoke-free. Smoking on the street is common.

Telephone

The country code for Taiwan is 886. Taiwan's telephone carrier for domestic and international calls is Chunghwa Telecom (www.cht.com.tw).

Area Codes

Do not dial the area code when calling within that area code.

The number of digits in telephone numbers varies with the locality, from eight in Taipei to five in the remote Matsu Islands.

Mobile Phones

Most foreign mobile (cell) phones can use local SIM cards with prepaid plans, which you can purchase at airport arrival terminals and top up at telecom outlets or convenience stores.

SIM Cards & Operators

➡ The main mobile operators are Chunghwa (www.cht.com.tw), Taiwan Mobile (www.taiwanmobile.com) and Far EasTone (www.fetnet.net).

➡ Both Chunghwa and Far EasTone require foreigners to have two forms of photo ID in order to register for a SIM card, so you will also need a driving licence or an ID card, as well as your passport. If you only have a passport, buy your SIM from Taiwan Mobile.

➡ Costs vary slightly between operators, but expect to pay around NT$300 for a new SIM with about NT$100 worth of call time and 1.2GB of data. Calls to a user on the same network cost between NT$3 and NT$6 a minute, while calls to users under another network cost between NT$7 and NT$10 per minute.

Time

Taiwan is eight hours ahead of GMT/UTC and on the same time zone as Beijing and Hong Kong. When it is noon in Taiwan, it is 2pm in Sydney, 4am in London, 11pm the previous day in New York and 8pm the previous day in Los Angeles. A 24-hour clock is used for train schedules.

Toilets

➡ Taiwan is fantastic for toilets. Free and usually spotlessly clean facilities are available in parks, transport stations, shopping malls, public offices, museums, temples and rest areas.

➡ While most public toilets are the squat style, there are usually at least one or two stalls with western-style sit-down toilets. They often also have toilet paper.

➡ Restaurants and cafes usually have bathroom facilities, and western-style toilets are standard in apartments and hotels.

➡ It is handy to remember the characters for men (男, *nán*) and women (女, *nǚ*).

➡ Many places ask you not to flush toilet paper but to put it in the wastebasket beside the toilet.

GOVERNMENT TRAVEL ADVICE

The following government websites offer travel advisories and information on current hotspots:

Australian Department of Foreign Affairs www.smartraveller.gov.au

British Foreign Office www.gov.uk/foreign-travel-advice

Canadian Department of Foreign Affairs www.travel.gc.ca

Japanese Ministry of Foreign Affairs www.mofa.go.jp

Netherlands Government www.government.nl

New Zealand Department of Foreign Affairs www.safetravel.govt.nz

US State Department http://travel.state.gov

Tourist Information

Visitor information centres are present in most city train stations, High Speed Rail (HSR) stations, popular scenic areas and airports. They stock English- and Japanese-language brochures, maps, and train and bus schedules, and usually staff can speak some English.

Welcome to Taiwan (www. taiwan.net.tw) The official site of the Taiwan Tourism Bureau; the Tourist Hotline (📞0800-011 765) is a useful 24-hour service in English, Japanese and Chinese.

Alishan National Scenic Area (www.ali-nsa.net)

East Coast National Scenic Area (www.eastcoast-nsa.gov.tw)

East Rift Valley National Scenic Area (www.erv-nsa.gov.tw)

Maolin National Scenic Area (www.maolin-nsa.gov.tw)

Matsu National Scenic Area (www.matsu-nsa.gov.tw)

North Coast & Guanyinshan National Scenic Area (www. northguan-nsa.gov.tw)

Northeast & Yilan Coast National Scenic Area (www. necoast-nsa.gov.tw)

Penghu National Scenic Area (www.penghu-nsa.gov.tw)

Sun Moon Lake National Scenic Area (www.sunmoonlake. gov.tw)

Tri-Mountain National Scenic Area (www.trimt-nsa.gov.tw)

Visas

Tourists from most European countries, Canada, USA, New Zealand, South Korea and Japan are given visa-free entry for stays of up to 90 days (www.mofa.gov.tw).

Visitor, Work & Other Visas

Those coming to Taiwan to study, work or visit relatives for an extended period of time should apply at an overseas mission of the Republic of China (ROC) for a visitor visa, which is good for 60 to 90 days.

If you're planning to stay longer than six months, the law requires you to have an Alien Resident Certificate (ARC). See the Bureau of Consular Affairs (www.boca. gov.tw) website for more information.

Visa Extensions

➡ Applications to extend visas should be made at the nearest National Immigration Agency Office (www. immigration.gov.tw).

➡ Only citizens of the UK and Canada are currently permitted to extend landing visas. They may extend their stay by another 90 days; the application must be made 30 days before the current visa expires.

Volunteering

Animal help groups often hire volunteers to work at shelters, walk dogs, participate in fundraisers and also foster dogs and cats (something you can do even if you are in Taiwan for a short time). Contact Taiwan SPCA (台灣防止虐待動物協會; www.spca. org.tw).

You can also volunteer at an organic farm through WWOOF (www.wwooftaiwan. com).

Women Travellers

Safety

Taiwan is a very safe place for solo female travellers. That said, be sensible and take precautions such as avoiding walking alone in a dark alley at night. Some stations on the Taipei metro have nocturnal women-only wait zones.

With a female president in power in May 2016, Taiwan is fairly progressive when it comes to gender issues; even so, society still borders on the conservative: women who dress in a particularly revealing manner, drink or smoke could garner stares.

Health

Supplies of sanitary products (including tampons) can be found in big supermarkets, pharmacy chains such as Watson's and Cosmed, and convenience stores.

Birth-control options may be limited so bring supplies of your own contraception.

Work

To work legally in Taiwan you generally need to enter on a visitor visa, have your company apply for a work permit, apply for a resident visa after you receive your work permit, and apply for an alien resident certificate (ARC) after receiving your resident visa.

Visitor visas are issued at any overseas Taiwan trade office or foreign mission, although it will be easier to apply in your home country since you often need to provide notified documentation.

Once in Taiwan, you apply for a resident visa from the Bureau of Consular Affairs (www.boca.gov.tw). The ARC is issued by the National Immigration Agency (www.immigration.gov.tw). For short-term employment rules see the BOCA website or visit your local Taiwan trade office or overseas mission.

Job listings can be found at Forumosa's (www. forumosa.com/taiwan) work classifieds and TEALIT (www. tealit.com).

Teaching English is not what it once was and there are fewer openings. The most popular website for teaching and tutoring jobs is TEALIT and Dave's ESL Cafe (www. eslcafe.com). Note that it's illegal to teach English at kindergartens.

Transport

GETTING THERE & AWAY

As an island, the most common way to enter Taiwan is by flight, arriving at **Taiwan Taoyuan International Airport** (☎03-273 3728; www.taoyuan-airport.com), just outside Taipei.

Flights, cars and tours can be booked online at lonely planet.com/bookings.

Entering Taiwan

Immigration is usually hassle free. Fingerprints are electronically scanned on entry and exit, and you will often be asked to provide the address of where you will stay when you first arrive. Most officials speak some English.

Visas

Visa information is covered in p392 of the Directory A–Z.

Air

Airports & Airlines

Taiwan Taoyuan International Airport (☎03-273 3728; www.taoyuan-airport.com) The main international airport is in

Taoyuan, 40km (45 minutes' drive) west of central Taipei.

Taichung Airport (www.tca.gov.tw) In Taichung, for domestic flights to the outer islands and Hualien, and to Japan (Okinawa), Korea (Incheon), China, Hong Kong, Macau and Vietnam.

Tainan Airport (www.tna.gov.tw/tw) A small civil and military airport that has several flights a week to Hong Kong, Japan and mainland China.

Siaogang Airport (www.kia.gov.tw) In Kaohsiung, Siaogang Airport has domestic flights to Hualien and the outer islands, as well as direct flights to China, Hong Kong, Thailand and other Asian destinations.

Taipei Songshan Airport (www.tsa.gov.tw) In Taipei county, this airport handles domestic flights to Hualien, Taitung and the outer islands; internationally it has direct flights to China, Japan and Korea.

Taiwan has two major international airlines. Eva Air (www.evaair.com) started operation in 1991 and has had no fatalities to date. China Airlines (www.china-airlines.com) was somewhat infamous for a number of crashes in the 1990s and early 2000s. Since 2010 or so, the airline has improved by bringing in new training and safety standards.

Land

It is not possible to travel here by land.

Sea

There are daily ferries from/to Xiamen (Fujian province, China) and Kinmen Island, as well as Matsu Island and Fuzhou (Fujian province, China). There are also weekly fast ferries with Cosco Taiwan (www.coscotw.com.tw) from Taichung, Keelung and Kaohsiung to Xiamen.

If travelling from Taiwan to China, you must have a Chinese visa in your passport.

GETTING AROUND

Cities and most tourist sites in Taiwan are connected by efficient and cheap transport. Because of the central spine of mountains down the island, there are far fewer options to go across the island, compared with up or down.

Air

Taiwan's domestic carriers have a poor safety record. One of the most recent accidents was in 2015, when a TransAsia flight crashed into a river in Taipei because of pilot error, killing 43 people.

Bicycle

Long-distance and recreational cycling has taken off in Taiwan and quite a lot of routes, especially in scenic

AIRLINES IN TAIWAN

The excellent train network renders domestic air travel, except to the outer islands, a bit pointless.

Domestic flights from Taipei leave from Songshan Airport and not Taoyuan.

Flights to outlying islands are often cancelled because of bad weather, especially on the east.

AIRLINE	WEBSITE	PHONE	DESTINATIONS
Daily Air Corporation	www.dailyair.com.tw	07-801 4711	Kaohsiung to Penghu; Taitung to Green Island & Lanyu
Far Eastern Air Transport (FAT)	www.fat.com.tw	02-8770 7999	Flights between Taipei, Kaohsiung, Penghu, Taichong & Kinmen
Mandarin Airlines	www.mandarin-airlines.com	02-412 8008	Taipei to Kinmen, Penghu & Taitung; Kaohsiung to Hualien; Taichung to Kinmen & Penghu
Uni Air	www.uniair.com.tw	02-2508 6999	Flies to Chiayi, Kaohsiung, Kinmen, Penghu, Matsu, Taichung, Tainan, Taipei, Taitung, Green Island & Lanyu

tourist areas, have designated cycle lanes. The east coast is especially popular and beautiful to cycle.

This means there are plenty of bike rental places. Bikes can be shipped by regular train one day in advance, or carried with you in a bag on the HSR trains and all slow local trains. You'll have no problems bringing bicycles into the country. The main enemies of the cyclist on regular roads and highways are bus drivers and motorcyclists. Note some stretches of the east-coast road are considered treacherous.

In the city, keep in mind that you are not allowed to cycle on pedestrian pavements or in public parks without cycling lanes.

See p38 for more information on cycling in Taiwan.

Boat

There are regular ferry routes to Penghu, Lanyu and Green Island (and between Lanyu and Green Island as well) in summer, and to Little Liuchiu Island year-round. Sailings to Green Island, Lanyu and Matsu are subject to weather conditions, however. Expect cancellations in bad weather and winter schedules to change frequently.

Bus

Buses are reliable, cheap and comfortable. Some companies offer very large, cosy aeroplane-style reclining seats. Reservations are advisable on weekends and holidays. Buses are severely air-conditioned so pack a blanket or warm clothes. The easiest way to buy a ticket is either from the bus station itself or from a convenience store, such as 7-Eleven.

For routes and companies see Taiwan Bus (www.taiwanbus.tw). Two of the biggest companies are Kuo Kuang (www.kingbus.com.tw) and UBus (www.ubus.com.tw).

Intercity Buses

There's an extensive network from Taipei to Kenting National Park and across the north as far as Yilan. Service from the west coast to the east coast is limited to a few buses a day from Taichung across to Hualien and Kaohsiung to Taitung. Service is also limited within the east area (from Hualien to Taitung).

On the west coast there are very frequent departures (some 24-hour operations), with midweek and late-evening discounts. Most companies serve the same west-coast routes. The main transit points are Taipei, Taichung, Tainan and Kaohsiung.

Rural Buses

The network is wide, but there are few daily departures except to major tourist destinations (such as Sun Moon Lake). In most cases you are better off taking the tourist shuttle buses.

Taiwan Tourist Shuttle

Taiwan has an excellent system of small shuttle buses with well-planned routes that connect major and minor tourist sites and destinations. The buses usually leave hourly on weekdays and half-hourly on weekends.

Single fares or one-day unlimited tickets are available. Children under 12, seniors and student card holders travel for half price.

See www.taiwantrip.com.tw for information on timetables, fares and routes.

Fares

Fares vary by city. For example, a single zone fare in Taipei is NT$15, while in Kaohsiung it's NT$12. The cost of travelling in two zones is double the price of a one-zone fare.

Sometimes you pay when you get on and sometimes when you get off. If you cross a zone, you pay when you get on and again later when you get off. As a general rule, follow the passengers ahead of you or look for the characters 上 or 下 on the screen to the left of the driver. The character 上 (up) means pay when you get on; 下 (down) means pay when you get off. If you make a mistake the driver will let you know (or likely just shrug it off).

Car & Motorcycle

Having your own vehicle, either a car or a scooter, is particularly useful on the east coast and in mountain areas.

Driving in Taiwan

By the standards of many countries, driving in Taiwan can be chaotic and dangerous. Always be alert for approaching cars driving in your lane (especially when going around blind corners).

You're not advised to drive in cities or medium-sized towns until you're familiar with conditions.

FUEL & SPARE PARTS

Petrol stations and garages are widely available for parts and repairs for scooters and cars. Check out www.forumosa.com for a thread on reliable and trustworthy mechanics.

ROAD CONDITIONS

Roads are generally in good shape, though washouts are common in mountain areas and roads are often closed. Most road signage is bilingual.

ROAD TOLLS

Several routes charge a toll, which is paid electronically through a system called eTag. Check with your rental company whether you pay this when you return the vehicle or if it's included in the rental fee. The toll is based on distance travelled.

The first 20km is free, the next 200km is NT$1.20 per kilometre; anything exceeding 200km on a single day is charged at NT$0.90 per km.

Driving Licences

INTERNATIONAL DRIVER'S PERMIT (IDP)

An International Driver's Permit (IDP) is valid in Taiwan for up to 30 days. With an ARC (Alien Resident Certificate) you can apply to have your permit validated at a local Motor Vehicles Office. You will need your IDP or local driving licence validated by a Taiwanese mission in your home country.

LOCAL DRIVING LICENCE

Driving licences are issued by county, and if you have an ARC you can apply. Tests include a written and driving section, and also include a health test.

Some Asian countries and US states have a reciprocal agreement with Taiwan so that a Taiwanese licence is issued just by showing your home licence and passport.

Vehicle Hire

CAR HIRE

Day rates start at NT$2400, with multiday and long-term discounts available.

All airports, and most HSR stations, have car-rental agencies (or free delivery).

Car Plus (☏0800-222 568; www.car-plus.com.tw) Good reputation with island-wide offices.

Easy Rent (☏0800-024 550; www.easyrent.com.tw) Island-wide locations including central Taipei, major airports and HSR stations.

INSURANCE

Third-party liability insurance and comprehensive insurance, with an NT$10,000 deduction for damages, is included in rental costs. In the case of theft or loss, renters are charged 10% of the value of the car.

SCOOTER HIRE

On average, scooter hire costs NT$400 to NT$800

ROAD DISTANCES (KM)

	Chiayi	Hsinchu	Hualien	Ilan	Kaohsiung	Keelung	Kenting	Taichung	Tainan	Taipei	Taitung
Hsinchu	169										
Hualien	339	240									
Ilan	270	101	139								
Kaohsiung	103	272	337	373							
Keelung	264	95	185	46	367						
Kenting	203	372	306	473	100	467					
Taichung	86	83	253	184	189	178	289				
Tainan	63	232	373	333	40	327	140	149			
Taipei	239	70	170	31	342	25	442	153	302		
Taitung	272	407	167	306	170	352	132	348	210	337	
Taoyuan	215	46	194	55	318	49	418	129	278	24	361

per day. Some places will allow you to rent with an IDP, while others require a local scooter licence.

In some tourists areas, eg Kenting, electric scooters, which have a top speed of 50km/h, can be rented without a licence.

Hitching

Hitching is never entirely safe, and we don't recommend it. Travellers who hitch should understand that they are taking a small but potentially serious risk.

At times, such as getting to or from a mountain trailhead, hitching may be your only option if you don't have a vehicle. Taiwanese are usually more than happy to give you a lift. Money is almost never asked for.

Local Transport

Mass Rapid Transit

Taiwan's two major cities, Taipei and Kaohsiung, both have Mass Rapid Transit (MRT) metro systems. They are clean, safe, convenient and reliable. All signs and ticket machines are in English. English signs around stations indicate which exit to take to nearby sights. Posters indicate bus transfer routes.

Check out the stations' websites, which both feature excellent maps of areas around each station.

Kaohsiung MRT (www.krtco. com.tw) Two lines, 38 stations, 53.3km of track. Connects with the international and domestic airports. On average trains leave every four to eight minutes.

Taipei MRT (www.metro.taipei) Five lines, 117 stations and 131.1km of track. New lines in the works. Connects with Taipei (Songshan) Airport, Taoyuan International Airport via Taoyuan Airport MRT. On average trains leave every three to eight minutes.

Taichung's MRT is scheduled to begin operation at the end of 2020.

Taxi

Taxis are ubiquitous in all of Taiwan's cities. Surcharges may apply for things such as luggage and reserving a cab (as opposed to hailing one).

Outside urban areas, taxi drivers will either use meters or ask for a flat rate (the smaller the town, the more likely the latter). In these areas, taxis are not that abundant, so it's a good idea to get your hotel to call first, and then to keep the driver's number for subsequent rides.

Uber vehicles are available in Taipei, Taichung and Kaohsiung. Tighter regulations were imposed from late 2019, potentially making it more difficult for Uber to run, but negotiations between the service provider and the government for more flexibility are under way.

Train

Taiwan Railway Administration (TRA; www.railway.gov. tw) has an extensive system running along both the east and west coasts. There are no services into the Central Mountains, except tourism branch lines.

Trains are comfortable, clean, safe and reliable, with few delays. Reserved seating is available, and food and snacks are served. All major cities are connected by train. For fares and timetables, see the TRA website.

Classes

Chu-kuang (莒光; Jǔguāng) & **Fu-hsing** (復興; Fùxīng) Most trains belong to these two classes; they're comfortable but not speedy. The fare is about 20% to 40% cheaper than Tze-chiang.

Local Train (區間車; Qūjiānchē) Cheap and stops at all stations; more like commuter trains; no reserved seating.

Tze-chiang (自強; Zìqiáng) These are express trains and are therefore faster and more expensive.

Taroko Express (太魯閣; Tàilǔgé) This is a special tilting train under the Tze-chiang class that takes you from Taipei to Hualien in two hours. There is no standing ticket for this service.

Puyuma Express (普悠瑪; Pǔyōumǎ) Named after Taiwan's Puyuma people, this is another tilting train under the Tze-chiang class. It is TRA's fastest train at 150km/h. There is no standing tickets.

Booking & Paying for Tickets

You have three main options for buying tickets. Tickets can be booked 14 days in advance online or 12 days in advance in person at a train station.

Online You can book on the TRA website (www.railway.gov.tw) by entering your passport number. Take your booking number to any train station or a convenience store to pay within two days of booking.

Convenience store Use an ibon kiosk (Chinese only) at a 7-Eleven to book your train ticket. Take the printed slip of paper with your booking number and pay at the counter.

Train station Go to any train station and book your ticket directly. Bring your passport with you.

For fast trains, especially on weekends or holidays, it is advisable to buy your tickets well in advance.

All classes of Tze-chiang train are priced the same for the same journey even though, for example, the Puyuma is the fastest.

Don't throw your ticket away – you'll need it to exit the station at your destination.

High-Speed Rail

The bullet service on the Taiwan High Speed Rail (HSR; www.thsrc.com.tw) zips between Taipei and Kaohsiung in as fast as 96 minutes. Tickets are a little less than double the price of a standard train but it takes less than half the time.

The trains offer aeroplane-like comfort, and reserved seating is available. Food and snacks are also available.

There are 12 stations on the route: Nangang, Taipei, Banciao, Taoyuan, Hsinchu, Miaoli, Taichung, Changhua, Yunlin, Chiayi, Tainan and Zuoying (for Kaohsiung).

For timetables and fares, see the HSR website. In general, there are at least three trains per hour. All stations have visitor information centres with English-speaking staff to help with bus transfers, hotel bookings and car rentals.

CLASSES

There are two classes: standard and business. Business fares are about 50% higher than the price of standard, and offer larger seats and 110V electrical outlets.

RESERVATIONS & FARES

You can buy tickets up to 28 days in advance. It is advisable to book if you are travelling on a weekend or holiday.

You have four main options for buying tickets (you'll need your passport number to book a ticket).

App You can book through the HSR's app TEXpress; instructions are bilingual and you can pay electronically or in person at a convenience store or at the station.

Online You can book on the HSR website. Take your booking number to any HSR station or a convenience store to pay within two days of booking.

Convenience store Use an ibon kiosk (Chinese only) at a 7-Eleven to book your train ticket. Take the printed slip of paper with your booking number and pay at the counter.

HSR station Go to any HSR station and book your ticket directly, either from the counter or the ticket machines.

There are small discounts for unreserved seating areas and 'early bird' discounts of 10% to 35% when booking eight to 28 days in advance. Tickets for seniors, children and people with disabilities are half the standard fare.

Tourism Branch Lines

Trree small branch lines are maintained for tourist purposes: Alishan, Jiji and Pingxi.

Tours

Taipei-based MyTaiwanTour (www.mytaiwantour.com) operates dozens of tours weekly all over the island; it also offers customised tours for individuals and groups.

Language

The official language of Taiwan is referred to in the west as Mandarin Chinese. The Chinese call it Pǔtōnghuà (common speech) and in Taiwan it is known as Guóyǔ (the national language). Taiwanese, often called a 'dialect' of Mandarin, is in fact a separate language and the two are not mutually intelligible. Today at least half the population speaks Taiwanese at home, especially in the south and in rural areas. However, travellers to Taiwan can get by without using any Taiwanese, as virtually all young and middle-aged people speak Mandarin. Hakka, another Chinese language, is spoken in some areas, and Taiwan's indigenous tribes have their own languages, which belong to a separate language family from Chinese.

WRITING

Chinese is often referred to as a language of pictographs. Many of the basic Chinese characters are in fact highly stylised pictures of what they represent, but most (around 90%) are compounds of a 'meaning' element and a 'sound' element. It is estimated that a well-educated, contemporary Chinese person might use between 6000 and 8000 characters. To read a Chinese newspaper you will need to know 2000 to 3000 characters, but 1200 to 1500 would be enough to get the gist.

Theoretically, all Chinese dialects share the same written system. In practice, however, Taiwan doesn't use the system of 'simplified' characters like China does. Instead, Taiwan has retained the use of traditional characters, which are also found in Hong Kong.

WANT MORE?

For in-depth language information and handy phrases, check out Lonely Planet's *Mandarin Phrasebook*. You'll find it at **shop.lonelyplanet.com**, or you can buy Lonely Planet's iPhone phrasebooks at the Apple App Store.

PINYIN & PRONUNCIATION

In 1958 the Chinese adopted a system of writing their language using the Roman alphabet, known as Pinyin. Travellers to Taiwan are unlikely to encounter much Pinyin other than for names of people, places and streets. The new signs tend to be in one of two different systems: Hanyu Pinyin, which is used in China (and has become the international standard for Mandarin), and Tongyong Pinyin, a home-grown alternative created in the late 1990s. Although the central government has declared Tongyong Pinyin to be Taiwan's official Romanisation system for both Hakka and Mandarin (but not for Taiwanese), it left local governments free to make their own choices. Taipei has selected to use Hanyu Pinyin and has applied the system consistently, but in most of the country progress towards standardisation in any form of Pinyin is slow.

In this chapter we've provided Hanyu Pinyin alongside the Mandarin script.

Vowels

a	as in 'father'
ai	as in 'aisle'
ao	as the 'ow' in 'cow'
e	as in 'her', with no 'r' sound
ei	as in 'weigh'
i	as the 'ee' in 'meet' (or like a light 'r' as in 'Grrr!' after c, ch, r, s, sh, z or zh)
ian	as the word 'yen'
ie	as the English word 'yeah'
o	as in 'or', with no 'r' sound
ou	as the 'oa' in 'boat'
u	as in 'flute'
ui	as the word 'way'
uo	like a 'w' followed by 'o'
yu/ü	like 'ee' with lips pursed

Consonants

c	as the 'ts' in 'bits'
ch	as in 'chop', but with the tongue curled up and back
h	as in 'hay', but articulated from further back in the throat
q	as the 'ch' in 'cheese'
r	as the 's' in 'pleasure'
sh	as in 'ship', but with the tongue curled up and back
x	as in 'ship'
z	as the 'dz' in 'suds'
zh	as the 'j' in 'judge' but with the tongue curled up and back

The only consonants that occur at the end of a syllable are n, ng and r.

In Pinyin, apostrophes are occasionally used to separate syllables in order to prevent ambiguity, eg the word píng'ān can be written with an apostrophe after the 'g' to prevent it being pronounced as píngān.

Tones

Chinese is a language with a large number of words with the same pronunciation but a different meaning. What distinguishes these words is their 'tonal' quality – the raising and the lowering of pitch on certain syllables. Mandarin employs four tones – high, rising, falling-rising and falling, plus a fifth 'neutral' tone that you can all but ignore. Tones are important for distinguishing meaning of words – eg the word ma can have four differ-ent meanings according to tone, as shown below.

Tones are indicated in Pinyin by the follow-ing accent marks on vowels:

high tone	mā (mother)
rising tone	má (hemp, numb)
falling-rising tone	mǎ (horse)
falling tone	mà (scold, swear)

BASICS

When asking a question it is polite to start with qǐng wèn – literally, 'may I ask?'.

Hello.	您好.	Nín hǎo.
Goodbye.	再見.	Zàijiàn.
Yes.	是.	Shì.
No.	不是.	Bùshì.
Please.	請.	Qǐng.
Thank you.	謝謝.	Xièxie.
You're welcome.	不客氣.	Bùkèqì.
Excuse me, ...	請問, ...	Qǐng wèn, ...

What's your name?
請問您貴姓?   Qǐngwèn nín guìxìng?

My name is ...
我叫 ...   Wǒ jiào ...

Do you speak English?
你會講英文嗎?   Nǐ huì jiǎng yīngwén ma?

I don't understand.
我聽不懂.   Wǒ tīngbùdǒng.

ACCOMMODATION

I'm looking for a ...	我要找 ...	Wǒ yào zhǎo ...
campsite	露營區	lùyíngqū
guesthouse	賓館	bīnguǎn
hotel	旅館	lǚguǎn
youth hostel	旅社	lǚshè

Do you have a room available?
你們有房間嗎?   Nǐmen yǒu fángjiān ma?

Where is the bathroom?
浴室在哪裡?   Yùshì zài nǎlǐ?

I'd like (a) ...	我想要 ...	Wǒ xiǎng yào ...
double room	一間 雙人房	yījiān shuāngrénfáng
single room	一間 單人房	yījiān dānrénfáng
to share a dorm	住宿舍	zhù sùshè

How much is it ...?	... 多少 錢?	... duōshǎo qián?
per night	一個 晚上	Yīge wǎnshàng
per person	每個人	Měigerén

DIRECTIONS

Where is (the) ...?
... 在哪裡?   ... zài nǎlǐ?

What is the address?
地址在哪裡?   Dìzhǐ zài nǎlǐ?

Could you write the address, please?
能不能請你把
地址寫下來?   Néngbùnéng qǐng nǐ bǎ dìzhǐ xiě xiàlái?

Could you show me (on the map)?
你能不能(在地圖
上)指給我看?   Nǐ néng bùnéng (zài dìtú shàng) zhǐ gěi wǒ kàn?

Go straight ahead.
一直走.   Yīzhí zǒu.

at the next corner
在下一個轉角   zài xià yīge zhuǎnjiǎo

at the traffic lights
在紅綠燈   zài hónglùdēng

SIGNS

入口	Entrance
出口	Exit
詢問處	Information
開	Open
關	Closed
禁止	Prohibited
廁所	Toilets
男	Men
女	Women

behind	後面	hòumiàn
far	遠	yuǎn
in front of	前面	qiánmiàn
near	近	jìn
opposite	對面	duìmiàn
Turn left.	左轉.	Zuǒ zhuǎn.
Turn right.	右轉.	Yòu zhuǎn.

EATING & DRINKING

I'm vegetarian.
我吃素.   Wǒ chī sù.

I don't want MSG.
我不要味精.   Wǒ bú yào wèijīng.

Not too spicy.
不要太辣.   Bú yào tài là.

Let's eat.
吃飯.   Chī fàn.

Cheers!
乾杯!   Gānbēi!

KEY WORDS

bill (check)	買單/結帳	mǎidān/jiézhàng
chopsticks	筷子	kuàizi
cold	冰的	bīngde
fork	叉子	chāzi
hot	熱的	rède
knife	刀子	dāozi
menu	菜單	càidān
set meal (no menu)	套餐	tàocān
spoon	調羹/湯匙	tiáogēng/tāngchí

TAIWANESE DISHES

clear oyster soup with ginger	蚵仔湯	kézǎi tāng
coffin cakes	棺材板	guāncái bǎn
congealed pig's blood	豬血糕	zhū xiě gāo
oyster omelette	蚵仔煎	ô-á-chian
stinky tofu	臭豆腐	chòu dòufu
tea egg	茶葉蛋	cháyè dàn
turnip cake	蘿蔔糕	luóbuó gāo

BREAD, BUNS & DUMPLINGS

baked layered flatbread	燒餅	shāobing
boiled dumplings	水餃	shuǐjiǎo
pot stickers/pan-grilled dumplings	鍋貼	guōtiē
steamed buns	饅頭	mántou
steamed meat buns & meat sauce	小籠湯包	xiǎo lóng tāng bāo
steamed vegetable buns	素菜包子	sùcài bāozi

SOUP

clam & turnip soup	蛤蠣湯	gě lì tāng
cuttlefish potage	魷魚羹	yóu yú gēng
hot & sour soup	酸辣湯	suānlà tāng
soup	湯	tāng
Taiwanese meatball soup	貢丸湯	gòng wán tāng
wonton soup	餛飩湯	húntún tāng

NOODLE DISHES

bean & mince-meat noodles	炸醬麵	zhájiàng miàn
fried noodles with pork	肉絲炒麵	ròusī chǎomiàn
fried noodles with vegetables	蔬菜炒麵	shūcài chǎomiàn
noodles (not in soup)	乾麵	gān miàn
noodles (in soup)	湯麵	tāngmiàn
sesame-paste noodles	麻醬麵	májiàng miàn
soupy beef noodles	牛肉麵	niúròu miàn
soupy noodles with chicken	雞絲湯麵	jīsī tāngmiàn
wonton with noodles	餛飩麵	húntún miàn

RICE DISHES

fried rice with chicken	雞肉炒飯	jīròu chǎofàn
fried rice with egg	蛋炒飯	dàn chǎofàn
fried rice with vegetables	蔬菜炒飯	shūcài chǎofàn
steamed white rice	白飯	báifàn
sticky rice	筒仔米糕	tǒngzǎi mǐgāo
watery rice porridge (congee)	稀飯/粥	xīfàn/zhōu

PORK DISHES

deep-fried pork chop with rice	炸排骨飯	zhà páigǔ fàn
deep-fried pork-mince buns	肉圓	ròu yuán
diced pork with soy sauce	醬爆肉丁	jiàngbào ròudīng
pork mince in soy sauce with rice	魯肉飯	lǔròu fàn
sweet & sour pork	咕嚕肉	gūlū ròu

BEEF DISHES

beef braised in soy sauce	紅燒牛肉	hóngshāo niúròu
beef steak platter	鐵板牛肉	tiěbǎn niúròu
beef with rice	牛肉飯	niúròu fàn

POULTRY DISHES

diced chicken braised in soy sauce	紅燒雞塊	hóngshāo jīkuài
diced chicken in oyster sauce	蠔油雞塊	háoyóu jīkuài
sweet & sour chicken	糖醋雞丁	tángcù jīdīng
congealed duck blood	鴨血糕	yāxiě gāo
duck with rice	鴨肉飯	yāròu fàn

SEAFOOD DISHES

clams	蛤蠣	géli
crab	螃蟹	pángxiè

QUESTION WORDS

How?	怎麼?	Zěnme?
What?	什麼?	Shénme?
When?	什麼時候?	Shénme shíhòu?
Where?	在哪裡?	Zài nǎlǐ?
Which?	哪個?	Nǎge?
Who?	誰?	Sheí?

diced shrimp with peanuts	宮爆蝦仁	gōngbào xiārén
fish braised in soy sauce	紅燒魚	hóngshāo yú
lobster	龍蝦	lóngxiā
octopus	章魚	zhāngyú
squid	魷魚	yóuyú

VEGETABLE & TOFU DISHES

clay pot tofu	砂鍋豆腐	shāguō dòufu
omelette with pickled radishes	菜脯蛋	càifǔ dàn
smoked tofu	滷水豆腐	lǔshuǐ dòufu
sweet & sour lotus root cakes	糖蓮藕	táng liánǒu
tofu	豆腐	dòufu

DRINKS

beer	啤酒	píjiǔ
black tea	紅茶	hóng chá
coconut juice	椰子汁	yēzi zhī
coffee	咖啡	kāfēi
green tea	綠茶	lǜ chá
Kaoliang liquor	高梁酒	gāoliáng jiǔ
jasmine tea	茉莉花茶	mòlihuā chá
milk	牛奶	niúnǎi
milk tea with tapioca balls	珍珠奶茶	zhēnzhū nǎi chá
mineral water	礦泉水	kuàngquán shuǐ
oolong tea	烏龍茶	wūlóng chá
orange juice	柳丁汁	liǔdīng zhī
red wine	紅葡萄酒	hóng pútao jiǔ
rice wine	米酒	mǐjiǔ
soft drink	汽水	qìshuǐ
soybean milk	豆漿	dòujiāng
tea	茶	chá
water	水	shuǐ
white wine	白葡萄酒	bái pútao jiǔ

EMERGENCIES

Help!	救命啊!	Jiùmìng a!
I'm lost.	我迷路了.	Wǒ mílùle.
Leave me alone!	別煩我!	Bié fán wǒ!
Call ...!	請叫 ...!	Qǐng jiào ...!
a doctor	醫生	yīshēng
the police	警察	jǐngchá
There's been an accident.		
發生意外了.		Fāshēng yìwài le.

NUMBERS

1	一	yī
2	二, 兩	èr, liǎng
3	三	sān
4	四	sì
5	五	wǔ
6	六	liù
7	七	qī
8	八	bā
9	九	jiǔ
10	十	shí
20	二十	èrshí
30	三十	sānshí
40	四十	sìshí
50	五十	wǔshí
60	六十	liùshí
70	七十	qīshí
80	八十	bāshí
90	九十	jiǔshí
100	一百	yībǎi
1000	一千	yīqiān

I'm ill.
我生病了. — Wǒ shēngbìngle.

It hurts here.
這裡痛. — Zhèlǐ tòng.

I'm allergic to (antibiotics).
我對(抗生素)
過敏. — Wǒ duì (kàngshēngsù) guòmǐn.

SHOPPING & SERVICES

I'd like to buy ...
我想買 ... — Wǒ xiǎng mǎi ...

I'm just looking.
我只是看看. — Wǒ zhǐshì kànkan.

Can I see it?
能看看嗎? — Néng kànkàn ma?

I don't like it.
我不喜歡. — Wǒ bù xǐhuān.

How much is it?
多少錢? — Duōshǎo qián?

That's too expensive.
太貴了. — Tài guìle.

Is there anything cheaper?
有便宜一點的嗎? — Yǒu piányí yīdiǎn de ma?

Do you accept credit cards?
收不收 信用卡? — Shōu bùshōu xìnyòngkǎ?

Where can I get online?
我在哪裡可以
上網? — Wǒ zài nǎlǐ kěyǐ shàngwǎng?

I'm looking for ... 我在找 ... — Wǒ zài zhǎo ...
an ATM 自動
櫃員機/
提款機 — zìdòng guìyuánjī/ tíkuǎnjī
the post office 郵局 — yóujú
the tourist office 觀光局 — guānguāngjú

TIME & DATES

What's the time? 幾點? — Jǐ diǎn?
... hour ...點 — ... diǎn
... minute ...分 — ... fēn
in the morning 早上 — zǎoshàng
in the afternoon 下午 — xiàwǔ
in the evening 晚上 — wǎnshàng
yesterday 昨天 — zuótiān
today 今天 — jīntiān
tomorrow 明天 — míngtiān

Monday 星期一 — Xīngqíyī
Tuesday 星期二 — Xīngqí'èr
Wednesday 星期三 — Xīngqísān
Thursday 星期四 — Xīngqísì
Friday 星期五 — Xīngqíwǔ
Saturday 星期六 — Xīngqíliù
Sunday 星期天 — Xīngqítiān

January 一月 — Yīyuè
February 二月 — Èryuè
March 三月 — Sānyuè
April 四月 — Sìyuè
May 五月 — Wǔyuè
June 六月 — Liùyuè
July 七月 — Qīyuè
August 八月 — Bāyuè
September 九月 — Jiǔyuè
October 十月 — Shíyuè
November 十一月 — Shíyīyuè
December 十二月 — Shí'èryuè

TRANSPORT

PUBLIC TRANSPORT

What time does the ... leave/arrive? ... 幾點 開/到? — ... jǐdiǎn kāi/dào?
boat 船 — chuán
city bus 公車 — gōngchē

intercity bus	客運	kèyùn
minibus	小型	xiǎoxíng
	公車	gōngchē
plane	飛機	fēijī
train	火車	huǒchē

I'd like a ... ticket.	我要一張 ... 票.	Wǒ yào yìzhāng ... piào
one-way	單程	dānchéng
platform	月台票	yuètái piào
return	來回	láihuí

I want to go to ...
我要去 ...　Wǒ yào qù ...

The train has been delayed/cancelled.
火車(晚點了/取消了).　Huǒchē (wǎndiǎn le/qùxiāo le).

When's the ... bus?	... 班車 什麼 時候來?	... bānchē shénme shíhòu lái?
first	頭	tóu
last	末	mò
next	下	xià
airport	機場	jīchǎng
left-luggage room	寄放處	jìfàng chù
long-distance bus station	客運站	kèyùn zhàn
platform number	月台號碼	yuètái hàomǎ
subway (underground)	捷運	jíeyùn
subway station	捷運站	jíeyùn zhàn

ticket office	售票處	shòupiào chù
timetable	時刻表	shíkèbiǎo
train station	火車站	huǒchē zhàn

DRIVING & CYCLING

I'd like to hire a ...	我要租一輛 ...	Wǒ yào zū yíliàng ...
bicycle	腳踏車	jiǎotàchē
car	汽車	qìchē
motorcycle	摩托車	mótuōchē

diesel	柴油	cháiyóu
petrol	汽油	qìyóu

Does this road lead to ...?
這條路到 ... 嗎?　Zhè tiáo lù dào ... ma?

Where's the next service station?
下一個加油站在哪裡?　Xià yíge jiāyóuzhàn zài nǎlǐ?

Can I park here?
這裡可以停車嗎?　Zhèlǐ kěyǐ tíngchē ma?

How long can I park here?
這裡可以停多久?　Zhèlǐ kěyǐ tíng duōjiǔ?

I need a mechanic.
我需要汽車維修員.　Wǒ xūyào qìchē wéixiūyuán.

The car has broken down (at ...).
車子 (在…) 拋錨了.　Chēzi (zài ...) pāomáo le.

I have a flat tyre.
輪胎破了.　Lúntāi pòle.

I've run out of petrol.
沒有汽油了.　Méiyǒu qìyóu le.

GLOSSARY

Amis – Taiwan's largest indigenous tribe; lives on the coastal plains of eastern Taiwan

ARC – Alien Resident Certificate; foreign visitors must apply for one if planning to stay for long-term work or study

Atayal – Taiwan's second-largest indigenous tribe; lives in mountainous regions of the north

Bao chung – type of oolong tea grown around Pinglin

Běnshěngrén – Taiwanese people whose ancestors came to Taiwan prior to 1949

Bunun – Taiwan's third-largest indigenous tribe; lives in Central Mountains

chá – tea, especially Chinese tea

Chu-kuang (*Jǔguāng*) – 2nd-class regular train

cochin pottery (also *koji*) – colourful decorative art for temples

congee – rice porridge

cūn – village

dàgēdà (literally 'big-brother-big') – mobile phone

dǒugǒng – special bracketing system for Chinese architecture

DPP – Democratic Progressive Party; Taiwan's first opposition party

fēnxiāng – spirit division, or the process by which branch temples are founded

Forest Recreation Area – similar to a state or provincial park in the West

Fu-hsing (*fùxīng*) – 2nd-class regular train

Fujianese – people originally from Fujian province in China who migrated to Taiwan; the Taiwanese dialect is derived from that of southern Fujian

gǎng – harbour/port
gōng – Taoist temple

Hakka – nomadic subset of the Han Chinese, the Hakka were among the first Chinese to settle in Taiwan; many prominent Taiwanese are also Hakka people
Hanyu Pinyin – system of Romanisation used in mainland China; though there is some crossover, most signs in Taiwan outside Taipei use the *Tongyong Pinyin* or *Wade-Giles* systems
HSR – High Speed Rail, Taiwan's 'bullet train'

Ilha Formosa – the name Portuguese sailors gave Taiwan, meaning 'beautiful island'

jiǎnniàn – mosaic-like temple decoration
jiǎotàchē zhuānyòng dào – bike path
jié – festival
jiē – street

Kaoliang – sorghum liquor; made in Matsu and Kinmen
KMRT – Kaohsiung's MRT system
KMT – Kuomintang; Nationalist Party of the Republic of China

líng – divine efficaciousness; a god's power to grant wishes
Lu Tung Pin – one of the eight immortals of classical Chinese mythology; couples avoid his temples as he likes to break up happy lovers

Matsu (*Mǎzǔ*) – Goddess of the Sea, the most popular deity in Taiwan; also the name of one of the Taiwan Strait Islands
miào – general word for temple
Minnan – used to refer to the language, people, architecture etc of southern China (especially Fujian)
mínsù – B&B, homestay
mountain permit – special permit you pick up from local police stations to allow you to enter restricted mountainous areas
MRT – Mass Rapid Transit

National Trail System – a system of hiking trails running over the entire island

One China – the idea that mainland China and Taiwan are both part of one country: People's Republic of China
oolong (also *wulong*) – semi-fermented tea
opera (Taiwanese) – also known as Beijing or Chinese opera, an art form that has been an important part of Chinese culture for more than 900 years
Oriental Beauty – heavily fermented tea, first grown in Taiwan

Paiwan – small indigenous tribe; lives south of Pingtung
PFP (People First Party); offshoot of *KMT* started by James Soong
PRC – People's Republic of China
pùbù – waterfall
Puyuma – small indigenous tribe; lives on Taiwan's southeast coast

qiáo – bridge
qū – district/area

ROC – Republic of China; covered all of China before the *PRC* was established
Rukai – small indigenous tribe; lives on Taiwan's southeast coast

Saisiyat – very small indigenous tribe; lives in mountains of Miaoli County
Sakizaya – very small indigenous tribe; lives around Hualien
Sediq – small indigenous tribe; lives in Nantou
sēnlín – forest
shān – mountain
sì – Buddhist temple
Sinicism – Chinese method or customs
suòxī – river tracing; sport that involves walking up rivers with the aid of nonslip shoes

taichi – slow-motion martial art
Taipeiers – people from Taipei

Taroko – a sub-branch of the indigenous Atayal tribe, recognised in 2004
Thao – very small indigenous tribe; lives around Sun Moon Lake
Three Small Links – the opening of cross-Strait trade between China and Taiwan's offshore islands
Tieguanyin (Iron Goddess of Compassion) – type of oolong tea
tongpu – a type of multi-person room with no beds, just blankets and floor mats
Tongyong Pinyin – system of Romanisation used in parts of Taiwan
Truku – small indigenous Atayal tribe; lives around Hualien
Tsou – small indigenous tribe; lives around Kaohsiung
Tze-Chiang (*Zìqiáng*) – the fastest and most comfortable regular train

VAT – Value-Added Tax

Wade-Giles – a Romanisation system for Chinese words; widely used until the introduction of *Hanyu Pinyin*
Wàishěngrén – Taiwanese who emigrated from mainland China following the *KMT* defeat in the Chinese civil war
Wang Yeh – a Tang-dynasty scholar, said to watch over the waters of southern China; worshipped all over the south
wēnquán – hot spring
White Terror – a large-scale campaign started by the KMT to purge the island of political activists during the 1950s; one of the grimmest times in Taiwan's martial-law period

xiàng – lane

Yami – A small indigenous tribe inhabiting Lanyu Island
yèshì – night market

zhàn – station

Behind the Scenes

SEND US YOUR FEEDBACK

We love to hear from travellers – your comments keep us on our toes and help make our books better. Our well-travelled team reads every word on what you loved or loathed about this book. Although we cannot reply individually to your submissions, we always guarantee that your feedback goes straight to the appropriate authors, in time for the next edition. Each person who sends us information is thanked in the next edition – the most useful submissions are rewarded with a selection of digital PDF chapters.

Visit **lonelyplanet.com/contact** to submit your updates and suggestions or to ask for help. Our award-winning website also features inspirational travel stories, news and discussions.

Note: We may edit, reproduce and incorporate your comments in Lonely Planet products such as guidebooks, websites and digital products, so let us know if you don't want your comments reproduced or your name acknowledged. For a copy of our privacy policy visit lonelyplanet.com/privacy.

OUR READERS

Many thanks to the travellers who used the last edition and wrote to us with helpful hints, useful advice and interesting anecdotes:

Adam Kimbrough, Andrew G Moncrieff, Birgit Jansen, Elenna Shih, Felix Gallenmüller, Gary S Harrold, Johan Peuron, K C Chen, Kathi Dresen, Lis Dunham, Lola Rodriguez, Maximus Sandler, Nico Scherer, Raphael Sammut, Shao-Yang Liao, Ronald Steenstra, Susan Mink, Tekke Terpstra, Tim Laslavic and Yishay Yafeh.

WRITERS' THANKS

Piera Chen

Special thanks to Alvin Tse, Keira Yeh, Trista, Nato, Kiwi and Scott for much-needed assistance. Gratitude also goes to my cowriters Dinah, Tom and Mark. And finally a big thank you to my husband and my daughter for their love and support.

Mark Elliott

A great part of what makes Taiwan such a fabulous place to visit is the unobtrusive helpfulness and generosity of so many kind people. Amongst many others, heartfelt thanks go to Sonam, Yung Chieh, Jia Chen and Mimi in Chisheng, May and Vikky at Wisdom Garden, Momo, Jacob in Magong, Jessica and Joshua in Hualien, Jeremy and Mark in Taitung, Lulu on Green Island, Jill and Edwina on Lanyu plus

Roxana and Nancy at Wawa, Lachy and crew in Kinmen, Mr Tsai at Tzu Chi, Ojun Liang at Sanxiantai, Daong in Qimei, Daniel at Bulowan, Su Kai and Yun Li in Matsu, Chun-Yi, Chris and Nikki, Mindi on Beigan, Mark and Robert at 497, the 'Mr Buster' Canadians, Dinah, Angie, and – especially – Sally for her intelligence, company, insight and love.

Dinah Gardner

My greatest thanks go to the Taiwanese people, who are so warm, welcoming and respectful. They made updating this edition such a joy. Individuals from Taiwan and elsewhere who were especially helpful were Carina Rother, Olivia Wu, Kaishiang Ho, Mengzhou Wu, and Robert Edwards and my editor Megan Eaves. Thanks also to fellow Lonely Planet writer Mark Elliott and the lovely Sally Kingsbury for seeing Taiwan through fresh and wise eyes! Not to forget Huaxi, the world's sweetest if laziest dog. Also Miguel Fialho, who asked to be included.

Thomas O'Malley

Thanks to the lovely folk of Formosa for making Taiwan such an easy pleasure. Special gratitude to Catherine Chen, Ching Yi Wu, Candy, and Pinyu. Thanks also to the kindly motorist offering me a lift but muddling his English, asking, 'Can you help me?' Confusion ensued. Thanks to my esteemed editor Megan for slotting me in on this project. And thanks, most of all, to Ophelia (and Almond), the best travel companions of all.

ACKNOWLEDGEMENTS

Climate map data adapted from Peel MC, Finlayson BL & McMahon TA (2007) 'Updated World Map of the Köppen-Geiger Climate Classification', *Hydrology and Earth System Sciences*, 11, 1633–44.

Cover photograph: Temple rooftop, Anakin Tseng / Getty Images ©

THIS BOOK

This 11th edition of Lonely Planet's *Taiwan* guidebook was curated by Piera Chen and researched and written by Piera, Mark Elliott, Dinah Gardner and Thomas O'Malley. The previous edition was also written by Piera and Dinah, and the 9th edition was written by Robert Scott Kelly and Chung Wah Chow. This guidebook was produced by the following:

Destination Editor
Megan Eaves
Senior Product Editor
Anne Mason
Regional Senior Cartographer Julie Sheridan
Cartographer Hunor Csutoros
Product Editor
Amanda Williamson
Book Designers Virginia Moreno, Wibowo Rusli
Assisting Editors Peter Cruttenden, Jodie Martire, Lou McGregor, Kate Morgan,

Charlotte Orr, Susan Paterson, Mani Ramaswamy, Sam Wheeler
Assisting Book Designer
Mazzy Prinsep
Cover Researcher
Meri Blazevski
Thanks to Ronan Abayawickrema, Imogen Bannister, Jess Boland, Hannah Cartmel, James Hardy, Karen Henderson, Andi Jones, Katie O'Connell, Guan Yuanyuan

Index

LONELY PLANET IN THE WILD

Map Legend

Sights
- Beach
- Bird Sanctuary
- Buddhist
- Castle/Palace
- Christian
- Confucian
- Hindu
- Islamic
- Jain
- Jewish
- Monument
- Museum/Gallery/Historic Building
- Ruin
- Shinto
- Sikh
- Taoist
- Winery/Vineyard
- Zoo/Wildlife Sanctuary
- Other Sight

Activities, Courses & Tours
- Bodysurfing
- Diving
- Canoeing/Kayaking
- Course/Tour
- Sento Hot Baths/Onsen
- Skiing
- Snorkelling
- Surfing
- Swimming/Pool
- Walking
- Windsurfing
- Other Activity

Sleeping
- Sleeping
- Camping

Eating
- Eating

Drinking & Nightlife
- Drinking & Nightlife
- Cafe

Entertainment
- Entertainment

Shopping
- Shopping

Information
- Bank
- Embassy/Consulate
- Hospital/Medical
- Internet
- Police
- Post Office
- Telephone
- Toilet
- Tourist Information
- Other Information

Geographic
- Beach
- Gate
- Hut/Shelter
- Lighthouse
- Lookout
- Mountain/Volcano
- Oasis
- Park
- Pass
- Picnic Area
- Waterfall

Population
- Capital (National)
- Capital (State/Province)
- City/Large Town
- Town/Village

Transport
- Airport
- Border crossing
- Bus
- Cable car/Funicular
- Cycling
- Ferry
- Metro/MRT/MTR station
- Monorail
- Parking
- Petrol station
- Skytrain/Subway station
- Taxi
- Train station/Railway
- Tram
- Underground station
- Other Transport

Note: Not all symbols displayed above appear on the maps in this book

Routes
- Tollway
- Freeway
- Primary
- Secondary
- Tertiary
- Lane
- Unsealed road
- Road under construction
- Plaza/Mall
- Steps
- Tunnel
- Pedestrian overpass
- Walking Tour
- Walking Tour detour
- Path/Walking Trail

Boundaries
- International
- State/Province
- Disputed
- Regional/Suburb
- Marine Park
- Cliff
- Wall

Hydrography
- River, Creek
- Intermittent River
- Canal
- Water
- Dry/Salt/Intermittent Lake
- Reef

Areas
- Airport/Runway
- Beach/Desert
- Cemetery (Christian)
- Cemetery (Other)
- Glacier
- Mudflat
- Park/Forest
- Sight (Building)
- Sportsground
- Swamp/Mangrove

OUR STORY

A beat-up old car, a few dollars in the pocket and a sense of adventure. In 1972 that's all Tony and Maureen Wheeler needed for the trip of a lifetime – across Europe and Asia overland to Australia. It took several months, and at the end – broke but inspired – they sat at their kitchen table writing and stapling together their first travel guide, *Across Asia on the Cheap*. Within a week they'd sold 1500 copies. Lonely Planet was born.

Today, Lonely Planet has offices in Franklin, London, Melbourne, Oakland, Dublin, Beijing and Delhi, with more than 600 staff and writers. We share Tony's belief that 'a great guidebook should do three things: inform, educate and amuse'.

OUR WRITERS

Piera Chen

Southern Taiwan, Western Taiwan Piera is a Hong Kong native based in Taipei. She has written more than a dozen travel guides on Hong Kong, Macau, Taiwan and China, and also writes poetry.

Piera also wrote the Plan, Understand and Survival Guide chapters.

Mark Elliott

Eastern Taiwan & Taroko National Park, Taiwan Strait Islands Mark had already lived and worked on five continents when he started writing travel guides. He has since written (or co-written) around 70 books including dozens for Lonely Planet. He also acts as a travel consultant, occasional tour leader, video presenter, public speaker, art critic, wine taster, interviewer and blues harmonicist.

Dinah Gardner

Taipei Dinah is a freelance writer covering travel and politics. During the past decade she has lived in Vietnam, Tibet, China, Hong Kong, Nepal and Bhutan, but has now been happily based in Taiwan, which she calls one of Asia's most charming and courteous countries, since 2015.

Thomas O'Malley

Northern Taiwan A British writer based in Beijing, Tom is a world-leading connoisseur of *hutong* dives, hangovers and donkey-meat sandwiches. He has contributed stories to everyone from the *BBC* to *Playboy*, and reviews hotels for the *Telegraph*. Tom likes the Great Wall, train travel, heritage buildings, beer and mutton. Under another guise, he is a comedy scriptwriter. Follow him by walking behind at a distance. Or at www.tomfreelance.com.

Published by Lonely Planet Global Limited
CRN 554153
11th edition – March 2020
ISBN 978 1 78701 385 8
© Lonely Planet 2020   Photographs © as indicated 2020
10 9 8 7 6 5 4 3 2 1
Printed in Singapore